Information Systems: Devices and Technologies

Information Systems: Devices and Technologies

Edited by Roberts Goddings

Clanrye International
www.clanryeinternational.com

Clanrye International,
750 Third Avenue, 9th Floor,
New York, NY 10017, USA

ISBN: 978-1-63240-598-2

Cataloging-in-Publication Data

Information systems : devices and technologies / edited by Roberts Goddings.
p. cm.
Includes bibliographical references and index.
ISBN 978-1-63240-598-2
1. Management information systems. 2. Information technology. 3. Computer networks.
4. Electronic information resources. 5. Information resources. I. Goddings, Roberts.
T58.6 .I54 2017
658.403 8--dc23

For information on all Clanrye International publications
visit our website at www.clanryeinternational.com

CLANRYE
INTERNATIONAL

Printed in the United States of America.

Contents

Preface

Every book is initially just a concept; it takes months of research and hard work to give it the final shape in which the readers receive it. In its early stages, this book also went through rigorous reviewing. The notable contributions made by experts from across the globe were first molded into patterned chapters and then arranged in a sensibly sequential manner to bring out the best results.

This book on information systems deals with the organization, processing and distribution of information, especially in the business sector. Information systems are an important factor in modern decision making and business performance. They require specific hardware and software for their efficient functioning. Research in this field seeks to constantly upgrade existing components of information systems as well as enhance their security. Topics included in this book discuss the conceptual, algorithmic and technical aspects of intelligent system manufacturing. This book is a complete source of knowledge on the present status of this important discipline. As this field is emerging at a fast pace, this book will help the readers to better understand the concepts of information systems.

It has been my immense pleasure to be a part of this project and to contribute my years of learning in such a meaningful form. I would like to take this opportunity to thank all the people who have been associated with the completion of this book at any step.

Editor

A novel artificial bee colony algorithm with an overall-degradation strategy and its performance on the benchmark functions of CEC 2014 special session

Bai Li[1, 2, 3]

[1]School of Control Science and Engineering, Zhejiang University, Hangzhou, 310027, China
[2]School of Advanced Engineering, Beijing University of Aeronautics and Astronautics, Beijing, 100191, China
[3]Department of Chemical Engineering, National Tsing Hua University, Hsinchu, 30013, Taiwan

Email address:
libai@zju.edu.cn

Abstract: The artificial bee colony (ABC) algorithm has been a well-known swarm intelligence algorithm, which assimilates the cooperating behavior of bees when seeking for nectar sources. Aiming to improve the conventional ABC algorithm, we focus on the re-initialization phase. In this paper, an overall-degradation-oriented artificial bee colony (OD-ABC) algorithm is proposed, pursuing to fight against premature convergence. This is achieved through re-initializing majority of the employed bees at one time, rather than generating at most one scout bee in each iteration. In this work, our OD-ABC algorithm is compared against the conventional ABC algorithms using 24 benchmark functions that origin from the CEC 2014's competition on single objective real-parameter numerical optimization. The numerical results show that the OD-ABC algorithm is effective and thus can be employed to fight against premature convergence.

Keywords: Artificial Bee Colony, Numerical Optimization, CEC 2014 Competition, Overall Degradation Strategy, Evolutionary Algorithm

1. Introduction

Investigations on evolutionary algorithms have been the focus of research for decades [1], which are designed in general for the derivation of optimal or near-optimal solutions of the objective functions [2].

The Artificial bee colony (ABC) is a swarm intelligence algorithm inspired by the foraging behavior of honey bees [3]. In this algorithm, the bee swarm mainly consists of three components, namely the employed bees, onlooker bees, and scout bees. In each cycle of iteration, the employed bees first carry out a global exploration. Those "qualified" employed bees then attract the onlooker bees to follow them. Due to the roulette selection strategy adopted in ABC, the relative qualification of each employed bee is related to its corresponding probability of being followed by onlooker bees. At the end of each iteration, "unqualified" employed bee will perish and then a randomly re-initialized scout bee will take their places. It is worthwhile to notice that in the conventional ABC algorithm at most one scout bee can emerge in each iteration.

Several previous research studies on the basis of different numerical benchmark tests have confirmed that the ABC algorithm is competitive comparing to some other well-known evolutionary algorithms (e.g., genetic algorithm, differential evolution algorithm, ant colony optimization algorithm and particle swarm optimization algorithm) [4]. In addition, the framework of ABC is relatively simple and clear, making it easy to acquire satisfactory results at a low computational cost. Such merits have given rise to applications of ABC spanning across various areas, such as trajectory planning [5-7], structure optimization [8-10], clustering [11], machine learning [12], scheduling [13-16], image recognition [17-20] etc.

Regarding the modifications ever made for the conventional ABC, from the author's viewpoint, the prevailing ways can be broadly classified into three categories. Methods in the first category usually adopt some strategies or theories from the outside world (e.g., see Refs. [21] and [22]). Those so-called hybridized algorithms that combine ABC with exterior techniques fall in this category as well. The methods in the second category mainly focus on making some small changes on the search equations of the conventional ABC (e.g., see Refs. [23-25]). Regarding the modifications in the third category, some changes in the algorithm's framework should be carried out (e.g., see Refs. [8, 10, 17, 19, 26, 27]). Here in this work, our interest is focused on improving the conventional ABC algorithm using a strategy that falls in the third category.

We notice that the conventional re-initialization process in ABC is not competent to handle premature convergence, especially when a "super individual" in a swarm emerges, which denotes a discovered local optimal location that attracting nearly all the bees to search around. In our enhanced re-initialization procedure, we do not restrict it to generate only one scout bee at each time. We intend to accumulate such inefficiency convergence information and make the required changes all at once. We call this an overall-degradation strategy. In this work, we proposed a hybrid ABC algorithm combined with such overall-degradation strategy (namely the OD-ABC algorithm).

The remainder of this paper is organized as follows. In Section 2, we review the fundamental principle of the conventional ABC algorithm. In Section 3, we present the motivation that has inspired us to improve the conventional ABC algorithm. Then in Section 4, we describe our OD-ABC algorithm, followed by Section 5 where the numerical tests as well as experimental results are presented. Thereafter, we discuss our findings in Section 6, and finally, the concluding remarks are provided in the last section.

2. Conventional ABC algorithm

The conventional ABC algorithm employs three kinds of bees: scout bees searching for nectar sources randomly, employed bees associated with specific nectar sources, and onlooker bees following the guidance of employed bees. Typically, half of a bee colony would consist of the employed bees and the other half the onlooker bees [28].

At the very beginning, the scout bees are set out to randomly search for nectar sources. Thereafter, they are replaced by employed bees responsible for global exploration. During the global exploration procedure, those employed bees can share information (i.e., nectar source quality and the current location) with companions by means of "dancing". Then the onlooker bees select the nectar sources that the employed bees have discovered to exploit. It is worth pointing out that relatively higher-quality nectar sources are more likely to be chosen by the onlooker bees to exploit (as a natural consequence of utilizing the roulette selection strategy). If an employed bee finds no better nectar source than the one that it has previously discovered within a certain cycle, it turns into a scout bee again, which implies that its position will be randomly initialized in the search space.

A location of a nectar source represents a feasible solution to the problem, and the nectar quantity is reflected by the objective function value. Let $\mathrm{X}=(X^1,X^2,\cdots,X^D)_{1\times D}$ represent a solution in the feasible solution space, $fun(\cdot)$ be the objective function that needs to be minimized, $rand(m,n)$ be a random number between m and n obeying the uniform distribution, and SN be the population size of a bee swarm. As aforementioned, the number of onlooker bees in a bee colony is $SN/2$, equalling that of the employed bees.

At first, as many as $SN/2$ scout bees are randomly initialized in the feasible solution space. Equation (1) shows how the jth element of the ith scout bee's location X_i is calculated:

$$X_i^j \leftarrow X_{\min}^j + rand(0,1)\cdot(X_{\max}^j - X_{\min}^j),\quad i\in\left\{1,2,...,SN/2\right\},\ j\in\{1,2,...,D\}, \tag{1}$$

where $X_{\min}^j$ and $X_{\max}^j$ denote the lower and upper boundaries of this jth element, and D denotes the dimension of a feasible solution. Thereafter, the $SN/2$ scout bees will become the employed bees and an iterated process begins from here.

In each cycle of iteration, an employed bee will share information with a randomly chosen companion and change one randomly chosen element of its location vector from X_i^j to X_i^{*j} using the following equation:

$$X_i^{*j} \leftarrow X_i^j + rand(-1,1)\cdot(X_k^j - X_i^j),\quad k\in\left\{1,2,\dots,SN/2\right\},\ j\in\{1,2,\dots,D\},\ k\neq i. \tag{2}$$

It is necessary to note that j and k are both randomly selected integers. When all the employed bees arrive at their new nectar sources X_i^* $i\in\left\{1,2,\dots,SN/2\right\}$, they evaluate the quality of these new nectars and then decide whether to stay at the new location or the previous one by means of a greedy selection strategy. Specifically, if the ith employed bee finds that $fun(\mathrm{X}_i^*) < fun(\mathrm{X}_i)$, it will go to the new location X_i^*, i.e., $\mathrm{X}_i \leftarrow \mathrm{X}_i^*$; otherwise, it remains at the previous location X_i.

When all the employed bees have decided on their locations, a roulette selection strategy will direct the onlooker bees to select "qualified" employed bees to follow. A probability index P is calculated according to Equations (3) and (4) to reflect the relative quality of nectar sources at which the employed bees are located.

$$P(i)=\frac{fitness(i)}{\sum_{j=1}^{SN/2} fitness(j)},\ i\in\left\{1,2,\ldots,SN/2\right\}, \quad (3)$$

$$fitness(i)=\begin{cases}\dfrac{1}{1+fun(X_i)} & \text{if } fun(X_i)\ \geq 0\\ 1+\left|fun(X_i)\right| & \text{if } fun(X_i)\ <0\end{cases}. \quad (4)$$

Each onlooker bee will search locally around an employed bee. For some ith onlooker bee, a comparison is made between a random number $rand(0,1)$ and $P(j)$. If $P(j)\geq rand(0,1)$, this onlooker bee will search around the jth employed bee; otherwise, a comparison between $rand(0,1)$ and $P(j+1)$ will be made. If even $P(SN/2)$ happened to be smaller than $rand(0,1)$, such a comparison process is repeated from the first employed bee's $P(1)$ again until a larger $P(j)$ is found. Then, the corresponding jth employed bee will be chosen. The following equation (i.e., Equation (5)) shows the location of the ith onlooker bee $Y_i=\left(X_j^1,\ldots,X_j^{k-1},Y_i^k,X_j^{k+1},\ldots,X_j^D\right)_{1\times D}$ that searches locally around the selected jth employed bee.

$$Y_i^k \leftarrow X_j^k + rand(-1,1)\cdot(X_m^k - X_j^k),\quad m\in\left\{1,2,\ldots,SN/2\right\},\ k\in\{1,2,\ldots,D\},\ m\neq j. \quad (5)$$

Note that in this equation m and k are randomly selected integers as well. When all the $SN/2$ onlooker bees have determined their locations, a greedy selection strategy is implemented. This time, however, a comparison is made between $fun(X_j)$ and $fun(Y_i)$, $i\in\left\{1,2,\ldots,SN/2\right\}$. If $fun(Y_i)$ is smaller than $fun(X_j)$, the jth employed bee will discard its current location X_j and fly to Y_i, i.e., $X_j \leftarrow Y_i$; otherwise, the jth employed bee remains at X_j.

It is interesting to point out that every time the greedy selection is carried out, it involves one central employed bee. There is an index that is associated with each of the employed bees, namely $trial$, which memorizes inefficient search times that concerns each of the employed bees. Specifically, $trial(i)$ records the number of times that the ith employed bee has searched inefficiently. That is, $trial(i)$ is incremented by one each time when the condition $fun(X_i^*)\geq fun(X_i)$ or $fun(Y_j)\geq fun(X_i)$ is satisfied. At the beginning, each $trial(i)$ is set to zero. As the iteration goes on, when $trial(i)$ reaches a predefined threshold $Limit$, the ith employed bee will turn into a scout bee again.

3. Motivation

In this section, we elaborate on the reason why it is advisable to make some changes in the re-initialization phase of ABC [1].

At the end of each iteration, having just one scout bee at most to be generated during the re-initialization phase limits the capability of the algorithm to overcome premature convergence. As a matter of fact, it has been confirmed in some numerical experiments that directly discarding the scout bees will not necessarily deteriorate the convergence performance [29].

Particularly, when a "super individual" (i.e., a discovered local optimal location that attracting nearly all the bees to search around) emerges in a swarm, such re-initialization process is not efficient at all to overcome. Once an employed bee is re-initialized in one iteration, it is likely to be attracted back to the same local optimal location again since other companions are still gathering around that place.

The emergence of super individuals is one cause of premature convergence in swarm intelligence algorithms. Another chief cause may be that the search domain is too large, thus making the optimization process slow to converge. In such cases, re-initializating a majority (but not all) of bees in the colony will be a feasible way to improve the situation.

In the next section, we will introduce the OD-ABC algorithm in detail.

4. Overall-degradation ABC Algorithm

The OD-ABC is different from the conventional ABC algorithm in the re-initialization phase. Here, before a new iteration begins (i.e., at the end of each iteration), any $trial(i)$ that has exceeded $Limit$ will be reset to $Limit$ (rather than 0). Thereafter, average value of $trial$ (i.e., $\frac{2}{SN}\sum_{i=1}^{SN/2} trial(i)$) is compared to $\alpha_{odr}\cdot Limit$, where $\alpha_{odr}\in(0,1)$ is a user-specified scalar. If $\alpha_{odr}\cdot Limit$ is smaller than $\frac{2}{SN}\sum_{i=1}^{SN/2} trial(i)$, the whole swarm is considered to be not working efficiently to a degree of α_{odr}. Then, as many as $\text{round}\left(\alpha_{odr}\cdot SN/2\right)$ randomly selected employed bees will be re-initialized according to Equation (1). At the same time, their corresponding $trial$ indices should be reset to zero. If $\frac{2}{SN}\sum_{i=1}^{SN/2} trial(i)$ is smaller, the current iteration is terminated directly and a new iteration will begin.

The pseudo-code and a flowchart (see Fig. 1) of the OD-ABC algorithm are given as follows [1].

Algorithm 1. OD-ABC Algorithm

1. Set the population size SN, overall degradation rate α_{odr}, and maximum cycle number MCN; Set the invalid trial time counter $trial(\cdot) \leftarrow 0 \quad (i \in \{1, 2, \ldots, SN/2\})$;
2. Randomly initialize locations of $SN/2$ scout bees using Equation (1);
3. For $iter = 1$ to MCN, do
4. For $item = 1$ to $SN/2$, do *% the employed bee phase*
5. Generate X^*_{item} for the $item$-th employed bee to search according to Equation (2);
6. If $fun(X^*_{item}) < fun(X_{item})$, then *% implement the greedy selection*
7. $X_{item} \leftarrow X^*_{item}$, and set $trial(item) \leftarrow 0$;
8. Else
9. $trial(item) \leftarrow trial(item)+1$;
10. If $trial(item) > Limit$, then
11. $trial(item) \leftarrow Limit$
12. End if
13. End if
14. End for
15. For $i = 1$ to $SN/2$, do *% prepare for the roulette selection*
16. Calculate $P(i)$ using Equations (3) and (4);
17. End for
18. Set $j = 1$;
19. Set $item = 0$;
20. While $item < SN/2$, do *% implement the roulette selection*
21. If $P(j) > rand(0,1)$, then *% the onlooker bee phase*
22. $item \leftarrow item + 1$;
23. Choose the jth employed bee to follow, and then generate Y_{item} using Equation (5);
24. If $fun(Y_{item}) < fun(X_j)$, then *% implement the greedy selection*
25. $X_j \leftarrow Y_{item}$, and set $trial(j) \leftarrow 0$;
26. Else
27. $trial(j) \leftarrow trial(j)+1$;
28. If $trial(j) > Limit$, then
29. $trial(j) \leftarrow Limit$
30. End if
31. End if
32. End if
33. $j \leftarrow j+1$;
34. If $j > SN/2$, then
35. Set $j \leftarrow 1$;
36. End if
37. End while
38. If $\frac{2}{SN}\sum_{i=1}^{SN/2} trial(i) > \alpha_{odr} \cdot Limit$, then *% implement the overall degradation strategy*
39. Randomly re-initialize as many as $\mathrm{round}\left(\alpha_{odr} \cdot SN/2\right)$ employed bees' locations according to Equation (1);
40. Set their corresponding scalars $trial(\cdot) \leftarrow 0$;
41. End if
42. Memorize the best solution;
43. End for
44. Output the best solution;

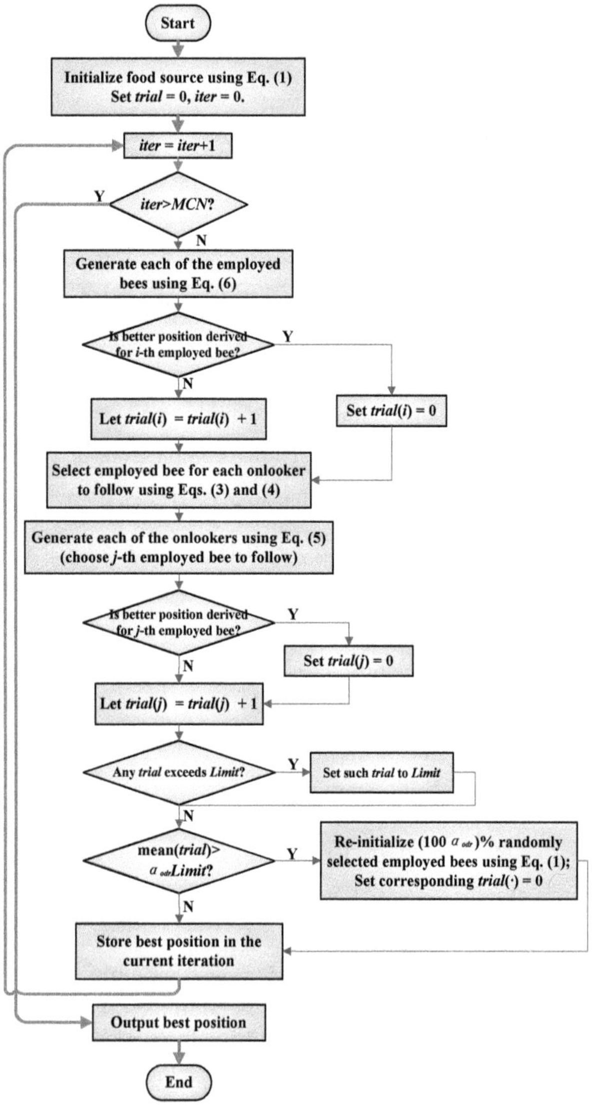

Fig 1. A flowchart of OD-ABC algorithm.

5. Experiments and Results

In order to see the performance of the OD-ABC algorithm in comparison with the conventional ABC algorithm, we systematically conducted a number of comprehensive simulation experiments (i.e., the first 24 benchmark functions for the competition of the CEC 2014 Special Session [30]). In all our computational experiments, the maximum number of cycles MCN was constantly set to 5000 and the swarm population (i.e., $2 \cdot SN$) was set to 40 for both algorithms involved. Each of the experiments was repeated for 30 times with different random seeds. The search range is constantly set to $[-100,100]^{Dim}$, where $Dim = 50$ refers to the dimension of the benchmark problems in this work. All the simulations were carried out in a Matlab R2011b environment and executed on a Intel Core 2 Duo CPU with 2GB RAM running at 2.53 GHz under the Microsoft Windows XP operating system.

The experimental results are listed in Table 1, where "Mean" denotes the average value at the 500th iteration from the 30 runs and S.D. is the corresponding standard deviation.

In the last columns of this table, we report the statistical significance level of the difference of the means of the results produced by the best and the second best algorithms (with respect to their final accuracies). Note that here "p value" reveals the chance if the null hypothesis (the differences between OD-ABC and ABC can form a normal distribution) is true. '+' indicates the OD-ABC works better than ABC at a 0.10 level of significance by two-tailed test; '-' indicates the ABC works better than OD-ABC at a same level of significance; while '.' indicates the two algorithm show no difference in statistics.

Three-dimensional visualization of a selected number of two-dimensional benchmark functions are illustrated in Figs. 2-10.

Table 1. *Result comparisons of ABC and OD-ABC on 24 benchmark functions in CEC 2014's competition.*

Test Function	ABC		OD-ABC		p-value	Significance
	Mean	S.D.	Mean	S.D.		
f1	6114570.5025	2419997.7581	6724954.4722	3359427.9062	0.3493	.
f2	530.5217	581.4641	755.1771	1232.0369	0.2134	.
f3	1818.6106	1719.7908	1355.3680	791.5116	0.1779	.
f4	445.8312	29.4235	446.6215	31.2563	0.8774	.
f5	520.1571	0.0236	520.0829	0.0186	0.0000	+
f6	614.8564	1.5735	615.1491	1.5120	0.5716	.
f7	700.0009	0.0049	700.0006	0.0032	0.9426	.
f8	800.0000	0.0000	800.0000	0.0000	1.0000	.
f9	996.6754	14.1212	990.5091	14.9428	0.1846	.
f10	1000.6780	0.5567	1000.7694	0.5598	0.6143	.
f11	3255.2904	213.0970	3138.9450	311.3926	0.0656	+
f12	1200.1958	0.0349	1200.1587	0.0245	0.0001	+
f13	1300.2369	0.0362	1300.2237	0.0366	0.1529	.
f14	1400.1969	0.0227	1400.2157	0.0184	0.0011	-
f15	1508.6140	1.5702	1508.9653	1.3481	0.5440	.
f16	1609.9398	0.3453	1610.0154	0.3368	0.6143	.
f17	2408523.2800	956030.9703	1841845.1394	1105817.4900	0.0300	+
f18	2731.6489	749.3723	2480.4172	633.9575	0.3286	.
f19	1907.3927	0.8670	1907.4452	0.7566	0.7655	.
f20	11923.4498	5260.5395	17061.2679	7256.6336	0.0111	-
f21	272118.8254	149638.8018	178289.7058	118298.2170	0.0098	+
f22	2502.2540	129.5824	2570.8483	112.8751	0.0387	-
f23	2615.3930	0.2305	2615.4770	0.4185	0.2134	.
f24	2626.3521	6.6572	2628.2003	2.0630	0.0060	-

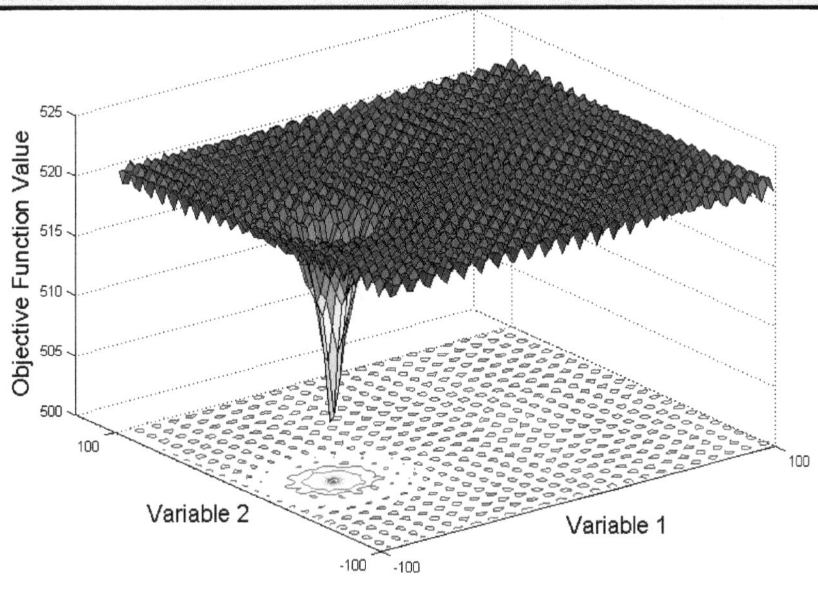

Fig 2. *3-D visualization for2-D benchmark function 5.*

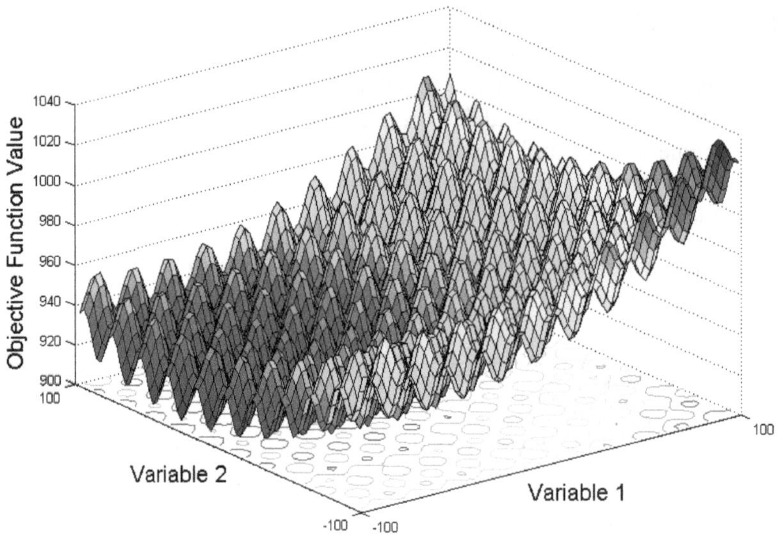

Fig 3. 3-D visualization for 2-D benchmark function 9.

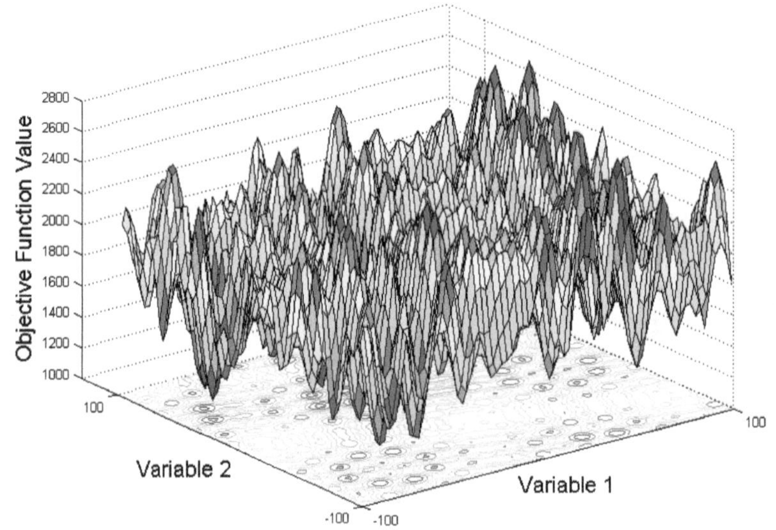

Fig 4. 3-D visualization for 2-D benchmark function 11.

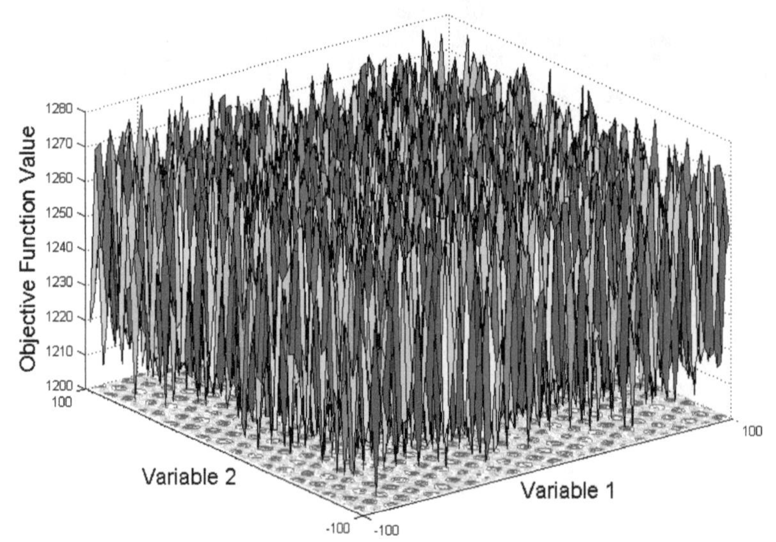

Fig 5. 3-D visualization for 2-D benchmark function 12.

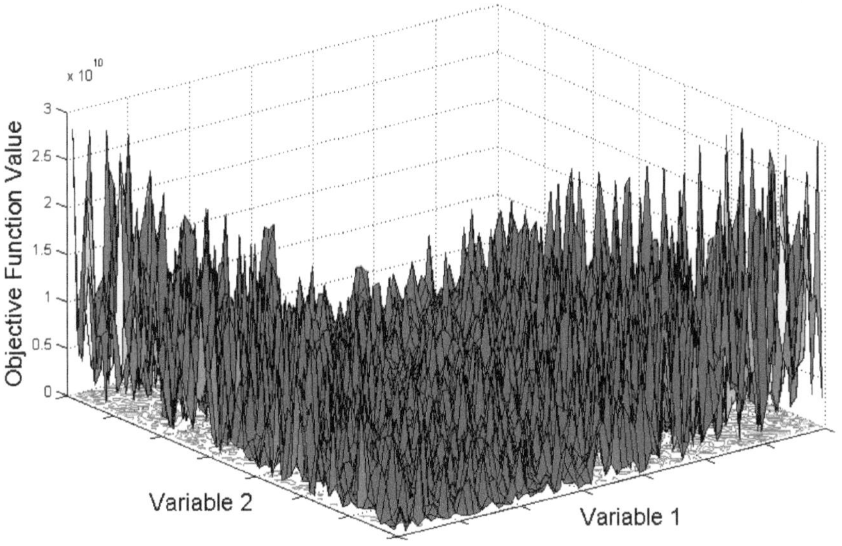

Fig 6. *3-D visualization for 2-D benchmark function 17.*

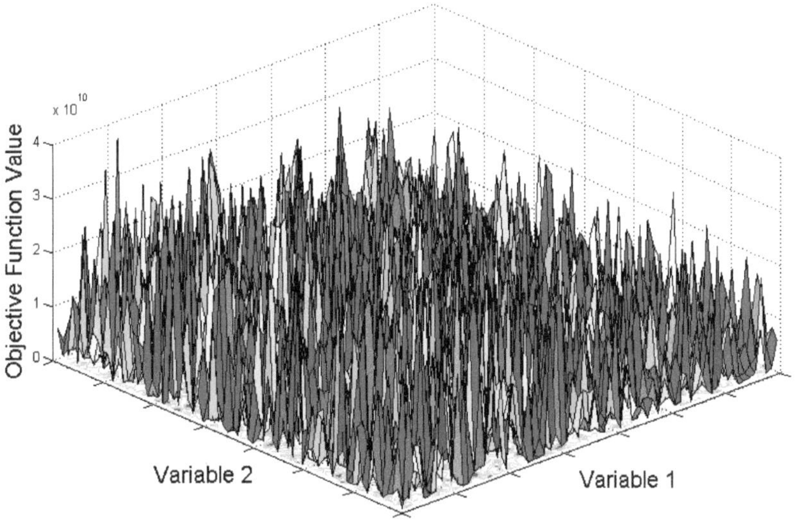

Fig 7. *3-D visualization for2-D benchmark function 21.*

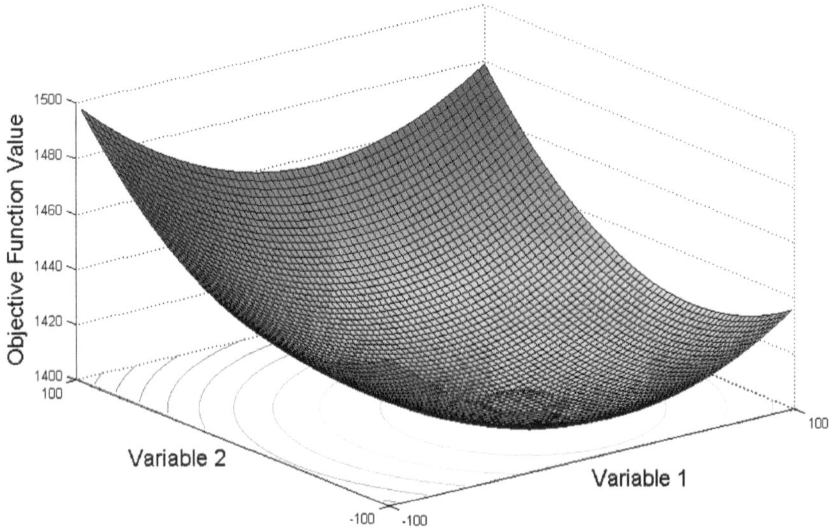

Fig 8. *3-D visualization for 2-D benchmark function 14.*

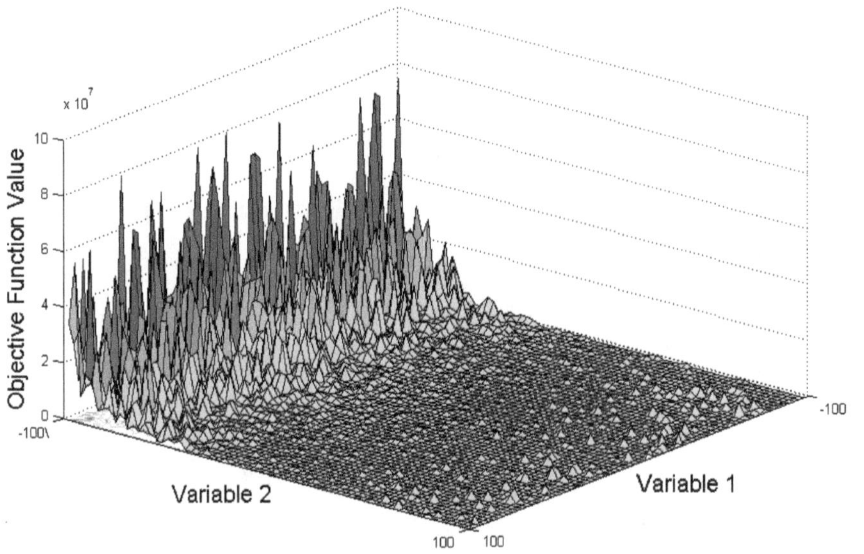

Fig 9. 3-D visualization for 2-D benchmark function 22.

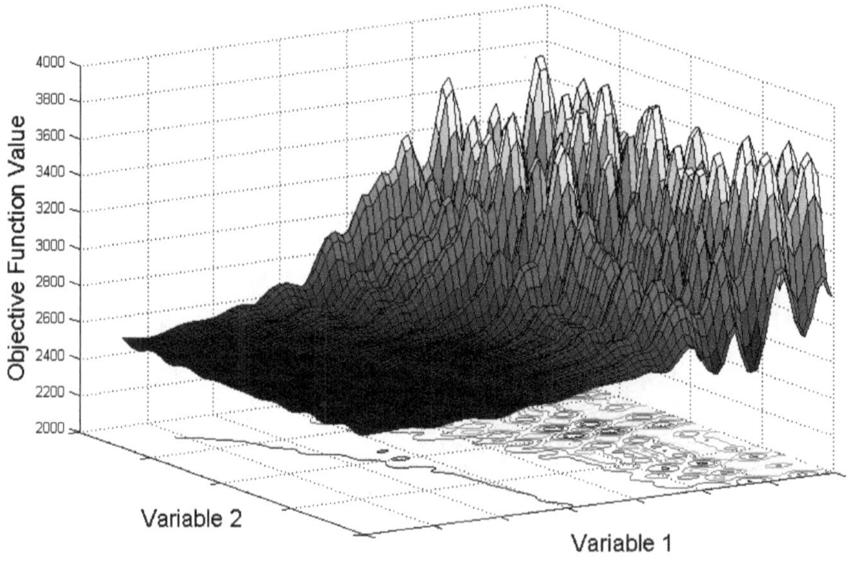

Fig 10. 3-D visualization for 2-D benchmark function 24.

6. Discussion

According to the results listed in Table 1, we find that in most cases, the OD-ABC algorithm cannot outperform the conventional ABC algorithm with statistical significance. However, it is worthwhile to notice that the several benchmark functions that OD-ABC works better on (see Figs. 2-7) are far more complicated than the ones that ABC works better on (see Figs. 8-10). As in Figs. 2-7, there are in general a large number of local minimums around the global optimum, making it difficult to overcome premature convergence. In contrast, local minimums are not so close to the global optimums in the cases of benchmark functions 14, 22 and 24. All the mentioned above indicate that, the OD-ABC algorithm works well to handle the objective functions that are more challenging.

7. Conclusion

In this paper, we have proposed an OD-ABC algorithm, the main idea of which is to provide a more efficient re-initialization phase in the algorithm's framework. The innovations and highlights of in this work can be summarized as follows.

First, we have pointed out a critical issue that deserves well considered in the framework of the conventional ABC algorithm. Then, we provide a modification solution to this issue accordingly. Second, we adopt a state-of-the-art set of benchmark functions to test the performance of the concerns algorithms. The experimental results we obtained support our conclusion that the OD-ABC algorithm is efficient to fight against premature convergence.

Despite these highlights and innovations, we confess there is still room for improvement since OD-ABC becomes inefficient when tested on some unimodal and/or simple multimodal benchmarks. As a feasible suggestion, combining such overall-degradation strategy with other existing strategies may work (e.g., see Refs. [1, 7, 31]).

After all, we believe that the unique and promising idea behind our OD-ABC algorithm is worth pursuing further.

Acknowledgements

The author declares that there is no conflict of interests regarding the publication of this paper. This work was supported in part by the 6th National College Students' Innovation & Entrepreneurial Training Program in China under Grant No. 201210006050.

References

[1] B. Li, R. Chiong and R. Zhang, Balancing Exploration and Exploitation: An Analysis of the Balance-Evolution Artificial Bee Colony Algorithm, unpublished.

[2] D. Dasgupta and Z. Michalewicz (Eds.). Evolutionary algorithms in engineering applications. Springer Berlin Heidelberg, 1997.

[3] D. Karaboga and B. Akay, A modified artificial bee colony (ABC) algorithm for constrained optimization problems, *Applied Soft Computing*, Vol. 11, No. 3, pp. 3021-3031, 2011.

[4] D. Karaboga and B. Basturk, A powerful and efficient algorithm for numerical function optimization: artificial bee colony (ABC) algorithm, Journal of global optimization, Vol. 39, No. 3, pp. 459-471, 2007.

[5] B. Li, L. G. Gong and C. H. Zhao, Unmanned combat aerial vehicles path planning using a novel probability density model based on Artificial Bee Colony algorithm, In *2013 Fourth International Conference on Intelligent Control and Information Processing* (*ICICIP 2013*), pp. 620-625, IEEE, 2013.

[6] H. Duan, S. Shao, B. Su and L. Zhang, New development thoughts on the bio-inspired intelligence based control for unmanned combat aerial vehicle, *Science China Technological Sciences*, Vol. 53, No. 8, pp. 2025-2031, 2010.

[7] B. Li, L. G. Gong and W. L. Yang, An improved Artificial Bee Colony algorithm based on balance-evolution strategy for unmanned combat aerial vehicle path planning, *The Scientific World Journal*, Vol. 2014, No. 23704, pp. 1-10, 2014.

[8] B. Li, L. G. Gong and Y. Yao, On the performance of internal feedback artificial bee colony algorithm (IF-ABC) for protein secondary structure prediction. In *2013 Sixth International Conference on Advanced Computational Intelligence* (*ICACI 2013*), pp. 33-38, IEEE, 2013.

[9] H. Sun, H. Luş and R. Betti, Identification of structural models using a modified Artificial Bee Colony algorithm, *Computers & Structures*, Vol. 116, pp. 59-74, 2013.

[10] B. Li, Y. Li and L. G. Gong, Protein secondary structure optimization using an improved artificial bee colony algorithm based on AB off-lattice model, *Engineering Applications of Artificial Intelligence*, Vol. 27, pp. 70-79, 2014.

[11] R. J. Kuo, Y. D. Huang, C. C. Lin, Y. H. Wu and F. E. Zulvia, Automatic kernel clustering with bee colony optimization algorithm, *Information Sciences*, Vol. 283, pp. 107-122, 2014.

[12] B. Li, Research on WNN modeling for gold price forecasting based on improved Artificial Bee Colony algorithm, *Computational intelligence and neuroscience*, Vol. 2014, No. 270658, pp. 1-10, 2014.

[13] Q. K. Pan, M. Tasgetiren, P. N. Suganthan and T. J. Chua, A discrete artificial bee colony algorithm for the lot-streaming flow shop scheduling problem, *Information sciences*, Vol. 181, No. 12, pp. 2455-2468, 2011.

[14] J. Q. Li, Q. K.Pan and K. Z. Gao, Pareto-based discrete artificial bee colony algorithm for multi-objective flexible job shop scheduling problems, *The International Journal of Advanced Manufacturing Technology*, Vol. 55, pp. 1159-1169, 2011.

[15] L. Wang, G. Zhou, Y. Xu, S. Wang and M. Liu, An effective artificial bee colony algorithm for the flexible job-shop scheduling problem, *The International Journal of Advanced Manufacturing Technology*, Vol. 60, No. 4, pp. 303-315, 2012.

[16] M. F. Tasgetiren, Q. K. Pan, P. N. Suganthan and A. H. Chen, A discrete artificial bee colony algorithm for the total flowtime minimization in permutation flow shops, *Information Sciences*, Vol. 181, No. 16, pp. 3459-3475, 2011.

[17] B. Li, L. G. Gong and Y. Li, A Novel Artificial Bee Colony Algorithm Based on Internal-Feedback Strategy for Image Template Matching, *The Scientific World Journal*, Vol. 2014, No. 906861, pp. 1-14, 2014.

[18] C. Chidambaram and H. S. Lopes, An improved artificial bee colony algorithm for the object recognition problem in complex digital images using template matching, *International Journal of Natural Computing Research*, Vol. 1, No. 2, pp. 54-70, 2010.

[19] B. Li and Y. Yao, An edge-based optimization method for shape recognition using atomic potential function, *Engineering Applications of Artificial Intelligence*, Vol. 35, pp. 14-25, 2014.

[20] C. Xu and H. Duan, Artificial bee colony (ABC) optimized edge potential function (EPF) approach to target recognition for low-altitude aircraft, *Pattern Recognition Letters*, Vol. 31, No. 13, pp. 1759-1772, 2010.

[21] W. F. Gao, S. Y. Liu and L. L. Huang, A novel artificial bee colony algorithm with Powell's method, *Applied Soft Computing*, Vol. 13, No. 9, pp. 3763-3775, 2013.

[22] F. Kang, J. Li and Z. Ma, Rosenbrock artificial bee colony algorithm for accurate global optimization of numerical functions, *Information Sciences*, Vol. 181, No. 16, pp. 3508-3531, 2011.

[23] G. Zhu and S. Kwong, Gbest-guided artificial bee colony algorithm for numerical function optimization, *Applied Mathematics and Computation*, Vol. 217, No. 7, pp. 3166-3173, 2010.

[24] G. Q. Li, P. Niu and X. Xiao, Development and investigation of efficient artificial bee colony algorithm for numerical function optimization, *Applied soft computing*, Vol. 12. No. 1, pp. 320-332, 2012.

[25] W. L. Xiang and M. Q. An, An efficient and robust artificial bee colony algorithm for numerical optimization, *Computers & Operations Research*, Vol. 40, No. 5, pp. 1256-1265, 2013.

[26] A. Alizadegan, B. Asady and M. Ahmadpour, Two modified versions of artificial bee colony algorithm, *Applied Mathematics and Computation*, Vol. 225, pp. 601-609, 2013.

[27] B. Li and Y. Li, Y, BE-ABC: hybrid artificial bee colony algorithm with balancing evolution strategy, In *2012 Third International Conference on Intelligent Control and Information Processing* (*ICICIP 2012*), pp. 217-222, IEEE, 2012.

[28] B. Li, R. Chiong and L. G. Gong, Search-Evasion Path Planning for Submarines Using the Artificial Bee Colony Algorithm, In *Proceedings of the IEEE Congress on Evolutionary Computation* (*CEC 2014*), pp. 528-625, IEEE, 2014.

[29] D. Karaboga and B. Basturk, B, On the performance of artificial bee colony (ABC) algorithm, *Applied soft computing*, Vol. 8, No. 1, pp. 687-697, 2008.

[30] J. J. Liang, B. Y. Qu and P. N. Suganthan, Problem definitions and evaluation criteria for the CEC 2014 special session and competition on single objective real-parameter numerical optimization, Technical Report 201311, Computational Intelligence Laboratory, Zhengzhou University, Zhengzhou China and Technical Report, Nanyang Technological University, Singapore, 2013..

[31] B. Li and Y. Li, A novel image matching method via lateral inhibition using balance-evolution artificial bee colony (BE-ABC) algorithm, submitted.

2

A modified kneed biped real robot based on parametric excitation principle

Yoshihisa Banno[1], Kouichi Taji[1], Yuji Harata[2], Kyohei Seta[1]

[1]Department of Mechanical Science and Engineering, Graduate School of Engineering, Nagoya University, Furo, Chikusa, Nagoya, 464-8603, Japan

[2]Division of Mechanical Systems and Applied Mechanics, Faculty of Engineering, Hiroshima University, 1-4-1, Kagamiyama, Higashi-Hiroshima, 739-8527, Japan

Email address:

y_banno@nuem.nagoya-u.ac.jp (Y. Banno), taji@nuem.nagoya-u.ac.jp (K. Taji), harata@hiroshima-u.ac.jp (Y. Harata), k_seta@nuem.nagoya-u.ac.jp (K. Seta)

Abstract: Parametric excitation walking is one of the bipedal gait generation methods on level ground. This method was first applied to a biped robot with telescopic legs and later to a kneed biped robot. An experimental robot with telescopic legs was also developed and it was verified that the robot could walk more than eight steps by the parametric excitation walking. Recently, we have developed an experimental kneed biped robot and have shown the robot can walk more than fifteen steps stably in inverse bending fashion. But the robot has a deficiency in that the robot does not have a ground sensor and the robot is controlled only in open-loop fashion. In this paper, we modify and improve the robot by using a ground sensor and shock absorbing material to enable to control in closed-loop fashion and hence, to improve the gait performance. The experiments are performed and the walking performance of the robot is investigated. The experimental results are compared with the numerical results, and the validity of the numerical simulation is verified.

Keywords: Parametric Excitation, Biped Robot, Passive Dynamic Walking, Experimental Robot, Walking Demonstration

1. Introduction

In recent two decades, the passive dynamic walking proposed in [1] has received much attention and has been studied extensively by many researchers. In passive dynamic walking, a robot walks down a slope stably and sustainably without any actuator, and passive dynamic walking has thought to be energy efficient. Inspired by passive dynamic walking, several walking method on level ground have been proposed, such as energy tracking control [2], virtual passive dynamic walking [3] and so on [4, 5].

The parametric excitation is another way of realizing passive dynamic-based walking on level ground. Parametric excitation is the principle to increase amplitude of vibration by changing a parameter periodically, and the principle is utilized to restore the energy lost by collision between a foot and the ground, and hence, sustainable walking is realized.

Reference [6] first applied the principle to the biped robot with telescopic legs which made the center of mass of swing leg up-and-down by pumping a leg, and showed that the robot walked sustainably on level ground. Later in [7], bending and stretching a swing leg was shown to have the same effect of pumping a telescopic leg, and the parametric excitation walking for a kneed biped was proposed and was shown to walk sustainably on level ground. Reference [8] proposed the parametric excitation based inverse bending walking in which the knee of swing leg was bent in inverse direction to human movement. Reference [8] also showed that inverse bending was more energy efficient than forward bending like human movement by numerical experiments.

An experimental robot based on parametric excitation principle with telescopic legs was developed in [9], and the robot could walk about five steps on level ground. The robot was improved in [10] by adding a counterweight, which enabled the robot walking more than eight steps. Recently, an experimental kneed biped robot based on parametric excitation principle has developed in [11]. The robot has actuated knee joints, and [11] has shown that the robot can walk more than fifteen steps stably in inverse bending fashion.

But there is a big difference between the developed robot in [11] and simulation model in that the robot does not have a sensor to detect heel strike. In parametric excitation walking, it is known [7, 8, 12] that walking performance strongly depends on a reference trajectory of a swing leg knee joint, and a reference trajectory is designed to start at heel strike. Hence, in our previous experiments [11], both knee joints were controlled only to track a simple periodic reference trajectory in an open-loop control fashion.

In this paper, we improve the kneed biped robot developed in [11] by introducing a ground sensor and show new experimental results. The purpose of introducing a ground sensor is to detect the instance of heel strike, which makes the robot close to the simulation model and enables to control knee joints in a closed-loop way. Moreover, the ground sensor enables to change the start time of bending, which causes to the changes of walking speed and walking period for the same reference trajectory. This has already shown by simulation in [7, 8] and might improve stability and efficiency, but has not been verified by an experimental robot so far.

This paper is organized as follows. In Section 2, we introduce the model of a kneed biped robot dealt with in this paper and the control input for the robot to realize parametric excitation walking. In Section 3, we first introduce the experimental robot developed in [11], and then explain the improve points in detail. Experimental results are shown in section 4. Finally in Section 5, we conclude this paper.

2. Parametric Excitation Walking for a Kneed Biped Robot

Fig. 1 illustrates a biped robot model based on which we have developed an experimental robot. The model has five point masses, and has semicircular feet whose centers are on each leg. Semicircular feet were shown to have the same effects of equivalent ankle torque, and to decrease energy dissipation at heel strike [13]. We assume that only knees are actuated.

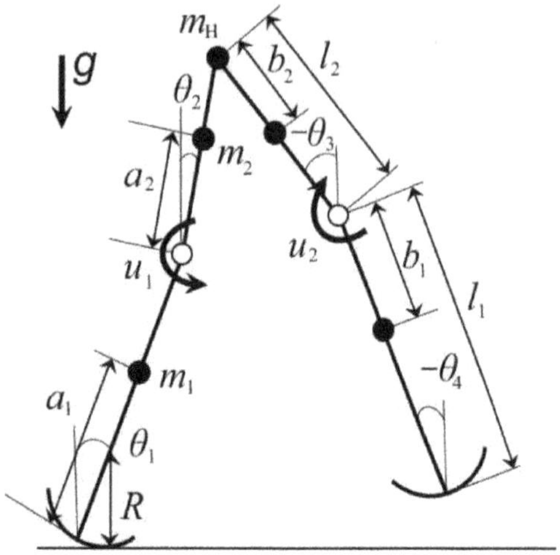

Fig. 1. Model of planar of kneed biped robot with semicircular feet.

The robot gait consists of the following two phases.

- Single support phase: A support leg rotates around the contact point between a semicircular foot and ground.
- Double support phase: This phase occurs instantaneously, and a support leg and the swing leg are exchanged after heel strike.

The dynamics of a robot during single support phase obeys the following equation of motion:

$$M(\theta)\ddot{\theta} + C(\theta, \dot{\theta})\dot{\theta} + g(\theta) = u, \tag{1}$$

where $\theta = [\theta_1\ \theta_2\ \theta_3\ \theta_4]^T$ is the generalized coordinate vector, M is the inertia matrix, C is the Coriolis force and the centrifugal force, and g is the gravity vector. The knee torque u is designed to realize parametric excitation walking.

The angular velocities $\dot{\theta}^-$ and $\dot{\theta}^+$, immediately before and after the double support phase respectively, are related by the impact equation

$$\dot{\theta}^+ = J(\theta)\dot{\theta}^-, \tag{2}$$

where J is the translation matrix. The detail and the derivations of (1) and (2) are described in [14].

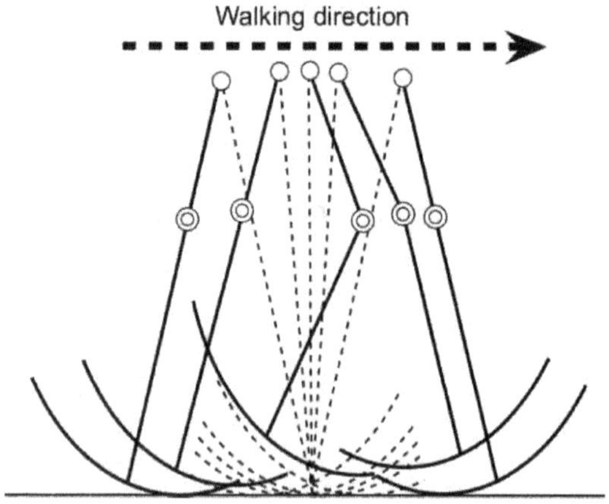

(a) Forward bending

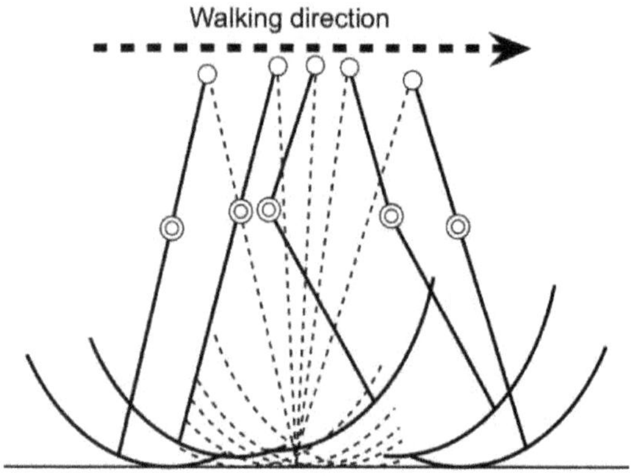

(b) Inverse bending

Fig. 2. Forward and inverse bending walking

In parametric excitation walking, the up-and-down motion of the center of mass by bending and stretching the swing leg knee restores mechanical energy lost at heel strike. Hence, it is important to control the relative angle of the swing leg knee exactly according to the given relative knee angle. Because the control input u completely tracking the given relative knee angle was made by a partial feedback linearization method [7], it is sufficient to determine the appropriately designed the reference trajectory $h(t)$ of the relative angle $\theta_3 - \theta_4$ of the swing leg knee. To design the control input u according to the trajectory $h(t)$ is also described in [14]. We note that, in the developed experimental robot, the knee joints are controlled by servomotors according to the given relative knee angle.

Reference [9] proposed the inverse bending walking in which a knee was bent in inverse direction to human movement. Stick diagrams of the forward bending and the inverse bending are shown in Fig. 2. In Fig. 2, the solid line represents a swing leg and the dashed line represents a support leg. The inverse bending walking was shown to restore larger energy than forward bending for the same reference trajectory in [9]. Because of this, we will compare the experimental results of the developed real robot with those of simulation results in the inverse bending walking only.

3. The Developed Kneed Biped Robot and its Modifications

In this section, we first introduce the experimental robot originally developed in [11], and then explain the improve points in detail.

3.1. The Experimental Robot Developed in [11]

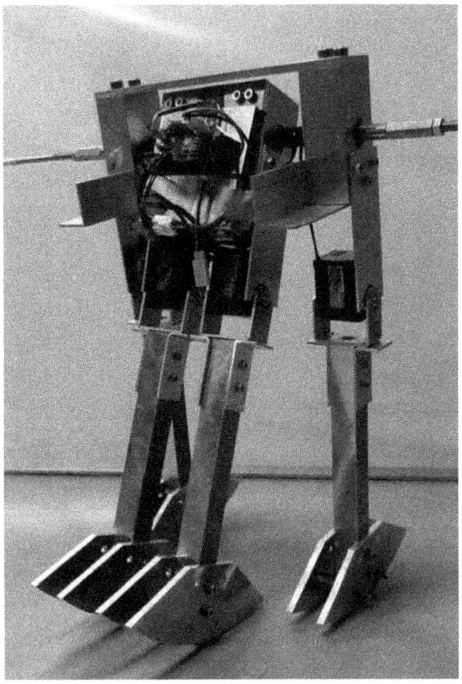

Fig. 3. Experimental robot

The experimental biped robot developed in [11] is shown in Fig. 3. The robot has four parallel legs. Each leg has a semicircular foot and a knee joint with a servomotor. To restrict the robot movement in sagittal plane, the inside two legs and the outside two legs are synchronized, respectively. Upper legs are synchronized by structural constraint, of which the inside two upper legs and the outside two upper legs are connected by bars respectively, and lower legs are synchronized by control input with servo motors. A hip joint is free and has no actuators. Battery and controller are implemented on the inside two upper legs. To balance the inside two legs with the outside two legs, we put counterweights on the outside legs. A counterweight was shown to improve gait performance in [10]. Moreover, counterweights prevent the control board from damage when the robot falls down. The semicircular foot and counterweights of the robot are also shown in Fig. 3 and the physical parameters of the robot are shown in Table 1. Table 2 presents the control devices of the robot and the characteristics of the servomotor are shown in Table 3.

Table 1. *Physical Parameters of the Robot*

Upper leg length	0.10m
Lower leg length	0.22m
Foot radius	0.15m
Upper leg mass	0.10kg
Lower leg mass	0.35kg
Hip mass	1.25kg
Total mass	3.05kg

Table 2. *Control devices (Manufactured by Kondo Kagaku Co.,Ltd.)*

Devices	Product Name
Servo motor	KRS-4013HV
Control board	RCB-3HV
Battery	ROBO powercell

Table 3. *The Performance of the servomotor*

Maximum torque	2.65Nm
Maximum speed	83.3rpm
Weight	0.065kg

3.2. Improved Points

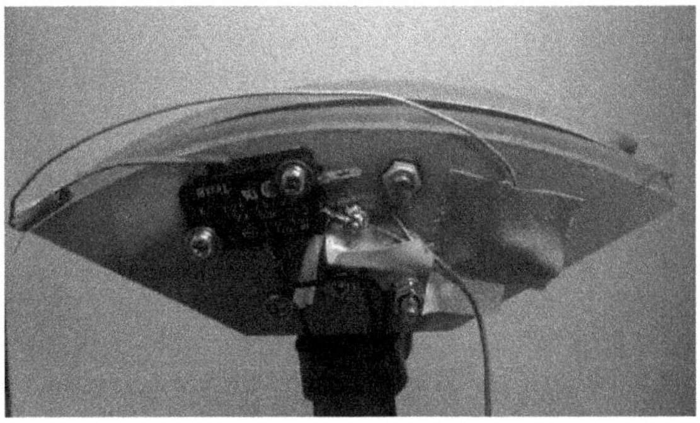

Fig. 4. Attached ground sensor and GEL tape

The improved points are two. One is to introduce a ground sensor. The experimental robot in [11] did not have a sensor to detect heel strike, and hence, both knee joints were controlled in an open-loop way. The ground sensor is made by micro switch (vx-53k-1A2, Omron Co. Ltd.) with a short wire, and is attached on a semicircular foot. The attached ground sensor is shown in Fig. 4. In the figure, the wire is used to enlarge the region of landing detected by the micro switch.

We note that the function of the ground sensor is to send the signal to start bending another knee, rather than to detect the instant of heel strike. However, the experimental results in the later show that the instant of heel strike is detected almost exactly.

Another improved point is to attach the shock absorbing material on a semicircular foot. The parametric excitation walking proposed in [7, 8] has assumed that the semicircular foot of a support leg rolls on a ground without slipping. It has also assumed that the collision at heel strike is completely inelastic, that is, a swing leg lands without bouncing. Because the semicircular foot of the robot has been made by an aluminum board, we have required the specially equipped experimental road for demonstration experiments in [11]. The experimental road used in [11] consisted of a rubber sheet avoiding slipping and a shock absorbing material avoiding bouncing.

Instead of using the experimental road, we put the shock absorbing material, GEL Tape GT-5 (Taica co. [15]), on the arc of a semicircular foot. A GEL Tape is a very good material to resolve two issues simultaneously, slipping on a ground and bouncing at heel strike. The thickness of the GEL tape is only 3mm, and hence, we can ignore the change of a radius of semicircular foot. In Fig. 4, a GEL tape can be seen as translucent thin material on the arc.

Finally, we note that the use of GEL tape has practical meaning rather than theoretical one, in that it make the robot possible to walk on everywhere of flat and firm floor.

4. Experimental Results

In this section, we first present the overview of the experiment methodology and then we show the experimental results.

4.1. Overview of Experiment

To perform walking experiment, we first should design the reference trajectory of the relative angle, $\theta_3 - \theta_4$, for a swing leg knee. In the numerical simulation, the reference trajectory has been designed by sufficiently smooth curves, such as, the cubic sinusoid [7, 8] and quartic spline [12]. But the controller and the servo motor used in the developed robot can only control the certain angle to the target angle, the angle velocity between these two angles and the starting time of rotation by the signal of the attached grounding sensor. Hence, the designed reference trajectory is determined by five parameters: the starting time t_0 of bending a swing leg from the heel strike, the relative angle A_0 of a support leg knee, the maximum bending angle A_m of a swing leg knee, the duration time t_m of maintaining the maximum bending and the times t_b and t_s of bending time from A_0 to A_m and stretching time from A_m to A_0, respectively.

In the demonstration experiments, the angle A_0 is fixed as $A_0 = 0.30$rad, and the times t_b, t_m and t_s are fixed as $t_b = 0.21$s, $t_m = 0.015$s and $t_s = 0.21$s, respectively. We test for three maximum bending angles, $A_m = 1.20, 1,35$ and 1.50rad, and for each A_m, the starting time t_0 is changed as $t_0 = 0.075, 0.090$ and 0.105s, that is, we test for nine reference trajectories. We note that the reason to introduce the positive support leg angle $A_0 = 0.30$rad is for a knee to avoid bending oppositely, and hence, the knee of the robot is always bending. The values of the parameters are set as the robot can walk, which are determined by trial and error in the experimental robot.

The lower, upper and relative knee angles during walking demonstration are measured by 3D motion capture system, OPTOTRAK Certus (Northern Digital Inc.). The motion capture system measures the positions of infrared-ray markers attached on the robot in 3D space by a camera and the markers invisible from the camera are not measured. Hence, we only measure the outside leg motion using four markers attached as shown in Fig. 5 with the 100Hz sampling rate.

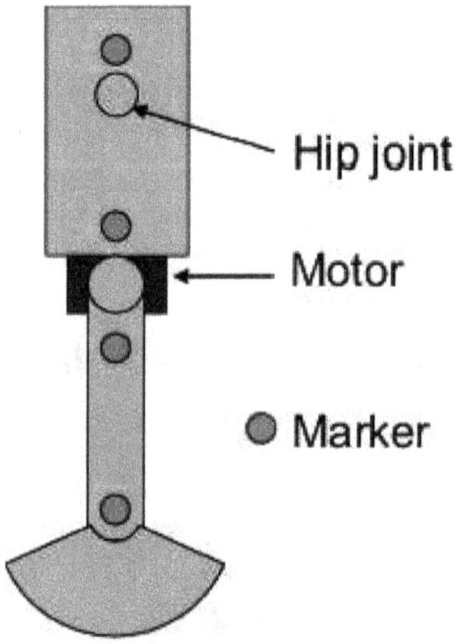

Fig. 5. *Marker positions*

To walk the robot, it is necessary to give an appropriate initial condition corresponding to a reference trajectory. This is very difficult in the simulations. But, in our demonstration experiment, this is resolved by the following simple method: the robot is held by hand until the gait becomes stable. In fact, the gait of the developed robot converges rapidly to steady gait within about seven or eight steps in our demonstration experiment, and hence the angles are measured after the first ten steps.

For the comparison purpose, we also perform numerical simulation. The reference trajectories of simulation are made with quartic spline to be close to the measured relative knee angles in demonstration experiment. We note that the reference trajectories used in simulation do not coincide with those in experiment by the limitation of the performance of a servo motor.

All experiments were performed on a wood board covered

by rubber sheets to avoid uneven road and make flat road.

4.2. Experimental Results

For the nine reference trajectories explained above, we perform five walking trials for each case and measure walking data. The results of numerical simulations are summarized in Table 4. In the table, we present the walking speed, the walking period and the step sizes for nine reference trajectories. All data are the average of measured data of the five trials for each reference trajectory. The results of numerical simulations are summarized in Table 5.

Table 4. *The Results of Experiment*

Maximum bending angle A_m[rad]	Bending time t_0	Walking speed [m/s]	Waling period [s]	Step size [m]
1.20	0.075	0.259	0.559	0.145
	0.090	0.289	0.572	0.166
	0.105	0.294	0.578	0.170
1.35	0.075	0.331	0.559	0.185
	0.090	0.341	0.578	0.197
	0.105	0.342	0.586	0.200
1.50	0.075	0.370	0.568	0.209
	0.090	0.375	0.580	0.216
	0.105	0.378	0.588	0.222

Table 5. *The Results of Simulation*

Maximum bending angle A_m[rad]	Bending time t_0	Walking speed [m/s]	Waling period [s]	Step size [m]
1.20	0.075	0.331	0.524	0.173
	0.090	0.343	0.541	0.185
	0.105	0.350	0.554	0.194
1.35	0.075	0.354	0.536	0.190
	0.090	0.363	0.552	0.201
	0.105	0.369	0.566	0.209
1.50	0.075	0.375	0.546	0.205
	0.090	0.382	0.563	0.215
	0.105	0.386	0.578	0.223

In all results, the robot walks more than twenty steps and the experimental results are the average of the measured five steps after than the first ten steps for each case. From the Table 4, we can observed that the walking speed, walking period and the step sizes of the experimental results are increasing as either the maximum bending angle is larger or the starting time of bending is later. These results are supported by the simulation results shown in Table 5. In particular, the differences of the results in the starting time $t_0 = 0.075s$ and those of $t_0 = 0.090s$ are larger than the differences between the results of $t_0 = 0.090s$ and those of $t_0 = 0.105s$, for all three maximum bending angle in both experiments and simulations.

But there are differences between the experimental results and simulation results in that the walking speed and the step sizes of simulation results are larger than those of experiments, while the walking periods of both results are almost same. This is because some physical parameters, such as, inertia moments of legs are different between the simulations and experiments, and some friction in the hip joint and between foot and road does not taken in consideration in the simulation. To resolve the influences of these facts are one of the future research theme.

To see the results more in detail, we present the measured results of relative knee angles in Fig. 6, and the upper and the lower angles in Fig. 7 of the case of the maximum bending angle $A_m = 1.35$rad. In the Figs. 6 and 7, case (a) represents the results of starting time $t_0 = 0.075s$, case (b) represents $t_0 = 0.090s$ and case (c) represents $t_0 = 0.105s$, and the blue solid lines denote the results of experiments and the red dotted lines denote those of simulation.

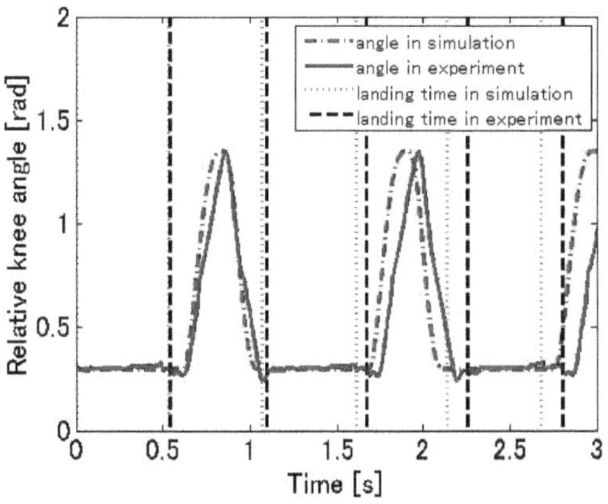

(a) $A_m = 1.35$rad and $t_0 = 0.075$s

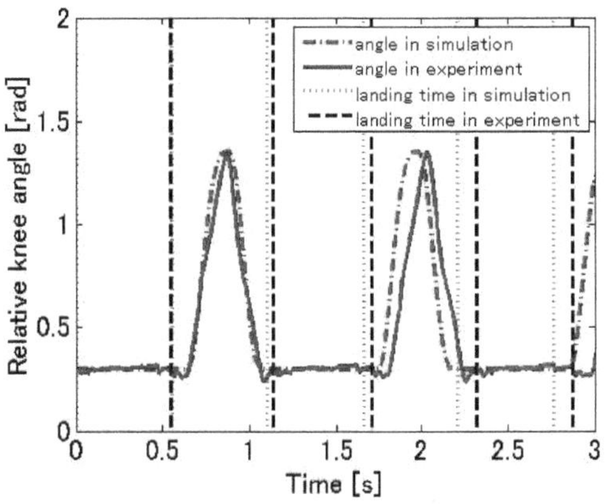

(b) $A_m = 1.35$rad and $t_0 = 0.090$s

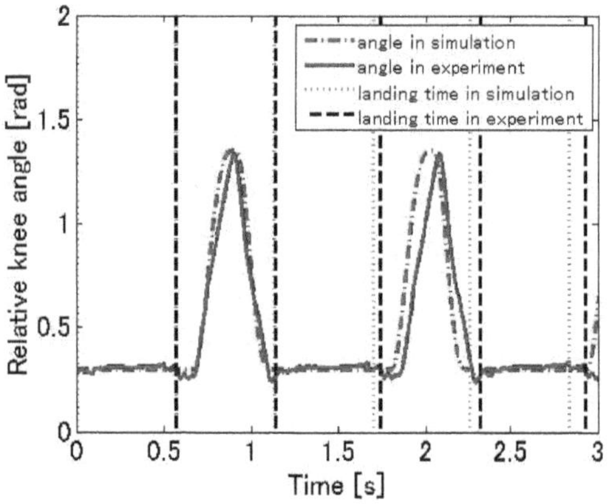

(c) $A_m = 1.35\text{rad}$ and $t_0 = 0.105\text{s}$

Fig. 6. Results of relative knee angles

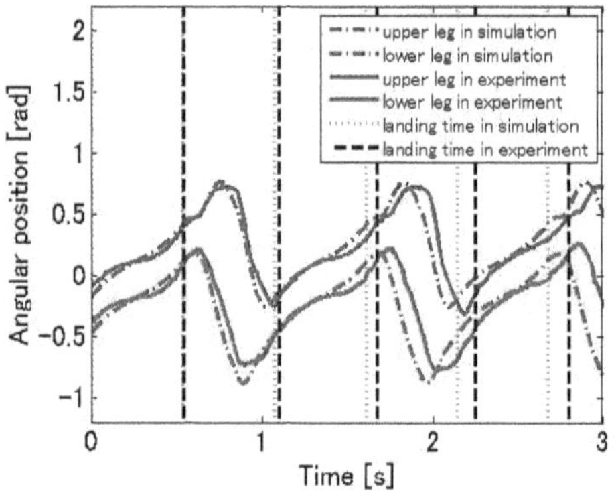

(a) $A_m = 1.35\text{rad}$ and $t_0 = 0.075\text{s}$

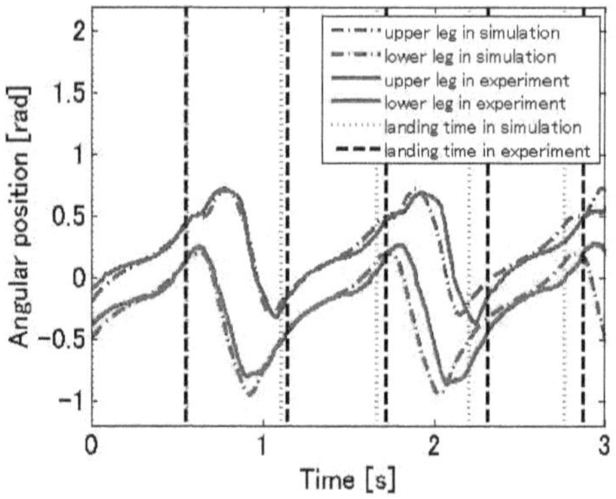

(b) $A_m = 1.35\text{rad}$ and $t_0 = 0.090\text{s}$

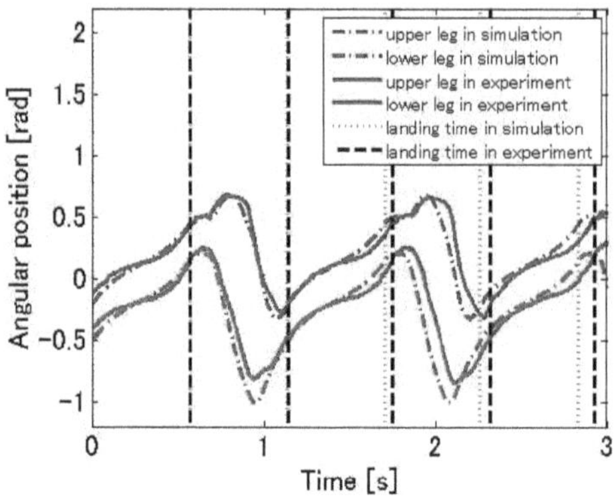

(c) $A_m = 1.35\text{rad}$ and $t_0 = 0.105\text{s}$

Fig. 7. Results of angular positions

We also illustrate the instant of heel strike in the Figs. 6 and 7. In the figures, the instant of heel strike is denoted as follows: The black dotted lines denote the experimental results, and the green dotted lines denote simulation results. From Fig. 6, it is observed that the reference trajectories of the swing leg knee angle are followed exactly by servo motors. Furthermore, the starting time of bending coincides with the given starting time exactly for all three cases. This indicates that the attached grounding sensor can detect the instant of landing almost exactly. On the other hand, the results of experiment get delayed step by step because the period of experiment is longer than that of simulation. This is also observed in Fig. 7 in that the leg angles of experiments are very close to those of simulations, but after one or two steps, their differences are observed.

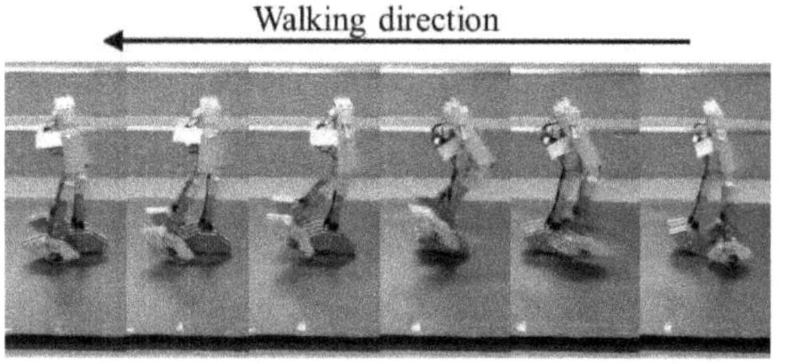

Fig. 8. Snapshots of walking demonstration

Finally, Fig. 8 represents the snapshots of the walking demonstration. Fig. 8 shows the serial photograph of one step of the case of $A_m = 1.35\text{rad}$ and $t_0 = 0.090s$. Some movies of walking demonstrations are available at [16].

5. Conclusion

Parametric excitation-based inverse bending gait has been realized on level ground by modifying the previous biped real robot. The experimental results were compared with numerical results. These results can be summarized as follows:

(1) The modification of the developed robot makes the gait generation based on parametric excitation principle on flat and firm ground without the experimental road consisted of a rubber sheet and a shock absorbing material.

(2) Introducing the bending time by detecting heel strike improves walking speed and enlarges step size.

(3) The experimental results were in good agreement with the numerical results, and the validity of the numerical was verified.

In the future, the parametric excitation-based walking on slope or uneven ground will be realized. In addition, reference trajectory where forward bending walking can be generated will be designed and the resultant walking compared with inverse bending walking.

We conclude the paper by giving remarks on the semicircular feet. Reference [13] has shown that a semicircular foot has two advantages, such as, a rolling effect corresponding to ankle torque and the reduction of dissipation energy at heel strike, and hence, many robots with semicircular feet have been developed. But a robot with semicircular feet has a difficulty in that the robot cannot stand upright stance. To overcome this and simultaneously to realize energy efficiency, [17, 18] have proposed a robot with flat feet and ankle springs, [19] has proposed a robot with inerter in ankle joints. The primal purpose of the paper was to realize the parametric excitation walking with a real robot, and hence, we adopted the most simple foot configuration in the developed robot.

References

[1] T. McGeer, "Passive dynamic walking," International Journal of Robotics Research, vol. 9, no. 2, pp. 62-82, 1990.

[2] A. Goswami, B. Espiau and A. Keramane, "Limit cycles in a passive compass gait biped and passivity-mimicking control laws," Journal of Autonomous Robots, vol. 4, no. 3, pp. 273-286, 1997.

[3] F. Asano, M. Yamakita and K. Furuta, "Virtual passive dynamic walking and energy-based control laws," Proceedings of the IEEE International Conference on Robotics and Systems, Takamatu, Japan, vol. 2, pp. 1149-1154, 2000.

[4] S. Collins, A. Ruina, R. Tedrake and M. Wisse, "Efficient bipedal robots based on passive-dynamic walkers," Science, vol. 307, pp.1082-1085, 2005.

[5] E. Dertien, "Dynamic walking with dribbel," IEEE Robotics and Automation Magazine, vol. 13, no. 3, pp. 118-122, 2006.

[6] F. Asano, Z. W. Luo and S. Hyon, "Parametric excitation mechanisms for dynamic bipedal walking," Proceedings of the IEEE International Conference on Robotics and Automation, pp. 611-617, 2005.

[7] Y. Harata, F Asano, Z. W. Luo, K. Taji and Y. Uno, "Biped gait generation based on parametric excitation by knee-joint actuation," Robotica, vol. 27, no. 7, pp. 1063-1073, 2009.

[8] Y. Harata, F. Asano, K. Taji and Y. Uno, "Parametric excitation-based inverse bending gait generation," Robotica, vol. 29, no. 6, pp. 831-841, 2011.

[9] F. Asano, T. Hayashi, Z. W. Luo, S. Hirano and A. Kato, "Parametric excitation approaches to efficient bipedal walking," Proceedings of the IEEE/RSJ International Conference on Intelligent Robotics and Systems, pp. 2210-2216, 2007.

[10] T. Hayashi, F. Asano, Z.W. Luo, A. Nagano, K. Kaneko and A. Kato, "Experimental study of a parametric excited dynamic bipedal walker with counterweights," Proceedings of the IEEE/RSJ International Conference on Intelligent Robots and Systems, pp. 81-86, 2009.

[11] Y. Banno, Y. Harata, K. Taji and Y. Uno, "Development and experiment of a kneed biped walking robot based on parametric excitation principle," Proceedings of the 2011 IEEE/RSJ International Conference on Intelligent Robots and Systems, pp. 2735-2740, 2011.

[12] K. Taji, Y. Banno and Y. Harata, "An optimizing method for a reference trajectory of parametric excitation walking," Robotica, vol. 29, no. 4, pp. 585-593, 2011.

[13] F. Asano and Z.W. Luo, "Efficient dynamic bipedal walking using effects of semicircular feet," Robotica, vol. 29, no. 3, pp. 3512-365, 2011.

[14] Y. Harata, Y. Banno and K. Taji, "Parametric excitation based bipedal walking: control method and optimization," Numerical Algebra, Control and Optimization, vol. 1, no. 1, pp. 171-190, 2011.

[15] http://www.taica.co.jp/gel-english/

[16] http://www.uno.nuem.nagoya-u.ac.jp/~taji/index-e.html

[17] T. Narukawa, K. Yokoyama and M. Takahashi, "Numerical and Experimental Studies of Planar Passive Biped Walker with Flat Feet and Ankle Springs," Journal of System Design and Dynamics, vol. 4, no. 6, pp. 848-856, 2010.

[18] M. Wisse, D. G. E. Hobbelen, R. J. J. Rotteveel, S. I. Anderson and G. J. Zeglin, "Ankle springs instead of arc-shaped feet for passive dynamic walkers," Proceedings of IEEE-RAS International Conference on Humanoid Robots, pp. 110-116, 2006.

[19] Y. Hanazawa and M. Yamakita, "High-Efficient Biped Walking Based on Flat-Footed Passive Dynamic Walking with Mechanical Impedance at Ankles,"Journal of Robotics and Mechatronics, vol. 24, no. 3, pp. 498-506, 2012.

A new method to detect circles in images based on genetic algorithms

Navid Khalili Dizaji[1, *], Nazila Masoudi[1], Aidin Sakhvati[2]

[1]Department of Mechatronics Engineering, Tabriz Branch, Islamic Azad University, Tabriz, Iran
[2]Department of Electrical Engineering, Tabriz Branch, Islamic Azad University, Tabriz, Iran

Email address:
navidkhalili@yahoo.com (Navid K. D.), nazila_masudi@yahoo.com (Nazila M.), aidin_sakhavati@yahoo.com (Aidin S.)

Abstract: Object detection is one of the key issues in digital image processing. Over the years, many algorithms have been created for detecting meaningful objects on the image which are based on specific characteristics of object or complex mathematical methods. Circle detection is one of these types of methods. One of the best methods for circle detection on digital images and discussion of machine vision is the Hough transform. The Hough transform can be described as the transformation of a point in the x-y-plane to the parameter space. Parameter space can be defined by the shape of the object. Using the special character of each image in space, we are able to retrieve and extract the image circle. Importantly, this method is time consuming and a large amount of memory is required for the image. The undesirable features have reduced the popularity of this method. The idea of using genetic algorithm for detecting a circle in the picture is very attractive and functional. This method can be used in Robot Soccer, targeting systems and iris recognition. In this method, accuracy and speed are among important parameters. For example, in the case of robot, it should detect ball in monochromatic and sometimes crowded areas (due to accumulation of other bots around the ball). Using a genetic algorithm for circle detection on images, Hough transform weaknesses have been removed. It also increases the computation speed and accurate detection of circle. In this paper, the Hough transform method will be presented and then we will describe the process of implementing genetic algorithms to find a circle in the picture.

Keywords: Hough Transform, Image Processing, Digital Image

1. Introduction

A common problem in determining the location is the number or the orientation of specific objects in image. For example, it can be the determination of direct roads in aerial imagery. This problem can be solved using the Hough transform for these lines. Most interesting, objects have other forms such as circle, oval or any other shape. Despite the enhancement of Hough transform complexity along with increasing the number of parameters required to describe the desired shape, Hough ordinary transform can be used on any shapes [2].

Circular Hough transform algorithm is summarized as follows [2]:

1 Find the edges
2 For each edge point "Hough transform begins»
3 A circle of radius r centered at the edge point is drawn and all the coordinates the circumference of the circle passes will be increased.
4 Maximum points are found in the storage. "The Hough transform will be finished"
5 Found parameters (r, a, b) are determined on the original image in accordance to the maximum points.

2. Hough Transform for Circle Detection

2.1. Parametric Display

The Hough transform is described as the transformation of a point in the x-y-plane to the parameter space. Parameter space can be defined by the shape of the object. A straight line which passes the points of (x1, x1) and (x2, y2) in the x-y-plane is defined as follows:

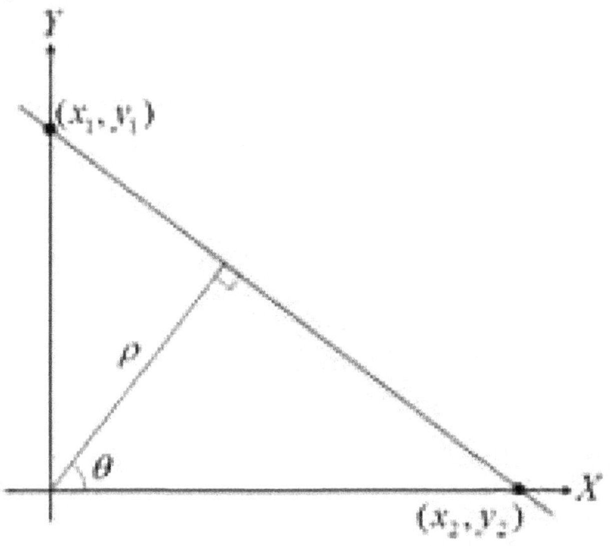

Figure 1. *Showing a line in Cartesian coordinates*

The relation is an equation for the straight line in a Cartesian coordinate system where 'a' and 'b' are the line parameters. Since the line perpendicular to the vector x has an infinite value leading to infinite volume of 'a' and 'b', the Hough transform of line does not use this relation. Instead of displaying the line as above, the line the parameter space can be displayed as below:

$$\begin{cases} a = -\dfrac{\cos\theta}{\sin\theta} \\ b = \dfrac{\rho}{\sin\theta} \end{cases} \Rightarrow y = \left(-\frac{\cos\theta}{\sin\theta}\right)x + \left(\frac{\rho}{\sin\theta}\right)$$

$$\rightarrow \rho = x.\cos\theta + y.\sin\theta$$

Equation 1. *Parameter space*

In this case, the parameter space includes and which is called limited volume

$$r^2 = (x-a)^2 + (y-b)^2$$

Equation 2. *limited volume*

Circle in Cartesian coordinates can be expressed as follows:

$$x = a + r.\cos\theta$$

$$y = b + r.\sin\theta$$

Equation 3. *Circle in Cartesian coordinates*

Compared to lines, circles in parameter space can be expressed more easily because circle parameters can be directly sent to the parameter space. In the above equation, 'a' and 'b' are coordinates of the circle center along the center line of 'x' and 'y'. 'r' is the radius of the circle. Parametric display of above equation is as follows:

It is clear that the parameter space of the circle is and the parameter space of the line is . With increasing the number of parameters required to describe the desired shape and the R size enhancement of the parameter space, the Hough transform complexity increases. To simplify the parameter space of the circle, the radius is recorded as a fixed number in this space [2].

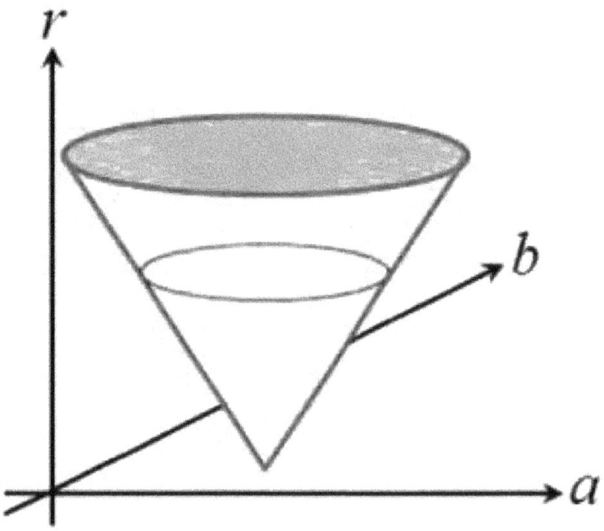

Figure 2. *The parameter space of the circle after the Hough transformation*

2.2. Storage

The process of finding the circle in an image using Hough transform is as follows:

First of all, all edges in the image are identified. It has no relevance to the Hough transform and all preferred technique of edge detection such as Sobel and Kenny can be used [3].

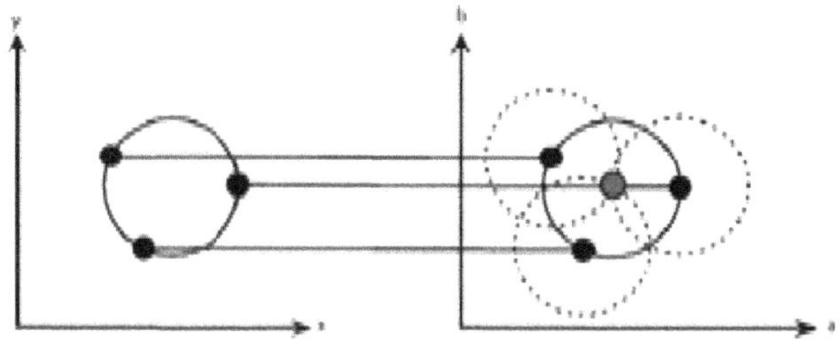

Figure 3. *Conversion of a circle from the x-y area (left) to the parameter space (right) for constant radius*

Furthermore, at each edge point, a circle centered at that point is drawn with desired radius. This circle is drawn in the parameter space in such a way that the x-axis, y-axis and z-axis model the components of 'a', 'b' and circle radius respectively. In coordinates which are drawn for the circumference of the circle, matrix storage value, which has equal sizes with parameters space, is increased. In this way, all edge points of the original image are investigated through drawing the circles with desired radius and increasing amounts in the storage. After that, the storage contains numbers presenting the number of passing circles from a unique coordinate. Therefore, the larger numbers which are selected intelligently based on the radius, correspond to the centers of the circles in the original image.

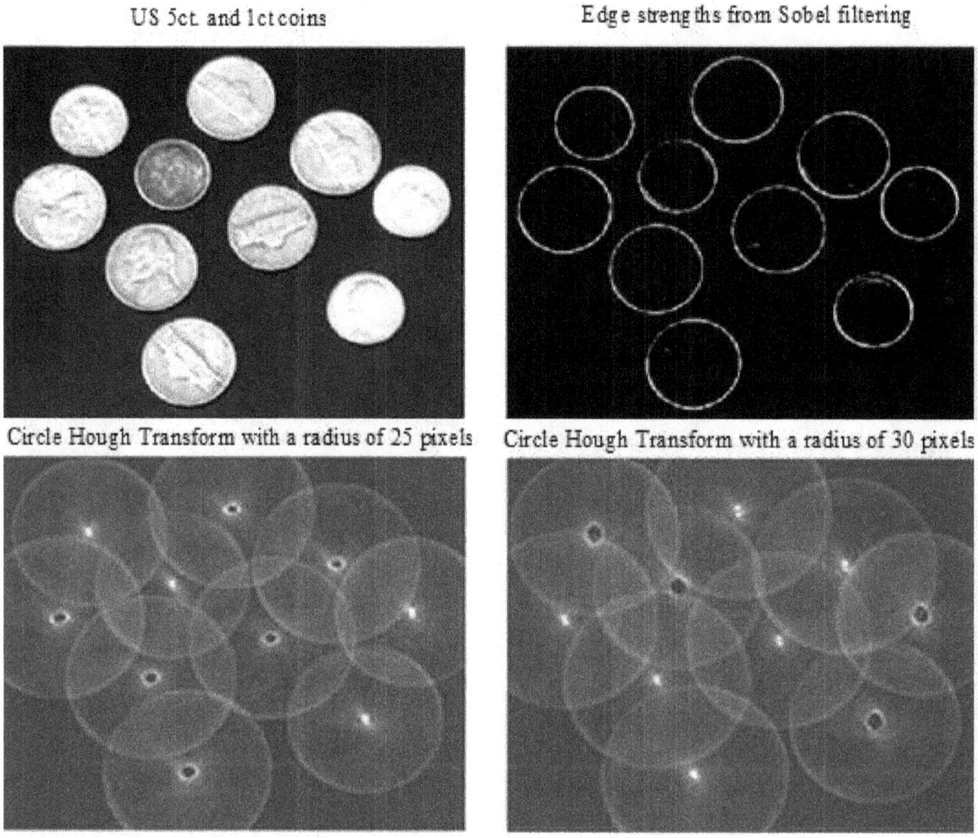

Figure 4. *Example of the storage operation using actual data which shows the Hough transform for two radius values*

2.3. Hough Transformation Algorithm

The process flow of Hough transformation algorithm is enumerated as below:

I. Find the edges
II. For each edge point "Hough transform begins»
III. A circle of radius r centered at the edge point is drawn and all the coordinates the circumference of the circle passes will be increased.
IV. Maximum points are found in the storage. "The Hough transform will be finished"
V. Found parameters (r, a, b) are determined on the original image in accordance to the maximum points.

3. Implementation

According to the algorithm presented in the previous section, the algorithm implementation can be conducted. However, before this, few points should be considered.

3.1. How can the Data be Stored

F If the radius is not fixed, the three-dimensional storage array can grow very fast in terms of stored data. The size of this array depends on the number of radius values and more importantly the size of the image. The computational cost to compute all the circles associated with the edge points will increase with the edge point's enhancement. The number of edge points is usually a function of image size. The calculation of total time of Hough transform for circles of large images with a lot of edge points can reach the unbridled amount of time rapidly.

3.2. How to Draw a Circle in the Discrete Space

A circle in the discrete space can be drawn using the Equation 3. However, the problem is. How to choose the discrete values with resolution of ? One solution is to use high resolution of and make the values rounded. But it may lead to draw the edge pixels more than once or, in the case of large radius values, it may lead to lack of pixels. The other solution is to round sine and cosine after multiplying the values by radius.

To ensure that all pixels are drawn, resolution of must be high. This will increase the computational cost. One method that can reduce computing cost is the quick calculation of values for sine and cosine functions using a lookup table. Although the discussed methods are feasible, but there are still better solutions [4].

Instead of using Equation 3, Bresenham's algorithm [4] can be used to draw a circle. The algorithm is designed to draw a line or a circle for a digital monitor. This algorithm has no problem in drawing a pixel more than once and it is appropriate for circular Hough transformation. An interesting feature of this algorithm is the determination of the pixels' actual number used to draw the circle. This information is appropriate when the center of the circle is to be found from the storage data.

3.3. How can the Circle be Found from the Hough Transform Data

Although this discussion is not related to the Hough transform, but it is useful for circles information extraction from the storage data. If there is no information about the number of circles and their radiuses, this process will be very cumbersome. One approach is to find the peaks of a and b planes each corresponding to a specific radius as shown in Figure 5.

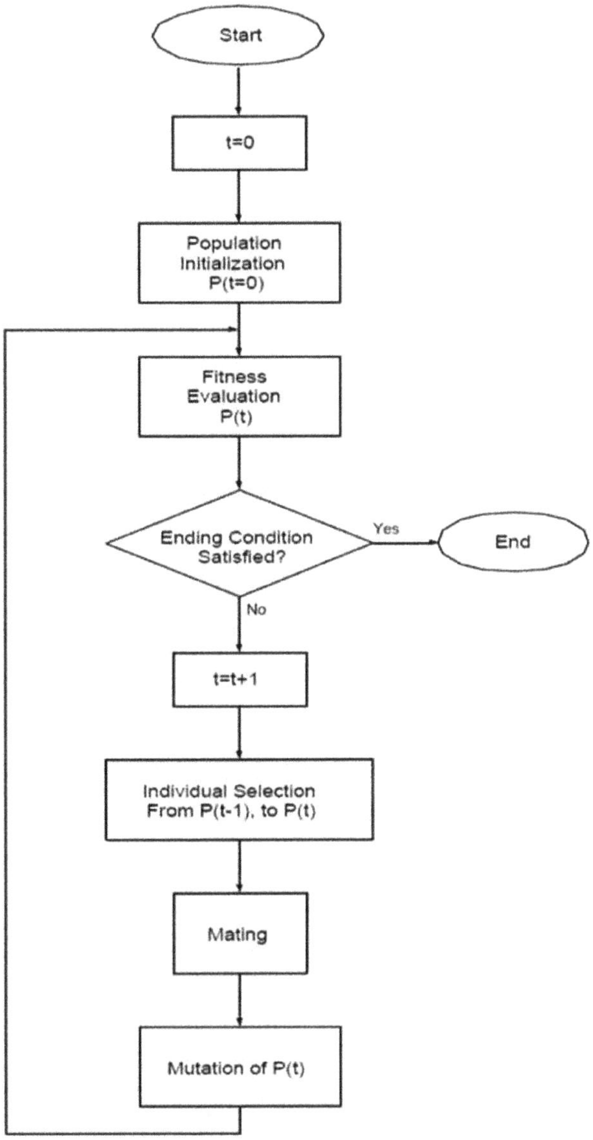

Figure 5. *Block diagram of a simple Genetic Algorithm (SGA)*

If the height of the peaks are equal compared to the number of edge pixels of the circle with a certain radius, peaks coordinates may correspond to the center of this circles. In the case of incomplete circle or oval shape, the center of the circle can be displayed with a height less than the number of the edge pixels. Eventually, if there is any difficulty in peaks determining, data storage can be paved.

4. Genetic Algorithm

Genetic Algorithm (GA) is a searching technique in computer science and artificial intelligence to find the optimal solution for the searching issues [5]. Genetic Algorithm is one of the Evolutionary Algorithms which is inspired by science of biology such as inheritance, mutation, sudden selection, natural selection and composition. It is briefly stated that Genetic Algorithm (GA) is a programming technique which uses genetic evolution as a model of problem solving. Most of the time, when the term of "struggle for survival" is used, its negative value comes to our mind. However, to rest assured, you can think that strongest was not always the winner. Despite their massive size and power, dinosaurs have ceded the survival game and having generation during a quite natural process, while much weaker creatures have continued their lives. It seems that the nature chooses the bests not only based on the size. In fact, it is more correct to say the nature chooses the fittest not the best. In the law of natural selection, having descendant is limited to some population's species which have the best features. Those who do not possess these characteristics will gradually disappear over time. For example, suppose a certain kind of people which are much more intelligent than the rest of the colony. In normal conditions, these people will improve more and have a relatively higher welfare. This welfare will lead to longer life and better reproduction. If intelligence is inheritable, the number of intelligent offspring will be more in the next generation of that community. If this trend continues, you will see that our sample population becomes smarter over the generations. In this way, a natural simple mechanism has managed to remove low-intelligent people of community. In addition, the average intelligence of community is constantly increasing [5].

Thus, we can see that the nature is able to improve each generation in terms of different features, using a simple mechanism; gradual elimination of undesirable species and reproduction of optimal species. The solutions are typically represented as binary 0 and 1, but there are other ways to display it. Evolution is started from a random set of entities and repeated in subsequent generations. In each generation, the fittest is selected not the best. One solution to this problem is shown by a list of parameters called chromosome or genome. Generally, chromosomes are displayed as a simple string of data. Other types of data structures can be used. At first, several features are produced randomly to create the first generation. During each generation, each feature is evaluated and the fitness value is calculated by fitness function. Typically the genetic algorithms have a number of possible connections which is between 0.6 and 1. It indicates the possibility of children creation. Organisms are combined together with this possibility. Two chromosomes connection creates the child which is added to the next generation. These are done until the appropriate candidates for response in the generation are emerged. The next step is to change the new children. Genetic algorithms have a fixed and small transition probability which is about 0.2 or less. Based on this possibility, child chromosomes are randomly changed or mutated.

The next step is to create a second generation of community. It is conducted by genetic operators (Chromosomes connected to each other and changed) based on the selection processes and production of selected features. For each individual, a pair of parents is selected. The selections are in such a way that the best elements are selected so that the weakest elements have the chance to be selected to prevent achieving the local response. This process creates a new generation of chromosomes which is different from previous generation. The whole process is repeated for the next generation. Pairs are selected for combination. The third generation population comes to existence and so on.

This process is repeated until we reach the last stage.

Terminating conditions of genetic algorithms include [5]

1 To reach a fixed number of generations.
2 Allocated funds to be finished (computation time / money).
3 One person (the produced child) to be found who meet minimum (lowest) criteria.
4 To reach the highest degree of children process and not to yield better results.
5 Manual inspection.
6 High combinations.

Figure 5 shows a flowchart of a simple Genetic Algorithm (SGA) [5].

Stored as a binary two level matrix. To extract the edges with the width of a pixel, Gaussian edge detection.

Figure 6 shows the Gaussian operator output for a gray image [6, 7].

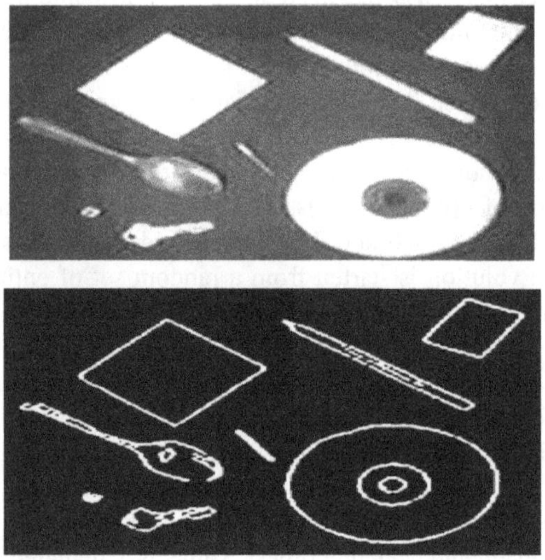

Figure 6. *Input image (upper) and a binary image of the Gaussian edge detection operator*

5. Circle Detection Using the Genetic Algorithm

According to the quadratic equation, each circle can be passed from three points in the image edge space. In simple terms, given the coordinates of three points, we can make a circle passing through it and extract the circle equation (If these three points have the potential to form a circle and not to be in a row). Preprocessed images have been used in our study. These images have been extracted by MATLAB and All edge points of the binary image should be stored in an array called v, with the following structure.

$$V = \{V\_1, V\_2, \ldots, V\_m\}$$

Equation 4. *Edage array*

Where 'm' is the total number of edge points in the image. It should be noted that the number of edge pixels in the image varies in accordance to the image size and texture. When listing the Edge values in the array V, the coordinates (x_i, y_i) of each edge pixel Vi should be stored in the edge vector. By changing any addresses form 1 to 'm' to a binary form and using three indicators of i_1, i_2 and i_3 for the edge points, the circle passing through the three points V_{i1} and V_{i2} and V_{i3} has the potential to detect circle in the image. A number of triple candidates which have the potential to solve circle is used for the initial population production in algorithm.

5.1. Type of Representation

Each individual circle can be revealed by three edge pixels on a chromosome (Figure 7). In this method, the address of edge points of the image in the genes is stored in accordance to it place in the edge array V (Figure 8). In this case, each chromosome has address of three edge points in the edge array V which are stored in three sequential genes.

$$(x - x_0)^2 + (y - y_0)^2 = r^2$$

Equation 5. *Genotype circle equation*

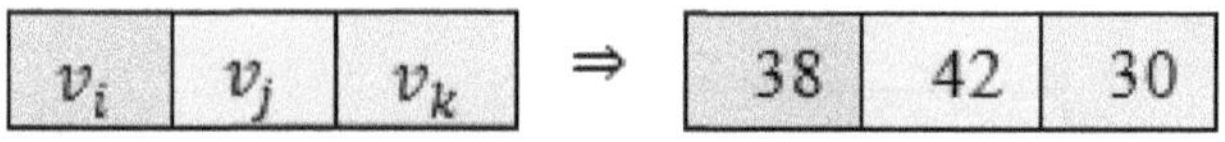

Figure 7. *A chromosome contains three gene to describe the circle edge pixel*

$$x_0 = \frac{\begin{vmatrix} x_j^2 + y_j^2 - (x_i^2 + y_i^2) & 2(y_j - y_i) \\ x_k^2 + y_k^2 - (x_i^2 + y_i^2) & 2(y_k - y_i) \end{vmatrix}}{4\left((x_j - x_i)(y_k - y_i) - (x_k - x_i)(y_j - y_i)\right)}$$

Equation 6. *Transformations X*

$$y_0 = \frac{\begin{bmatrix} 2(x_j - x_i) & x_j^2 + y_j^2 - (x_i^2 + y_i^2) \\ 2(x_k - x_i) & x_k^2 + y_k^2 - (x_i^2 + y_i^2) \end{bmatrix}}{4\left((x_j - x_i)(y_k - y_i) - (x_k - x_i)(y_j - y_i)\right)}$$

Equation 7. *Transformations Y*

According to the above equations, it can be called T transfer function with input edge indices of i, j and k.

	i	1	2	3	4	...	100
V=	v_i	v_1	v_2	v_3	v_4	...	V_m
		↓	↓	↓	↓	↓	↓
	$v(i,1)$	X=7	X=67	X=54	X=34	...	X=2
	$v(i,2)$	Y=5	Y=88	Y=55	Y=78	...	Y=44

Figure 8. *The number of each gene points out a cell address of the array V. The coordinates of the edge pixels are recorded in this cell.*

Each circle is coded to three edge points of the image. The phenotype surface of each circle is indicated by three parameters of X0 and Y0 and r. is coordinate of the center of the circle and r is circle radius. For conversion of Genotype to Phenotype, the following equations are used. In fact, center and radius of the circle passing through the three edge points are estimated using the following equation [8].

$$[x_0, y_0, r] = T(i, j, k)$$

Equation 8. *Transfer function*

With T transfer function, the circle of each chromosome in a discrete space can be easily estimated.

5.2. Fitness Function

To calculate the fitness of each chromosome, coordinates of the circle passing through the edge pixels of the chromosome should be computed using the T transfer function (equation 6, 7 and 8). Actually we should obtain three parameters of, and r. Then, coordinates of the edge points in V should be computed. The number of these points is designated as test set and shown as. Function of is a number of Matrix V points which apply in the coordinates of the circle passing through three points. Our goal is to make the C value close to the maximum value. The larger the value, the better the answer for circle candidate is. The optimization process can be stopped due to the number of generations or the threshold value of the fitness. With regard to the issue, each of these methods can be employed. In this paper, the number of generations is the stop condition of the algorithm [9, 10].

5.3. Selection Operator

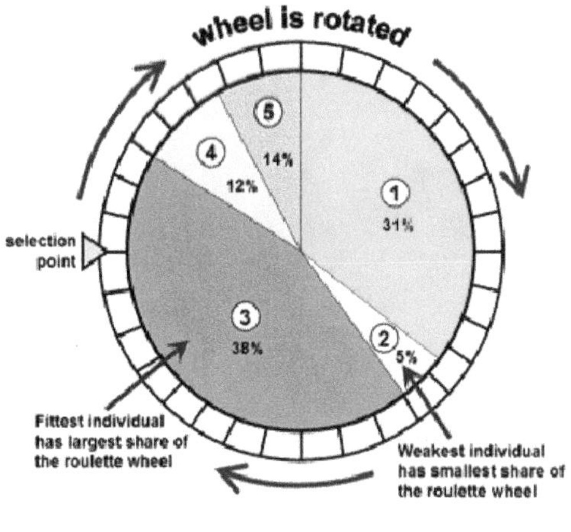

Figure 9. *The Roulette Wheel [8]*

At this stage, an appropriate number of paired chromosomes are selected based on their fitness level to be used in the next stage. Chromosomes with high fitness values can be selected several times during the production phase. Chromosomes with low fitness values may not be selected. For this step, the selection method of random pairs is used as a roulette wheel model of weighted ranking. In this model, the surface of wheel is divided into segments whose number is equal to the population members. The surface of each section is appropriate to the fitness value of each chromosome. Then the wheels circulate to be stopped in a point accidentally. This point specifies the selected chromosome. Figure 9 shows the roulette wheel.

This type of selection increases the number of optimal chromosomes in the population over time so that the average fitness value of the population increased compared to the past population.

5.4. Blending Operator

At this stage, cross operator acts on the parent chromosomes with Pc probability and produces new chromosomes with their combinations. In this paper, the single point blending is used.

5.5. Mutation Operator

In this paper, the mutation rate operator of 20% is used. In this step, the mutation is done on displacement chromosome with Pm probability. Each chromosome is randomly selected with a same probability and a random chromosome of V collection is substituted.

The following table shows the parameter values of the genetic algorithm for circle detection problem [10].

Table 1. *Parameters of the genetic algorithm for circle detection problem in an image*

Parameter	Value
Population size	100
Crossover probability	0.5
Mutation probability	0.2
Number of elite individuals	2
Selection method	Roulette wheel
Crossover method	Crossover
Population size	100

6. Discussion and Conclusion

In this paper, a method for detecting objects in images is proposed. To this end, the characteristics of the Hough transform method and genetic algorithm classifier are used. With improving the estimation method of initial points, a higher percentage of detection can be achieved. Another important issue is the dependence of the classification capabilities of the network to the collection combination of training images. For example, with a big number of images, the amount of output neurons will be reduced and it causes the output to be less than the threshold value in the images. In this regard, we can study the composition of the sample. The feature selection can also help to improve process because, in this method, all features of feature extraction phase have been used.

In some cases, where the preprocessing is done in windows with linear functions, weights convolution of the input layer of genetic algorithm with image can be used to speed up.

References

[1] Tahir Rabbani and Frank van den Heuvel,"Efficient Hough transform for automatic detection of cylinders in point clouds." in Proceedings of the 11th Annual Conference of the Advanced School for Computing and Imaging ,The Netherlands, June 2005.

[2] Just Kjeldgaard Pedersen, Simon," Circular Hough Transform." Aalborg University, Vision, Graphics, and Interactive Systems. November 2007.

[3] B. Jahne, H. Scharr, and S. Körkel, "Principles of filter design,"In Handbook of Computer Vision and Applications. Academic Press, 1999.

[4] Bresenham, J. E. (1), "Algorithm for computer control of a digital plotter," IBM Systems Journal, pp25–30 January 1965.

[5] Bies, Robert R, Muldoon, Matthew F., Pollock, Bruce G, Manuck, Steven, Smith, Gwenn, Sale, Mark E, "A Genetic Algorithm-Based, Hybrid Machine Learning Approach to Model Selection,"Journal of Pharmacokinetics and Pharmacodynamics, pp 196–221, 2006.

[6] G. Eason, B. Noble, and I. N. Sneddon, "On certain integrals of Lipschitz-Hankel type involving products of Bessel functions," Phil. Trans. Roy. Soc. London, vol. A247, pp. 529–551, April 1955.

[7] G. Kendall and G. Whitwell, "An evolutionary approach for the tuning of a chess evaluation function using population dynamics," In Proceedings of the 2001 Congress on Evolutionary Computation, pp 995–1002. IEEE Press, World Trade Center, Seoul, Korea, 2001.

[8] Shah, S.M.; Thaker, C. S, Singh, D, " Multimedia based fitness function optimization through evolutionary game learning,"Emerging Trends in Networks and Computer Communications (ETNCC), 2011 International Conference, page(s): 164- 168,2011.

[9] H.A.Rowley, S.Baluja, T.Kande, "Rotation invariant neural network-based face detection," Computer Science Technical Report, CMU-CS-97-201, CMU, Pittsburgh, 1997.

[10] H.Schneiderman, "T.Kande. Probabilistic modeling of local appearance and spatial relationships for object recognition,"IEEE Conference on Computer Vision and Pattern Recognition, 45-51, Santa Barbara, 1998.

[11] T.K.Leung, M.C.Burl, P.Perona. "Finding faces in cluttered scenes using random labeled graph matching," International Conference on Computer Vision, p: 637-644, Cambridge, MA, 1995.

A discrete-time quasi-theoretical solution of the modified Riccati matrix algebraic equation

Tahar Latreche

Magistère in Civil Engineering, B.P. 129 Salem Lalmi, 40003 Khenchela, Algeria

Email address:
latrache.tahar@yahoo.ca

Abstract: In this paper, based on MacLaurin's series and the Riccati equation, an algebraic quadratic equation will be developed and hence, its two roots, which represent the minimizing and maximizing optimal control matrices, would be deducted easier. Otherwise, a step-by-step algorithm to compute the control matrix for every step of time according to the preceding responses and a new signal pick will be explained. The proposed method presents a new discrete-time solution for the problem of optimal control in the linear or nonlinear cases of systems subjected to arbitrary signals. As an example, a system (structure) of three degrees of freedom, subjected to a strong earthquake is analyzed. The displacements versus time and the stiffness forces versus displacements of the system, for the two uncontrolled and controlled cases are graphically shown. Therefore, the curves of variations of the elements of the optimal control matrix versus discrete-time are also presented and clearly show the effect of the nonlinearity, of the system, which is the cause of the great responses in the uncontrolled case, and that it is optimally treated by the proposed solution. The results obtained clarify a great reduction of the controlled system results, in comparison with the uncontrolled system ones. The percentage of the differences between the controlled and uncontrolled results (displacements or stiffness forces) could even surpass 90 %, which demonstrates that the adopted solution is good even than that of the original ones of the differential or the algebraic Riccati equation.

Keywords: Optimal Control, Modified Riccati Equation, Quasi-Theoretical Solution, Discrete-Time Algorithm, Nonlinear Systems

1. Introduction

It is well known that the QR is a widely used method for the optimal control of systems in engineering analysis and design practices. The method indeed, is based on the determination of the optimal control matrix, which is practically and optimally reduce the effect of the signals for which the systems are subjected. Moreover, the interest to resolve the Riccati matrix equation is appear clarify in the literature since decades, and several simple or complex algorithms are proposed [1-15 and17-23], an iterative algorithm [18], a numerical algorithm using the iterative Newton-Raphson method [1], an algorithm and a software using the Eigen-solution [6], an iterative algorithm using the iterative Newton method [8] and a step-by-step algorithm for the resolution of the differential Riccati equation [12], present some from which is published in this domain.

Otherwise, based on the matrix algebraic equation of Riccati and the MacLaurin's series, a quadratic algebraic equation will be developed, such that its two roots which represent the closed-loop minimize and maximize optimal control matrices will be deducted easily. The deducted control matrices are computed for every so small step of time and for a given system proper matrices (deducted from the previously step of time). Therefore, the step-by-step algorithm proposed, means that the system behaves linearly during every step of time; but changing its properties from step to step in terms of the responses computed previously, so actually the proposed algorithm could be considered as a nonlinear algorithm and resolve nonlinear problems, such that the results of this method stretching well to the exact solution as-well-as the time step taken should be refined as possible.

As testing numerical example, to demonstrate the efficiency of the proposed method, a nonlinear structure of three degrees of freedom, subjected to El-Centro earthquake was analyzed, in the two uncontrolled case and controlled one using the proposed method. The curves of the responses and the acted stiffness forces on every degree of freedom show the great reductions of the results in the case of the controlled structure, compared with the others of the same uncontrolled one. Moreover, the variations of the optimal control matrix elements versus time are also shown.

Firstly, we start in the second section to transform the classical Riccati algebraic equation to a quadratic one, and therefore, we deduct in the third section, the two quasi-theoretical minimize and maximize optimal control matrices and force vector. The fourth section is appearing in the numerical example to present the results which could the proposed method offers. The following sections dealing with the explanation of results and the conclusion.

2. The Transformation of the Riccati Equation

The state space formulation of a controlled dynamic system is stated by the ordinary differential equation

$$\dot{Z}(t) = A(t)Z(t) + Bf_e(t) + Bf_c(t) \quad (1)$$

Where, $f_c(t)$ is the controlled force vector deducted after computing the optimal control matrix, $f_e(t), Z(t), A(t), B$ are respectively, the seismic force vector, the state space response vector, and the state space matrices, given by

$$f_e(t) = -M\Gamma a_g \qquad Z(t) = \begin{Bmatrix} U(t) \\ \dot{U}(t) \end{Bmatrix}$$

$$A(t) = \begin{bmatrix} 0 & I \\ -M^{-1}K(t) & -M^{-1}C(t) \end{bmatrix} \qquad B = \begin{Bmatrix} 0 \\ M^{-1} \end{Bmatrix}$$

I represents the unity matrix, Γ a unity vector and a_g the ground acceleration.

Suppose that the optimal control matrix $P(t)_{2n\times 2n}$ (such that n represents the number of the structure's degrees of freedom), is related by

$$P(t) = \lambda(t)Z^{-1}(t) \quad (2)$$

By differentiating the Hamiltonian function we conclude the vector relations

$$\begin{cases} \dot{\lambda}(t) = -A^T(t)\lambda(t) - Q(t)Z(t) \\ \dot{Z}(t) = -BR^{-1}B^T\lambda(t) + A(t)Z(t) \\ f_c(t) = -R^{-1}B^T\lambda(t) = -R^{-1}B^TP(t)Z(t) \end{cases} \quad (3)$$

Expressions, such that $R_{n\times n}$ and $Q_{2n\times 2n}$ represent the weighting matrices.

The first equation of the expressions (3) can be rewritten, after replacing $\lambda(t)$ by its expression (2), and differentiating according to t

$$\dot{P}(t)Z(t) + P(t)\dot{Z}(t) = -A^T(t)P(t)Z(t) - Q(t)Z(t) \quad (4)$$

Replacing $\dot{Z}(t)$ by its relation (3) and simplifying by $Z(t)$, we can getting then

$$\dot{P}(t) - P(t)BR^{-1}B^TP(t) + P(t)A(t) = -A^T(t)P(t) - Q(t) \quad (5)$$

Therefore, the differential matrix equation of Riccati, could be concluded as following

$$\dot{P}(t) = P(t)BR^{-1}B^TP(t) - P(t)A(t) - A^T(t)P(t) - Q(t) \quad (6)$$

Assuming that $\dot{P}(t) = F(P) = 0$, hence we could write

$$F(P) = PBR^{-1}B^TP - PA - A^TP - Q \quad (7)$$

According to MacLaurin's series, the equation (7) would be developed as follows

$$F(P) = F(0) + F_{,P}(0)P + F_{,PP}(0)\,P^2/2 \quad (8)$$

$$\begin{cases} F(0) = 0BR^{-1}B^T0 - 0A - A^T0 - Q = -Q \\ F_{,P}(0) = BR^{-1}B^T0 + 0BR^{-1}B^T - (A + A^T) = -(A + A^T) \\ F_{,PP}(0) = 2BR^{-1}B^T \end{cases} \quad (9)$$

Replacing $F(0)$, $F_{,P}(0)$ and $F_{,PP}(0)$ by their values (9), we get hence

$$\dot{P}(t) = BR^{-1}B^TP^2(t) - \big(A(t) + A^T(t)\big)P(t) - Q(t) \quad (10)$$

The solution of the differential equation (10) couldn't indeed extends a minimize solution, because is appearing as a mixed solution, and to separate between the minimize and maximize solutions we suppose that $\dot{P}(t) = 0$. Therefore, the following algebraic equation will be deducted

$$BR^{-1}B^TP^2 - (A + A^T)P - Q = 0 \quad (11)$$

This equation represents a transformation of the matrix algebraic equation of Riccati. Therefore, the two roots of this equation represent clearly and optimally the minimizing and maximizing solutions. These roots of this equation could then be deducted easier as it is will be demonstrated in the following section for every step of time and in terms of the proper matrices of the system, computed by the step which precedes.

3. The Optimal Control Matrices and Force Vector

The two matrix roots of the above equation (11), are given by the following expressions, which are represent the minimize and maximize optimal control matrices respectively

$$\begin{cases} P_1(t) = [2BR^{-1}B^T]^{-1}\left[\big(A(t) + A^T(t)\big) - \left[\big(A(t) + A^T(t)\big)^2 + 4BR^{-1}B^TQ(t)\right]^{1/2}\right] \\ P_2(t) = [2BR^{-1}B^T]^{-1}\left[\big(A(t) + A^T(t)\big) + \left[\big(A(t) + A^T(t)\big)^2 + 4BR^{-1}B^TQ(t)\right]^{1/2}\right] \end{cases} \quad (12)$$

Otherwise, the matrix $BR^{-1}B^T$ couldn't have an inverse such that it has the form

$$BR^{-1}B^T = \begin{bmatrix} 0 & 0 \\ 0 & M^{-1}R^{-1}M^{-1} \end{bmatrix} \quad (13)$$

Therefore, we should to proceed approximately. The proposed approximation procedure can be stated as follows

The square matrix $(BR^{-1}B^T+I)^2$ could be developed by the relation

$$(BR^{-1}B^T+I)^2=(BR^{-1}B^T)^2+2BR^{-1}B^TI+I^2$$

Multiplying lefty the two sides of this equation by the term $(BR^{-1}B^T)^{-1}$, we get

$$(BR^{-1}B^T)^{-1}(BR^{-1}B^T+I)^2=BR^{-1}B^T+2I+(BR^{-1}B^T)^{-1}I^2$$

After simplification, this equation becomes

$$(BR^{-1}B^T)^{-1}[(BR^{-1}B^T+I)^2-I^2]=BR^{-1}B^T+2I$$

The matrix $[(BR^{-1}B^T+I)^2-I^2]$ has the same form as $BR^{-1}B^T$, and couldn't also have an inverse. Approximately, we propose to take the term μI instead of I^2, such that the coefficient μ is a, as possible, stretching to the unity but not equals the strictly unity. According to the precision of the computer and/or the programming language used, we can take μ precise as possible. For example we can take $\mu=0.9999999999999999$. Then we can get approximately

$$(BR^{-1}B^T)^{-1}=[BR^{-1}B^T+2I][(BR^{-1}B^T+I)^2-\mu I]^{-1} \quad (14)$$

Replacing $(BR^{-1}B^T)^{-1}$ by its expression (14) in the two matrix roots (12), the minimize and maximize optimal control matrices which should to be computed for every step of time are then becomes

$$\begin{cases} P(t)=0.5[BR^{-1}B^T+2I][(BR^{-1}B^T+I)^2-\mu I]^{-1} \\ \left[(A(t)+A^T(t))-\left[(A(t)+A^T(t))^2+4BR^{-1}B^TQ(t)\right]^{1/2}\right] \\ P(t)=0.5[BR^{-1}B^T+2I][(BR^{-1}B^T+I)^2-\mu I]^{-1} \\ \left[(A(t)+A^T(t))+\left[(A(t)+A^T(t))^2+4BR^{-1}B^TQ(t)\right]^{1/2}\right] \end{cases} \quad (15)$$

The matrix $\left[(A(t)+A^T(t))^2+4BR^{-1}B^TQ(t)\right]^{1/2}$ can be computed using the iterative method [16], supposing that

$$X^2-\left[(A(t)+A^T(t))^2+4BR^{-1}B^TQ(t)\right]=0$$

Such that X is the matrix square root needed.

The optimal control matrix is computed in terms the system proper matrices computed from the preceding step, such that they are in turns following the system nonlinearity laws in function of the responses computed. The optimal control forces acted to every degree of freedom of the system, for any step of time, are ranked in the vector of the third equation (3) in terms of the last step responses.

Therefore, the proposed method is summarized, for every step of time, in the following steps:

1. Computing the proper matrices of the system, according to the previously results (responses)
2. Computing, according the case, the minimize or the maximize optimal control matrix
3. Deducting the optimal control force vector and adding it to the new exterior force vector
4. Resolving the ordinary differential state space equation of the system to get the responses of this step of time
5. According to the results found from the step (4.), starting a new loop with a new step of time

4. Numerical Example

The chosen numerical example, for the evaluation of the efficiency of the proposed method to reduce optimally the results of the systems subjected to arbitrary signals, is imitated in a structure of three degrees of freedom with concentrates masses at the level of every degree of freedom, and subjected to the Modified El-Centro Earthquake. The stiffness behavior of the material, which the structural elements has been fabricated, is assumed to be following a bilinear model, for which it consists of two branches, an elastic branch with the stiffness equals k_e and a plastic branch such that the stiffness equals k_p. The mass, stiffness and damping matrices for the chosen structure are given by

$$M=\begin{bmatrix} m & 0 & 0 \\ 0 & m & 0 \\ 0 & 0 & m \end{bmatrix} \quad K=\begin{bmatrix} k_1 & -k_1 & 0 \\ -k_1 & k_1+k_2 & -k_2 \\ 0 & -k_2 & k_2+k_3 \end{bmatrix}$$

$$C=\alpha M+\beta K$$

$m=1\,kg$ and $k_{1\,or\,2\,or\,3}$ can take the values: $k_e=25\,N/m$ (for the elastic linear branch) and $k_p=k_e/3$ (for the plastic branch), α and β represent the Rayleigh damping coefficients which are given in terms of the frequencies of the linear elastic structure ω_1 and ω_2 and the damping coefficient ξ. Assuming that the damping coefficient $\xi=0.05$, then

$$\beta=0.1\,(\omega_2-\omega_1)/({\omega_2}^2-{\omega_1}^2)=0.006559$$

$$\alpha=\omega_1\omega_2\beta=0.368488$$

The elastic limit displacement, with which the material stiffness transferring from the elastic to the plastic branch, is chosen to be equals $0.025\,m$, this limit indeed, that deciding if the proper structural stiffness and damping matrices changing or no from any step of to another. The ground acceleration variations are shown in Figure 1, such that the step of time separates two peaks is $0.02\,s$. The weighting matrices are chosen to be giving by

$$R=\begin{bmatrix} 0.1 & 0 & 0 \\ 0 & 0.1 & 0 \\ 0 & 0 & 0.1 \end{bmatrix} \quad Q=\begin{bmatrix} 0 & 0 \\ 0 & -MRM(CM^{-1})^2 \end{bmatrix}_{6\times 6}$$

The displacements curves of the three floors (degrees of liberty), for the two uncontrolled and controlled cases, versus time are shown by the Figure 2, 3 and 4. The hystereses of the stiffness forces acted on the three degrees of freedom versus the displacements variations are clarified by the three figures 5, 6 and 7. To show the effect of the nonlinearity behavior of the system, some of the optimal control matrix elements variations versus time are be clearing in figures 8, 9, 10 and 11.

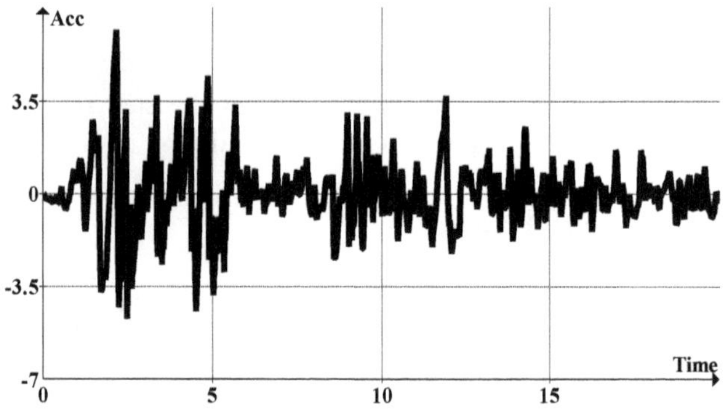

Figure 1. *The acceleration of the ground* (m/s^2)

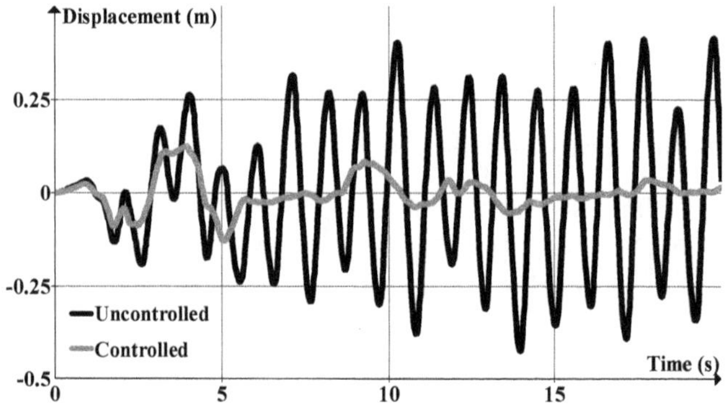

Figure 2. *The first floor displacement vs. time*

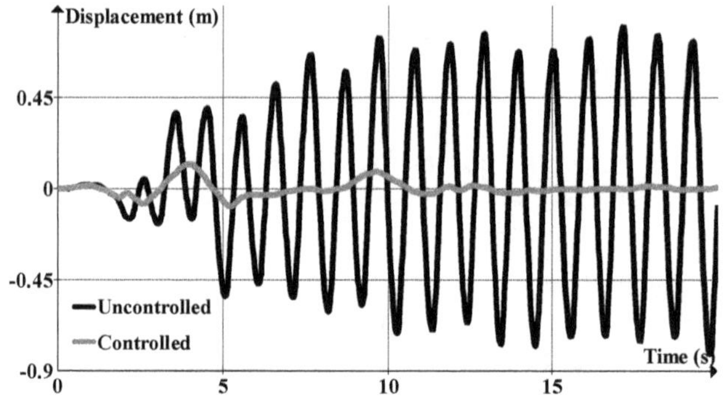

Figure 3. *The second floor displacement vs. time*

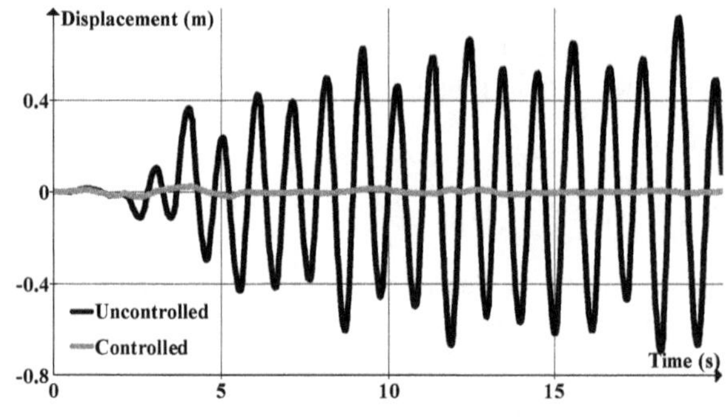

Figure 4. *The third floor displacement vs. time*

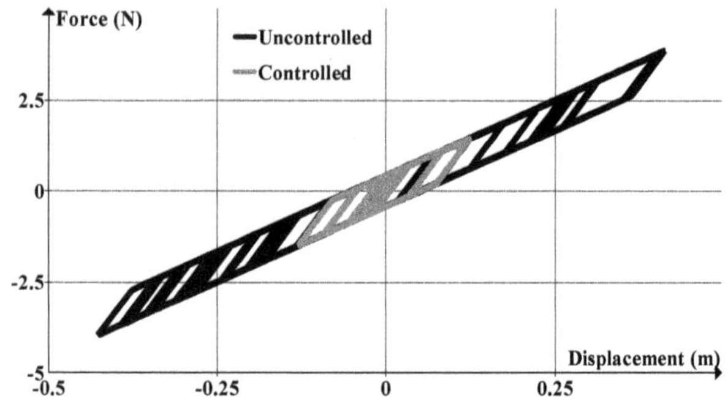

Figure 5. *The first floor stiffness force vs. Displacement*

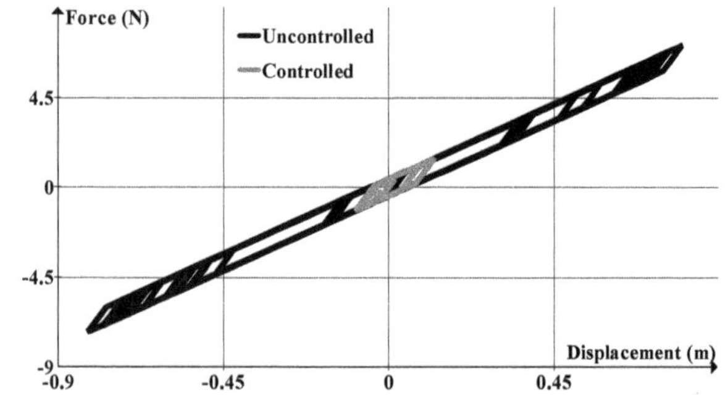

Figure 6. *the second floor stiffness force vs. displacement*

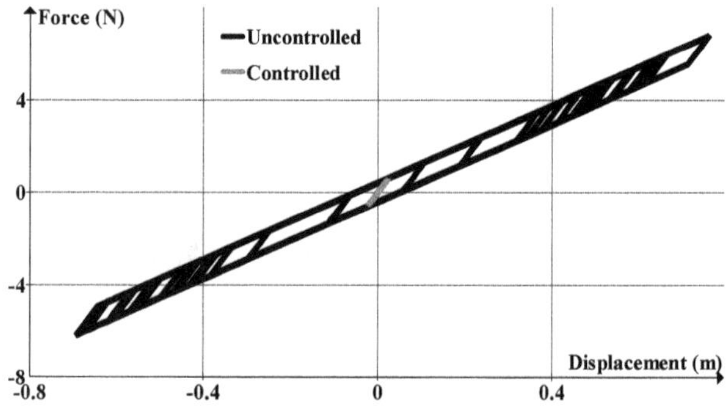

Figure 7. *The third floor stiffness force vs. displacement*

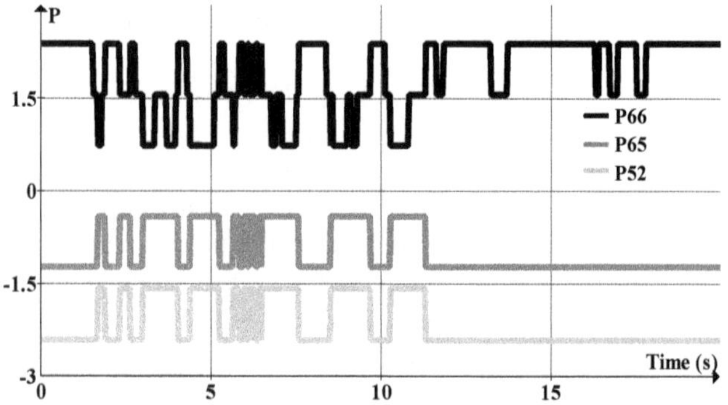

Figure 8. *The P66, P65 and P52 elements of the optimal control matrix*

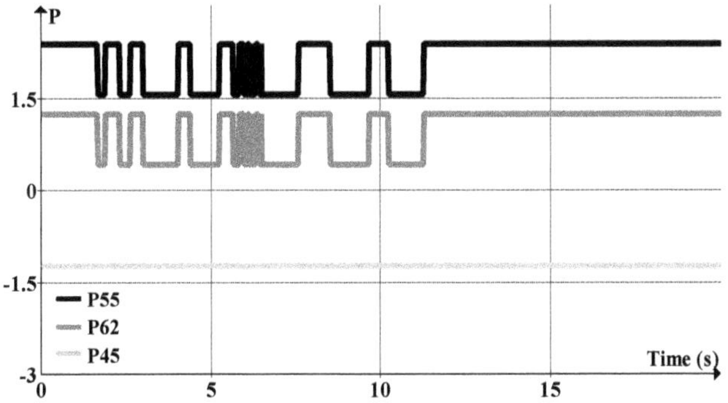

Figure 9. *The P55, P62 and P45 elements of the optimal control matrix*

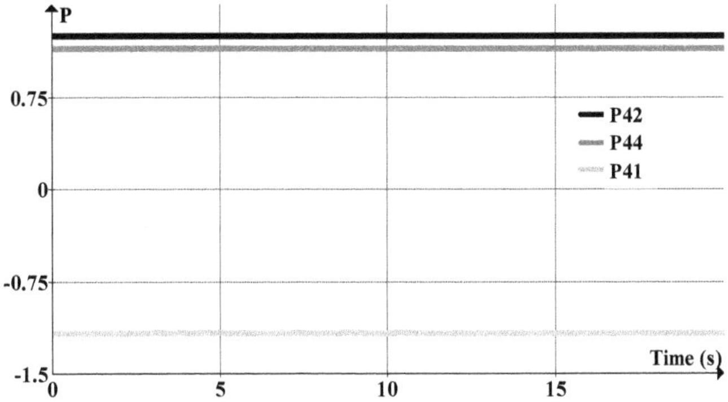

Figure 10. *The P42, P44 and P41 elements of the optimal control matrix*

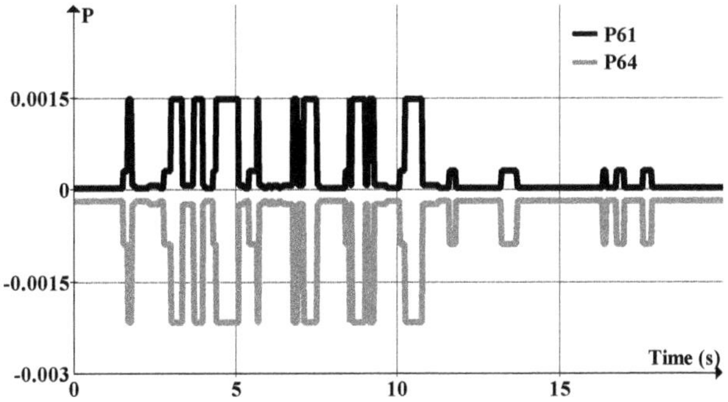

Figure 11. *The P61 and P64 elements of the optimal control matrix*

5. Results and Discussion

By perceiving of the figures 2, 3 and 4 and Table1, we can remark the grand differences between the displacements of the three floors of the analyzed structure. Despite that the analyzed structure is subjected to a so strong earthquake, and the uncontrolled responses are so considerable (40 to 80 cm), we can see that the controlled responses are so moderate (3 to 13 cm) despite the fact that the elastic displacement adopted is so small too (2.5 cm), and the percentage of the differences of the three degrees of freedom displacements has being about 71 %, 85 % and 97 % from the first to the third degree of freedom respectively. The differences between the stiffness forces, for the uncontrolled and controlled cases, are also considerable, such that we can observe, by the examination of the figures 5, 6, 7 and Table 2, that the stiffness forces for the uncontrolled case are fluctuate between 4 N and 7.2 N, while these forces for the controlled case, alternate between 0.6 N and 1.5 N, and such that the percentage of the differences are ranged between 62 % and 92 % for the first and the third degree of freedom.

Table 1. *The maximal Uncontrolled, Controlled displacements and their fraction*

Floors	Uncontrolled max. displacements	Controlled max. displacements	% Cont./Uncont.
1	0.426	0.124	29.11
2	0.816	0.121	14.83
3	0.763	0.024	3.15

Table 2. *The maximal Uncontrolled, Controlled forces and their fraction*

Floors	Uncontrolled max. forces	Controlled max. forces	% Cont./Uncont.
1	3.968	1.493	37.63
2	7.218	1.418	19.65
3	6.774	0.566	8.36

6. Conclusion

The proposed method could be summarized in determining firstly, the minimize and maximize optimal control matrices (according the case) which are the matrices roots of the quadratic equation developed herein and secondly, to compute the roots by a discrete-time algorithm which aimed to evaluate the optimal control matrix for every step of time according to the nonlinear behavior of the analyzed system which in turn (the behavior of the system), is a function of the previously responses (the displacements and velocities in the case of structural engineering). This proposed method of the optimal control of systems subjected to arbitrary signals indeed, possesses the ability to offer a good control and a so sufficiently results. Furthermore, the method allows the analysis of nonlinear systems (i.e. real systems), because it is resolved for every step of time and according to the state of the system. The figures 8-11, clearing show the effect of the nonlinearity of the structure adopted as an example, on the variations of the optimal control matrix.

The results (displacements and stiffness forces curves) of the proposed example show the efficiency of the getting solution. As it is seen by the figures and tables, the controlled results are very considerably reduced, which can surpass 90 % of percentage of the differences between uncontrolled and controlled displacements and acted stiffness forces. In spite that the ground motion acceleration are very high, and this effect is shown by the uncontrolled structure responses; but the controlled results are too moderate and sufficiency, and for the third floor, the element was not plasticized even as shown by Figure 7, despite that the limit elastic displacement adopted is very small.

These excellent controlled results indeed, demonstrate the effect of the optimal control of structures using the Quadratic Regulator method, and the obtained solution of the optimal control matrix formulated and the effect of the nonlinear behavior of the system adopted.

References

[1] H. M. Amman, H. Neudecker, "Numerical solutions of algebraic Riccati equation", J. of Economic Dynamics and Control, no. 21, pp. 363 - 369, 1997.

[2] B. D. O. Anderson, J. B. Moore, *Linear optimal control.* Prentice-Hall, 1971.

[3] B. D. O. Anderson, J. B. Moore, *Optimal Filtering.* Prentice-Hall, 1979.

[4] B. D. O. Anderson, J. B. Moore, *Optimal control, linear quadratic methods.* Prentice-Hall, 1989.

[5] Y. Arfiadi, *Optimal passive and active control mechanisms for seismically excited buildings.* PhD Thesis, University of Wollongong, 2000.

[6] W. F. Arnold, A. J. Laub, "Generalized eigenproblem algorithms and software for algebraic Riccati equations", Proceedings of IEEE, vol. 72, no. 12, 1984.

[7] A. Astolfi, L. Marconi, *Analysis and design of nonlinear control systems.* Springer Publishers, 2008.

[8] P. Benner, J-R. Li and P. Thilo, "Numerical solution of large-scale Lyapunov equations, Riccati equations, and linear-quadratic optimal control problems", Numerical Linear Algebra with Applications, no. 15, pp. 755 – 777, 2008.

[9] D. L. Elliott, *Bilinear control systems.* Springer Publishers, 2009.

[10] P. H. Geering, *Optimal control with engineering applications.* Springer Publishers, 2007.

[11] M. S. Grewal, A. P. Andrews, *Kalman Filtering: Theory and practice.* John Wiley, 2008.

[12] L. Grune, J. Pannek, *Nonlinear model predictive control.* Springer Publishers, 2011.

[13] A. Isidori, *Nonlinear control systems 2.* Springer Publishers, 1999.

[14] P. L. Kogut, G. R. Leugering, *Optimal control problems for practical differential equations on reticulated domains.* Springer Publishers, 2011.

[15] T. Latreche, "A discrete-time algorithm for the resolution of the Nonlinear Riccati Matrix Differential Equation for the optimal control", American J. of Civil Engineering, no. 2, pp. 12-17, 2014.

[16] T. Latreche, "A numerical algorithm for the resolution of scalar and matrix algebraic equations using Runge-Kutta method", Applied and Computational Mathematics, no. 3, pp. 68-74, 2014.

[17] A. Locatelli, *Optimal control: an introduction.* Birkhäuser Virlag, 2004.

[18] T. K. Nguyen, "Numerical solution of discrete-time algebraic Riccati equation", Website: http://www.ictp.trieste.it/~pub-off

[19] A. Preumont, *Vibration control of active structures: An Introduction.* Kluwer Academic Publishers, 2002.

[20] I. L. Vér, L. L. Beranek, *Noise and vibration control engineering.* John Wiley, 2006.

[21] S. L. William, *Control system: Fundamentals.* Taylor and Francis, 2011.

[22] S. L. William, *Control system: Applications.* Taylor and Francis, 2011.

[23] S. L. William, *Control system: Advanced methods.* Taylor and Francis, 2011.

5

Color image encryption by code image and hill algorithm

Ali Moradmard*, Mohammad Tahghighi Sharabiani

Department of Computer Engineering, Islamic Azad University, Zanjan Branch, Zanjan, Iran

Email address:
a.moradmard@gmail.com (A. Moradmard), mtahghighi@yahoo.com (M. T. Sharabiani)

Abstract: Today in a digital world, protection of information plays an essential role in message exchange and trading. Encryption is used to meet the security needs of safe transaction. Regarding the importance of the issue and the shift of traditional stage to digital stage, familiarity with encryption methods seems necessary. Different data have different methods of encryption. Images are also one type of data for which encryption is critically needed to prevent impermissible access. In this article, first a primary image is selected, then, based on the proportion of the image needing encryption, pixels from code image are picked and is being encrypted by a function. In the next stage, this proportion is being XOR-ed by the pixel proportion of the image needing encryption, and eventually the final proportion is encrypted by Hill Algorithm. MATLAB software has been used for studying the project, and efficiency of this method, in comparison to Hill Algorithm as a standard algorithm, is investigated. At the end, maintaining the image quality after decryption is evaluated by standards such as PSNR and SSID. The results indicate high efficiency of this method.

Keywords: Hill Algorithm, Security, Image Encryption, Efficiency

1. Introduction

A safe data exchange between source and target has al-ways been one of the big challenges in data transmission. The challenge seems more serious whenever the confidentiality of transmitted data is higher. One of the important data in information transmission is digital images. Transmitted images can have military, trading, or even medical applications, but regardless of the field, the security and preventing impermissible access of images is indisputable [1,12].

With the growth of social networks, huge data such as audio files, video files, and images can easily be transmitted to the internet. Therefore it is necessary to protect them from impermissible access. One way of keeping secret data transmission secure is encryption. Encryption, in fact, is the knowledge of changing message body or information by the help of a code key and an encryption algorithm so that only the person who knows keys and algorithm can extract the original information from encrypted information; and a person who does not know one or both cannot have access to them. Regarding image properties, especially high volume of images data, using encryption methods such as RSA [2], DES [3], and AES [4] are not directly applicable for image encryption, because encryption of high volume of image data via above methods is very time-consuming and practically is impossible in immediate usages. On the other hand, we face with the problem of key length in these methods. Since there is a high volume of encrypted data, using a key with a limited length leads to method vulnerability against the attacks of cipher text. To overcome the problems, many articles have been written about the image encryption in which the necessity of changes in the preliminary structure of the provided algorithms is admitted. However the methods are different due to images types.

Generally, images can be divided into many types like gray-scale and color images. Images are composed of units called pixels. Each pixel can show 256 different surfaces, which means an interval of 0 to 255. These surfaces are so-called image brightness. Gray scale images are composed of one matrix. Each house of this matrix saves one number inside. While color images are composed of three color matrix: red, green, and blue. Each pixel gains its own color by mixing these three colors. The encrypted images in this paper are color images.

Encryption Algorithm is divided into two types, symmetrical and asymmetrical. In symmetrical algorithm two sides of sender and receiver use the same key for encryption and decryption [5, 6]. In this case, data decryption and encryption are two reverse processes.

In this article, first we produce a random matrix to the number of transmitted image pixels by the help of provided encrypted image algorithm, and then, by using extended Hill Algorithm we complete the encryption. To have the best form of encryption, we used all three layers (red, green, blue) and their solidarity in forming the final image caused more encryption of it. Visual analysis, quality analysis, and Histogram analysis have been used for evaluation of the provided method. The analysis results confirm the quality improvement of encrypted image by the proposed algorithm in comparison to the Hill Algorithm.

The research history and literature will be mentioned in the second section. In the third section definitions and the methods used will be discussed. The proposed algorithm will be in the fourth section and section five will include analyzing the proposed algorithm. Section six, the results and findings of the research are discussed.

2. Literature

According to literature about encryption, the history of the science goes back to 1900 B.C. Based on available documents, an Egyptian expressed pictorial texts by unusual images. But most works in digital encryption images have been done in 1990s [7]. Different image encryptions can be divided into two main groups [8]:

a) Chaotic encryption method

b) Non-chaotic encryption method

In most works done by the previous studies, the proposed encryption algorithm could only be implemented on some special formats such as BMP, JPG, TIFF, and just a few of them were applicable for different formats of images.

Kuang TsanLin [1] proposed using Fourier method an image encryption method for transmitting an image between the source and target. Xiaofeng Liao [9] used sound waves for image encryption. In this method the image had been dividing into two parts in which the first part used the other for image encryption. C. J. Tay [10] used two methods for image encryption. In the first method, they separated different parts of color image, which means three layers of red, green, and blue by special lenses, and each of them was encrypted by a special method. In the second method, the image is divided into two parts, image matrix and color map, and color map is encrypted by proposed method. Yicong Zhou [11] used Fibonacci series to image encryption and pixel displacement and compared its quality to original image after decryption by SSIM method. Xingyuan Wang [12] used chaotic function to encrypt color images and simultaneously encrypted all three matrix of red, green, and blue color and showed that the relationship between these three color factors brings about resistance against different attacks.

3. Definition and Methods

In this article, Hill Algorithm will be explained shortly and finally a proposed algorithm for image encryption based on Hill Algorithm will be illustrated.

3.1. Hill Encryption

Hill encryption was introduced by Lester Hill [13] to encrypt text in 1929. The core of encryption was using a matrix for multiplication in numerical equivalent in order to change it to a code and using inverse matrix (as a key) for decryption of numerical equivalent of the text. In the picture below, assuming 3*3 encrypted matrix, mathematical operations of encryption and decryption are shown.

3.1.1. Encryption Stages in Hill

In this example, we assumed that the matrix is 3*3. The procedure of encryption is based on Figure 1.

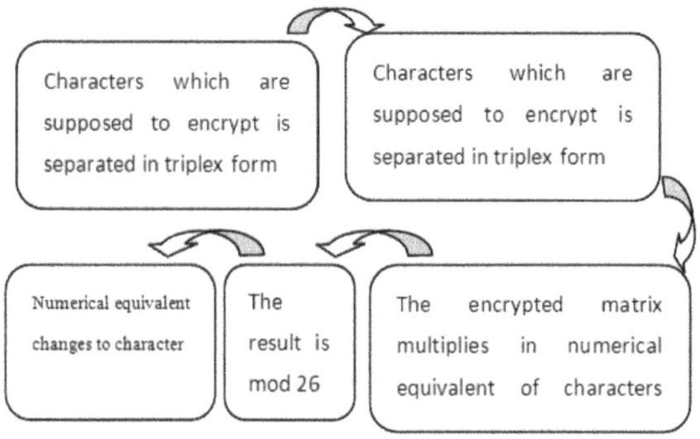

Figure 1. Encryption stages in Standard Hill.

$$\begin{pmatrix} c1 \\ c2 \\ c3 \end{pmatrix} = \begin{pmatrix} 17 & 17 & 5 \\ 21 & 18 & 21 \\ 2 & 2 & 19 \end{pmatrix} \begin{pmatrix} 15"p" \\ 0"A" \\ 24"Y" \end{pmatrix} = \begin{pmatrix} 375 \\ 819 \\ 486 \end{pmatrix} Mod26 = \begin{pmatrix} 11 \\ 13 \\ 18 \end{pmatrix} = "LNS"$$

As it was shown in formula (1), three first letters of (PAY) changed to three letters (LNS) after encryption.

3.1.2. Decryption Stages in Hill

Now the procedure of decryption in the source based on the same matrix 3*3 will be explained. The procedure can be seen in Figure 2.

$$\begin{pmatrix} p1 \\ p2 \\ p3 \end{pmatrix} = \begin{pmatrix} 4 & 9 & 15 \\ 15 & 17 & 6 \\ 24 & 0 & 17 \end{pmatrix} \begin{pmatrix} 11"L" \\ 13"N" \\ 18"S" \end{pmatrix} Mod26 = \begin{pmatrix} 15"P" \\ 0"A" \\ 24"Y" \end{pmatrix}$$

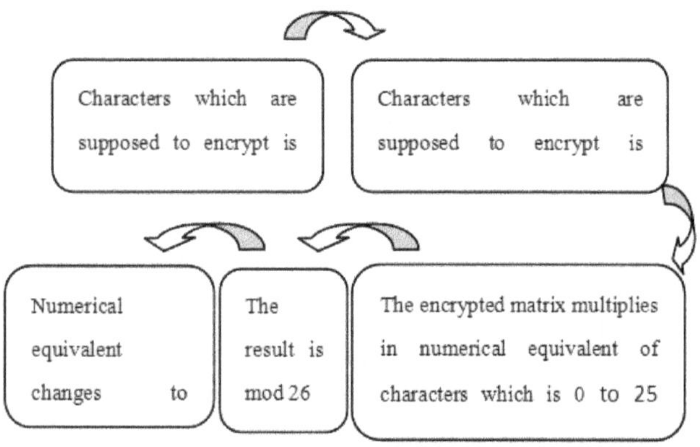

Figure 2. Decryption stages in Standard Hill

3.2. Using Encrypted Image Matrix

In this method, first an image will be shared between sender and receiver as a key. Now we select pixels from this picture (key) according to the number of pixels of the image which we want to encrypt.

Then, it will convert to the original encrypt picture by the mentioned equation.

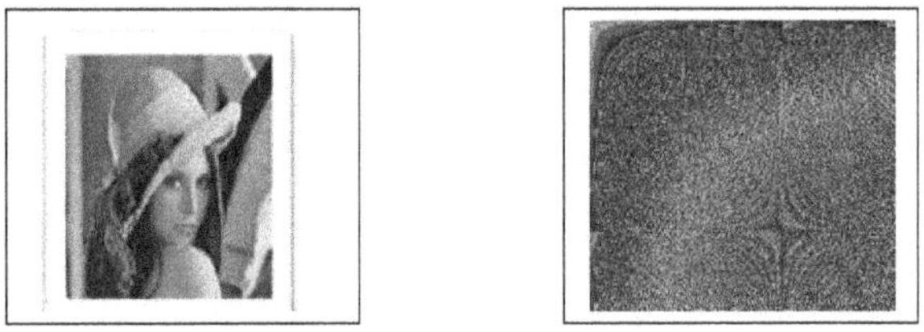

Figure 3. *Encrypted image Lena*

4. The Proposed Algorithm

In the proposed algorithm, first an image will be shared between the sender and receiver. Then, the image we want to encrypt is XOR-ed by key image. In the stage of pixel changing for image encryption, numerical equivalence of pixels in all three levels (blue, red, green) must be multiplied by encrypted matrix. In this article, we used the same multiplication matrix 3*3, and one pixel of each layer has been selected for encryption, and this number will be put instead of numerical equivalent in Hill method.

In Figure 4, you can see peppers image after encryption by preliminary Hill Algorithm by matrix 3*3. Some parts of the encrypted image are not uniform in this encryption, and the primary image is visible in the encrypted one.

Since one of the important factors in encryption quality is image uniformity after decryption, we propose some solutions to improve it.

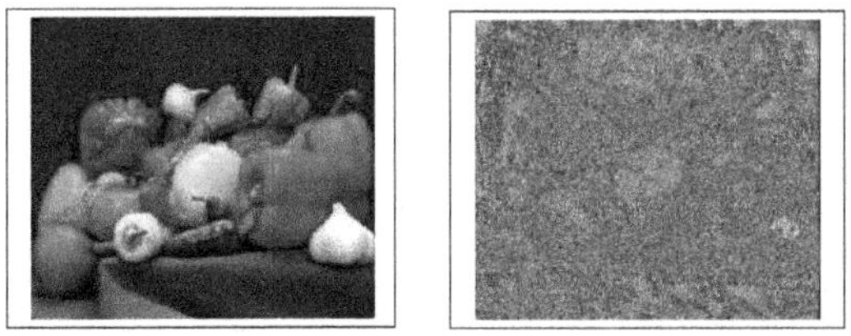

Figure 4. *Primary and encrypted image by Standard Hill Algorithm*

In Figure 5, the spots which were not completely encrypted has been shown in Hill Algorithm, were well covered by the proposed algorithm.

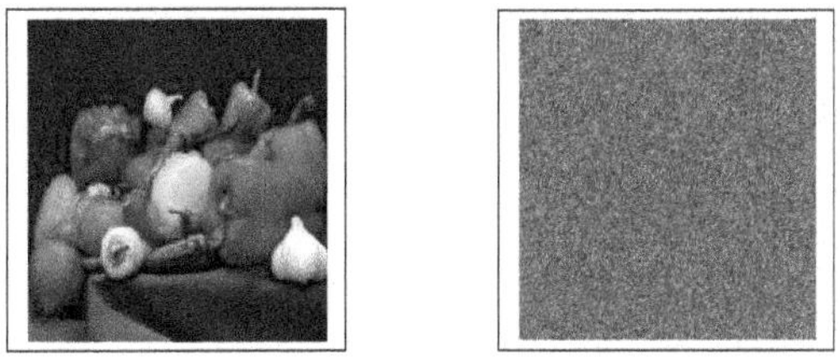

Figure 5. *Primary and encrypted image by the proposed algorithm.*

5. Efficiency Analysis (Result Evaluation)

5.1. Visual Analysis

In this section, to have a better comparison of the two mentioned methods, we used images in which adjacent pixels are very similar to each other because Hill Algorithm has a high efficiency drop in this condition [14] and we can have a better evaluation.

By the help of proposed combined method in this article, it was shown in the visual test that images which were encrypted just by Hill method are largely recognizable Figure 6, but some improvements can be seen in the visual test after using the proposed combined algorithm Figure 7.

Figure 6. *Decrypted image by Standard Hill algorithm.*

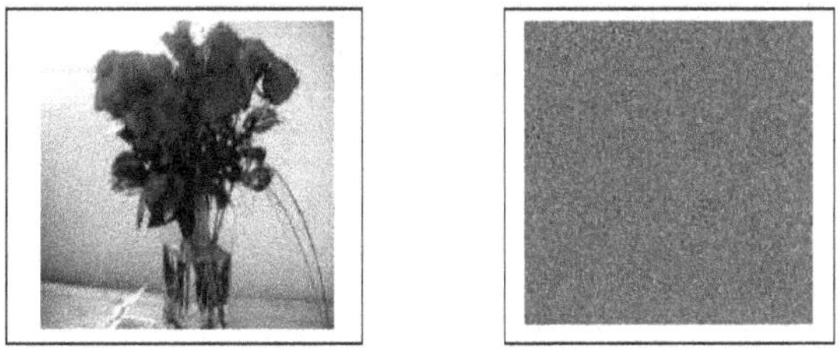

Figure 7. *Decrypted image by the proposed algorithm.*

5.2. Histogram Analysis

One of the most important image encryption principles to avoid information leakage and invaders' attack is that there should not be any statistical similarities between the encrypted image and the original image. Using repetition rate of each pixel in the image, Histogram analysis shows the distribution manner of pixels in it. [15] The more uniformity in the chart surface would bring about the more dispersion of the pixels. The peppers image, which is among available images on MATLAB, has been used for the test. The Histogram comparison of encrypted image (Fig.8) with the original image (Fig.9) shows that these two pictures are totally different and there is no statistical similarity between them. Finally, the comparison of decrypted image with the original image shows the quality of decrypted image.3

Table 1. *The features of quality analysis*

	Image	PSNR	MSE	SSID
1	Encrypted image(Lena)	11,08	5,06	0,09
2	Original image(Lena)	43,29	3,04	0,99
3	Encrypted image(peppers)	10,47	5,82	0,08
4	Original image(peppers)	39,42	6,76	0,99
5	Encrypted image(Flowers)	9,97	6,54	0,19
6	Original image(Flowers)	45,86	1,68	0,99

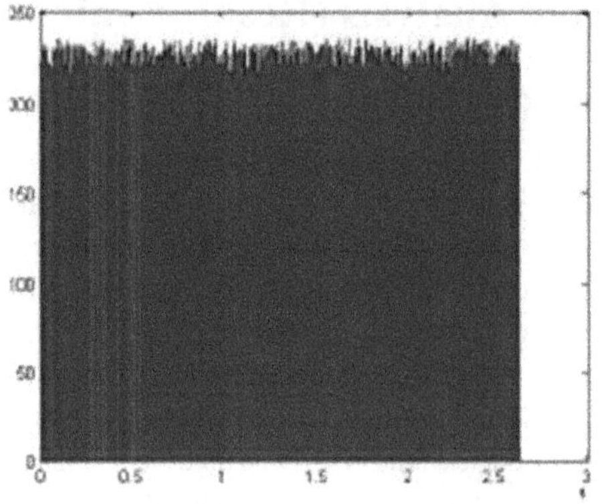

Figure 8. Histogram of the encrypted image.

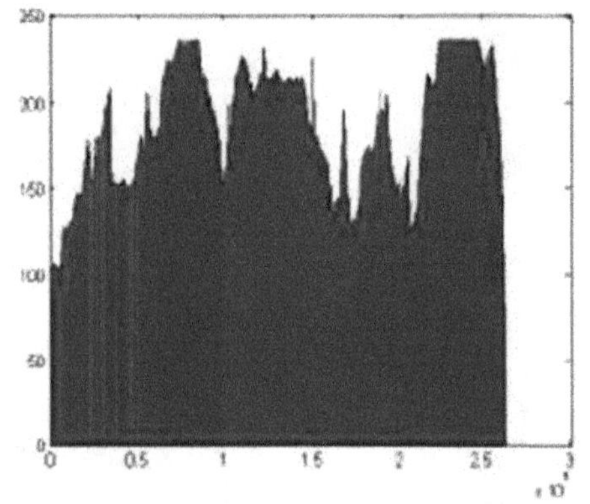

Figure 9. Histogram of the original image.

5.3. Quality Analysis

The measure of quality change between the encrypted image and original image:

Structural similarity (SSIM), proposed by Wang [16], is a quality test to measure the similarities between two images. Peak signal-to-noise ratio is used to calculate quality change between two images and two images are more similar to each other when the number is closer to 50 [16].

For testing the similarity between two images in both methods of quality analysis, MATLAB is used.

6. Discussion and Conclusion

In this article, a simple and efficient way for image encrypting by the use of Hill Encryption Algorithm was proposed. In this method, first the original image with N*M pixels was XOR-ed to N*M size by created pixels by produced values of a shared image between the sender and receiver, and the result was encrypted by Hill Algorithm. In Hill Algorithm, pixels values were used for encryption (each time, one red layer, one green layer, and one blue layer). The selected image, with regard to the relationship of these pixels for making related pixel, was encrypted. Three tests named visual test, Histogram analysis, and quality change algorithms were used to compare the original image and decrypted image (PSNR, SSID) and the result of visual test showed an improvement in encrypted images via proposed method comparing to the previous method. Moreover, in evaluating Histogram analysis, there was no similarity between the original image and the encrypted image. In the encrypted image quality test, there is a little difference between the images after decryption comparing to the original images.

References

[1] Kuang Tsan Lin, " Binary encoding method to encrypt Fourier-transformed", information OF 15th Annu. Conf. IEEE EMBS, pp. 778-780, 1993.

[2] R.L. Rivest, A. Shamir, and L. Adleman, "A Method for Obtaining Digital Signatures and Public-Key Cryptosystems", Communications of the ACM, pp.120-126, 1978.

[3] Eli Biham, Adi Shamir, "Differential cryptanalysis of DES-like cryptosystems", Springer, Volume 4, Issue 1, pp.3-72, 1991.

[4] Joan Daemen, Vincent Rijmen, "The Design of Rijndael: AES The Advanced Encryption Standard", Springer, p.238, February 2002.

[5] R.Kusters and MTuengerthal, "Universally Composable Symmetric Encryption", 2nd IEEE Computer Security Foundations Symposium (CSF '09), pp. 293-307, July 2009.

[6] H Jin, Z.Liao, D.Zou, and C.Li, "Asymmetrical Encryption Based Automated Trust Negotiation Model", The 2nd IEEE International Conference on Digital Ecosystems and Technologies (DEST 2008), pp.363-368, Feb. 2008.

[7] Shiguo Lian, "Multimedia Content Encryption Techniques and Applications", CRC Press,p.3.

[8] Ratinder Kaur, V. K. Banga, "Image Security using Encryption based Algorithm", International Conference on Trends in Electrical, Electronics and Power Engineering (ICTEEP'2012) Singapore, July 15-16, 2012.

[9] Xiaofeng Liao, Shiyue Lai, Qing Zhou, "A novel image encryption algorithm based on self-adaptive", Digital Signal Processing Principles, New York Macmillan, 1992.

[10] C.J. Tay, C. Quan, W. Chen, Y. Fu, "Color image encryption based on interference and virtual optics", Optics & Laser Technology, pp. 409–415, 2010.

[11] Yicong Zhou, Karen Panetta, SosAgaian, C.L. Philip Chen," Image encryption using P-Fibonacci transform and decomposition","Optic s Communications", 285 (2012) 594–608

[12] Xingyuan Wang, Lin Teng, Xue Qin, "A novel colour image encryption algorithm based on chaos", Signal Processing, pp.1101–1108, 92 (2012).

[13] Lester S. Hill, "Cryptography in an Algebraic Alphabet", The American Mathematical Monthly" ,Vol.36, pp. 306–312, June–July 1929.

[14] J.Zillami and D. G. Manolakis, "Encryption Based On Advance Hill, Algorithms and Applications", New York Macmillan, 2008.

[15] Ahmed A. Abd El-Latif, Li Li, Ning Wang, Qi Han, Xiamu Niu, "A new app roach to chaotic image encryption based on quantum chaotic system, exploiting color spaces Signal Processing", Volume 93, pp.387-397, 2013.

[16] Z. Wang, A.C. Bovik, H.R. Sheikh, E.P. Simoncelli, " Image Quality Assessment: From Error Visibility toStructural Similarity", Transactions on Image Processing IEEE, pp.600-612, 13 (2004).

Automatic Persian text summarizer using simulated annealing and genetic algorithm

Elham Mahdipour, Masoumeh Bagheri

Computer Engineering Department, Khavaran Institute of Higher Education, Mashhad, Iran

Email address:
Mahdipour@khi.ac.ir (E. Mahdipour), M_bagheri3000@yahoo.com (M. Bagheri)

Abstract: Automatic text summarization is a process to reduce the volume of text documents using computer programs to create a text summary with keeping the key terms of the documents. Due to cumulative growth of information and data, automatic text summarization technique needs to be applied in various domains. The approach helps in decreasing the quantity of the document without changing the context of information. In this paper, the proposed Persian text summarizer system employs combination of graph-based and the TF-IDF methods after word stemming in order to weight the sentences. SA-GA based sentence selection is used to make a summary, and once the summary is created. The SA-GA is a hybrid algorithm that combines Genetic Algorithm (GA) and Simulated Annealing (SA). The fitness function is based on three following factors: Readability Factor, Cohesion Factor, and Topic-Relation Factor. Evaluation results demonstrated the efficiency of the proposed system.

Keywords: Automatic Text Summarization, Stemming, TF-IDF, Genetic Algorithm, Simulated Annealing

1. Introduction

Nowadays with increase of information, users need to have access to effective methods in order to search for the requested information. In most cases, people study the summary of a document rather than the whole. Automatic text summarization is a solution for this issue. Automatic text summarization is a process to reduce the volume of text documents; using computer programs to create a text summary with keeping the key points and important documents. This approach shortens the information content of a text file while preserving the original contents [1].Summarizing large documents is a difficult task for human. One approach to respond to the cumulate growth of information is to use automatic text summarization to decrease the volume of information and increase speed of accessibility to important notes.

Research studies on automatic text summarization started at mid-1950s [2] and is an old challenge that needs attention of text mining researchers in the field of computational intelligence, machine learning and natural language processing, and various methods such as neural networks, decision trees, semantic graphs, regression models, fuzzy logic, swarm Intelligence [3]. Research studies show that the content of summaries depends on the input source, nature of the text, purpose and target of readers. Overall automatic text summarization consists of three main steps: 1) identifying keywords of the document as well as the most important pieces of information in the text; 2) interpreting the content of the document, extracting two or more topics, then combining them to one or more concepts; 3) creating a good summary with formulating the extracted sentences and combining them with the concepts [2].

In this paper we have proposed Phoenix Summarizer for development of Parsina summarizer [2, 4] and designed for improving the quality of text extraction. This paper is structured as follows. Section 2 introduces concepts of summarization. In section 3, the previous automatic text summarizer is reviewed. In section 4, the proposed automatic text summarization system, known as Phoenix, is introduced. Section 5 evaluates the proposed Phoenix system. Finally in section 6, the results and comparison of Phoenix and Parsina text summarization systems are discussed.

2. The Concepts of Automatic Text Summarization

The important factors in text summarization include: input factors, output factors, and target factors [5, 6].

Input factors are listed as follow:

1 Input form, such as:
   a. Length of input text: short text (1 or 2 pages), long text (more than 50 pages).
   b. Text structures: text structures that impact on text process such as: paragraph, entity, and predicate.
   c. Text language: such as single language and multiple languages.
   d. Text type: such as single document or multiple documents.

2 Text topic, such as:
   a. Normal text: the subjects have vast knowledge domain such as scientific, sport, and farming.
   b. Special text: the topics depend on knowledge of reader such as computer and medical.
   c. Limited text: the special topics pertain to organization or society such as news and technical reports.

Output factors are listed as follow:

1 Content: this factor pertains to normal summary or response, extracted summary or abstract. Also when summary is normal, content included the most important information.
2 Format: text format may be having figures, tables, diagrams and etc.
3 Style: summary style can be predication or advisement.

The targets factors depend to field of application text and cause of summary and determined based on three factors:

1 Listeners: The level of listener's knowledge about the summary text field directly affects the results.
2 Conditions: the conditions or purpose determine means of the summary. When summary field is vast and identified, can remove the details.
3 Application: Depending on the application of the summary, the approach for creating summary text could change. As an example, will the summary be used for retrieving the whole text? Or is it a replacement for the input text? Or it could even be an overview of a reviewed document. In general terms, the application could be divided into public and interrogative categories.

In Addition, the summarizer system can be divided into three categories: [7]:

1 Category based on form and organization: Overall summaries based on form and organization can be divided into extraction and abstract. In extraction, summary based on statistical information of text, determination of the important sentences, and selection of the most important items to create the summary. The abstract methods attend to relationship between difference parts of text, terms concepts and semantics. For large documents, using extraction methods are easier and more flexible. However, the results might be incoherent and un-related. On the other hand, the abstract method presents the summary of important parts and key points. In this method the compress rate is high due to summary hint to the content of text. Also, the resulting text would be coherent. Therefore abstract systems are stronger than extraction systems.
2 Category based on process level: we can divide summaries based on process level to superficial and deep categories. The superficial method, displays information based on superficial properties such as statistical conditions, place conditions, terms, and special domain. The summaries of this category are created by extraction method. The deep methods, employs natural language processing and needs to perform semantic analysis such as syntax and semantic relationships. The summary of this category creates combination of extraction and abstract methods.
3 Category based on addressee: the summaries based on addressee could be divided into three categories: public, based on query, and special topic. Purpose of public summary is for widespread society of readers and generally all topics are important. The application of summary based on query is related to one question such as "what is the cause of incidence?". The purpose in special topic summary is the user revenue and emphasis on special topic or single document and multiple document categories, or single language and multiple language categories.

2.1. Summarization Methods

There are many methods for text summarization such as information retrieval (IR) [6], clustering [8], graph theory [9], machine learning [10], Latent semantic analysis [6], and TF-IDF [2, 11]. We describe TF-IDF methods because the proposed system uses this because it is easy and accurate. Also the combination of TF-IDF and graph based methods is more applicable.

The TF-IDF weighting system is used with some adoptions which is similar to IR model. TF-ISF weights are computed for each sentence (equation (1) and (2)), where $tf_{i,j}$ is term frequency of ith index term in the jth sentence, and isf_i is inverse sentence frequency of ith index term. Also N is the number of all sentences and n_i is the number of sentences which contain i^{th} index term [2, 11].

$$tf_{i,j} = \frac{freq_{i,j}}{\max_i freq_{i,j}} \quad (1)$$

$$isf_i = \log\frac{N}{n_i} \quad (2)$$

The corresponding weight is therefore computed as equation (3).

$$W_{i,j}=tf_{i,j}*isf_i \quad (3)$$

3. Related Works

Research studies in non-Persian languages domain considers challenges of automatic text summarization and related works to 2009 [3].

Some research studies improve the summarization by using fuzzy logic. As an example, in [12] summary sentences were extracted using fuzzy rules and sets. They extracted the important features for each sentence of the document represented as the vector of features consisting of the following elements: title feature, sentence length, term weight, sentence position, sentence to sentence similarity, proper noun, thematic word and numerical data. They had done experiments with 125 dataset, comparing our summarizer with Microsoft Word 2007 and baseline using precision, recall and f-measure built by ROUGE. The results show that the best average precision, recall and f-measure to summaries produced by the fuzzy method. Certainly, the experimental result is based on fuzzy logic could improve the quality of summary results that based on the general statistic method. In conclusion, they proposed that using combination of fuzzy logic and other learning methods and extract the other features could provide the sentences more important.

In another study an automatic multiple document text summarizers has been presented [13]. Research was first started naively on single document abridgement but recently information is found from various sources about a single topic in different website, journal, newspaper, text book, etc., for which multi-document summarization is required. In [13], automatic multiple documents text summarization task is addressed and different procedure of various researchers are discussed. They compared various techniques that have done for multi-document summarization. Some promising approaches are indicated and particular concentration is dedicated to describe different methods from raw level to similar like human experts, so that in future one can get significant instruction for further analysis.

In addition, there are some studies done in Persian text summarization such as FarsiSum [14] which is inspired by SweSum [15]. This system works based on statistical properties and does not consider text linguistics and special Persian language challenges such as find synonyms, words stemming and etc.

Shamsfard and Karimi [16] propose summarizers based on lexical chain and graph theory that each sub graph show the discrete subject in document. In this method summaries are created based on query and selected of special sub graph, whereas in public summaries the sentences can be selected from all sub graphs.

Furthermore, the Parsina text summarizer employs combination of TF-IDF, graph-based methods and genetic algorithm (GA) [2].

Riahi et. al, [17] propose automatic text summarization using artificial neural networks (ANN) for the weighting system. In this system, importance of parameters are determined using ANN and creates final summary by pruning artificial neural networks.

Bazqandi et. al, [8] have clustered Persian sentences using binary particle swarm optimization where semantic distance of two vectors are used instead of Euclidean distance. The results show that their proposed method assessors, the use of semantic clustering PSO to determine the optimal number of clusters, better accuracy in terms of clustering is compared with other methods.

In this paper we use combine research studies related to Parsina [2], and SA-GA hybrid algorithm [18]. Therefore, the next sub-section describes SA-GA and Parsina text summarizer system, respectively.

3.1. SA-GA Hybrid Algorithm

In this method, we use combination of genetic algorithms (GA) and simulated annealing (SA) to present a new method called SA-GA [18].

In genetic algorithms, chromosomes with three crossover operator, mutation and selection in successive iterations converge to the best solution in the search space. However, while there is variation in population genetic algorithm, convergence to optimality is not guaranteed [18].

Simulated annealing algorithm is an optimization method that finds the optimal locations using random search. In this method, particles with an initial temperature and proceeded to search the solution space are determined. For each particle, r1 parameter ranges specified in the operating position (Present) by equation (4) where α is random number between zero and one [18].

$$Present[i+1] = Present[i] + r_1 - r_1 * 2 * \alpha \quad (4)$$

The SA-GA hybrid algorithm employs SA for crossover operation in GA. This method uses the concept of SA for crossover the chromosomes. We have used of real version of Genetic Algorithm (Real-GA). For crossover operation using statistical averages and equation (4) the proposed equation (5) is created.

$$Present[i] = \frac{(Present[i] + Present[i+1])}{2} + r_1 - r_1 * 2 * \alpha \quad (5)$$

Where the Present [i] and Present [i + 1] are two combined parents, r1 and α similar to equation (4) are set. Researchers demonstrate performance of these algorithms on complex mathematical functions [18].

3.2. Parsina Text Summarizer

The Parsina text summarizer uses combination of graph-based methods and genetic algorithms [11, 2, 4]. A directed graph is produced after weighting sentences and creates the similarity matrix. The sentences included in the summary based on topic relation factor, cohesion and readability factors are selected. The fitness function in GA, evaluate the sentences. Chromosome length of genetic algorithms is the number of sentences in the summary. The genes per chromosome in population GA represent the number of sentences that there are in summary. This system uses the

Krovetz stemming for noun and verb stemming [19, 20]. Also this system detects the synonym words. The Parsina text summarizer steps are as follows.

Firstly, it detects synonym and stop words with the use of databases. Also performs stemming all words such as nouns and verbs. Secondly, the frequency of words using TF-IDF (equation (1) and (2)), is calculated. The weight of each word according to equation (3) is also calculated. It should be noted that weighting the title words and keywords of the equation (6) is calculated.

$$W_{i,j} = (0.5 + \frac{0.5 * freq_{i,q}}{\max_l freq_{l,q}}) * isf_i \quad (6)$$

Where q represents the user's title or keyword. Third step is the construction of a similarity matrix using equations (7) and (8). In equation (7) similarity of sentence with title is computed. In equation (8) similarity of two sentences together is calculated.

$$sim(s_j, q) = \frac{\sum_{i=1}^{t} w_{i,j} * w_{i,q}}{\sqrt{\sum_{i=1}^{t} w_{i,j}^2} * \sqrt{\sum_{i=1}^{t} w_{i,q}^2}} \quad (7)$$

$$sim(s_m, s_n) = \frac{\sum_{i=1}^{t} w_{i,m} * w_{i,n}}{\sqrt{\sum_{i=1}^{t} w_{i,m}^2} * \sqrt{\sum_{i=1}^{t} w_{i,n}^2}} \quad (8)$$

After constructing the similarity matrix, a weighted graph is composed. In fact, the weight of an edge, connecting two vertices, is the similarity of the corresponding sentences (equation (9)).

$$\forall (s_i, s_j) \in E, W(s_i, s_j) = sim(s_i, s_j)$$
$$\forall i < N : sim(s_i, s_i) = 0, \forall i, j < N : sim(s_j, s_i) = 0 \quad (9)$$

A good summary contains sentences that are similar to the text title. Now that the similarities are computed, we can define the Topic Relation Factor (TRF) [2, 4, 11]. A simple method is to consider the average similarity of sentences in the summary, divided by the maximum average. Let TR be the average similarity to title in a summary (s). Using TR, we compute TRF using equation (10). Where max is computed among all possible summaries of length S. To find the max, we should simply average top greater S similarities of all sentences with the topic. TRF shows the similarity of the created summary to the document title. In summaries where sentences are closely related to the title, TRF is close to 1. But in summaries which are constructed by the sentences far from the title, TRF tends to zero.

$$TR_s = \frac{\sum_{s_j \in summary} sim(s_j, q)}{S}, TRF_s = \frac{TR}{\max_{\forall summary}(TR)} \quad (10)$$

Cohesion Factor (CF) is a measure to determine whether sentences in the summary talk about the same information or not. Suppose C be the average of similarities of all sentences in a summary, it is clear that, C is the average of weights of all edges in the summary sub graph. Where Ns is the total number of edges in summary sub graph and can easily be computed. Suppose summary nodes are $S_{S_1}, S_{S_2}, \ldots, S_{S_S}$, and S is the total number of sentences in the summary. Then Ns is the number of edges from S_{S_1} to S_{S_j}, 1<j≤S, plus number of edges from S_{S2} to S_{S_j}, 2<j≤ S, therefore:

$$C_s = \frac{\sum_{\forall s_i, s_j \in summarysubgraph} W(s_i, s_j)}{N_s}$$

$$CF_s = \frac{\log(C*9+1)}{\log(M*9+1)}, M = \max_{i,j \le N} sim_{i,j}$$

$$N_S = (S-1)+(S-2)+\ldots = \frac{(S)*(S-1)}{2} \quad (11)$$

CF should show how summary sentences are close in total, and is defined as equation (11) [2, 4, 11]. M is the maximum weight in the graph, i.e. M is the maximum similarity of sentences. If most of the sentences in the extract talk about same topic, CF grows and on the other hand if they are mostly far from each other, CF tends to 0. Readable extracts are hard to be achieved. A readable document is a document which sentences are highly related to their proceeding sentences. First sentence and second sentence are related to each other with a high similarity, same for second and third sentences, and so on. In fact a readable summary, as we define, is made up of sentences which form a smooth chain of sentences. Suppose the readability of summary s with length S, say Rs. Therefore, the readability factor of summary s is computed such as equation (12).

$$R_s = \sum_{0 \le i < S} W(s_i, s_{i+1}), RF_s = \frac{R_s}{\max_{\forall i} R_i} \quad (12)$$

It should be noted that we have made the assumption that the summary length is fixed and the maximum is computed among all possible summaries of that summary length. Finding this maximum can be done in polynomial time. Suppose the summary length is S, so the goal of finding the most readable summary is equal to finding a path of length S with maximum weight in the document graph. To have such a fitness function we use a function which is the weighted average of three factors such as equation (13) [11, 2, 4].The fitness function is a flexible one, which means, it has parameters to be adjusted by the user need. One may desire a summary with the highest readability while another may like to have a summary in which sentences are highly related to the topic, and readability is not a matter at all.

$$F = \frac{\alpha * TRF + \beta * CF + \gamma * RF}{\alpha + \beta + \gamma} \quad 0 \le \alpha \le 1, 0 \le \beta \le 1-\alpha, \gamma = 1-\alpha-\beta \quad (13)$$

α, β and γ are real numbers and are defined by user. TRF; CF; RF are all between 0, 1, so this composition of them results a real number between 0 and 1. Finally, we perform the genetic algorithm to find the best summary.

4. Phoenix: The Proposed Automatic Text Summarizer System

The proposed system known as Phoenix is the extended version of Parsina text summarizer system [2, 4]. The system aims to improve the quality of summaries produced by using the SA-GA hybrid algorithm. In order to improve the quality of summaries produced by the proposed method the following tasks have been considered: 1) providing a faster method of coding for word stemming krovetz method, 2) Extending the dictionary of words and their synonymous, roots of verbs and nouns to cover more aspects of the text and the increasing use of software in various fields of scientific, artistic, political, or social, and 3) Using SA-GA hybrid algorithm for evaluating the quality of the produced summary.

There is a preprocessing phase in Phoenix system, such as Parsina, to solve the problem bipartite compound words and integration them. The preprocessing phases in phoenix text summarizer system, which display main structure of text, include the following:

1. Identifying the boundaries of sentences: In the Phoenix system for identify boundaries of Persian sentences of point, question mark, semicolon are used.
2. Removing stop words: words that have no meaning and we cannot collect information about them, such as conjunctions and adverbs that have no role in the concept of sentences.
3. Stemming: Finding the root of the derivational words is called stemming. The stemming phases in Phoenix system is similar to Parsina, and uses Krovetz algorithm that have a dictionary of morphological methods for examining the roots [19, 20]. Also the Phoenix system uses an optimized krovetz algorithm. Experimental results show that the stemming method in Parsina is time consuming because of the nested IF statements used in the code. However, In Phoenix system, the Krovetz stemming algorithm is implemented using a function and nested condition statements have been removed. This procedure has improved performance in the stemming phase, and increased its speed compared to Parsina system.

First step in the processing phase of Phoenix system is to compute the effective properties and relation of sentences As well as the TF-IDF weight allocated to sentences. The final score of each sentence are then determined by using an equivalent weight. The best sentences are ranked and selected for the final summary.

The authors have used binary crossover operator in Real-GA for Parsina system, but in the Phoenix system they have used a combination of binary crossover and SA-GA methods in crossover operator. Therefore, the crossover point according to equation (14) for two parents in crossover operator is determined.

$$\text{Crossover Point} = r - r * 2 * \alpha \tag{14}$$

Where r is the temperature in the SA formula and initial value is a random number between one and the numbers of sentences in the text. Alpha (α) is a random number between zero and one. After determining the crossover point at random and using the SA formula, we perform crossover such as binary crossover.

Generally there are three units in Phoenix system named: initializing, scoring and summarizing unit.

Initializing unit includes pre-processing, segmentation and stemming. Scoring unit consists of weighted words (equations (1), (2), (3) and (6)) and constructs the similarity matrix (equations (7), (8) and (9)). The summarizing unit includes the following stages: computing the number of summary sentences, calculating the percentage of Topic Relation Factor (equation (10)), Cohesion (equation (11)), and Readability (equation (12)); and implementing the SA-GA hybrid algorithm.

The SA-GA hybrid algorithm in Phoenix text summarizer system uses SA algorithm in GA crossover operator. In fact the crossover point in chromosome is determined using the concept of SA. The SA-GA algorithm implementation steps are as follows [18]:

1. Begin
2. Create and initialize a random population.
3. Select the best population with elitism.
4. Create a new generations using of crossover point (equation (14)) and crossover rate equal with 0.7.
5. Perform Mutation with mutation rate 0.1.
6. The above steps until you reach the appropriate level of fitness, repeated (Go to 3).
7. End

5. Evaluation of the Phoenix Text Summarizer System

The Phoenix summarizer assessment questionnaire		
Question	Phoenix Summarizer	Parsina Summarizer
Category Name		
File Name		
Text Title		
Keywords		
Topic Relation Factor (Percentage)		
Cohesion Factor (Percentage)		
Readability Factor (Percentage)		
Satisfaction with the summaries generated for compress 10%:		
Satisfaction with the summaries generated for compress 25%:		
Satisfaction with the summaries generated for compress 50%:		
Satisfaction with the summaries generated for compress 75%:		
Satisfaction with the summaries generated for compress 90%:		
Mean satisfaction with the summaries produced:		

Figure 1. *The Phoenix summarizer assessment questionnaire.*

In this section we evaluate the Phoenix text summarizer, by using 6 text categories in various fields such as: scientific, cultural, social, economic, political and artistic. Also the Phoenix and Parsina text summarizers are compared together. Each category includes 5 text files with different lengths, so a total 30 texts were compared. The purpose is to evaluate the quality of text summaries from a human perspective; therefore a team of people are required to evaluate both softwares. We used 10 persons for this work. Each person evaluates the produced summary of Phoenix and Parsina for 30 texts with compress percentages 10%, 25%, 50%, 75% and 90%. We use questionnaire (Figure 1) to register results of both software. Also we considered results in the same conditions. So we used the same title, keywords, topic relation factor, cohesion, readability, and compress percentage for each text in each category.

Results from the questionnaire showed that the average accuracy of the Phoenix automatic text summarization system for each category is as table 1.

Table 1. *Average accuracy of the Phoenix and Parsina systems.*

Category Name	Phoenix	Parsina
Scientific	80.56%	74.78%
Cultural	51.11%	64.44%
Social	60%	44.44%
Economic	58.89%	60%
Political	61.67%	57.22%
Artistic	73.89%	58.33%

So in the Phoenix the average of quality and accuracy is 64.35% while in the Parsina is 59.86%.This proves that the SA-GA hybrid algorithm increases the quality of text summarization. The results show that the Phoenix text summarizer is faster than Parsina text summarizer for short text; but for longer texts is a bit slower than Parsina system with the advantages of having more quality for summary of text compared to Parsina. Figure 2 compares the average quality of text in Phoenix and Parsina text summarizers for various documents show.

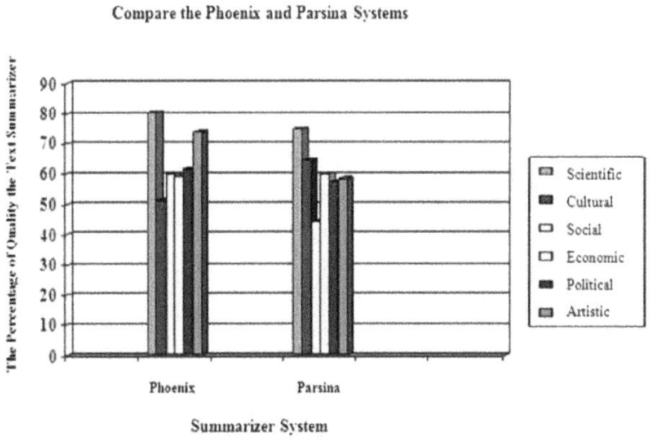

Figure 2. *Comparison chart between Phoenix and Parsina systems.*

6. Discussion and Conclusion

In this paper we proposed an extended version of Parsina automatic text summarization called as Phoenix. The main differences between Phoenix and Parsina are: 1) providing a faster way of coding for Krovetz method in word stemming phase, 2) Extending the dictionary of morphological methods for examining the roots have been found, to cover more aspects of the text and improving the applicability of software in various fields such as scientific, cultural, social, economic, political, and artistic fields, 3) Phoenix employs SA-GA hybrid algorithm for determining the sentences of the summary and evaluation of the Summary producer. The results show that the SA-GA hybrid algorithm increases the quality of the text summary in the Phoenix system (64.35%) rather than Parsina system (59.86%).

Future works include suing Wordnet for Persian language and develop the Phoenix text summarizer system for more applications and multiple documents.

References

[1] Karen Sparck Jones, "Automatic summarizing: factors and directions, in: Advances in Automatic Text Summarization", MIT Press, pp. 1–12, 1999.

[2] Bahrepour Majid, Mahdipour Elham, Ghalibaf. K. Azadeh, Amiri Malihe, Tahmaseby Aida, Akbarzadeh T. Mohammad Reza, "Automatic Persian Text Summarization",14th Annual Conference of Computer Society of Iran, Amirkabir Universityof Technology (Tehran Polytechnic), 2009. (Persian) Available on: http://www.civilica.com/Paper-ACCSI14-ACCSI14_082.html

[3] Oi Mean Foong, Alan Oxley and Suziah Sulaiman, “Challenges and Trends of Automatic Text Summarization”, IJITT, Vol. 1, Issue 1, ISSN: 0976–5972, 2010.

[4] Mahdipour Elham, Bahrepour Majid, Amiri Malihe, Tahmaseby Aida, "Parsina: Automatic Persian Text Summarizer", Registered software in the development center of information technology and digital media, Register Number: 10.308, Register Date: 2010, Identification Number: 8-00202-000269. Iran, Tehran (Persian)

[5] Hassel,M.,"Resource Lean and Portable Automatic TextSummarization",Stockholm,Sweden.p.144,2007.

[6] Jen-Yuan Yeh, H.-R.K, Wei-Pang Yang, I-HengMeng, "Text Summarization using a trainable summarizer and latent semantic analysis", Information Processing & Management, Vol. 41, Issue 1, pp:75-95, 2005.

[7] Karel Jezek, Josef Stainberger, "Automatic Text Summarization (The state of the art 2007 and new challenges)", Vaclav Snasel(Ed.): Znalosti 2008, pp.1-12, ISBN 978-80-227-2827-0, FIIT STU Brarislava, Ustav Informatiky a softveroveho inzinierstva,, 2008.

[8] Bazqandi Mahdi, Taday'ounTabriziQamarnaz," Clustering the sentences based on swarm intelligence", 4th Iranian Conference on Electrical and electronic, Islamic Azad University of Gonabad, 2011. (Persian) Available on: http://www.civilica.com/Paper-ICEEE04-ICEEE04_153.html

[9] Ohtake,K.,Okamoto,D.,Kodama,M.,Masuyama,S.,"Yet another summarization system with two modules using empirical knowledge", In Proceeding of NTCIR Workshop2 Meeting,2001.

[10] Neto, J., Freitas, A., Kaestner, "Automatic text summarization using machine learning approach", Proc. 16th Brazilian Symp. On Artificial Intelligence (SBIA-2002). Lecture Notes in Artificial Intelligence 2507, pp 205-215, 2002.

[11] Qazvinian,Vahed.,SharifHassnabadi,Leila.,Halavati, Ramin.,"Summarizing Text With a Genetic Algorithm-Based Sentence Extraction", Int. J. Knowledge Management Studies, Vol. 2, No. 4, pp:426-444, 2008, Available on: http://citeseerx.ist.psu.edu/viewdoc/download?doi=10.1.1.130.2201&rep=rep1&type=pdf.

[12] Ladda Suanmali, Naomie Salim and Mohammed Salem Binwahlan,"Fuzzy Logic Based Method for Improving Text Summarization", (IJCSIS) International Journal of Computer Science and Information Security, Vol. 2, No. 1, 2009.

[13] Md. Majharul Haque, Suraiya Pervin, and Zerina Begum, "Literature Review of Automatic Multiple Documents Text Summarization", International Journal of Innovation and Applied Studies, ISSN 2028-9324 Vol. 3 No. 1, pp. 121-129, 2013.

[14] Mazdak,N., Hassel,M.,"FarsiSum-a Persian Text Summarizer", Master Thesis, Department of Linguistics, Stockholm University, 2004.

[15] Dalianis,H.,"SweSum- A Text Summarizer for Swedish, Technical Report", TRITANA-p0015, IPLab-174,NADA, KTH, 2000.

[16] ShamsFard Mehrnoush, Karimi Zohre, "The automatic Persian text summarization system", 12th Annual Conference of Computer Society of Iran, Tehran, 2007. (Persian) Available on: http://www.civilica.com/Paper-ACCSI12-ACCSI12_377.html

[17] Riahi Noushin, Ghazali Fatemeh, Ghazali Mohammad Ali, "Improved the Persian text summarizer performance using pruning algorithm of neural networks", 1th conference of Line processing and Persian language, Department of Electrical and Computer Engineering, Semnan, Iran, 2011. (Persian) Available on: http://conf.semnan.ac.ir/uploads/conferance_khat/Persian/110.pdf

[18] Mahdipour Elham, Bahrepour Majid, Mohammad Kazemi Farhad, Akbarzadeh T. Mohammad Reza, "A novel method for hybrid of genetic algorithm and simulated annealing", 2nd Joint Congress on Fuzzy and Intelligent Systems, Malek Ashtar University of Technology, Tehran, Iran, 2009. (Persian) Available on: http://www.civilica.com/Paper-FJCFIS02-FJCFIS02_016.html

[19] R. Krovetz, "Viewing morphology as an inference process", Proc.16th ACM SIGIR, 1993.

[20] Hessami Fard Reza, Ghasem sany Gholamreza, "Design of a stemming algorithm for Persian", 11th Annual Conference of Computer Society of Iran, Tehran, 2006. (Persian) Available on: http://www.civilica.com/Paper-ACCSI11-ACCSI11_066.html

7

Software development for identifying Persian text similarity

Elham Mahdipour, Rahele Shojaeian Razavi, Zahra Gheibi

Computer Engineering Department, Khavaran Institute of Higher Education, Mashhad, Iran

Email address:
Mahdipour@khi.ac.ir (E. Mahdipour), rahil.razavi@gmail.com (R. S. Razavi), zgdayana184@yahoo.com (Z. Gheibi)

Abstract: The vast span of nouns, words and verbs in Persian language and the availability of information in all fields in the form of paper, book and internet arises the need of a system to compare texts and evaluate their similarities. In this paper a system has been presented for comparing the text and determining the degree of Persian (Farsi) text similarities. This system uses TF-IDF method to give weight to sentences. Moreover, the roots of the nouns have been found and identical score has been given to synonyms and word families. The results gained from implementation indicate that the proposed system has a desired efficiency in comparing short texts.

Keywords: Text Similarity, TF-IDF, Semantic Similarity, Stemming

1. Introduction

Nowadays the information is growing and persons have collision problems with unauthorized or unrelated use of information. One of the problems in this regard is the deficiency of effective methods for evaluating the degree of similarities of the texts. Text mining- the extraction of the words features and comparing them with each other is the basic technology to respond to this problem. One of its applications is the evaluation of text similarity which has gained lots of attention in various applications nowadays. For instance, comparing the similarity of one paper to other papers and determining whether it is repetitive or not is one of the most usages of assessing similarity of the text in conference and journal publications.

Text comparison is the process of studying the degree of similarities and differences of the texts with each other by a computer program. Evaluating the similarity between two pieces of short texts is a highly significant task in applied researches and programs like: text-mining, text extraction, information retrieval in web and search engines. In this case, evaluating the similarity or differences between two short texts or two sentences is a main step for the system's better function [1]. For instance, in an interactive question and answer system, evaluating the similarity between two short texts like two questions, is a basic step in classifying questions as well as the suggested questions. In the case of documents retrieval in web, it has been proved that evaluating the similarity between two texts holds a great significance. For instance, when the page headings are used to display documents in the page using the same name for finding a special task [2]. In text mining, evaluating the similarity in short texts is a helpful method to discover the hidden knowledge from the database [3].Studying the similarities of short texts is also applicable in wide range of programs like formulas search [4].

Generally, different methods exists for text mining and evaluating the text similarity including: Information retrieval, clustering, graphs theory, machine learning, latin semantic analysis (LSA), N-gram, part of speech tagging (POS), singular values decomposition (SVD), machine translation and TF-IDF [2, 5, and 13].

For this purpose, the manner the natural language processor functions can be applied to evaluate text similarity in which the system receives a full sentence (preferably ended with a punctuation mark) and then processes the word through stages [5]. For instance the following general steps can be considered:

First, the words which have been separated by a space are recognized using database and the functions for recognizing combined words and provide the required data for the processor. In this stage, the phonemic form of the words is also formed.

In this stage the surveyor recognizes the type of sentence

and determines the structural features of the words and the phonemically form in adjective and noun modifiers.

Stemming is the process of weighting the words and sentences, computing the scores and creating the similarity matrix.

The results evaluated the text similarity matrix for the two related texts.

Using graph-based methods and TF-IDF, a software system has been created in this paper to compare the similarity of Persian texts. Accordingly, the structure of the paper is in this way: Section 2 has a review on primary topics of text similarity evaluation. Section 3 investigates what has been done in the field of comparing text similarity, Section 4 studies the suggested software of text similarity called as "Iranian Persian Text Similarity System". In section 5, the experimental result by performing the software is assessed.

2. The Primary Concepts of Evaluating Text Similarity

The semantic word similarity is used to introduce a degree of similarity between the words used in unique information of a big structure. In order to calculate the semantic similarity two measuring ways can be used: 1) Mutual point to point information [6] and 2) latent semantic analysis [7].

One of the simple ways to find the similarity between two parts of the text is to use lexical adaptation. That is, the similarity is determined based on the number of lexical units which exists in both parts of the text. Aas and Eikvil [8], made some changes in the stages of this simple method as: Stemming, omitting the stop words, marking a part of speech, the longest sequence adaptation as different weights and factors normalization [8]. The text-based semantic similarity which is widely used is in fact an estimation of some inquiries made as information retrieval or using latent semantic analysis which gains the text similarity by operating the relations of second rank words which have been automatically gained from the big collections. The procedure includes a method for formalizing the translation and interpretation which is normally used for aligning the sentences in case of sudden changes or an interpretation of a generation which uses distributive similarity in the route of dependency trees [9].

The evaluations related to semantic similarity has traditionally been defined between the words or concepts and textual parts consist of two or some words. One of the indices of word to word similarity is the accessibility of the resources which encode the relation between words and concepts. In addition to this derivation, measuring the text to text similarity begins with a word based on semantic similarity may have no step forward. Mainly, the most of what has been done in the field is the applied programs of the traditional model of vector space which sometimes develops to N-gram language model. Considering the two parts of input text, a score indicating similarity in the semantic level is automatically determined and as a result, simple lexical adaptation method is applied for this purpose. The fact is that a comprehensive index of the text semantic similarity should be considered in its structure. To solve this problem, first a piece of the text is chosen and for modeling, the semantic similarity of the text is regarded as a function of semantic similarity of part of the word. This is done with the indices of word to word similarity and that group of a word features which are considered as a potential good formula for semantic similarity of two input texts [10].

What can be concluded so far is that first of all, we should act to divide the words and their meaning. This demands using stemming algorithms.

2.1. Stemming

Words in each language are divided into two groups of simple and derivational. The words which are derived from other words are called derivational. Simple words are those which have not been derived from any other word. Finding the root of the derivational words is called stemming. Due to developments in natural language processing, stemming has found lots of applications. Generally, there are two main applications for stemming of the words.

Stemming in Machine Translators: It is clear that words accompanied with their derivations give significant variety to the words which practically makes sentence translation difficult. In this method by using stemming, the complexity of the translation is decreased.

Stemming in Information Retrieval Systems: Information retrieval and text process is regarded as one of the growing applications of the recent. Processing and classifying the news, processing scientific texts and alike, are regular today. In information retrieval systems, there is usually a very huge database on which information retrieval and process has to be done. The more precise and developed the semantic networks extracted from these information are, the more convenient will be to access the extracted information. One of the applications of stemming is to provide more developed semantic networks in text process system and information retrieval.

In spite the fact that the problems in two above-mentioned applications are similar, words stemming in them has different demands. In translator systems, we often try to find the roots of the words whose derivation does not make any change in its type of that word (verb, noun, etc.).When the type of the word changes, its equivalent in the target language changes a lot and this practically ends to a translation of low quality. While in text process systems, discovering all relations is very important. Therefore, in machine translations, the emphasis is mostly on the cases where there is no change in the function of the words like verbs conjugation .Of course, this does not mean that stemming has no applicability in cases of translation systems, rather, by considering current means of translation systems which are mostly applicable in the level of words structure and not in the level of concept, stemming has to be directed in the same direction.

One of the algorithms of stemming, whose Persian version has been used in this paper, is Krovetz algorithm [11]. This algorithm applies morphological methods and a dictionary for trying found roots. This algorithm has shown a desirable efficiency in languages in which compound words structure is rule–governed. Hungarian and Hebrew languages are placed in this category. Krovetz algorithm studies the prefixes and suffixes of the words and has shown an acceptable efficiency in translator machines. In Persian language in which word derivation is systematic, stemming is well capable to become mechanized. As noted before, for languages that have more morphological derivations, the capabilities of Krovetz algorithm are more evident. Persian and Arabic languages are placed in this category. Similar methods have only used linguistic structures .As a result, their results can be improved. Krovetz algorithm and Krovetz2 have been developed for verbs stemming in Persian language [12].

After stemming the words, considering the frequency and abundance of each word, a weight is assigned to it. In this paper TF-IDF method [13] is used to give weight to words.

2.2. TF-IDF Weighting

TF-IDF method equals the index of term frequency – inverse document frequency in the method of information retrieval. In this method, weight giving tf-isf is calculated for each sentence, in a way that $tf_{i,j}$ is said to the frequency of ith word in j^{th} sentence and isf_i is the inverse of document frequency of ith word. Where N is the number of all sentences and n_1 the number of sentences containing i^{th} word [13] (Equation 1).

$$isf_i = \log\frac{N}{n_i} \quad tf_{i,j} = \frac{freq_{i,j}}{\max_i freq_{i,j}} \qquad (1)$$

Thus the weight of the words is calculated in the following way (Equation 2):

$$W_{i,j}=tf_{i,j}*isf_i \qquad (2)$$

3. Related Works

The current available text similarity systems are for other languages except Persian and there has been no comprehensive language for evaluating Persian language text similarities. Among available systems for other languages, the following tasks have been studied.

In Rada et al. [14] knowledge-based methods have been used to measure semantic similarity of the texts. Since a great part of the information available today include short texts (scientific papers abstracts, notes on the pictures, descriptions of the products), their paper studies the semantic similarity of short texts. It offers methods for measuring semantic similarity of the texts using information and trivial similarity between them, as well as methods for extracting similarity as text to text and semantic similarity in knowledge-based method. Their results indicate that the semantic similarity methods based on simple lexical adaptation has caused 13% error reduction to the evaluation methods based on vector space.

In Toral et, al, [15] the ambiguous and unambiguous relationship between the nouns in Word net and Wikipedia have been evaluated based on text similarity methods. They consider a combination of supervised and unsupervised methods. The gold standard with disambiguated links is publicly available. The results range from 64.7% for the first sense heuristic, 68% for an unsupervised combination, and up to 77.74% for a supervised combination.

In [16] a new method has been presented for measuring the similarity between two short texts by comparing each of them with probable subjects. Their goal is to find discrimination between two short texts and compare them with series of probable subject's extracted using Gibbs sampling method. The conditions of short text discrimination are gained by studying their probabilities under subjects that have been discovered in that field. The similarity between two textual short abstracts is gained based on their normal conditions as well as relationship between their differences. Extensive tests in the ground of questions interpretation and categorizations indicate that the suggested method can perform a more precise computation for evaluating the degree of similarity compared to other methods that use TF-IDF.

4. Persian Text Similarity System

The programming language of Persian text similarity system is C#.net and uses Microsoft Access database. The reason why it uses Access database is that the program is easily used in each system with no need to SQL Server. Moreover, since during the performance, the database of the program do not face any changes including inserting, deleting and editing, the speed of performing the operation in SQL database has no benefit for the system, Access database was used.

Generally, a text similarity system is made of segmentation, stemming and scoring sections. Persian text similarity system holds two actors of user and text similarity method and two units of initializing and scoring. The initializing unit includes pre-process and segmentation. The scoring unit includes weight giving and creating the matrix of similarity. Accordingly, the stages of implementing the Persian text similarity system are as follows.

First, a collection of general knowledge on natural languages (NLP) has to be presented in order to facilitate text segmentation to the desired extracted unites. In a coherent text a word may usually appear in several different forms. These forms of derivation if in the form of plural or singular are controlled by the text. After the process of stemming, each word is shown with its root. In most cases, the different forms of the word have a similar semantic interpretation and hence can be acted as synonyms for a large number of information management. Thus in the first stage, using database, the synonyms, special and redundant and the algorithm of stemming all words and verbs are root-found and prepositions, plural markers and unimportant words are omitted.

In the second stage, the frequency of the words is gained using TF-IDF, Equation (1). Then the weight of each word in the sentence is calculated by Equation (2). The third stage is making matrix of similarity using Equation 3 in which the similarity of two sentences with each other is calculated.

$$sim(s_m, s_n) = \frac{\sum_{i=1}^{t} w_{i,m} * w_{i,n}}{\sqrt{\sum_{i=1}^{t} w_{i,m}^2} * \sqrt{\sum_{i=1}^{t} w_{i,n}^2}} \quad (3)$$

Where m refers to the sentences of the first text and n refers to the sentences of the second text. $W_{i,m}$ is the weight of ith word in the first text in m^{th} sentence of the first text. Similarly, $W_{i,n}$ is the weight of ith word in the first text in n^{th} sentence of the second text . Using Equation (3), the similarity matrix is formed. It is a m*n matrix in which m refers to the number of sentences in the first sentence equal to matrix rows and n is the number of sentences of the second text or the columns of the matrix. After making the similarity matrix, the weight graph is formed in which the weight of each edge for two joint vectors is the degree of similarity of two sentences to each other.

Furthermore, in order to get familiar with the manner of implementing the Persian text similarity system, its algorithm is defined below:

1. Receiving the first text.
2. Receiving the second text.
3. Segmenting the sentences of the first and second texts.
4. Separating the words of the first and second texts.
5. Stemming of the first and second texts.
6. Calculating the frequency of the words of the first text based on TF-IDF weight giving system.
7. Calculating the frequency of the words of the first text in the second text based on TF-IDF weighting system.
8. Scoring the sentences of the first and second texts.
9. Making similarity matrix according to Equation (3).
10. After making the similarity matrix, each matrix element refers to the degree of similarity of each sentence of the first text with each sentence of the second text. Now, in order to calculate the percentage of similarity of the two texts, primarily, for each sentence of the first text, the average of its similarity with all sentences of the second text is gained that is, the average of each row of similarity matrix is calculated. Then again an average is taken from all the averages in each row so that the percentage of total similarity is gained and announced to the user.

Figure 1 shows the flowchart of Persian text similarity system.

5. The Experimental Results

Figure 2 shows the software environment of the Persian text similarity system. Working with this software is very simple and facile. In order to work with this software, first click on the icon of open and choose the desired text. Do the same for the second text as well. The click "run" button to execute the software and see the result (Figures 2-4).

In order to evaluate the degree of accuracy of the text similarity declared by the software, manpower has been used in this research. Five volunteers studied the degree of textual similarities for 20 sample texts compared mutually. The satisfaction degree of each volunteer of the software outputs was recorded and finally the average of the volunteers' satisfaction was measured. The findings showed that the average of man's satisfaction of text similarity announced by the software is 64.31%. This criterion indicates the preciseness of Persian text similarity system.

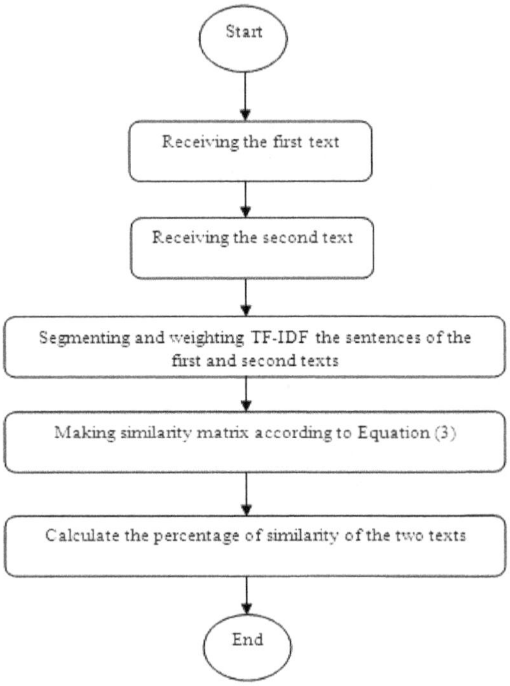

Figure 1. *Flowchart of Persian text similarity software steps.*

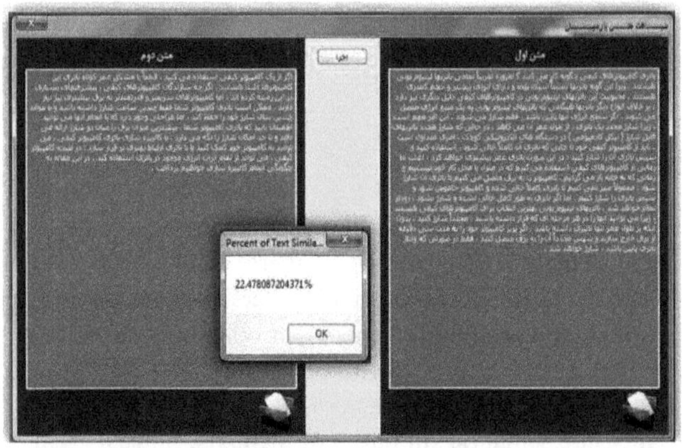

Figure 2. *Two different texts with some similar words.*

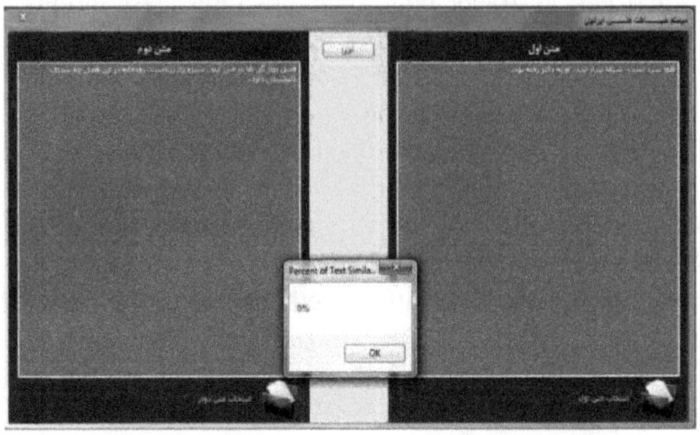

Figure 3. *Two complete different texts (No Similarity).*

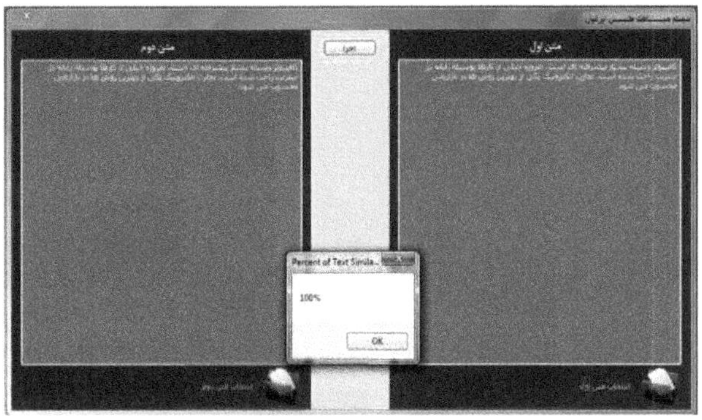

Figure 4. Two Same texts (complete similarity).

6. Discussion, Conclusion and Future Work

The methods used in evaluating text similarity can be classified into two general groups. The first group is the statistical methods based on information retrieval (IR) which acts in lexical level and puts the statistical characteristics into consideration such as the frequency of the word due to neglecting the semantic relation between sentences, this method affects the text readability. The other approach existing in this evaluation gets benefit from natural language process and information extraction, thus tries to understand the subject and the relations between different parts of the text. The methods that use this approach, generally use syntactic-semantic analysis like LSA, lexical chain, random indexing and so on in order to discover the relations between entities. These methods use the word features of concurrence, co-reference, lexical similarity and semantic analysis. The results gained from the methods following this approach are usually of a higher quality. Usage of weight giving TF-IDF system is also a highly efficient way to gain frequency and other features of the words.

In the present paper, the similarities between two Persian texts were discovered using TF-IDF method. In order to calculate text similarity, the words were root found and the synonyms were accurately recognized and identical scores were assigned to them. The results gained by implementing this software indicate that by developing the database of this software, it can be used for larger texts as well.

The Persian text similarity system gained the human satisfaction average degree of 64.31% for evaluating the similarity of short texts and abstracts in all fields which indicates the preciseness of the offered system. Comparing the text of web pages including photos and link also needs a program to understand the layers and frames of the web pages so that it can extract the words and their features. The authors plan to upgrade the Persian text similarity system in order to compare long texts and the texts of web pages. Hence, it is planned to put the related information extensively in database.

References

[1] WenyinL, Hao TY, ChenW, FengM "A web-based platform for user interactive question answering". World Wide Web: Internet Web Inform Syst (2009) 12(2):107–124, 2009.

[2] Park EK, Ra DY, Jang MG, "Techniques for improving web retrieval effectiveness". Inform Process Manag 41:1207–1223, 2005.

[3] Atkinson-Abutridy J, Mellish C, Aitken S, "Combining information extraction with genetic algorithms for text mining", IEEE Intelligent Systems, pp: 22-30, 2004, Available on: http://homepages.abdn.ac.uk/c.mellish/pages/papers/atkinsonieee.pdf.

[4] K Metzler D, Dumais S, Meek C, "Similarity measures for short segments of text". In: Proceedings of the 29th European conference on information retrieval (ECIR 2007). Lecture notes in computer science,vol 4425, Springer, Berlin , pp 16–27, 2007.

[5] Hassel, M., Resource Lean and Portable "Automatic Text Summarization", Stockholm, Sweden. p. 144, 2007.

[6] Turney, P. "Mining the web for synonyms: PMI-IR versus LSA on TOEFL". In Proceedings of the Twelfth European Conference on Machine Learning, 2001, Available on: http://www.extractor.com/turney-ecml2001.pdf.

[7] Landauer T. K., Foltz P., and Laham D, "Introduction to latent semantic analysis". Discourse Processes 25, 1998.

[8] K. Aas and L. Eikvil, "Text Categorisation: A Survey", 1999, Available on: http://citeseer.nj.nec.com/aas99text.html.

[9] Wu Z., Palmer M., "Verb semantics and lexical selection". ACL' 94 Proceedings of the 32nd Annual Meeting of the Association for Computational Linguistics, pp: 133-138, 1994. Available on: http://dl.acm.org/citation.cfm?id=981751.

[10] Voorhees E., "Using WordNet to disambiguate word senses for text retrieval", SIGIR '93 Proceedings of the 16th annual international ACM SIGIR conference on research and development information retrieval, pp: 171-180, 1993, Available on: http://dl.acm.org/citation.cfm?id=160715.

[11] R. Krovetz, "Viewing morphology as an inference process", Proc. 16th ACM SIGIR Conference, Pittsburgh, June 27-July 1, pp. 191-202, 1993.

[12] Hessami Fard Reza, Ghasem sany Gholamreza, "Design of a stemming algorithm for Persian", 11th Annual Conference of Computer Society of Iran, Tehran, 2006. (Persian) Available on: http://www.civilica.com/Paper-ACCSI11-ACCSI11_066.html

[13] Qazvinian,Vahed.,SharifHassnabadi,Leila., Halavati, Ramin.,"Summarizing Text With a Genetic Algorithm-Based Sentence Extraction", Int. J. Knowledge Management Studies, Vol. 2, No. 4, pp:426-444, 2008, Available on: http://citeseerx.ist.psu.edu/viewdoc/download?doi=10.1.1.130.2201&rep=rep1&type=pdf.

[14] Rada Mihalcea, Courtney Corley, Carlo Strapparava, "Corpus-based and Knowledge-based measures of text semantic similarity", AAAI '06 Proceeding of the 21st national conference on Artificial intelligence, Vol. 1, pp: 775-780, 2006.

[15] Antonio Toral, Oscar Ferrandez, Eneko Agirre, Rafael Munoz, "A study on linking Wikipedia categories to Wordnet synsets using text similarity", International Conference RANLP 2009, Borovets, Bolgaria, pp: 449-454, 2009.

[16] Xiaojun Quan, Gang Liu, Zhi Lu, Xingliang Ni, Liu Wenyin, "Short text similarity based on probabilistic topics", Knowl Inf Syst, 25, pp:473-491, DOI:10.1007/s10115-009-0250-y, 2010.

Presenting an algorithm for choosing an optimum local service based on the qualitative feature of combining

Aalia Hemmati, Sima Emadi

Computer Engineering department. Islamic Azad university of Meybod, Yazd, Iran

Email address:
Aaliahemmati64@gmail.com (A. Hemmati), au_emadi@yahoo.com (S. Emadi)

Abstract: The combination of web services is the result of complex and increasing needs of the users and disability of single web services in resolving the users' needs. One of the important challenges in the field of web 2.0 is the combination of web services based on their qualitative features. Since it is probable that there would be several different combinations of services for achieving a specific goal, choosing the service is based on some qualitative features like combining, availability, acceptability, service cost and security. One of the important issues is the quantitative survey of combining rate of the two services shared on the combination. So in this research, in the first stage, for measuring the combining rate, the effective factors on this feature would be surveyed. In the second stage, for choosing the optimum service based on the qualitative feature of combining, the local strategy is used. The proposed algorithm in local strategy selects services that their combining rate is more than a specific threshold. The implementations and analysis show that the proposed algorithm presents the optimum service in user's view with an acceptable combining capability. Also, the analysis of results and an evaluation with a case study show the optimized results of the local proposed algorithms compared to existing methods.

Keywords: Web Service, Qualitative Feature of Service, Combining

1. Introduction

Service-oriented systems have special importance because of the possibility of working in heterogeneous distributed environments. The users of such systems use the web services that provide system components. In some cases, the needs of the users are not met with the single web service. However, each combination of services is not always the best possible solution and some criteria and features of the new combined service such as the quality of the new service can be a criterion for choosing the appropriate service. In fact, one of the important challenges in the field of web services is the combination of web services considering their quality. The need to combine web services is the result of complex and increasing requirements of users and disability of web services in responding to the goals of the users. Since it is likely that there would be several different combinations of services in achieving to a specific goal, choosing the service is based on some qualitative features like combining, availability, acceptability, service cost and security. One of the important issues that has been noted less is the accuracy quantitative survey of combination rate of the two services shared on the combined platform.

This feature brings the rate of services' adaptation with each other for combining without causing a problem in the runtime. After that the user applies for the required service, the component identifies the basic services with the combination of which it can get to the desired service and search for them inside the service store. Because of the diversity of different producers and services, it's likely that several candidate services be found for each desired efficiency.

For choosing the optimum service, we can consider the optimization in two ways: local and global. According to the conditions of the issue, the local optimality is used for choosing the optimum service based on the quality rate of combining. In [1], a framework is presented for choosing the service in terms of qualitative features in which the combination rate of services is focused. In [10], the combining feature is surveyed absolutely or with the use of local strategy, in this way that the two services are combined with each other or not. In [10], the optimization of services' combining has been done based on the local and global algorithm combination without considering services' combining.

In this research, by surveying the available weaknesses in the presented method in [10], a more accurate amount is obtained for combining feature and the optimum local optimization algorithm and an optimum service based on the combining rate is selected. While the most similar tasks have been spent on surveying the only effective factors on combining and the different ways of choosing the optimized compound service as local or global without considering the combining rate of services. . Some existing methods have more focused on similarities of services' input and output for surveying the combining rate of the two services and in cases that the other effective factors on combining is surveyed, no metric has been presented for its measuring. The presented model in this article has used the local optimality in comparison with the existing method and is done dynamically and in phase. It has evaluated the more number of parameters including cost, performance time, acceptability, reliability and combining in comparison with the other methods. As it goes on, the structure of the article is in this way that in the second chapter the combining rate is measured. In the third chapter, the proposed algorithm based on the qualitative feature of services' combining is presented. In the fourth chapter, simulation and results' analysis are stated and in the fifth chapter conclusion and future activities are proposed.

2. Measuring the Qualitative Feature of Combining

In this article, web service is considered as a black box and there is access only to its interface. And when the service is implemented as a web service, WSDL descriptions are the most common documents of service description. Since the available web services use WSDL, a semantic description in OWL-S language has been added to these services. OWL-S description of service is in three part of service profile, service model and service support [10].

Here, service profile part that includes input, output, name and service description and service support that includes transfer protocol and web service address are considered more. Also, it is supposed that services based on SOAP protocol communicate with each other [10].

The stages of measuring the qualitative feature of combining is in this way that in the first stage, the effective criteria on services' combining are surveyed in atomic terms. In the second stage, metric is obtained for the effective criteria. In the third stage, an appropriate weight for each criterion is obtained and their relationships with each other are determined. And finally, a metric for measuring the combining feature of services is presented.

Effective factors on combining are in two groups. One of them are the factors that are obtained of the communication between the desired candidate service with the previous existing service of the combination, like the surveying parameters of the similarity level of input- output parameters, effects and preconditions and the other are the factors surveyed on candidate atomic service. Table 1 is retrieved of [10] and shows the effective factors on combining in atomic terms with this difference that the importance level and the two qualitative parameters of reusability and adaptability is added in order that a more accurate rate of combining would be obtained.

Table 1. *Effective criteria for qualitative feature of combining and metrics.*

Effective factors	Metric	_ importance level
Reusability [7]	$\lambda_1(S_1)$ = -0.5 * Coupling + 0.61 * ServiceGranularity + 0.61 * Parameter Granularity	Medium
Adaptability[6]	$\lambda_2(S_1)=Num_{Consumers\ Satisfied\ Variants}/\ Num_{TotalApplicableConsumers}$	High
Granularity[5]	$\lambda_3(S_1)$= 1/number of "atomic process" in owls file	
Availability [4]	$\lambda_4(S_1)$=WSOT/(WSOT+WSRT)	
Loosely-Coupled [9]	$\lambda_6(S_1)$=1/(α_x :number of Complex data types + β_x Number of service calls)	Medium
Well-defined Interfaces [10]	$\lambda_6(S_1)=\sum_{i=0}^{4} Xi$ $x_i \in \{0,0.2\}$ $xi = \begin{cases} 0.2, hasparameter \\ 0, no\ parameter \end{cases}$ x_0 = input, x_1=output, x_2=precondition, x_3=result, x_4=category	High
Study of Quality of Service [10]	$\lambda_7(S_1)=\left(\sum_{Qi\in neg} W_i \frac{Q_i^{max}-Q_i}{Q_i^{max}-Q_i^{min}} + \sum_{Qi\in pos} W_i \frac{Q_i-Q_i^{min}}{Q_i^{max}-Q_i^{min}}\right)$	

2.1. Metric for Measuring the Combining Feature

This metric is presented for measuring the combining rate of the two continuous service that are combined with each other. The input of the issue is a workflow including some duties that are to be performed by the real services. These services are shown as S_1 S_2.

Assume that for the duty x_1 a real service called s_1 has been found. Now, the issue is that among the candidate services for the duty x_2, which real service is better to be selected. The choosing criterion is the service that would have a higher combining capability with the real service s_1. This metric is computed by relation 1 [10]:

$$\text{Composability } (S_1) = \lambda(S_1) \tag{1}$$

$$\lambda(S_1)=\begin{cases} 0, if\ \prod_i \lambda_i(S_1) = 0 \\ \sum a_i \lambda_i (S_1), \text{if } \prod_i \lambda_i (S_1) \neq 0 \end{cases} \tag{2}$$

In which, I is the number of effective factors, i ={1…7}, a_i is the weight allocated to each criteria (between 0 and 1) $\sum_{i=1}^{n} ai = 7$.

Finally, the obtained amount for combining is divided into the number of effective factors in formula so that the obtained number be normal. $\lambda_i(S_1)$ shows the amount of each mentioned parameters for service combining. $\lambda(S_1) \in [0,1]$ is the combining rate of the desired candidate service. In order to normalize the acquired amount for combining, $\lambda(S_1)$ is divided into $\sum_{i=1}^{n}$ ai.

And finally, from among the candidate services, the service is selected that the combining rate of it be more than the defined threshold for combining. The combining threshold is the minimum amount that a service must have in order that face no problem in runtime when combining with other services. In this research, the combining threshold has determined 0.6 in the normal situation.

3. The Proposed Model

Optimizing can be considered in two local and global ways. In local optimality, for each action, a service of the highest quality from among the whole candidate services is chosen. Therefore, it is performed very fast but it doesn't provide a warranty for presenting a general optimum compound service. In global optimality, the services are chosen for each action that of their putting together the quality of compound service has the highest amount [10]. In proposed algorithm the local optimality is used for choosing the service based on the combining feature. It's needed to be noted that the algorithm does not operate voraciously because in global algorithm, several candidate service is needed for each action with the combining rate higher than the threshold in order that the general optimum compound service be presented in user's view. As it goes on, we state the details of this algorithm.

4. Proposed Local Algorithm

```
Output of this algorithm includes groups of the services
that have the acceptable rate of combining. Input:
Q.com, (S1, S2,..., Sn)
Output: (S'1, S'2,..., S'n)
1) For each sij in Si {
// computes the combining rate of service
2) sij. com= Compute-Compose(sij );
// rate of combining threshold
3) Q.com=0.6;
4) If (sij. com < Q.com)
5){ Si =Si - {sij };
Return;}}
6) S'i = Si; }
7) Return (S'1, S'2,..., S'n)
```

Figure1. Local strategy.

In local algorithm, the base of the task is the rate of the combining feature which is itself the combination of several other qualitative features like availability, cost, runtime, etc. Therefore, it is necessary that the combining rate of the single existing based services be surveyed. When choosing the services from among the different services, the state is chosen that has an acceptable rate of combining and finally, leads to an optimized compound service. Stages of the proposed local algorithm according to the code-alike of Table 1 are as follows:

1. Environment of the system is determined. When a compound workflow enters the system, it is assumed that in the services' store, as for each existing action in workflow, there is a group of candidate services which perform that action.
2. The algorithm computes the combining rate of each candidate service for each action.
3. Rate of combining threshold would be considered 0.6 and combining rate of candidate services would be compared to the threshold amount.
4. From each group, the services which have the combining rate of less than the amount of threshold are deleted and the related group becomes updated.
5. The outputs of this algorithm are the groups of the services that have an acceptable rate of combining.

5. Evaluation and Analysis of the Results

The case study is considered as a way for evaluating the presented metric. In this regard, a real sample of the compound services is shown. A case study on "reserving a hotel" scenario was performed and the possibility of computing the presented formula for combining is surveyed. Finally, the accuracy of the function of the presented method was evaluated and compared with a valid method. Also, in the local algorithm, the time is spent on choosing the optimum service and the comparison of it with the local algorithm of the valid method and there are comparisons in this field with the existing methods. Stages of reserving a hotel are shown in Figure 2 in the form of a workflow.

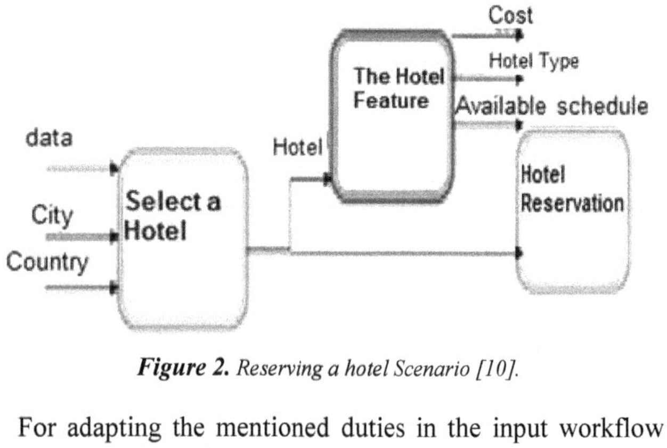

***Figure 2.** Reserving a hotel Scenario [10].*

For adapting the mentioned duties in the input workflow with real services, the stores were searched in order to find the services that did each of these functions. Finally, for each of these duties, some candidate services were found that performed the function. The user requests that discovered services for doing these duties had the following qualitative features, as in Table 2.

Table 2. Qualitative features [1]

Qualitative features	Renges
Execution time	0< exe < 10s
Reliability	90 <rel < 100
Reputation	70 < rep < 100
Price	0< p < 1000$

In this research, the real existing services in method [10] that were taken from the service store sws_tc were used for doing the case study in order for the results to be closer to reality. Finally, the results were compared with method [10].

5.1. Comparing the Combining Rate of Candidate Services in Atomic Terms

Computing the combining rate of discovered services for the task "choosing a hotel" is given in Table 3. All the effective criteria on combining is surveyed and computed. Finally the combining rate of each service for "choosing a hotel" is obtained according to relation 1.

Table 3. Computing the combining rate of services for the task "reserving a hotel"

Services	λ_1(gran)	λ_2(ava)	λ_3(cou)	λ_4(reus)	λ_5(adap)	λ_6(inte)	λ_7(qos)	Com
WorldwideHotel InfoService	1	0.75	1.5	0.35	1	0.4	0.32	0.76
CityCountryHotel Service	1	0.97	1.7	0.25	1	0.6	0.36	0.84
CityHotelService	1	0.9	1.6	0.3	1	0.4	0.225	0.77
Cityhotels	1	0.85	1.2	0.5	1	0.6	0.154	0.75

5.2. Comparing the Function of Proposed Metric with the Existing Method Based on Combining Rate

In this chapter, we spend time on comparing the obtained amounts for combining in the proposed method with method [10] in atomic terms. Table 3 shows the obtained combining rate in both methods for the task "choosing a hotel".

Table 4. Comparing the combining rate of services for the task "reserving a hotel" in both methods.

Candidate services	combining rate in offered method	combining rate in presented method[10]
WorldwideHotel InfoService	0.76	0
CityCountaryHotelService	0.84	0.68
CityHotelService	0.77	0.57
CityHotels	0.75	0.63

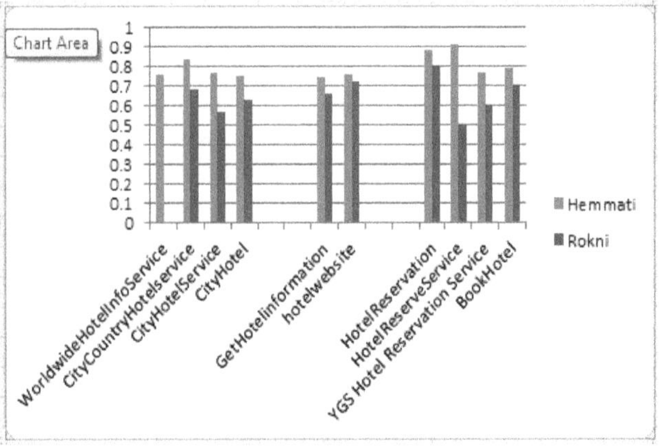

Figure 3. Comparing the obtained combining rate in the proposed method and presented method in [10].

The chart in Figure 3 shows a comparison between the obtained combining rate in the proposed method and presented method in [10]. As seen in Figure 3, in the presented method, by adding the two effective factors of "reusability" and "adaptability", a more accurate rate was obtained for combining feature of candidate services in comparison to method [10].

The chart in Figure 3 shows a comparison between the obtained combining rate in the proposed method and presented method in [10]. As seen in Figure 3, in the presented method, by adding the two effective factors of "reusability" and "adaptability", a more accurate rate was obtained for combining feature of candidate services in comparison to method [10].

5.3. Comparing the Proposed Local Algorithm with the Local Algorithm of Existing Method Based on the Combining Rate

As it was stated before, according to the proposed local algorithm, from among the candidate services for each action, the service which has the combining rate of more than the threshold would be selected as the optimum service but in method [10], optimality of choosing the service is done only locally and voraciously and the service is selected as the optimum service that has a higher rate of combining. The chart in Figure 3 demonstrates a comparison between the proposed local algorithm output and the method presented in [10].

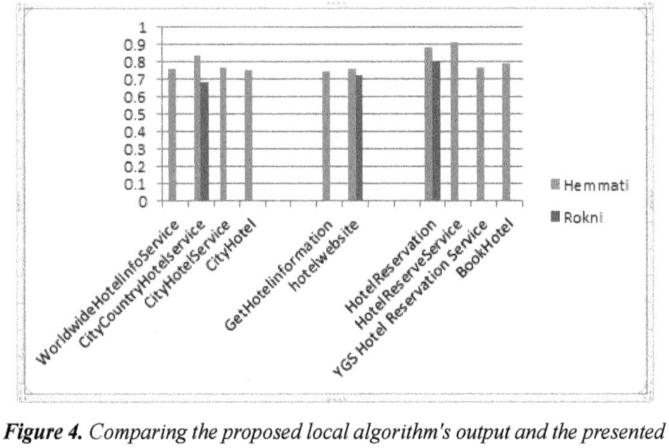

Figure 4. Comparing the proposed local algorithm's output and the presented method in [1].

As observed in the chart of Figure 4, in method [10],

because of performing voraciously, for the task of choosing hotel, the service "CityCountryHotelservice", for the task of surveying hotel information, the service “hotelwebsite” and for the task reserving a hotel, the service “HotelReservation” is selected. Also, because of performing voraciously, a service is likely to be selected that, after combining with other selected services, cannot finally obviate users' needs. In the proposed local method, a service choosing was done based on an acceptable rate of combining in order that, in the implementation time for combining with other services, it did not get into trouble. In this case study, all the candidate services obtained the acceptable rate of combining and were selected.

6. Discussion, Conclusion and Future Works

In this article, by surveying the existing weaknesses in method [10] and the more number of effective factors on the combining feature, a more accurate amount is obtained. Then, a local algorithm based on the combining rate of the services is presented for optimality of choosing services locally. This algorithm was designed in such a way that can be combined with global algorithm in future and finally a general optimized compound service was presented. While in method [10], in local optimality, because of performing voraciously, presenting a general optimized compound service in user’s view wan not warrantied. Most of the similar tasks survey the only effective factors on combining and no metric is presented for them. Also, some different methods have spent time on choosing the optimized compound service locally or globally without considering the combining rate of the services. In line with this research, we can evaluate the other qualitative parameters in addition to the combining rate in future and present a metric for it. A more accurate surveying on weights allocated to each of combining parameters is another job that can be surveyed in future.

References

[1] Q. Yu, M. Rege, A. Bouguettaya,B. Medjahed, M. Quzzani , A Two-Phase Framework For Quality-Aware Web Service Selection, Service Oriented Computing and Applications Journal, Vol 4, No.2, pp. 63-79, 2010.

[2] M., M., Akbar, M., S., Rahman, M., Kaykobad, E., G, Manninga, G., C., Hoja, Solving the Multidimensional Multiple-choice Knapsack Problem by Constructing Convex Hulls, Computers & Operations Research Journal, Vol. 33, pp. 1259- 1273, 2006.

[3] S. Choi, S. Jin Sun and S. D. Kim, QoS Metrics for Evaluating Services from the Perspective of Service Providers, in IEEE International Conference, e-Business Engineering, ICEBE (2007), pp. 622-625, 2007.

[4] J. Fang, S. Hu and Y. Han, A Service Interoperability Assessment Model for Service Composition, in Proceedings of the 2004 IEEE International Conference on Services Computing, IEEE Computer Society, pp. 153-158, 2004.

[5] R. Sindhgatta, B. Sengupta and K. Ponnalagu, Measuring the Quality of Service Oriented Design, in Proceedings of the 7th International Joint Conference on Service-Oriented Computing, Springer-Verlag: Stockholm, pp. 485-499, 2009.

[6] S. Choi and S. Kim, A Quality Model for Evaluating Reusability of services in SOA, 10th IEEE Conference on E-commerce Technology and the Fifth IEEE Conference on Enterprise Computing, E-Commerce and EServices,2008.

[7] B. Shim, S. Choue, S. Kim and S .Park, A Design Quality Model for Service Oriented Architecture, 15th Asia Pacific Software Engineering Conference, pp.403-410, 2008.

[8] G. Feuerlicht, Design of Composable Services, in Service-Oriented Computing, ICSOC Workshops, 2009.

[9] N.M. josuttis, SOA in practice the Art of distributed system design, oreilly: united state. pp. 35-46, 2007.

[10] Z. Rokni, “ choosing the service in service-based architecture based on qualitative features” MA thesis, Shahid Beheshti university, 2011

Modeling and prediction of changes in Anzali Pond using multiple linear regression and neural network

Farshad Parhizkar Miandehi*, Erfan Zidehsaraei, Mousa Doostdar

Department of Computer Engineering, Zanjan Branch, Islamic Azad University, Zanjan, Iran

Email address:
Farshad.parhizkar@gmail.com (F. P. Miandehi), Erfan.Zidesaraei@gmail.com (E. Zidehsaraei), doustdar55@yahoo.com (M. Doostdar)

Abstract: Iranian ponds and water ecosystems are valuable assets which play decisive roles in economic, social, security and political affairs. Within the past few years, many Iranian water ecosystems such asUrmia Lake, Karoun River and Anzali Pond have been under disappearance threat. Ponds are habitats which cannot be replaced and this makes it necessary to investigate their changes in order to save these valuable ecosystems. The present research aims to investigate and evaluate the trend of variations in Anzali Pond using meteorological data between 1991-2010 by means of GMDH, which is based upon genetic algorithm and is a powerful technique in modeling complex dynamic non-linear systems, and linear regression technique. Input variables of both methodsinclude all factors (inside system and outside system factors) which affect variations in Anzali Pond. Exactness of linear regression method was 78% and exactness of GMDH neural network method was more than 97%. As as result, exactness of GMDH neural network method is significantly better than regression model.

Keywords: Anzali Pond, Regression Analysis, GMDH Neural Network

1. Introduction

Investigation of conditions of natural ecosystems like jungles, range, lakes and ponds is of great importance in every country [3]. At present, Iran uses its natural resources 3.6% more than its normal use.Iranian environment will be disappeared if this trend continues[2]. Within the past few years, many Iranian natural ecosystems like Urmia Lake, Arasbaran jungles and Anzali Pond have received irreparable harms and are prone to complete disappearance [1]. Ponds are important natural ecosystems which cannot be replaced and they cannot be revived if they are not safeguarded. This makes it necessary to investigate the trend of their changes [4]. One of the uninvestigated points about ponds is absence of attention to non-linear changes and behavioral nature of them, which can be affected by many factors [10]. Therefore, the present research tries to model the trend of ponds changes using linear regression and GMDH neural network methods and compare their prediction exactness. It is necessary to understand and model relationship between input-output data in order to model any system. Fuzzy logic, neural networks and genetic algorithm are good techniques in solving complex non-linear systems [9-15-16]. Numerous studies have been conducted on prediction of ntural ecosystems changes in different spots of the world [8]. Most of them have used aerial images or satellite images for evaluation. One of the main studies in this case is titled "trend of ecosystems changes in general and ponds changes in particular" [11]. In this research, the author believes that understanding of the trend of changes in natural ecosystems and especially ponds can be useful in prediction of future status of them. Another research tried to investigate the trend of changes in South African ponds and then identify factors which affect these changes and interactions between the factors using satellite images and geoGraphicalInformation Systems (GIS) [11]. Prediction of natural ecosystems changes in Iran started when Urmia Lake went under crisis and many studies dealt with the reduction of the volume and area of UrmiaLake using visual analysis of satellite images and meteorological data [9-12-13]. In a similar study [17], researchers used image processing and recognition of Urmia Lake textures and identification of salt sections and calculation of increase in these sections around UrmiaLake to investigate bioenvironmental threats on this lake and then used linear regression to evaluate the present status of the lake. In the present research, table of factors affecting area and depth changes was created first of all. Then, we analyzed the trend of changes in area and depth of Anzali Pond using linear regression. In the next step, we predicted a time series for changes in Anzali pond using GMDH neural network based on genetic algorithm and used all factors affecting changes in the pond. 70% of data were used as input and 30% were used as test. Results showed that exactness of prediction of area and depth in regression analysis was 78% and in GMDH neural network method was 98%. General structure of this paper is as follows:

In the second part, we review definitions and methods. In the third section, factors influencing on changes in Anzali Pond are introduced. In the fourth section, the influence of the factors on the trend of pond changes is investigated and in the fifth section, we will investigate the implementation and evaluation of the trend of changes using linear regression and GMDH neural network method. In the sixth section, we present conclusions and recommendations.

2. Definitions and Methods

2.1. Multiple Linear Regression

These models are the most widely used of all regression methods. There are two or more predictor variables that may be measurement or qualitative (dummy) variables. Some multiple regression models may contain one measurement variable in multiple forms.

More often, the response variable is influenced by more than one predictor variable. For example, its diameter, height, species, age, and soil fertility may affect timber volume or crown surface of a tree. The crop yield may be affected by amount of irrigation as well as fertilizer.

Unlike simple linear regression, where the response is a straight line, the response may be a curvilinear or multi-dimensional, represented by a hyper-plane or a more complex surface.

Multiple implies more than one predictor variable and linear means linear in the regression coefficients being additive. Examples of two variable linear models are

$$Y = \beta_0 + \beta_1 X_1 + \beta_2 X_2 + \varepsilon \quad (1)$$

a first order linear model with two predictor variables; First order model implies that there is no interaction and the effects of changes in predictor variables are additive. And

$$Y = \beta_0 + \beta_1 X + \beta_2 X^2 + \varepsilon \quad (2)$$

polynomial regression model with one variable with higher power.

$$Y = \beta_0 + \beta_1 X + \beta_2 (1/X) + \varepsilon \quad (3)$$

with transformed predictor variable (1/X).

$$\log(Y) = \beta_0 + \beta_1 X_1 + \beta_2 X_2 + \varepsilon \quad (4)$$

with X_2 qualitative response variable;

$$Y = \beta_0 + \beta_1 X_1 + \beta_2 X_2 + \varepsilon \quad (5)$$

where X_2 is a qualitative indicator variable such as gender (male, female). Indicator variables that take on the values of 0 or 1 are used to identify the class of a qualitative variable.

2.2. GMDH Neural Network

The GMDH algorithm uses estimates of the output variable obtained fromsimple primeval regression equations that include small subsets of input variables. To elaborate on the essence of the approach, we adhere to the following notation. Let the original data set consist of a column of the observed values of the output variable y and N columns of the values of the independent system variables, that is x = x1; x2; . . , X_n . The primeval equations form a PD which comes in the form of a quadratic regression polynomial

$$z = A + Bu + Cv + Du^2 + Ev^2 + Fuv$$

In the above expression A; B; C;D; E; and F are parameters of the model, u; v, are pairs of variables standing in x whereas z is the best fit of the dependent variable y.

The generation of each layer is completed within three basic steps [5-6-7]:

Step 1. In this step we determine estimates of y using primeval equations.

Here, u and v are taken out of all independent system variables x1, x2,.., X_n. In this way, the total number of polynomials we can construct via (1) is equal to Z_m. The resulting columns $Z_m$of values, m = 1,2,…,N(N-1)/2.contain estimates of y resulting from each polynomial that are interpreted asnew "enhanced" variables that may exhibit a higher predictive power than the original variables being just the input variables of the system, x1, x2, . . . , X_n .

Step 2. The aim of this step is to identify the best of these new variables andeliminate those that are the weakest ones. There are several specific selectioncriteria to do this selection. All of them are based on some performance index (mean square, absolute or relative error) that express how the values (Z_m)follow the experimental output y. Quite often the selection criterion includes an auxiliary correction component that "punishes" a network for its excessive complexity. In some versions of the selection method, we retain the columns (Z_m) for which the performance index criterion is lower than a certain predefined threshold value. In some other versions of the selection procedure, a prescribed number of the best $Z_m$is retained. Summarizing, this step returns a list of the input variables. In some versions of the method, columns of x1, x2; . . . ,. $X_n$are replaced by the retained columns of z1, z2, . . . , zk , where k is the total number of the retained columns. In other versions, the best k retained columns are added to columns x1; x2; . . . ,X_n to form a new set of the input variables. Then the total number N of input variables changes to reflect the addition of $Z_m$values or the replacement of old columns X_n with Z_m new total number of input variables.

If Step 2 is completed within the generation of the current layer (or thecurrent iteration) of the design procedure, the iteration of the next layer (or the next iteration) begins immediately by repeating step 1 as described above, otherwise we proceed with step 3.

Step 3 consists of testing whether the set of equations of the model can befurther improved [14]. The lowest value of the selection criterion obtained duringthis iteration is compared with the smallest value obtained at the previous one.

If an improvement is achieved, one goes back and repeats steps 1 and 2,otherwise the iterations terminate and a realization of the network has beencompleted. If we were to make the necessary algebraic substitutions, we would have arrived at a very complicated polynomial of the form which is also known as the Ivahnenko polynomial

$$y = a_0 + \sum_{i=1}^{n} b_i x_i + \sum_{i=1}^{n}\sum_{j=1}^{n} c_{ij} x_i x_j + \sum_{i=1}^{n}\sum_{j=1}^{n}\sum_{k=1}^{n} d_{ijk} x_i x_j x_k + \cdots \quad (6)$$

where a, b_i, c_{ij}, d_{ijk} and so forth are the coefficients of the polynomial.

2.3. Criteria for Prediction Power Measurement

Different criteria have been introduced for measuring prediction power of different models. The followings are several of these criteria:

Root square mean error (RSME):

$$\text{RMSE}=\sqrt{\sum_{t=T+1}^{T+h} t(\hat{y_t} + y_t)^2} \quad (7)$$

Mean absolute error (MAE):

$$\text{MAE}=\sum_{t=T+1}^{T+h} \left|\hat{y_t} + y_t\right| /h \quad (8)$$

Mean absolute prediction error (MAPE):

$$\text{MAPE}=\sum_{t=T+1}^{T+h} \left|\frac{\hat{y_t}+y_t}{y_t^a}\right| /h \quad (9)$$

3. Factors Affecting the Trend of Changes in Anzali Pond

Thepresent research aims to model and predict the trend of changes in area and depth of Anzali pond. Table 1 shows factors affecting changes in area of the pond and table 2 shows factors affecting changes in the depth of the pond.

Table 1. *Independent and dependent variables for modeling and prediction of changes in area of the pond [3].*

variables	constants	Intended atmospheric parameters
X1	B1	Precipitation-independent
X2	B2	Water discharged in river-independent
X4	B4	Temperature-independent
Y		Pond surface area-dependent

Table 2. *dependent and independent variables for modeling and prediction of depth of water in the pond [3].*

variables	constants	Intended atmospheric parameters
X_1	B_1	Precipitation-independent
X_2	B_2	Water discharged in river-independent
X_3	B_3	Temperature-independent
X_4	B_4	Debris-independent
Y		Pond depth-dependent

4. Investigation of Factors Affecting the Trend of Changes in Lake

4.1. Using Multiple Linear Regression

In regression analysis, the depth and surface area of the pond were considered as dependent variables and atmospheric parameters were considered as independent variables and the regression equation is as follows:

Y=B0+B1X1+B2X2+B3X3+B4x4+...

Xs are atmospheric parameters and Bs are calculated in a way that least squares index is satisfied.

On the other hand, comparison of B coefficients reveals the rank and impact size of each of the factors.

4.1.1. Depth Investigation

As it was mentioned in section 3, atmospheric data are independent variables in linear regression and elevation of pond level is as presented in table 2. We reach the following equation after investigation of data and variables. the calculated determination coefficient is equal to 0.72.

Y=124.36+0.0551X1+0.00291X2-0.3658X3

4.1.2. Surface Area Investigation

Investigation of the data and variables leads us to the following equation and coefficients. The corresponding determination coefficient is equal to 0.83.

Y=1265.1202.3X1+0.987X2-217.0074X3 (10)

tities and variables, but not Greek symbols. Use a long dash

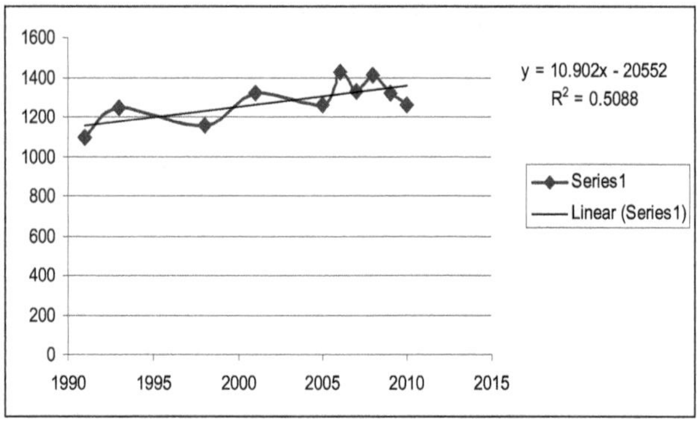

Figure 1. *trend of changes in precipitation level in 1991-2010.*

Table 3. data needed for GMDH neural network.

Year	Volume of discharged debris (tons)	Volume of discharged water (million cubic meters)	rain(mm)	evaporation(MM)	Pond surface area (Km^2)
1991	974.44	1600	1095	1100	57.84
1993	990.759	1700	1246	950	58
1998	1073.616	3100	1154	1020	81.87
2001	1175.728	1900	1324	900	66.9
2005	1273.572	1800	1257	850	66.5
2006	1273.189	1700	1425	800	66
2007	1273.158	2000	1326	900	64.5
2008	1272.214	1900	1411	800	62.09
2009	1271.144	1800	1324	1000	60.39
2010	1291.52	1700	1264	900	56.91

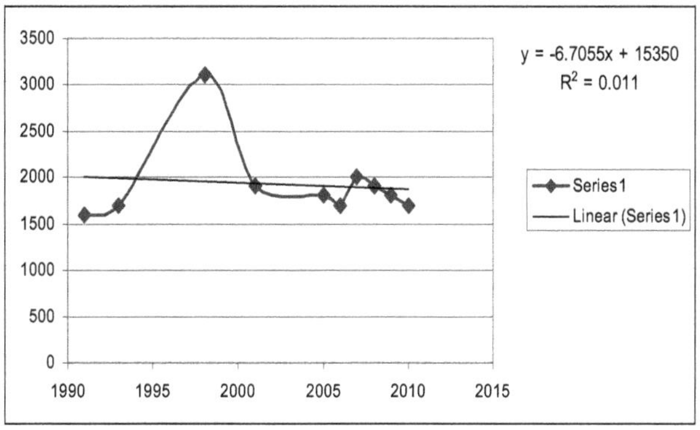

***Figure 2**. trend of changes in the volume of water discharged in Anzali Pond in 1991-2010.*

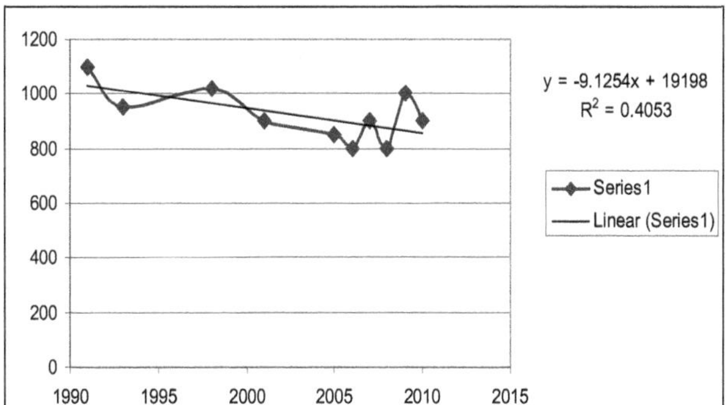

***Figure 3.** trend of temperature changes in 1991-2010.*

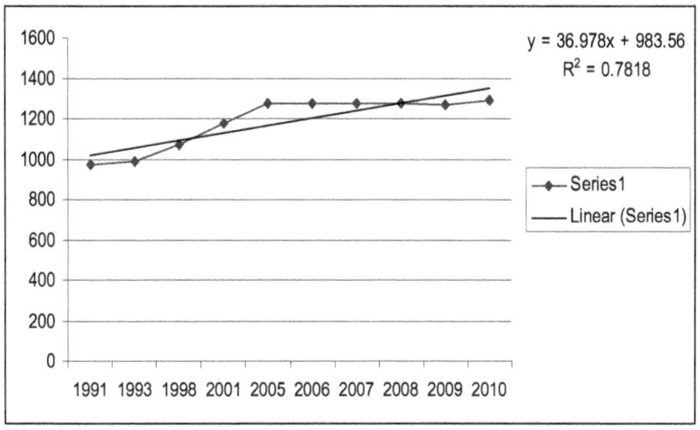

***Figure 4.** level of debris inserted into Anzali Pond in 1991-2010.*

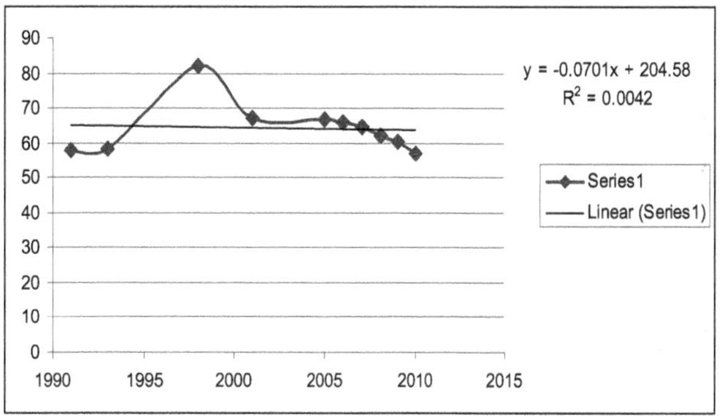

***Figure 5.** changes in the pond's surface area in 1991-2010.*

4.2. Modeling and Prediction of Changes in Anzali Pond Using GMDH Neural Network

Primary assumptions in GMDH neural network analysis are as follows:

- The number of latent layers is equal to 3.
- Percentage of the samples considered for test is equal to 30%. in the first layer yields 6 answers and combination of these 6 answers in the second layer yields 21 answers and in the third layer, we obtain 231 layers. For the case of 4 variables for pond depth calculation, we obtain 1540 answers. However, it is necessary to select the best answers out of all answers in order to avoid neural network's divergence. Therefore, training error and prediction error was calculated for all final combinations. Selection of optimal answers seeks two targets: minimization of modeling error and prediction. Another point in selection of optimal final input is observation of the order of selected variables to avoid scattering. As it can be seen in figures (4) and (5), 10 samples were selected for estimation of surface area of the pond and 7 samples were selected for estimation of pond depth using genetic algorithm. Rows 5 and 8 were considered for calculation of the trend of changes due to maintaining the order of input variables.

Table 4. *table of selection of variables for surface area.*

Row	Variables index								Prediction error	Trainingerror
1	3	3	2	1	2	1	1	2	0.015425	0.000159
2	3	1	3	2	2	1	1	2	0.025124	0.000541
3	3	2	2	1	1	2	2	2	0.065321	0.002124
4	3	3	3	3	3	1	2	3	0.025413	0.251256
5	3	1	2	1	3	3	2	2	0.025125	0.002514
6	3	2	2	1	1	1	2	2	0.365214	0.000215
7	2	2	2	3	3	2	3	3	0.895636	0.005112
8	1	3	1	2	1	1	2	3	0.021212	0.000113
9	2	2	2	3	3	3	1	1	0.521545	0.008955
10	2	1	1	2	2	1	3	3	0.854123	0.005455

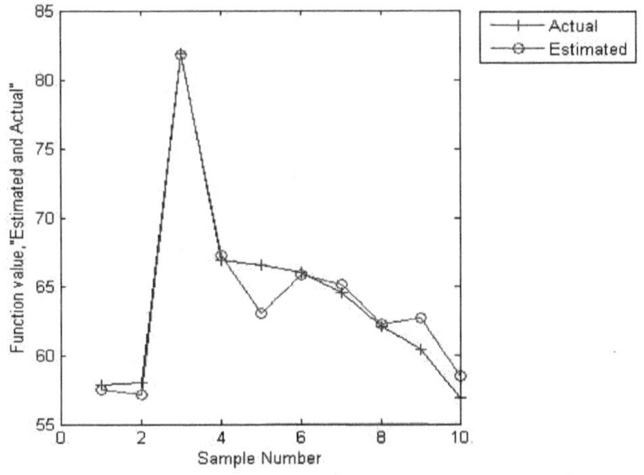

Figure 6. *trend of temperature changes in 1991-2010.*

Table 5. *table of selection of variables for depth.*

Row	Variables index								Prediction error	Trainingerror
1	4	1	2	3	2	1	1	4	0.013333	0.002154
2	4	3	3	2	1	2	4	1	0.025214	0.251546
3	4	2	1	1	3	4	3	2	0.032565	0.003251
4	1	2	3	3	3	4	3	2	0.026566	0.022212
5	3	2	4	1	1	2	3	4	0.025556	0.251561
6	4	4	3	2	2	1	1	1	0.251254	0.225511
7	3	4	2	1	1	2	3	4	0.254136	0.000215

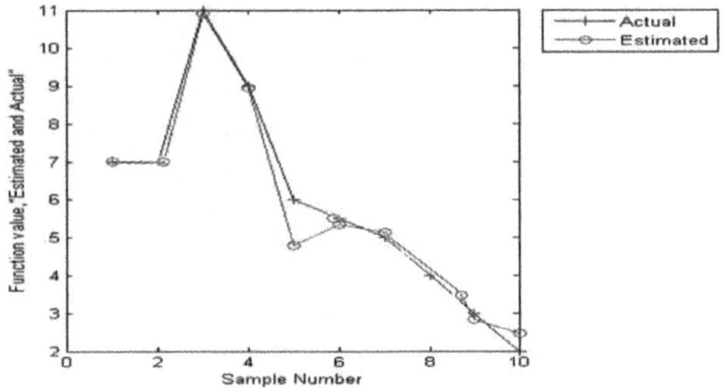

Figure 7. *trend of temperature changes in 1991-2010.*

Inputs were classified in two categories: training data (including at least 70% of data) and test data (30% of data). tables 6 and 7 indicate the exactness of depth and surface area evaluation.

Estimations of the coefficients of this model were presented in the previous sections. Prediction of the estimated model by means of linear regression in the time period using equations (7) and (8) reveals that error percentage of the linear regression model for prediction of trend of depth changes is 9.3% and also RMSE for surface area was 7.3%. real data and predicted data using both methods can be observed in figures (8) and (9).

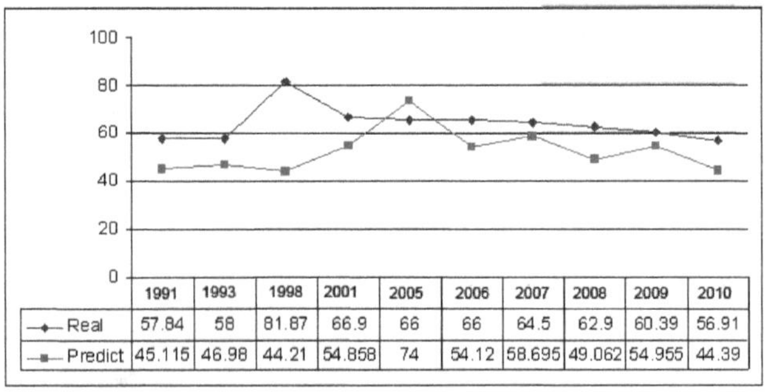

Figure 8. *real data graph and linear regression line equation figure for pond surface area.*

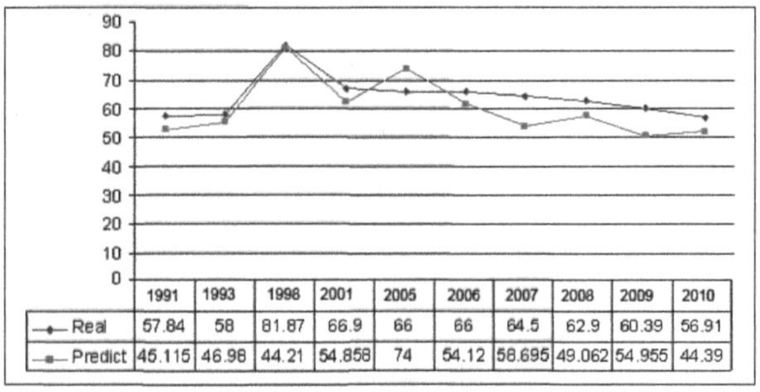

Figure 9. *real data figure and GMDH neural network for pond surface area.*

5. Discussion and Conclusion

In the present research, we modeled and predicted the trend of changes in Anzali pond using linear regression and GMDH neural network based on genetic algorithm and using table of factors affecting changes in Anzali pond in 1991-2010 and investigated the impact of each of the factors on depth and surface area of Anzali Pond. Results of GMDH neural network modeling analysis on all factors which affect changes in the pond's surface area (as inputs, 10 inputs) proved the serious reduction in surface area (from 82 square kilometers in 1998 to 57 square kilometers in 2010) and its prediction exactness is more than 97%. Using linear regression method, this value was equal to 69 square kilometers. Further, results of analyses conducted on input data (7 inputs) indicated serious reduction in the pond's depth. Further, exactness above 98% for prediction of changes in pond's depth verifies the results of this prediction.

References

[1] Tavakkoli, B and SabetRaftar, K. investigation of the impact of area, population and population compression factors of water basin on rivers discharging Anzali Pond, journal of environmental studies: special notes on Anzali pond: 51 to 57, 2007.

[2] Zebardast, L, Jafari, H. R, evaluation of the trend of changes in Anzali Pond using remote sensing and presentation of a managerial solution, journal of environmental studies, 57-64, 2011.

[3] Jamalzad, F, determination of the level of sensitivity of different areas of Anzali Pond using GIS, master degree thesis, environment faculty, Tehran University, page 52, 2008.

[4] Ghahraman, A and Attar, F. Anzali Pond in death coma (an ecological-floristic investigation). Journal of environmental studies: special notes on Anzali Pond: 1 to 38.

[5] Abrishami, Hamid and Moeeni, Ali and Mehrara, Mohsen and AHrari, Mahdi and SoleimaniKia, Fatemeh (2008), "modeling and prediction of gasoline price using GMDH neural network", quarterly of Iranian economic studies, 12th year, number 36, pp: 37-58.

[6] Sharzei, Gholam Ali and AHrari, Mahdi and Fakhraee, Hasan (2008), "structural models, time series and GMDH neural network", journal of economic studies, number 84, pp: 151-175.

[7] Abrishami, Hamid and Mehrara, Mohsen and Ahrari, Mahdi and Mir Ghasemi, Soudeh (2009), "modeling and prediction of Iranian economic growth with a GMDH neural network approach", journal of economic studies, number 88, pp: 1-24.

[8] Ozesmi, S. L., E. M., Bauer. "Satellite Remote Sensing of Wetlands. Wetlands Ecology and, Management", Vol.10, pp.381-402, 2002.

[9] Abbaspour, M. and Nazaridoust, "Determination of Environmental Water Requirements of Lake Urmia, Iran: an Ecological Approach", International Journal of Environmental Studies, Vol.64, pp.161-169, 2007.

[10] Zhaoning, G., et al. "Using RS and GIS to Monitoring Beijing Wetland Resources Evolution", IEEE International, Vol.23, pp.4596 – 4599, 2007.

[11] De Roeck, E., Jones, K., "Integrating Remote Sensing and Wetland Ecology: a Case Study on South African Wetlands", pp.1-5, 2008.

[12] Yung, J.L., "Sustainable Wetland Management Strategies under Uncertainties", the Environmentalist, Vol.19, pp. 67-79, 2008.

[13] van Stappen, G., Bossier, P., Sepehri, H., Lotfi, V., RazaviRouhani, S., Sorgeloos, P., "Effects of Salinity on Survival,Growth, Reproductive and Life Span Characteristics of Artemia Populations from Urmia Lake and Neighboring Lagoons", Journal of Biological Sciences, Vol.11, pp.164-172, 2008.

[14] Howland. J.C, Voss. M.S. "Natural Gas Prediction Using the Group Method of Data Handling", ASC. . (2003)

[15] Ivakhnenko.G.A (1995),"The Review of Problems Solvable by Algorithms of the Method of Data Handling (GMDH)", Pattern Recognition and Image Analysis, Vol.5, No.4, PP 527-535.

[16] Ivakhnenko. G.A and Muller. J.A. (1996). "Recent Development of Self-Organizing Modeling in Prediction and Analysis of Stock Market", Available in URL Address: http://www.inf.kiev.ua/GMDH Home/Articles.

[17] Ahmadi, R., Mohebbi, F., Hagigi, P., Esmailly, L., Salmanzadeh, R. Macro-invertebrates in the Wetlands oftheZarrineh "estuary at the south of Urmia Lake. International Journal of Environmental Restoration", 5(4), 1047-1051. (2011).

Integrating type-1 fuzzy and type-2 fuzzy clustering with k-means for pre-processing input data in classification algorithms

Vahid Nouri[1, *], Mohammad Reza Akbarzadeh[2], Tootoonchi, Alireza Rowhanimanesh[3]

[1] Department of Computer Engineering, Islamic Azad University, Mashhad Branch, Mashhad, Iran
[2]Department of Electrical Engineering, University of Neyshabur, Neyshabur, Iran
[3]Departments of Electrical and Computer Engineering, Center of Excellence on Soft Computing and Intelligent Information Processing (SCIIP), Ferdowsi University of Mashhad, Mashhad, Iran

Email address:
vahid.nouri@mshdiau.ac.ir (V. Nouri), akbarzadeh@ieee.org (M. R. Akbarzadeh), rowhanimanesh@ieee.org (A. Rowhanimanesh)

Abstract: In several papers, clustering has been used for preprocessing datasets before applying classification algorithms in order to enhance classification results. A strong clustered dataset as input to classification algorithms can significantly improve the computation time. This can be particularly useful in "Big Data" where computation time is equally or more important than accuracy. However, there is a trade-off between computation time (speed) and accuracy among clustering algorithms. Specifically, general type-2 fuzzy c-means (GT2 FCM) is considered to be a highly accurate clustering approach, but it is computationally intensive. To improve its computation time we propose a hybrid clustering algorithm called KFGT2FCM that combines GT2 FCM with two fast algorithms k-means and Fuzzy C-means algorithm for input data preprocessing of classification algorithms. The proposed algorithm shows improved computation time when compared with GT2 FCM on five benchmarks from university of California Irvine (UCI) library.

Keywords: Classification, Input Data Preprocessing, Clustering, General Type-2 Fuzzy Logic, Fuzzy C-Means (FCM), K-Means

1. Introduction

Classification is a common problem in data mining [20] where datasets are mapped into predefined groups called classes. Classes are defined according to the similarity of characteristics or features of data [15]. Since the classes are determined before applying the real data, this method is known as a supervised learning algorithm. Classification is used in many fields and sciences such as, image segmentation [1, 2], geology [3], robot control [4, 5], bio-informatics [6], genetics [8], biology [7] and healthcare [9].

Several researches have shown that the speed improvement of a classification algorithm is enhanced if the input data is first clustered before classification. This is particularly applicable when handling big data, where low computation time is equally or more important than classification accuracy. The class information also improves the accuracy of clustering [10]. In order to have the advantages of clustering and classification, many hybrid algorithms have been developed [10]. For example in both [11] and [10], first the criterion is preprocessed and optimized by a clustering algorithm and then in the next step the classification criterion is applied to the achieved clustering results to enhance the accuracy of classification algorithms.

Generally, accuracy and computation time of clustering algorithms are in contrast with each other, i.e. the higher the accuracy, the more computation time. Two well-known clustering algorithms are k-means and FCM. FCM and k-means are fast but have low accuracy [15]. General type-2 fuzzy clustering (GT2 FCM) is a new method that has high accuracy but is computationally intensive. In [18], a general type-2 fuzzy clustering algorithm is introduced that is based on α-planes. This algorithm has high accuracy and can deal with the uncertainty in datasets, while k-means and FCM, which are fast clustering algorithms, cannot handle the uncertainty in a dataset.

There are several works that concentrate on improving the computation time of type-2 fuzzy clustering. A modified version of type-2 fuzzy system was proposed in [21] to improve the speed (computation time) of type-2 fuzzy clustering. Also, in other studies [12, 13, and 14] interval type-2 fuzzy is used instead of general type-2 fuzzy for clustering, because interval type-2 is faster than general type-2 fuzzy.

In addition Yang worked on similarity metrics of type-2 fuzzy clustering algorithms on fuzzy datasets [23-26]. In these studies, Yang redefined new similarity metrics based on union maximum. These new similarity metrics affect type-2 fuzzy clustering efficiency.

The hybrid clustering algorithm which is proposed in this paper is used for data input preprocessing of classification algorithms to address the high computation time of general type-2 fuzzy clustering algorithm. The proposed hybrid method is based on a combination of general type-2 fuzzy, which is an accurate algorithm and k-means, which is a fast algorithm. We call the proposed approach KFGT2FCM. KFGT2FCM has the advantages of general type-2 fuzzy, k-means and FCM clustering algorithms, i.e. it has high accuracy and low computation time. The results are compared with GT2 FCM clustering algorithms for different datasets. Unlabeled datasets are used for clustering algorithms, however, labeled datasets are used for classification algorithms. While, we use classification datasets in our experiments, we can measure the accuracy of our clustering algorithm. The paper is organized as follows: section 2 discusses the proposed hybrid algorithm. The results and conclusion are presented in sections 3 and 4, respectively.

2. Proposed Method

Our method is based on k-means, Fuzzy C-means and general type-2 fuzzy clustering. General type-2 fuzzy clustering was presented in [18]. First, a general overview of type-2 fuzzy is presented, and then the proposed method is described.

There are two kinds of type-2 fuzzy sets which are used in clustering algorithms: 1) interval and 2) general. In interval type-2 fuzzy, the secondary membership function always equals one, while in general type-2 fuzzy it is a value in the interval of [0,1].

General type-2 fuzzy clustering is based on FCM (Fuzzy C-Means) algorithm. Like FCM, it initializes the centers randomly. The FCM algorithm uses linguistic terms such as "Small", "Medium" or "High", modeled by type-1 fuzzy sets for the fuzzifier parameter M (Figure 1). The FCM algorithm is used by the GT2 FCM cluster membership functions. The general type-2 fuzzy clustering proposed in [18] uses α-planes. The uncertainty of general type-2 fuzzy sets is managed by α-planes. The GT2 FCM algorithm exploits the linguistic fuzzifier M for its secondary membership functions of the general type-2 fuzzy partition matrix $\tilde{u}_j$ as shown in Equation 1. In addition, Equation 2, that is a membership grade $\tilde{u}_j(x_i)$ is expressed as type-1 fuzzy sets, which is used to describe the membership degree of pattern x_i to cluster v_j.

$$\tilde{u}_j = \sum_{x_i \in X} \tilde{u}_j(x_i) \tag{1}$$

$$\tilde{u}_j(x_i) = \bigcup_{\alpha\in[0,1]} \alpha / S_{\tilde{u}_j}(x_i|\alpha) = \bigcup_{\alpha\in[0,1]} \alpha / [S^L_{\tilde{u}_j}(x_i|\alpha), S^R_{\tilde{u}_j}(x_i|\alpha)] \tag{2}$$

Where $s^R_{\tilde{u}_j}(x_i \mid \alpha)$ and $s^L_{\tilde{u}_j}(x_i \mid \alpha)$ are calculated by (3) and (4):

$$s^R_{\tilde{u}_j}(x_i|\alpha) = max\left(\frac{1}{\sum_{l=1}^{c}(d_{ij}/d_{il})^{2/(s^L_M(\alpha)-1)}}, \frac{1}{\sum_{l=1}^{c}(d_{ij}/d_{il})^{2/(s^R_M(\alpha)-1)}}\right) \tag{3}$$

$$s^L_{\tilde{u}_j}(x_i|\alpha) = min\left(\frac{1}{\sum_{l=1}^{c}(d_{ij}/d_{il})^{2/(s^L_M(\alpha)-1)}}, \frac{1}{\sum_{l=1}^{c}(d_{ij}/d_{il})^{2/(s^R_M(\alpha)-1)}}\right) \tag{4}$$

Based on [18], centroid $C_{\tilde{u}j}$ can be calculated as a weighted composition of the interval centroids of individual

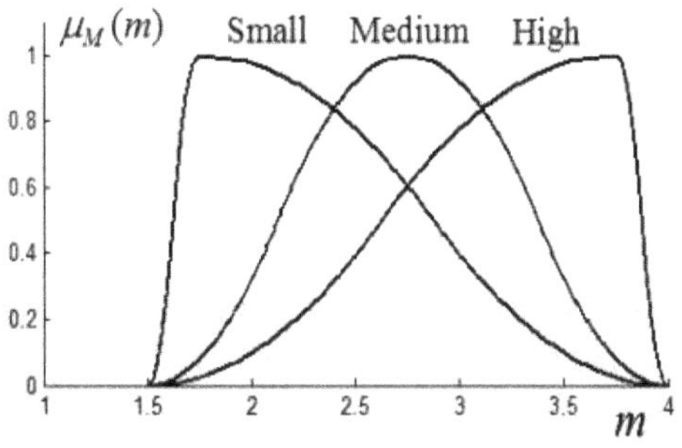

Figure 1. Linguistic variables for initializing the membership functions [18]

α-planes using Equation 5. The input of Equation 5 is $\tilde{u}_j$. Here, d_{ij} is the distance of ith data from jth centroid. Initial centroids are used for the first iteration. s^R_M and s^L_M are obtained as shown in Figure 2 for each α-planes and c is the number of clusters.

To compute the precise cluster position, Equation 6 is used to defuzzify the cluster centroid $C_{\tilde{u}j}$.

$$C_{\tilde{u}j} = \bigcup_{\alpha\in[0,1]} \alpha / [c^L_{\tilde{u}j}(\alpha), c^R_{\tilde{u}j}(\alpha)] \tag{5}$$

$$v_j = \frac{\sum_{i=1}^{K} y_i C_{\tilde{u}_j}(y_i)}{\sum_{i=1}^{K} C_{\tilde{u}_j}(y_i)} \quad (6)$$

In Equation 6, K shows the number of steps that the domain of the centroid has been discretized into and y_i is the position vector of i_{th} discretized step. According to [18], the hard-partitioning is done based on the defuzzified value of the type-1 fuzzy membership grade. So, the following rule is used for hard-partitioning:

$$\text{If } \left(\tilde{u}_j(x_i)\right) > (\tilde{u}_k(x_i)))), \text{ k=1,...,c, k≠j} \quad (7),$$

Then belongs to cluster j

The authors, in [18] use Equation 8 for hard-partitioning instead of Equation 7. In Equation 7, since the Euclidian distance norm is used to calculate the membership of pattern x_i to cluster j in the multidimensional space, it seems redundant to separately aggregate identical membership values for each dimension.

Therefore, in [18] the authors use Equation 8 for hard-partitioning:

$$\text{If} (c\left(\tilde{u}_j(x_i)\right) > c(\tilde{u}_k(x_i)))), \text{ k=1,...,c , k≠j} \quad (8)$$

Then belongs to cluster j

The centroid of the type-1 fuzzy membership grade $c(\tilde{u}_j(x_i))$ can be calculated using Equation 9:

$$c\left(\tilde{u}_j(x_i)\right) = \frac{\sum_{i=1}^{K} y_i \tilde{u}_j(y_i)}{\sum_{i=1}^{K} \tilde{u}_j(y_i)} \quad (9)$$

In this equation, K and y_i have the same definitions as in Equation 6, where $c(\tilde{u}_j(x_i))$ is the centroid of the jth cluster.

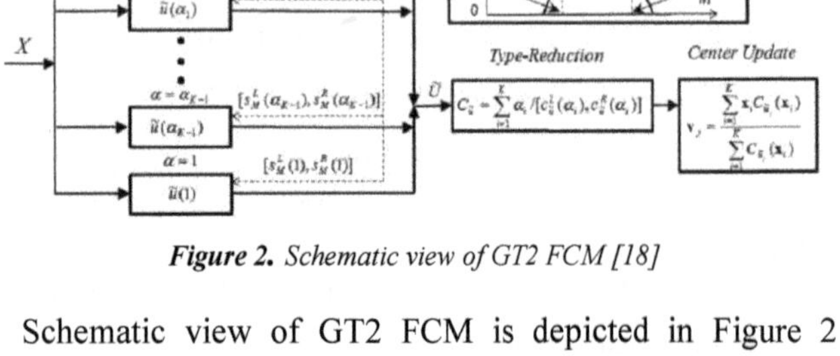

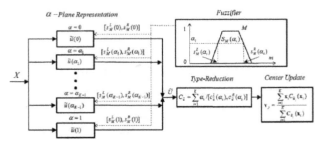

Figure 2. *Schematic view of GT2 FCM [18]*

Schematic view of GT2 FCM is depicted in Figure 2 Because of initial centroids are selected randomly the algorithm has more number of iterations, hence, more computation time (lower speed). So, if a clustering algorithm, such as FCM, finds the centers one step before GT2 FCM and passes them to GT2 FCM, the computational time of GT2 FCM will be reduced. But, FCM clustering algorithm has higher computational time against a simple clustering algorithm same as k-means. Therefore, in order to make FCM faster than standard FCM, a k-means clustering algorithm is run before FCM and finds the centers. K-means is used to determine the centroids of input data and then calculate the distances of each data from all centroids. The normalized distances are assumed as initial values of membership functions of input data of FCM. By doing so, FCM would have a better starting point and it helps to reduce the execution time and iterations of FCM. This algorithm is called KFGT2FCM.

k-means is one of the most common algorithms in clustering. In this method, k denotes the number of clusters. k-means algorithm has three steps including:

Step 1) k cluster centers are specified, randomly i.e. one center for each cluster, step 2) for each input, and distance from each cluster center is calculated. The data belongs to the cluster which has the minimum distance from the center. This step is repeated for all dataset, and step 3) the barycenters of clusters (which are generated in step 2) are calculated and considered as new cluster centers and then the algorithm goes to step 2 [15]. These steps are repeated until centers do not change for the two consecutive iterations. The algorithm minimizes its cost function to achieve the target. Its cost function denoted as Equation 10 [15].

$$J = \sum_{i=1}^{n} \sum_{j=1}^{K} \left\| x_i - c_j \right\|^2 \quad (10)$$

Here, n shows the number of samples, K is the number of clusters, c_j shows the jth cluster and x_i is ith sample of pattern.

In this paper we use Euclidian distance which is a traditional metric for distance measurement of k-means. Euclidian distance is presented in Equation (11) [16]:

$$d(x, y) = \sqrt{\Sigma (x_i - y_i)^2} \quad (11)$$

D_{ij} is the Euclidian distance between ith sample with jth cluster.

Also, in FCM clustering algorithm the cluster numbers (c) are determined before clustering, same as K-means. The objective function of FCM is denoted as Equation 12:

$$J_0 = \sum_{i=1}^{d} \sum_{j=1}^{c} \mu_{ij}^m \left\| x_i - v_j \right\|^2 \| \quad (12)$$

In Equation 12, m is a real number which is greater than one and by default is equal to two.

X_i is the ith sample and V_j is the jth cluster's centroid. Parameter of μ_{ij} shows the membership function of ith sample of jth cluster. The sign of ||*|| denotes the similarity of the sample with the cluster centroid which can be implemented using different functions. The similarity function that is used in this paper is the Euclidean distance. The μ_{ij} are elements of a two dimensional matrix called μ. The μ_{ij} values are numbers between zero and one [6, 9]. To calculate the value of μ and centroids of clusters, the Equations 13 and 14 are used, consecutively.

$$\mu_{ij} = \left[\sum_{k=1}^{c} \left(\frac{\|x_i - v_j\|^2}{\|x_i - v_k\|^2}\right)^{1/(m-1)}\right]^{-1} \quad (13)$$

$$vj = \frac{\sum_{i=1}^{d} u_{ik}^{m} x_i}{\sum_{i=1}^{d} u_{ij}^{m}} \quad (14)$$

In GT2 FCM, the centroids are initialized using random values, similar to k-means and FCM. In the proposed method, first, k-means is applied to the dataset using Euclidean distance to cluster the input dataset. We use K-means instead of FCM due to its higher speed, however it has lower accuracy against FCM. Therefore, with higher speed and lower accuracy the center of clusters are detected. The obtained centers of k-means are applied to the FCM for initializing the centroids, but, in FCM, first the membership function degree of dataset must be initialized. Usually, in the standard FCM the membership function degrees are initialized using random values.

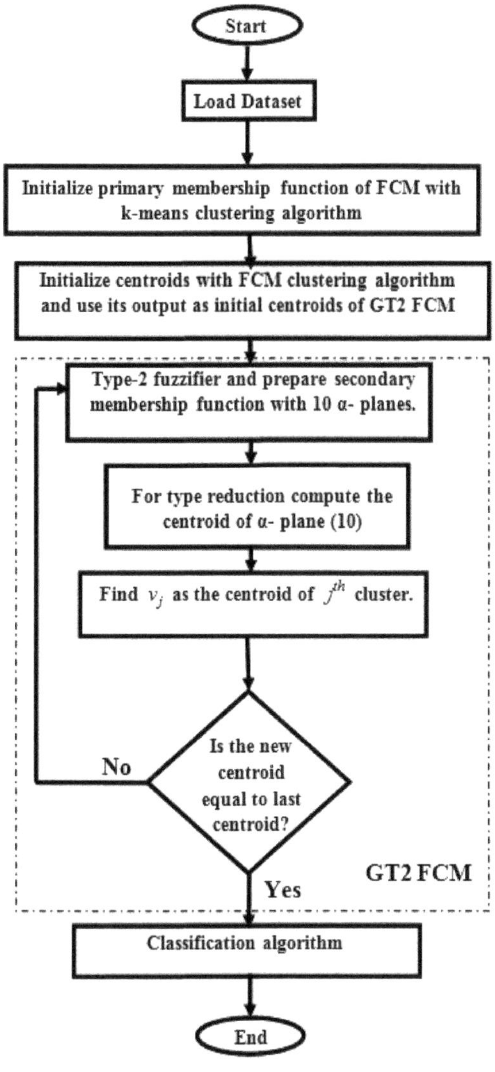

Figure 3. *Flowchart of proposed KFGT2FCM*

In the proposed method, after using k-means at the beginning of algorithm, the distance of each data to each cluster is calculated, normalized and used as initial centroids of FCM. Therefore, the FCM clustering becomes faster. In the next step, the obtained centroids of FCM are used as initial centroids of GT2 FCM. Then, the type-2 fuzzifier function calculates the secondary membership functions based on α-planes and using Equation 3, Equation 4 and "Medium" linguistic term for secondary membership function as depicted in Figure 1. We use 10 α-planes. Furthermore, EKM [1] algorithm [22] is used for type reduction and finding the centroids of α-planes. EKM was introduced by Mendel and Wu to enhance the computation time of KM. EKM is 39% faster than KM algorithm and saves about two iterations while KM find the answer usually between two to six iterations [22]. In this paper, Equation 5 which is based on EKM algorithm is used for type reduction to find the centroids of 10 α-planes. In this way, the type-2 fuzzy membership function reduces to a primary membership function which is type-1 fuzzy. To find the precise center of each cluster, the centroids should be determined using Equation 6. The centroids calculated by Equation 6 are compared to the previous centroids of each cluster. If they are not equal, the algorithm recalculates the secondary membership function using new centroids. Then the previous steps are repeated. Otherwise, the algorithm finishes (Figure 3).

The centroids which are applied to GT2 FCM are closer to optimal centroids compared to random centroids. Therefore, the required time for GT2 FCM to find the optimal centroids is decreased. Actually, k-means makes FCM faster and FCM makes GT2 FCM faster, consecutively. The flowchart of KFGT2FCM is depicted in Figure3.

3. Simulation Results

In this section the experimental setup and simulation results are presented.

3.1. Experimental Setup

Table 1. *List of datasets that used for experiments*

Dataset	Attributes	Size	Clusters
Iris	4	150	3
Wine	13	178	3
Pima Indian	8	768	2
Magic	10	19,020	2
Shuttle	9	43,500	2

In this paper, five standard datasets of university of California Irvine (UCI) are selected, including Iris, Wine, Pima Indians, Shuttle and Magic which have been listed in table 1 [19]. The Shuttle data has been divided into two classes. One class (class 1) includes the most numerous data class which is 80% of data and the second class (class 2) contains the remaining less numerous data classes which is the 20% of data. All of the datasets of Table 1 are applied to GT2 FCM,

[1] Enhancement Karnik Mendel

KFGT2FCM 50 times. The system used for doing the experiments and simulations is an Acer 5750G system with an Intel Core i7-2630QM@2.00GHz and 6.00 GB RAM and running Windows 7. MATLAB software has been used for implementing the algorithms. For fair comparisons of computation time of the two algorithms, the target accuracy has been assumed the same for both algorithms (i.e. GT2 FCM, KFGT2FCM) are based on GT2 FCM [18], and use the same membership functions. Since initial centroids of k-means and GT2 FCM are selected randomly, we run each algorithm for 50 iterations, i.e. with 50 sets of random initial centroids, to show that the random initial centroids have trivial effects on the results. For our experiments we use 30% and 70% of each dataset. In this way, the effect of number of samples is observed better.

3.2. Experimental Results

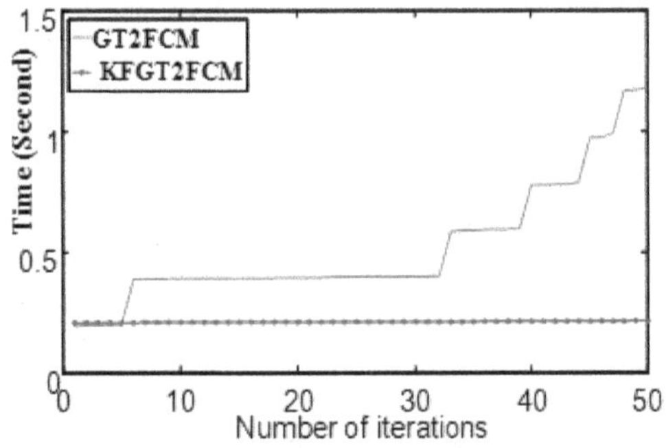

Figure 4. *Comparison of computation time for 50 iterations of both algorithms with a target accuracy of 60% for 230 data of Pima Indians dataset*

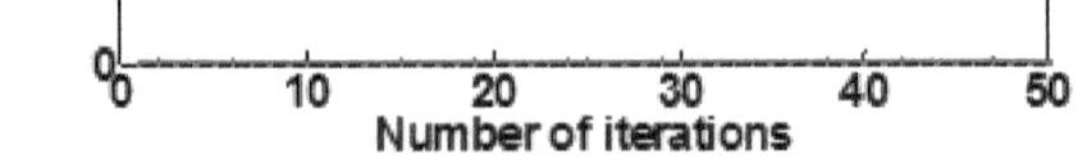

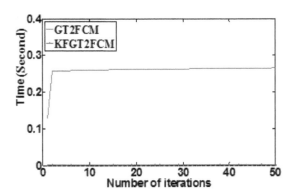

Figure 5. *Comparison of computation time for 50 iterations of both algorithms with a target accuracy of 66% for 53 data of Wine dataset*

The computation time of two algorithms are shown in Figure 4, Figure 5, Figure 6 and Figure 7. The 30% of Pima Indians dataset which have been selected randomly is applied to the two algorithms while the target accuracy is assumed to be 60% for both. In Figure 4 the results of this experiment is depicted. In another experiment which is shown in Figure 5, 30% of Wine dataset which have been selected randomly is applied to the both algorithms while the target accuracy is assumed to be 66% for two algorithms.

Comparing Table 2 and Table 3, reveals that KFGT2FCM outperforms GT2 FCM significantly for low target accuracies. For the experiments performed for generating results of Table 2 and 3, 30% and 70% of each dataset which selected randomly were used, respectively. However, for the experiments done for generating results of Figure 4, Figure 5, Figure 6 and Figure 7, 30% or 70% of each dataset, which selected randomly, were exploited.

As both pictures illustrate the computation time of KFGT2FCM is less than GT2 FCM. Also, in Figure 6 and Figure 7, 70% of Iris and 30% of Wine dataset are applied to both algorithms, respectively. The comparison shows that proposed method is faster that GT2 FCM.

Tables 2 and 3 show that for 60% of cases the proposed method (KFGT2FCM) is faster than GT2 FCM. Also, for 40% of cases where KFGT2FCM is slower for them than GT2FCM, the computation time difference of these algorithms is little.

In Table 2 and 3 Acc shows the target accuracy for each dataset in 50 iterations. Also, each the best results in each table are bolded. All of the results are calculated in seconds.

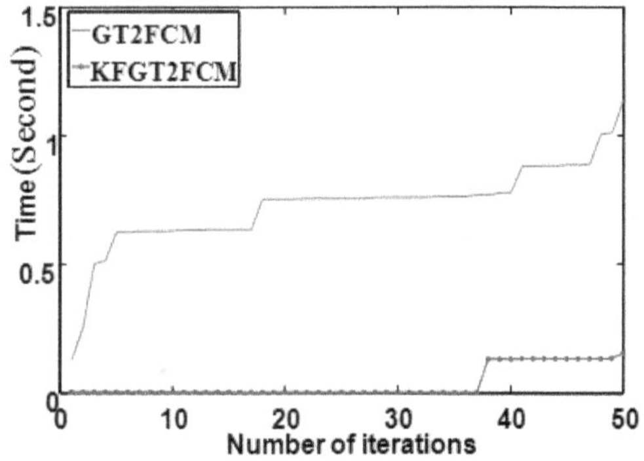

Figure 6. *Comparison of computation time for 50 iterations of both algorithms with a target accuracy of 75% for 105 data of Iris dataset*

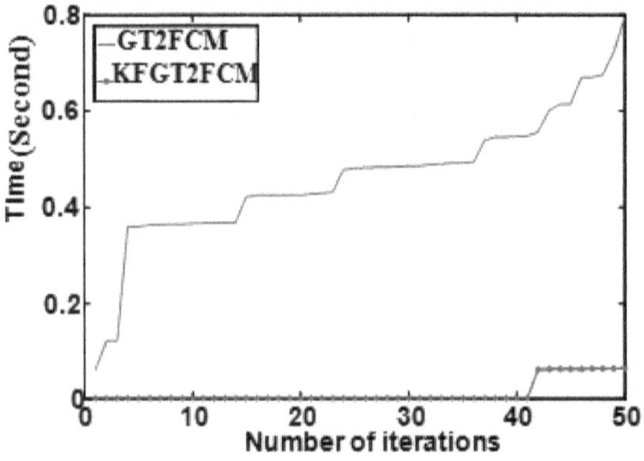

Figure 7. *Comparison of computation time for 50 iterations of both algorithms with a target accuracy of 80% for 45 data of Wine dataset*

Table 2. *Comparing computation time (in seconds) of two algorithms on 30% of datasets*

	Iris Acc:70%	Wine Acc:60%	Pima Indians Acc: 62.5%	Shuttle Acc: 55%	Magic Acc: 50%
GT2 FCM	0.1459	0.26	3.1795	2.32e-4	2.13e-5
KFGT2FCM	1.61e-5	1.55e-5	0.8244	2.8e-5	2.32e-5

Table 3. Comparing computation time (in seconds) of two algorithms on 70% of datasets

	Iris Acc:70%	Wine Acc:60%	Pima Indians Acc: 62.5%	Shuttle Acc: 55%	Magic Acc: 50%
GT2 FCM	1.1	0.53	1.63e-5	2.32e-4	1.29e-4
KFGT2FCM	0.04	1.64e-5	1.75e-5	2.33e-4	1.37e-4

4. Discussion and Conclusion

Recently, several works have used clustering and classification in sequential structures to improve the efficiency of classification algorithms. As indicated, the performance of classification learning is enhanced if the input data is first clustered and then used for classification. However, there is a trade-off between computation time (speed) and accuracy of clustering algorithms. In this paper, a new clustering method is introduced to improve the computation time of a classification algorithm by preprocessing classification dataset. To address the conflict of high computation time and high accuracy of clustering algorithm, we propose a hybrid clustering algorithm called KFGT2FCM.

This hybrid algorithm is a combination of high accuracy general type-2 fuzzy C-means (GT2 FCM) that can handle the uncertainty via using α-planes with low computation time k-means algorithm for input data preprocessing of classification algorithms. The proposed algorithm improves the speed of GT2 FCM. It has been evaluated using five datasets of UCI for clustering with different target accuracy.

For cases were 30% and 70% of data of each dataset are used, KFGT2FCM obtains better results compared to the GT2 FCM when target accuracy is low or features size are small. Also, results show that the number of clusters affects computation time of both algorithms.

The results depict that the proposed method is significantly faster than GT2 FCM, also in the 70% of case studies KFGT2FCM is faster than both GT2 FCM and in remaining 30% of case studies the difference of computation time of KFGT2FCM is not very high. According to Table 1, KFGT2FCM is more suitable for the most kind of low accuracy target of datasets than GT2 FCM.

Acknowledgements

We thank Dr. Ondrej Linda from Idaho University, for his generosity and support.

References

[1] Ting liu, Jurrus, E., Seyedhosseini, M., Ellisman, M., Tasdizen, T.,Watershed merge tree classification for electron microscopy image segmentation. 21st International Conference on Pattern Recognition (ICPR), 11-15 Nov. 2012.

[2] Zhang Bin,Ma, Guorui,Zhang, Zhi,Qin, Qianqing, Region-based classification by combining MS segmentation and MRF for POLSAR images , Journal of Systems Engineering and Electronics. 2013 (Volume:24, Issue:3).

[3] Zhou Q. ,Tong G. ,Xie D. ,Li B. , A Seismic-Based Feature Extraction Algorithm for Robust Ground Target Classification . Signal Processing Letters, IEEE. 2012 (Volume: 19, Issue: 10).

[4] Garcia Bermudez, F.L., Julian, R.C., Haldane, D.W., Abbeel P., Performance analysis and terrain classification for a legged robot over rough terrain , International Conference on Intelligent Robots and Systems (IROS), 2012 IEEE/RSJ.7-12. 2012, Vilamoura, Portugal.

[5] Nasrollahi P., Jafari S. , Ebrahimi, M., Action classification of humanoid soccer robots using machine learning , 16th CSI International Symposium on Artificial Intelligence and Signal Processing (AISP), 2-3 May 2012, Shiraz, Iran.

[6] B., H.B., N., J.C., Hierarchical classification using a Competitive Neural Network , Eighth International Conference on Natural Computation (ICNC), 2012. 29-31 May 2012, Chongqing ,China.

[7] W. Yang , K. Wang , W. Zuo, Prediction of protein secondary structure using large margin nearest neighbor classification . Advanced Computer Control (ICACC), 2011 3rd International Conference, 18-20 Jan. 2011, Harbin, China.

[8] Yuvaraj, N. ,Vivekanandan, P., An efficient SVM based tumor classification with symmetry Non-negative Matrix Factorization using gene expression data, International Conference on Information Communication and Embedded Systems (ICICES), 2013. 21-22. 2013, Chennai, India.

[9] Swangnetr, M.,Kaber, D.B., Emotional State Classification in Patient–Robot Interaction Using Wavelet Analysis and Statistics-Based Feature Selection, IEEE Transactions on Human-Machine Systems (Volume:43,Issue:1),.2013.

[10] W Cai ;S. Chen ;D. Zhang. A Multi-objective Simultaneous Learning Framework for Clustering and Classification . IEEE Transactions on Neural Networks, Volume: 21 , Issue: 2 2010.

[11] E. R., Pfahringer, B., Holmes, G., Clustering for classification . Information Technology in Asia (CITA 11), 2011 7th International Conference on Digital Object Identifier: 10.1109/CITA.2011.5998839. 2011 , Page(s): 1 – 8.

[12] A. Shahi, R. Binti Atan and M-D. Nasir Sulaiman, An effective fuzzy c-mean and type-2 fuzzy logic for weather forecasting . Journal of Theoretical and Applied Information Technology. 2009, Vol. 5 Issue 5, p550 . Malaysia.

[13] Q. Liang and J. Mendel, Decision Feedback Equalizer for Nonlinear Time-Varying Channels Using Type-2 fizzy Adaptive Filters . Fuzzy Systems, 2000..

[14] G. Zhengetal, A Similarity Measure between Interval Type-2 Fuzzy Sets . Proceedings of the 2010 IEEE, International Conference on Mechatronics and Automation 2011.

[15] Kimito Funatsu and Kiyoshi Hasegawa, New fundamental technologies in data mining. First published January, 2011. Printed in India.

[16] Rui Xu, Donald Wunsch II, Survey of Clustering Algorithms . IEEE TRANSACTIONS ON NEURAL NETWORKS, VOL. 16, NO. 3, 2005.

[17] Huaxiang Zhang , Jing Lu , Creating ensembles of classifiers via fuzzy clustering and deflection . Fuzzy Sets and Systems, Volume 161, Issue 13, 1 2010, Pages 1790–1802.

[18] Ondrej Linda, Milos Manic, General Type-2 Fuzzy C-Means Algorithm for Uncertain Fuzzy Clustering . Fuzzy Systems, IEEE Transactions. 13 2012, ISSN : 1063-6706.

[19] Frank, A. Asuncion, UCI Machine Learning Repository [http://archive.ics.uci.edu/ml], Irvine, CA: University of California, School of Informatics and Computer Science.

[20] R. Athauda, M. Tissera, C. Fernando. " Data Mining Applications: Promise and Challenges". Data Mining and Knowledge Discovery in Real Life Applications, ISBN 978-3-902613-53-0, pp. 438, 2009, I-Tech, Vienna, Austria.

[21] M. H. Fazel Zarandi, I. B. Turksen, O. Torabi Kasbi," Type-2 fuzzy modeling for desulphurization of steel process". Expert Systems with Applications 32 (2007) 157–171.

[22] D. Wu , J. Mendel." Enhanced Karnik-Mendel Algorithms for Interval Type-2 Fuzzy Sets and Systems". Fuzzy Information Processing Society, 2007. Annual Meeting of the North American.

[23] Der-Chen Lin, Miin-Shen Yang," A similarity measure between type-2 fuzzy sets with its application to clustering". Fourth International Conference on Fuzzy Systems and Knowledge Discovery, 2007

[24] Wen-liang Hung, Miin-shen Yang ," Similarity Measures Between Type-2 Fuzzy Sets". International Journal of Uncertainty, Fuzziness and Knowledge-Based Systems. Vol. 12, No. 6 (2004) 827-841.

[25] Miin-Shen Yang, Der-Chen Lin. "On similarity and inclusion measures between type-2 fuzzy sets with an application to clustering". Computers and Mathematics with Applications 57 (2009) 896_907.

[26] Hwang C.-M., Yang M.-S., Hung W.-L., "On similarity, inclusion measure and entropy between type-2 fuzzy sets". International Journal of Uncertainty, Fuzziness and Knowlege-Based Systems 2012. Volume 53, Issues 9–10.

Infrasound Source Identification Based on Spectral Moment Features

Zahra Madankan[1], Noushin Riahi[1], Akbar Ranjbar[2]

[1]Computer Engineering Department, Engineering Faculty, Alzahra University, Tehran, Iran
[2]Electronic Engineering Department, Engineering Faculty, Shahed University, Tehran, Iran

Email address:
z_madankan@yahoo.com (Z. Madankan), nriahi@alzahra.ac.ir (N. Riahi), Akranj@yahoo.com (A. Ranjbar)

Abstract: Infrasound signals have a frequency range below the human hearing frequency range, and originate from different sources. Since these waves contain useful information about the occurrence of some important event, in this paper we intend to present a method for the recognition of sources of these signals. In the present paper, by using the feature spectral moment along with Mel-frequency cepstral coefficients (MFCC) and linear prediction coefficients (LPC) and also selecting a subset from the feature which plays a more discriminative role for the signal sources, and then by using classifier ensembles, we reached a 98.1% precision in the infrasound source identification.

Keywords: Feature Extraction, Spectral Moment, Feature Selection, Recognition, Infrasound, Classifier Ensembles

1. Introduction

Infrasound is a technical term to identify acoustical waves with frequencies below 20Hz which is beyond human hearing capabilities with frequencies between 20Hz to 20KHz [1-4]. Infrasound waves propagate through the atmosphere around the earth and since they has a very low absorption characteristic, they travel very long distances [4-6].

Infrasound waves are generated by different kinds of natural and man-made sources including earthquakes, volcanoes, bolide, thunderstorms, chemical and nuclear explosions, airplanes, rockets and so on. Because various events produce infrasound by different mechanisms, the energy of the signals is also distributed in different frequency [7].

Thus we are surrounded by a world of non-perception sounds which include valuable information about their original sources and clearly determine the necessity of detection and the analysis of infrasound waves in the atmosphere.

On the other hand identifying some of the originating sources of the infrasound wave is the specific mission of CTBTO[1] and specific tasks for research institutes, therefore scientists and researchers have used different method to separate the infrasound waves and one of the best approaches to do so is the artificial intelligence approach.

Infrasound waves are collected by infrasound sensors or microbarographs which are set up by a special design in an array in infrasound network stations. The most important world wide spread infrasound stations operate under the International Monitoring System (IMS) which includes sixty stations worldwide to collect the infrasound waves for the International Data Center (IDC) in Vienna, Austria.

To identify the sources of infrasound signals, different steps should be taken. In preprocessing step, signals are normalized and noise is eliminated. In next steps, the feature vectors are extracted which best describe the signals. After that feature selection is done. Since the entire extracted feature vectors are not necessarily used for recognition in these signals, we are looking forward to using the methods to select the most important features which discriminate the signals propagating from different sources the best, so that we can use them in the recognition step. In the following, when all the trained data are available in this way, using the classifier ensembles method, the recognition step is going to be implemented. Finally, to test and evaluate the efficiency of the algorithms, cross validation method is used.

The block diagram of an infrasound source identification system can be seen in figure 1.

1Comprehensive Nuclear-Test-Ban Treaty Organization

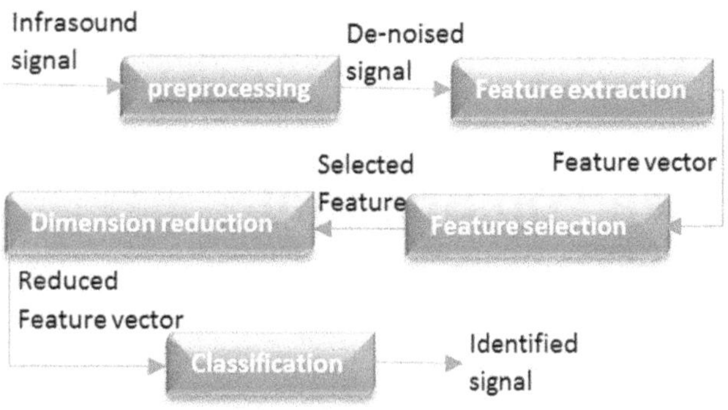

Figure 1. An infrasound source identification system block diagram.

In section 2 we present an overview of the related works. Section 3 presents our proposed method to extract the features. In section 4 we present our experimental results and section 5 offers our conclusions.

2. Related Works

Efforts to identify the infrasound signals have been done before. In 2005, F. M. Ham proposed a bank of Radial Basis Function (RBF) neural networks, to discriminate between six different man-made events [8]. Mel-Frequency Cepstral Coefficients (MFCC) feature set extracted for this method. He improved his method in [9] by a Parallel neural network classifier bank (PNNCB) with the same feature vector.

In 2008 a combination of Wavelet coefficients feature vector with a fuzzy K-means clustering method used to earthquake prediction [10].

In [11] a Hidden Markov Model (HMM) is used to detect the presence of elephants with Linear predictive coding method for extracting the formants of the elephant rumbles.

Another paper is published by F. M. Ham in 2011 that is focused on exploiting the infrasonic characteristics of volcanoes by extracting unique cepstral-based features from the volcano's infrasound signature. These feature vectors are then used by a neural-classifier to distinguish the ash-generating eruptive activity from three volcanoes [12].

X. Lui et. al. proposed a classification method based on Hilbert-Huang transform (HHT) and support vector machine (SVM) to discriminate between three different natural events [13]. The frequency spectrum characteristics of infrasound signals produced by different events, such as volcanoes, are unique, which lays the foundation for infrasound signal classification.

Feature extraction is an important block in any machine learning based system. Features extracted from signals can be divided into three categories: the time-domain features, the frequency-based features and time-frequency features. The time-domain features or temporal features are simply extracted and have easy physical interpretation, Energy of signal, zero crossing rate, maximum amplitude and minimum energy are some of the time-domain features. The frequency-based or spectral features are obtained by converting the time based signal into the frequency domain using Fourier transform, like: fundamental frequency, spectral centroid, spectral moments, etc. Time-frequency features describe a signal in both the time and frequency domains simultaneously. One of the most basic forms of time-frequency analysis is Short-Time Fourier Transform (STFT) and one more sophisticated technique is wavelet.

In recent researches the different and various sound and infrasound signals feature extraction methods, including cepstral coefficients method and spectral methods which describe the signal linear characteristics, are more common and used. One of the research challenges is dealing with the noisy environment of infrasound waves. As mentioned before these features, although they describe the signal the best, they are not robust in noisy environments. Thus we are trying to use other powerful methods for noisy environment to combine them with the feature extraction methods for improving our algorithm performance.

One of the feature extraction methods, which is more robust in noisy environments and has an ability to describe the nonlinear characteristics of the signal, is the spectral moment method. In the following, a short description of linear spectral features and spectral moment's features is presented.

Linear spectral features are features derived from power spectral density of a signal and they are able to extract the linear characteristics of a signal. These features include cepstral coefficients which result from discrete cosine transform over signal power spectral. Also the perceptual linear prediction has cepstral coefficients which are similar to the MFCC with one exception which is based on the human hearing perceptual model.

These features are used in some research [8, 9, 11, 12, 14] and usually used as a standard feature in the most of automatic speech recognition (ASR) systems. This set of features extract the linear speech signal information suitably, but it is not able to describe the nonlinear characteristics or higher order statistical features of the signal. Furthermore, one of the most important weaknesses of the spectral features is its low robustness in noisy environment. These features are very sensitive to additive noise [15].

To improve the robustness of these features, with respect to background noise and other distortions, an effort has been made to search for alternative features [16-20].

Since the upper sections of the spectral amplitude (such as formants) are less susceptible to noise, Paliwal [20] suggested spectral sub-band centroids (SCC) as new features to complete the cepstral coefficients features. These features are obtained by dividing the frequency band into some specific sub-bands and then finding sub-band centroids using the power spectral and Fourier transform methods. He tested these features over the recognition of English alphabets and showed that the centroids features is more robust due to the noise, but is still weaker compared to linear prediction cepstral coefficients (LPCC) in clean speech. This idea was improved in [21] and it was proved that these new features have a lot of capabilities for robust speech recognition.

The spectral sub-band centroids idea or the same first order spectral moments is extended to higher order normalized spectral sub-band moments (NSSM) [22].

3. The Proposed Method

We tried to extend the first order spectral moment to a higher-ordered one and while presenting a two-dimension definition of these features, we introduce the mixed moments and used them in our work.

The concept of moment is used to describe the features of a population. In general, the Kth moment centroid of a random variable with a single real variable X is defined as follow: [23]

$$\mu_k = E[(X - E[X])^k] \quad (1)$$

Moments could be defined in two centroid and non-centroid types. Unlike the non-centroid moments which are computed around zero, centroid moments are calculated around the average value and with respect to it.

Each two-dimensional probability density function could be described with sets of unlimited numbers. The lower order moments tend to describe the more generalized characteristics of distribution form. While the higher order moments describe the noise characteristics and their details. A two-dimensional density function could be considered as a two-dimensional shape which we supposed to extract its characteristics.

With the two-dimensional moment concept definition in hand, we can extend it to a two-dimensional distribution density function, and in such case, the two-dimensional spectral moments of this distributed density function describe its spectral form. On the other hand it presents a description of the spectrograph. The second dimension of the distribution function for our infrasound signals is the frames of the signal related to the specific event which has resulted from the implementation of the window function and of filter bank on the signal.

Two-dimensional Cartesian moments,m_{pq}, from the $p+q$ order, is defined with a distribution function $f(x,y)$, as bellow:

$$m_{pq} = \int_{-\infty}^{\infty}\int_{-\infty}^{\infty} x^p y^q f(x,y)dxdy \quad (2)$$

The two-dimensional moment for a digitized picture of $(M \times N)$ with a discrete distribution density $g(x,y)$ is as follows: [24]

$$m_{pq} = \sum_{x=0}^{M-1}\sum_{y=0}^{N-1} x^p y^q g(x,y) \quad (3)$$

m_{pq} is a set of n order moment including all moments so that $p+q \le n$, and includes $\frac{1}{2}(n+1)(n+2)$ elements.

The first order moments, $\{m_{10}, m_{01}\}$, are used for localizing the centroid of the shape mass. The coordinate of the centroid mass, $(\bar{x}, \bar{y})$, is determined by the following formulas:

$$\bar{x} = \frac{m_{10}}{m_{00}},\ \bar{y} = \frac{m_{01}}{m_{00}} \quad (4)$$

The second order moments, $\{m_{02}, m_{11}, m_{20}\}$ which are known as the moments of inertia are used to define the object principal axes. These principal axes are the pair of axes about which there is the minimum and the maximum second moment. The two third-order centroid moment, $\{\mu_{30}, \mu_{03}\}$, describe the image projection skewness. The skewness is a classic statistical measure of the degree of asymmetric of a symmetrical distribution around the average value.

The two fourth-order moments, $\{\mu_{40}, \mu_{04}\}$, are describing the kurtosis of a picture visualization. The kurtosis is a classical statistic measure of the peakedness of a distribution.

Moments beyond 4th-order moments are High-order moments. In [25], M. Vuskovic and S. Du analysed the impact of noise in temporal signals and found to be very high at higher order moments.

Now, by presenting a proposal about the moments, we expand them and extract more characteristics of the signal by moments named mixed moments.

Assuming $X = (X_1, X_2, \dots, X_n)$ is a multi-variables random vector with n dimensions, with the finite moments up to fourth order, the average vector $E[X] = (E[X_1, \dots, E[X_n]])$ briefly becomes a $\mu = (\mu_1, \dots, \mu_n)$. The nth order centroid moment's matrix is specified by $M_k[X]$ with $k = 2,3,4$.

The covariance, which is the extended concept of variance, is the measure of coordinate variations of the two random variables. The covariance matrix is a matrix whose elements show the correlation among the different parameters of the system. For k=2 the$n \times n$ covariance matrix is as follow:

$$M_2[X] = D[X] = (V_{ij}), 1 \le i,j \le n \quad (5)$$

The elements of the matrix are:

$$V_{ij} = E[(X_i - \mu_i)(X_j - \mu_j)] \quad (6)$$

Now the idea of extending the variance moment to covariance could be used to extend the skewedness and kurtosis moments to obtain the coskewness and cokurtosis matrices.

The coskewness matrices which is$n \times n^2$, is defined as follows:

$$M_3[X] = (S_{ijk}), 1 \le i,j,k \le n \quad (7)$$

Its elements are:

$$S_{ijk} = E[(X_i - \mu_i)(X_j - \mu_j)(X_k - \mu_k)] \quad (8)$$

Then the matrix $M_4[X] = (K_{ijkl}), 1 \le i,j,k,l \le n$ which is $n \times n^3$ and its elements are:

$$K_{ijkl} = E[(X_i - \mu_i)(X_i - \mu_j)(X_k - \mu_k)(X_l - \mu_l)] \quad (9)$$

is known as a cokurtosis matrix [26].

On the other hand, since we cannot ignore the features in which the power spectral function is extracted with regards to spectral specifications of the signal, we always use these features with the spectral moment features.

There are different methods to select the features from the feature space. An approach is a correlation-based feature selection [27]. In this approach we have to search the feature space and find subsets of features that are highly correlated with the class while having low intercorrelation. By scattering search method we first select some candidate subsets [28] and then evaluate the worth of a subset of attributes by considering the individual predictive ability of each feature along with the degree of redundancy between them.

4. Experiments

As was mentioned in the introduction, the infrasound waves originate from different sources. In this paper we have used the data released from six sources of infrasound from Defense Threat Reduction Agency (DTRA) data centre and it includes infrasound signals obtained from IMS and DoE arrays. The detailed information about these six events is shown in table 1.

Table 1. *Detailed infrasound data.*

Event name	Number of Signals
Bolide	15
Chemical Explosion	88
Earthquake	9
Suspected Mine Blast	279
Rocket Lunch	37
Volcano	179

After feature extraction and a subset selection from the proper features, we start the source identification process from the different available source signals through the classifier ensembles method [29].

The purpose of this algorithm is to make precise and diverse classifiers. The main idea is to implement the feature extraction over the subsets of features and to make one set with all features for each classification, so the PCA is used here.

Table 2. *Comparison of the proposed method results with some recent research.*

Feature extraction method	Classification method	Accuracy (%)
Wavelet coefficients	Multilayer perceptron (2007)	78
Wavelet coefficients	Decision table (2007)	60
Wavelet coefficients	RBF network (2007)	87
Wavelet coefficients	K-means clustering (2008)	96
LPC	Hidden Markov Model (2011)	90.5
MFCC	RBF network (2012)	96
HHT	SVM	97.7
Spectral moments	Rotation Forest	98.1

In methods that we use in this section for classification, to develop the trained data for a classifier, the features set is divide randomly into k-subsets (k is the algorithm parameter), and the PCA is applied to each subset. All PCAs are retained in order to preserve the variability information in the data. Thus k-axis rotations are executed to form the new features. The reason to use the decision trees for classification, here, is that they are sensitive to rotation of the feature axes. The purpose is to train multi-classifier systems based on uniform classification model over the different subsets.

Assume $x = \{x_1, \ldots, x_n\}^T$ is a sample with n described features, and we consider X as a set of data including trained data in the form of $N \times n$ matrix. We consider Y as a vector with a class label for the data as $Y = [y_1, \ldots, y_N]^T$ in such a way y_i adapts a value from class labels set $\{\omega_1, \ldots, \omega_c\}$. We also consider the classifications as a collective one in form of $D_1, \ldots, D_L$ and the feature set in form of F. All the classifiers can train in parallel.

After data preparation, we applied the algorithms to the data and the algorithms performances are evaluated by the 10-fold cross validation method.

5. Results

In this paper we used spectral moment features and combine them with the linear spectral features. Also, using a feature selection technique and a classifier ensembles method, produce a system which is able to recognize the infrasound signals propagated from different natural and man-made sources from each other. The system uses the spectral moment features to extract nonlinear features and higher order statistical specifications of the signals, and combine them with linear spectral features to have a proper linear description of the signal. Furthermore, by using the feature selection technique the system is able to obtain the smallest optimal feature vector which is able to have a better discrimination of the infrasound events. We obtained a recognition precision of 98.1% by using the classifier ensembles method.

References

[1] Rossing, T. D., *Springer handbook of acoustics*. 2007: Springer.

[2] Valentina, V., *Microseismic and Infrasound Waves*. Research Reports in Physics), Springer Verlag, New York, 1992.

[3] Pierce, A., *Acoustics: An Introduction to its Physical Principles and Applications, Acoustical Soc.* Am. Publ., Sewickley, PA, 1989.

[4] Bedard, A. and T. Georges, *Atmospheric infrasound*. Acoustics Australia, 2000. 28(2): p. 47-52.

[5] Liszka, L., *Infrasound: a summary of 35 years of infrasound research*. 2008: Swedish Institute of Space Physics.

[6] Bass, H., et al., *Atmospheric absorption of sound: Further developments*. The Journal of the Acoustical Society of America, 1995. 97(1): p. 680-683.

[7] D. Cárdenas-Peña, M. Orozco-Alzate, and G. Castellanos-Dominguez, "Selection of time-variant features for earthquake classification at the Nevado-del-Ruiz volcano," Computers & Geosciences, 2013, vol. 51, pp. 293–304.

[8] Ham, F. M., et al. *Classification of infrasound events using radial basis function neural networks*. in *Neural Networks, 2005. IJCNN'05. Proceedings. 2005 IEEE International Joint Conference on*. 2005. IEEE.

[9] Ham, F., et al. *Classification of infrasound surf events using parallel neural network banks*. in *Neural Networks, 2007. IJCNN 2007. International Joint Conference on*. 2007. IEEE.

[10] Wang, W., et al. *Fuzzy K-means clustering on infrasound sample*. in *Fuzzy Systems, 2008. FUZZ-IEEE 2008.(IEEE World Congress on Computational Intelligence). IEEE International Conference on*. 2008. IEEE.

[11] Wijayakulasooriya, J. V. *Automatic recognition of elephant infrasound calls using formant analysis and Hidden Markov Model*. in *Industrial and Information Systems (ICIIS), 2011 6th IEEE International Conference on*. 2011. IEEE.

[12] Iyer, A. S., F. M. Ham, and M. A. Garces. *Neural classification of infrasonic signals associated with hazardous volcanic eruptions* in *Neural Networks (IJCNN), The 2011 International Joint Conference on*. 2011. IEEE.

[13] X. Liu, M. Li, W. Tang, Sh. Wang, and X. Wu, *A New Classification Method of Infrasound Events Using Hilbert-Huang Transform and Support Vector Machine*, Hindawi Publishing Corporation, Mathematical Problems in Engineering, Volume 2014.

[14] Park, S., F. M. Ham, and C. G. Lowrie, *Discrimination of infrasound events using parallel neural network classification banks*. Nonlinear Analysis: Theory, Methods & Applications, 2005. 63(5): p. e859-e865.

[15] Indrebo, K. M., R. J. Povinelli, and M.T. Johnson, *Third-order moments of filtered speech signals for robust speech recognition*, in *Nonlinear Analyses and Algorithms for Speech Processing*. 2005, Springer. p. 277-283.

[16] Pitton, J. W., K. Wang, and B.-H. Juang, *Time-frequency analysis and auditory modeling for automatic recognition of speech*. Proceedings of the IEEE, 1996. 84(9): p. 1199-1215.

[17] Kim, D.-S., S.-Y. Lee, and R.M. Kil, *Auditory processing of speech signals for robust speech recognition in real-world noisy environments*. Speech and Audio Processing, IEEE Transactions on, 1999. 7(1): p. 55-69.

[18] Potamianos, A. and P. Maragos, *Time-frequency distributions for automatic speech recognition*. Speech and Audio Processing, IEEE Transactions on, 2001. 9(3): p. 196-200.

[19] Ghitza, O., *Auditory models and human performance in tasks related to speech coding and speech recognition*. Speech and Audio Processing, IEEE Transactions on, 1994. 2(1): p. 115-132.

[20] Paliwal, K. K. *Spectral subband centroid features for speech recognition*. in *Acoustics, Speech and Signal Processing, 1998. Proceedings of the 1998 IEEE International Conference on*. 1998. IEEE.

[21] Gajic, B. and K. K. Paliwal. *Robust feature extraction using subband spectral centroid histograms*. in *Acoustics, Speech, and Signal Processing, 2001. Proceedings.(ICASSP'01). 2001 IEEE International Conference on*. 2001. IEEE.

[22] Chen, J., et al. *Recognition of noisy speech using normalized moments*. in *INTERSPEECH*. 2002.

[23] Chan, T. F., G. H. Golub, and R. J. LeVeque, *Algorithms for computing the sample variance: Analysis and recommendations*. The American Statistician, 1983. 37(3): p. 242-247.

[24] Fujinaga, I. and B. Adviser-Pennycook, *Adaptive optical music recognition*. 1997: McGill University.

[25] Vuskovic, M. and S. Du, *Spectral moments for feature extraction from temporal signals*. International Journal of Information Technology, 2005. 11(10): p. 112-122.

[26] Jondeau, E., S.-H. Poon, and M. Rockinger, *Financial modeling under non-Gaussian distributions*. 2007: Springer.

[27] Hall, M. A., *Correlation-based feature selection for machine learning*, 1999, The University of Waikato.

[28] Laguna, M., R. Martín, and R. C. Martí, *Scatter search: methodology and implementations in C*. Vol. 24. 2003: Springer.

[29] Rodriguez, J. J., L. I. Kuncheva, and C. J. Alonso, *Rotation forest: A new classifier ensemble method*. Pattern Analysis and Machine Intelligence, IEEE Transactions on, 2006. 28(10): p. 1619-1630.

12

Analysis of information logistics in order management process - Focusing on make-to-order small and medium company

Reakook Hwang[1], Koichi Murata[2, *], Hiroshi Katayama[3]

[1]Industry & Strategy Department I, Samsung Economic Research Institute, Seoul, Korea
[2]Department of Industrial Engineering and Management, College of Industrial Technology, Nihon University, Chiba, Japan
[3]Department of Industrial and management Systems Engineering, Faculty of Science and Engineering, Waseda University, Tokyo, Japan

Email address:
murata.kouichi30@nihon-u.ac.jp (K. Murata)

Abstract: This paper discusses an analysis of an order management process (OMP) in a make to order production system. An inquiry process is particularly focused in this study. It is a delivery process of order information in OMP. The proposed procedure of this paper consists of the following five steps; 1) identification of inquiry process in OMP, 2) investigation of identified inquiry process, 3) creation of categories of attributes of identified inquiry process, 4) quantification of characteristic of identified inquiry process and 5) consideration of improvement of identified inquiry process. Through using the experimental result by the proposed procedure, a clarification of the characteristics of identified inquiry processes and a determination of the order of the processes to improve are possible.

Keywords: Information Logistics, Make to Order System, Small and Medium Company, Order Management Process, Process Analysis

1. Introduction

Order management process (OMP) is first step for realizing the product to satisfy customer requirement. OMP is considered as first process of order full process (OFP). It is a process which is from receiving orders to having the finished goods delivered. Lin (1998) summarizes main process of an OFP as follows;

- Order management, which receives orders from customers and commits order requests;
- Manufacturing, which includes production scheduling, material planning, capacity planning and shop floor control;
- Distribution, which considers the logistics such as inventory and transportation.

A reduction time for second process and third process has been eagerly tackled with in a production sector. On the other hand, a management for the first process is not focused too much. The reason is that there are many non-standard operations in the process. Examples are a product design with customer and a coordination of detail specification with trial and error and so on. As the result, it takes many times to proceed with the process caused by inefficient operations and losses in the operations. On the base of the recognitions, the purpose of this paper is a trial of OMP analysis.

'An inquiry process' is particularly focused as the analyzed object of this paper. It is important to communicate related information among organizations in OMP such as a) between a costumer and an order company, b) among business department, design department and production department within the order company. However it is found here and there that relevant operations are not smoothly proceeded to. For example, though a designer asks a salesperson/a customer about information for the product design, a response is taking a long time to come back and a progress of drawing and programming is stagnated. Also, because customer's final confirmation of the product specification before manufacturing the product is too late, the production preparation can't be set about. Moreover it is difficult to even obtain too busy boss's consent within one department. A waiting time in above examples lengthen the lead time from an ordering to a delivery of goods. And it causes a decline in a customer trust.

For the analysis, a systematic procedure is proposed in this paper. Most of methods used in the procedure are only traditional ones such as role activity diagram (RAD) (Ruth 2004), pairwise comparison (Saaty et al 1994) and quantification theory category III (Takakura 1962, Hayashi and Suzuki 1975, and Hayashi 1993). The idea of the proposed procedure is a combination use of these methods in one analysis flow to realize a systematic analysis of OMP. This paper will contribute a powerful use of them compared with a single use of each one.

On the other hand, an improvement of quantification theory category III is proposed. The method was originally proposed by Hayashi. It is one of the methods of multivariate analysis. The theory is a method of classification of samples based on the similarity of the response pattern with respect to attributes having several items. A response pattern is a pattern of items to which a sample belongs. In this paper, the analyzed data concern the relationship between improved inquiry processes in the OMP and attributes of an inquiry process. Quantification theory category III is a suitable solution methodology because most of the analyzed data are qualitative data and do not have external criteria. In this case, 'items' and 'sample' mean 'attributes of an inquiry process' and the 'inquiry process' respectively. However there are a few problems as follows.

- The attributes of an inquiry process are not weighted.
- It is difficult to extract different difficulties to improve a performance of an inquiry process from similar attributes.
- It is difficult to extract different difficulties to improve a performance of an inquiry process from similar processes.

In this paper, a model to resolve the problems is proposed by giving weighted-scores to attributes of an inquiry process and a simple case analysis is performed to confirm the utility of the proposed model.

2. Proposed Analysis Procedure

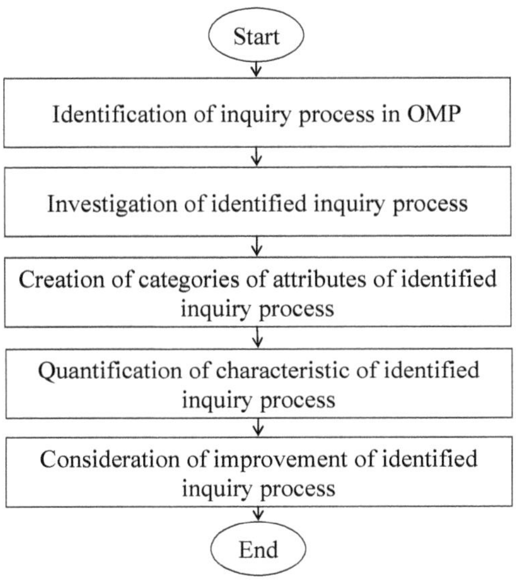

Figure 1. *A flowchart of proposed procedure*

Proposed procedure consists of five steps as shown in Figure 1; 1) identification of inquiry process in OMP, 2) investigation of identified inquiry process, 3) creation of categories of attributes of identified inquiry process, 4) quantification of characteristic of identified inquiry process and 5) consideration of improvement of identified inquiry process. A detail of each step is described as the following chapter.

2.1. Identification of Inquiry Process in OMP (Step 1)

The purpose of the step is an identification of inquiry processes in OMP. For the analysis, RAD is used. It describes processes in an intuitively straightforward way as a network of activities carried out by agents (Wastell et al 1994). Plural graphs like Figure 2 will be found from the analysis result by RAD. One graph means one inquiry process. A feature of the process is as follows.

- One sender and one recipient are in the analyzed process.
- A sender delivers some information to a recipient and receives processed information from a recipient.
- A recipient treats information received from a sender and returns processed information to a sender.

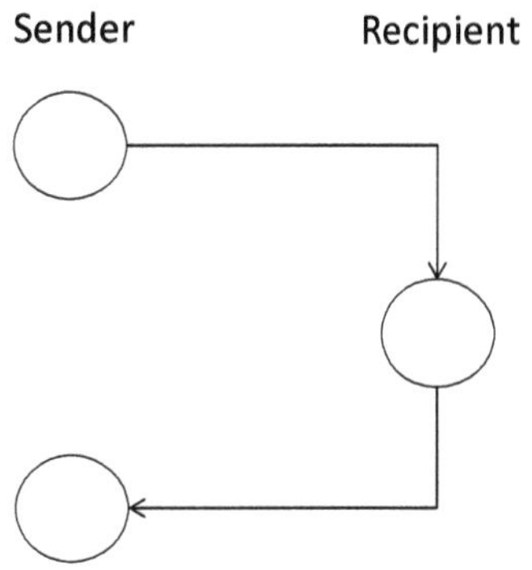

Figure 2. *Identified inquiry process*

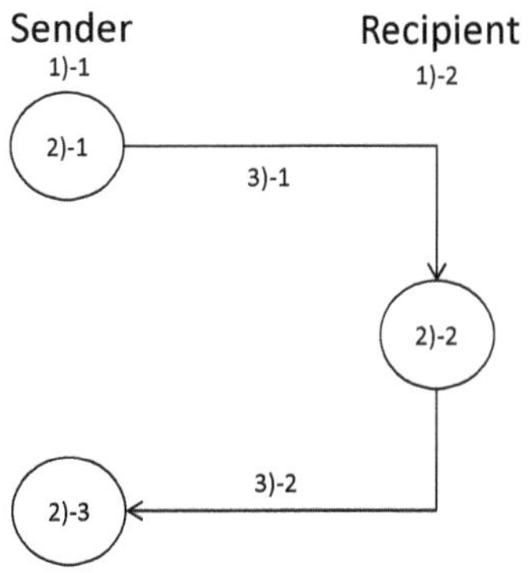

1) character information: role in OMP
2) circles: operation on OMP
3) arrows: direction of transmission for OMP

Figure 3. *Component of identified inquiry process*

A number of inquiry processes and their location in OMP can be clarified through finding the charts in the analysis result by RAD (Ruth 2004). Moreover, but the chart is simple, three kinds of components are included in the chart as shown in

Figure 3. The first component is a role of OMP by character information. The second component is an operation on OMP by circles information. And the third component is a direction of transmission for OMP by arrow information. However, there is a limit to clarify detail of each identified inquiry process better than this. Hence, detail of each identified inquiry process is analyzed in the next step.

2.2. Investigation of Identified Inquiry Process (Step 2)

In the step, an identified inquiry process is investigated by the proposed survey sheet as shown in Table 1. The table is systematically designed to realize smooth survey based on the above three components of an inquiry process as shown in Figure 3. In the part of the first component in the sheet, a sender's attribute and a recipient's attribute, i.e. a belonging, a position and an operation in charge, are described. In the part of the second component in the sheet, three operations are described; 1) a preparation for an inquiry process by a sender, 2) a response by a recipient and 3) a cleaning up after an inquiry process by a sender. And in the part of the third component in the sheet, how to transmit between a sender and a recipient is described. In addition, in order to understand an outline of an inquiry process, it is important the purpose of an inquiry process is summarized before three components are investigated.

Table 1. *Survey sheet of inquiry process*

No.	
Survey sheet of inquiry process	
< A survey framework > 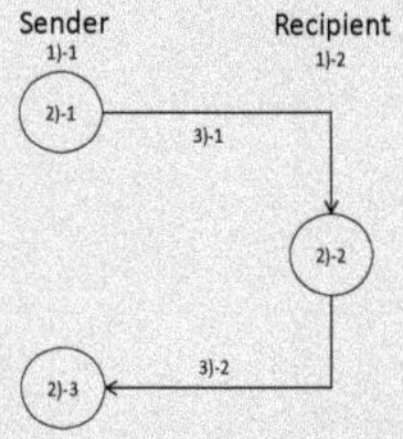	1) Role in OMP (Character information) 1)-1 Sender 1)-2 Recipient 2) Circles: Operation on OMP (Circles) 2)-1 Preparation for inquiry process by sender 2)-2 Response by recipient 2)-3 Cleaning up after inquiry process by sender
<Purpose of inquiry process>	3) Direction of transmission for OMP (Arrows) 3)-1 How to transmit from sender to recipient 3)-2 How to transmit from recipient to sender

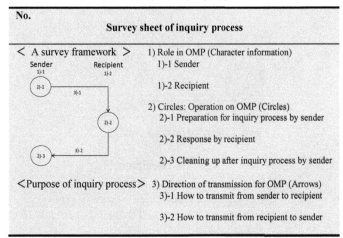

2.3. Creation of Categories of Attributes of Identified Inquiry Process (Step 3)

For the step, six attributes is prepared. Their names are 'combination type', 'preparation', 'response', 'clean up', 'transmission 1' and 'transmission 2'. A determination of them is systematic. To be concrete, each of them is related to three factors in the survey framework of an inquiry process as shown in Figure 3. 'Combination type' is obtained from 'role in OMP'. 'Preparation', 'response' and 'clean up' are obtained from 'operation on OMP'. 'Transmission 1' and 'transmission 2' are obtained from 'direction of transmission for OMP'. An illustration of each attributes is described in Table 2. And then the final output of the step is categories of each above attributes. A source for creating the output is the survey result of previous step and a relevant literature.

2.4. Quantification of Characteristic of Identified Inquiry Process (Step 4)

In the step, a relationship between identified inquiry processes and attributes of inquiry process is clarified by 0-1 variable. Through the analysis of the relationship data by an original qualification theory category III, the overall relationship, the similarity among categories of attributes and the similarity among processes can be quantified. Table 3 shows a form of the analyzed data. a_{kj} is defined as the value of category k of attribute j. b_i is defined as the value of inquiry process i. σ_{ikj} is 0-1 variable; If inquiry process i has category k of attribute j, σ_{ikj} is 1. If inquiry process i don't have category k of attribute j, σ_{ikj} is 0. i is a suffix of inquiry process, j is a suffix of attribute and k is a suffix of category. The objective function of the original model is the correlation coefficient between a_{kj} and b_i is maximized.

2.5. Consideration of Improvement of Identified Inquiry Process (Step 5)

In the step, the order of identified inquiry processes to improve is considered with the improved qualification theory category III. The analyzed data is illustrated from Table 4. Attributes are weighted from the viewpoint of the difficulty regarding performance improvement of inquiry process. Notation of weight j is w_j. A weighting is performed based on a pairwise comparison (Saaty et al 1994) which is one of the representative polite comparison methods. Also, when attributes is weighted, a value of the relationship between inquiry processes and attributes of inquiry process is not 0-1 variables but variables between 0 and 1. For corresponding to the change, the formulation for the proposed model is as the following formula (1) to formula (7).

Table 2. *Attribute of inquiry process*

Factor of survey framework	Attribute	Illustration of attributes
1) role in OMP	1)-1 combination type	a type of relationship between sender and recipient
2) operation on OMP	2)-1 preparation	a operation for making questions from a sender to a recipient
	2)-2 response	a operation for making responses to questions from a sender by a recipient
	2)-3 clean up	a operation for processing a design data based on created responses from recipient by a sender
3) direction of transmission for OMP	3)-1 transmission 1	a medium of a transmission from a sender to a recipient
	3)-2 transmission 2	a medium of a transmission from a recipient to a sender

Table 3. *Analyzed data by qualification theory category III*

		a_{11}	a_{k1}	a_{v1}		a_{1j}	a_{kj}	a_{vj}		a_{1m}	a_{km}	a_{vm}
	Process		Attribute *1*				Attribute *j*				Attribute *m*	
		Category *11*	Category *k1*	Category *v1*		Category *1j*	Category *kj*	Category *vj*		Category *1m*	Category *km*	Category *vm*
b_1	Process *1*	σ_{111}			...	σ_{11j}			...	σ_{11m}		
	...											
b_i	Process *i*		σ_{ik1}				σ_{ikj}				σ_{ikm}	
	...											
b_n	Process *n*			σ_{nv1}				σ_{nvj}				σ_{nvm}

Notation

a_{k_j} :value of category *k* of attribute *j* $(j=1,\ldots,m, k_j=1,\ldots,v_j)$

b_i :value of inquiry process *i* $(i=1,\ldots,n)$

δ_{ijk} :0-1 variables; If inquiry process *i* has category *k* of attribute *j*, δ_{ijk} is 1. If inquiry process *i* don't have category *k* of attribute *j*, δ_{ijk} is 0. $(i=1,\ldots,n, j=1,\ldots,m, k_j=1,\ldots,v_j)$

Table 4. *Analyzed data for weighted-qualification theory category III*

		a'_{11}	a'_{k1}	a'_{v1}		a'_{1j}	a'_{kj}	a'_{vj}		a'_{1m}	a'_{km}	a'_{vm}
	Process		Attribute *1*				Attribute *j*				Attribute *m*	
		Category *11*	Category *k1*	Category *v1*		Category *1j*	Category *kj*	Category *vj*		Category *1m*	Category *km*	Category *vm*
b'_1	Process *1*	$w_1\sigma_{111}$			...	$w_j\sigma_{11j}$			...	$w_m\sigma_{11m}$		
	...											
b'_i	Process *i*		$w_1\sigma_{ik1}$				$w_j\sigma_{ikj}$				$w_m\sigma_{ikm}$	
	...											
b'_n	Process *n*			$w_1\sigma_{nv1}$				$w_j\sigma_{nvj}$				$w_m\sigma_{nvm}$

Notation

w_j :weighting score of attribute *j* $(j=1,\ldots,m)$

a'_{k_j} : value of category *k* of attribute *j* $(j=1,\ldots,m, k_j=1,\ldots,v_j)$

b'_i : value of inquiry process *i* $(i=1,\ldots,n)$

δ_{ijk} : 0-1 variables; If inquiry process *i* has category *k* of attribute *j*, δ_{ijk} is 1. If inquiry process *i* don't have category *k* of attribute *j*, δ_{ijk} is 0. $(i=1,\ldots,n, j=1,\ldots,m, k_j=1,\ldots,v_j)$

Objective function

$$\max \rho = \frac{C_{a'b'}}{\sqrt{\sigma_{a'}^2 \sigma_{b'}^2}} \qquad (1)$$

(maximum correlation coefficient between inquiry processes and attributes of inquiry process) subject to,

$$b'_i = \frac{1}{\sum_{j=1}^{m} v_j} \sum_{k_j=1}^{v_j} w_{ik_j} a'_{k_j} \qquad (2)$$

(value of inquiry process *i*)

$$\overline{a'} = 0 \qquad (3)$$

(constrains the average values of the attributes of inquiry process)

$$\overline{b'} = 0 \qquad (4)$$

(constrains the average values of the inquiry processes)

$$\sigma_{a'}^2 = \frac{1}{T} \sum_{j=1}^{m} \sum_{k_j=1}^{v_j} \sum_{i=1}^{n} w_{ik_j} {a'_{k_j}}^2 \qquad (5)$$

(variance of the marginal distribution of the attribute value on the simultaneous distribution between inquiry processes and attributes of inquiry process)

$$\sigma_{b'}^2 = \frac{1}{T} \sum_{j=1}^{m} \sum_{k_j=1}^{v_j} \sum_{i=1}^{n} w_{ik_j} b_i'^2 \qquad (6)$$

(variance of the marginal distribution of the inquiry process value on the simultaneous distribution between inquiry processes and attributes of inquiry process)

$$C_{a'b'} = \frac{1}{T} \sum_{j=1}^{m} \sum_{k_j=1}^{v_j} \sum_{i=1}^{n} w_{ik_j} a'_{k_j} b'_i \qquad (7)$$

(covariance between the attribute values and the inquiry process values on the simultaneous distribution between inquiry processes and attributes of inquiry process).

Decision variables

ρ : correlation coefficient between inquiry process and attributes of inquiry process

a'_{k_j} : value of category *k* of attribute *j* $(j=1,\ldots,m, k_j=1,\ldots,v_j)$

b'_i : value of inquiry process *i* $(i=1,\ldots,n)$

Fixed variables

w_j : weighting score of attribute *j* $(j=1,\ldots,m)$

T : total number of inquiry processes × a number of categories $(n \times \sum_{j=1}^{m} v_j)$

3. Case Study for a Characteristic Analysis of Inquiry Processes in OMP

In this section, the utility of the proposed procedure is confirmed through its application to the OMP of the small and medium company in Japan. They have manufactured machine tool accessories and supplied to their customers who are mainly machine-tool makers. Their different products are different specifications and they have politely corresponded to each of their customer's requirements. In other words, their production system is typical make to order system.

The case company considers a time from order receipt to product delivery as shown in Figure 4. In other words, they divide the time into an order management time and a production/delivery time. Up to the present, they have tackled with a reduction of production/delivery time. On the other hand, OMP is not focused. However it becomes necessary to improve a performance of OMP in accordance with becoming higher level of their customer requirement.

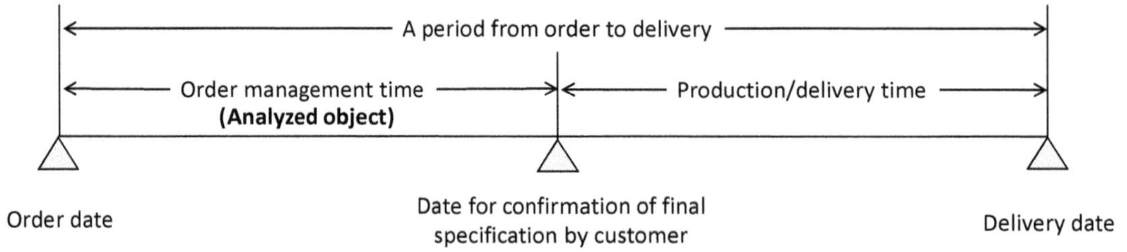

Figure 4. *A period from order to delivery in case company*

Table 5. *A part of analysis result of the OMP*

Order Process	*Customer*	*Business department*			*Development department*		*Manufacturing control department*	
		Manager	*Contact person*	*Office worker*	*Manager*	*Contact person*	*Manager*	*Contact person*
1. Issuing new order sheet								
1.1 Making new order sheet based on customer's inquiry information				○				
1.2 Transmitting new order sheet by e-mail				○				
1.3 Receiving new order sheet by e-mail			○					
…								

Table 6. *Identified inquiry process*

Process No.	Contents of each process
1	an approval of an acceptance of new customer order within business d.
2	a request of an offer of information to make a specification from development d. to business d.
3	a request of an offer of information to make a specification from business d. to a customer
4	an approval of an issuance of completed specification within development d.
5	a request of a confirmation of created specification from business d. to a customer
6	an approval of an issuance of completed specification within business d.

3.1. A trial of Identification of Inquiry Process in OMP (Step 1)

Analyzed object is OMP which contains plural sub-processes. Examples are an issuance process of new order sheet based on customer's requirement, a discussion process of details of the product through making a specification and a drawing etc. and a confirmation process of a final specification by a customer before the product is begun to manufacture. Related departments are a business department, a development department and a manufacturing department. In each department, one manager and one contact person are in charge of one customer order. But two contact persons are arranged in business department. One is salesman which can directly contact the customer. The other is in charge of the office procedure within the department. Table 5 shows a part of the analysis result of the analyzed object by RAD. Six inquiry processes are identified as shown in Table 6. They are put from an upstream of the OMP to a downstream of the OMP in numerical order.

3.2. A Trial of Investigation of Identified Inquiry Process (Step 2)

Each identified inquiry process was investigated by the proposed survey sheet. As one example, the survey result of the second inquiry process, 'A request of an offer of information to make a specification from development department to business department', is illustrated from Table 7. A noticeable point is how to transmit from a sender to a recipient in the survey sheet. Namely, different inquired contents have different communication tools. If inquired contents are a simple question and a delicate nuance for a design, a telephone is utilized. If inquired contents are numerical number information for a product design and a request which isn't given immediately, e-mail is utilized. Moreover a communication tool from a sender to a recipient is connected with a communication tool from a recipient to a sender. To be concrete, in case that a method from a sender to a recipient is a telephone, a method from a recipient to a sender is a telephone. In case that a method from a sender to a recipient is e-mail, a method from a recipient to a sender is e-mail.

3.3. A Trial of Creation of Categories of Attributes of Identified Inquiry Process (Step 3)

After details of all identified inquiry processes are surveyed, categories of attributes of inquiry process are established. The result is described in Table 8. Considered attributes is five items of prepared six items. They are 1) combination type, 2)-2 response, 2)-3 clean up, 3)-1 transmission 1 and 3)-2 transmission 2. In the case study, 2)-1 preparation is not considered because it is positively correlated with 3)-1 transmission 1 and a category of the former overlaps with a category of the latter.

Table 7. *Example of survey result of inquiry process (inquiry process 2)*

No. 2

Survey sheet of inquiry process

< A survey framework >

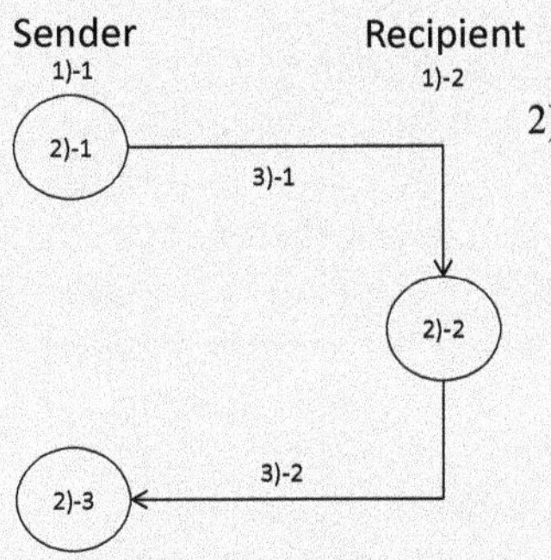

1) Role in OMP (Character information)
1)-1 Sender A person in charge of the development department
1)-2 Recipient A salesperson (A contact person with customer)

2) Circles: Operation on OMP (Circles)
2)-1 Preparation for inquiry process by sender
Concretely checking a shortage of information to make a specification and a drawing and its arrangement as a list of questions to a salesperson.
2)-2 Response by recipient
Answering questions from a person in charge of the development department. If a salesperson can't answer it, he may inquiry it to his customer again.
2)-3 Cleaning up after inquiry process by sender
Revising a specification and a drawing based on responded contents from a salesperson.

<Purpose of inquiry process>

Checking an order sheet before making a specification and a drawing

3) Direction of transmission for OMP (Arrows)
3)-1 How to transmit from sender to recipient
a. Telephone: In case of a simple question, a delicate nuance for a design etc.
b. Electronic mail: In case of an answer which isn't given immediately, numerical number information for a product design etc.

3)-2 How to transmit from recipient to sender
In case of a in 3)-1, Main method is a telephone
In case of b in 3)-2, Main method is an electronic mail.

Table 8. *Established category of attribute of inquiry process*

Factor of survey framework	Attribute's name	Categories of each attribute
1) role in OMP	1)-1 combination type	between customer and order company between departments within order company within one department
2) operation on OMP	2)-1 preparation 2)-2 response 2)-3 clean up	- (The category is not covered in this paper.) confirmation and recognition retrieval and examination additional operation simple operation
3) direction of transmission for OMP	3)-1 transmission 1 3)-2 transmission 2	face to face telephone passing round e-mail postal service the same category as 3)-1 transmission 1

Table 9. *Example of information richness*

Transmission tool	Speed of feedback	Expression way of information	Source of Information
face to face	fast		personal
		oral + alpha	
		oral + writing + alpha	
		oral	
telephone			personal
		writing	
passing round			impersonal
		writing	
e-mail			impersonal
		writing	
postal service	slow		impersonal

A category of first attribute is three items such as 'between customer and order company', 'between departments within order company' and 'within one department' followed by a relationship between sender's organization and recipient's organization. A category of second attribute is two items such as 'confirmation and recognition' and 'retrieval and examination' from the viewpoint of whether focused operation is typical or not. A category of third attribute is two items. One is 'additional operation' which is an alteration and a revision of relevant materials based on the processed information by a recipient. The other is 'simple operation' which is only a reception and a keeping of them. Categories of three attributes up to here are established based on the survey result. Categories of next two attributes are considered based on the following relevant literature. A category of fourth and fifth attributes are five items such as 'face to face', 'telephone', 'passing round', 'e-mail' and 'postal service'. They are founded on a characteristic of information richness (Daft et al. 1984) as shown in Table 9. For example, in case of 'face to face', it is useful for urgent inquiry and tough negotiation because a large volume of information is expected to be transmitted and a speed of feedback is fast. In case of 'postal service', it is useful for accurate inquiry because document materials are utilized.

3.4. A Trial of Quantification of Characteristic of Identified Inquiry Process (Step 4)

Table 10 illustrates categories of attributes of six identified inquiry processes which are chosen from established items as shown in Table 8. One identified inquiry process has one category set except second process and third process. The two processes have two category sets because two transmission patterns are extracted from the survey sheet in step 2.

Table 10 is quantified by 0-1 variable and a_{kj} and b_i are given from the quantified data by qualification theory category III. They are illustrated from Table 11 and Table 12. A coefficient of correlation is 0.87. a_{kj} indicates a similarity among seventeen categories. Five higher rank of a_{kj} are one and over score; 1.97 (passing round, transmission 1), 1.97 (passing round, transmission 2), 1.79 (simple operation, clean up), 1.62 (postal service, transmission 2) and 1.62 (postal service, transmission 1). It will be thought that a common point of five categories is a routine operation. On the other hand, three lower rank of a_{kj} are minus one and below score; -1.42 (telephone, transmission 2), -1.24 (between departments within order company, combination type), -1.14 (telephone, transmission 1). It will be thought that a common point of three categories is an operation including technical decision making. From the above discussion, a_{kj} means the standardization degree of the operation.

Moreover low score process will be guessed as a complicated process from the result of the interpretation of a_{kj}. When the value of b_i is actually checked in Table 12, low score processes are upstream processes in the OMP where many changes of the operation have occurred compared to downstream processes.

Table 10. *Assigned categories of identified inquiry processes*

Process No.	1) Role in OPM	2) Operation on OPM		3) Direction of transmission for OPM	
	-1 Combination type	-2 Response	-3 Clean up	-1 Transmission 1	-2 Transmission 2
1	within one department	confirmation and recognition	additional operation	e-mail	e-mail
2-1	between departments within order company	retrieval and examination	additional operation	telephone	telephone
2-2	between departments within order company	retrieval and examination	additional operation	e-mail	e-mail
3-1	between customer and order company	retrieval and examination	additional operation	telephone	e-mail
3-2	between customer and order company	retrieval and examination	additional operation	face to face	face to face
4	within one department	confirmation and recognition	additional operation	face to face	face to face
5	between customer and order company	confirmation and recognition	simple operation	postal service	postal service
6	within one department	confirmation and recognition	simple operation	passing round	passing round

Table 11. *Value of categories of attributes of inquiry process (a_{jk})*

Attribute	Category	a_{jk}
Transmission 1	Passing round	1.97
Transmission 2	Passing round	1.97
Clean up	Simple operation	1.79
Transmission 2	Postal service	1.62
Transmission 1	Postal service	1.62
Response	Confirmation and/or recognition	0.95
Combination type	Within one department	0.72
Combination type	Between customer and order company	0.11
Transmission 2	Face to face	-0.10
Transmission 1	Face to face	-0.10
Transmission 1	E-mail	-0.55
Clean up	Additional operation	-0.60
Transmission 2	E-mail	-0.65
Response	Retrieval and/or examination	-0.95
Transmission 1	Telephone	-1.14
Combination type	Between departments within order company	-1.24
Transmission 2	Telephone	-1.42

*a descending order of a_{kj}

Table 12. *Value of inquiry process (b_i)*

Process	b_i
Process 6	0.44
Process 5	0.36
Process 4	0.05
Process 1	-0.01
Process 3-2	-0.10
Process 3-1	-0.19
Process 2-2	-0.23
Process 2-1	-0.31

*a descending order of b_i

3.5. A Trial of Consideration of Improvement of Identified Inquiry Process (Step 5)

Table 13 shows the result of the pairwise comparison among attributes. In the comparison, each rating scale has five ranks, 5.00, 3.00, 1.00. 0.33 and 0.20.

Table 13. *Weighting score of each attribute*

A	1)-1	2)-2	2)-3	3)-1	3)-2
1)-1	1.00	0.20	0.20	0.20	0.20
2)-2	5.00	1.00	3.00	0.33	3.00
2)-3	5.00	0.33	1.00	0.20	0.33
3)-1	5.00	3.00	5.00	1.00	3.00
3)-2	5.00	0.33	3.00	0.33	1.00

1)-1 combination type, 2)-2 response, 2)-3 clean up, 3)-1 transmission 1, 3)-2 transmission 2

The consistency index of above pairwise comparison matrix: 0.12

Rating score:

5.00: Improvement of inquiry process from the viewpoint of attribute A is much easier than attribute B.

3.00: Improvement of inquiry process from the viewpoint of attribute A is easier than attribute B.

1.00: Improvement of inquiry process from the viewpoint of attribute A is as easy as attribute B.

0.33: Improvement of inquiry process from the viewpoint of attribute A is a little more difficult than attribute B.

0.20: Improvement of inquiry process from the viewpoint of attribute A is more difficult than attribute B.

w_j can be obtained through resolving the eigenvalue problem from equation (8) to equation (10). It is

$$H = [c_{jj}] \quad (j = 1, \dots, m) \quad (= \text{Table 13}) \tag{8}$$

$$A = \begin{bmatrix} w_1 \\ \vdots \\ w_j \\ \vdots \\ w_5 \end{bmatrix} \tag{9}$$

$$HA = \lambda A \tag{10}$$

Notation

w_j :weighting score of attribute j $(j = 1, \dots, m)$

$c_{j,}$:value of pairwise comparison of attribute j against attribute j $(j = 1, \dots, m)$

w_j of five attributes are as follows; 1)-1 combination type: 0.041, 2)-2 response: 0.257, 2)-3 clean up: 0.096, 3)-1 transmission 1: 0.441, 3)-2 transmission 2: 0.165. The relationship between inquiry processes and attributes of inquiry process is created utilized by the given w_j. And then a'_{kj} and b'_j are given by the proposed model. A coefficient of correlation is 0.46. Table 14 and Table 15 are the value of a'_{kj} and b'_j compared to the result by the conventional model. From the two tables, attributes of inquiry process which has larger of a'_{kj} is regarded as more effective objects of performance improvement. And inquiry process which has larger of b'_j is regarded as more effective objects of performance improvement too. For example, it is found that ranks of categories of 'transmission 1' by the proposed model are higher than the conventional model. In particular, the value of 'face to face, transmission 1' is changed from a negative number (-0.10 see Table 11) to a plus number (0.80 see Table 14). As the result, the value of fourth inquiry process (0.07 see Table 15) become near the value of fifth inquiry process and sixth inquiry process (0.08 see Table 15) which are attacked without difficulty. Actually, in fourth inquiry process, after a contact person explains the complicated specification to his manager within development department, it may be possible to revise it slightly. However the process is performed by face to face within one department. It is thought that an improvement of the process is not more difficult than the process between different departments.

Under the evaluation mentioned above, the proposed model provides three contributions.

- Decision of the order of inquiry processes to improve is systematic.
- The difficulty of performance improvement of inquiry process can be quantified by the proposed mathematical model.
- Analysis by both of the conventional model and the proposed model is an improved analysis by the conventional model from the viewpoint of a multistep analysis using both non weighting score and weighting score instead of non weighting score as the analyzed data.

Also, it is found that the proposed procedure is effective for an analysis of OMP through the above case study. In particular, inquiry processes are identified in the OMP, the attributes of them are clarified and the characteristics of them are quantified. It will be difficult to realize a systematic analysis of OMP without the propose procedure.

Of course, this paper is just an initial step towards realizing a systematic improvement of OMP. The following three tasks are mainly considered for future study; 1) actual performance improvement based on the result of the analysis, 2) analysis of more complicated inquiry process and 3) improvement of the performance of the proposed model to raise a coefficient of correlation.

Table 14. *Value of attributes of inquiry process (a'_{jk})*

Attribute	Category	Score	Change of ranking from conventional method to proposed one
Transmission 1	Passing round	1.05	Down (1→2)
Transmission 2	Passing round	0.65	Down (1→7)
Clean up	Simple operation	0.95	Down (3→4)
Transmission 2	Postal service	0.60	Down (4→8)
Transmission 1	Postal service	0.97	Up (4→3)
Response	Confirmation and/or recognition	2.61	Up (6→1)
Combination type	Within one department	0.75	Up (7→6)
Combination type	Between customer and order company	0.07	Down (8→11)
Transmission 2	Face to face	0.51	- (9→9)
Transmission 1	Face to face	0.84	Up (9→5)
Transmission 1	E-mail	0.25	Up (11→10)
Clean up	Additional operation	-0.21	- (12→12)
Transmission 2	E-mai	-0.30	- (13→13)
Response	Retrieval and/or examination	-1.42	Down (16→14)
Transmission 1	Telephone	-1.54	Down (17→15)
Combination type	Between departments within order company	-0.34	Up (16→14)
Transmission 2	Telephone	-0.49	Up (17→15)

*a descending order of a'_{kj}

Table 15. *Value of inquiry processes (b'_i)*

Process	Score	Change of ranking from conventional method to proposed one
Process 6	0.08	- (1→1)
Process 5	0.08	Up (2→1)
Process 4	0.07	- (3→3)
Process 1	0.04	- (4→4)
Process 3-2	0.00	- (5→5)
Process 3-1	-0.07	Down (6→7)
Process 2-2	-0.02	Up (7→6)
Process 2-1	-0.07	Up (8→7)

*a descending order of b'_i

4. Concluding Remarks

One proposal and one trial were presented in this paper. For the proposal, the analysis procedure of an order management process (OMP) was proposed. The purpose of the procedure is systematic clarification of characteristics of inquiry processes which are delivery processes of order information for accurately catching customer needs in OMP. Also, the capability of quantification theory category III utilized in the procedure was improved. Its technological essence is to obtain the optimal values that enable to obtain the maximum correlation coefficient between inquiry processes and attributes of inquiry process. For the trial, followed by the proposed procedure, the characteristics of identified inquiry processes are clarified and the order of the processes to improve is determined.

Acknowledgements

This research was undertaken with the support of Matsumoto Machine Co., Ltd., Japan. We sincerely thank President Mr. Kaname Matumoto and Ms. Mayumi Yoshida and their company for their kind support by managing regular joint research meetings to exchange data and ideas and support creative collaboration.

References

[1] Daft, R. L. and Lengel, R. H., 1984. Information richness: a new approach to managerial behavior and organization design. *Research in Organizational Behavior*, 4, 191-232.

[2] Hayashi, C., 1993. *Quantification: Theory and methodology*. Tokyo: Asakura Publishing Company [in Japanese].

[3] Hayashi, C. and Suzuki, T., 1975. Quantitative approach to a cross-societal research: a comparative study of Japanese character Part II. *Annals of the Institute of Statistical Mathematics*, 27 (1), 1–32.

[4] Saaty, T.L. and Vargas, L., 1994. *Fundamentals of decision making and priority theory with the analytic hierarchy process*, RWS Publications.

[5] Takakura, S., 1962. Some statistical methods of classification by the theory of qualification. *Journal of the Institute of Statistical Mathematics*, 9 (2), 81–105 [in Japanese].

[6] Lin, F. R., 1998. Reengineering the order fulfillment process in supply chain networks. *The international of Flexible Manufacturing System*, 10, 197-229.

[7] Ruth, S. A-S., 2004. Business process modeling: Review and framework. *International Journal of Production Economics*, 90, 129-149.

[8] Wastell, G. D, White, P. and Kawalek, P., 1994. A methodology for business process redesign: experiences and issues. *Journal of Strategic Information Systems*, 3(1), 23-40.

13

Diagnosis of production system of marine frozen products by inventory management theory - A case of blue fins

Koichi Murata[1,*], Nao Watanabe[2], Reakook Hwang[3], Seiichiro Isobe[1], Hiroshi Katayama[4]

[1]Department of Industrial Engineering and Management, College of Industrial Technology, Nihon University, Chiba, Japan
[2]Large Motors and Drives Department, Discrete Automation and Motion Division, ABB K.K., Tokyo, Japan
[3]Industry & Strategy Department I, Samsung Economic Research Institute, Seoul, Korea
[4]Department of Industrial and management Systems Engineering, Faculty of Science and Engineering, Waseda University, Tokyo, Japan

Email address:
murata.kouichi30@nihon-u.ac.jp (K. Murata)

Abstract: The purpose of this paper is a characteristic analysis of current production and inventory system for frozen products of blue fins under a fishery instability caused by the warming of the earth and an indiscriminate fishing. For the analysis, a simulation is performed quoted by Vassian's production management theory. The result of the analysis is that the current system is aimed at minimizing a variation of the inventory at the end of the period.

Keywords: Production and Inventory Planning System, Frozen Processing Industry, Simulation

1. Introduction

This paper proposes a simple diagnosis of current capability of actual production system by an inventory management theory. Objective system is a production system of blue fins frozen products in Japan. The reason is that Japan has the largest fishing and consumptions of them in the world. However a catch of blue fins has been decreased these past few years because of the warming of the earth and an indiscriminate fishing. Also, after 2011 Tohoku earthquake and tsunami, a development of a renewal production model has been required in the area. Applied theory is Vassian's production management theory (1954) which is one of the traditional and robust theories. It is mainly used to decide a production order with considering an inventory of the product. In this paper, an application of the theory is performed to check a capability of current production system. The challenge of this paper has two meaning. First, a use of the theory will be expanded from a determination of a production order to a diagnosis of a current production system. Second, a convenient method based on a theoretical approach is proposed to an actual production site for an intermediation between an academic field and an industry field.

2. Literature Review

Simon proposed one inventory management models by a servomechanisms theory. One of them is illustrated from Figure 1 (Simon 1952). It is a feedback control system by the block system. The optimum inventory θ_I is input data, the actual inventory θ_o is output data and the difference between two data ε ($=\theta_I - \theta_o$) is an error. An order θ_L is a disturbance of warehouse K_1 as a controlled object. An inventory controller K_2 determines a manipulated variable μ to minimize the difference ε and supplies to warehouse K_1.

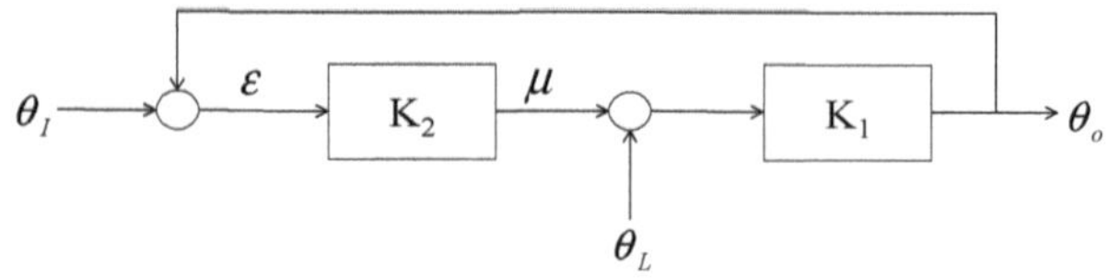

Figure 1. Inventory Management System (Simon 1952)

There have been researches about the production and inventory planning based on the model. He himself introduced a fixed interval ordering system in which production lead time was adapted to a manipulated variable μ of the model (Simon 1952). Vassian (1954) proposed a fixed interval ordering system quoted by a control theory too. In the model, a demand at period t is input and an inventory at the end of the period t is output. By the two assumptions, a block diagram can express the manufacturing flow which is an order, a production and an inventory in order. Equation (1) and Equation (2) are a mathematical model of the diagram. Equation (1) has four items such as a) accumulated demands predicated within next production lead time, b) production orders delivered for the future, c) inventories at the end of the period and d) safety inventories. The output is a production order of each period to minimize the variation of the inventory at the end of the period.

$$P_t = \sum_{i=1}^{L} \hat{D}_{t;t+i} + \sum_{i=1}^{L-1} P_{t-i} - I_t + S \qquad (1)$$

$$I_t = I_{t-1} + P_{t-L} - D_t \qquad (2)$$

<Notation>

D_t: Demand at the period t

I_t: Inventory at the end of the period t

P_t: Production order indicated at the period t. It is delivered at the period $t+L$.

$\hat{D}_{t;t+i}$: Future demand at the period $t+i$ predicated at the end of the period t

L: Production lead time+1

S: Safety inventory

Furthermore various studies have been performed based on Vassian's model. For example, Katayama (1986, 1998) and Nishijima (1999) developed sub-models of the model, i.e. methodologies of a demand forecasting or a production ordering. Hirakawa (2003) extended the model to a multistep system. These outputs are mainly applied to manufacturing industry. In addition, an application range of the studies has been spread in recent year. For example, Chiyoma (2013) utilized Vassian's model to a supply chain on agriculture industry. All investigated studies are only used to decide a production order as a matter of course. An idea of this study is that a decision model of a production order is used to diagnosis a type of a production system.

On the other hand, in this paper, a marine frozen production industry is focused. As for the industry, Pall (1988) is recognized as one of the previous studies. Focusing on a procurement activity of a processing factory under the influence of daily variation of fish catches in north Europe, it proposes a formularization of a production scheduling problem under the condition of the effect by linear programming. However, studies of a marine frozen production by the approach from a production management are not found except it under reviewing related literature up to the present.

3. Research Procedure

Research procedure of this paper consists of the four steps.

3.1. STEP1: Investigation of Statistical Data

From the annual report of statistical data on a distribution of aquatic products (Ministry of Agriculture, Forestry and Fisheries 2007, 2008, 2009, 2010 and 2012), three statistical data on a frozen production of blue fins, as the object of our research, are surveyed such as 1) a monthly amount of materials to plants, 2) a monthly amount of products from plants and 3) an inventory of products at the end of the month. The report is the result of the survey on a distribution of frozen aquatic products in the survey on a distribution of aquatic products. It is carried out by Ministry of Agriculture, Forestry and Fisheries in Japan. The object data of this paper are data from 2005 to 2009 before not only a modification of how to survey from 2010 but also the 2011 earthquake off the Pacific coast of Tohoku. A definition of blue fins is followed by the annual report. Namely, the category of blue fins consists of four kinds such as a long-finned tuna, a big eye tuna, a yellow fin tuna and others.

In order to analyze surveyed data, not only basic statistics but also a link relative is calculated to a monthly amount of materials to plants and a monthly amount of products from plants. Values of a link relative are given in the utilization process of a method of a link relative (Persons 1919). It is the ratio of each item at the period t of the series to the preceding item, which is item at the period $t-1$. A quantification of a change of an annual series' shape of the two surveyed data will be expected by the indicator.

3.2. STEP2: Construction of Constructed Models

Two constructed models are formularized to grasp the current of the object system. Previously, a performance of a production and inventory planning system is measured by a stability of input and/or output of the system. A representative indicator of the former is a variation of an indicated production order and that of the latter is a variation of an inventory at the end of the period (Nishijima 1999). Watanabe (2013) focuses on the facts and proposes a method to analyze the characteristic of the current system through the comparison among the current system, the model to minimize a variation of an indicated production order and the model to minimize a variation of an inventory at the end of the period. This paper applies to the analysis method too.

3.3. STEP3: Simulation of Production and Inventory System

In the simulation, a monthly amount of materials to plants investigated in Step 1 is considered as input data of two models constructed in Step 2. And an average and a standard deviation of an indicated production order and an inventory at the end of the period are calculated in the simulations by every model. Through the comparisons among current values and the results, a characteristic of the current system is analyzed.

3.4. STEP4: Discussion

Based on the result in the previous steps, the future direction of a production and inventory planning system of frozen blue fins products is discussed.

4. STEP1: Investigation of Statistical Data

4.1. A Monthly Amount of Materials to Plants

Figure 2 shows time series of a monthly amount of materials to plants from 2005 to 2009. It is found that the time series go down year by year. In particularly, the minimum amount is reduced every year. An average of the monthly amounts is 31,545 ton in 2009 which is 88% of 38,322 ton in 2005.

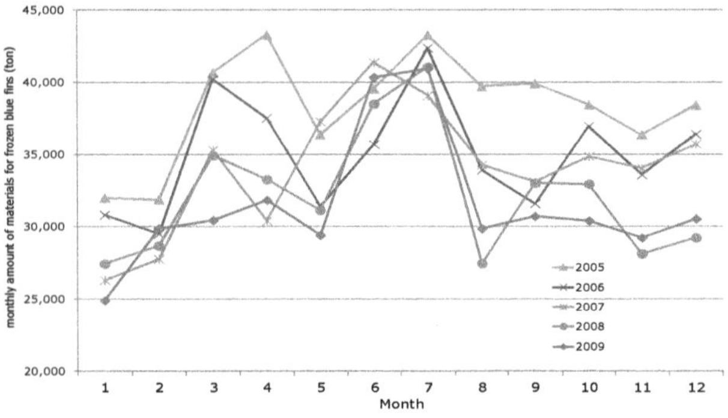

Figure 2. Time series of monthly amount of materials for frozen blue fins from 2005 to 2009

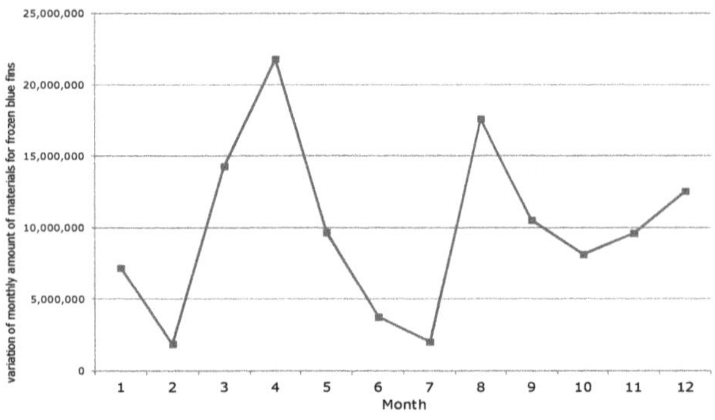

Figure 3. Time series of variation of monthly amount of materials for frozen blue fins among five years from 2005 to 2009

Table 1. Link relatives of monthly amount of materials for frozen blue fins from 2005 to 2009

Month	2005	2006	2007	2008	2009
1	-	0.80	0.72	0.77	0.85
2	1.00	0.96※	1.06※※	1.05	1.20
3	1.28	1.36	1.27	1.22	1.02
4	1.06	0.93※	0.86	0.95	1.05※※
5	0.84	0.84	1.23※※	0.94※	0.92
6	1.09	1.14	1.11	1.24	1.37
7	1.09	1.19	0.94※	1.07※※	1.01
8	0.92	0.80	0.88	0.67	0.73
9	1.00	0.93※	0.97	1.20※※	1.03
10	0.96	1.17※※	1.05	1.00	0.99※
11	0.95	0.91	0.98	0.85	0.96
12	1.06	1.08	1.05	1.04	1.04

※※: A link relative is less than 1.00 at a year but it is 1.00 and over at the preceding year.
※※: A link relative is 1.00 and over at a year but it is less than 1.00 at the preceding year.

There are some months which have large variation of the monthly amounts among five years. In particularly, the amounts on April and August in 2009 drop to a lower position but the amounts in 2005 are the most of amounts in five years. From the results, the variation of the monthly amount on each month is very large as shown in Figure 3.

Furthermore, Table 1 indicates link relatives every month among five years. It is found that a change of increase or decrease of the amount at a month against the amount at next month occurs during the investigated years.

Instability of the amount is confirmed based on the above analysis. A realization of maintenance of a capacity of a frozen processing line to overcome the burden will be needed.

4.2. A Monthly Amount of Frozen Products from Plants

Figure 4 show time series of a monthly amount of products from plants from 2005 to 2009. It is found that the time series go down year by year like a monthly amount of materials to plants. An average of the monthly amounts is 38,224 ton in 2009 which is 85% of 32,365 ton in 2005. On the other hand, in comparison with the time series among five years, there is little disturbance of the shape of the time series. From Table 2, it indicates to realize steady supply to the market every year. However, in case of July, a change of increase or decrease of the amount at a month against the amount at next month occurs during the investigated years.

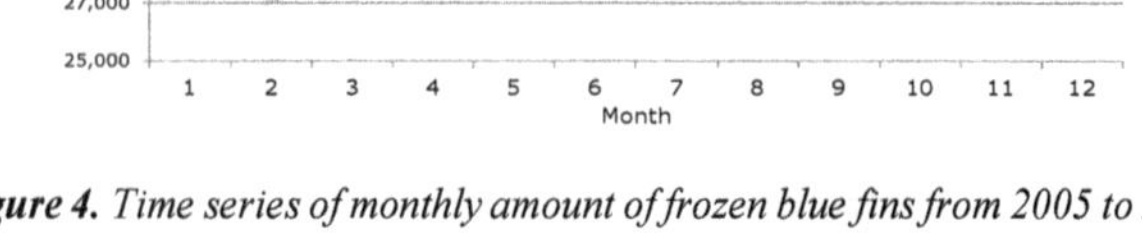

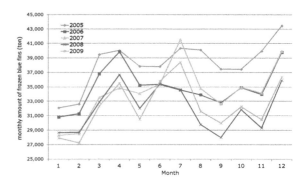

Figure 4. Time series of monthly amount of frozen blue fins from 2005 to 2009

Table 2. Link relatives of monthly amount of frozen blue fins from 2005 to 2009

Month	2005	2006	2007	2008	2009
1	-	0.71	0.71	0.72	0.78
2	1.02	1.01	1.01	1.00	0.98※
3	1.21	1.18	1.18	1.15	1.19
4	1.01	1.08	1.04	1.12	1.10
5	0.95	0.88	0.98	0.87	0.86
6	1.00	1.00	1.04	1.11	1.17
7	1.07	0.98※	1.18※※	0.98※	1.07※※
8	0.99	0.98	0.84	0.86	0.82
9	0.93	0.97	0.94	0.94	0.95
10	1.00	1.07	1.07	1.14	1.08
11	1.07	0.97※	0.98	0.92	0.94
12	1.09	1.17	1.17	1.22	1.19

※※: A link relative is less than 1.00 at a year but it is 1.00 and over at the preceding year.
※※: A link relative is 1.00 and over at a year but it is less than 1.00 at the preceding year.

In the tendency of quantitative reduction mentioned above, a ratio of a setup time to total processing time will be increased. It is necessary to maintain a productivity of a production system which is equal to the conventional system.

4.3. An Inventory of Products at the End of the Month

Figure 5 shows time series of an inventory of products at the end of the month from 2005 to 2009. It is found that the time series go down year by year like two kinds of the amounts mentioned above. Days of an inventory are illustrated from Figure 3. It is given a monthly amount of the products from plants divided by an inventory of the products at the end of the month. An average of the indicator increases from 1.77 in 2005 to 1.95 in 2009. It seems that a suitable reduction of an inventory of the products has not been performed. Furthermore a variance of the indicator increases from 0.22 in 2005 to 0.05 in 2009. It indicates the instability of the inventory of the products.

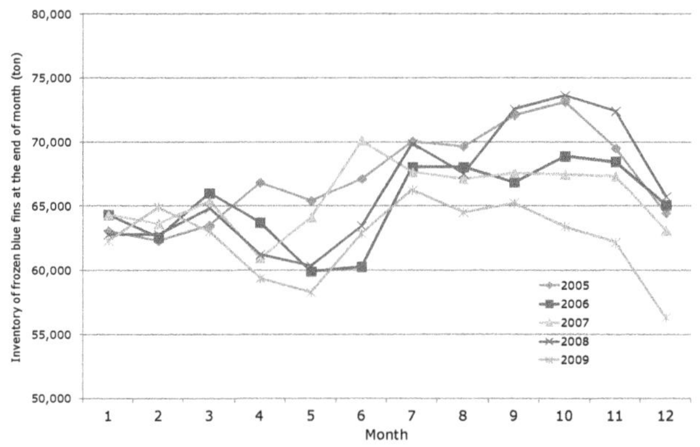

Figure 5. Time series of inventory of frozen blue fins at the end of month from 2005 to 2009

Table 3. Days of an inventory of frozen blue fins from 2005 to 2009 (Month)

Month	2005	2006	2007	2008	2009
1	1.97	2.09	2.27	2.19	2.23
2	1.91	2.00	2.23	2.19	2.38
3	1.61	1.80	1.95	1.97	1.95
4	1.67	1.60	1.75	1.67	1.67
5	1.73	1.70	1.88	1.89	1.91
6	1.78	1.71	1.98	1.79	1.76
7	1.74	1.97	1.63	2.02	1.73
8	1.74	2.01	1.93	2.27	2.04
9	1.92	2.04	2.07	2.59	2.18
10	1.95	1.97	1.93	2.31	1.97
11	1.74	2.02	1.97	2.47	2.04
12	1.48	1.64	1.58	1.83	1.55
Average	1.77	1.88	1.93	2.10	1.95
Variance	0.020	0.029	0.040	0.074	0.055

5. STEP2: Construction of Constructed Models

On the assumption that production lead time is one period, Equation (1) and Equation (2) become Equation (3) and Equation (4). Two models are proposed based on the two equations. In addition, followed by the situation of the object case, P_t means a monthly amount of materials to plants and D_t means regarded as a monthly amount of products from plants.

$$P_t = \hat{D}_{t;t+1} + \hat{D}_{t;t+2} - P_{t-1} - I_t + S \quad (3)$$

$$I_t = I_{t-1} + P_{t-2} - D_t \quad (4)$$

1) In case of a minimization of a variation of an inventory at the end of the period

The assumption that a monthly amount of products of term i ahead are given at the end of the period t is installed to Equation (3).

$$\hat{D}_{t;t+1} = D_{t+1} \quad (5)$$

$$\hat{D}_{t;t+2} = D_{t+2} \quad (6)$$

2) In case of a minimization of a variation of an indicated production order

The assumption that a monthly amount of products of each period is constant is installed to Equation (3).

$$P_t = C \quad (7)$$

6. STEP3: Simulation of Production and Inventory System

6.1. Precondition

In this step, the simulation is performed by the two proposed models. An outline of the simulation is as follows.

<Outline of the simulation>

- Input data: Actual data of the monthly amount of materials to plants
- Output data 1: Average and standard deviation of monthly amounts of materials
- Output data 2: Average and standard deviation of inventories at the end of month
- A number of simulation: Five times (from 2005 to 2009)
- Others
  - An inventory at the end of December in the preceding year: Actual data (In case of 2005, 2004's value is utilized.)
  - A monthly amount of materials to plants at November and December in the preceding year: Actual data (In case of 2005, 2004's value is utilized.)
  - A monthly amount of frozen products from plants in January and February of the next year: Actual data (In case of 2009, the following equation is utilized.)
    - The amount at January in 2010=The amount at January in 2009×(The amount at January in 2009-The amount at January in 2005)÷5
    - The amount at February in 2010=The amount at February in 2009× (The amount at February in 2009- The amount at February in 2005)÷5

- Safety inventory:
  Two month's average of actual monthly amount of products from plants during simulation term
- In case of minimization of a variance of a monthly amount of materials to plants, a monthly amount of materials to plants:
  Average of actual monthly amount of materials to plants during simulation term

6.2. Results

The results of the simulation are illustrated from Table 4, Table 5, Figure 6 and Figure 7. It is found that the current system is nearly a system to minimize a variance of an inventory at the end of the period. However it is considered that the system had a margin for a reduction of an inventory at the end of the period.

Table 4. *Results of the simulation (Materials to plants)*

Year	Minimization of a variance of an inventory at the end of the period		Current system		Minimization of a variance of an amount of materials to plants	
	Average	Standard deviation	Average	Standard deviation	Average	Standard deviation
2005	37,166	1,211	38,322	1,021	38,224	0
2006	33,892	1,044	35,002	1,086	34,940	0
2007	33,647	1,324	34,119	1,202	34,390	0
2008	30,850	1,236	32,147	1,214	31,990	0
2009	31,940	1,060	31,545	1,263	32,365	0

Table 5. *Results of the simulation (Inventory at the end of the period)*

Year	Minimization of a variance of an inventory at the end of the period		Current system		Minimization of a variance of an amount of materials to plants	
	Average	Standard deviation	Average	Standard deviation	Average	Standard deviation
2005	76,966	885	67,293	1,001	81,314	1,132
2006	70,505	583	65,212	859	72,036	710
2007	69,703	756	65,757	712	73,889	1,223
2008	65,313	954	66,456	1,292	69,692	945
2009	65,098	265	62,397	826	62,787	1,079

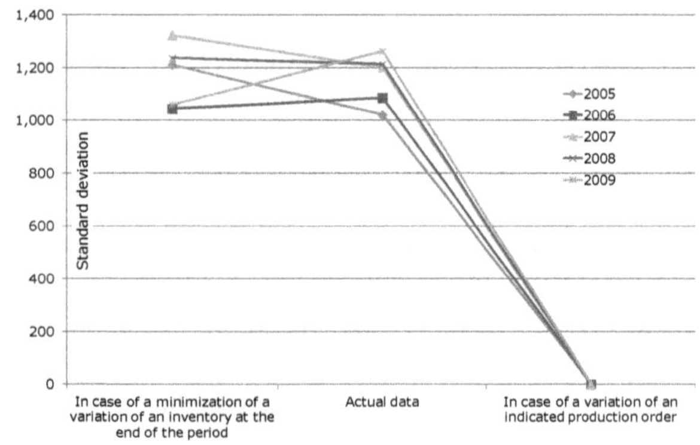

Figure 6. *Standard divisions of materials of conventional model and two proposed models*

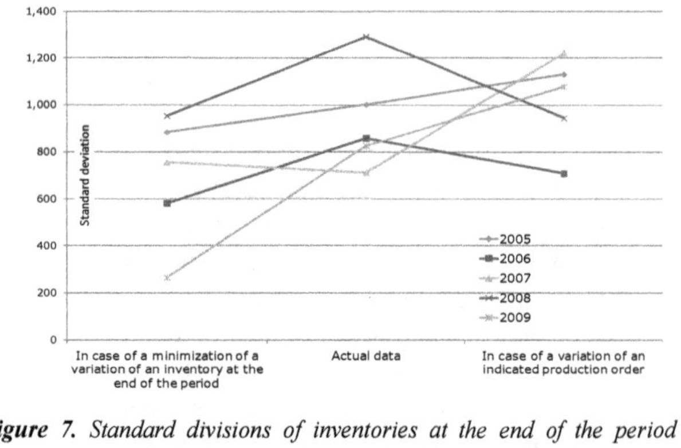

Figure 7. *Standard divisions of inventories at the end of the period of conventional model and two proposed models*

7. STEP4: Discussion

From the both results of the survey described in Step 2 and the simulation performed in Step 3, the following four future works are considered.

- Future work 1: Construction of the production system that absorbs an instability of amounts of materials to plants
- Future work 2: Improvement of a flexibility of the production line that corresponds to a reduction of amount of products from plants
- Future work 3: Compression of an inventory that corresponds to a reduction of amount of products from plants
- Future work 4: Equalization of two variances of amount of materials to plants and an inventory at the end of the period

For the first work, the amount of materials to plants is reduced and the expected amount will not be guaranteed on the basis of a stable fish catch. It is related to an excess and a deficiency of production capacity and become factors in an occurrence of opportunity loss and surplus cost. A shift of planned procurement of materials will be needed corresponding to market requirements.

For the second work, as a production scale become down, a ratio of setup time to total processing time will become up. Based on the internet survey about a frozen processing process of blue fins, in order to fillet one big blue fins to a shape of rectangles, several cutting process which are from a cutting of helmet-shaped head of blue fins to a removal of dark-colored meat is passed as shown in Figure 8 (Fukuichi Gyogyo 2014). An exchange time of a cutting tool is a stop time of production. It is important to shorten set up time in the process.

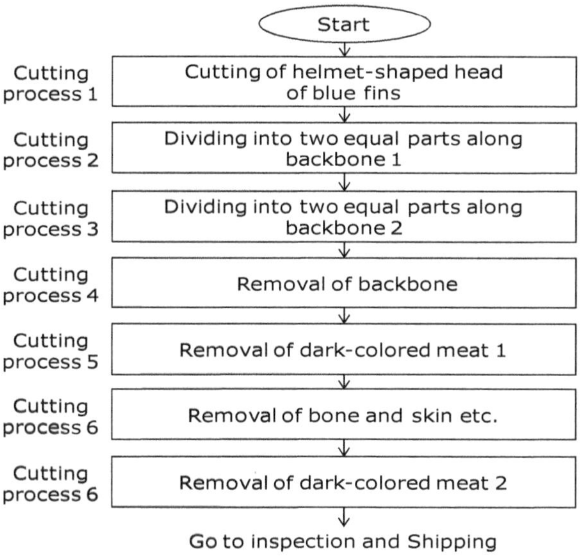

※Authors is made referred to Fukuichi Gyogyo (2014)

Figure 8. *Cutting Process in blue fins processing*

For the third work, in the survey of Step 2, a reduction ratio of an inventory at the end of the period is low against a reduction ratio of amount of materials/product to/from plants. Also, it is found that a variance of an inventory at the end of the period is increasing. In general, a surplus of an inventory becomes an increase factor of cost. Accordingly effective management of an inventory in the object system will seem needed.

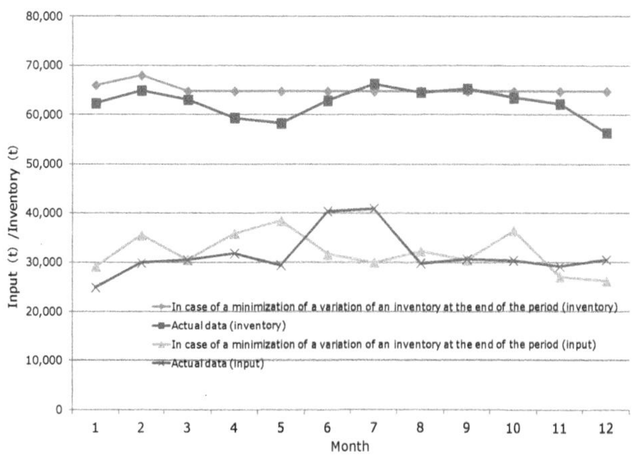

Figure 9. *Time series of an amount of materials to plants and inventories at the end of the period (In case of 2009)*

For the fourth work, Figure 9 shows time series of the monthly amount of materials to plants and an inventory at the end of the period provided from the simulation results described in Step 3. In case of a minimization of a variance of an inventory at the end of the period, a stationary state is kept in an inventory at the end of the period from March to December however transient characteristics are confirmed at January and February. Compared the simulated data with actual data, actual data is equal to or lower than the simulated data. On the other hand, as stated above, a variance of an inventory at the end of the period is increasing year by year. When an amount of materials to plants is checked, equalization of simulation results is better than that of actual data. Based on the results, a control of a variance of materials to plants is needed as one direction of the object system improvement. And a production and inventory system is more stabilized without becoming worse of current level of a variance of an inventory at the end of the period.

8. Concluding Remarks

In this paper, a characteristic analysis of current production and inventory planning system for frozen products of blue fins is performed under the instability of the fishery caused by the warming of the earth and an indiscriminate fishing. For the results, it is found that the current system is aimed at minimizing a variation of the inventory at the end of the period. Also, in order to correspond to the instability of a material procurement, the future works are discussed. For example, it is necessary to control a variance of amount of materials to plants and to reduce setup time, in particular an exchange of cutting tool, in total processing time without becoming worse of current level of a variance of an inventory at the end of the period.

References

[1] Chiyoma, H. and Katayama, H., 2013. "Model Building and Performance Analysis of Forward / Reverse: - Combined Logistics System in Agricultural Industry", *Proceedings of the 8th International Congress on Logistics and SCM Systems (ICLS2013)*, pp. 281-288, International Conference Center of Waseda University, Tokyo, Japan, 5th-7th August.

[2] Fukuichi Gyogyo Co. Ltd. Homepages, URL: http://www.maguro-fukuboh.jp/ (Access dat: 8th, April, 2014.)

[3] Herbert A. Simon, 1952. "On the Application of Servomechanism Theory in the Study of Production Control", *Econometrica*, Vol. 20, No. 2, pp. 247-268.

[4] Herbert J. Vassian, 1954. "Application of Discrete Variable Servo Theory to Inventory Control", *Journal of the Operations Research Society of America*, Vol. 3, Iss. 3, pp. 272-282.

[5] Hirakawa Y., Katayama, H., Hoshino K. and Soshiroda M., 2003. "A Hybrid Push/Pull Production Control System for Multistage Manufacturing Environments", *The Journal of The Japan Industrial Management Association*, Vol. 45, No. 3, pp. 194-201.

[6] Katayama, H., 1986. "On an Ordering System Using Orthogonal Elements of Moving Average Demand Model", *The Journal of The Japan Industrial Management Association*, Vol. 37, No. 2, pp. 73-79.

[7] Katayama, H., Soshiroda M. and Muramatsu R., 1988, "Analysis of Periodic Reordering System with Plural Moving Average Demands", *The Journal of The Japan Industrial Management Association*, Vol. 39, No. 4, pp. 218-225.

[8] Nishijima J., Goto M. And Tawara N., 1999, "A Study of Periodical Ordering System to Control the Cost Occurred from Variances", The Journal of The Japan Industrial Management Association, Vol. 50, No. 4, pp. 207-215.

[9] Ministry of Agriculture, Forestry and Fisheries, 2007. *The annual report of statistical data on a distribution of aquatic products (2007)*, Association of Agriculture and Forestry: Tokyo.

[10] Ministry of Agriculture, Forestry and Fisheries, 2008. *The annual report of statistical data on a distribution of aquatic products (2008)*, Association of Agriculture and Forestry: Tokyo.

[11] Ministry of Agriculture, Forestry and Fisheries, 2009. *The annual report of statistical data on a distribution of aquatic products (2009)*, Association of Agriculture and Forestry: Tokyo.

[12] Ministry of Agriculture, Forestry and Fisheries, 2010. *The annual report of statistical data on a distribution of aquatic products (2010)*, Association of Agriculture and Forestry: Tokyo.

[13] Ministry of Agriculture, Forestry and Fisheries, 2012. *The annual report of statistical data on a distribution of aquatic products (2012)*, Association of Agriculture and Forestry: Tokyo.

[14] Pall J., 1988. "Daily Production Planning in Fish Processing Firms", *European Journal of Operational Research*, Vol. 36, pp. 410-415.

[15] Warren M. Persons, 1919. "Indices of Business Conditions", *The Review of Economic Statistics*, pp. 18-31.

[16] Watanabe, N., Hwang R. K. and Katayama, H., 2013. "Analysis and Improvement of Production and Inventory Planning System for Process Industry", *Proceedings of The 16th Japan Society of Logistics Systems (JSLS) National Conference*, pp. 91-96, Nihon University, Narashino, Chiba, Japan, 11th-12th, May.

On-line scheduling algorithm for real-time multiprocessor systems with ACO

Cheng Zhao, Myungryun Yoo, Takanori Yokoyama

Department of Computer Science, Tokyo City University, Tokyo, Japan

Email address:
zcs88122@gmail.com (Cheng Zhao), yoo@cs.tcu.ac.jp (Myungryun Yoo), yokoyama@cs.tcu.ac.jp (Takanori Yokoyama)

Abstract: The Ant Colony Optimization algorithms (ACO) are computational models inspired by the collective foraging behavior of ants. By looking at the strengths of ACO, they are the most appropriate for scheduling of tasks in soft real-time systems. In this paper, ACO based scheduling algorithm for real-time operating systems (RTOS) has been proposed. During simulation, results are obtained with periodic tasks, measured in terms of Success Ratio & Effective CPU Utilization and compared with Kotecha's algorithm in the same environment. It has been observed that the proposed algorithm is equally optimal during underloaded conditions and it performs better during overloaded conditions.

Keywords: Real-Time Systems, Scheduling, ACO, EDF

1. Introduction

In recent year, applications of real-time systems are spreading. For example, the automotive, mobile phone, plant monitoring systems and air traffic control systems.

There are two types of real-time systems: *Hard real-time* systems and *Soft real-time* systems. *Hard real-time* systems are defined as those systems in which the correctness of the system depends not only on the logical result of computation, but also on the time at which the results are produced[1]. *Soft real-time* systems are missing an occasional deadline is undesirable, but nevertheless tolerable. Our interest in this question stems from the increasing prevalence of applications such as networking, multimedia, and immersive graphics systems that have only *Soft real-time* systems.

The objective of real-time task scheduler is to reduce the deadline of tasks in the system as much as possible when we consider soft real time system. To achieve this goal, vast researches on real-time task scheduling have been conducted. Mostly all the real time systems in existence use preemption and multitasking. Real time scheduling techniques can be broadly divided into two categories: Off-line and On-line.

Off-line algorithms assign all priorities at design time, and it remains constant for the lifetime of a task. On-line algorithms assign priority at runtime, based on execution parameters of tasks. On-line scheduling can be either with static priority or dynamic priority. RM (Rate Monotonic) and DM (Deadline Monotonic) are examples of On-line scheduling with static priority [2]. EDF (Earliest Deadline First) and LST (Least Slack Time First) are examples of On-line scheduling with dynamic priority. EDF and LST algorithms are optimal under the condition that the jobs are preemptable, there is only one processor and the processor is not overloaded [3][4]. But the limitation of these algorithms is, their performance decreases exponentially if system becomes slightly overloaded [5].

Several characteristics make ACO a unique approach: it is constructive, population-based meta-heuristic which exploits an indirect form of memory of previous performance. [6][7]. Therefore in this paper, the same approach has been applied for real-time operating systems.

The rest of this paper is organized as follows. In Sec. 2, our system model is presented. In Sec. 3, our proposed algorithm is described and discussed. In Sec. 4, a simulation-based evaluation of proposed algorithm and kotecha's algorithm[8] . Sec. 5 is conclusions.

2. System Model

The system knows about the deadline and required computation time of the task when the task is released. The task set is assumed to be preemptive. We have assumed that the system is not having resource contention problem. Moreover, preemption and the scheduling algorithm incur no overhead.

In soft real-time systems, each task has a positive value. The goal of the system is to obtain as much value as possible. If a task succeeds, then the system acquires its value. If a task fails, then the system gains less value from the task [8]. In a special case of soft real-time systems, called a firm real-time system, there is no value for a task that has missed its deadline, but there is no catastrophe either [9]. Here, we propose an algorithm that applies to firm real-time system. The value of the task has been taken same as its computation time required [10].

3. Related Work

3.1. Ant Colony Optimization

Social insects that live in colonies, such as ants, termites, wasps, and bees, develop specific tasks according to their role in the colony. One of the main tasks is the search for food. Real ants, when searching for food, can find such resources without visual feedback, and they can adapt to changes in the environment, optimizing the path between the nest and the food source. This fact is the result involves positive feedback, given by the continuous deposit of a chemical substance, known as pheromone.

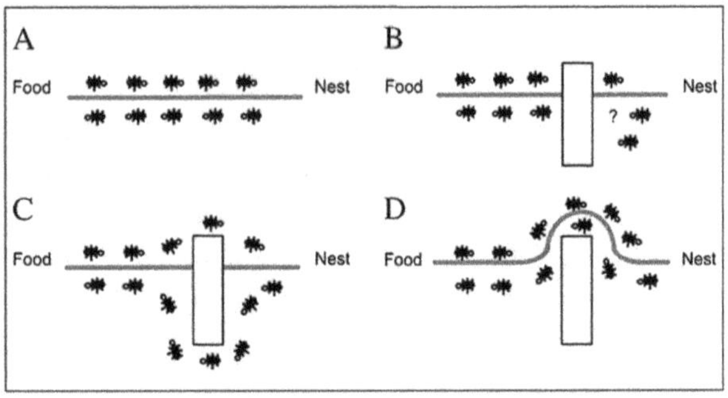

Figure 1. *Ant colony optimization.*

A classic example of the construction of a pheromone trail in the search for a shorter path is shown in Fig. 1 and was first presented by Colorni[11]. In Fig. 1A there is a path between food and nest established by the ants. In Fig. 1B an obstacle is inserted in the path. Soon, ants spread to both sides of the obstacle, since there is no clear trail to follow (Fig. 1C). As the ants go around the obstacle and find the previous pheromone trail again, a new pheromone trail will be formed around the obstacle. This trail will be stronger in the shortest path than in the longest path, as shown in Fig. 1D.

3.2. Kotecha's Algorithm

The scheduling algorithm is required to execute when a new task arrives or presently running task completes. The main steps of the proposed algorithm are given as following and the flowchart of the algorithm has been shown in Fig.2:

- Construct tour of different ants and produce the task execution sequence
- Analyze the task execution sequences generated for available number of processor
- Update the value of pheromone
- Decide probability of each task and select the task for execution

The detailed description of four main steps is as follows:

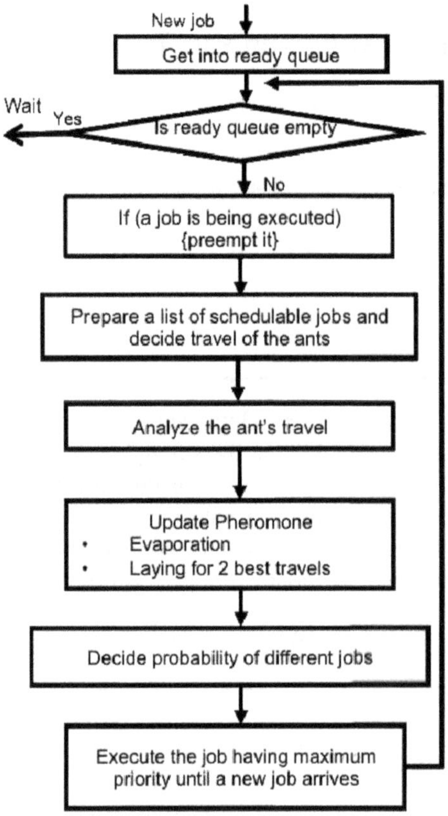

Figure 2. *Flowchart of algorithm*

3.2.1. Tour Construction

First, find probability of each node using (1). Each schedulable task is considered as a node and probability of each node to be selected for execution is decided using pheromone τ and heuristic value η.

$$p_i(t) = \frac{(\tau_i(t))^{\alpha} * (\eta_i(t))^{\beta}}{\sum_{l \in R1}(\tau_l(t))^{\alpha} * (\eta_l(t))^{\beta}} \quad (1)$$

where,

pi(t) is the probability of ith node at time t; i∈ N_1 and N1 is set of schedulable tasks at time t.

τi(t) is pheromone on ith node at time t.

η_i is heuristic value of ith node at t, which can bedetermined by (2)

$$\eta_i = \frac{K}{D_i - t} \quad (2)$$

Here, t is current time ,K is constant and Di is absolute deadline of ith node.

α and β are constants which decide importance of τ and η.

Ants construct their tour based on the value of p of each

node as per following:

Ant 1. Highest p > second highest p > third highest p >....
Ant 2. Second highest p > highest p > third highest p >....
Ant 3. Third highest p > second highest p > highest p >....
...

Suppose at time t, there are 4 schedulable tasks. As shown in Figure 1, each task will be considered as a node and from each node; one ant will start its journey. If we consider the priorities of all the nodes are in decreasing order of A, B, C, D; ants will traverse different nodes as per following:

Ant 1. A > B > C > D
Ant 2. B > A > C > D
Ant 3. C > A > B > D
Ant 4. D > A > B > C

3.2.2. Analyze the Journey

After all ants have completed their tour, evaluate the performance of different ants's travel. We have analyzed this based on ratio of number of success tasks and number of missed tasks. Find out maximum two best journeys of ants and update the value of pheromone accordingly.

3.2.3. Pheromone Update

Pheromone updating on each node is done in two steps:

- Pheromone Evaporation :Pheromone evaporation is required to forget bad travel of ants and to encourage new paths. Value of τ is updated using(3)

$$\tau_i(t+1) = (1-\rho)\tau_i(t) \qquad (3)$$

where,
ρ is a constant.
$i \in R_l$; R_l is set of all tasks.

- Pheromone Laying: Pheromone will be laid only for two best journeys of ants. Select the best journey and put pheromone depending on their order of visited node. Amount of pheromone (Δτ) laid will be different at each node i.e. the nearest node will get highest amount of pheromone and far most node will get least.

$$\tau_i(t+1) = \tau_i(t) + \Delta\tau_i \qquad (4)$$

where,
$i \in N_2$; N_2 is set of tasks executed by the ant.

$$\Delta\tau = \frac{ph}{s} \qquad (5)$$

Here,

$$ph = C * \frac{Number\ of\ Successed\ Jobs}{Number\ of\ Missed\ Jobs+1} \qquad (6)$$

s is sequence number of node visited by the ant during the best travel.

Value of C is constant (preferably 0.1)

3.2.4. Selection of Task for Execution

After updating pheromone, again find out probability of each node using (1) and select the task for execution having the highest probability value.

3.2.5. Important Points about the Algorithm

Each schedulable task is considered as a node, and it stores the value of τ i.e. pheromone. Initial value of τ is taken as one for all nodes.

Value of α and β decide importance of τ and η. During simulation, both values are taken as one.

Number of ants which construct the tour, is important design criteria. During simulation, number of ants taken is same as number of executable tasks the system is having at that time.

3.3. Proposed Algorithm

In Kotecha's algorithm ,The part of Tour Construction, the heuristic value ηi depend on absolute deadline that is most similar to EDF algorithm. However, EDF's performance decreases exponentially if system becomes slightly overloaded[12]. Since we consider the heuristic value should be depend on a ratio of remain execute time and absolute deadline at time t. This can make more helpful heuristic value to increase the Success ratio of jobs .

And in the part of pheromone evaporation, executable tasks and executed tasks without distinction when the stage of updating pheromone. We consider the search history of a previous time when scheduler startup is a reference value. The tasks are periodic, they are released by each period, when they exit run once , they should be released in the near future, Therefore, selected tasks have high probability be selected again. At the pheromone evaporation stage, we only chose the schedulable tasks to evaporate. The selected tasks are still with high pheromone until next period.

We proposed a new pheromone evaporation that don't make all tasks forget traveled nodes, only the task which schedulable at time t. It as follows :

3.3.1. New Tour Construction

First, find probability of each node using (7). Each schedulable task is considered as a node and probability of each node to be selected for execution is decided using pheromone τ and heuristic value η.

$$p_i(t) = \frac{(\tau_i(t))^{\alpha} * (\eta_i(t))^{\beta}}{\sum_{l \in R1}(\tau_i(t))^{\alpha} * (\eta_i(t))^{\beta}} \qquad (7)$$

where,

pi(t) is the probability of ith node at time t; i∈ N_1 and N1 is set of schedulable tasks at time t.

τi(t) is pheromone on ith node at time t.

ηi is heuristic value of ith node at t, which can be determined by (8),

$$\eta_i = \begin{cases} 0, & otherwise \\ \frac{K*D_i}{E_i(t)}, & if\ \frac{D_i}{E_i(t)} \le 1 \end{cases} \qquad (8)$$

Here, t is current time, K is constant and Di is absolute deadline of ith node, $E_i(t)$ is remain execute time of ith node.

α and β are constants which decide importance of τ and η.

3.3.2. New Pheromone Evaporation

Pheromone evaporation is required to forget bad travel of ants and to encourage new paths. Value of τ is updated using (9).

$$\tau_i(t+1) = (1-\rho)\tau_i(t) \quad (9)$$

where,

ρ is a constant.

$i \in N_1$; N_1 is set of schedulable tasks at time t.

4. Simulation and Results

We have implemented our algorithm & Kotecha's algorithm and have run simulations to accumulate empirical data. We have considered periodic tasks for taking the results. For periodic tasks, load of the system can be defined as summation of ratio of executable time and period of each task. For taking result at each load value, we have generated 200 task sets each one containing 3 to 9 tasks. The results for 5 different values of load are taken ($0.7 \le$ load ≤ 2.5) and tested on more than 35,000 tasks. Results are shown in Table 1 and Fig. 2.

The system is said to be overloaded when even a clairvoyant scheduler cannot feasibly schedule the tasks offered to the scheduler. A reasonable way to measure the performance of a scheduling algorithm during an overload is by the amount of work the scheduler can feasibly schedule according to the algorithm. The larger this amount the better the algorithm. Because of this, we have considered following two as our main performance criteria:

1) In real-time systems, deadline meeting is most important and we are interested in finding whether the task is meeting the deadline. Therefore the most appropriate performance metric is the Success Ratio and defined as (10) [5],

$$SR = \frac{Number\ of\ Jobs\ Successefully\ schedled}{Total\ number\ of\ Jobs\ arrived} \quad (10)$$

2) It is important that how efficiently the processors are utilized by the scheduler especially during overloaded conditions. Therefore, the other performance metric is Effective CPU Utilization (ECU) and defined as (11):,

$$ECU = \sum_{i \in R} \frac{V_i}{T} \quad (11)$$

Where,

V is value of task and

- value of a task = Computation time of a task, if the task completes within its deadline.
- value of a task = 0, if the task miss the deadline.

R is set of tasks, which are completed within their deadline.

T is total time of scheduleing.

An on-line scheduler has a competitive factor Cf if and only if the value of the schedule of any finite sequence of tasks produced by the algorithm is at least Cf times the value of the schedule of the tasks produced by an optimal clairvoyant algorithm [7]. Since maximum value obtained by a clairvoyant scheduling algorithm is a hard problem, we have instead used a rather simplistic upper bound on this maximum value, which is obtained by summing up the value of all tasks [14]. Therefore, we have considered value of ECU for clairvoyant scheduler is 100%.

Finally, the results are obtained, compared with Kotecha's algorithm in the same environment and shown in Fig.3 and Fig.4.

Table 1. *Results: Success Ratio of job*

Load	Kotecha's Algo	New Algo.
0.7	100%	100%
1.0	100%	100%
1.5	61.60%	66.70%
2.0	47.30%	54.70%
2.5	36.70%	48.80%

Fig.3 and Table1 shows the results achieved by the proposed algorithm and Kotecha's algorithm. We can obseve that the proposed Algorithm have a same performance with Kotecha's algorithm. However, we find that proposed algorithm is definitely more than 5% and12% when load values are 1.5 and 2.5.

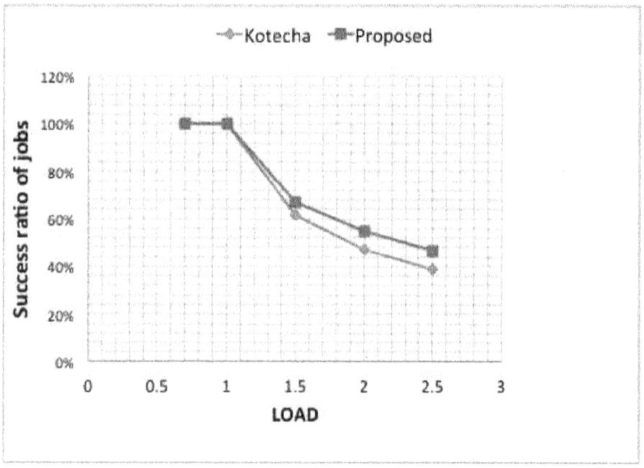

Figure 3. *Success ratio of jobs*

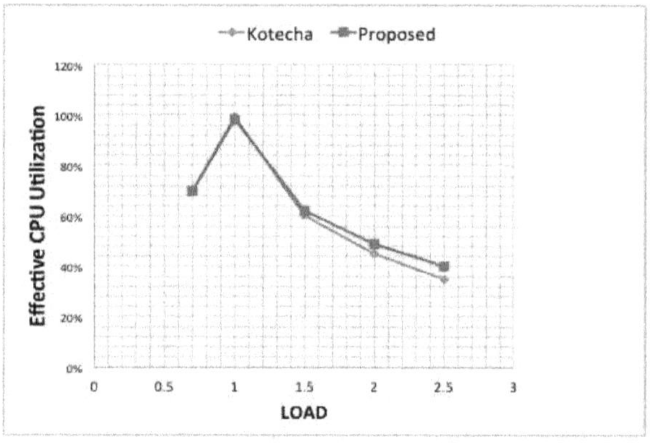

Figure 4. *Effective CPU Utilization.*

Fig. 4 and Table2 shows the results of Effective CPU Utilization achieved by the proposed algorithm and Kotecha's algorithm. We can observe that the proposed Algorithm have a same performance with Kotecha's algorithm. However, we find that proposed algorithm is definitely more than 5% and12% when load values are 1.5 and 2.5.

Table 2. RESULTS: Effective CPU Utilization

Load	Kotecha's Algo	New Algo.
0.7	100%	100%
1.0	100%	100%
1.5	61.60%	66.70%
2.0	47.30%	54.70%
2.5	36.70%	48.80%

5. Conclusions

The algorithm discussed in this paper is for scheduling of soft real-time system with single processor and preemptive task sets. For scheduling, the concept of ACO has been introduced. The algorithm is simulated with periodic task sets; results are obtained and compared with Kotecha's algorithm.

From the results of simulation we can conclude that the proposed algorithm performs equally optimal for single processor, preemptive environment when the system is underloaded. We can also observe that the proposed algorithm during overloaded conditions performance is better than Kotecha's algorithm.

Acknowledgements

This work is supported in part by JSPS KAKENHI Grant Number 24500046.

References

[1] K. Ramamritham and J. A. Stankovik, "Scheduling algorithms and operating support for real-time systems", Proceedings of the IEEE, vol. 82, pp. 56-76, January 1994.

[2] C. L. Liu and L. Layland, "Scheduling algorithms for multiprogramming in a hard-real-time environment", Journal of ACM, vol.20, pp: 46-61, January 1973.

[3] M. Dertouzos and K. Ogata, "Control robotics: The procedural control of physical process," Proc. IFIP Congress, pp. 807-813, 1974.

[4] A. Mok, "Fundamental Design Problems of Distributed Systems for the Hard-Real-Time Environment," Ph.d. thesis, MIT, Cambridge, Massachusetts, May 1983.

[5] G. Saini, "Application of Fuzzy logic to Real-time scheduling", Real-Time Conference, 14th IEEE-NPSS.pp.113-116, 2005.

[6] M. Dorigo and G. Caro, "The Ant Colony Optimization Metaheuristic in D. Corne, M. Dorigo and F. Glover(eds)", New Ideas in Optimization, McGraw Hill, 1999.

[7] V. Ramos, F. Muge, and P. Pina, "Self-organized data and image retrieval as a consequence of inter-dynamic synergistic relationships in artificial ant colonies", In Second International Conference on Hybrid Intelligent System, IOS Press, Santiago, 2002.

[8] Kotecha and A Shah, "Scheduling Algorithm for Real-Time Opeating Systems using ACO", 2010 Intelligence and Communication Networks, pp. 617–621, Nov 2010.

[9] C. D. Locke, "Best Effort Decision Making for Real-Time Scheduling", Ph.d. thesis, Computer Science Department, Carnegie-Mellon University, 1986.

[10] G. Koren and D. Shasha, "Dover: An optimal on-line scheduling algorithm for overloaded real-time systems", SIAM Journal of Computing, 24(2): 318-339 April 1995.

[11] A Shah, K Kotecha and D Shah, "Adaptive scheduling algorithm for real-time distributed systems", To appear in International Journal of Intelligent Computing and Cybernetics.

[12] A. Colorni, M. Dorigo, and V. Maniezzo, "Distributed optimization by ant colonies," In: Proceedings of European Conf. on Artificial Life. Elsevier, Amsterdam, pp. 134-142, 1991.

[13] K. Ramamritham, J. A. Stankovik, and P. F. Shiah, "Efficient scheduling algorithms for real-time multiprocessor systems", IEEE Transaction on Parallel and Distributed Systems, vol. 1, April 1990.

[14] S. Baruah, G. Koren, B. Mishra, A. Raghunath, L. Roiser, and D. Shasha, "On-line scheduling in the presence of overload," In FOCS, pp. 100–110 1991.

15

Evaluating reverse logistics networks with centralized centers: An adaptive genetic algorithm approach based on fuzzy logic controller

YoungSu Yun

Division of Management Administration, Chosun University, Gwangju, Korea

Email address:
ysyun@chosun.ac.kr

Abstract: This paper proposes an adaptive genetic algorithm (FLC-aGA) approach based on fuzzy logic controller (FLC) for evaluating the reverse logistics (RL) networks with centralized centers. For the FLC-aGA approach, an adaptive scheme using a fuzzy logic controller is applied to GA loop. Five components which are composed of customers, collection centers, recovery centers, redistribution centers, and secondary markets are used to design the RL networks. For the RL with centralized centers (RLCC), collection center, recovery center, redistribution center and secondary market will be opened alone. The RLCC will be formulated as a mixed integer programming (MIP) model and its objective function is to minimize the total cost of unit transportation costs, fixed costs, and variable costs under considering various constraints. The MIP model for the RLCC is solved by using the FLC-aGA approach. Three test problems with various sizes of collection centers, recovery centers, redistribution centers, and secondary markets are considered and they are compared the FLC-aGA approach with other competing approaches. Finally, the optimal solutions by the FLC-aGA and other competing approaches are demonstrated each other using some measures of performance.

Keywords: Adaptive Genetic Algorithm, Fuzzy Logic Controller (FLC), Reverse Logistics Network, Centralized Centers

1. Introduction

In general, supply chain management (SCM) considers two ways of its flow. First flow is a forward logistics network and it considers various components such as row material supply firms, manufacturing firms, distribution centers, retailers and customers. On the other hand, second flow is called as a backward (or reverse) logistics network and it consists of customers, collection centers, recovery centers, redistribution centers, and secondary markets. Of the two flows, especially, reverse logistics (RL) network have recently focused on many researchers since increasing interests in exhaustion of resources and environmental regulation have caused the effective treatment of used products [1-5].

The European working group on reverse logistics defined the RL as "the propose of planning, implementing and controlling flows of raw materials, in process inventory, and finished goods, from the point of use back to point of recovery or point of proper disposal" [1]. In a broader sense, the RL refers to the distribution activities involved in product return, source reduction, conservation, recycling, reuse, repair, disposal, refurbishment, and remanufacturing [6]. Various sides of the RL fields have been investigated by many researchers [7-12]. Of the sides, a few studies have addressed the problem of determining the optimal locations and numbers of the RL components such as collection centers, recovery centers, etc. [2, 5, 13].

Min *et al.* [2] proposed a nonlinear mixed integer programming (MIP) model to determine the optimal numbers and locations of initial collection centers and centralized return centers among RL components. The MIP model was solved using genetic algorithm (GA) approach. A similar study was performed by Aras and Aksen [13]. They suggested a mixed integer nonlinear programming (MINP) to determine the optimal numbers and locations of collection centers in the RL network. The MINP was solved by Tabu search method. Yun *et al.* [5] developed an aGA approach to solve the RL network which determines the optimal numbers and locations of collection center, remanufacturing centers, redistribution center and secondary markets. Two types of RL network were taken into consideration. One is to consider the single RL network with collection center, remanufacturing centers, redistribution center and secondary markets alone and the other is to use the multiple RL networks which collection center, remanufacturing centers, redistribution center and secondary markets can be opened more than one. They compared the single RL network with the multiple RL network using various measures of performance. Finally, the single RL network outperformed the multiple RL network.

The above studies concerning the optimal location and selection problem of RL components can be classified into two ways; the RL with centralized center (RLCC) and the RL with decentralized center (RLDC). In the RLCC, all used products are sent to each central facility, where they are collected, processed, and finally shipped to secondary markets. On the other word, in the RLCC, collection centers, recovery centers, redistribution centers and secondary markets will be opened alone. In the RLDC, however, all used products are sent to at least more than one facility, that is, several collection centers, recovery centers, redistribution centers and secondary markets can be opened. Between the RLCC and the RLDC, the performance of the former has been proved to be more effective than that of the latter [5].

Therefore, in this paper, we use the concept of the RLCC and its detailed components consist of collection centers, recovery centers, redistribution centers and secondary markets. The RLCC will be formulated by a MIP model and its objective is to minimize the total cost of transportation costs, fixed costs, and variable costs under considering various constraints. The MIP model will be solved by the proposed FLC-aGA approach with a fuzzy logic controller (FLC). Based on the above procedures, the objective of this paper is to develop an efficient MIP model and the FLC-aGA approach for the RLCC.

The focus of this paper is to design an adaptive genetic algorithm (FLC-aGA) approach based on fuzzy logic controller (FLC) for evaluating the reverse logistics (RL) networks with centralized centers. The paper is organized as follows: Section 2 introduces the detailed scheme of the reverse logistics networks with centralized centers (RLCC). A mixed integer programming (MIP) model is formulated for the RLCC problem in Section 3. For solving the RLCC problem, the FLC-aGA is proposed in Section 4. Three types of numerical experiments with various sizes of the RLCC problems are considered and they are solved for comparing by the FLC-aGA approach with other competing approaches in Section 5. Finally, conclusion and some remarks are outlined in Section 6.

2. Reverse Logistics Network with Centralized Centers (RLCC)

Since the RLCC is more efficient than the RLDC [5], we first define the correct status of the RLCC. Generally, the RLCC network consists of various components such as collection centers, recovery centers, etc. In the previous studies, Min et al. [2] considered only two components of initial collection centers and centralized return centers. Aras and Aksen [13] used one component of collection centers. On the other hand, Yun et al. [5] considered various components of collection centers, recovery centers, redistribution centers and secondary markets.

Among the conventional studies mentioned above, we use the basic concept of the RLCC network introduced in Yun et al. [5], since they considered various components in the flow of the RL network, but Min et al. [2] and Aras and Aksen [13] used only a few components in it. Therefore, the former is more acceptable concept in the RLCC network model than the latters. Figure 1 shows a conceptual model for the RLCC network used in this paper.

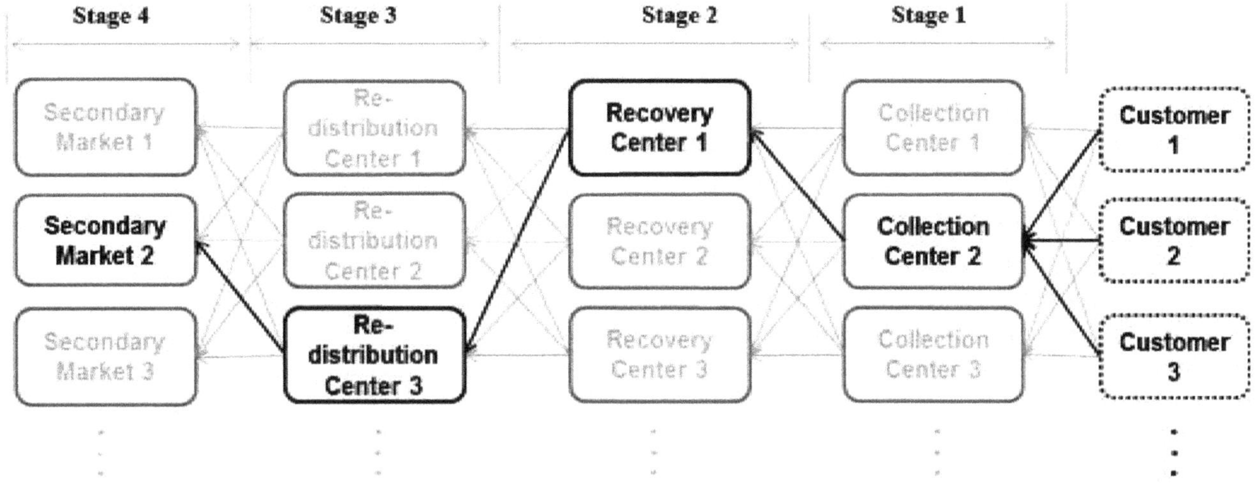

Figure 1. Conceptual model for the RLCC network

In Figure 1, the used products collected from customers are sent to a collection center, and after classifying them, the products available for reuse are sent to a recovery center. The recovery center revives or repairs them through proper treatments. The revived or repaired products are sent to a secondary market via a redistribution center and are then resold them to customers. The considerations under the RLCC network in Figure 1 are as follows:

- The locations of collection centers should be determined for effectively sending the used products collected from customers. The locations of recovery centers, redistribution centers, and secondary markets should also be determined for revival (or repair), redistribution and resale of the used products.
- The fixed costs required for the opening of the determined collection center, recovery center, redistribution center and secondary market, and their operation costs for treating unit product should be determined.
- The unit transportation costs required for transporting the products at each stage (customers → collection center → recovery center → redistribution center → secondary market) should be determined.

3. Mathematical Formulation

Before designing a mathematical model for the RLCC problem, several assumptions considered are as follows:

- This paper only considers the RL network for a single product.
- The number of customers is already known and each of them sends only one used product to a collection center opened. Therefore, the capacity of all customers is identical with the number of customers.
- The locations of customers, collection centers, recovery centers, redistribution centers, and secondary markets are displayed as site coordinates and their values of each location are known in advance.
- The fixed costs required for the opening of collection center, recovery center, redistribution center and secondary market are different each other and are already known.
- For the RLCC problem, the collection centers, recovery centers, redistribution centers and secondary markets will be opened alone respectively.
- Unit handling cost at same stage is identical, since each center (or market) at same stage performs same function.
- Unit transportation costs at each stage are calculated by the site coordinates of the collection center, recovery center, redistribution center and secondary market opened at each stage. For instance, if the site coordinates of the jth recovery center and the kth redistribution center are (x_j, y_j) and (x_k, y_k) respectively, then the unit transportation cost between the recovery center and the redistribution center is calculated by using the Euclidian distance as follows:

$$d_{jk} = \sqrt{(x_k - x_j)^2 + (y_k - y_j)^2} \tag{1}$$

Based on the assumptions mentioned above, we develop a mathematical model effectively representing the RLCC problem. The objective of this paper is to design their optimal networks which can minimize the total cost composed of fixed costs, variable costs and transportation costs. The minimization of the total cost is considered as an objective function and various constraints. The indices, parameters and decision variables used in the objective function and various constraints are set as follows:

Indices:

i : index of customer; $i \in I$

j : index of collection center; $j \in J$

k : index of recovery center; $k \in K$

l : index of redistribution center; $l \in L$

m : index of secondary market; $m \in M$

Parameters:

FC_j : fixed cost at collection center j

FM_k : fixed cost at recovery center k

FD_l : fixed cost at redistribution center l

FS_m : fixed cost at secondary market m

VC : unit handling cost at collection center

VM : unit handling cost at recovery center

VD : unit handling cost at redistribution center

VS : unit handling cost at secondary market

CC_{ij} : unit transportation cost from customer i to collection center j

CM_{jk} : unit transportation cost from collection center j to recovery center k

MD_{kl} : unit transportation cost from recovery center k to redistribution center l

DS_{lm} : unit transportation cost from redistribution center l to secondary market m

CU_i : capacity at customer l

Decision variables:

c_j : collection capacity at collection center j

m_k : treatment capacity at recovery center k

d_l : treatment capacity at redistribution center l

s_m : treatment capacity at secondary market m

$$x_j^C = \begin{cases} 1, & \text{if collection center } j \text{ is open} \\ 0, & \text{otherwise} \end{cases}$$

$$x_k^M = \begin{cases} 1, & \text{if recovery center } k \text{ is open} \\ 0, & \text{otherwise} \end{cases}$$

$$x_l^D = \begin{cases} 1, & \text{if redistribution center } l \text{ is open} \\ 0, & \text{otherwise} \end{cases}$$

$$x_m^S = \begin{cases} 1, & \text{if secondary market } m \text{ is open} \\ 0, & \text{otherwise} \end{cases}$$

Using the parameters and decision variables described

above, we develop a mathematical model for effectively representing the RLCC as follows:

$$\begin{aligned} \text{Minimize } Z = & \sum_{i}\sum_{j} CC_{ij}\cdot CU_i \cdot x_j^{C} + \sum_{j} FC_j \cdot x_j^{C} + VC(\sum_{j} c_j \cdot x_j^{C}) + \\ & \sum_{j}\sum_{k} CM_{jk}\cdot c_j \cdot x_k^{M} + \sum_{k} FM_k \cdot x_k^{M} + VM(\sum_{k} m_k \cdot x_k^{M}) + \\ & \sum_{k}\sum_{l} MD_{kl}\cdot m_k \cdot x_l^{D} + \sum_{l} FD_l \cdot x_l^{D} + VD(\sum_{l} d_l \cdot x_l^{D}) + \\ & \sum_{l}\sum_{m} DS_{lm}\cdot d_l \cdot x_m^{S} + \sum_{m} FS_m \cdot x_m^{S} + VS(\sum_{m} s_m \cdot x_m^{S}) \end{aligned} \quad (2)$$

subject to

$$\sum_{j} c_j - \sum_{k} m_k = 0 \quad (3)$$

$$\sum_{k} m_k - \sum_{l} d_l = 0 \quad (4)$$

$$\sum_{l} d_l - \sum_{l} s_m = 0 \quad (5)$$

$$\sum_{j} x_j^{C} = 1 \quad (6)$$

$$\sum_{k} x_k^{M} = 1 \quad (7)$$

$$\sum_{l} x_l^{D} = 1 \quad (8)$$

$$\sum_{m} x_m^{S} = 1 \quad (9)$$

$$x_j^{C} = \{0, 1\} \qquad \forall j \in J \quad (10)$$

$$x_k^{M} = \{0, 1\} \qquad \forall k \in K \quad (11)$$

$$x_l^{D} = \{0, 1\} \qquad \forall l \in L \quad (12)$$

$$x_m^{S} = \{0, 1\} \qquad \forall m \in M \quad (13)$$

$$c_j, m_k, d_l, s_m \geq 0 \quad \forall j \in J, \forall k \in K, \forall l \in L, \forall m \in M \quad (14)$$

The objective function (2) minimizes the sum of fixed costs, variable costs, and transportation costs resulting from each stage. Equation (3) ensures that the sum of the used products collected in whole collection centers is the same as that treated in whole recovery centers. As the same meaning, equations (4) and (5) ensure that the sums treated in whole recovery centers and redistribution centers are the same as those in redistribution centers and secondary markets, respectively. Equations (6), (7), (8) and (9) show that collection centers, recovery centers, redistribution centers and secondary markets should be opened alone. Equations (10), (11), (12) and (13) restrict the variables to integers 0 and 1. Equation (14) means non-negativity.

The mathematical model formulated in this paper is represented as a mixed integer programming (MIP) and the FLC-aGA approach is proposed in next Section.

4. FLC-aGA Approach

Since the network design such as the RL network problem has been known as NP-complete [14-15], conventional approaches are difficult to effectively find the optimal solution. Recently, a methodology using GA approach has been successfully adopted to effectively solve the RL network design problems [2, 4-5]. Unfortunately, however, conventional GA approaches have some weakness in the correct setting of genetic parameters such as crossover and mutation rates. Identifying the correct setting values of genetic parameters is not an easy task, because GA performance considerately relies on their setting values. Therefore, many studies have been performed to locate the correct setting values [16-20].

Most of the conventional studies mentioned above have recommended the use of adaptive scheme which can automatically regulate GA parameters. Since keeping a balance between exploitation and exploration in genetic search process highly affects locating the optimal solution, it has been generally known that, during its search process, the approach both with a moderate and various increasing and decreasing trends in its parameter values is more efficient than the approach with rapid increasing or decreasing trends or the approach with a constant value. Therefore, much time for the correct setting of the genetic parameters can be saved, and the search ability of GA can be improved in finding global optimal solution [21].

In this Section, therefore, we design an adaptive genetic algorithm approach based on fuzzy logic controller (FLC-aGA) approach. Firstly, representation, initialization and GA operators will be suggested. Secondly, an adaptive scheme based on a FLC will be followed.

4.1. Representation and Initialization

The most important thing when designing the RL network by GA is how to set a correct representation scheme, since whether collection centers, recovery centers, redistribution centers and secondary markets are opened or not should be automatically determined during genetic search process. Therefore, we design a new representation scheme as shown in Figure 2 to correctly represent the structure of the RLCC proposed in this paper.

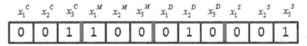

x_1^C	x_2^C	x_3^C	x_1^M	x_2^M	x_3^M	x_1^D	x_2^D	x_3^D	x_1^S	x_2^S	x_3^S
0	0	1	1	0	0	0	1	0	0	0	1

Figure 2. *An example of representation for the RLCC*

In Figure 2, the collection center 3 is opened ($x_3^{C} = 1$) and the collection centers 1 and 2 are not opened ($x_1^{C} = x_2^{C} = 0$). As a same meaning, the recovery center 1, the redistribution center 2, and the secondary market 3 are also opened, respectively. Therefore, whether collection center, recovery center, redistribution center and secondary market are opened or not is determined by randomly having 0 or 1 in order that the total cost should be minimized. By using the representation scheme, we can easily produce initial population. If population size is 5, then initial population can be generated as shown in Figure 3.

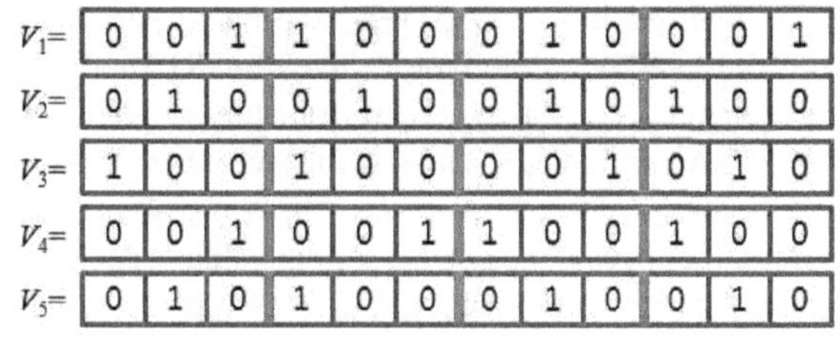

Figure 3. An example of initial population for the RLCC

4.2. Genetic Operators

4.2.1. Selection

The selection strategy is to choose the respective individuals from the current population. Therefore, the chosen individuals are considered as the population of the next generation. For selection, the elitist selection strategy in an enlarged sampling space [15] is used.

4.2.2. Crossover

For improving the solution quality during genetic search process, a crossover operator is needed for exchanging some genes between individuals. In this paper, we develop a new crossover operator for the RLCC. The detailed implementation procedure is as follows:

Step 1: two individuals are randomly selected in population.

Step 2: two genes in the selected individuals are randomly selected.

Step 3: the values of the selected genes are exchanged with each other. If the value of the selected gene is exchanged with 1 (the third genes of V_4* in Figure 4), then the gene with the value 1 among the other genes should have the value 0 instead of 1 (the second genes of V_4** in Figure 4). On the other hand, if the value of the selected gene is exchanged with 0 (the third genes of V_1* in Figure 4), then select randomly a gene among the other genes and then the value of the selected gene is exchanged with 1 (the second genes of V_1** in Figure 4).

These procedures of the crossover operators for the RLCC are summarized in Figure 4.

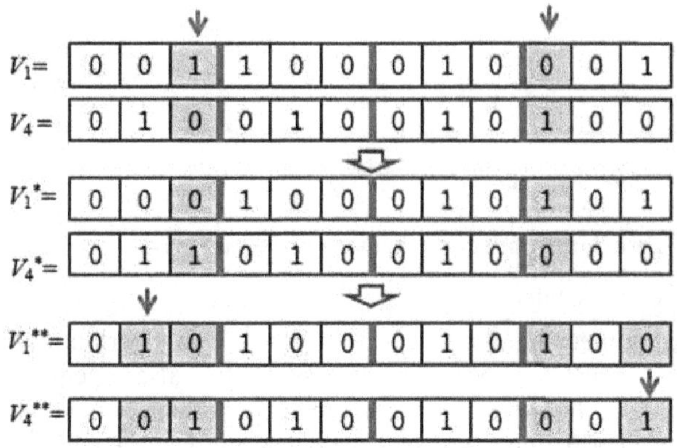

Figure 4. An example of crossover operator for the RLCC

4.2.3. Mutation

A new mutation operator for the RLCC problem is developed as follows:

Step 1: an individual is randomly selected in population.

Step 2: a gene in the selected individual is randomly selected.

Step 3: If the value of the selected gene is 0, then the value is exchanged with 1(the fifth genes of V_5* in Figure 5). In this case, the gene with the value 1 among the other genes should have the value 0 instead of 1 (the forth genes of V_5** in Figure 5). On the other hand, if the value of the selected gene is 1, then the value is exchanged with 0. In this case, a gene among the other genes is randomly selected and then the value of the selected gene is exchanged with 1.

These procedures of the mutation operators for the RLCC are summarized in Figure 5.

4.2.4. Repair Strategy for Infeasible Link

The physical link at each stage, representing the new individuals after crossover and mutation operators, may be infeasible, if the values of the genes of the new individuals are changed (e.g., 0 → 1, or 1 → 0). Therefore, a new repair strategy that the link at each stage can be feasible for the individuals with the changed values of the genes should be developed. In this paper, the following heuristic procedure is used for the repair strategy.

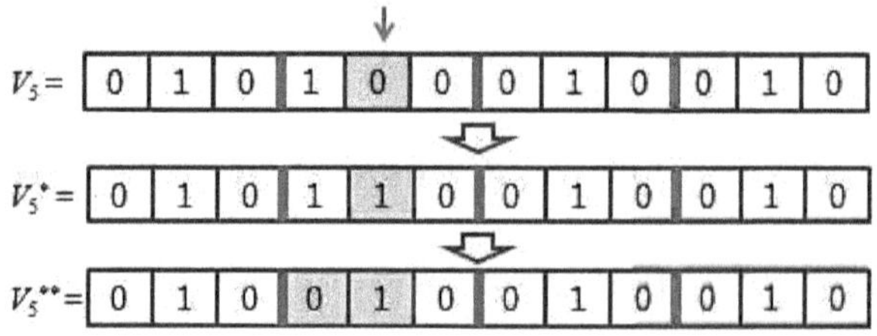

Figure 5. An example of mutation operator for the RLCC

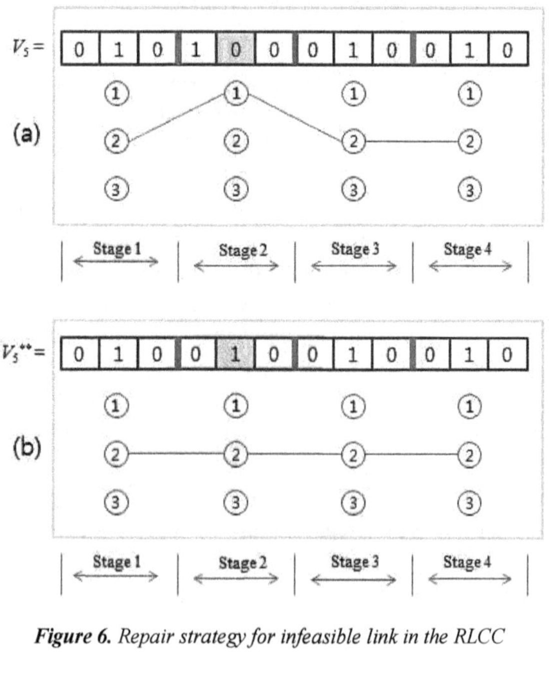

Figure 6. Repair strategy for infeasible link in the RLCC

Step 1: Select one individual with the changed values of the gene among the individuals resulting from crossover and mutation operators

Step 2: The gene with value 1 at previous stage is linked to the gene newly having value 1 at current stage. The linked gene at current stage is also linked to the gene with value 1 at the next stage. If all individuals have feasible links, then stop, otherwise go to Step 1.

These procedures of the repair strategy are summarized in Figure 6. The feasible link of the individual (V_5) is described in the representation (a) of Figure 6. If the newly generated individual after crossover and mutation operators is the V_5^{**} of Figure 6, then the link (a) is changed into infeasible one. Therefore, we have to generate a new feasible link using the V_5^{**}. The new generated feasible link (b) is just obtained by connecting the genes with the value 1 at each stage.

4.2.5. Fitness test

Each individual of the population in the FLC-aGA approach should be evaluated by measuring its fitness. The fitness values of each individual are computed by using the objective functions in the equation (2) under satisfying all constraints from the equations (3) through (14) for the RLCC.

4.3. Adaptive scheme by a FLC

The adaptive scheme used in the FLC-aGA approach is to automatically regulate the rates of the crossover and mutation operators. Many conventional studies have developed various adaptive schemes for regulating the rate [16-19, 22-26]. Of them, several adaptive schemes using FLCs have been successfully adopted for improving the performance of GAs [16,18, 27]. Gen and Cheng [18] surveyed various adaptive schemes using several FLCs. Subbu *et al.* [27] developed a fuzzy logic-controlled genetic algorithm (FLC-GA) using a fuzzy knowledge base. The developed FLC-GA automatically regulates the rates of the crossover and mutation operators. Song *et al.* [16] suggested the two FLCs to automatically regulate the rates of the crossover and mutation operators. The suggested two FLCs are used as the input variables of the GA. For successfully applying FLCs to GAs, Subbu *et al.* [27] and Song *et al.* [16] proposed the production of well-formed fuzzy sets and rules. Therefore, the GAs which are controlled by these types of FLCs are more efficient in terms of the search speed and solution quality than the GAs without them [16, 18, 27].

Based on the conventional studies using FLCs, we also use an FLC to adaptively regulate the rates of the crossover and mutation operators in this paper. We use the basic concept of Song *et al.* [16] and improve it in some aspects. The main idea behind the concept is to use the crossover FLC and the mutation FLC. These two FLCs are implemented independently to automatically regulate the rates of the crossover and mutation operators during the genetic search process. The heuristic updating strategy for regulating the rates is to consider the changes of the average fitness values over two successive generations in the FLC-aGA populations. That is, the rate of the crossover operator (P_C) and that of the mutation operator (P_M) should be increased, if better offspring through the changes are consistently yield. However, the P_C and P_M should also be decreased, if poorer offspring are continuously produced. This scheme encourages well-performing operators to produce more individuals, while also reducing the chance for poorly performing operators to destroy the respective individuals during genetic search process.

For example, when a minimization problem is assumed, we can set the change of the average fitness value at generation t, $Change\_AvgFit(t)$, as follows:

$$Change\_AvgFit(t) = (\overline{Fit_{par\_size}(t)} - \overline{Fit_{off\_size}(t)}) \times \alpha$$
$$= \left(\frac{\sum_{k=1}^{par\_size} Fit_k(t)}{par\_size} - \frac{\sum_{k=par\_size+1}^{par\_size+off\_size} Fit_k(t)}{off\_size}\right) \times \alpha \quad (15)$$

where k is the generation index and α is a scaling factor to normalize the average fitness value for applying defuzzification in the FLC. The α is varied according to the problem under consideration. The parameter, α, was not used in the original study [16]. However, the α is definitely required for normalizing the average fitness value since it is varied according to the problem under consideration. Both $Change\_AvgFit(t-1)$ and $Change\_AvgFit(t)$ are used to regulate p_C and p_M, as shown in Figure 7.

Procedure: regulation of p_C and p_M using average fitness value
begin
 if $\beta \le Change\_AvgFit(t-1) \le \gamma$ **and**
  $\beta \le Change\_AvgFit(t) \le \gamma$
  then increase p_C and p_M for next generation ;
 if $-\gamma \le Change\_AvgFit(t-1) \le -\beta$ **and**
  $-\gamma \le Change\_AvgFit(t) \le -\beta$
  then decrease p_C and p_M for next generation ;
 if $-\beta < Change\_AvgFit(t-1) < \beta$ **and**
  $-\beta < Change\_AvgFit(t) < \beta$
  then rapidly increase p_C and p_M for next generation ;
 end
end

Figure 7. *Regulation of* p_C *and* p_M *using average fitness value.*

In the above, β is a given real number in the proximity of zero, and γ and $-\gamma$ are given maximum and minimum values of a fuzzy membership function, respectively. The implementation strategy for the crossover FLC is as follows.

- Input and output for the crossover FLC.
  The inputs for the crossover FLC are $Change\_AvgFit(t-1)$ and $Change\_AvgFit(t)$. The output is the change in the crossover rate, $\Delta c(t)$.
- Membership functions of $Change\_AvgFit(t-1)$, $Change\_AvgFit(t)$, and $\Delta c(t)$.

The membership functions of the fuzzy input and output linguistic variables are shown in Figures 8 and 9, respectively. Both $Change\_AvgFit(t-1)$ and $Change\_AvgFit(t)$ are respectively normalized in the range, [-1.0, 1.0]. $\Delta c(t)$ is also normalized in the range of [-0.1, 0.1] with respect to the corresponding maximum values.

- Fuzzy decision table
  The fuzzy decision table developed in the conventional study (Song *et al.* 1997) is used.
- Defuzzification table for control actions
  The defuzzification table to simply represent the control action for the crossover FLC should be required. The defuzzification table developed in the conventional study [16] is used.

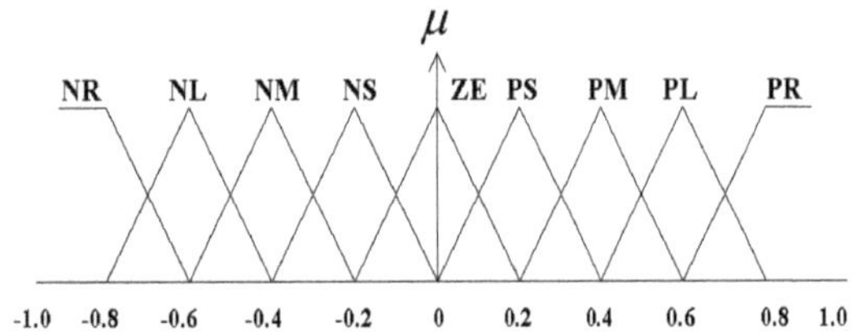

Figure 8. *Membership functions of* $Change\_AvgFit(t-1)$, $Change\_AvgFit(t)$

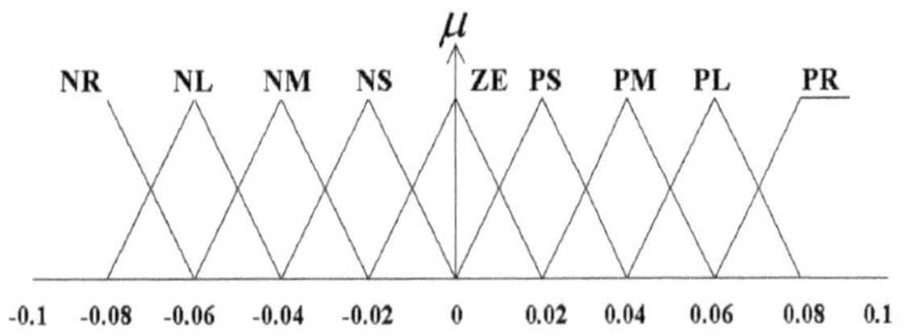

Figure 9. *Membership function of* $\Delta c(t)$

In the Figures 8 and 9, NR means Negative larger, NL Negative large, NM Negative medium, NS Negative small, ZE Zero, PS Positive small, PM Positive medium, PL Positive large, and PR Positive larger.

The inputs of the mutation FLC are the same as those of the crossover FLC and the output is the change in the mutation rate, $\Delta m(t)$. The regulating strategy of the crossover and mutation FLCs in the FLC-aGA is summarized in Figure 10.

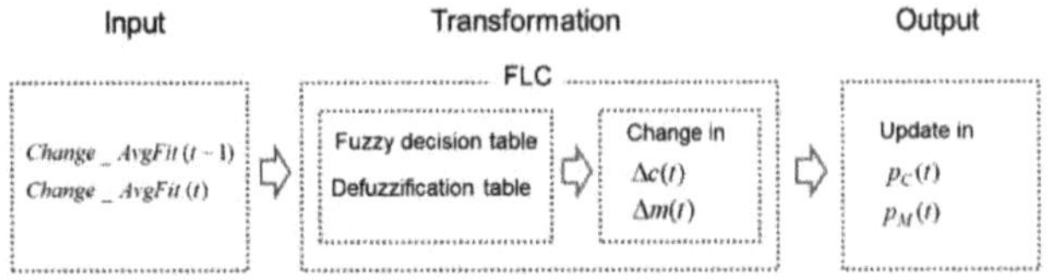

Figure 10. *Regulation strategy of the crossover and mutation FLCs*

The detailed procedure for its application is as follows.

Step 1: The input variables of the FLC for regulating the rates of the crossover and mutation operators are the changes in the average fitness value in two successive generations as follows:

$$Change\_AvgFit(t-1),\ Change\_AvgFit(t) \quad (16)$$

Step 2: After normalizing $Change\_AvgFit(t-1)$ and $Change\_AvgFit(t)$, assign these values to the indexes *i* and *j* corresponding to the control actions in the defuzzification table [16].

Step 3: Calculate $\Delta c(t)$ and $\Delta m(t)$ as follows:

$$\Delta c(t) = Z(i, j)\times 0.02 \qquad \Delta m(t) = Z(i, j)\times 0.002 \quad (17)$$

where the contents of $Z(i, j)$ are the corresponding values of $Change\_AvgFit(t-1)$ and $Change\_AvgFit(t)$ in the defuzzification table [16]. The values of 0.02 and 0.002 are given to regulate the increasing and decreasing ranges of the rates of the crossover and mutation operators.

Step 4: Update the changes in the rates of the crossover and the mutation operators by using the following equations:

$$p_C(t) = p_C(t-1) + \Delta c(t),$$

$$p_M(t) = p_M(t-1) + \Delta m(t) \quad (18)$$

The adjusted rates should lie between 0.5 and 1.0 for the $p_C(t)$ and between 0.0 and 0.1 for the $p_M(t)$.

4.4. Overall Procedure of the FLC-aGA Approach

The detailed metaheuristic procedure for the FLC-aGA approach is as follows.

Step 1: Representation
The representation method as shown in Figure 2 is used to effectively represent the RLCC.

Step 2: Initialization
The initial population is consisted of the individuals obtained by the representation procedure developed in this paper.

Step 3: Fitness test
Equation (2) is used for the fitness test.

Step 4: Genetic operators
Selection: The elitist strategy in an enlarged sampling space [18].
Crossover: The crossover operator shown in Section 4.2.2 is used.
Mutation: The mutation operator shown in Section 4.2.3 is used.

Step 5: Adaptation by FLC
The adaptive scheme using the FLC shown in Section 4.3 is used for automatically regulating the rates of crossover and mutation operators.

Step 6: Termination condition
If a pre-defined maximum number of generations is reached during the genetic search process, then all the steps are terminated; otherwise, go to Step 3.

5. Numerical Experiments

Three types of the RLCC problem scales are considered in numerical experiments. Each problem type has various sizes of collection centers, recovery centers, redistribution centers and secondary markets. Table 1 summarizes the sizes of these types. For each type, the fixed costs, unit handling costs and the site coordinate information at customers, collection centers, recovery centers, redistribution centers and secondary markets are listed in Appendixes 1 through 6. The graphical representation using site coordinate information for Type 1 is displayed Figure 11.

Table 1. *Three types of the RLCC*

Type	No. of Customer	No. of collection center	No. of recovery center	No. of redistribution center	No. of secondary market
1	30	5	2	3	3
2	30	10	4	7	5
3	30	15	6	9	7

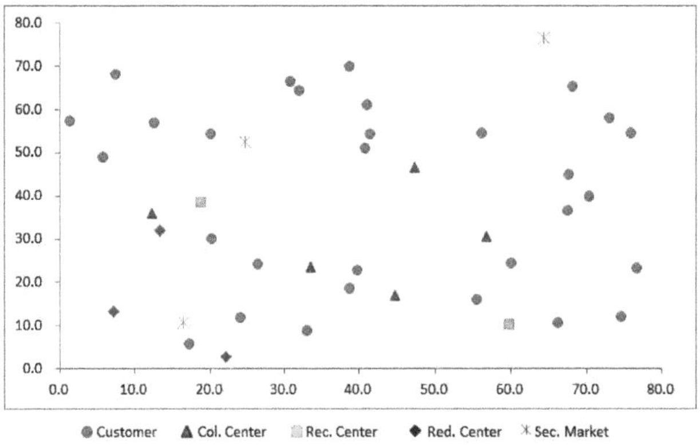

Figure 11. *Graphical representation using site coordinate information for Type 1*

For various comparisons, two conventional approaches are used here and their performances are compared with the FLC-aGA approach. They are summarized in Table 2. The aGA approach shown in Table 2 has a heuristic for adaptive scheme (Mak *et al.* 2000).

Table 2. *Approaches for comparison*

Approach	Description
GA	Conventional GA without any adaptive scheme
aGA	aGA with the adaptive scheme used in Mak *et al.* [19]

All the approaches shown in Table 2 were programmed in Visual Basic version 6.0 and ran on the environment of IBM compatible PC Pentium 4 processor, CPU 3.2GHz, 2GB RAM and Window-XP. The parameter settings for the two conventional approaches (GA and aGA) and the FLC-aGA approach are as follows: total generation number is 10,000, population size is 20, crossover rate is 0.5, and mutation rate is 0.05. The crossover and mutation rates in the GA approach are fixed, but the rates in the aGA and the FLC-aGA approaches are automatically regulated, during genetic search process. Altogether 20 independent runs are made to eliminate the randomness of each approach. All the approaches are compared with each other using some measures of performance shown in Table 3.

In Table 3, the CPU time is averaged over 20 independent runs. The optimal solution and the optimal setting mean the best result when each approach reaches to a pre-defined maximum number of generations.

Table 3. *Measures of performance*

Measure	Description
CPU time	Average CPU time (in Sec.)
Optimal Solution	The value of minimizing the sum of fixed cost, variable cost, and transportation cost resulting from each stage.
Optimal setting	Fixed cost, variable cost, transportation cost, opening/closing decision at collection centers, recovery centers, redistribution centers, secondary markets in the optimal solution

Table 4. *Performance results for Type 1*

			GA	aGA	FLC-aGA
CPU Time			0.47	0.38	0.39
Optimal solution			3272.5	3020.4	3020.4
Optimal Setting	Col. Center	Fixed Cost	25.5	25.5	25.5
		Var. Cost	75.0	75.0	75.0
		Transp. Cost	1227.8	1227.8	1227.8
	Rec. Center	Fixed Cost	32.5	32.5	32.5
		Var. Cost	135.0	135.0	135.0
		Transp. Cost	210.0	210.0	210.0
	Red. Center	Fixed Cost	23.2	20.1	20.1
		Var. Cost	96.0	96.0	96.0
		Transp. Cost	1080.0	834.0	834.0
	Sec. Market	Fixed Cost	25.5	25.5	25.5
		Var. Cost	48.0	48.0	48.0
		Transp. Cost	294.0	291.0	291.0
	Col. Center 1	Opening/Closing	Closing	Closing	Closing
	Col. Center 2	"	Closing	Closing	Closing
	Col. Center 3	"	Opening	Opening	Opening
	Col. Center 4	"	Closing	Closing	Closing
	Col. Center 5	"	Closing	Closing	Closing
	Rec. Center 1	"	Closing	Closing	Closing
	Rec. Center 2	"	Opening	Opening	Opening
	Red. Center 1	"	Closing	Closing	Closing
	Red. Center 2	"	Opening	Closing	Closing
	Red. Center 3	"	Closing	Opening	Opening
	Sec. Market 1	"	Closing	Closing	Closing
	Sec. Market 2	"	Closing	Closing	Closing
	Sec. Market 3	"	Opening	Opening	Opening

Table 4 shows various performance results of each approach for Type 1. Especially, for more detailed comparison, various costs and opening/closing decisions at each collection center, recovery center, redistribution center, and secondary market are shown in terms of the optimal setting.

In terms of the CPU time of Table 4, the GA approach is the slowest, but the aGA and the FLC-aGA approaches have almost the same result and the quickest, which means that the aGA and the FLC-aGA approaches appropriately control their search processes rather than the GA approach since the formers have adaptive schemes to automatically regulate a balance between exploitation and exploration during genetic search process. The appropriate control of the search process in the aGA and the FLC-aGA approaches has influence on their performances, that is, the performances of the aGA and the FLC-aGA approaches are more efficient in terms of the optimal solution than that of the GA approach. In terms of the optimal setting, except for the fixed cost and the transportation cost at the redistribution center and the transportation cost at the secondary market, all of the costs in the GA, the aGA and the FLC-aGA approaches have the same values, since the redistribution center 2 in the GA approach is opened, whereas, the redistribution center 3 in the aGA and the FLC-aGA approaches are opened.

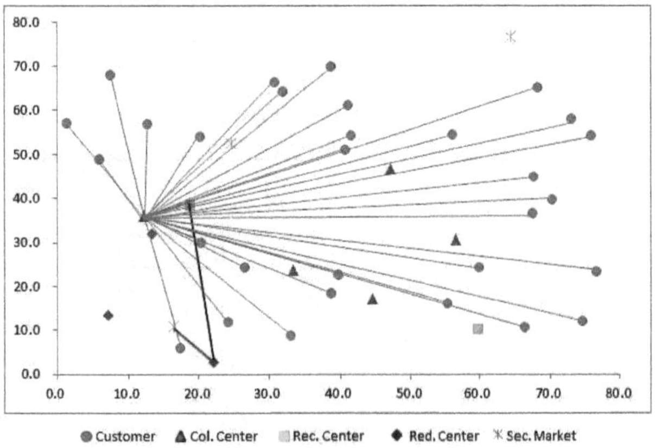

Figure 12. Graphical representation according to opening/closing decisions of the GA approach for Type 1

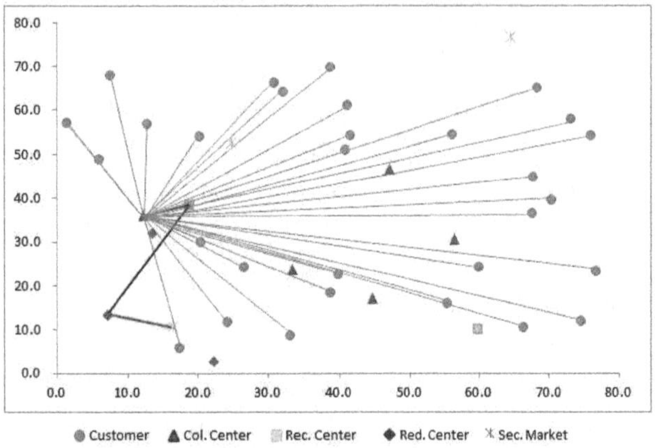

Figure 13. Graphical representation according to opening/closing decisions of the aGA and the FLC-aGA approaches for Type 1

Figures 12 and 13 show the graphical representation according to the opening and closing decisions of each collection center, recovery center, redistribution center, and secondary market, when each approach reach to the optimal solution.

In Figures 12 and 13, the opening decisions of collection centers, recovery centers, redistribution centers and secondary markets are represented as a link among them.

In Figs 12 and 13, the used products collected from all the customers are sent to the collection center 3, the recovery center 2 and the secondary market 3 for classifying, repairing and selling them, respectively, which process is happened under the same situation regardless of the GA, the aGA and the FLC-aGA approaches. However, in the opening and closing decision of redistribution centers, the GA approach opens the redistribution center 2, while, the aGA and the FLC-aGA approaches open the redistribution center 3, thus, the former and the latter show different graphical representation. These different site coordinates highly affect the fixed cost and transportation cost. Finally, the optimal solutions of the GA and the two adaptive GAs (aGA and FLC-aGA) approaches have different results.

Table 5. Performance results for Type 2

			GA	aGA	FLC-aGA
CPU Time			0.98	0.70	0.72
Optimal solution			5614.3	5498.4	4927.2
Optimal Setting	Col. Center	Fixed Cost	12.8	12.5	10.2
		Var. Cost	105.0	105.0	105.0
		Transp. Cost	1482.0	913.4	974.5
	Rec. Center	Fixed Cost	36.5	36.5	36.5
		Var. Cost	324.0	324.0	324.0
		Transp. Cost	825.0	1278.0	648.0
	Red. Center	Fixed Cost	10.5	10.5	10.5
		Var. Cost	192.0	192.0	192.0
		Transp. Cost	795.0	795.0	795.0
	Sec. Market	Fixed Cost	10.5	10.5	10.5
		Var. Cost	75.0	75.0	75.0
		Transp. Cost	1746.0	1746.0	1746.0
	Col. Center 1	Opening/Closing	Closing	Closing	Opening
	Col. Center 2	"	Closing	Opening	Closing
	Col. Center 3	"	Closing	Closing	Closing
	Col. Center 4	"	Closing	Closing	Closing
	Col. Center 5	"	Closing	Closing	Closing
	Col. Center 6	"	Closing	Closing	Closing
	Col. Center 7	"	Opening	Closing	Closing
	Col. Center 8	"	Closing	Closing	Closing
	Col. Center 9	"	Closing	Closing	Closing
	Col. Center 10	"	Closing	Closing	Closing
	Rec. Center 1	"	Closing	Closing	Closing
	Rec. Center 2	"	Closing	Closing	Closing
	Rec. Center 3	"	Opening	Opening	Opening
	Rec. Center 4	"	Closing	Closing	Closing
	Red. Center 1	"	Closing	Closing	Closing
	Red. Center 2	"	Closing	Closing	Closing
	Red. Center 3	"	Closing	Closing	Closing
	Red. Center 4	"	Closing	Closing	Closing
	Red. Center 5	"	Closing	Closing	Closing
	Red. Center 6	"	Opening	Opening	Opening
	Red. Center 7	"	Closing	Closing	Closing
	Sec. Market 1	"	Closing	Closing	Closing
	Sec. Market 2	"	Closing	Closing	Closing
	Sec. Market 3	"	Closing	Closing	Closing
	Sec. Market 4	"	Opening	Opening	Opening
	Sec. Market 5	"	Closing	Closing	Closing

Table 5 shows the performance results for Type 2. In terms of the CPU time, the aGA and the FLC-aGA approaches are slightly quicker than the GA approach. In terms of the optimal setting, the GA and the aGA approaches open the collection centers 7 and 2, respectively, whereas, the FLC-aGA approach opens the collection center 1. Each collection center opened has different fixed costs and different site coordinates. Therefore, the fixed costs at each approach are different each other, and the transportation costs between all the customers and each collection center opened are also different. The difference of the transportation costs between each collection center opened and each recovery center opened is interpreted by the difference among the site coordinates at each collection center opened. These differences on the fixed cost, transportation cost, and site coordinates at each approach have greatly influence on the optimal solution, that is, the performance of the FLC-aGA approach is superior to those of the GA and the aGA approaches.

For Type 3, the performance results of each approach are shown in Table 6. Similar to the result analysis of Table 5, the aGA and the FLC-aGA approaches are slightly quicker than the GA approach in terms of the CPU time. The optimal solutions of each approach are greatly influenced by the fixed costs, variable costs, and transportation costs resulting from the collection centers, recovery centers, redistribution centers and secondary markets opened. By the influence, the performance of the FLC-aGA approach has the best result in terms of the optimal solution.

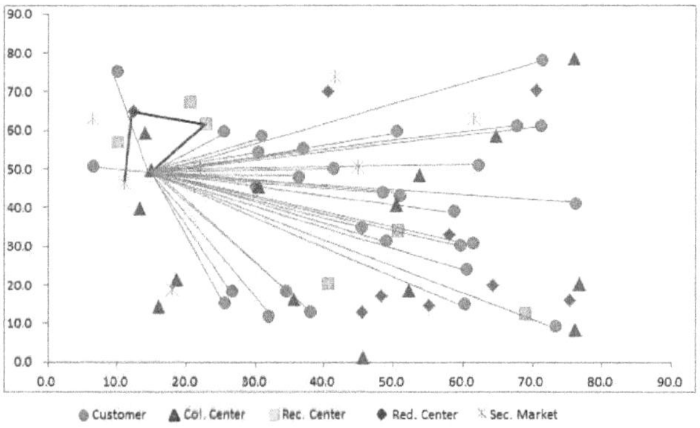

Figure 14. *Graphical representation according to opening/closing decisions of the GA approach for Type 3*

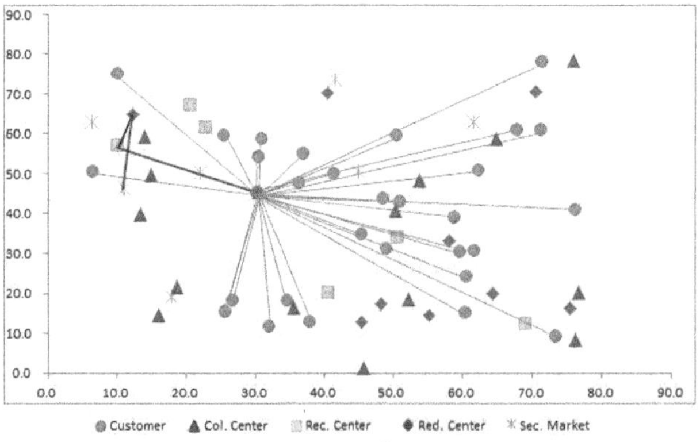

Figure 15. *Graphical representation according to opening/closing decisions of the aGA approaches for Type 3*

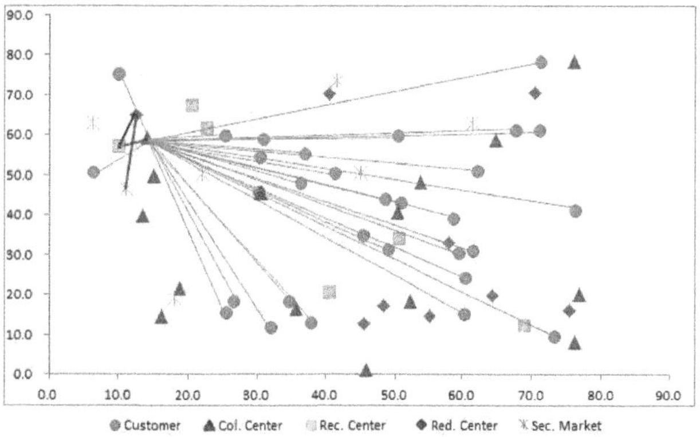

Figure 16. *Graphical representation according to opening/closing decisions of the FLC-aGA approaches for Type 3*

Figures 14, 15 and 16 show the graphical representation according to opening and closing decisions of each collection center, recovery center, redistribution center, and secondary market, when each approach reach to the optimal solution. In the Figures, the GA, the aGA and the FLC-aGA approaches open the collection centers 10, 1 and 12, respectively. Therefore, the former and the latter have different site coordinates and show different graphical representation in Figures 14, 15 and 16, which has greatly influence on the fixed cost and transportation cost at the collection centers and recovery centers opened. By the influence, the optimal solutions of each approach have different results as shown in Table 6.

Figure 17 shows the convergence process of each approach for Type 3, until each approach reaches a pre-defined maximum number of generations (in our case, 10,000). Each approach show fast convergence processes during the initial generations. However, after these generations, the GA and the aGA approaches does not show any convergence behaviors, whereas, the FLC-aGA approach shows a convergence behavior after about the generations of 2,200. By the difference of these convergence behaviors, we can confirm that the performance of the FLC-aGA approach is significantly superior to those of the GA and the aGA approaches as shown in Table 6.

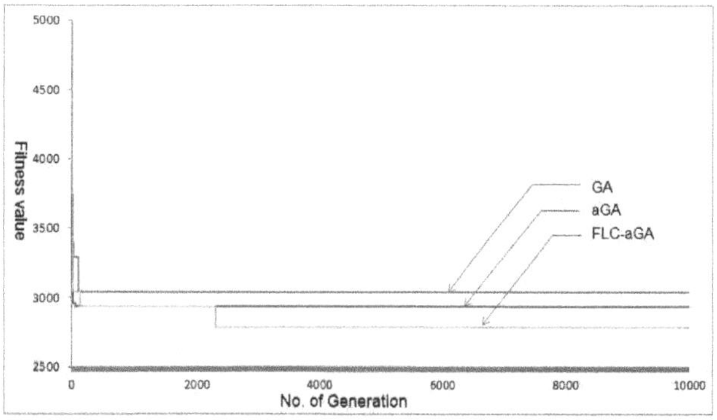

Figure 17. *Convergence processes of each approach for Type 3*

Table 6. Performance results for Type 3

			GA	aGA	FLC-aGA
CPU Time			1.20	0.91	0.92
Optimal Solution			3039.5	2941.0	2787.1
Optimal Setting	Col. Center	Fixed Cost	19.3	20.5	25.2
		Var. Cost	75.0	75.0	75.0
		Transp. Cost	1147.1	832.4	1246.8
	Rec. Center	Fixed Cost	22.2	36.2	36.2
		Var. Cost	156.0	156.0	156.0
		Transp. Cost	432.0	711.0	138.0
	Red. Center	Fixed Cost	23.6	23.6	23.6
		Var. Cost	144.0	144.0	144.0
		Transp. Cost	324.0	246.0	246.0
	Sec. Market	Fixed Cost	24.3	24.3	24.3
		Var. Cost	114.0	114.0	114.0
		Transp. Cost	558.0	558.0	558.0
	Col. Center 1	Opening/Closing	Closing	Opening	Closing
	Col. Center 2	"	Closing	Closing	Closing
	Col. Center 3	"	Closing	Closing	Closing
	Col. Center 4	"	Closing	Closing	Closing
	Col. Center 5	"	Closing	Closing	Closing
	Col. Center 6	"	Closing	Closing	Closing
	Col. Center 7	"	Closing	Closing	Closing
	Col. Center 8	"	Closing	Closing	Closing
	Col. Center 9	"	Closing	Closing	Closing
	Col. Center 10	"	Opening	Closing	Closing
	Col. Center 11	"	Closing	Closing	Closing
	Col. Center 12	"	Closing	Closing	Opening
	Col. Center 13	"	Closing	Closing	Closing
	Col. Center 14	"	Closing	Closing	Closing
	Col. Center 15	"	Closing	Closing	Closing
	Rec. Center 1	"	Closing	Closing	Closing
	Rec. Center 2	"	Closing	Closing	Closing
	Rec. Center 3	"	Closing	Closing	Closing
	Rec. Center 4	"	Opening	Closing	Closing
	Rec. Center 5	"	Closing	Closing	Closing
	Rec. Center 6	"	Closing	Opening	Opening
	Red. Center 1	"	Closing	Closing	Closing
	Red. Center 2	"	Closing	Closing	Closing
	Red. Center 3	"	Closing	Closing	Closing
	Red. Center 4	"	Closing	Closing	Closing
	Red. Center 5	"	Closing	Closing	Closing
	Red. Center 6	"	Closing	Closing	Closing
	Red. Center 7	"	Closing	Closing	Closing
	Red. Center 8	"	Opening	Opening	Opening
	Red. Center 9	"	Closing	Closing	Closing
	Sec. Market 1	"	Closing	Closing	Closing
	Sec. Market 2	"	Closing	Closing	Closing
	Sec. Market 3	"	Closing	Closing	Closing
	Sec. Market 4	"	Closing	Closing	Closing
	Sec. Market 5	"	Closing	Closing	Closing
	Sec. Market 6	"	Opening	Opening	Opening
	Sec. Market 7	"	Closing	Closing	Closing

According to the above mentioned various analysis results using Types 1, 2 and 3, we can conclude the following:

- The aGA and the FLC-aGA approaches with adaptive schemes are more efficient in terms of the CPU times and the optimal solutions than the GA approach without any adaptive scheme, since the formers are well regulate the genetic search process to reach their optimal solutions rather than the latter does.
- Of the aGA and the FLC-aGA, the adaptive scheme using the FLC in the FLC-aGA approach outperforms that using the heuristic in the aGA approach.
- The FLC-aGA approach more effectively represents various types of the RLCC than the GA and the aGA approaches.

6. Conclusion

This paper has proposed a FLC-aGA approach to effectively solve various types of the RLCC problems. For the FLC-aGA approach, a new representation, crossover operator, mutation operator and repair strategy have been employed, and a FLC has been used for an adaptive scheme. The used FLC can automatically regulate the rates of crossover and mutation operators during genetic search process.

For designing the RLCC network model, four stage networks have been considered and they are composed of customers, collection centers, recovery centers, redistribution centers, and secondary markets. Various constraints including unit transportation costs, fixed costs, and variable costs have been considered at each stage. Since the objective of designing the RLCC network model is to minimize the total cost resulting from each stage, we have suggested a mathematical model using mixed integer programming.

In numerical experiment, three types of the RLCC problem with various sizes of collection centers, recovery centers, redistribution centers, and secondary markets have been suggested and they have been solved using the GA approach without any adaptive scheme, the aGA with an adaptive scheme using the conventional heuristic, and the proposed FLC-aGA approach with an adaptive scheme using the FLC. Some measures of performance have been used for comparing the efficiency among each approach. Finally, the FLC-aGA approach has been proved to be more efficient than other competing approaches (GA and aGA).

For our future study, much larger sized problems of the RLCC network model will be considered to compare the performance the FLC-aGA with other competing approaches.

Appendix

Appendix 1. Fixed cost and unit handling cost for Type 1

	Fixed cost	Unit handling cost
Col. Center 1	32.0	2.5
Col. Center 2	28.1	”
Col. Center 3	25.5	”
Col. Center 4	29.2	”
Col. Center 5	20.0	”
Rec. Center 1	35.3	4.5
Rec. Center 2	32.5	”
Red. Center 1	28.4	3.2
Red. Center 2	23.2	”
Red. Center 3	20.1	”
Sec. Market 1	20.8	1.6
Sec. Market 2	28.2	”
Sec. Market 3	25.5	”

Appendix 2. Site coordinates information for Type 1

No.	Customer		Col. Center		Rec.Center		Red. Center		Sec. Market	
	x	y	x	Y	x	y	x	y	x	y
1	31.9	64.4	56.6	30.7	59.7	10.2	13.4	32.0	24.7	52.6
2	12.6	57.1	44.6	17.2	18.7	38.6	22.1	2.7	64.4	76.6
3	39.7	22.9	12.2	36.0			7.1	13.3	16.5	10.8
4	75.9	54.5	47.1	46.7						
5	1.3	57.3	33.4	23.7						
6	32.9	8.9								
7	67.4	36.7								
8	38.6	18.6								
9	24.0	11.9								
10	41.0	61.3								
11	38.6	70.1								
12	66.2	10.7								
13	40.7	51.2								
14	73.1	58.2								
15	41.4	54.4								
16	56.0	54.6								
17	55.4	16.2								
18	70.3	39.9								
19	17.2	6.0								
20	67.5	45.0								
21	26.4	24.4								
22	7.4	68.2								
23	20.1	54.3								
24	74.5	12.1								
25	30.7	66.5								
26	76.6	23.4								
27	5.8	49.0								
28	68.1	65.3								
29	20.2	30.1								
30	59.9	24.4								

Appendix 3. Fixed cost and unit handling cost for Type 2

	Fixed cost	Unit handling cost
Col. Center 1	10.2	3.5
Col. Center 2	12.5	“
Col. Center 3	13.6	“
Col. Center 4	11.8	“
Col. Center 5	12.1	“
Col. Center 6	11.5	“
Col. Center 7	12.8	“
Col. Center 8	11.4	“
Col. Center 9	12.0	“
Col. Center 10	11.1	“
Rec. Center 2	35.2	10.8
Rec. Center 2	36.5	“
Rec. Center 3	36.5	“
Rec. Center 4	35.1	“
Red. Center 1	10.5	6.4
Red. Center 2	11.6	“
Red. Center 3	10.4	“
Red. Center 4	11.1	“
Red. Center 5	11.8	“
Red. Center 6	10.5	“
Red. Center 7	10.5	“
Sec. Market 1	10.5	2.5
Sec. Market 2	10.2	“
Sec. Market 3	10.8	“
Sec. Market 4	10.5	“
Sec. Market 5	10.5	“

Appendix 4. Site coordinates information for Type 2

No.	Customer		Col. Center		Rec.Center		Red. Center		Sec. Market	
	x	y	X	y	x	y	x	y	x	y
1	50.4	19.1	24.5	27.2	59.9	57.5	19.5	36.2	7.5	28.4
2	14.2	18.1	50.5	33.5	76.0	39.3	74.9	37.9	28.4	40.9
3	53.3	35.0	71.3	52.4	8.7	41.9	50.3	12.7	23.6	0.8
4	2.4	72.8	1.0	41.7	56.4	47.6	58.6	44.2	28.4	72.6
5	45.1	5.5	60.0	72.2			45.0	31.8	52.4	1.9
6	13.9	10.7	30.3	30.6			14.7	16.1		
7	65.6	26.1	13.4	69.0			75.3	5.6		
8	34.7	38.2	71.0	18.3						
9	78.9	16.7	36.0	26.3						
10	51.8	36.4	64.4	14.3						
11	7.4	25.8								
12	47.6	20.3								
13	45.3	76.3								
14	78.3	34.9								
15	74.4	52.7								
16	6.4	7.0								
17	54.2	78.2								
18	57.8	12.7								
19	37.3	55.1								
20	57.9	42.8								
21	8.5	71.0								
22	14.0	11.2								
23	8.2	71.8								
24	70.8	54.2								
25	29.7	5.7								
26	25.3	41.2								
27	59.3	35.8								
28	34.7	32.8								
29	9.4	28.3								
30	25.7	24.6								

Appendix 5. Fixed cost and unit handling cost for Type 3

	Fixed cost	Unit handling cost
Col. Center 1	20.5	2.5
Col. Center 2	25.5	"
Col. Center 3	18.9	"
Col. Center 4	15.8	"
Col. Center 5	12.4	"
Col. Center 6	14.5	"
Col. Center 7	20.6	"
Col. Center 8	22.7	"
Col. Center 9	21.8	"
Col. Center 10	19.3	"
Col. Center 11	22.4	"
Col. Center 12	25.2	"
Col. Center 13	24.1	"
Col. Center 14	22.4	"
Col. Center 15	24.1	"
Rec. Center 2	33.9	5.2
Rec. Center 2	34.7	"
Rec. Center 3	35.5	"
Rec. Center 4	22.2	"
Rec. Center 5	35.1	"
Rec. Center 6	36.2	"
Red. Center 1	22.5	4.8
Red. Center 2	25.4	"
Red. Center 3	26.3	"
Red. Center 4	22.1	"
Red. Center 5	25.2	"
Red. Center 6	26.4	"
Red. Center 7	18.5	"
Red. Center 8	23.6	"
Red. Center 9	22.7	"
Sec. Market 1	22.4	3.8
Sec. Market 2	24.6	"
Sec. Market 3	25.7	"
Sec. Market 4	27.8	"
Sec. Market 5	23.3	"
Sec. Market 6	24.3	"
Sec. Market 7	21.1	"

Appendix 6. Site coordinates information for Type 3

No.	Customer		Col. Center		Rec.Center		Red. Center		Sec. Market	
	x	y	X	y	x	y	x	y	X	y
1	30.1	45.6	30.5	45.5	20.5	67.5	70.5	70.5	45.0	50.6
2	34.5	18.5	50.4	40.6	40.5	20.5	40.5	70.2	22.0	50.2
3	45.4	35.0	52.2	18.5	50.6	34.2	48.3	17.2	18.0	18.9
4	58.7	39.2	13.3	39.9	22.7	61.8	55.2	14.6	6.4	63.0
5	9.9	75.4	45.8	1.3	68.8	12.5	45.5	12.9	61.5	63.0
6	30.3	54.5	76.2	8.3	9.9	57.2	64.3	19.9	11.1	46.4
7	31.8	12.0	64.8	58.6			75.4	16.2	41.6	73.6
8	60.2	15.3	35.6	16.4			12.4	65.0		
9	61.5	31.0	18.7	21.5			58.0	33.0		
10	71.2	78.4	14.9	49.6						
11	26.5	18.5	16.0	14.4						
12	36.9	55.4	14.1	59.3						
13	67.6	61.2	76.0	78.5						
14	76.1	41.3	76.8	20.2						
15	50.4	59.8	53.8	48.2						
16	37.9	13.2								
17	71.1	61.2								
18	62.2	51.1								
19	6.4	50.9								
20	50.9	43.2								
21	41.3	50.4								
22	73.3	9.5								
23	36.3	47.9								
24	30.8	58.9								
25	25.3	59.8								
26	60.5	24.3								
27	48.9	31.3								
28	48.5	44.1								
29	59.5	30.5								
30	25.5	15.5								

References

[1] REVLOG (2004) Available at: http://www.fbk.eur.nl/OZ/REVLOG/PROJECTS/TERMINOLOGY/def-reverselogistics.html.

[2] Min, H., Ko, H. J. & Ko, C. S. (2006). A genetic algorithm approach to developing the multi-echelon reverse logistics network for product returns, *Omega*, 34, 56-69.

[3] Tuzkaya, G. & Gulsun, B. (2008). Evaluating centralized return centers in a reverse logistics network: An integrated fuzzy multi-criteria decision approach, *International Journal of Environment Science Technology*, 5(3), 339-352.

[4] Lee, J. E., Gen, M. & Rhee, K. G. (2009). Network model and optimization of reverse logistics by hybrid genetic algorithm, *Computers & Industrial Engineering*, 56, 951-964.

[5] Yun, Y. S., Gen, M. & Hwang, R. K. (2013). Adaptive genetic algorithm to multi-stage reverse logistics network design for product resale, *Information: An International Interdisciplinary Journal*, 15(12), 6117-6138.

[6] Stock, J. K. (1992). *Reverse logistics, White paper*, Council of logistics management. IL: Oak Brook.

[7] Kroon, L. & Vrijens, G. (1995). Returnable containers: An example of reverse logistics, *International Journal of Physical Distribution & Logistics Management*, 25(2), 56–68.

[8] Barros, A., Dekker, I. & Scholten, V. A. (1998). A two-level network for recycling sand: A case study, *European Journal of Operational Research*, 110(2), 199–214.

[9] Brito, M. P., Dekker, R. & Flapper, S. D. P. (2003). Reverse Logistics: a review of case studies, *ERIM Report Series Reference No. ERS-2003-012-LIS*, http://ssrn.com/abstract=411649.

[10] Fleischmann, M., Bloemhof-Ruwaard, J. M., Dekker, R., Vander Laan, E., Van Numen, J. A. E. E. & Van Wassenhove, L. N. (1997). Quantitative models for reverse logistics: A review, *European Journal of Operational Research*., 103(1), 1-17.

[11] Fleischmann, M., Krikke, H. R., Dekker, R. & Flapper, S. D. P. (2000). A characterization of logistics networks for product recovery, *Omega*, 28(6), 653-666.

[12] Pati, R. K., Vrat, P. & Kumar, P. (2008). A goal programming model for paper recycling system, *Omega*, 36(3), 405–417.

[13] Aras, N. & Aksen, D. (2008). Locating collection centers for distance- and incentive-dependent returns, *International Journal of. Production Economics*, 111(2), 316-333,

[14] Savaskan, R. C., Bhattacharya, S. & Van Wassenhove, L. N. (2004). Closed-loop supply chain models with product remanufacturing, *Management Science*, 50, 239-252.

[15] Gen, M. & Cheng, R. (1997). *Genetic algorithms and engineering design*, John Wiley & Son, New York.

[16] Song, Y. H., Wang, G. S., Wang, P. T. & Johns, A. T. (1997). Environmental/economic dispatch using fuzzy logic controlled genetic algorithms. *IEEE Proceedings on Generation, Transmission and Distribution*, 144(4), 377-382.

[17] Wu, Q. H., Cao, Y. J. & Wen, J. Y. (1998). Optimal reactive power dispatch using an adaptive genetic algorithm. *Electrical Power and Energy Systems*, 20(8), 563-69.

[18] Gen, M. & Cheng, R. (2000). *Genetic Algorithms and Engineering Optimization*. New York: John-Wiley & Sons.

[19] Mak, K. L., Wong, Y. S. & Wang, X. X. (2000). An adaptive genetic algorithm for manufacturing cell formation. *International Journal of Manufacturing Technology*, 16, 491-97.

[20] Yun, Y. S. & Gen, M. (2003). Performance analysis of adaptive genetic algorithms with fuzzy logic and heuristics. *Fuzzy Optimization and Decision Making*, 2(2), 161-75.

[21] Yun, Y. S. (2010). Reliability optimization problems using adaptive genetic algorithm and improved particle swarm optimization, Nova Science Publisher, Inc., New York,. pp. 1-34.

[22] Srinivas, M. & L. M. Patnaik (1994). Adaptive probabilities of crossover and mutation in genetic algorithms, *IEEE Transaction on Systems, Man and Cybernetics*, 24(4), 656-667

[23] Wang, P. T., G. S. Wang & Z. G. Hu (1997). Speeding up the search process of genetic algorithm by fuzzy logic, *Proceedings of the 5th European Congress on Intelligent Techniques and Soft Computing*, 665-671.

[24] Hong, T. P., H. S. Wang, W. Y. Lin & W. Y. Lee, (2002). Evolution of appropriate crossover and mutation operators in a genetic process, *Applied Intelligence*, 16, 7-17.

[25] Yun, Y. S., (2002). Genetic algorithm with fuzzy logic controller for preemptive and non-preemptive job shop scheduling problems, *Computers and Industrial Engineering*, 43(3), 623-644.

[26] Yun, Y. S., M. Gen * S. L. Seo, (2003). Various hybrid methods based on genetic algorithm with fuzzy logic controller, *Journal of Intelligent Manufacturing*, 14(3-4), 401-419.

[27] Subbu, R., A. C. Sanderson & P. P. Bonissone, (1988). Fuzzy logic controlled genetic algorithms versus tuned genetic algorithms: an agile manufacturing application, *Proceedings of the 1999 IEEE International Symposium on Intelligent Control (ISIC)*, 434-440

16

Control systems design based on classical dynamics

Wang Funing[1], Kai Pingan[2]

[1]Ningdong Power Plant, Gouhua Power Group, Ningdong town, Ningxia, P. R. C.
[2]Energy Research Institute, Development and Reformation Committee of State, Beijing, P. R. C.

Email address:
wangfn7119@163.com (Wang Funing), pingank@aliyun.com (Kai Pingan)

Abstract: The paper presents unity between control systems and classical dynamics. A state observer is constructed based on uniformly accelerated motion. It is known F = ma in Newtonian motion equation is considered as a control input force which functions on the controlled plant process. The designed control system is of good robust performance.

Keywords: Uniformly Accelerated Motion, Newtonian Mechanics, State Observer, Kalman Filter, Robust Performance

1. Introduction

Design control systems in modern control theory always needs a mathematics model of controlled plant , however the model is not exactly obtained and the model is uncertain in general, these limits led to the poor control system performance.

The paper designs a control system based on Classical dynamics without exact plant model, and the systems are of good robust performances.

2. State Observer Based on Uniformly Accelerated Motion

When a motion (/response) velocity of controlled plant process (/ body) is greatly less than velocity of light, we can describe its motion using uniformly acceleration motion:

$$S = S_0 + V_0 t + 0.5at^2$$

$$\dot{S} = V = V_0 + at \tag{1}$$

$$\ddot{S} = \dot{V} = a$$

where S, V, a are respectively the position, velocity and acceleration of the body/process motion.

Assume a controlled second system with the random disturbance $v(t)$:

$$\ddot{y} = f(y, \dot{y}, v(t)) + bu \tag{2}$$

the system in state space is:

$$\dot{y}_1 = y_2$$

$$\dot{y}_2 = f(y_1, y_2, v(t)) + bu \tag{3}$$

$$y = y_1$$

For a controlled plant process, assuming $z(1)$, $z(2), \cdots, z(k)$, the k measurement output data are obtained from the controlled plant output $y(k)$, sample(/control) period is t_s , the measurement equation is

$$z(k) = y(k) + v(k) , \tag{4}$$

where: $E[v^2(k)] = r_2$, $E[v(k)] = 0$

$v(k)$ is white noise, we can estimate the controlled plant output $y(k)$ using Exp. (1) based on $z(1)$, $z(2), \cdots, z(k)$, when t_s is very short,

$$\begin{aligned} \hat{y}(k) &= \hat{y}(k-1) + t_s \dot{\hat{y}}(k-1) + 0.5t_s^2 \ddot{\hat{y}}(k-1) \\ \dot{\hat{y}}(k) &= \dot{\hat{y}}(k-1) + t_s \ddot{\hat{y}}(k-1) \\ \ddot{\hat{y}}(k) &= \ddot{\hat{y}}(k-1) \end{aligned} \tag{5}$$

where $\hat{y}(k)$, $\dot{\hat{y}}(k)$ and $\ddot{\hat{y}}(k)$ are respectively the estimated values of $y(k)$, $\dot{y}(k)$ and $\ddot{y}(k)$ at time k .

let $\hat{Y}(k) = \begin{bmatrix} \hat{y}(k) \\ \dot{\hat{y}}(k) \\ \ddot{\hat{y}}(k) \end{bmatrix}$ and $\phi = \begin{bmatrix} 1 & t_s & t_s^2/2 \\ 0 & 1 & t_s \\ 0 & 0 & 1 \end{bmatrix}$ (6)

Exp. (5) can be written as:

$$\hat{Y}(k) = \phi \hat{Y}(k-1) \quad (7)$$

To improve estimate accuracy, the compensating for random disturbance is into acceleration estimate $\ddot{\hat{y}}(k)$:

$$\ddot{\hat{y}}(k) = \ddot{\hat{y}}(k-1) + w(k-1) \quad (8)$$

where: $E[w(k)] = 0$, $E[w^2(k)] = r_1$

Exp.(7) becomes:

$$\hat{Y}(k) = \phi \hat{Y}(k-1) + \Gamma w(k-1) \quad (9)$$

where: $\Gamma = [0 \ \ 0 \ \ 1]^T$

measurement equation (4) is written as:

$$z(k) = c\hat{Y}(k) + v(k) , \quad (10)$$

where: $c = [1 \ \ 0 \ \ 0]$

Kalman filter theory can be used for state equation (9) and measurement equation(10), ϕ and Γ are constant matrixes, meet $rank(\phi,\Gamma) = n$, $rank(\phi,c) = n$, so the system is completely controllable and observable in Kalman filter theory(the proof is given the following lemma), when t_s is very short and filtering time is very long, the covariance matrix,

$$\lim_{k\to\infty} P(k) = P ,$$

gain matrix

$$\mathop{Lim}_{k\to\infty} K(k) = K ,$$

$$K(k) \to K = [\alpha, \beta, \gamma]^T .$$

We have the following time discrete observer to an unknown controlled plant:

$$\begin{cases} \hat{y}(k) = \hat{y}(k-1) + t_s\dot{\hat{y}}(k-1) + 0.5t_s^2\ddot{\hat{y}}(k-1) + \alpha t_s(z(k) - \hat{y}(k-1)) \\ \dot{\hat{y}}(k) = \dot{\hat{y}}(k-1) + t_s\ddot{\hat{y}}(k-1) + \beta t_s(z(k) - \hat{y}(k-1)) \\ \ddot{\hat{y}}(k) = \ddot{\hat{y}}(k-1) + \gamma t_s(z(k) - \hat{y}(k-1)) \end{cases} \quad (11)$$

$F = ma$ in the classical dynamics. Referencing Exp.(3), the control input u is considered as a force which functions on the controlled plant, $u = F$, and $a = \theta u$, where F is the force and a is the acceleration.

As $\ddot{\hat{y}}(k) = (\dot{\hat{y}}(k) - \dot{\hat{y}}(k-1))/t_s$ is an estimate to the acceleration of the system,

$$\ddot{\hat{y}}(k) = (\dot{\hat{y}}(k) - \dot{\hat{y}}(k-1))/t_s = \theta u(k-1)$$

so, $\dot{\hat{y}}(k) = \dot{\hat{y}}(k-1) + t_s\theta u(k-1)$

Relate Exp.(11),

$\dot{\hat{y}}(k) = \dot{\hat{y}}(k-1) + t_s\ddot{\hat{y}}(k-1) + \beta t_s(z(k-1) - \hat{y}(k-1))$, we have

$$\dot{\hat{y}}(k) = \dot{\hat{y}}(k-1) + t_s\ddot{\hat{y}}(k-1) + \beta t_s(z(k-1) - \hat{y}(k-1)) + t_s\theta u(k-1)$$

Exp.(11) becomes:

$$\begin{cases} \hat{y}(k) = \hat{y}(k-1) + t_s\dot{\hat{y}}(k-1) + 0.5t_s^2\ddot{\hat{y}}(k-1) + \alpha t_s(z(k) - \hat{y}(k-1)) \\ \dot{\hat{y}}(k) = \dot{\hat{y}}(k-1) + t_s\ddot{\hat{y}}(k-1) + \beta t_s(z(k) - \hat{y}(k-1)) + t_s\theta u(k-1) \\ \ddot{\hat{y}}(k) = \ddot{\hat{y}}(k-1) + \gamma t_s(z(k) - \hat{y}(k-1)) \end{cases} \quad (12)$$

Exp.(12) is a time discrete observer with control input u for the control system (3)

Using the transformation

$$I + At + 0.5A^2t^2 = \phi$$

We have the following time continuous observer of an unknown controlled plant

$$\begin{cases} \dot{\hat{y}}_1 = \hat{y}_2 + \alpha(z - \hat{y}) \\ \dot{\hat{y}}_2 = \hat{y}_3 + \beta(z - \hat{y}) + \theta u \\ \dot{\hat{y}}_3 = \gamma(z - \hat{y}) \end{cases} \quad (13)$$

where $\hat{y}_1 = \hat{y}$; $\hat{y}_2 = \dot{\hat{y}}$; $\hat{y}_3 = \ddot{\hat{y}}$, t_s is sample(/control) period, u is control input to the plant system, $l \le \theta \le h$,. l and h are real boundary numbers.

Exp. (13) is the time continuous observer of an unknown controlled plant with control input u for the control system (3), Exp. (13) is simply called OCICD(Observer with Control Input based on Classical Dynamics).

Lemma. Discrete systems (9) and (10) are completely controllable and observable.

Proof. The state matrix ϕ is time-invariant, as t_s is determined in systems (9), we calculate

$$(\phi,\Gamma) = [\Gamma \mid \phi\Gamma \mid \phi^2\Gamma] = \begin{bmatrix} 0 & t_s^2/2 & 2t_s^2 \\ 0 & t_s & 2t_s \\ 1 & 1 & 1 \end{bmatrix}$$

$$(\phi,c) = [c^T \mid \phi^T c^T \mid (\phi^T)^2 c^T] = \begin{bmatrix} 1 & 1 & 1 \\ 0 & t_s & 2t_s \\ 0 & t_s^2/2 & 2t_s^2 \end{bmatrix}$$

$rank(\phi,\Gamma) = 3$, $rank(\phi,c) = 3$; so discrete systems (9) and (10) are completely controllable and observable.

Theorem 1. Time continuous observer system (13) is consistent asymptotic stable.

Proof. We have proved discrete systems (9) and (10) are completely controllable and observable, time discrete observer (12) is obtained by Kalman filter, so time discrete observer (12) is consistent asymptotic stable when α, β and γ are rightly selected. Time continuous observer (13) is obtained by transforming time discrete observer (12), so time continuous observer (13) is also consistent asymptotic stable, when α, β and γ are rightly selected. From characteristic equation $|sI - A| = s^3 + \alpha s^2 + \beta s + \gamma$ of time continuous observer (13), if

$$\alpha > 0, \beta > 0, \gamma > 0 \text{ and } \alpha\beta > \gamma, \tag{14}$$

then time continuous observer system (13) is consistent asymptotic stable, based on Routh and Hurwitz's stability criterion.

We set

$$\alpha = 1/t_s, \beta = 0.5/t_s^2, \gamma = 0.088/t_s^3 \tag{15}$$

in time continuous observer system (13) based on Exp. (14) and our experience.

Exp. (15) is only related to a sample (/control) period t_s, and independents from a controlled plant.

Theorem 2. $\hat{y}_3$ in time continuous observer system (13) is unbiased estimate value to $f(x_1, x_2, v(t))$ in a second order state space model (3) :

Proof. It is known, Kalman filter is an unbiased estimator, time discrete observer (12) and time continuous observer system (13) are the special applications of Kalman filter, and second system (3) is completely controllable and observable, so time discrete observer (12) and time continuous observer system (13) are unbiased estimators to system (3).

Let

$$x_3 = f(x_1, x_2, v(t)) \tag{16}$$

System (3) is written as:

$$\begin{cases} \dot{x}_1 = x_2 \\ \dot{x}_2 = x_3 + bu \\ \dot{x}_3 = \dot{f}(x_1, x_2, v(t)) \\ y = x_1 \end{cases} \tag{17}$$

Comparing Exp. (17) with Exp. (13):

$$\begin{cases} \dot{\hat{y}}_1 = \hat{y}_2 + \alpha(z - \hat{y}) \\ \dot{\hat{y}}_2 = \hat{y}_3 + \beta(z - \hat{y}) + \theta u \\ \dot{\hat{y}}_3 = \gamma(z - \hat{y}) \\ \hat{y} = \hat{y}_1 \end{cases}$$

Because time continuous observer system (13) is unbiased estimator to system (3), we have:

$$\hat{y}_1 \to x_1 = y,\ \hat{y}_2 \to x_2, \hat{y}_3 \to x_3 = f(x_1, x_2, v(t)) \tag{18}$$

We have proven $\hat{y}_3$ in time continuous observer system (13) is unbiased estimate value to $f(x_1, x_2, v(t))$ in a second system (16).

We have the following observer system for a controlled plant process with acceleration $a = 0$:

$$\dot{\hat{y}}_1 = \hat{y}_2 + \alpha(z - \hat{y}) + \theta u; \quad \dot{\hat{y}}_2 = \beta(z - \hat{y}) \tag{19}$$

$$\hat{y} = \hat{y}_1$$

where $\alpha = 1/t_s, \beta = 0.5/t_s^2$

We have the following observer system for a controlled plant process with varying acceleration a

$$\begin{bmatrix} \dot{\hat{y}}_1 \\ \dot{\hat{y}}_2 \\ \dot{\hat{y}}_3 \\ \dot{\hat{y}}_4 \end{bmatrix} = \begin{bmatrix} -\alpha & 1 & 0 & 0 \\ -\beta & 0 & 1 & 0 \\ -\gamma & 0 & 0 & 1 \\ -\theta & 0 & 0 & 0 \end{bmatrix} \begin{bmatrix} \hat{y}_1 \\ \hat{y}_2 \\ \hat{y}_3 \\ \hat{y}_4 \end{bmatrix} + \begin{bmatrix} \alpha & 0 \\ \beta & 0 \\ \gamma & \lambda \\ \theta & 0 \end{bmatrix} \begin{bmatrix} z \\ u \end{bmatrix} \tag{20}$$

$$\hat{y} = \hat{y}_1$$

where $\alpha = 1/t_s, \beta = 0.5/t_s^2\ \gamma = 0.088/t_s^3, \theta = 0.01/t_s^4$.

3. Control System Design with OCICD and Removing Uncertain

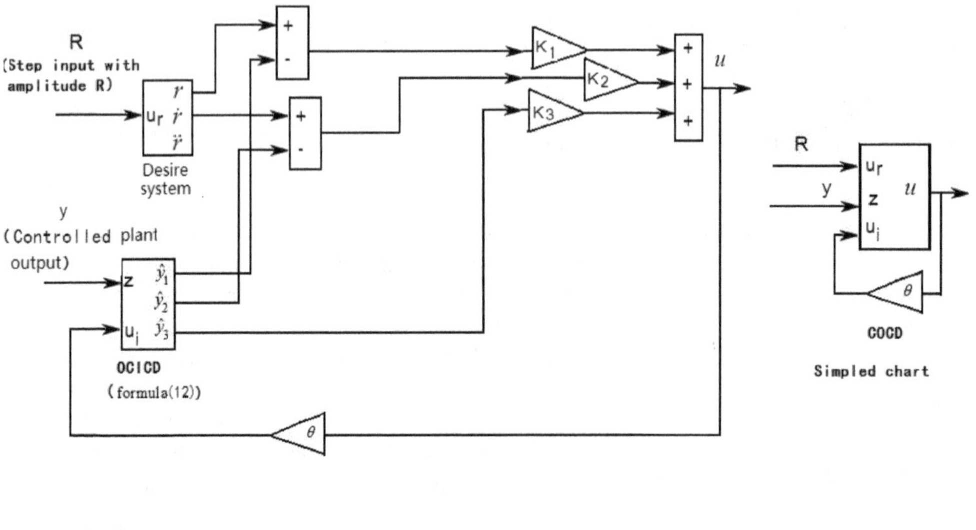

Fig 1. *COCD (Controller with Observer based on Classical dynamics).*

A controller and control system with OCICD are respectively designed shown in Fig.1 and Fig.3. The position, velocity and acceleration of control system output are negative feedback function in system. The controlled plant is a second order state space model (3), the second order system is of general model in process control system.

The controller of Fig.1 is called as COCD (Controller with Observer based on Classical dynamics), it consists of setting desire system output locus, OCICD and controller output. The control system of Fig.3 is called as CSCOCD (Control System with COCD).

3.1. Setting Desire System Output Locus

The desire system output y is designed in COCD,

$$y = R/(as^2 + bs + 1) = G_r(s)R;$$

$$G_r(s) = 1//(as^2 + bs + 1) \quad (21)$$

where R is the amplitude of step input,

$$a = 1/w_n^2, b = 2\varsigma / w_n; \quad (22)$$

w_n is the undamped natural frequency, ς is the damping coefficient.

The desire transient process time T is defined as the time in which y approaches to $0.98*R$ for the closed loop system, and T is related to Exp. (22) , (23) and (24).

$$\varsigma = 1, \ w_n = 7/T, \quad (23)$$

then the desire system is determined, it is configured in state space model shown in Fig,2, $f_1 = 1/a, f_2 = b/a$ in Fig,2.

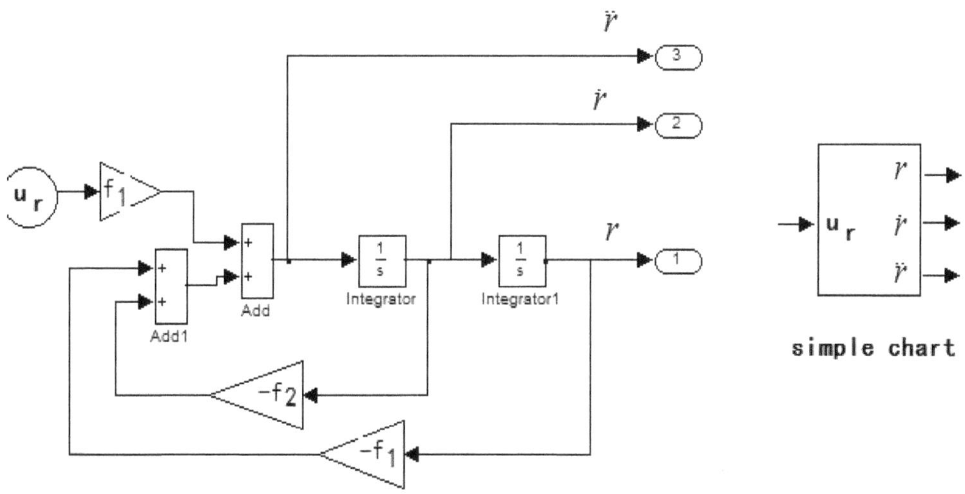

Fig 2. *Desire system.*

3.2. Determining Parameters of OCICD

The sample t_s is determined by the sample theory and our experience:

$$t_s = T/n, \ n \in [1000 \ \ 2000] \quad (24)$$

where T is the desire transient process time, the α, β and γ are calculated by Exp. (15).

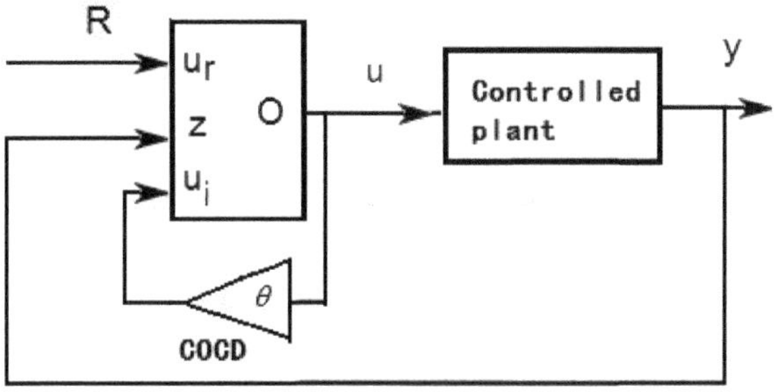

Fig 3. *CSCOCD(Control system with COCD).*

3.3. Controller Output

If the value b in controlled plant state space model (17) is known, let

$$u = (u_0 - f(x_1, x_2, v(t)))/b \quad (25)$$

then controlled plant state space model (16) is changed to

$$\begin{cases} \dot{x}_1 = x_2 \\ \dot{x}_2 = u_0 \\ y = x_1 \end{cases}$$

A suitable u_0 is selected, the transform function $G_a(s)$ between y and u_0

$$G_a(s)=[1,0]\left[\begin{bmatrix} s & 0 \\ 0 & s \end{bmatrix}-\begin{bmatrix} 0 & 1 \\ 0 & 0 \end{bmatrix}\right]^{-1}\begin{bmatrix} 0 \\ 1 \end{bmatrix}=1/s^2,$$

If $f(x_1,x_2,v(t))$ in controlled plant state space model (3) is uncertain, then the uncertain $f(x_1,x_2,v(t))$ including unknown disturbance $v(t)$ are completely removed. We have proven that $\hat{y}_3$ in time continuous observer system (13) is unbiased estimate value to $f(x_1,x_2,v(t))$ in Theorem 2, so we select $K_3=1/b$, and

$$u=K_1(r-\hat{y}_1)+K_2(\dot{r}-\hat{y}_2)-K_3\hat{y}_3=u_0-\hat{y}_3/b \qquad (26)$$

where $u_0=K_1(r-\hat{y}_1)+K_2(\dot{r}-\hat{y}_2)$.

If controlled plant space model (16) is known, then

$$\theta=b,\ K_3=1/\theta, \qquad (27)$$

and K_1 and K_2 can be obtained by the solution of optimal linear-quadratic Gaussian algorithm(LQG) for the controlled plant space model (3).

If the plant state space model (17) is unknown, assuming

$$l\le b\le h, \qquad (28)$$

we set firstly:

$$\theta=(l+h)/2,\ K_3=1/\theta,\ K_1\in[1\ \ 1.5],\ K_2\in[0.5\ \ 2] \qquad (29)$$

then we can determine θ, K_1, K_2, K_3 by several times tests based on the golden section.

It is important to determine desire transient process time T without the mathematics model of controlled plant . Control engineers must estimate the motion (/response) velocity and completing time of controlled plant process based on analysis and understanding for a controlled plant process, just as the time program to plan a trip, we must estimate velocity and completing time of a vehicle.

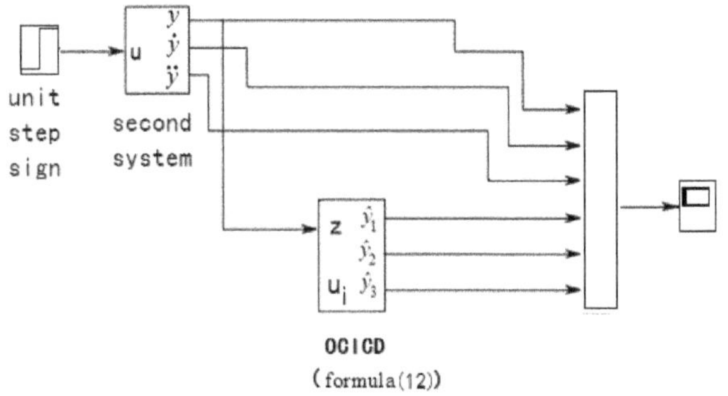

Fig 4. Inspecting the OCICD efficiency.

4. Simulation and Application Examples with COCD

4.1. Simulation Example

Fig.4 is simulated with Matlab to inspect the OCICD efficiency. The second system transfer function $G_p(s)=1/(0.21s^2+0.37s+1)$ is configured as Fig.2, where $f_1=4.76, f_2=1.76$, R=1, . T=1(sec),$t_s=0.001, \alpha=1000$, $\beta=500000, \gamma=88000000$ in OCICD.

The simulated curves of OCICD outputs and the second system outputs are shown in Fig.5, the OCICD outputs are very close to the second system outputs, Fig.5 confirms OCICD (13) which is an unbiased estimator to a system.

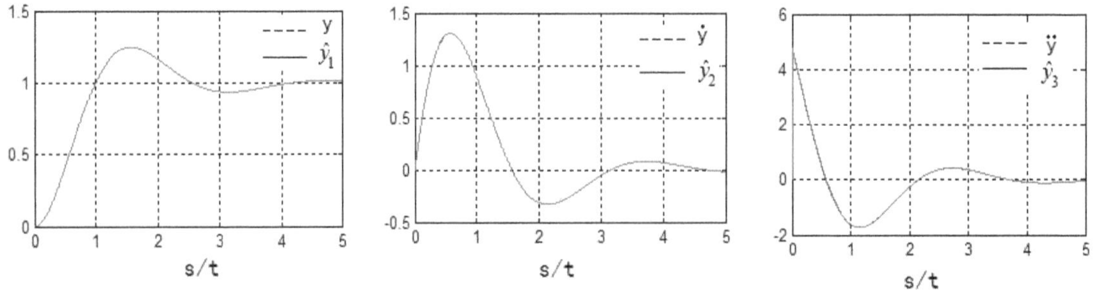

Fig 5. Comparing outputs of OCICD and the second system.

4.2. Application Example

CSCOCD of Fig.3 is used to control the time-varying controlled plant with the transfer function $G_{p1}(s)=0.8/(0.21s^2+0.37s+1)$ and $G_{p2}(s)=1.3/(0.06s^2+0.17s+1)$ in some steel factory. The same parameters are selected for the time-varying controlled plants $G_{p1}(s)$ and $G_{p2}(s)$:

T=1(sec),$t_s=0.001, \alpha=1000$, $\beta=500000, \gamma=88000000$ in OCICD; R=1, $f_1=45, f_2=13.5$ in the desire system of Fig.2; $K_1=1, K_2=1.5, K_3=0.007$, $\theta=145$.

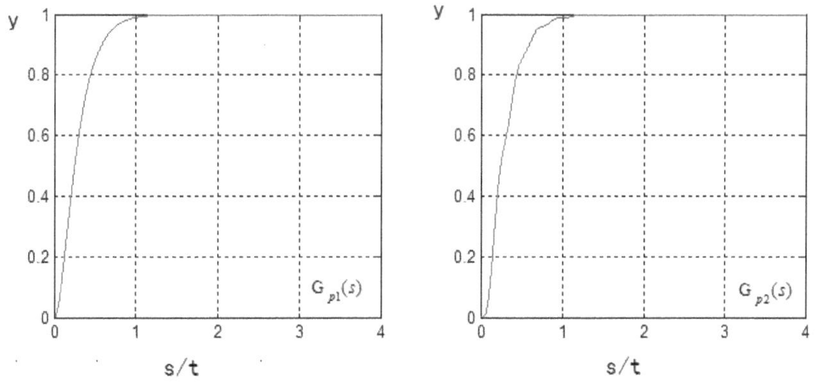

Fig 6. Outputs of the closed loop system of $G_{p1}(s)$ *and* $G_{p2}(s)$.

The closed loop system outputs of $G_{p1}(s)$ and $G_{p2}(s)$ with the same control parameters are shown in Fig.6, and Fig.6. confirms good robust performance of CSCOCD.

5. Conclusion

(1) The paper designs the control system based on classical dynamics and explains classical dynamics philosophy of the control system design.
(2) The control system is of good robust performance, it can overcome the uncertain of a controlled plant and remove disturbances into the system in the paper.
(3) The design of control system needs not an exact mathematics model of the controlled plant. If we can estimate the values T in Exp. (24) and l, h in Exp. (29), we can design the control system without an exact mathematics model of the controlled plant.

References

[1] Kalman, R. E., 'On the general theory of control systems', Ire Transactions On Automatic Control (1959) Volume: 4, Issue: 3, Publisher: Butterworth, London, pp. 110-110.

[2] Kudva, P., Viswanadham, N., Ramakrishna, A., 'Observers for linear systems with unknown inputs', IEEE Trans. Automat. Control, 1980. pp.113~115.

[3] [3] R. E. Kalman, R. S. Bucy, 'New results in linear filtering and prediction theory', J. Basic Eng, 1961 [7]. pp.111-145.

[4] Corless. M, Tu.J State/input estimation for a class of uncertain system system,Automatica, 1998, 34(6); pp.757-764.

[5] Jingqing Han, 'Nonlinear State Error Feedback Control', Control and Decision (Chinese), Vol.10, No.3, Nov., 1994, pp.221-225.

[6] Kai Pingan etc., 'Advanced control technology in fire power plant', (Chinese), China Electric Power Publishing House, 4, 2010. pp.65-76.

17

Performance models preventing multi-agent systems from overloading computational resources

Petr Kadera[1, *], Petr Novak[1, 2], Vaclav Jirkovsky[1, 3], Pavel Vrba[1]

[1]Czech Institute of Informatics, Robotics and Cybernetics, Czech Technical University in Prague, CZ-169 00, Prague, Czech Republic
[2]Christian Doppler Laboratory for Software Engineering Integration for Flexible Automation Systems, Vienna University of Technology, A-1040, Vienna, Austria
[3]Rockwell Automation Research and Development Center, CZ-150 00, Prague, Czech Republic

Email address:
petr.kadera@fel.cvut.cz (P. Kadera), novakp46@fel.cvut.cz (P. Novak), jirkova@fel.cvut.cz (V. Jirkovsky), pavel.vrba@ciirc.cvut.cz (P. Vrba)

Abstract: Multi-Agent Systems (MASs) suffer from low immunity against burst of arrival requests which can result in a permanent outage of such systems. This factor limits the suitability of MASs for control of real-world manufacturing systems with strict requirements on performance and reliability. This manuscript explains the origins of the performance degradation of MASs based on Contract-Net Protocol and proposes a method that protects the systems against the destructive effect of temporal overloads. The proposed method continuously observes the communication among agents and analyzes it in order to identify possible saturation of a system resource. If triggering a new action saturates a system resource, the carrying out of the action will be postponed. The impacts of the method are demonstrated on a test-bed consisted of six mini-computers Raspberry Pi. It shows that the proposed method avoids overloading of the system and thus guarantees a specific system throughput effectively and efficiently.

Keywords: Holonic Systems, Multi-Agent Systems, Robustness, Reconfigurable Systems, Software Agents

---

1. Introduction

Multi-Agents Systems (MASs) have provided a new abstraction paradigm for designing distributed and flexible industrial control systems emphasizing attributes such as autonomy, robustness, survivability, adaptation, and reconfiguration [1][1][3]. Agents find optimal solutions at runtime, which eliminates the need for preparing control strategies for all possible scenarios in advance.

A shift of MASs from laboratory research to real world deployment is slower than expected. This is caused by multiple factors; one of them is a group of performance-related problems of MASs caused by overload of computational resources. This causes hardly predictable delays or even prevents the MASs from converge to a solution due to expired communication timeouts. This manuscript proposes a method that protects the MASs based on Contract-Net Protocol (CNP) against overloading caused by bursts of requests. Providing such a protection is of the highest importance because even a temporal burst of requests can transfer the MAS to such a state from which the system is not able to recover. Many concurrent actions overload resources and prolong the execution times. This may lead to the expiration of the negotiation timeouts. Then, agents usually invoke new attempts to cooperate, but it repetitively ends up with not passing the timeouts due to the reoccurring overloads. This forms a never ending loop, from which the agents cannot escape. In practice, this situation frequently occurs in the system setup mode, when the initial state has to be reflected in agent actions, as well as in the operation mode, when external events come with excessive frequency.

In general, these problems are caused by saturation of computational resources. Overloaded resources decrease the agent responsiveness which might end up with exceeding the communication timeouts. This fact closely corresponds with another problem of MASs: it is difficult to find the optimal setup of communication timeouts, which the agents use to bound their waiting for responses. Too long timeouts decrease the performance by waiting for messages that never come (e.g. from a broken agent). On the other hand, the communication timeouts cannot be too short either, because it might disallow the system to converge to the best solution as have been many times experienced during the work on the Chilled Water System (CWS) application [4]. Moreover, the optimal setup is specific for each system configuration (including number of agents, computational performance of used hardware, and system load). Thus, any hardware or software change of the well-tuned system has to be followed by a new timeout setup.

This manuscript proposes a method which replaces the fine tuning of communication timeouts by a congestion control mechanism that prevents the system from entering overloaded operational regimes. The method breaks the relation between timeout settings and the current system load. This is achieved by the observation of the agent communication and its analysis which provides information how each initial request loads each of the system resources (e.g. a CPU). These parameters form a Loading matrix, which is used as input for the Operational analysis. It is an analytical method that identifies among all resources potential system bottlenecks. The saturation load in terms of the frequency of arrival requests is then identified for the bottleneck candidates.

The low computational complexity makes this method applicable at runtime, where it extends capabilities of the regular Directory Facilitator (DF). Consequently, the extended DF can spread the possible burst of request into a longer time period, in order to prevent any part of the system against saturation. The method is directly applicable to MASs utilizing the Contract-Net Protocol (CNP) [5] or its extension Plan Commit Execute (PCE) protocol [6], because the cooperation in such systems forms chains, where initiators can be identified and then the successors can be traced in order to estimate the overall impact of the initial request. The method is further limited only to such systems that use DFs for starting cooperation between agents.

Utilization of the method is demonstrated on a segment of CWS containing one service agent (requests cold water), four valve agents (connect water piping sections), and one chiller agent (provides cold water). The experimental evaluation was done on the test-bed consisted of six minicomputers Raspberry Pi Model B (see Figure 1), which host Jade agents.

Figure 1. Testbed containing six minicomputers Raspberry Pi Model B.

2. Related Work

This section introduces selected methods, approaches, and tools that increased the acceptance of MASs and distributed embedded systems by industrial enterprises.

2.1. Methodologies for MASs

A lot of attention in the area of the development of a methodology for holonic systems was paid within the research program for Intelligent Manufacturing Systems (IMS). Within its activities, two holonic architectures were developed – PROSA [7] and ADACOR [8]. Both introduce sets of guidelines to decompose manufacturing control functions into communities of autonomous and cooperative entities called holons. Recently, methods for validation of agent-based manufacturing systems have become investigated. ANEMONA [9] presents means for functional validation of multi-agent architectures in conformance with specific trade requirements.

2.2. Model-Based Diagnostics

MABLE [10] is a conventional imperative programming language which is extended by constructs from MASs. The agents designed in MABLE maintain their social knowledge using linear temporal belief-desire-intention logic. The major advantage of this approach is the ability to formally prove that any interaction of agents will not lead to a fault state. On the other hand, the fundamental disadvantage and perhaps the stopper for the wider spread of this technique is the limited set of constructs that an agent can use. In other words, the agent has to be designed in the way suitable for MABEL from the very beginning.

2.3. Formal Time Analysis for Embedded System

The domain of embedded systems is facing a dramatic increase of the network complexity. For example, modern automotive control systems contain more than fifty electronic control units (ECUs) that are produced by various suppliers [11]. The units are inter-connected via a communication network representing a shared resource. It is necessary to assure that a potential conflict in usage of the shared resource would not lead to a dangerous situation. It means, for example, the function of the Anti-lock braking system (ABS) in a car must not be harmed by increased communication of other systems. Similar problem and requirements come from the aircraft industry and also from the designers of multi-processor systems [12]. In general, networked or distributed systems can be characterized by observing a high amount of data flows within the network. To address the challenges posed by the increased network complexity the Network Calculus [13] and its extension Realtime calculus [14] were introduced. Network Calculus enables evaluation of timing properties of data flows in communication networks. Realtime Calculus extends this concept to make it suitable for real-time embedded systems. The basic idea behind these two approaches is to substitute individual events by data flows called event streams. The validation problem is then transformed into the examination of flows, which can be solved by efficient methods.

2.4. Qualitative and Quantitative Analysis of Industrial Multi-Agent Systems

The investigation of methods for validation of MASs was addressed by the EU FP7 research project GRACE [15]. One of the project outputs is the methodology for qualitative analysis based on Petri net modeling notation. The behavior of each agent is represented as a single Petri net which can be verified by the regular methods to find out whether the model is bounded (the resource can only execute one operation at time), reversible (the agent can reinitiate by itself) or out of deadlocks (the agent can make at any state an action). The extension of these models with concept of time provides methods for quantitative analysis of multi-agent systems. The transitions are extended with the time parameters to capture the times of transition activations. Such a simulation shows the evolution of the tokens over places and over the time. The complete information about the progress of the agent behavior is summarized with a Gantt chart. Unfortunately, the development of the Petri net models is a time-consuming process, which requires specialized skills.

2.5. Supportive Tools for Development of Multi-Agent Systems

Debugging and tuning of MASs is a challenging process that cannot be tackled by methods used for monolithic applications such as debuggers and profilers. Particularly, the multi-agent applications cannot be debugged step by step due to the asynchronous communication between components. Instead, logging mechanisms are used to capture the time-lines of system events that are afterwards analyzed by the programmer. Technically, a log is captured by a specialized meta-agent that is usually called sniffer. A basic sniffer is part of the Jade platform. Advanced features to visualize the workflows provides Java Sniffer [16].

3. Scheduling of Operations in MASs

The prevention of MASs from entering overloaded operational regimes is based on observation of communication among agents. The fundamental part of the method is the automated identification of loading matrices from communication logs. In more details, the entire method consists of six steps. First, the communication produced by a MAS is logged and divided into groups according to the initial events, i.e., every group consists of messages that are successors of the same initial event. Second, the messages in each group are causally ordered (from initiators to participants) into tree structures. Such trees are called workflows and the initial events are their roots. Third, the workflows are analyzed to identify the loading matrix. Fourth, operational analysis is utilized in order to identify the bottleneck candidates. Fifth, the DF is extended by scheduling features which prevent the system from triggering too many activities in parallel. Sixth, the comparison of the original and the improved MASs are presented to illustrate the contribution of the method.

3.1. Communication Analysis

Many MAS platforms including JADE and Autonomous Cooperative System (ACS) support logging (sniffing) messages sent among agents. The proposed method builds on this feature and develops a new sniffer that observes the overall agent communication in a similar way as other sniffers, but it adds the time analyzes of the logged messages, whereas regular sniffers focus mainly on the visualization of the communication. The new sniffer analysis causal relations and timing of messages in order to obtain workflows, i.e., knowledge what are the initial messages and what are their successors.

The global behavior of MASs emerges from local interactions between components. These interactions have a causality defined by roles of communicating agents: initiator → participant. Because the participants can also become to be initiators to re-distribute the received requests, the interactions form cooperation chains called workflows. It is necessary to identify these workflows to understand the impact of the beginning request on the whole system. These initial events are called Primary actions because they are triggered by internal events in agents. They drive the agent's proactivity as they cause that the agents initiate new conversations as reactions to perceptions done inside of the agents. A typical example from the industrial domain is an agent that receives notifications from the low-level control about a change of a data tag value. It causes a reaction of the agent in terms of creating a new conversation with other agents. The Secondary actions are reactions on received messages coming from either Primary or another Secondary action.

Messages sent among agents are composed according to the FIPA ACL specification [17]. This specification defines a set of mandatory parameters that each message contains. These parameters are used to identify who the sender is and which conversation the message belongs to. Such an identification is necessary to enable agents to work on multiple tasks in parallel without mixing up messages coming from different conversations. To enable the backward communication traceability, agents use parameter "Reply With" to add additional pieces of information into messages. The content of this field is composed iteratively by all agents participating on the particular negotiation. The original seed of the parameter creates the initiator of the communication and stores in it its name and the number of the conversation, in which this agent takes part (e.g.: svc1@100:0). The next participant extends the content of this field by the "~" character and its own identifier (e.g. svc1@100:0~acp@100:310) and so on. This annotation is sufficient for the reconstruction of the workflows.

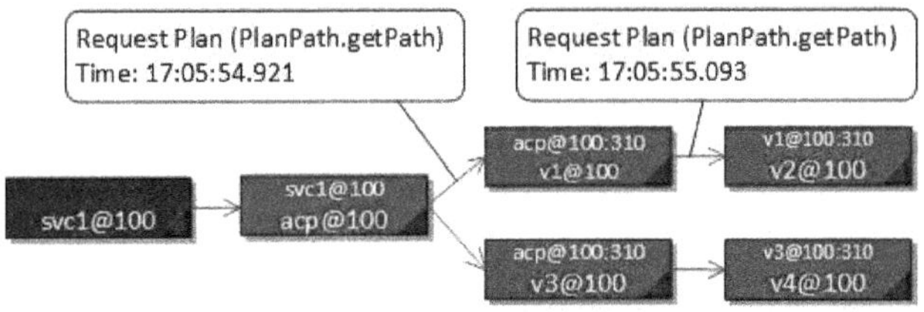

Figure 2. Example of a workflow that illustrates a piece of negotiation in CWS application. The bubble labels highlight parts of the messages sent between agents.

In general, a communication log consists of multiple workflows. The first step of the communication analysis is the organization of the messages into individual workflows. Using terminology of the graph theory, a workflow is a tree (see Figure 2) and the whole communication is a forest of such trees. The root of each workflow is the initiator of the particular communication. Intermediate nodes represent agents that are not capable to satisfy the received request on their own, but are able to inquire other agents. Finally, workflow leafs represent agents, who (i) can fully satisfy the request or (ii) cannot and even are not able to involve into the negotiation process any other participants.

The next step is the computation of the loading matrix. It is a table (see Figure 3) containing information how each initial request (Customer class in terminology of performance models) Cr loads a resource (Job Center in terminology of performance models) Ji. The load is derived from time differences between input and output messages.

	C_1	C_2	$\cdots$	C_R
J_1	L_{11}	L_{12}	$\cdots$	L_{1R}
J_2	L_{21}	L_{22}	$\cdots$	L_{2R}
$\vdots$			$\ddots$	
J_M	L_{M1}	L_{M2}	$\cdots$	L_{MR}

Figure 3. Loading Matrix.

The computation of a cell of the Loading Matrix is illustrated on a concrete example. First, the communication is captured by Sniffer. Second, the messages are organized into workflows. Third, the load is computed from the time differences. For example, the cell in the matrix corresponding to the column for customer "Request from SVC1@100" and the row representing resource which hosts agent "v1@100" contains value 0.172 (17:05:55.093 - 17:05:54.921), i.e., time in seconds representing the time distance between the input and output message. The matrix is constructed row by row and each row represents a workflow. If the workflow for a specific initial request is received again, to old value are overwritten by the new ones. Whenever the Loading Matrix is changed, the updated values are sent to the DF.

3.2. The DF for Prevention against Overload

The proposed method benefits from a DF overview of ongoing activities, because the DF enabled to start all of them. This is combined with the loading matrix communicated from the sniffer and serves as input for the Operational analysis in details described in the next paragraphs.

The Operational analysis [18][19] based on operational laws is the most straightforward analytic technique for performance considerations. It outperforms other approaches in the speed, it is simple for implementation and does not require any specialized skills. On the other hand, this notation can be used only for systems with homogeneous workload, i.e. the behavior of system components (jobs, resources) is time invariant. Beside this, operational laws cannot describe any notion of synchronization or exclusive access.

Utilization law: The utilization is equal to the product of the throughput and the mean service time.

Because the method proposed in this paper uses only the utilization law, we will not introduce the other two operational laws (i.e., Little's law and Forced flow law) in detail.

The operational analysis was selected due to its low computational complexity. The operational laws, as they were introduced in [18], are directly applicable only in single-class case, but the multi-class cases require extension of the notation to handle various load coming from various customer classes. This work adopts and further extends method introduced by Casale [20].

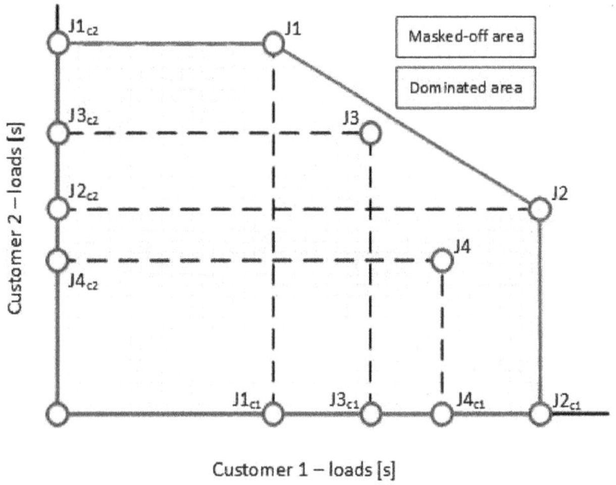

Figure 4. Graphical representation of a loading matrix meaning.

The key idea of the proposed method is that all system resources should be prevented from entering a saturated operational mode, which decreases the throughput of the particular resource and consequently of the whole system. To achieve this, the loading matrix, respectively its graphical representation, is used. Figure 4 depicts graphical representation of a loading matrix of a system with two customer classes. Points J1, J2, J3, and J4 represent individual job centers (in this case CPUs hosting agents). Their x- resp. y-coordinate represents the load imposed by customer of class 1 resp. 2. It is worth noticing, that the non-bottleneck JCs can be of two types. The first are dominated by another JC (e.g. J4 is dominated by J2) or they might be masked off by a combination of other centers (e.g. J3 is masked off by the combination of J1 and J2). The method constructs the convex hull around all job centers. The job centers placed on a facet of the hull are the first ones facing the danger of saturation, therefore it is sufficient to keep out of the saturation these ones to guarantee that no other JC becomes saturated. The formal definition of this statement and its proof can be found in [20].

The transformation to the λ-space, where λ_r denotes the arrival frequency of r-customer class, is needed for further analysis.

$\lambda=\{\lambda_1,\lambda_2,\cdots,\lambda_r\}$ is the vector of arrival frequencies of all customer classes. The transformation is based on the following equation:

$$U_i(\lambda) = \lambda_r * L_{ir} \quad (1)$$

For non-saturated stations holds:

$$U_i(\lambda) \leq 1 \quad (2)$$

where i iterates over the set of all bottleneck candidates as were identified in the previous step.

The set of equations (2) defines the region, for which holds that none of the resources is saturated.

3.3. Scheduling Extension of the DF

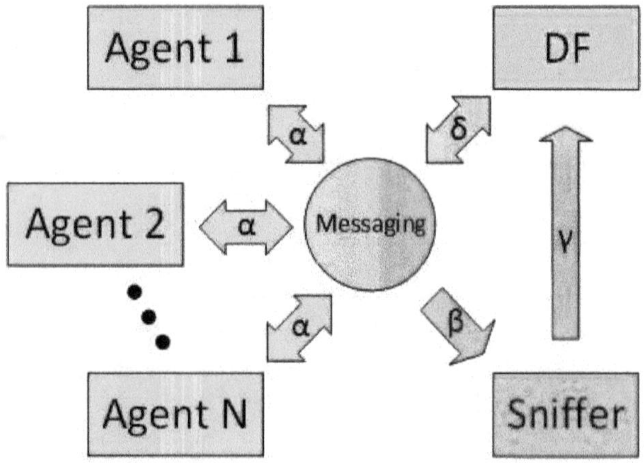

Figure 5. Architecture of a MAS with Sniffer and Extended DF, which postpones the impracticable actions.

Attention was paid to the interoperability of the designed method with existing systems. The final implementation comprehends extension of two meta-agents — Sniffer and DF (see Figure 5). The first one is an extension of the Java Sniffer, which logs the messages and analyzes them in order to derive the loading matrix *L*. The matrix is then communicated via the regular messaging channel to the DF. This meta-agent utilizes the matrix to detect, whether the series of requests arriving to the system causes saturation of any JC — in this case it is a computer hosting an agent. If the danger of saturation is detected, the request is postponed to match the maximum frequency under given conditions.

The Sniffer's part contains the regular and freely available Java Sniffer, which is responsible for capturing the messages, and further the newly developed extension, which computes the load matrix from the timestamps of corresponding messages. Beside this, the extension communicates its observations to the DF. All components of this part are written in pure Java and use only common libraries.

The DF's part extends the standard Jade's DF in three main parts. The first one is the register implemented as a HashMap, where keys are the request types and the values are timestamps denoting the time of the last occurrence of the request. A request type is a unique combination of an agent and the requested service. For instance, if agent "A1" requests service "cooling" then the request type is "$A1_{cooling}$." The second part is related to the computation of the convex hull. The computation itself is done in Matlab. The Matlab version R2014a provides function for computation of convex hull in n-dimensional space:

The input L is the loading matrix (the number of rows is the number of JCs, columns refer to the dimension of the space) and the output K is a matrix[x,y] - x is number convex hull facets, y is the dimension. In other words, the first row of matrix K contains indices of points from L that demarcate the first facet. The bottleneck candidates are such points that appears among the facet members. Set of constraints for these possible bottlenecks is created according to the set of equations (2).

When the DF is requested by an agent for a provider of a particular service, the current **λ** is computed as follows:

For the currently received request — of n-th customer class,

$$\lambda_i = 1/(t_{now} - t_{iL1}),\ i = n \quad (3)$$

$$\lambda_i = 1/(\max(t_{now} - t_{iL1}, t_{iL1} - t_{iL2})),\ i \neq n \quad (4)$$

where t_{now} is the current time, t_{iL1} is the time, when the task i was triggered last time and t_{iL2} is the time, when the task i was triggered before the last occurrence. The procedure is illustrated in Figure 6.

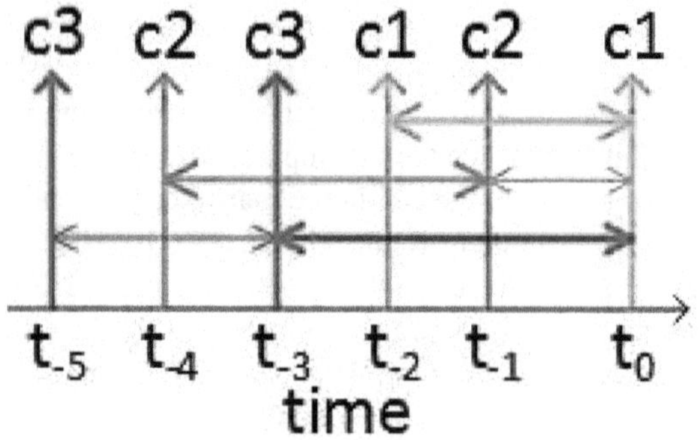

Figure 6. Computation of arrival frequencies.

Afterwards, the satisfaction of all constrains is tested. If none of them is violated, the request is handled immediately. Otherwise, the DF repeats the test after a relaxation time T until all constrains are satisfied.

4. Experimental Evaluation

The first experiment confirms that the behavior of the real distributed systems is coherent with the simulation results. Using the test bed, we set up system with six Jade agents representing a part of the CWS application. One agent represents a service (the agent asking for cooling water), one agent represents a chiller (the agent providing cooling water) and four valve agents (the agents interconnecting segments of the water-piping system). The cooperation schema is depicted in Figure 2. The initiator of the communication is the service agent *svc1*. It asks the DF for contacts to agents providing cooling water. The DF provides contact (i.e., an agent id used for addressing messages within the JADE platform) to the chiller *acp*. The chiller communicates with the valves (*v1*, *v2*, *v3*, and *v4*) in order to arrange the transport of the cooling water to the *svc1*.

The plot (see Figure 7) depicts the relation between frequency of request entering the system (Input Frequency) and the frequency of finishing the jobs - system throughput. The measured characteristic confirms the existence of the throughput maximum.

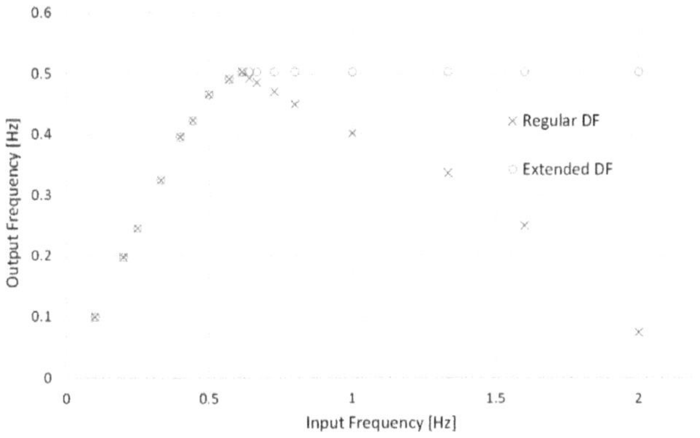

Figure 7. *Throughput with One Customer Class.*

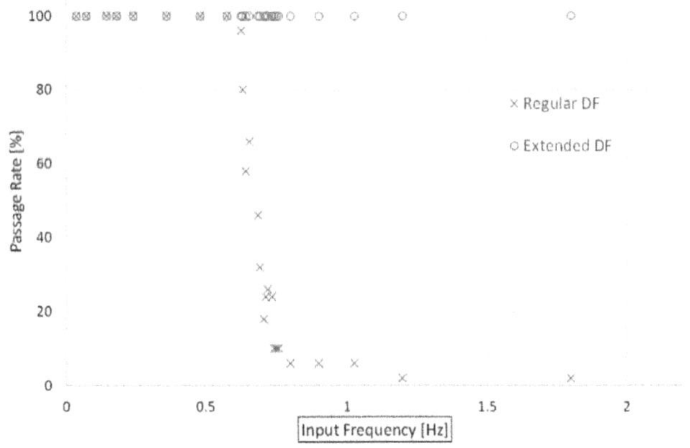

Figure 8. *Passage Rate*

The positive impact of using the extended version of the DF is clearly shown in Figure 8. The points marked by crosses represents measurements done with the regular JADE system and it demonstrates that after crossing a certain frequency the amount of jobs passed by a certain deadline steeply decreases. On the other hand, the modified version of the DF regulates the frequency of the input jobs, which leads the preserving the passing rate at 100 %.

The further experiments were focused on systems with more customer classes. We present the contribution of the proposed approach on a 2-customer system, i.e., on a system, where two types of customer requests occur. It was created by extending the previous 1-customer experiment by a new type of request, but still using the same test bed. The measurements go along with the previous results regarding the performance degradation, but on top of that also demonstrates the strong influence across input frequency of individual classes (see Figure 9 and Figure 10).

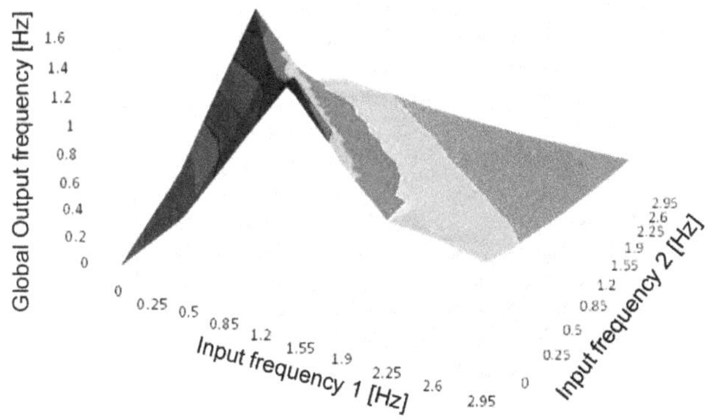

Figure 9. *Throughput with Two Customer Classes - Regular DF.*

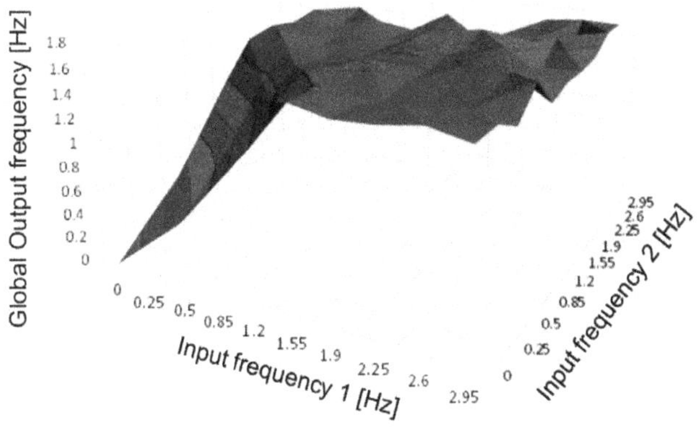

Figure 10. *Throughput with Two Customer Classes - Extended DF.*

5. Conclusion

This manuscript proposes a method to fill the gap in the design methodology for MASs related to the performance and responsiveness of the system. The method prevents a MAS from entering such operational regimes that would saturate a system resource. To achieve this, the communication between agents is observed (i) to obtain the loading matrix and (ii) to observe the frequency of tasks arriving to the MAS. Based on the analysis of the derived loading matrix, the method excludes from the further consideration such resources that cannot become bottlenecks. The loading parameters of the potential bottlenecks generate a set of constrains on frequencies of arriving tasks that cannot be exceeded unless some resources are saturated. The extended DF provides features to guarantee fulfillment of all constrains by delaying new tasks if needed. The experiments have confirmed the contribution of the method to the overall system performance.

The methods provide many opportunities for future development. First of all, they can be generalized for an arbitrary event-based system. Next, the limiting requirement to trigger primary event by primary event to distinguish their impacts can be eliminated by an advanced method for estimating impacts of individual tasks that are influenced by other tasks statistically from multiple observations. Currently, the loading matrix is estimated at the beginning, since it is assumed that its values do not change in time. However, this assumption can be in some cases difficult to fulfill and an adaptation mechanism for the loading matrix might be requested in the future.

Acknowledgements

This work was supported by the Grant Agency of the Czech Technical University in Prague, grant No. SGS12/188/OHK3/3T/13; and by the Christian Doppler Forschungsgesellschaft, the Federal Ministry of Economy, Family and Youth, and the National Foundation for Research, Technology and Development – Austria.

References

[1] M. Pěchouček, S. Thompson, J. Baxter, G. Horn, K. Kok, C. Warmer, R. Kamphuis, V. Mařík, P. Vrba, K. Hall, F. Maturana, K. Dorer, M. Calisti, Agents in industry: the best from the AAMAS 2005 industry track, IEEE Transactions on Intelligent Systems, 21(2), 86 (2006). DOI 10.1109/MIS.2006.19J.

[2] P. Vrba, V. Mařík, P. Siano, P. Leitao, G. Zhabelova, V. Vyatkin, T. Strasser, A Review of Agent and Service-oriented Concepts applied to Intelligent Energy Systems, IEEE Transactions on Industrial Informatics (99), 1 (2014). DOI 10.1109/TII.2014.2326411

[3] O. Yildirim, G. Kardas, A multi-agent system for minimizing energy costs in cement production, Computers in Industry 65(7), 1076 (2014). DOI 10.1016/j.compind.2014.05.002

[4] P. Kadera, P. Tichý, Chilled water system control, simulation, and visualization using Java multi-agent systém, Information Control Problems in Manufacturing, vol. 13 (2009), vol. 13, pp. 1808-1813

[5] R.G. Smith, The Contract Net Protocol: High-Level Communication and Control in a Distributed Problem Solver, IEEE Transactions on Computers (12), 1104 (1980)

[6] P. Kadera, P. Tichy, Plan, commit, execute protocol in multi-agent systems, Holonic and multi-agent systems for manufacturing (Springer, 2009), pp. 155 – 164

[7] H.V. Brussel, J. Wyns, P. Valckenaers, L. Bongaerts, P. Peeters, Reference architecture for holonic manufacturing systems: PROSA, Computers in Industry 37(3), 255 (1998). DOI 10.1016/S0166-3615(98)00102-X

[8] P. Leitao, F. Restivo, ADACOR: A holonic architecture for agile and adaptive manufacturing control, Computers in Industry 57(2), 121 (2006). DOI 10.1016/j.compind.2005.05.005

[9] A. Giret, V. Botti, Engineering Holonic Manufacturing Systems, Computers in Industry 60(6), 428 (2009). DOI 10.1016/j.compind.2009.02.007

[10] M. Wooldridge, M. Fisher, M.P. Huget, S. Parsons, Model checking multi-agent systems with MABLE, in Proceedings of the first international joint conference on Autonomous agents and multiagent systems: part 2 (ACM, 2002), pp. 952-959

[11] S. Schliecker, J. Rox, M. Negrean, K. Richter, M. Jersak, R. Ernst, System Level Performance Analysis for Real-Time Automotive Multicore and Network Architectures, IEEE Transactions on Computer-Aided Design of integrated Circuits and Systems, 28(7), 979 (2009)

[12] K. Richter, M. Jersak, R. Ernst, A formal approach to MpSoC performance verification, Computer 36(4), 60 (2003)

[13] R. L. Cruz, A calculus for network delay, IEEE Transactions on Information Theory, 37(1), 114 (1991)

[14] L. Thiele, S. Chakraborty, M. Naedele, Real-time calculus for scheduling hard real-time systems, in Proceedings of IEEE International Symposium on Circuits and Systems, vol. 4 (2000), pp. 101-104

[15] P. Leitao, N. Rodrigues, Modelling and validating the multi-agent system behaviour for a washing machine production line, in Proceedings of IEEE International Symposium on Industrial Electronics (ISIE) (2012), pp. 1203-1208. DOI 10.1109/ISIE.2012.6237260

[16] J. Kubalík, P. Tichý, R. Šindelář, R.J. Staron, Clustering Methods for Agent Distribution Optimization, IEEE Transactions on Systems, Man, and Cybernetics, Part C: Applications and Reviews, 40(1), 78 (2010)

[17] FIPA. Fipa ACL message structure specification (2002)

[18] P.J. Denning, J.P. Buzen, The operational analysis of queueing network models, ACM Computing Surveys (CSUR) 10(3), 225 (1978)

[19] V. Cortellesa, A. D. Marco, P. Inverardi, Model-based software performance analysis, Springer, 2011

[20] G. Casale, G. Serazzi, Bottlenecks identification in multiclass queueing networks using convex polytopes, in Proceedings of The IEEE Computer Society's 12th Annual International Symposium on Modeling, Analysis, and Simulation of Computer and Telecommunications Systems, 2004. pp. 223-230.

Maximum Power Point Tracking (MPPT) Using Artificial Bee Colony Based Algorithm for Photovoltaic System

Hassan Salmi*, Abdelmajid Badri, Mourad Zegrari

EEA&TI Laboratory, Faculty of Sciences and Techniques, Hassan II Casablanca University, Mohammedia, Morocco

Email address:

salmi.hassan91@gmail.com (H. Salmi), abdelmajid_badri@yahoo.fr (A. Badri), mourad_zegrari@yahoo.fr (M. Zegrari)

Abstract: The Artificial Bee Colony based algorithm (ABC) studied in this paper is assigned as an intelligent control of photovoltaic system. The output power of a photovoltaic panel depends on solar irradiation and temperature. Therefore, it is important to operate the photovoltaic (PV) panel in its maximum power point. In this aim, the ABC consists to track the optimal duty cycle of the electronic converter, in order to lead to the Maximum Power Point (MPP) of the PV system. Moreover, the classical method Perturb and Observe (P&O) [1-2] is studied in the sake of comparison with the ABC method in Matlab/Simulink, by taking into consideration the efficiency, the speed and the robustness performance when the meteorological conditions change.

Keywords: Maximum Power Point, Artificial Bee Colony, P&O, Matlab/Simulink

1. Introduction

Photovoltaic (PV) systems have generated immense market and research interests recently due to the abundance of raw materials and their noiseless and environment friendly power-generating process [3-4]. The electrical energy produced by a photovoltaic system stored or used directly by static converters is not maximized. The maximum power point (MPP) is achieved by adjusting the operating point of the PV array using a DC–DC converter. In this context, an increasing interest has been given to the methods of tracking the maximum power of the PV system named Maximum Power Point Tracker (MPPT) [5].

Different techniques to track the MPP have been presented in literatures. These techniques are dedicated to find the optimal duty cycle of the boost, we can distinguish the conventional P&O which known by oscillation in the steady state and the inability to provide the appropriate MPP when the meteorological condition change. In this work an intelligent approach using Artificial Bee Colony has introduced to track the maximum power point of the photovoltaic panel.

We studied the methods of P&O and ABC in order to compare the performances. The results are obtained using Simulink environment. The system is presented in Fig. 1.

This paper is organized as follows: In section II, description of the photovoltaic system. Maximum power point tracking control is described in section III. The simulation and results are presented in section IV. Conclusion is given in the last section.

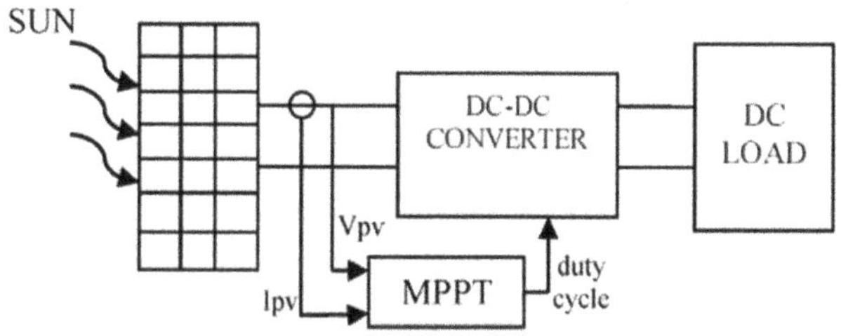

Figure 1. General diagram of the photovoltaic system.

2. Description of the Photovoltaic System

2.1. Characteristics of PV Module

A PV array is formed of several PV modules connected in series and/or parallel and the total power is a combination of the power derived from each PV module. [6]. The fundamental equation for PV panel is given by:

$$IPV = npIPh - npIs\left[\exp\left(\frac{V_{Pv}+R_S I_{Pv}}{nsV_{th}}\right) - 1\right] - \frac{V_{Pv}+R_S I_{Pv}}{R_{sh}} \quad (1)$$

$$Is=Ir\,(\frac{T}{T_r})3\ expo(\frac{qE_g}{KqA}(\frac{1}{T_r}-\frac{1}{T})) \quad (2)$$

$$IPh=[I_{Sc}+K_I(T-T_r)]\frac{G}{1000} \quad (3)$$

where:

Table 1. *Parameters of a PV.*

I_{PV}	Output current
V_{PV}	Output voltage
T	Cell temperature (K).
G	Solar irradiance (W/m2).
I_{Ph}	Light-generated current.
Is	PV cell saturation current.
Ir	saturation current at Tr.
Isc	Short-circuit current at reference condition.
Tr	Reference temperature.
KI	Short-circuit temperature coefficient.
q	Charge of an electron.
K	Boltzmann's constant.
Eg	Band-gap energy of the material.
A	Ideality factor.

The behavior of the PV module is shown in two characteristics I_{PV}(VPV) and PPV(VPV) for different irradiation and temperature values can be plotted.

The following curves give an example of these characteristics for two different irradiance (G) and temperature:

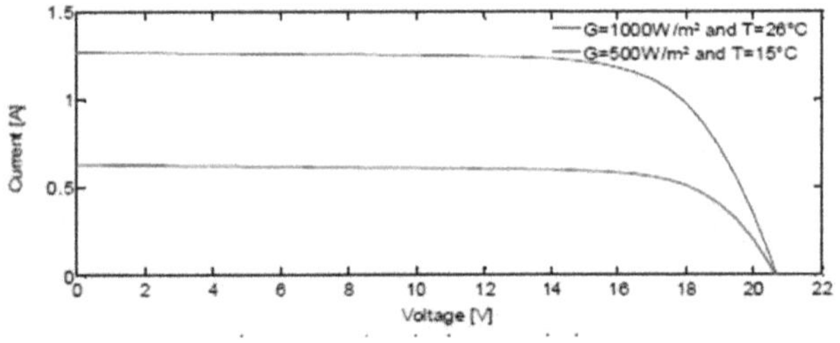

Figure 2. *PV Characteristics of the photovoltaic Panel $I_{PV}(V_{PV})$.*

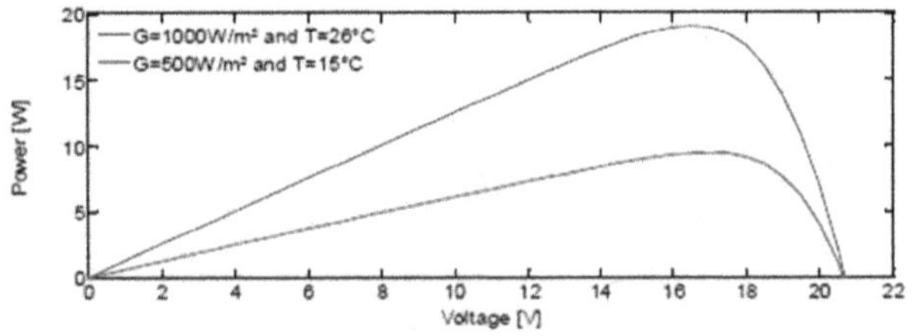

Figure 3. *$P(V_{PV})$ Characteristic.*

The specification of the photovoltaic module used are:

Table 2. *The specification of the photovoltaic module used.*

Pmax (W)	20.0W.
Voc (V)	20.8V.
Isc (A)	1.27A.
Vmp(V)	17.1V.
Imp(A)	1.17A.

2.2. Boost DC-DC

A boost chopper is one of power converters used in photovoltaic systems. In this aim we will insert this converter 'boost' between the photovoltaic system and the load in order to bring this load to function optimally. The control of the converter is managed by the duty cycle which itself needed to be adjusted to its optimal value. This adjustment is actually directed by MPPT methods. The boost converter is composed of inductor, capacitor, and a power switch often is a mosfet transistor. The boost circuit is depicted in Fig. 4 [7].

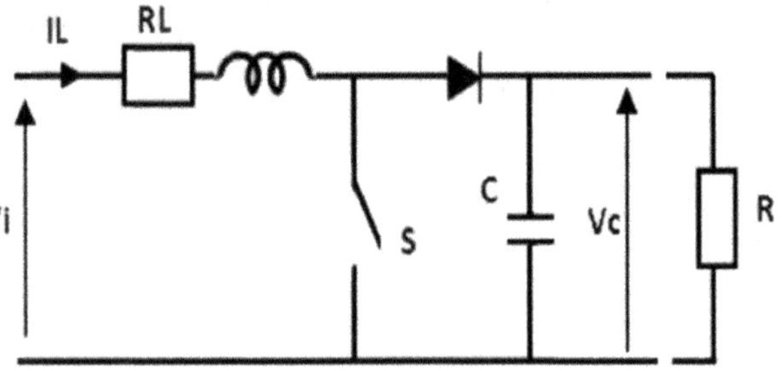

Figure 4. *Boost Converter circuit.*

2.3. Maximum Power Point Tracking

Maximum power point tracking (MPPT) technique is used to extract the maximum power delivered by the solar panel. Indeed there are several algorithms to extract the maximum power. The most famous is Perturb & Observe (P & O).In this section we offer a new controller based on ABC.

1) Perturb and Observe:

Perturb and observe approach is the most used method to pursue the maximum power point of a photovoltaic generator. The principle is to disrupt the voltage or duty cycle and calculating the power terminal of the PV module.

- When p(k-l)<p(k), the voltage is increased.
- When p(k-l) > p(k), the voltage is decreased.

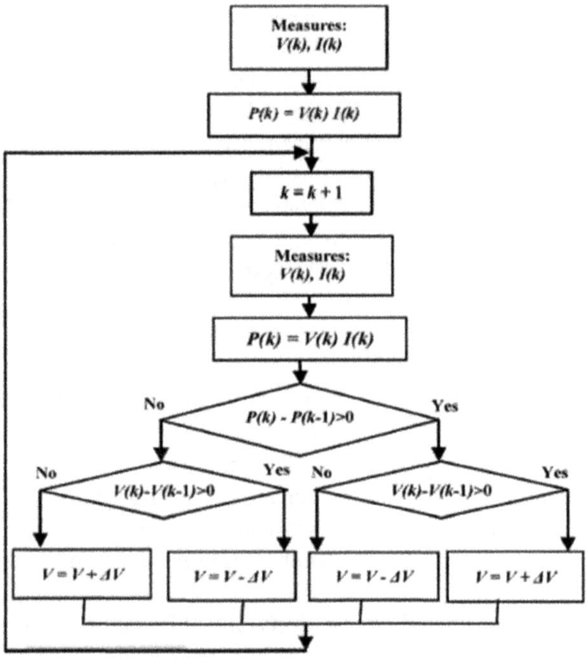

Figure 5. *Flowchart for conventional Perturb and Observe algorithm.*

2) Principle of ABC algorithm:

The artificial bee colony (ABC) algorithm was introduced for solving optimization problems proposed by Tereshko and Loengarov [8–9].

The ABC consists of three groups of artificial bees: employed, onlooker and scouts. Every group has a different task in the optimization process [10].

The employed bee is currently searching for food and carry the data about food source back to the hive. A bee waiting in the hive for making decision to select a food source is called as an onlooker. Whenever a food source is exploited fully, all the employed bees associated with it abandon the food source, and become scout. The number of food sources is equal to the number of employed bees and also equal to the number of onlooker bees. The flowchart of the proposed ABC algorithm is given in Fig. 6.

The steps of the ABC algorithm are outlined as follows:

1. At the initialization phase, the ABC generates a randomly distributed initial population of ns solutions (duty cycle). Each solution is produced within its limits [0, 1] according to the equation below:

$$X^j = X_{min} + rand[0, 1]*(X_{max}- X_{min})\ i=1, 2,\ldots, SN \quad (4)$$

Where xmin and xmax represent respectively the minimum and the maximum of the parameter j.

2. Each employed bee leaves to a food source and locates a neighbor source vi according to Eq. (5) and then estimates its fitness fiti:

$$V_i= X_i+ \phi_i *(X_i - X_K) \quad (5)$$

Where k ∈ {1, 2,..., SN} and j ∈{1, 2,., D } are randomly chosen indexes.

Although k has to be different from I and ϕ_{ij} Є [-1, 1].

3. Each onlooker observes the nectar of employed bees and chooses one of their sources depending on the probability Pi defined as:

$$Pi=\frac{Fit_i}{\sum_{n=1}^{SN} Fit_n} \quad (6)$$

where fiti is the fitness value of the solution xi (Power).

The fitness of each new produced candidate solution vij is com-pared with that of its old one. If the new solution has an equal or better fitness than the old solution, it replaces the old one in the memory. Otherwise, the old one is retained in the memory. In other words, a greedy selection mechanism is employed in the selection operation between the old and the candidate one.

4. At the end of each search cycle, if the fitness of a solution cannot be improved and the predetermined number of trials, which is called "limit", is exhausted, then the solution will be abandoned by scout bee and a new solution is randomly searched.

The main advantage of the ABC-based algorithm is that it does not require expending more effort in tuning the control parameters, as in the case of GA [56-59], and other evolutionary algorithm. This feature marks the proposed ABC-based algorithm as being advantageous for implementation.

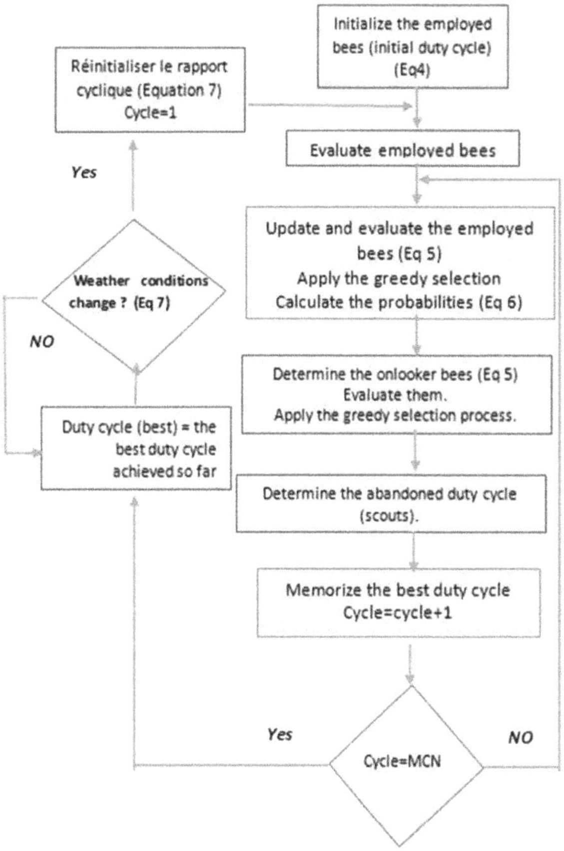

Figure 6. *Flowchart of the proposed ABC-based MPPT.*

3. Results and Discussions

In this section we will compare the performance of P&O which has a fixed Δd (representing the step size) to those of the ABC.

For T=25°C and G=1000W /m²

1) P&O algorithm with a fixed step size Δd=0.025 and Ts=0.002s:

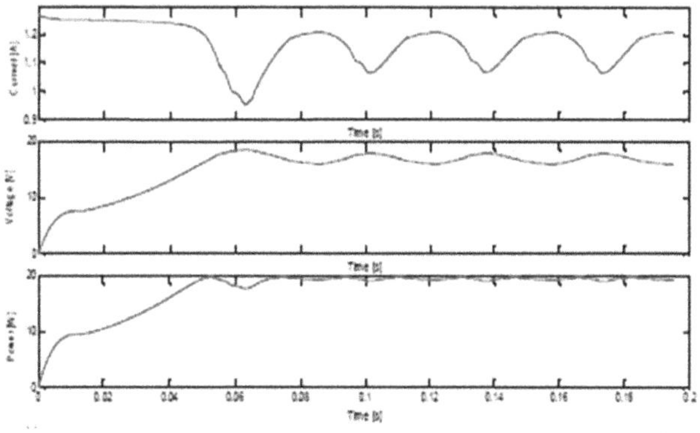

Figure 7. *Trend of IPV, VPV and PPV for P&O algorithm.*

As we observe that the P&O with a fixed Δd=0.02, oscillate at the steady state around the MPP. These oscillations is due to the unstable values of duty cycle « d » which does not allow the algorithm to lead the PV module to reach the maximum power point effectively.

2) ABC Algorithm:

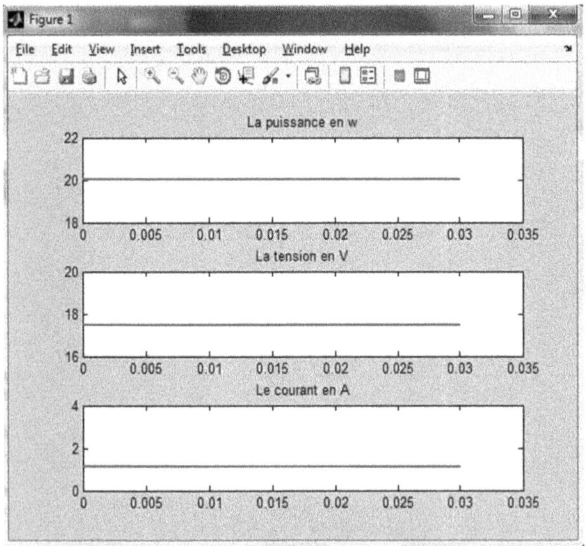

Figure 8. *Trend of I_{PV}, I_{PV} and P_{PV} for ABC method.*

The ABC algorithm find the maximum power point (MPP) at t=0s while P&O find the value of the same point at t= 0.053s and the ABC can track the MPP quickly and effectively without any oscillations in the steady state.

During a change in temperature or irradiation, the ABC algorithm resets (we control the fluctuation of weather conditions through equation 7) then converges to the new maximum power which makes our more robust algorithm.

$$\frac{P_{pv(new)}-P_{pv(Old)}}{P_{pv(new)}} \geq \Delta P \quad (7)$$

4. Conclusion

In this paper we clearly see that the ABC algorithm which is considered as an intelligent control outperforms the method of MPPT P&O in tracking the MPP. We have shown through the simulation of photovoltaic system in simulink that the technique of ABC under variable irradiation conditions is more robust and has satisfactory results. In addition, the proposed algorithm requires only two control parameters; its convergence is not dependent on the initial condition.

Beside all of that, it provides just one optimal value of duty cycle, in contrast P&O find many values of duty cycle which causes in the end of their convergence an instability and oscillations in the steady state.

Acknowledgements

This work returns the framework of the research project SISA1 "Mini intelligent Power plant" began between research center SISA and our University. We are anxious to think the Hassan II University of Casablanca for the financing of this project.

References

[1] E. M. Ahmed and M. Shoyama, "Variable Step Size Maximum Power Point Tracker Using a Single Variable for Stand-alone Battery Storage PV Systems," Journal of Power Electronics, Vol. 11, No. 2, March 2011, pp. 218-227.

[2] N. Femia, G. Petrone, G. Spagnuolo and M. Vitelli, "Optimization of Perturb and Observe Maximum Power Point Tracking Method," IEEE TRANSACTIONS ON POWER ELECTRONICS, Vol. 20, No. 4, July 2005, pp. 963-973.

[3] S. Mekhilef, R. Saidur, and A. Safari, "A review on solar energy use in industries," *Renew. Sustain. Energy Rev.*, vol. 15, no. 4, pp. 1777–1790, May 2011.

[4] S. Mekhilef, A. Safari, W. E. S. Mustaffa, R. Saidur, R. Omar, and M. A. A. Younis, "Solar energy in Malaysia: Current state and prospects, "*Renew. Sustain. Energy Rev.*, vol. 16, no. 1, pp. 386–396, Jan. 2012.

[5] M. A. Eltawil and Z. Zhao, "MPPT techniques for photovoltaic applications," Renewable and Sustainable Energy Reviews, Vol. 25, 2013, pp. 793-813.

[6] Salhi, Mohamed, and Rachid El-Bachtri. "Maximum Power Point Tracker using Fuzzy Control for Photovoltaic System." International Journal of Research and Reviews in Electrical and Computer Engineering 1.2 (2011): 69-75.

[7] Guang Yi Cao, «Mathematical Models of Dc-Dc Converters», Journal of Zhejiang University, pp263-270, China, 2009

[8] V. Tereshko, T. Lee, How information mapping patterns determine foraging behaviour of a honeybee colony, Open Syst. Inf. Dyn. 9 (2002) 181–193.

[9] V. Tereshko, A. Loengarov, Collective decision-making in honeybee foraging dynamics, Comput. Inf. Syst. J. 9 (2005) 1–7.

[10] A. S. Oshaba, E. S. Ali and S. M. Abd Elazim "Artificial Bee Colony Algorithm Based Maximum Power Point Tracking in Photovoltaic System" WSEAS TRANSACTIONS on POWER SYSTEMS (2015) 126-127.

An introduction to software-defined networking

Babak Darabinejad[1], Seyed Rasoul Mousavi Fayyeh[2]

[1]Department of Computer Engineering, Mehrarvand International Institute of Technology, Abadan, Iran
[2]Department of Computer Engineering, Science and Research Branch, Islamic Azad University, Tehran, Iran

Email address:
b.darabi@gmail.com (B. Darabinejad), sr.mousavi@srbiau.ac.ir (S. R. M. Fayyeh)

Abstract: Although computer networks have spread worldwide, organizations that use networking technologies, have complained about the fact that no new feature has been added. Due to their newly emerged needs, they also prefer to automate many tasks. Moreover, they prefer their networks to be developed using software, rather than expensive and new hardware. Software-defined networking and Open Flow protocol separate data level from control level which makes the network smarter and more manageable. Network's main infrastructure is also separate from applications. This makes organizations to program, automate, and control networks more efficiently. In this paper we will introduce this technology by reviewing the literature.

Keywords: Software Defined Networking, Protocol, Open Flow, Overlay Networks

1. Introduction

By the development of portable devices and accessories, server virtualization, and the emergence of cloud systems, the revision of network architecture is made necessary. Many network architectures are traditional and hierarchical which are comprised of nodes in Ethernet switches in a tree structure. In client-server communications architecture, this is more evident. This static architecture, however, does not meet the requirements of dynamic communications and organizations' needs regarding data center and media servers [1].

It is almost impossible to meet the emergent needs of market using common network architectures. Information technology (IT) companies make use of management tools at machine and manual-level processing to deal with financial crisis or budget cuts.

Telecommunication service providers are also faced by similar issues. It is due to the fact that there is an increasing demand for dynamic networks bandwidths. At the same time, however, their profits decrease due to the costs of central equipment and a decrease in their income. Network architectures are not designed in a way to meet the current requirements of companies, telecommunication service providers, and users. In other words, network designers mislead IT technology due to limitations, such as complexity, contradictory policies, lack of scalability, dependence on the seller [1], and lack of coordination between market needs and network capabilities. In order to prevent these, software-defined networking was introduced along with its standards.

2. The Idea of Software Defined Networking

The idea of Software Defined Networking (SDN) is not a new one and it was introduced more than a decade ago. An efficient definition of SDN describes it as the separation of routers' data and controlling operations as well as other infrastructures of the second layer using a programming interface [2]. The foundations of the current SDN model which includes projects, such as active networking, form the basis of many network infrastructures that could be programmed by custom services [3, 4]. Open signaling (OPENSIG) in 1995 started to be used for making ATM and cell phone networks and the Internet as an extendable and programmable SDN [5]. Network configuration (NETCONF) was proposed as a management and adjustment modification protocol in network devices in 2006 [6].

The foundations of new SDNs were laid by two scholars in computer sciences. Nick Mckeown of Stanford, Scott Shenker of Berkley, and a group of students redefined SDN in 2008 [2, 7]. Their project, named Ethane, had started 15 years earlier. The aim of Ethane was to improve network security using a series of flow-based protocols [2, 8].

3. SDN Architecture

SDN is a newly emerged network architecture in which network control is separate from traffic exchange and is directly programmed. This immigration which used to be limited to hardware, makes virtual machines and network infrastructure to define and provide new services. It also makes them capable of communicating with a new range of applications for more network flexibility and widespread access to exchanged data [1].

Figure 1 illustrates an overview of SDN architecture. Logically, the smart layer of the network, which maintains the overall network structure, lies in the center of SDN software controllers. Therefore, applications consider the network as a unified logical switch. Using SDN, companies and telecommunication operators can control the network using a unified central controller, regardless of its hardware and its manufacturer. It makes network designing and its exploitation much easier. Moreover, SDN simplifies devices and machines used in a network, since there is no need for identifying and processing thousands of protocol standards. Orders are only issued by the SDN controller [1].

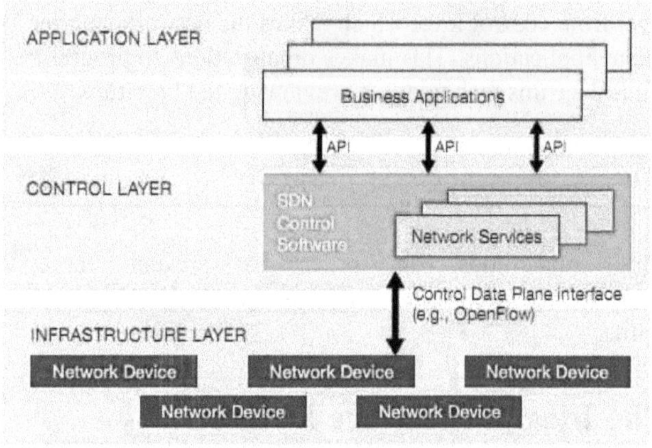

Figure 1. *SDN architecture[1]*

3.1. SDN Network Components

3.1.1. Controllers

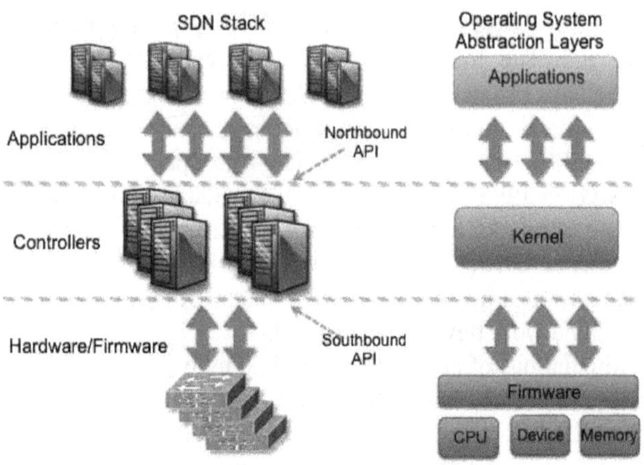

Figure 2. *Controllers in SDN[10]*

One of the major ideas behind SDNs is that a device, called controller, directly communicates with all devices on a network domain, is aware of network's topology, and programs the network from a central point. An SDN controller changes network programming from a distributed state to a centralized one. Figure 2 illustrates an SDN network as firmware. It also shows a connection through a controller. A connection with lower rank devices which is called a southbound connection and a connection with higher ranks which is called a northbound connection are also depicted.

3.1.2. Virtual Switches

The emergence of server virtualization technologies, that are exploited using hyper wires, highlighted the role of virtual switches in connecting virtual servers using virtual network adapters, traffic congestion, and in sending the traffic outside hyper wires in physical networks. Hardware and software switches play a role in SDN, since they are directly responsible for sending scheduled tables using controllers [11, 12].

3.1.3. Overlay Networks

Overlay networks are virtual networks that jointly use the same physical network platform, but are logically independent. Some SDN controllers use overlay networks for their communications in dispersed data centers and selecting from various virtual hosts.

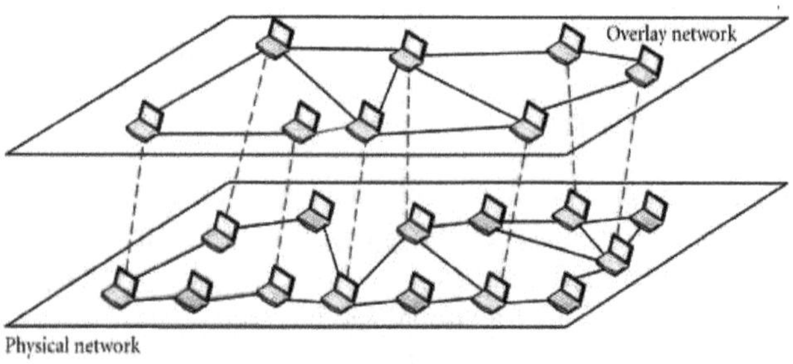

Figure 3. *Overlay networks structure*

4. Open Flow Protocol

Open Flow protocol is the first standard communication interface that lies between control layer and sending layer in an SDN [1]. Open Networking Foundation (ONF) started in 2011 with the aim of promoting a new form of SDN networks compatible with Open Flow protocol [13]. To this end, ONF took the responsibility of standardizing Open Flow protocol [1]. Unlike most other groups or industrial consortia for IT standardization, ONF was not founded by infrastructure suppliers. It was, in fact, founded by companies that were willing to use this technology, such as Google, FaceBook, Microsoft, Yahoo!, and 19 other companies [14].

Open Flow protocol facilitates direct access and changing network accessory sending programs, such as switches and routers, both physically and virtually based on hyper wires. The lack of an open interface in sending data programs led today's networks into becoming integrated, closed, and semi-centralized processing. No other standard protocol can carry out the tasks of Open Flow protocol. A similar protocol is needed to get the network out of switch's control and directs it to the central controller software [1].

Open Flow protocol first defines the central controller. Then, it determines how it can safely connect to network devices and control them. It then determines how incoming packages are manipulated, processed, and forwarded. Before Open Flow protocol, there was no standard for manipulating and forwarding network routing table. Therefore, SDN was bound to run independently which faced it with shortcomings in network performance [15].

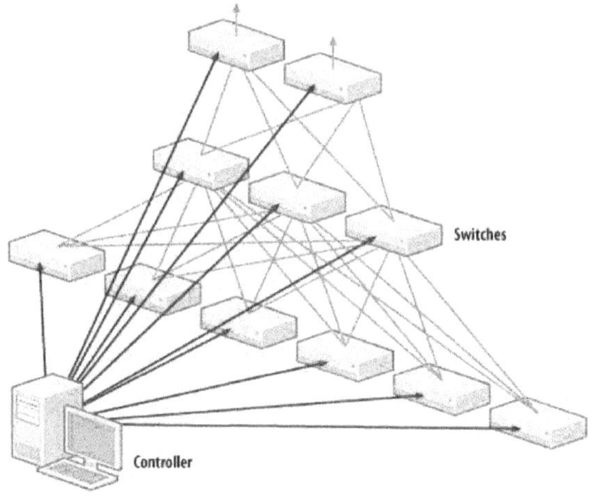

Figure 4. *A network with a centralized controller[15]*

As Figure 4 shows, SDN focuses on network controlling unit which makes it possible for users and IT managers to control routing and data traffic in switches through defining rules and policies for the central controller. In those networks, sending units and data units are maintained distributively between Open Flow-based switches and routers. The smartness of network lies in the central controller [15].

Routing flow tables are comprised of flow gateways. As Figure 5 shows, each gateway is comprised of matching fields, counter fields, and instruction fields [17].

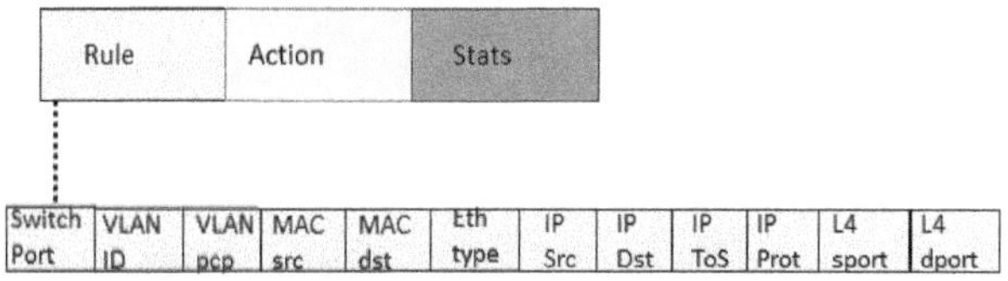

Figure 5. *Flow routing table in Open Flow [17]*

There may be multiple flow gateways for determining the mode of each packet. The gateway with the highest number of modes for a packet is finally chosen for matching. Then, the input instruction is applied on gateway's instructions. A packet may be assigned an address by a physical or virtual port. Packets may be sent for the controller, flood the controller, or get referred to the switch. Moreover, packets may be sent to virtual ports in flood or normal mode [16].

5. Conclusion

SDN is not a product or hardware/software concept, but rather a new architecture and approach for enhancing networks flexibility and controllability, facilitating the use of various applications, services, and software services on current networks. It reduces the tasks and lowers the highlighted role of hardware and network devices, while simplifies networking management and control and highlights the roles and tasks of software layers of a network. The way in which SDN can help improve network highly depends on the problems that are to be solved. Exploiting appropriate SDN solutions can simplify operational processes, decrease human error, and control traffic based on uncommon ways that are defined by the unique criteria of a particular organization. In short, it enhances performance and flexibility.

References

[1] White paper, Software-Defined Networking: The New Norm for Networks, Open Networking Foundation, April 13, 2012. Retrieved August 22, 2013.

[2] David Strom, 100Gbps and beyond: What lies ahead in the world of networking, www.arstechnica.com, Feb 19 2013.

[3] D. Tennenhouse, J. Smith, W. Sincoskie, D. Wetherall, and G. Minden. A survey of active network research. Communications Magazine, IEEE, 35(1):80-86, 1997.

[4] D. Tennenhouse and D. Wetherall. Towards an active network architecture. In DARPA Active Networks Conference and Exposition, 2002. Proceedings, pages 2-15. IEEE, 2002.

[5] A. Campbell, I. Katzela, K. Miki, and J. Vicente. Open signaling for atm, internet and mobile networks (opensig'98). ACM SIGCOMM Computer Communication Review, 29(1):97-108, 1999.

[6] R. Enns. NETCONF Configuration Protocol. RFC 4741 (Proposed Standard), Dec. 2006. Obsoleted by RFC 6241.

[7] Scott Shenker, Gentle Introducton to Softwaer- Defined Networking, Technion lecture, The 2nd Annual International TCE Conference Networking, Cloud and Beyond, June 6-7 2012

[8] M. Casado, M. Freedman, J. Pettit, J. Luo, N. McKeown, and S. Shenker. Ethane: Taking control of the enterprise. ACM SIGCOMM Computer Communication Review, 37(4):1-12, 2007.

[9] N. Gude, T. Koponen, J. Pettit, B. Pfaff, M. Casado, N. McKeown, and S. Shenker. Nox: towards an operating system for networks. ACM SIGCOMM Computer Communication Review, 38(3):105-110, 2008.

[10] Brent Salisbury, The Northbound API- A Big Little Problem, www.networkstatic.net, June 12 2012

[11] G. Lu, R. Miao, Y. Xiong, and C. Guo. Using cpu as a traffic co-processing unit in commodity switches. In Proceedings of the first workshop on Hot topics in software defined networks, HotSDN '12, pages 31-36, New York, NY, USA, 2012. ACM.

[12] J. C. Mogul and P. Congdon. Hey, you darned counters!: get off my asic! In Proceedings of the first workshop on Hot topics in software defined networks, HotSDN '12, pages 25-30, New York, NY, USA, 2012. ACM.

[13] John Markoff, Open Networking Foundation Pursues New Standards, The New York Times, www.nytimes.com/2011/03/22/technology, March 22, 2011

[14] Katherine Noyes, Google and other titans form Open Networking Foundation, www.computerworld.com.au, 23 March 2011

[15] Open Flow Tutorial: Next-Gen Networking Has Much To Prove, www.techweb.com, Oct 17, 2011

[16] Jeff Doyle, Strategy: Inside Open Flow, informationweek,October,2011, http://reports.informationweek.com/abstract/19/8351/Network-Infrastructure/Strategy:-Inside-OpenFlow.html

[17] Srini Seetharaman , Open Flow/SDN tutorial , March, 2012,http://www.yuba.stanford.edu/~sd2/ Open Flow Tutorial_O FC2012.ppt

An XCS-Based Algorithm for Classifying Imbalanced Datasets

Hooman Sanatkar, Saman Haratizadeh

Faculty of New Sciences and Technologies, University of Tehran, Tehran, Iran

Email address:

hooman.sanatkar@ut.ac.ir (H. Sanatkar), haratizadeh@ut.ac.ir (S. Haratizadeh)

Abstract: Imbalanced datasets are datasets with different samples distribution in which the distribution of samples in one class is scientifically more than other class samples. Learning a classification model for such imbalanced data has been shown to be a tricky task. In this paper we will focus on learning classifier systems, and will suggest a new XCS-based approach for learning classification models from imbalanced data sets. The main idea behind the suggested approach is to update the important parameters of the learning method based on the information gathered in each step of learning, in order to provide a fair situation for the minor class, to contribute in building the final model. We have also evaluated our approach by testing it with real-world known imbalanced datasets. The results show that our new algorithm has a high detection rate and a low false positive rate.

Keywords: Imbalanced Dataset, Evolutionary Algorithm, XCS

1. Introduction

Learning from imbalanced datasets are among the most important challenges in machine learning issues. In such data sets the share of one class of samples from the data is much more than that of the other classes. In such a situation, a classification algorithm will not lose much accuracy even if it completely ignores the samples from the minor class. Hence, if the learning algorithm is not used with cautions, usually the resulting model will be biased toward the major class. This can be a very serious problem, because most of the times, detecting an unlabeled sample from the minor class (like a patient being infected by a rare disease) is the main goal of the prediction. Different approaches to solve the problem of unbalanced data has been taken in statistics and machine learning domain [1] [2].

Learning classifier systems (LCS) are a set of learning methods that use evolutionary approaches like genetic algorithms to generate rule-based classifiers [10]. In these methods a rule or a set of rules is coded as chromosome and a population of chromosomes is subject of an evolutionary process. There are two classes of LCS's: Pittsburgh and Michigan. The difference between the two, lies in the way they evolve the classifiers: in Pittsburgh approach, each chromosome is a candidate rule set while in Michigan approach, each chromosome is a single rule and the whole population forms the classifier rule set [3].

Like other learning methods, LCS's are not very good at classification of imbalanced data. Some methods has been proposed for dealing with imbalanced data when using LCS's for learning, but most of them have focused on Pittsburgh methods. On the other hand, it seems that Michigan class of LCS's has some interesting features that make it a very flexible method compared to most of other learning methods [4].

In Michigan approach, the model is built gradually while it experiences the training data over and over, and has the chance to refine and update every single rule, based on its performance so far. So the learning process can focus on any classification rule or any sample in the data set that needs more attention during the learning process [5]. This is a very useful feature and we will use it to improve the performance of a basic algorithm called XCS in generating models from imbalanced data sets.

The rest of this paper is organized as follows. We will review the related works in section 2. In section 3, we will describe the architecture and implementation of our algorithm. Section 4 presents the evaluation results of the proposed system on various imbalanced datasets and we conclude in section 5.

2. Related Works

There are several approaches to constructing a prediction model based on the imbalanced datasets. One of the most popular approaches is resampling which has some different approaches, like over-sampling, under-sampling and random sampling. For using with evolutionary algorithms, some variations of resampling have been suggested [6] [7] [8] [7] [8].

In XCS-based approaches some other techniques have been suggested. For example, Orriols [9] [10] [11] has showed that using smaller learning rates on XCS will improve the performance of XCS on imbalanced datasets. That experiment, also shows that low values of GA threshold in the beginning and incrementing it slowly during the learning process can make improvements on classification quality [12].

There are some methods for handling imbalance data sets using multi objective optimization in Pittsburg evolutionary algorithms. These methods follow 2 objectives: maximizing classification accuracy for majority samples and maximizing classification accuracy for minority samples. NSGA, NPGA, and PESA are some Pittsburg evolutionary algorithms that are used in this category [13] [14] [15].

3. Minor Grabber

In this section, we illustrate a new classifier system, Minor Grabber, whose goal is to improve the classification's accuracy on imbalanced datasets using an XCS-based evolutionary algorithms.

3.1. Overview

Minor grabber is a new version of XCS, designed to improve the performance of XCS in imbalanced datasets. We will first explain the XCS algorithm briefly and discuss some of its characteristics which may cause some problems when dealing with imbalanced datasets.

3.2. XCS

XCS is the most famous Michigan evolutionary algorithm with a good performance in data classification. Like all evolutionary algorithms XCS is based on evolution of a population of chromosomes. In XCS each chromosome is a classification rule while the whole population forms a classification model. The main cycle of XCS is as follows:

1. A data sample is presented to the population
2. All rules whose "if" part match the sample are gathered in a set "M" called match set. Each rule suggests a label and predicts a reward that shows how much reward it expects to receive by suggesting that label.
3. Based on the reward prediction of the rules in "M" and the fitness of the rules, a label is selected. All the rules suggesting that label are gathered in a set "A" called action set.
4. The suggested label is compared to the real label of that data sample. If they are the same, a high reward is given to the rules in "A", and if not, the rules in "A" receive a low reward. The reward prediction of the rules are updated based on their current value and this last reward value.
5. In every few cycles, a GA process will be run over the chromosomes in the action set and new rules will be generated and added to the population, possibly causing some old and low quality rules being removed. The fitness measure used for rules, is usually a value proportional to the preciseness of the rules in predicting rewards

3.3. XCS Shortcomings for Imbalanced Datasets

As we know, minority samples are rare in the training set so they will not be presented to XCS as frequently as majority samples. This means that the action set is often containing rules that recommend the label of the majority class. So, the rules that classify a sample as the majority class have a higher chance to reproduce in the population of the rules. This means that the minority class has a little chance to form appropriate set of rules in the population. As a result the population gets biased toward the majority class. In addition if the XCS manages to keep some rules for the minority class in the population, these rules will rarely find a way in to the action set. So XCS will not have enough experiment with these rules to refine them. That means the population will find a mature set of rules suggesting the majority class early in the process while the minority class rules are still young and unable to compete with other rules. Because of this phenomenon, XCS usually can not find a good set of rules when facing a skewed data set.

Minor grabber improves XCS algorithm to deal with imbalanced datasets. In the main loop of algorithm, Minor Grabber counts the number of times that the action set belongs to each class. So, after every cycle of the algorithm, that is one pass through the training set, and at the beginning of next learning cycle, we calculate the percentage of times that the action set has suggested each class of the samples. One can expect that if the rules are formed correctly, this ratio, for each class, should be equal to the ratio of instances of that class in the training data set used in that cycle. Based on this intuition, we adaptively set the number of training sample from each class for the next run as follows:

$$SR_{t+1}(c) = SR_t(c) + \alpha\big(SR_t(c) - RR_t(c)\big) \qquad (1)$$

In this equation $SR_t(c)$ shows the ratio of samples of class "*c*" at cycle "*t*" and $RR_t(c)$ stands for the ratio of times "*c*" is the label suggested by the action set at cycle "*t*" of the algorithm.

This equation updates the number of instances of each class for every cycle of the algorithm. For the first cycle, the number of instances are set proportional to the number of them in the whole data set. If the number of needed samples of each class is more than its total number of samples, over-sampling will be applied and if this value is less than total number of samples in that class, then, under-sampling will happen. So we will have a self-adaptive system that controls the XCS's learning process by adaptively updating its input training data. Picking a small value for alpha will cause a smooth change of the number of training samples in each class, and will give the system enough time to evaluate its current population of rules. It's worth mentioning that since during the learning process Minor Grabber will use exploration steps, this method can't possibly lead to a situation that one class takes over the whole training set forever.

In essence, the adaptive resampling does the same for every class of the data and the whole process adjusts the ratio of samples in the training data in each cycle so that XCS receives more samples for the classes that have not been learnt well yet. For the special case of skewed data, adaptive resampling puts more samples from minority class in the training samples of the next run, to give the XCS the chance to experience the minority class well.

The remaining problem is that although adaptive resampling adjusts the number of samples of each class in the training data, it does not say anything about which samples in the class need to be in the training set. It is important to pick the samples wisely because the performance of the classifier for each class may not be the same in different parts of the feature space. In other words, XCS may be able to classify some samples of a class correctly and still misclassify those samples from the same class that are in a different part of space.

The intuition used for solving this problem is to give higher chances to those samples that have a higher rate of misclassification by XCS. We will do it here using a sample weighting process. In order to give a sample a resampling weight, Minor Grabber looks at the match set formed for that sample. If there is a close competition among the rules present in the match set for finding a way in to the action set, it concludes that the prediction model for this sample is still immature. So this sample will probably will need more time to be learned well. Minor Grabber will give a higher chance to this sample for being included in the training data of the next cycle by increasing its resampling weight. It is important to note that all the classifiers in the match set are in a neighboring space, because they all match the same sample. So by giving a high weight to a sample we are saying that it lies in a part of feature space in which the prediction model is not mature yet.

Based on resampling weights assigned to samples, and sample ratio of each class calculated by adaptive resampling, one can use a method like roulette-wheel to pick the sample for the training set of the next learning cycle.

Table 1. *Datasets statistics.*

Row	Dataset	Num. of Samples	Imbalanced Ratio	Minority Samples	Majority Samples	Number Of Attributes	Attributes Type
1	CAR_EVAL_4	1377	25.6	56	1321	7	Nominal
2	KR_VS_K_THREE_VS_ELEVEN	2935	35.3	81	2854	7	Nominal
3	KR_VS_K_ZERO_VS_EIGHT	1460	53.7	27	1433	7	Nominal
4	KR_VS_K_ZERO_VS_FIFTEEN	1702	80.22	21	1681	7	Nominal

4. Experiments

To evaluate the performance of Minor Grabber, we have tested it on several skewed datasets, including datasets with low, medium and high imbalanced ratio.

Table 2. *Variables default values.*

Variable	Default Value
Population Size	150
Max Iteration Number	30000
Learning Rate	0.1
Cross Over Probability	0.8
Experience Probability	0.8
Sharp Probability	0.6-0.7
Mutation Probability	0.02
Deletion Threshold	20
GA Threshold	35
Delta	0.1
μ	0.01
P0	0.01
E0	0.01
F0	0.01
alpha	0.1

Clearly generating a good prediction model from a highly imbalanced data set is usually harder and we have chosen data sets with different imbalance ratios to test the performance of the Minor Grabber against problems with different degrees of difficulty. Datasets are gathered from Georgia University repository and California Irvine machine learning repository. The chosen data sets and their specifications are summarized in Table 1.

We have implemented the Minor Grabber and evaluated the accuracy of the resulted model in prediction of the test data for each data set. Table 2 summarizes the default values of the variables in our system.

In order to show how the innovations added to the general XCS algorithm have improved the performance of this algorithm on the skewed data sets we have tested XCS with the same parameter values presented in Table 2. The classification accuracy of XCS on different data sets has been shown in Table 3.

Table 3. *XCS results.*

Dataset	Classification Accuracy
Dataset1	0.9652
Dataset2	0.9709
Dataset3	0.9793
Dataset4	0.9840

According to these results one can see that the

classification accuracy on XCS on datasets is high. However, as shown in figure 1, XCS can't learn the minor (positive) class and the true positive rate does not increase as the learning process proceeds. The performance of the XCS is basically the same for all the data sets and figure 1 shows the typical convergence process.

Figures 2-5 show the learning procedure of proposed algorithm for each dataset. The results are the average of 15 runs for each dataset.

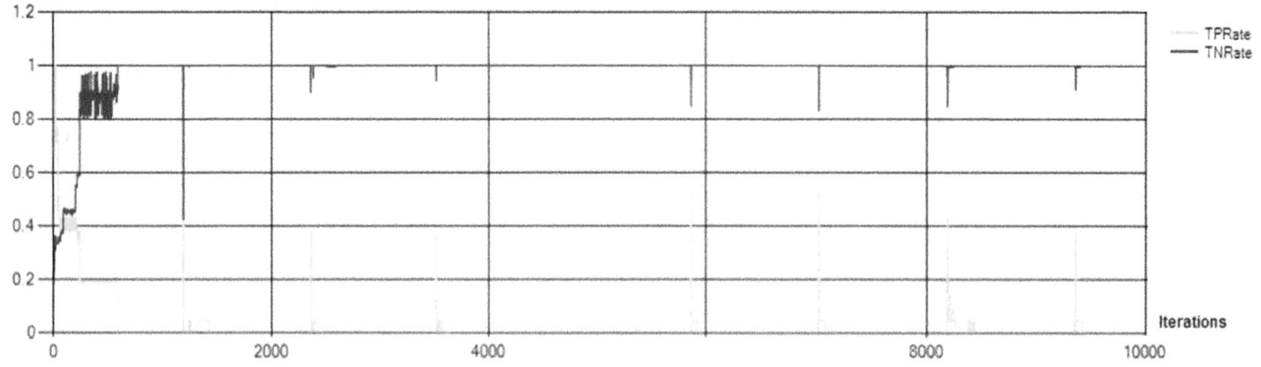

Figure 1. *Typical convergence process of XCS.*

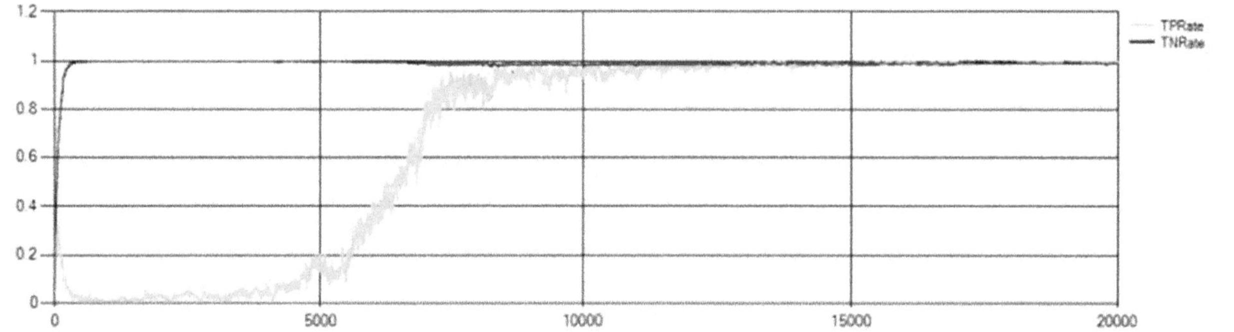

Figure 2. *Convergence process of the new method on dataset 1.*

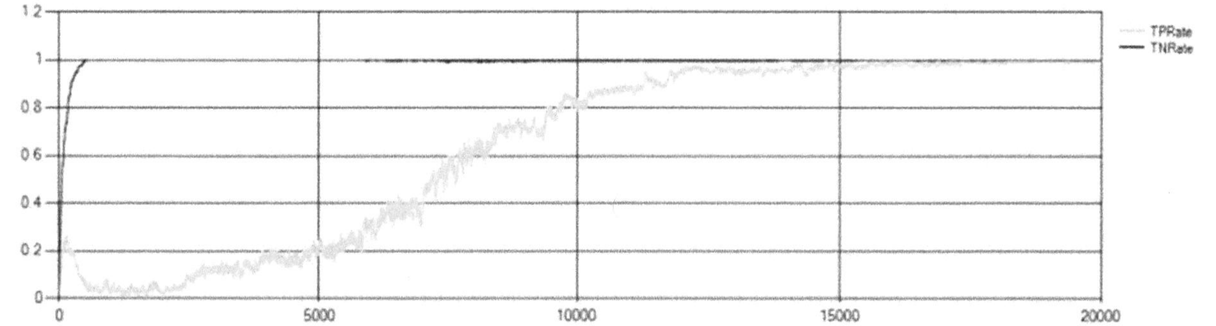

Figure 3. *Convergence process of the new method on dataset 2.*

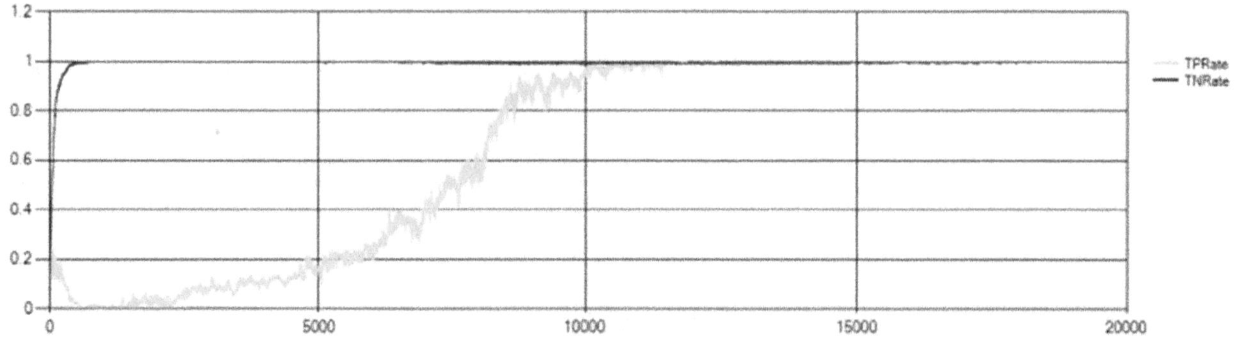

Figure 4. *Convergence process of the new method on dataset 3.*

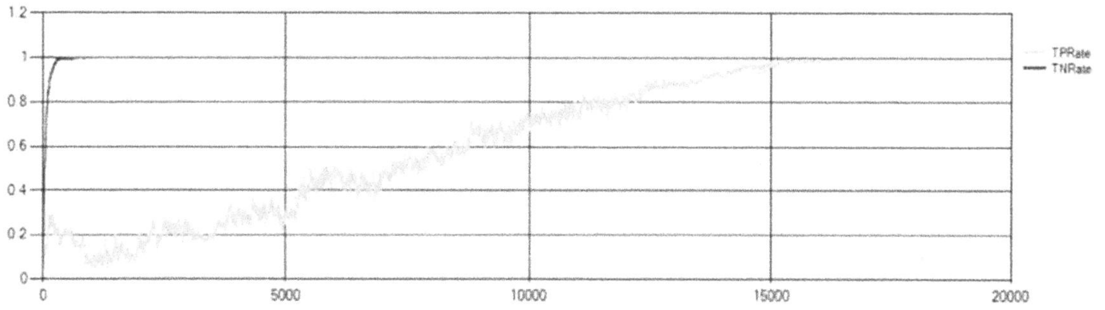

Figure 5. *Convergence process of the new method on dataset 4.*

Table 4. *Minor Grabber results.*

Dataset	TP	TN	Classification Accuracy
Dataset1	0.9960	0.9851	0.9845
Dataset2	1	0.9985	0.9984
Dataset3	0.9833	0.9982	0.9986
Dataset4	1	0.9998	0.9999

Figures 2-5 present the convergence of Minor Grabber on different skewed data sets and Table 4 compares the performance of Minor Grabber with that of XCS. As can be seen in these results, Minor Grabber not only has achieved higher classification accuracies than XCS in all data sets but also has been able to learn the minority class (positive) samples as well. As presented in figures 3-6 the true positive rate improves in all data sets as the algorithm proceeds and finally converges to 1. Although this convergence happens later for the minor class, the important fact is that Minor Grabber can eventually find the correct prediction model while the XCS is unable to do that.

5. Conclusion

In this paper, we presented Minor Grabber, an XCS-based learning classifier system improved by two techniques called adaptive resampling and sample weighting. These two methods help the algorithm to wisely choose samples for the training sets used in each learning cycle. Using this approach the algorithm can adaptively focus on classes that have not been learnt yet, and experiment suitable training instances to improve the model for those classes. The algorithm has been tested against different skewed data sets with imbalanced ratios from 11 to 80, and has shown a quite good performance in learning prediction models for those data sets.

References

[1] A. Bria, N. karssemeijer and F. Tortorella, "Learning from unbalanced data: A cascade-based approach for detecting clustered microcalcifications," *Medical image analysis,* 2014.

[2] Xue, Jing-Hao and P. Hall, "Why Does Rebalancing Class-unbalanced Data Improve AUC for Linear Discriminant Analysis," *Pattern Analysis and Machine Intelligence,IEEE Transactions on* , pp. 1109-1112, 2015.

[3] M. Butz, "Learning classifier systems," in *Springer Handbook of Computational Intelligence*, Berlin , Springer , 2015, pp. 961-981.

[4] P. L. Lanzi, "Learning classifier systems: a gentle introduction," in *companion on Genetic and evolutionary computation companion*, 2014.

[5] L. Bull, "A brief history of learning classifier systems: from CS-1 to XCS and its variants," *Evolutionary Intelligence,* 2015.

[6] N. CHAWLA, K. Bowyer, L. Hall and W. Kegelmeye, "SMOTE: Synthetic minority over-sampling technique," *Journal of Artificial Intelligence Research,* vol. 15, pp. 321-357, 2002.

[7] N. Japcowicz and S. Stephen, "The Class Imbalance Problem:A Systematic Study," *Intelligent Data Analisis,* 2002.

[8] Wang, Shuo, L. Leandro, Minku and Xin Ya, "Resampling-Based Ensemble Methods for Online Class Imbalance Learning," *Knowledge and Data Engineering, IEEE Transactions on,* pp. 1356-1368, 2015.

[9] A. Orriols-Puig, "Facetwise Analysis of Learning Classifier Systems in Imbalanced Domains," Ramon Liull University, 2006.

[10] A. Orriols-Puig and E. Bernad´o-Mansilla, "Evolutionary rule-based systems for imbalanced datasets," *Soft Computing Journal,* vol. 13, no. 3, pp. 213-225, 2009.

[11] A. Orriols-Puig and E. Bernad´o-Mansilla, "Bounding XCS parameters for unbalanced datasets," in *Genetic and Evolutionary Computation Conference*, 2006.

[12] A. Orriols-Puig and E. Bernad´o-Mansilla, "The Class Imbalance Problem in Learning Classifier Systems:A Preliminary Study," in *Genetic and Evolutionary Computation Conference*, 2005.

[13] K. Deb, A. Pratap , S. Agarwal and T. Meyarivan, "A fast and elitist multiobjective genetic algorithm: NSGA-II.," *Evolutionary Computation,* vol. 6, no. 2, pp. 182-197, 2002.

[14] M. Erickson, A. Mayer and J. Horn, "Multi-objective optimal design of groundwater remediation systems: application of the niched Pareto genetic algorithm (NPGA)," *Advances in Water Resources,* vol. 25, no. 1, pp. 51-65, 2002.

[15] D. Corne, N. R. Jerram, J. D. Knowles and M. J. Oates, "Corne, David W., et al. "PESA-II: Region-based selection in evolutionary multiobjective optimization," in *Genetic and Evolutionary Computation Conference*, 2001.

21

Optimization of closed-loop supply chain problem for calculation logistics cost accounting

Lee Jeongeun, Rhee Kyonggu

Department of Accounting, Dongeui University, Busan, Korea

Email address:
leeje@deu.ac.kr (Lee J.), rhee@deu.ac.kr (Rhee K.)

Abstract: This paper aims to build closed loop supply chain model (CLSCM) and propose a multi-objective genetic algorithm. This paper designs the method of calculation for a solution using optimization algorithms with the priority-based genetic algorithm (priGA), and Adaptive Weight Approach (AWA).In this paper, we present a multi-objective closed loop supply chain model in integrated logistics system. We formulated a mathematical model with two objectives functions: (1) minimize transportation cost, open cost, inventory cost, purchase cost, disposal cost and saving cost of integrated facilities of CLSCM, (2) minimize the delivery time tardiness in all periods. Finally, a simulation is investigated to demonstrate the applicability of the proposed multi-objective closed loop supply chain model (CLSCM) and solution approaches.

Keywords: Closed-Loop Supply Chain, Logistics Cost Accounting, Genetic Algorithm

1. Introduction

Reverse Logistics, which is the logistics activity covering over the produce recovery, recycling, waste disposal and etc., has received considerable attention due to the following two reasons. First, the seriousness of environmental problem has been embossed in corporate logistics activity and the environmental logistics problem has been international issue by Government Resolutions and etc. Second, the resources have been exhausted all over the world.

In the recent years due to the ever-increasing development of the competitive environment, the researchers have paid attention to the supply chain network problem. This problem has a key importance role in long-term decisions/performance and requires to be optimized for efficiency of the whole supply chain [1].

In the following, we introduce research papers associated with closed-loop supply chain model (CLSCM).

Ma and Wang [2] consider a closed-loop supply chain (CLSC) with product recovery, which is composed of one manufacturer and one retailer. The retailer is in charge of recollecting and the manufacturer is responsible for product recovery. The system can be regarded as a coupling dynamics of the forward and reverse supply chain.

Chuang et al. [3] study closed-loop supply chain models for a high-tech product which is featured with a short life-cycle and volatile demand. They focus on the manufacturer's choice of three alternative reverse channel structures (i.e., manufacturer collecting, retailer collecting, and third-party firm collecting) for collecting the used product from consumers for remanufacturing: (1) the manufacturer collects the used product directly; (2) the retailer collects the used product for the manufacturer; and (3) the manufacturer sub contracts the used product collection to a third-party firm.

Lee et al. [4] is also proposed multi-objective closed-loop supply chain model. However, they only consider a limited logistics cost (e.g., transportation cost and open cost). We propose the improved model considering minimization of total cost (e.g., transportation cost, open cost, inventory cost, purchase cost, disposal cost and saving cost of integrated facilities) and minimization of total delivery tardiness.

This paper is organized as follows: in Section 2, the mathematical model of the multi-objective reverse logistics network is introduced; in Section 3, the priority-based encoding method and adaptive weight approach (AWA) are explained in order to solve this problem; in Section 4, numerical experiments are presented to demonstrate the efficiency of the proposed method; finally, in Section 5, concluding remarks are outlined.

2. Problem Definition

2.1. Mathematical Model of CLSC

The model is a multi-objective problem considered the multi echelon, multi period, and multi product in closed-loop supply chain. We formulated the CLSCM as a multi-objective 0-1 mixed integer linear programming model.

The following assumptions are made in the development of the model:

A1. Only one product is treated in closed loop supply chain model.

A2. The inventory factor is existed over finite planning horizons.

A3. The requirement by manufacturer and the quantity of collected products is known in advanced.

A4. The maximum capacities about echelons are known.

A5. All of inventory holding costs of processing centers are same.

A6. In the case of transportation from processing center to manufacturer, the lot size is 100 and the lead time is not considered.

The parameters, decision variables, objective functions, and restrictions in this closed-loop supply chain model are as follows.

(1) Indices

i index of manufacturer (i=1,2,…, I)
j index of distribution center (j=1,2,…, J)
k index of retailer (k=1,2,…, K)
l index of customer (l=1,2,…, L)
$k`$ index for returning center ($k`$=1,2,…, $K`$)
m index of processing center (m=1,2,…, M)
t index of time period (t=1,2,…, T)

(2) Parameters

I number of manufacturers
J number of distribution centers
K number of retailers
L number of customers
$K`$ number of returning centers
M number of processing centers
N disposal center
S supplier
T planning horizons
a_i capacity of manufacturer i
b_j capacity of distribution center j
u capacity of retailer k
$u_{k`}$ capacity of returning center $k`$
u_m capacity of processing center m
d_i demand of manufacturer i
c^1_{ij} unit cost of transportation from manufacturer i to distribution center j
c^2_{jk} unit cost of transportation from distribution center j to retailer k
c^3_{kl} unit cost of transportation from retailer k to customer l
$c^4_{lk`}$ unit cost of transportation from customer $l$ to returning center $k`$
$c^5_{k`m}$ unit cost of transportation from returning center $k`$ to processing center m
c^6_{Mn} unit cost of transportation from processing center m to disposal N
c^7_{mi} unit cost of transportation from processing center m to manufacturer i
c^8_{Si} unit cost of transportation from supplier S to manufacturer i
c^O_j open cost of distribution center j
c^O_k open cost of retailer k
$c^O_{k`}$ open cost of returning center k`
c^H_j unit holding cost of inventory per period at distribution center j
c^H_k unit holding cost of inventory per period at retailer k
$c^H_{k`}$ unit holding cost of inventory per period at returning center $k`$
c^H_m unit holding cost of inventory per period at processing center m
r_N disposal rate
d_{ij} delivery time from returning center i to processing center j
d_{jM} delivery time from processing center j to manufacturer M
p_j processing time for reusable product in processing center j
t_E expected delivery time by customers

(3) Decision variables

$x^1_{ij}(t)$ amount shipped from manufacturer i to distribution center j in period t
$x^2_{jk}(t)$ amount shipped from distribution center j to retailer k in period t
$x^3_{kl}(t)$ amount shipped from retailer k to customer l in period t
$x^4_{lk`}(t)$ amount shipped from customer $l$ to returning center $k`$ in period t
$x^5_{k`m}(t)$ amount shipped from returning center $k`$ to processing center m in period t
$x^6_{mN}(t)$ amount shipped from processing center m to disposal N in period t
$x^7_{mi}(t)$ amount shipped from processing center m to manufacturer i in period t
$x^8_{Si}(t)$ amount shipped from supplier S to manufacturer i in period t
$y_j(t)$ inventory amount at distribution center j in period t
$y_k(t)$ inventory amount at retailer k in period t
$y_{k`}(t)$ inventory amount at returning center $k`$ in period t
$y_m(t)$ inventory amount at processing center m in period t

2.2. Mathematical Formulation

The first objective function, f_1 consists of the total cost.

$$\text{Minimize} \quad \{f_1,f_2\} \tag{1}$$

Min

$$f_1 = \text{TC} + \text{OC} + \text{IC} + \text{PC} + \text{RTC} + \text{ROC} + \text{RIC} + \text{DC} - \text{SC} \quad (1)^a$$

The cost components in the objective function F_1 can be calculated by using the following relations:

Forward logistics transportation costs

$$\mathrm{TC} = \left[\sum_{i=1}^{I}\sum_{j=1}^{J} c_{ij}^{1} x_{ij}^{1}(t) + \sum_{j=1}^{J}\sum_{k=1}^{K} c_{jk}^{2} x_{jk}^{2}(t) + \sum_{k=1}^{K}\sum_{l=1}^{L} c_{kl}^{3} x_{kl}^{3}(t) \right]$$

Forward logistics open costs

$$\mathrm{OC} = \sum_{j=1}^{J} c_{j}^{\mathrm{O}} z_{j}(t) + \sum_{k=1}^{K} c_{k}^{\mathrm{O}} z_{k}(t)$$

Forward logistics inventory costs

$$\mathrm{IC} = \sum_{j=1}^{J}\sum_{k=1}^{K} c_{j}^{\mathrm{H}} y_{j}(t) + \sum_{k=1}^{K}\sum_{l=1}^{L} c_{k}^{\mathrm{H}} y_{k}(t)$$

Forward logistics purchase costs

$$\mathrm{PC} = \sum_{i=1}^{I} c_{Si}^{8} x_{Si}^{8}(t)$$

Reverse logistics transportation costs

$$\mathrm{RTC} = \sum_{l=1}^{L}\sum_{k`=1}^{K`} c_{lk`}^{4} x_{lk`}^{4}(t) + \sum_{k`=1}^{K`}\sum_{m=1}^{M} c_{k`m}^{5} x_{k`m}^{5}(t) + \sum_{m=1}^{M}\sum_{i=1}^{I} c_{mi}^{7} x_{mi}^{7}(t)$$

Reverse logistics open costs

$$\mathrm{ROC} = \sum_{k`=1}^{K`} c_{k`}^{O} z_{k`}(t)$$

Reverse logistics inventory costs

$$\mathrm{RIC} = \sum_{k`=1}^{K`}\sum_{m=1}^{M} c_{k`}^{\mathrm{H}} y_{k`}(t) + \sum_{m=1}^{M}\sum_{i=1}^{I} c_{m}^{\mathrm{H}} y_{m}(t)$$

Reverse logistics disposal costs

$$\mathrm{DC} = \sum_{m=1}^{M} c_{mN}^{6} x_{mN}^{6}(t)$$

Saving cost from integrating retailer/returning center

$$\mathrm{SC} = \sum_{k=1}^{K}\sum_{k`=1}^{K`} c_{k}^{\mathrm{O}} z_{k}(t) z_{k`}(t)$$

The second objective function, f_2 is total delivery tardiness.
min f_2

$$f_2 = \sum_{t=0}^{T}\left[\sum_{i=1}^{I}\sum_{j=1}^{J} d_{ij} x_{ij}(t) + \sum_{j=1}^{J} (d_{jM} + p_j) x_{jM}(t) \right] - t_E d_M(t) \qquad (1)^{\mathrm{b}}$$

Subject to
- open cost

$$1 - z_j(t-1) = z_j(t) \qquad \forall j \in J, t \in T \qquad (2)$$

$$1 - z_k(t-1) = z_k(t) \qquad \forall k \in K, t \in T \qquad (3)$$

- inventory costs

$$y_j(t) = x_{ij}^{1}(t) + x_{jk}^{2}(t-1) \qquad \forall j \in J, t \in T \qquad (4)$$

$$y_k(t) + y_{k`}(t) = x_{jk}^{2}(t) + x_{kl}^{3}(t-1) + x_{lk`}^{4}(t) + x_{k`m}^{5}(t-1) \quad \forall k \in K, k`\in K`, t \in T \qquad (5)$$

$$y_m(t) = x_{k`m}^{5}(t) + x_{mi}^{7}(t-1) - x_{mN}^{6}(t) \qquad \forall m \in M, t \in T \qquad (6)$$

- disposal costs

$$\sum_{m=1}^{M} x_{mN}^{6}(t) = \sum_{k`=1}^{K`}\sum_{m=1}^{M} x_{k`m}^{5}(t) r_N \qquad \forall t \in T \qquad (7)$$

- capacity constraints

$$\sum_{j=1}^{J} x_{ij}^{1}(t) \le a_i \qquad \forall i \in I, t \in T \qquad (8)$$

$$\sum_{k=1}^{K} x_{jk}^{2}(t) + y_j(t-1) \le b_j z_j(t) \qquad \forall j \in J, t \in T \qquad (9)$$

$$\sum_{l=1}^{L} x_{kl}^{3}(t) + y_k(t-1) + \sum_{m=1}^{M} x_{k`m}^{5}(t) + y_{k`}(t-1) \le u_k z_k(t) + u_{k`} z_{k`}(t) \quad \forall k \in K, k`\in K`, t \in T \qquad (10)$$

- demand constraints

$$x_{mi}^{7}(t) + x_{Si}^{8}(t) + x_{ij}^{1}(t) = d_i \qquad \forall t \in T \qquad (11)$$

$$\sum_{j=1}^{J} x_{jM}(t) \le d_M(t), \qquad \forall t \qquad (12)$$

- non-negativity constraints

$$x_{ij}^{1}(t), x_{jk}^{2}(t), x_{ij}^{3}(t), x_{lk`}^{4}(t), x_{k`m}^{5}(t), x_{mN}^{6}(t), x_{mi}^{7}(t), x_{Si}^{8}(t) \ge 0 \quad \forall i \in I, j \in J, k \in K, l \in L, m \in M, t \in T \qquad (13)$$

- binary constraints

$$z_j(t) = \{0,1\} \qquad \forall j \in J, t \in T \qquad (14)$$

$$z_k(t) = \{0,1\} \qquad \forall k \in K, t \in T \qquad (15)$$

$$z_{k`}(t) = \{0,1\} \qquad \forall k`\in K`, t \in T \qquad (16)$$

$$\sum_{i=1}^{I} x_{ij}(t) + y_j^{\mathrm{H}}(t-1) \le b_j z_j, \qquad \forall j,\ t \qquad (17)$$

$$y_j^{\mathrm{H}}(t-1) + \sum_{i=1}^{I} x_{ij}(t) - x_{jM}(t) = y_j^{\mathrm{H}}(t), \qquad \forall j, t \qquad (18)$$

$$x_{ij}(t),\ x_{jM}(t), y_j^{\mathrm{H}}(t) \ge 0, \ \forall i, j, t \qquad (19)$$

3. Optimization of the Closed-Loop Supply Chain with the Genetic Algorithm

3.1. Priority-Based Encoding Method

For a transportation problem, a chromosome consists of priorities of sources and depots to obtain transportation tree and its length is equal to total number of sources m and depots n, *i.e.* $m+n$. The transportation tree corresponding with a given chromosome is generated by sequential arc appending between sources and depots [5]. At each step, only one arc is added to tree selecting a source (depot) with the highest priority and connecting it to a depot (source) considering minimum cost [6].

3.2. Adaptive Weight Approach

While we consider multiobjective problem, a key issue is to determine the weight of each objective. Gen *et al.*[7] proposed an Adaptive Weight Approach (AWA) that utilizes some useful information from the current population to readjust weights for obtaining a search pressure toward a positive ideal point[8]. In this study, we are using the following objectives:

(1) Minimization of the total cost (c_T)

(2) Minimization of the delivery tardiness. (c_D)

$$\max \{f_1 = \frac{1}{f_1(v_k)} = \frac{1}{c_T}, f_2 = \frac{1}{f_2(v_k)} = \frac{1}{c_D}\} \quad (20)$$

For the solutions at each generation, z_q^{max} and z_q^{min} are the maximal and minimal values for the qth objective as defined by the following equations:

$$z_q^{max} = \max\{f_q(v_k),\ k = 1,2,\ \dots,\ popSize\},\ q = 1,2$$
$$z_q^{min} = \min\{f_q(v_k),\ k = 1,2,\ \dots,\ popSize\},\ q = 1,2 \quad (21)$$

The adaptive weights are calculated as

$$w_q = \frac{1}{z_q^{max} - z_q^{min}},\ q = 1,2 \quad (22)$$

The weighted-sum objective function for a given chromosome is then given by the following equation

$$eval(v_k) = \sum_{q=1}^{2} w_q (f_q(v_k) - z_q^{min}),\ k = 1,2,\dots,popSize \quad (23)$$

4. Simulation

In this section, multiobjective hybrid genetic algorithm and CPLEX software is used to compare the results of small-size problems. All the test problems are solved on a Pentium 4, 3.20GHz clock pulse with 1GB memory. The data in test problems were also randomly generated to provide realistic scenarios.The 3 test problems were combined, as shown in Table 1.

Table 1. *The size of test problems (Rhee et al. [9])*

Problem No.	Period	returning centers(I)	processing centers(J)	No. of constraints	No. of variables
1	4	5	3	264	120
2	4	10	6	852	404
3	4	20	15	2988	1452

We ran the procedure for 20 times for each problem considering following parameters:

Population size, *popSize*=100;

Maximum generations, *maxGen*=1000;

Crossover probability, p_C=0.7;

Mutation probability, p_M=0.3

4.1. Numerical Results

In this paper, we compared percentage gap of CPLEX, Priority-based encoding method with Adaptive Weight Approach (pri-awGA) and multiobjective hybrid genetic algorithm (mo-hGA).

In order to compare the non-dominated solutions of the two methods, the value of the second objective function (f_2) of each solution obtained by mo-hGA is insesrted into the model formulation as a new constraint.

$$\text{gap}(\%) = 100(\text{GA}f_1 - \text{CPLEX}f_1)/\ \text{CPLEX}f_1 \quad (24)$$

In table 2, we explain the simulation results for 3 test problems with 20 instances in each. We use the percentage gap between optimum solution and heuristic solutions, which are pri-awGA and mo-hGA. And we also compare CPLEX f_1 and GAs f_1 and Pareto solutions (f_1, f_2) at the same time.

Table 2. *The comparison of CPLEX, pri-awGA and mo-hGA with Optimality Gaps*

Problem No.	CPLEX	pri-awGA		mo-hGA		Optimalaty Gaps (%)			
						pri-awGA		mo-hGA	
	f1	f1	(f1, f2)	f1	(f1, f2)	f1	(f1, f2)	f1	(f1, f2)
1	201020	201020	(202600, 94500)	201020	(202600, 94500)	0.00	0.79	0.00	0.79
2	290866	290866	(296245, 1510500)	290866	(293205, 1405100)	0.00	1.85	0.00	0.80
3	643928	651655	665655, 326220)	651655	(651972, 326430)	1.20	3.37	1.20	1.25
Average						0.40	2.00	0.40	0.95

When the GAs f_1 are compared with respect to average gap over all 3 problems, the result are same CPLEX, pri-awGA and mo-hGA in problem 1 and 2. On the other hand, the average gap in pri-awGA and mo-hGA are 1.20% over CPLEX in problem 3.

When the Pareto solutions (f_1, f_2) are compared with respect to average gap over all 3 problems, it is seen that the mo-hGA exhibits the best performance with the average gap of 0.95%. While the average gap for pri-awGA is 2.00%, which is a small value.

The comparison is first done according to the computation time and it is seen that the computation time needed for mo-hGA is less than pri-awGA in all problems. Next, according to the number of Pareto solutions, both methods found the same number for problem 1, and they are slightly same for problem 2. But for problem 3, the number of Pareto solutions found by pri-awGA are less than that found by mo-hGA. Finally the improvement rate according to each time period are shown in the last column of Table 3. When comparing number of Pareto solutions, the results are same in problem 1 and 2. On the other hand, the result using mo-hGA is better in problem 3.

Table 3. *The experimental results of pri-awGA and mo-hGA*

No.	Time period	Computational time[sec]			No. of Pareto solutions [S_j]		
		pri-awGA	mo-hGA	Improvement Rate(%)	pri-awGA	mo-hGA	Improvement Rate(%)
1	*t*=1	4,537	3,546	21.84	3	3	0.00
	t=2				5	5	0.00
	t=3				2	2	0.00
	t=4				4	4	0.00
2	*t*=1	4,596	3,596	21.76	5	6	20.00
	t=2				7	7	16.67
	t=3				6	8	33.33
	t=4				9	8	-11.11
3	*t*=1	4,646	3,656	21.31	7	13	85.71
	t=2				6	9	50.00
	t=3				6	10	66.67
	t=4				8	9	12.50

Fig. 1~3 represents Pareto solutions obtained from CPLEX, pri-awGA and mo-hGA for test problems. In this figure, the corresponding solutions on CPLEX and pri-awGA and mo-hGA Pareto optimal solutions with the same f_2 values are labeled with the same letters.

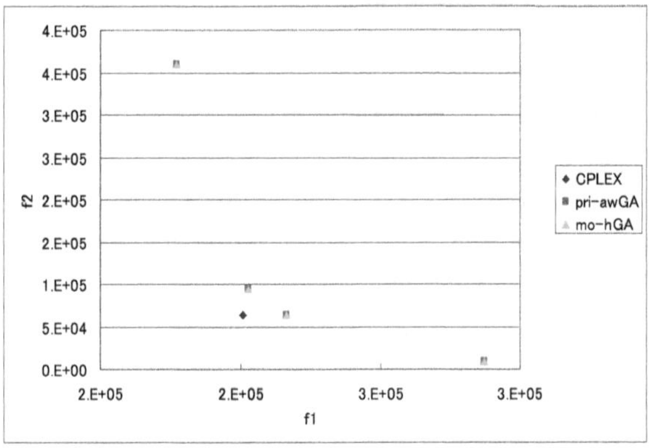

Figure 1. *Pareto solutions (Problem 1)*

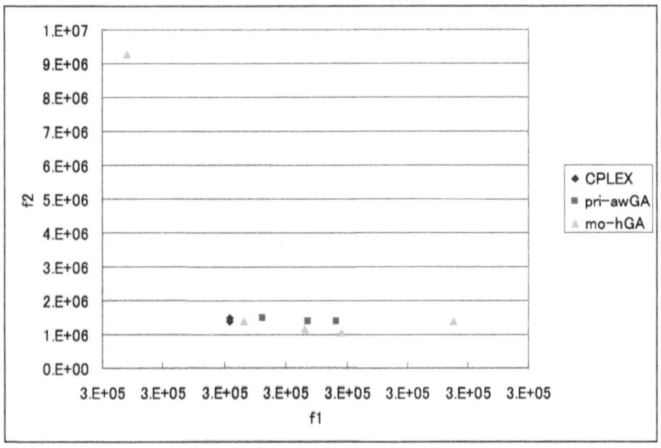

Figure 2. *Pareto solutions (Problem 2)*

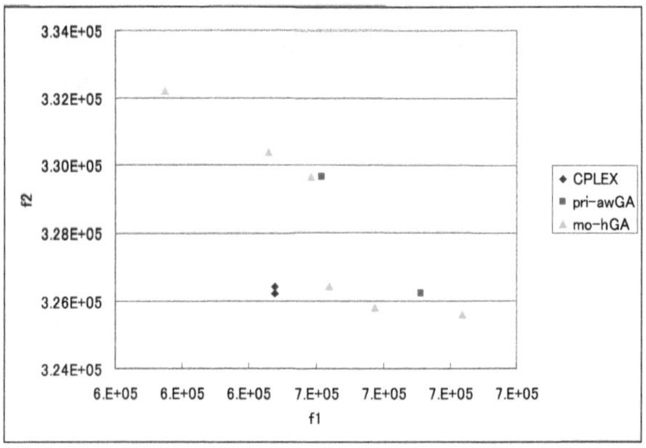

Figure 3. *Pareto solutions (Problem 3)*

5. Conclusion

In this paper, we presented 0-1 mixed-integer linear programming model for multi-objective optimization of CLSCM and a genetic algorithm approach.

We propose the improved model considering minimization of total cost (e.g., transportation cost, open cost, inventory cost, purchase cost, disposal cost and saving cost of integrated facilities) and minimization of total delivery tardiness.

Finally, through the comparison of percentage gap of CPLEX, Adaptive Weight Approach (pri-awGA) and multi-objective hybrid genetic algorithm (mo-hGA), the effectiveness of the proposed method was demonstrated.

References

[1] Majid Ramezani, Ali Mohammad Kimiagari, Behrooz Karimi, "Closed-loop supply chain network design: A financial approach", Applied Mathematical Modelling, Vol. 38, No. 15–16, 2014, pp. 4099-4119.

[2] Junhai Ma, Hongwu Wang, "Complexity analysis of dynamic noncooperative game models for closed-loop supply chain with product recovery", Applied Mathematical Modelling, Vol. 38, No. 23, 2014, pp. 5562–5572.

[3] Chia-Hung Chuang, CharlesX.Wang , YabingZhao, "Closed-loop supply chain models for a high-tech product under alternative reverse channel and collection cost structure"s, International Journal of Production Economics, Vol. 156, 2014, pp. 108-123.

[4] Lee, J. E. Chung, K. Y., Lee, K. D. and Gen, M., "A multi-objective hybrid genetic algorithm to minimize the total cost and delivery tardiness in a reverse logistics", Multimedia Tools and Applications, published online, 03 August 2013.

[5] Syarilf, A. and Gen, M., "Double Spanning Tree-based Genetic algorithm For Two Stage Transportation Problem", International Journal of Knowledge-Based Intelligent Engineering System, Vol. 7, No. 4, 2003, pp. 388-389.

[6] Gen, M. and Cheng, R., Genetic Algorithms and Engineering Optimization, John Wiley and Sons, New York, 2000.

[7] Gen, M., Cheng, R. and Lin, L., Network Models and Optimization: Multiobjective Genetic Algorithm Approach, Springer, 2008.

[8] Altiparmak, F., Gen, M., Lin, L. and Paksoy, T., "A genetic algorithm approach for multi-objective optimization of supply chain networks", Computers & Industrial Engineering, Vol. 51, No. 1, 2006, pp. 197-216.

[9] Rhee, K. G., Lee, J. E. and Lee, K. D., "Multiobjective Reverse Logistics Model considering Inventory Systems with Backordering", The Korean Academic Association of Business Administration, Vol. 25, No. 1, 2012, pp. 613~625.

The magnetic induction communications for the wireless underground sensor networks

Farzam Saeednia[1, *], Shapour Khorshidi[2], Mohssen Masoumi[3]

[1]Department Of Electrical Engineering, Kazerun Branch, Islamic Azad University, Kazerun, Iran
[2]Air-Sea Science and Technology Academic Complex, Shiraz, Iran
[3]Department Of Electrical Engineering, Jahrom Branch, Islamic Azad University, Jahrom, Iran

Email address:
Farzam_2958@yahoo.com (F. Saeednia),khorshidy@yahoo.com(S. Khorshidi), maesoumi@jia.ac.ir (M. Masoumi)

Abstract: The most important difference between the wireless underground sensor networks (WUSNs) andthe wireless ground sensor networksis the propagation environment of the signal .In fact, the underground environments consist of soil, rock and water instead of the air. The challenging reasons of these environments to propagate the wireless signal via the Electro Magnetic (EM) 2waves are considered as: the high path loss, channel dynamic conditions and the high size of antenna. At the present study, the details of Bit Error Rate (BER) 3 for 2PSK modulation, path loss and the bandwidth of the Magnetic Induction (MI) 4Systems and Electro Magnetic (EM) Waveguide in the underground environment areevaluated. Meanwhile, a new method isintroduced via MI waveguide that provided the constant conditions of channel by the small inductive coils. At the end of this study,itisfounded that the transmission range in MI waveguide system would be raised and the path loss in that system would be declined severely.

Keywords: Channel Modulation, MI Waveguide Method, Underground Communications, Wireless Sensor Networks, Magnetic Induction

1. Introduction

The Wireless Underground Sensor Networks (WUSNs) have the wireless sensors that are buried underground. WUSNs have so many applications such as the coverage, easy to use, appropriate data, reliability and the cover density. The other applications are the control of the soil conditions, earthquake, landslides forecast, the underground substructures control, the landscapes management and security [1, 2].

It can be mentionedthat the underground propagation environment consists of soil, rock and water instead of the air that confront us with three challenges if it is applied for the wireless communications via the Electro-Magnetic (EM) Waves: The high path loss, channel dynamic conditions, and Antenna size [3].

Akyilidizet.al,[2]evaluated the wireless communications networks installed in the underground and also the propagation via electromagneticwaves. Meanwhile,years later, Zhi Sun and Akyilidiz [9] compared the traditional methods and MI systems of the wireless underground communications.At the end of this study, the wireless underground communications were evaluated by a new method called “MI Waveguide” [9].

In the second part, the theoretical structure of a new methodcalled MI Waveguide was presented that used some inductive coil.The third section of simulation considered the theory of second section and the comparison of communication methods.

2. The MI Waveguide Characteristics

As the underground route is limited in many WUSN applications such as the control of underground structure,the sensors must be placed in the earth depths. The Magnetic Induction (MI) is a physical layer method for WUSN in high depths of soil[4]. Although the magnetic permeability of the soil, water and air is same, the MI channel conditions will be remained the same because the magnetic fields create slight changes in the loss of wave's strengthin the soil and water to the air. Furthermore, the transmission and reception of MI waveguide are conducted by some small wire cores called as induction coils (there is no multipath disappearance in MI waveguide) due to the low resistance of the irradiation in the coil inductance [2, 5, 6].

For MI Waveguide Method,some multiple factors were applied such as the soil properties, soil size, number of rotations in each ring of coil, coil resistance in the operational frequency [6].Our analyses indicate that MI Typical Systems has a higher transmission range and lesser bandwidth than EM waveguides systems. But neither MI typical system nor EM waveguide system is able to provide enough communication range for the practical applications of WUSN.

3. The MI Waveguide for the Underground Communications

The propagation characteristics of Electro Magnetic (EM) waves in the underground environment (soil, water, rock) were presented in fig.3. The analyses indicate that the path loss is much higher than the ground cases and its reason is the absorption in the elements of the underground environment. The success in the communications dependson the combination of operational frequency and soil. Thus, as the operational frequency decreases, the path loss is decreased too but we need a larger antenna [3]. One suggested solution is to apply some antenna with 0.3m length to receive 300 MHz signals. Meanwhile, the signal transmission rangeof these antennas is about 4 meter. Recently, the Magnetic Induction method has been used as a new physical layer method for the wireless communications but it has disadvantages as the high path loss and Low bandwidth.MI can be considered as an alternative communication method in Bluetooth. For the first time, MI was introduced in wireless underground communications. According to the previous studies, MI transmission isn't influenced by the soil type, combinations, concentration or the moisture [7].

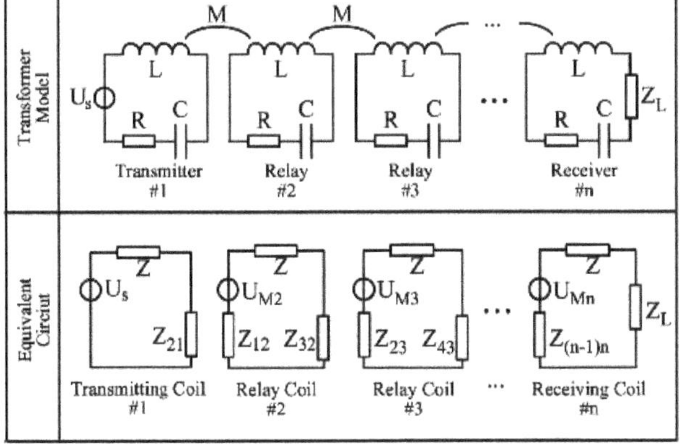

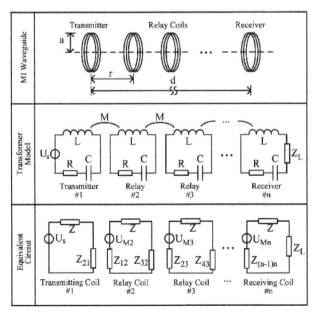

Fig. 1. Communication Channels Model for MI Waveguide.

Although the channel is constant and the transmission range of the MI typical system is more than EM, its transmission range is still short for the operational applications. One suggested solution is to apply several simple relay inductioncoilswithout any energetic resourceandprocessing machine between the receiver and transmitter to conduct MI waves by EM Waves method. The procedure is that at first, the sinusoidal current in the transmitter'scoil loop induces a sinusoidal current in the primary relay induction coil point .Then this sinusoidal current in the coil loop of the primary relay induces another sinusoidal current in the secondary loop and this procedure continues until to reach the receiver. As it is shown in the first row in fig.1, a typical structure of n-2 coil loops has been placed between the axis of receiver and transmitter. Thus, n,the total number of coil loop;r,the distance between the adjacentcoil loops/ringsand d is the distance between the receiver and transmitter. D=(n-1)r ; a is the radius of coil loops. According to the second row in fig.1, it can be said that each relay coil consists of the receiver and transmitter's coil loop that is loaded via a capacitor, C. In order to transmit the magnetic signals, an appropriate design should be presented for the capacitor value and the effective value of the resonant coil loop to create the mutual induction among each pair of coil loop that depends on the proximity of the loops. In the underground communications, we considered the distance between two relay loops as 5meters. But that distance was higher than the maximum of the communication range in EM waves system. Despite this, the application of relay loop instead of the underground devices in MI system reduces the costs. In the next part, an appropriate distance is obtained by analyzing the distance of MI waveguide relay loop. The distance of loops in comparison with the relay loop 0.15m is high enough and it causes that the coils only have a mutual self-induction with their neighbors.

3.1. System Modeling

For modeling the MI waveguide, all loops must have the same parameters (resistance, mutual inductance and self-inductance). M is the mutual inductance between the adjacent coils, U_a is the voltage of transmitter battery, L, the self-inductance of the coils, R is the coil resistance, C is the loaded capacitors in each coil and Z_L is the impedance of the load in the receiver .The equivalent circuit of the multistep transformer shown in the third row in fig.1 is as follow:

$$Z = R + j\omega L + \frac{1}{j\omega C}$$

$$Z_{i(i-1)} = \frac{\omega^2 M^2}{Z + Z_{(i+1)i}} \left(i = 2,3, \ldots, n-1 \text{ and } Z_{n(n-1)} = Z_L\right)$$

$$Z_{(i-1)i} = \frac{\omega^2 M^2}{Z + Z_{(i-2)(i-1)}} \left(i = 3,4, \ldots . n \text{ and } Z_{12} = \frac{\omega^2 M^2}{Z} \right)$$

$$U_{Mi} = -j\omega M \frac{U_{M(i-1)}}{Z + Z_{(i-2)(i-1)}} \left(i = 2,3, \ldots . n \text{ and } U_{M1} = U_s\right) \quad (1)$$

whereas $Z_i(i-1)$ is the effect of ith coil on $(i-1)^{th}$ loop andvice versa. Then the received power in receiver is calculated as:

$$P_r = Re\left\{\frac{Z_L . U_{Mn}^2}{\left(Z_{(n-1)n}+Z+Z_L\right)^2}\right\} \quad (2)$$

3.2. System Optimization

If the coil loops are resonated, U_{Mn}value as the induced voltage in the receiver will be reached to its maximum value that makes the received power to reach to its maximum on the basis of equ.1.Therefore, we should design a capacitor to prevent from reducing the actual value of received power severely because of self-induction in the coil loops $(jwL + \left(\frac{1}{jwL}\right) = 0$

By the self-induction in equ.7, the capacitor value is calculated as:

$$C = \frac{2}{\omega^2 N^2 \mu\pi a} \quad (3)$$

When the coil loops are resonated,the received power, U_{Mn} can be extended as:

$$U_{Mn} = U_s * -\frac{j\omega M}{R} * -\frac{j\omega M}{R+\frac{\omega^2 M^2}{R}} * -\frac{j\omega M}{R+\frac{\omega^2 M^2}{R+\frac{\omega^2 M^2}{R}}} \ldots\ldots$$

$$= U_s * (j)^{n-1} * \frac{1}{x_1} * \frac{1}{x_2} * \ldots\ldots\frac{1}{x_{n-1}} \quad (4)$$

According to the above-mentioned equations, it can be said that the multiplying operation, $x_1, x_2, x_3, \ldots, x_{n-1}$is n-1 degree from $x_1 = R/\omega M$ written as $\xi\left(\left(\frac{R}{wM}\right), n-1\right)$, the following equation is :

$$\zeta\left(\frac{R}{\omega M}, n-1\right) = b_{n-1}\left(\frac{R}{\omega M}\right)^{n-1} + b_{n-2}\left(\frac{R}{\omega M}\right)^{n-2} + \cdots + b_2\left(\frac{R}{\omega M}\right)^2 + b_1\left(\frac{R}{\omega M}\right) + b_0 \quad (5)$$

Whereas, $\{b_i, i = 1,2,\ldots,n-1\}$ are the polynomial coefficients that aren't influenced by the parameter for an special and constant n. Since the coil loop has been resonant, it causes that the load impedance is matched with the pure strength. So, the load impedance is regarded as $Z_L = \overline{Z_{(n-1)n} + R}$. Finally,in MI waveguide if the receiver is d meter away from the transmitter and there is some loops with n-2 relay coil between them,the received power will be written as:

$$P_r(d) = \frac{1}{4(Z_{(n-1)n}+R)} \cdot \frac{U_s^2}{\zeta^2\left(\frac{R}{\omega M}, n-1\right)} \quad (6)$$

Whereas, d is the transmission range, d= (n-1) r. Like MI typical system, the transmitted and received powers in MI system are reduced simultaneously as the transmission distanceincreased. Thus, MI waveguide loss, L_{MIG} is defined as:

$$L_{MIG}(d) = -10\log\frac{P_r(d)}{P_t(r_0)}$$

$$\cong 10\log\left(\frac{4(Z_{(n-1)n}+R)}{R} + 20\log\zeta\left(\frac{R}{\omega M}, n-1\right)\right)$$

$$= 10\log 4\left[1 + \frac{1}{\left(\frac{R}{\omega M}\right)^2 + \frac{1}{1+\frac{1}{\left(\frac{R}{\omega M}\right)^2 + \frac{1}{1+\cdots}}}}\right]$$

$$+20\log\left[b_{n-1}\left(\frac{R}{\omega M}\right)^{n-1} + \cdots + b_1\left(\frac{R}{\omega M}\right) + b_0\right] \quad (7)$$

Whereas, $P_t(r_D)$ isdefinedas the transmission power when the transmitter is very close to the receiver and there is no induction coil.On the basis of equ.7, the path loss in MI waveguide system is a function from $R/\omega M$. Meanwhile, $\xi\left(\left(\frac{R}{wM}\right), n-1\right)$ is a polynomials that has a significant effect on the path loss. Thus, the path loss is a monotonic function with the increased performance from R/ωM. Thus, in order to reduce the path loss, R/ωM must be reduced to the minimum value. By the wire resistance, R and the mutual inductance, M in equ.4 and equ.6 [4],R/ωM is expressed as [9]:

$$\frac{R}{\omega M} = \frac{4R_0}{\omega N\mu\pi} \cdot \left(\frac{r}{a}\right)^3 \quad (8)$$

Note that, the relay distance, r is 1/ (n-1) of the total transmission range, d.

By this method, the effect of Cubic functionfor the path loss can be decreased. With regard to this scheme, it is possible to decrease the path loss by considering the following items:

- The decrease of relay distance to the coil radius, r/a.

-The increase of operational frequency, ω and the number of loops in the coil, N.

- The decrease of wire resistance, R_D

-But there are some other factors to minimize the path loss (the relay distance to radius). In order to facilitate the deployment of coils, it is expected to have a decrease in the total transmission range. In this section, in order to keep the advantages of the above case on the underground EM waveguide system, the relay distance is restricted to the minimum value, 4 m to have the maximum release in the transmission range. With regard to the coil radius, 0.15 meters, the relay distance to coil radius is very high.

-There are other factors included in to this law and there isn't possibleto increase the operational frequency and the number of rotations in the coil loop. Thus, these two parameters can be restricted by equ.3. The capacitors with loads in each resonant coil should be more than 10PF.

Furthermore, the decrease of coil resistance can reduce the total path loss. In order to obtain the practical value of the resonant capacitors in each resonant coil, it isn't possible to maximize N and ω. Furthermore, very high operational frequency and the high number of coil rotations causes the severe operation arising from Parasitic Capacity[22].In this section, the operational frequency is 10 MHz,the number of rotations is 5 for each coil and the capacitor value is 35PF.

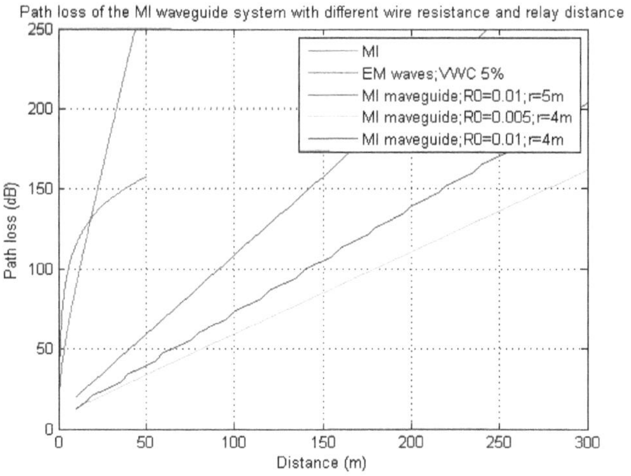

Fig. 2. the comparison of the path loss in MI waveguide with EM,MI wave systems.

Although the decrease of coil resistance can reduces the path loss, two problems may occur: 1) in order to decrease the coil resistance, the wire diameter must be raised. It causes the costs increase and the loop becomesheavier. 2) The decrease of coil resistance causes some fluctuations in the received signal that make problems in receiving the signal in the receiver. In this study, the coil was made of copper with 0.45mm diameter. With regard to the AWG standard[8], the resistance of unit length, $R_D$is 0.01$\frac{\Omega}{m}$.

3.3. Numerical Analysis

3.3.1. Path Loss

The path loss in the MI waveguide system in Equ.7 were evaluated viaMATLAB software. The results were shown in fig.2. In order to have a better comparison, the path loss of EM waves system with the operational frequency, 300MH in the soil with VWC, 0.5 and the path loss of typical MI system with the operational frequency, 10MHz were drawn. According to the mentioned discussions in the fourth section, MI system operation can't influence on the soil properties. The soil environment has the permeability as the air ($4\pi * 10^{-7} H/m$). So in evaluating MI waveguide, there is no need to consider the environmental parameters. Except the evaluation of the effects of special parameters , all available loops in the transmitter , receiver and relay points have some default values: radius, a=0.15m and the number of rotationsin system , N=5.The resistance of unit length for the natural coil and the low resistance coils are R0=0.01Ω/m and R0=0.005Ω/m respectively. The operational frequency is set on 10MHz. The relay distance, r is also 5m.The total number of coil loops, n is determined by the transmission distance, where d= (n-1)r. The path loss of MI waveguide system, dB with the different transmission distances, d, the different relay distance, r and different coil resistance, R_D have been shown in fig.2. It can be found that MI waveguide system has a lower path loss in 100 dB and even with the transmission distance, 250m to EM magnetic and MI typical systems. But its path loss increases in more than 100 dB with the distance, 5 m. Furthermore, the path loss can be obtained via decreasing the relay distances and the coil resistance.

3.3.2. Bit Error Rate

The BER and MI waveguide characteristics were evaluated in fig.7. The analyses of third section with 2PSK modulation were shown as the Scheme Modulation .Two noise levels were considered which the noise moderatelevel, P_n was regarded in low parasite scenario, -103dBmwhile in high noise scenario, P_n is -83 dBm. The transmission power value,P_t is also set on 10 dBm. In fig.7, BER in MI waveguide system has been shown as a function of transmission distance, d with the different relay distances, r and different wire resistance, R_D.In fact, EM waveguide system and MI typical system has been drawn for comparison. by comparing the low transmission range of two other methods (lower than 10m) , it can be said that even in high parasite scenarios , the transmission range of wave is about 250m.. It means that in comparison with two other systems, the transmission range in MI waveguide system will be raised for more than 25 times.In compliance with the analyses in the path loss, the transmission range of MI waveguide can be increased by decreasing the relay distance and resistance of the coil.

3.3.3. Bandwidth

Assuming that there is only one frequency in the transmission signals, thepath loss in high levels and in the transmission range of MI waveguide system is calculated. According to this central frequency, all coils can be resonated.But if there is any kind of deployment from the central frequency, the resonance status of each coil will be disappeared. So, it is necessary to analyze the band width in MI waveguide system. In fig.2, the frequency response of MI waveguide system was shown with different relay distances, r and different wire resistance, R_D. The number of relay coilwas shown by constant 7.The results indicate that when the operational frequency is 10MHz, the band width 3dB in MI waveguide system will be placed in a same range as MI typical system that is about 1 kHz to 2 kHz. Although the lower coil resistance can decrease the path loss in the central frequency, thefluctuations of the frequency response is such a serious problem that may make some problems in the transferring the power to the receiver. The band width can be increased as the relay distance reduces. But for a special transmission range, it can be said that the reduction of relay distance means that we need more relay loops. Two possible operational parameters are as follow:

1. The relay distance , r=5m and the resistance of unit length, R_D,R_D=0.01Ω/m that make the system conductor in operation in 10KHz frequency ,the radius, 250m and the band width,1KHz.
2. The relay distance , r=4m and the resistance of unit

length, R_D,R_D=0.01Ω/m that make the system conductor in operation in 10KHz frequency,the radius, 400m and the band width,2 KHz.

3.3.4. The Deployment Effect

It must be mentioned that the high operation of MI waveguide system is ideal in placement of the coils. All relay coils are placed in it carefully as relay coil, N-2 is distributed in the transmission range uniformly between the transmitter and receiver that exactly consists of the same distances .the transmission range to temporal intervals is divided to N-1. Thus, the mutual inductances between the coils are the same. But in the operational applications, these conditions aren't operated because of the two following reasons: 1.in theinitial stage of placement, it isn't possible to place the coil in its exact position due to some restrictions such as stones or rocks. 2. Perhaps, the position of loops is changed due to the ground pressure on the network or the soil motions. Thus, the operational status was analyzed in figs.3, 4. It is assumed that the relay coil loops isn't placed in the accurate positions. So, the relay loop, n-2 between the receiver and transmitter is applied. Their designed positions are as $\left\{i.\frac{d}{n-1}\right.$,$i = 1,2,...n-2$

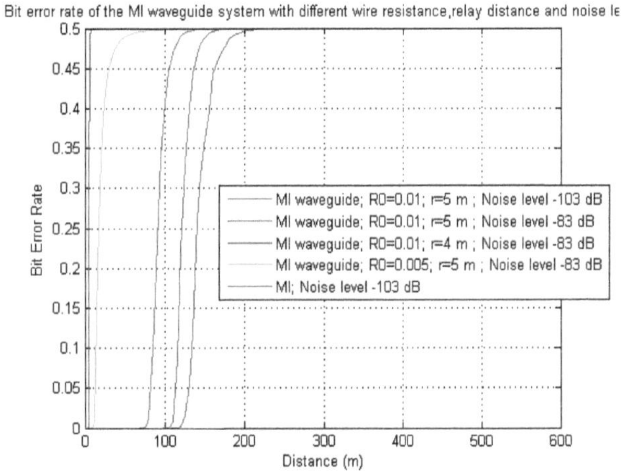

Fig. 3. The Comparison of Bit Error Rate of MI Waveguide with Different Relay Distances and Noises for EM and MI waves system.

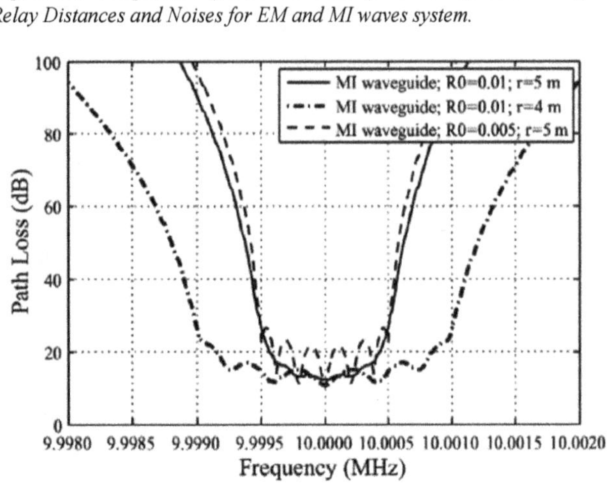

Fig. 4. The Frequency Response of MI Waveguide System with Different Wire and Remote Relay Resistances.

$X_j$in the relay loop, i is a Gaussian random variable with the mean, i.d/(n-1) and the standard deviation , σ_r. After that, it can be said that the transmission distance, d is dividable to n-1 intervals with r_1,r_2,r_{n-1} whereas $r_i = x_i - x_{i-1}$ are the transmitter and receiver positions respectively. Itwas assumed that the standard deviation had been designed for the relay distances 5%,10% or 20%. The other simulation parameters were set on the default values. The results were obtained from 100 samples in average. Both the moderate value and the standard deviation were drawn in the figure. It can be said that operationally, there is also an additional path loss. Furthermore, when the standard deviation is 20% , the band width decreases severely.The level of additional path loss and the reduction of band width are determined by the standard deviation. The higher standard deviation makes more problems in the system. Furthermore, as the transmission distance increases, the additional path loss will be raised too. When the deployment increases, the standard deviation of the path loss and the band width are also raised severely.This indicates that as the deployment occurs, the reliability of MI waves system is also reduced. Meanwhile, as the standard deviation is lesser than 10%, we can ignore the effect of deployment on the operation of MI waves system.

4. Discussion and Conclusion

In the underground wireless communications, the traditional methods via EM waves have three major challenges: the high path loss because of the material absorption, the channel dynamic conditions because of the various properties of the soil and the very high size of the antenna.

MI is an alternative method with the same channel conditionsand it can accomplish the communications with the small cores .At the present study, one analytic model was shown that indicated the communicational underground channel characteristics of MI. According to the channel analysis, we presented one MI wave method that increased the transmission range. Our analysis indicated the following results:

MI method has the constant conditions of channel because the path loss only depends on the permeability of propagation environment. When the environment is the air, it remains the same but if the environment is the water or more kinds of soils and rocks, this value is the same. The materials absorption is one of the most important parts in the path loss of EM system that may change in the various soil conditions. In the underground environments, the path loss of MI system is slightly lower than EM wave system in the natural and wet soils. But because of the high path loss, both systems can provide one transmission range that is more than 10m.Although the band width of MI systemand MI waves system is only 1 to 2KHz (more lesser than EM waves system), these values are enough for monitoring few data in the WUSNS applications. One of the other advantages of MI waves system is that as the transmission range increases, the transmission power decreases simultaneously with regard to the received power.This is ideal for WUSNS restricted energy. MI Waves Method decreases the path loss effectively. It must be mentioned that the cores of relay coil don't consume energy. hence, their costs are very low. The band width of MI system is similar to one MI typical system. In comparison with MI typical system and EM waves, the transmission range of MI waves increases severely.

References

[1] I. F. Akyildiz, W. Su, Y. Sankarasubramaniam, and E. Cayirci, "Wireless sensor networks: A survey," *Computer Networks.*, vol. 38, no. 4, pp. 393–422, March 2002.

[2] I. F. Akyildiz and E. P. Stuntebeck, "Wireless underground sensor networks: Research challenges," Ad Hoc Networks (Elsevier),vol. 4, pp. 669–686, Jul. 2006.

[3] L. Li, M. C. Vuran, and I. F. Akyildiz, "Characteristics of underground channel for wireless underground sensor networks," presented at the Med-Hoc-Net'07, Corfu, Greece, Jun. 2007.

[4] T. A. Milligan, Modern Antenna Design, 2nd ed. Piscataway, NJ: IEEE Press, 2005.

[5] N. Jack and K. Shenai, "Magnetic induction IC for wireless communication in RF-impenetrable media," presented at the IEEE Workshop on Microelectronics and Electron Devices (WMED 2007), Apr. 2007.

[6] J. J. Sojdehei, P. N. Wrathall, and D. F. Dinn, "Magneto-inductive (MI) communications," presented at the MTS/IEEE Conf. and Exhibition (OCEANS 2001), Nov. 2001.

[7] A. R. Silva and M. C. Vuran, "Development of a testbed for wirelessunderground sensor networks," EURASIP J.WirelessCommun.Netw.(JWCN)[Online].Available:http://cse.unl.edu/~mcvuran/ugTestbed.pdf

[8] Standard Specification for Standard Nominal Diameters and Cross- Sectional Areas of AWG Sizes of Solid Round Wires Used as Electrical Conductors, ASTM Standard B 258-02, ASTM International, 2002.

[9] Sun, Z. and Akyildiz, I. F.,"Magnetic Induction Communications for Wireless Underground Sensor Networks,"IEEE Transactions on Antenna and Propagation, vol. 58, no. 7, pp. 2426-2435, July 2010.

Utilizing automatic recognition and classification of images for pattern recognition

Mohammad Hadi Yousofi[1, *], Habib Yousofi[2], Sayyed Amir Mohammad Razavi[3]

[1]Department of Mechatronics, Postgraduate School, Islamic Azad University of Kashan, Kashan, Iran
[2]School of Medicine, Kashan University of Medical Sciences, Kashan, Iran
[3]Department of Electrical and Computer, Islamic Azad University of Kashan, Kashan, Iran

Email address:
Mhu320@yahoo.com (M. H. Yousofi), Ha_usofi@yahoo.com (H. Yousofi), Mohammadrazavi@yahoo.com (S. A. M. Razavi)

Abstract: Pattern recognition is a scientific approach for categorizing objects to class or subject numbers. These subjects need to be classified based on their applications (can be image, signal or any other type of measurements). Occupation, automation, military information, communication, industry and commercial applications and many other fields can benefit from Pattern recognition approaches. Perhaps, one the most important reasons that lead to pattern recognition prominent place in today's research studies, is the role of image auto-classifications. In this research, we investigate recent literatures about image auto-classification and image processing to identify patterns.

Keywords: Pattern Recognition, Images Auto-Classification, Image Processing, Support Vector Machine

1. Introduction

The simplicity that we recognize a portrait, understand words , read manuscripts, identify car keys with hands in our pocket leads to less attention to operation complexity which is done in these process as pattern recognition . Pattern recognition is a scientific method that aims to categorize objects to class or subject numbers. These subjects need to be classified depending on their applications (can be image, signal or any other type of measurements). Like other fields, progress in computer science led to increasing need of pattern recognition practical applications and as a result led to spread projects in this field. Atomization of works and role of pattern recognition in the research is one of the most important reasons that cause pattern recognition to have a prominent place in today's researches.

We can say that pattern recognition is receiving raw data and deciding based on data grouping. More research studies about pattern recognition are related to "supervised learning " or " non – supervised learning ", which we explain in the next sections. Pattern recognition methods separate special patterns from data collection via previous knowledge about patterns or statistical information. Those patterns which are classified in this way are groups of measurements or observations that form determined areas in a multidimensional space. This characterization is the main difference of pattern recognition with pattern matching, where patterns are identified base on a determined pattern and accurate real cases. Pattern recognition and matching pattern are main sections of image process discussion especially in machine vision.

Nowadays, there are more attentions to improved information systems because information is a main element in decision-making and the amount of information in the world is increasing in different forms with different complexity. One of the main issues in designing modern information systems is automated pattern recognition. Recognition is a leading characteristic of being human. A pattern is a description of an object [1]. Humans have high level informational system that is due to developed pattern recognition ability. According to nature of recognized patterns, recognition operation is divided into two main species.

2. Materials and Methods

2.1. Supervised and Un-Supervised Pattern Recognition

In most cases, representative pattern from every class are

available. In these situations, we can apply supervised pattern recognition, and the basis of this approach is a collection of identified practical patterns to classify and perform a suitable learning method. In some applications, maybe there is a collection of un-identified practical patterns to category. In these situations, we can apply un-supervised portrait recognition techniques. As mentioned before, supervised pattern recognition introduced by this matter are when correct group of every practical pattern is clear [2]. In un-supervised cases, however, we deal with learning matters in presented pattern classes. This issue is known as an un-supervised learning approach [3].

2.2. Classification Algorithms (Algorithms with a Predictor Supervisor)

The selected algorithm for recognizing patterns depend on the type of output, with or without supervision, and the static or dynamic nature of algorithms. Static algorithms are divided to two difference categories: differentiate and generative. In the following, we investigate different algorithms for recognizing patterns.

2.2.1. Decision Tree

Decision tree is a tool to support decision and employs various trees to make a model. Decision tree is usually used in research in operation. Especially it is used to determine strategy with a high probability to reach an aim in decision analysis. Description of conditional probability computations are the other applied area of decision trees [4].

Supervised decision tree, in usual statics method, is used more in data mining [5]. In decision analysis, a decision tree is used as a tool to draw and analyze decisions where the predicted amounts are computed from competitions frequently [6].

One decision tree has three types of groups:

1 Decision group; usually shown by square.
2 Random group; shown by circle.
3 Final group; shown with triangle.

The advantages of decision trees are as follows:

1 Simple understanding: every human can learn the work style of decision tree with little study and practice.
2 works with big and complex data: in spite of simplicity, decision tree can work with huge data easily and make a decision base on them.
3 Simple re-use: when a decision tree is made for one problem, we can compute different samples of that problem with the same tree.
4 Combination with other methods: we can combine the results of decision tree with other decision techniques and gain better results.

The disadvantage of decision tree is that it becomes big exponentially.

2.2.1.1. Support Vector Machine

Support Vector Machine (SVM) is one the relatively modern methods that has showed high efficiently in recent years compared to older methods for classification including perceptron nervous systems. Work basis of SVM classification is data linearly classification and in linear division, we try to select a line that has more reliable edge. To solve this equation, we should find optimum line for data by quadratic programming QP methods that are determined methods to solve limited problems. Before line division, we take data to higher dimensions via phi function to classify data with higher complexity in machine. We apply Lagrange Duality Theorem to transform minimization problem to duality form where we use simple function called core function that is vector coefficient of Phi function to solve a problem with very high dimensions. We can use different core functions including exponential cores, vector and Sigmund.

Therefore, we define learning data collection 'D' including 'n' member as follow:

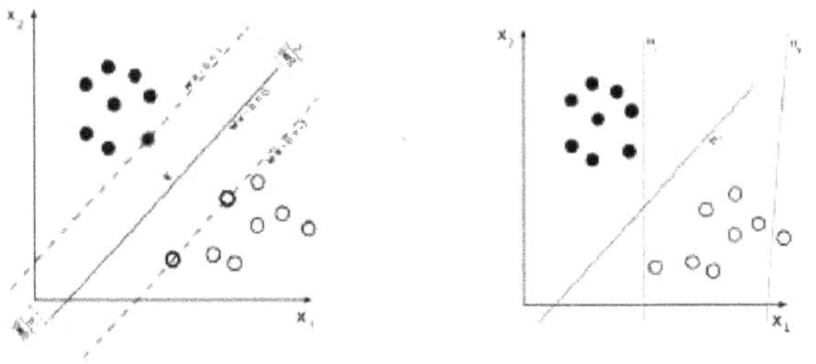

$$\mathcal{D} = \{(\mathbf{x}_i, y_i) \mid \mathbf{x}_i \in \mathbb{R}^p,\ y_i \in \{-1,1\}\}_{i=1}^{n}$$

Figure 1. Maximum-margin hyperplane and margins for an SVM trained with samples from two classes. Samples on the margin are called the support vectors.

Where y is equal to 1 or -1 and every Xi is equal to real vector of –p dimensional. The aim is to find separator hyper plane with a most distance from marginal areas that separate areas with y_i =1 from y_i=-1. Every cloud page can be a set of points that satisfies the following condition wrote:

W.X-b=0

Where (.) is the multiply symbol. W is a normal vector that is vertical to hyper plane. We want to select W and b in a way that provide the most distance among parallel hyper plane which separate data from each other. These hyper planes are defined as follow (Equation 1):

$$\mathbf{w}\cdot\mathbf{x} - b = 1 \quad (1)$$

And

$$\mathbf{w}\cdot\mathbf{x} - b = -1. \quad (2)$$

If the separative supervised data W is linear, then we can have two hyper planes in point's edge so that they do not have any common point and try to maximize their distance. Given the geometry, the distance of these two plane is $\frac{2}{\|w\|}$. So we should minimize $\|w\|$. In order to avoid entering the margin, we add the following conditions. For every 'i':

$$\mathbf{w} \cdot \mathbf{x}_i - b \geq 1 \qquad \text{for } \mathbf{x}_i \text{ of the first class}$$

$$\mathbf{w} \cdot \mathbf{x}_i - b \leq -1 \qquad \text{for } \mathbf{x}_i \text{ of the second class} \tag{3}$$

It can be written as follows:

$$y_i(\mathbf{w} \cdot \mathbf{x}_i - b) \geq 1, \quad \text{for all } 1 \leq i \leq n. \tag{4}$$

2.2.1.2. Nonlinear Support Vector Machine

The optimum separator was first presented by Vapnik in 1963 that was a linear category. In 1992, Bernhard, Boser, Guyon, Isabelle and Vapnik suggested a way to provide non-linear grouper via placing core to find hyper plane with more edge [7, 8]. The achieved algorithm look same, except all of points multiplies was placed with a nonlinear core function. This led the algorithm to be suitable for hyper plane with the most edge in a transformed space [9].

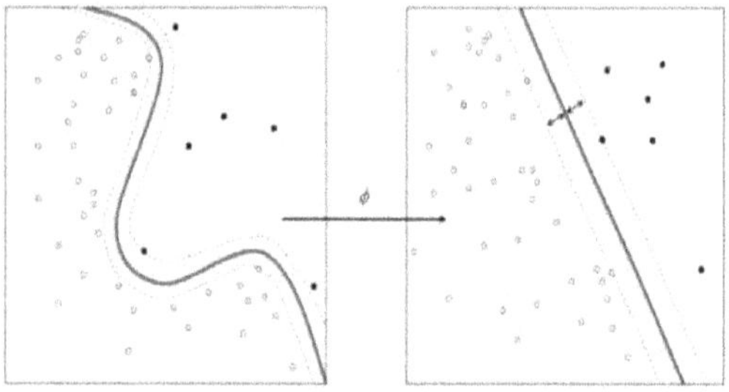

Figure 2. *Kernel machine*

Perhaps if the transform is nonlinear, the transformed spaces have a higher dimension. However, the grouper is a hyper plane in characterize space with high dimensions that it may be nonlinear in input space. If we use core with Gusin function, corresponding property space is a infinite Hilbert space. The rouper of the most edge, is in good – arrange, so infinite dimensions do not destroy the result. The common cores are as follow:

- The polynomial (homogeneous):

$$k(\mathbf{x_i}, \mathbf{x_j}) = (\mathbf{x_i} \cdot \mathbf{x_j})^d \tag{5}$$

- The polynomial (inhomogeneous):

$$k(\mathbf{x_i}, \mathbf{x_j}) = (\mathbf{x_i} \cdot \mathbf{x_j} + 1)^d \tag{6}$$

- Gusin:

$k(\mathbf{x_i}, \mathbf{x_j}) = \exp(-\gamma \|\mathbf{x_i} - \mathbf{x_j}\|^2)$ for $\gamma > 0$. Some (7)

Times parametrized using $\gamma = 1/2\sigma^2$

- Hyperbolic tangent

$k(\mathbf{x_i}, \mathbf{x_j}) = \tanh(\kappa \mathbf{x_i} \cdot \mathbf{x_j} + c)$, for some (not every) $\kappa > 0$ and $c < 0$ (8)

2.2.1.3. Multiclass Support Vector Machine

Basically, SVM is a binary separator. Therefore, we explain theory basis of SVM for grouping of two classes. One multi-class pattern recognition can be reached via multi-classes SVM combination. Usually, there are two visions for this aim. One is the strategy of "one against all" for classifying every pair and remained classes. The other strategy is "one against one" to classify every pair. When first classification leads to vague classification, the general approach for multi-classes is minimized to multi-classes problems and several binaural problems. Every problem is solved with one binary separator. Then, SVM binary seperator output combines together and in this way the multiclasses problem can be solved [10, 11].

The advantages of this approach are:

1 The supervision is relatively simple.
2 Unlike the neural network, it does not get stuck in a local maximum.
3 For high dimensional data, it has relatively good answer.
4 Reconciliation between grouper complexity and error amount can be controlled clearly.

The disadvantage is that we need to Select a good kernel function parameter C.

2.2.2. Perceptron

Perceptron is a binary separator that corresponds X self input (a vector from real numbers) to output amount f(x), (one scalar from real numbers) that compute as follow:

$$f(x) = \begin{cases} 1 & \text{if } w \cdot x + b > 0 \\ 0 & \text{otherwise} \end{cases} \tag{9}$$

Where w is a vector from weights with real amounts and < . > is a point coefficient (that compute the total weight). "b" is a bias ; a fix sentence that do not relate to input.

$f(x)$ sign to classify x to a positive or negative sample and it is used in binary classification problems. Bias can be considered as an action function adjustor or every amount for basis for action of output neuron "b" is negative, inputs weighted combination should be a positive amount higher than, to place a grouper neuron in a condition higher than zero threshold . [12]

3. Discussion and Conclusion

In this article, we have considered different group of pattern recognition algorithms. Considering the advantages and disadvantages of the discussed, we cannot rely to specific algorithm permanently. The decision about which algorithm with less computation, less time and best results could be different based on the situation and applications.

Based on our analysis from different methods, we should try to use combination system with a combination of pattern recognition algorithms to reach minimum computation and less time, as possible.

References

[1] Milewski, Robert; Govindaraju, Venu (31 March 2008). "Binarization and cleanup of handwritten text from carbon copy medical form images". Pattern Recognition 41 (4): 1308–1315. doi:10.1016/j.patcog.2007.08.018.

[2] Richard O. Duda, Peter E. Hart, David G. Stork (2001) Pattern classification (2nd edition), Wiley, New York, ISBN 0-471-05669-3

[3] R. Brunelli, Template Matching Techniques in Computer Vision: Theory and Practice, Wiley, ISBN 978-0-470-51706-2, 2009.

[4] Quinlan, J. R., (1986). Induction of Decision Trees. Machine Learning 1: 81-106, Kluwer Academic Publishers

[5] Rokach, Lior; Maimon, O. (2008). Data mining with decision trees: theory and applications. World Scientific Pub Co Inc. ISBN 978-9812771711.

[6] Barros R. C., Cerri R., Jaskowiak P. A., Carvalho, A. C. P. L. F., A bottom-up oblique decision tree induction algorithm. Proceedings of the 11th International Conference on Intelligent Systems Design and Applications (ISDA 2011).Conference Location :Cordoba. DOI:10.1109ISDA.2011.6121697

[7] Cortes, Corinna; and Vapnik, Vladimir N.; "Support-Vector Networks", Machine Learning, 20, 1995.

[8] Aizerman, Mark A.; Braverman, Emmanuel M.; and Rozonoer, Lev I. (1964). "Theoretical foundations of the potential function method in pattern recognition learning". Automation and Remote Control25: 821–837.

[9] Boser, Bernhard E.; Guyon, Isabelle M.; and Vapnik, Vladimir N.; A training algorithm for optimal margin classifiers. In Haussler, David (editor); 5th Annual ACM Workshop on COLT, pages 144–152, Pittsburgh, PA, 1992. ACM Press. doi:10.1145/130385.130401. ISBN 089791497X.

[10] Duan, Kai-Bo; and Keerthi, S. Sathiya (2005). "Which Is the Best Multiclass SVM Method? An Empirical Study". Proceedings of the Sixth International Workshop on Multiple Classifier Systems. Lecture Notes in Computer Science 3541: 278. doi:10.1007/11494683_28. ISBN 978-3-540-26306-7.

[11] Hsu, Chih-Wei; and Lin, Chih-Jen (2002). "A Comparison of Methods for Multiclass Support Vector Machines". Neural Networks, IEEE Transactions on (Volume:13 , Issue: 2). DOI:10.1109/72.991427.

[12] Liou, D.-R.; Liou, J.-W.; Liou, C.-Y. (2013). "Learning Behaviors of Perceptron". ISBN 978-1-477554-73-9. iConcept Press.

24

Solving quadratic assignment problem using water cycle optimization algorithm

Maryam Parhizgar, Farhad Mortezapour Shiri

Department of Computer Engineering, Sience and Research Branch, Islamic Azad University, Qazvin, Iran

Email address:
mail.parhizgar@Gmail.com (M. Parhizgar), farhad.mortezapour.sh@Gmail.com (F. M. Shiri)

Abstract: The Quadratic Assignment Problem (QAP) is one of combinatorial optimization problems which devote some facilities to some locations. The aim of this problem is assignment of each facility to a location which minimizes total cost. Because the QAP is NP-hard, so it couldn't be solved by exact methods. In recent years, meta-heuristic algorithms are used in solving NP-hard optimization problems increasingly. In this article Water Cycle Optimization Algorithms (WCO) is used to solve QAP. The implementation of proposed algorithms on standard test functions and also its result comparison with other meta-heuristics algorithms express algorithm`s desirable quality and its prominence to other meta-heuristics algorithms.

Keywords: Quadratic Assignment Problem, Combinatorial Optimization Problems, Water Cycle Optimization Algorithms, Meta-Heuristics Algorithms

1. Introduction

The Quadratic Assignment Problem (QAP) is one of combinatorial optimization problems that, in many firms have done various researches in order to devote some facilities to some locations. The most important thing in this process is assignment costs, which this type of costs become minimized. The computation of optimized solutions is really hard and difficult for most of optimization problems observed in many operational and practical fields. The solutions for optimization problems include two groups of exact and heuristics methods. The exact methods gain optimized solution and guarantee optimizing condition [1]. Heuristics methods produce high qualified solutions in sensible time, but didn't guarantee to find the thorough optimized solution [2]. The QAP is a problem with exponential complexity. Totally, problems with larger than 20 dimensions aren`t solvable through exact methods otherwise from the view point of time they aren`t economical. Therefore, meta-heuristics methods are used in these cases. Indeed meta-heuristics algorithms is one of heuristics optimization algorithms types which have outgo mechanisms from local optimization and are applicable in many different problems [3]. Various types of these algorithms are developed during recent decades. The meta-heuristics algorithms which used in solving QAP are Annealing algorithm [4], Tabu Search [5, 6], Genetics algorithm [7], Ant Colony Optimization algorithm [8, 9], Harmony Search algorithm [10], Imperialist competitive algorithm [11], Artificial Bee Colony algorithm [12], and Cuckoo algorithm [13].

In presented design, the syntax of WCO meta-heuristics algorithms are used to solve QAP. Implementation of proposed algorithm on standard test functions and also its comparison with other meta-heuristics algorithms express desirable quality and its prominence to other meta-heuristics algorithms. The structure of the reminder of this paper is as follows: Section 2 is an introduction to QAP. In section 3 an introduction to WCO algorithm is given. In section 4, we describe the proposed algorithm based on WCO algorithm to solve the problem. Section 5 and 6 are dedicated to describe experimental results and paper conclusion, respectively.

2. Definition of Quadratic Assignment Problem

The QAP is one of combinatorial optimization problem which devote a category of facilities to a category of locations, along with cost that is function of distance and the flow among facilities in addition to relevant costs to facilities which located in specified location. The aim of this problem is assignment of each facility to each location in way that total cost becomes minimized. General model of QAP is presented below.

$$\min \sum_{i=1}^{n} \sum_{j=1}^{n} \sum_{k=1}^{n} \sum_{l=1}^{n} f_{ij} d_{kl} x_{ik} x_{jl} \quad (1)$$

$$\text{s.t. } \sum_{i=1}^{n} x_{ij} = 1 \quad 1 \le j \le n \quad (2)$$

$$\sum_{j=1}^{n} x_{ij} = 1 \quad 1 \le i \le n \quad (3)$$

Where f_{ij} is the flow between I and j facilities, and $d_{kl}$is the distance among k and l locations [14]. If pay attention to activities assignment to locations, general model of QAP is like below.

$$\min \sum_{i=1}^{n} \sum_{j=1}^{n} \sum_{k=1}^{n} \sum_{l=1}^{n} f_{ij} d_{kl} x_{ik} x_{jl} + \sum_{i} \sum_{k} C_{ik} x_{ik} \quad (4)$$

Kopmans and Beckman introduced QAP for the first time in 1957 as a mathematic model which is relevant to economic activities [15]. This problem has many different applications from that time up to now. One of the main usages of QAP is in Placement theory, which F= (fij) is a flow matrix. The aim of this problem is finding an assignment of all facilities to all locations with minimized cost. Other usages of it is sorting constructions in hospitals, warehouses management and distribution strategies, minimizing wire`s cables length in electronic circuits, assignment of some factories to some locations, wiring the circuit problem, controlling panels and typist keyboards designing.

3. Water Cycle Optimization Algorithm

WCO Algorithm [16] is a meta-heuristics algorithm which is inspired from water cycle in nature. In presented scheme, there have been attempt to introduce a new algorithm using water cycle in nature. The aim of this problem is benchmarking WCO like raining, the population of each generation has suitable diversity and scattering, and also by simulation of falling water drops motion process toward river, algorithm has a high convergence speed to gain thorough optimum. In addition to benchmark saturated pits during raining, escaping designed local optimum make algorithm to have suitable search in problem space and doesn't trap into local optimum. This algorithm includes a set of primary values for each parameters of problem. In each cycle of performing this algorithm, some values are selected based on a priority for each parameter of problem and make a smaller category, then by considering values competence, several solution will be generated by incorporating values of each parameter. After that each solution of problem located in its local optimum using local search algorithm. Each local optimum according to its propriety receives a capacity that explains the survival of that answer in consecutive performances and also the probability of being candidate to move other answers towards itself. In each cycle of performance, the answers which should be exited out of problem move towards answers with better competence and reach to local optimum that chose by themselves, if they didn't meet any more competence answer during path. Each cycle one of problem solutions with the most competence reminds constant and at the end of each cycle, values of each parameter of problem solution enter to set of primary values. After ending n cycle, the best solution of nth cycle is optimum solution of problem.

4. Water Cycle Algorithm Steps to Solve QAP

Water-cycle algorithm has 5steps which include:

4.1. Initialization

Such as many evolutionary algorithms, this algorithm also initializes with set of random primary values. In first performance of it, ocean initialized by random primary values. It assumed for discrete problem solution, the answer is a permutation of 1 to n (problems with n variables).

Ocean and initialization: it is a n*n matrix that its initial value will be $(Ocean\ Size)/n$, that Ocean size expresses size of ocean. In an example with 5 variables, ocean is a 5*5 matrix and initial values of all its elements will be $200/5 = 40$. this values will change in river`s water entrance into ocean. In this matrix, columns present a variable (tiny drop) of problem. Rows show the probability of locating one variable in location of 1 to n.

4.2. Evaporation Step Out of Ocean and Formation of Cloud Droplets

In this step some droplets should be selected for evaporation or formation of drop. This means that according to figures in each column, a droplet is selected in a way that more figure for a droplet, has more probability to choose. A simple solution can be in this way that sum first column droplets values, then generate a random value between 1 and sum of droplets value. This random value placed in intervals of each droplet, the droplet will be selected. Finally with n droplet, one drop will be formed.

4.3. Local Search

In local search a drop should immigrate to its better neighbor. Three types of neighborhood are defined for permutation problems.

4.3.1. Replacing Two Quantities

Two locations selected randomly and their quantities replace with each other.

Example: 1 5 4 2 3, elements 1 and 4 are selected and result will be 1 3 4 2 5

4.3.2. Inverting a Limited Area

Two randomly quantities are generated and the limited area between them will be inverted.

Example: 1 5 4 2 3 numbers of 1 and 4 are selected and

result will be 1 3 2 4 5

Tow random quantities are generated and the first one converts to next element after second quantity.

Example: 1 5 4 2 3 numbers of 1 and 4 are selected and result will be 1 5 3 2

4.4. Surface Runoff

The way of falling water motion from the origin pit to destination pit is in this way that a permutation of numbers from 1 to n are generate randomly and based on that permutation, the droplet equal with the droplet on destination pit on that location, founded in origin pit and replaces with droplet in origin pit on that location.

Origin pit: 2 4 5 3 1

Destination pit: 4 3 2 1 5

Generated permutation: 3 2 4 5 1

The origin pit after one step movement: 1 3 2 4 5 the first number which generated by permutation is 3, the third number of destination pit is 2, that should be located in its main location in origin pit, it means that 2 replaces with 5.

The origin pit after one step movement: 5 3 2 4 1

The origin pit after one step movement: 5 3 2 1 4

The origin pit after one step movement: 4 3 2 1 5

Surface runoff to n-1 steps are needed.

4.5. River Water Entry to Ocean

The numbers inside ocean change like below in each step:

$$s_{ij} = s_{ij} - (\propto\times s\_ij)/(Osean\ Sizae) \quad (5)$$

$$s_{r_{i}i} = s_{r_{i}i} + \propto \quad (6)$$

Where S is ocean itself, α is a coefficient which delivered after entry and r is river.

5. Experiments and Simulation Results

This study addresses the general form of QAP and its purpose is to evaluate the WCO in solving QAP so that its applicability is confirmed and it can then be used in solving specific real cases in next studies. For this reason, those problems are chosen which are more famous and have been used for testing other algorithms. Therefore, the most credible reference of QAPs, QAPLIB [17], was used which is prepared by Peter Hann, Berkard, Chella, Randal, and Karisch who are mathematics professors that specialize in QAP. In QAPLIB, different QAPs of different sizes are defined and solved by scientists such as Berkard, Al-Shaafi, Steinburg, etc. using exact, heuristic, and meta-heuristic methods.

The results of experiments and simulations are presented in Tables 1, 2 and 3 and graphically in Figures 1 and 2. First, we determine the results for a small population. Then, the resulting error percent is calculated and compared to the genetic and honeybee and water cycle improved algorithms.

Table 1. *Results of running the program with 200 repeats for the problems chosen from qaplib. errors are in percent.*

Problem Name	Problem Size	Best Solution Found So Far	Solution Method	Errors of Previous Methods	HBMO Error	COA Error	WCO Error
Lipa30a	30	13178	Exact		3.74	2.01	1.31
Lipa60a	60	107218	Exact	-	2.25	0.95	0.58
Lipa90a	90	360630	Exact	-	1.67	0.39	0.28
Sko49	49	23386	RO-TS	5.91	16.11	3.56	0.10
Sko56	56	34458	RO-TS	5.37	18.49	4.39	1.04
Sko64	64	48498	RO-TS	5.7	16.91	4.47	1.41
Sko72	72	66256	RO-TS	5.38	14.34	4.85	1.34
Sko81	81	90998	GA	5/41	13.57	4.332	1.38
Sko100a	100	152002	GA	6/41	12.74	12.95	1.48

Table 2. *Results of running the program with 500 repeats for the problems chosen from qaplib. errors are in percent.*

Problem Name	Problem Size	Best Solution Found So Far	Solution Method	Errors of Previous Methods	HBMO Error	COA Error	WCO Error
Lipa30a	30	13178	Exact		3.78	2.00	1.08
Lipa60a	60	107218	Exact	-	2.3	0.96	0.48
Lipa90a	90	360630	Exact	-	1.65	0.38	0.19
Sko49	49	23386	RO-TS	5.91	18.82	3.55	0.14
Sko56	56	34458	RO-TS	5.37	15.88	4.38	0.05
Sko64	64	48498	RO-TS	5.7	14.36	4.45	0.86
Sko72	72	66256	RO-TS	5.38	13.78	4.78	0.85

Table 3. Results of running the program for the problems chosen from qaplib with large population.

Problem Name	Problem Size	Optimized Solution	Error of the Best GA Solution (%)	Error the Best HBMO Solution (%)	Error of the Best COA Solution (%)	Error of the Best WCO Solution (%)
Esc32a	32	130	21.69	54.86	10.769	3.70
Esc32b	32	168	20.75	50.56	16.66	1.75
Esc32c	32	642	0	9.7	0	0
Esc32d	32	200	0	29.57	0	0
Esc32e	32	2	0	0	0	0
Esc32h	32	438	1.79	22.06	0.9132	0.4235

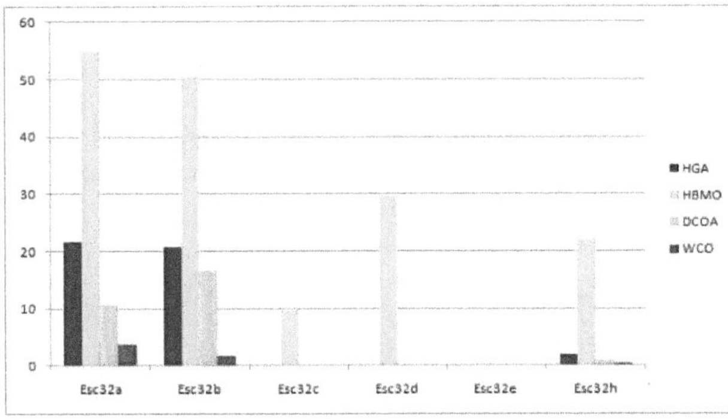

***Figure 1.** Comparison of Algorithms results for low-level.*

WCO the problems and the weak points of other optimization algorithms (such as GA, HBMO and the other new methods like colonial completion algorithm) are not seen in this method, therefore WCO method has high capability to converge to the optimized solution faster than the other algorithms and also has this ability to find overall optimized points with higher accuracy. The ability of WCO method was examined for problems with high dimensions and the results showed that this method works very well in this issue.

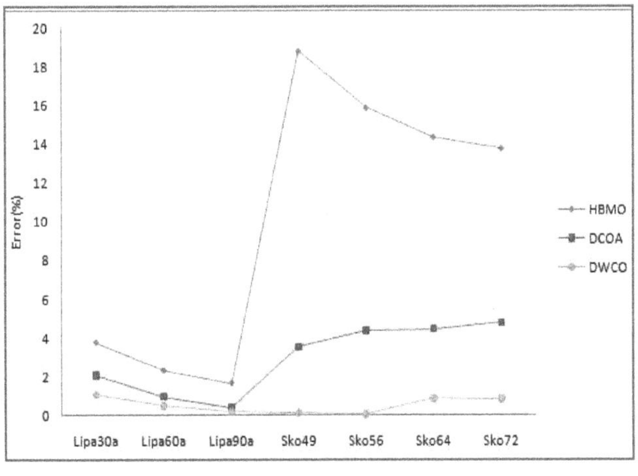

***Figure 2.** WCO algorithm accuracy for sko* problems.*

6. Discussion and Conclusion

In this article the idea of WCO algorithm to solve QAP problem was studied. Results were gained for low, medium and large population. The effects of increasing optimization repeats in enhancement of algorithm`s answering precision are also investigated. The results indicate that water-cycle optimization algorithm performs better than Genetics, Cuckoo and Bee Colony algorithms, and in most comparisons, has better performance to other evolutionary algorithms in different test functions to find the best solution. Therefore, it has very fast convergence capability and the power of finding optimum points will be more precise. This algorithm generates appropriate solutions for problems with large dimensions. While the error of Genetics and Bee Colony algorithms are increased by problem with medium dimensions.

References

[1] E.Loiola, N.de Abreo, P.boaventura-nett, P.Hahn, T.Querido, “Asurvay for the Quadratic assignment problem, ” Eur J Oper Res 176:657-690, 2007.

[2] RE.Burkard, T.Bonniger, “A hurestic for quadratic boolean programs with applications to quadratic assignment problems, ” European J, Oper.res, 13:374-86, 1983.

[3] Li.Yong, M.Panos Pardalos, and G.C.Mauricio Resende, “A Greedy Randomized Adaptive Search Procedure for the Quadratic Assignment Problem, ” DIMACS Series in Discrete Mathematics and Theoretical Computer Science, May 20-21, 1993.

[4] Ghandeshtani, Mollai, Seyedkashi, and Neshati, “New Simulated Annealing Algorithm for Quadratic Assignment Problem, ” The Fourth Internatinal Conference on Advanced Engineering Computing and Applications in Sciences, 2010.

[5] J.Skorin-Kapov, “Tabu search applied to the quadratic assignment problem, ” ORSA J. Comput. 1990;2:33-45. R.K. Ahuja et al. Computers & Operations Research 27,917-934, 2000.

[6] E.Taillard, Robust, “tabu search for the quadratic assignment problem, ” Parallel Comput,17,443-55, 1991.

[7] C.Fleurent, JA.Ferland, “Genetic hybrids for the quadratic assignment problem, ” DIMACS Series in Discrete Mathematics and Theoretical Computer Science, vol. 16, Providence, RI: American Mathematical Society, pp, 173-87, 1994.

[8] T.Stutzle, M.Dorigo, “ACO algorithms for the quadratic assignment problem, ” In: Corne, D., Dorigo, M., Glover, F. (Eds.), New Ideas for Optimization. McGraw-Hill, pp, 33–50, 1999.

[9] L.Gambardella, E.Taillard, M.Dorigo, "Ant Colonies for the QAP, " Tech. Report IDSIA,4-97, IDSIA, Lugano, Switzerland, 1997.

[10] Z.W. Geem, J.-H. Kim, G.V. Loganathan, "A new heuristic optimization algorithm: harmony search," Simulation,76 (2) 60–68, 2001.

[11] A.Safari Mamaghani,and M.Reza Meybodi, "An Application of Imperialist Competitive Algorithm to Solve the Quadratic Assignment Problem," 6th international conference on internet technology and secured translation, 11-14, 2011.

[12] M.Mirzazadeh, Gh.Hasan Shirdel AND B.Masoumi,"A Honey Bee Algorithm to Solve Quadratic Assignment Problem," Journal of Optimization in Industrial Engineering (2011) 27-36.

[13] R. Rajabioun, "Cuckoo Optimization Algorithm, " In: Applied Soft Computing journal, vol. 11, pp, 5508-5518, 2011.

[14] E.M.Loiola, N.M.Maia de Abreu, P.O.Boaventura-Netto, P.Hahn and T.Querido, "A survey for the quadratic assignment problem," European Journal of Operational Research, 176, 657–690, 2007.

[15] T. C. Koopmans and M. J. Beckmann, "Assignment problems and the location of economic activities," Econometrica, 25, 53-76, 1957.

[16] M.Hosseini, M.Sadri, " A new evolutionary algorithm based on the water cycle in nature," 4th Conference on Electrical and Electronics Engineering, University GONABAD,7-9 August 2001.

[17] RE.Burkard, SE.Karisch, F.Rendl. "QAPLIB - A quadratic assignment program library," J.Global Optim.;10:391-403,1997.

Packet switch scheduler for increasing sending packet

Kazunori Omori, Myungryun Yoo, Takanori Yokoyama

Information Engineering, Tokyo City University, Tokyo, Japan

Email address:
g1381501@tcu.ac.jp (K. Omori), yoo@cs.tcu.ac.jp (M. Yoo), yokoyama@cs.tcu.ac.jp (T. Yokoyama)

Abstract: Recently, the need of the high speed packet switch is increased. The Re-2DRR scheduling algorithm based on 2DRR scheduling algorithm provides high throughput communication on a packet switch. However, computer network is using many cases, that huge data communication, complex, and other. This paper proposes a new method to increase choices in algorithm variation for three specific systems and more easily implementation than Re-2DRR. The effectiveness of the proposed algorithm is shown through simulation studies.

Keywords: Packet Switch Scheduling algorithm; 2DRR; High-Throughput

1. Introduction

In recent years, the number of traffic packet network is on the increase [1], [2]. And they are making many kinds of systems on a computer networks, and they use to a computer network for special use for example, multimedia communications [3], [4], and other. They are needed more the high speed packet switch scheduler for special use [5]. Richard presented the basic two Dimensional Round Robin (2DRR) scheduling algorithm [6]. The four matrixes, Request Matrix (RM), Pattern Matrix (PM), Scheduling Matrix (SM), and Allocation Matrix (AM) are used in the basic 2DRR. Each matrix size is N x N, where N means the number of inputs and outputs [7]. The basic 2DRR provides high throughput, fair access [8], [9] and simple working on a packet switch. However, few input and output node could not be permissioned in some timeslots because the basic 2DRR use only value of PM to running scheduling. It occurs decreasing throughput and some transmission delay.

The Repetitive two Dimensional Round Robin (Re-2DRR) scheduling algorithm provides higher throughput than that of the basic 2DRR scheduling algorithm [10]. The Re-2DRR is using new matrix about Sub-AM. It is solve the 2DRR delay point. Although the Re-2DRR do making Sub-AM many times, and it hindered an implementation.

In this paper, we propose two method based on Re-2DRR. And we increase choices in algorithm for special use. First method is changing to making Sub-AM operation that the basic Re-2DRR was remaking many times at it have empty packets. If this method recognize an empty packet at AM, that just made Sub-AM group once time. It is suppression a repeat operation. Second method is making priority port in Re-2DRR. It enables high throughput at specific port.

2. Related Works

2.1. The Basic Two Dimensional Round Robin (2DRR)

In an N x N switch (Fig.1), up to N different requests can be simultaneously served by the switch in one time slot such that no two requests are in the same row or column in the request matrix. In order to select such N elements of the request matrix, RM, the basic 2DDR examines elements of RM that belong to generalized diagonals.

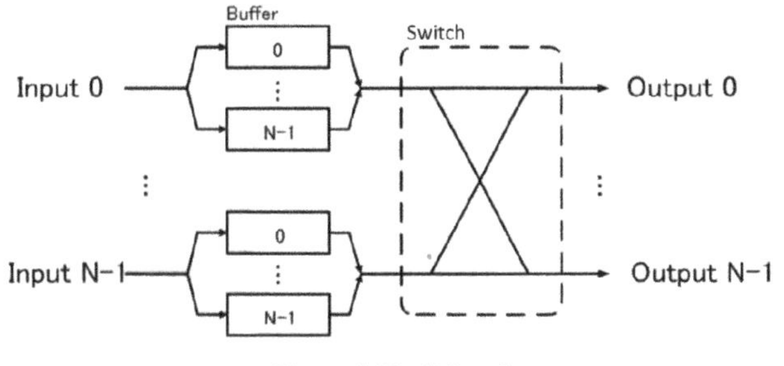

***Figure 1.** N x N Switch*

Definition 1: A generalized diagonal is a set of N elements in an N x N matrix, such that no two elements are in the same row or column.

There are *N!* different generalized diagonals in an *N* x *N* matrix. The basic 2DRR algorithm uses only *N* of these diagonals by selecting one basic diagonal and then generating the remaining *N-1* ones by shifting the basic diagonal across the matrix (so that each matrix element is covered by one of the *N* diagonals). That is, by sweeping a generalized diagonal pattern of length *N* through the request matrix, all N^2 input output pairs in the request matrix can be satisfied in *N* time slots. This property is used to guarantee a minimum amount of service to each input/output queue.

The basic 2DRR scheduling algorithm operates in repeating cycles of *N* time slots in which the time slots of each cycle are indexed by the variable *L*, which takes on values from 0 through *N–1*. The following 4 matrices are assumed.

1) Request Matrix (RM)

Each entry RM[R, C] is binary with the semantics:

RM[R, C] = 1, if there is at least one request for
a connection from output R to
output C
0, otherwise

2) Scheduling Matrix (SM)

Each entry SM[R, C] contains an integer between 0 and N–1 inclusive where

$$SM[R,C]=(C-R)\bmod N$$

If SM[R, C] = K, then RM[R, C] is covered by diagonal pattern K.

3) Pattern Sequence Matrix (PM)

Each entry PM[I, J] is an integer between 0 and N–1 inclusive with the semantics:

PM[I, J] = K implies that when the timeslot index L of a cycle is equal to J, then the I-th diagonal pattern in the sequence applied by the algorithm is the one numbered K in the diagonal pattern matrix. The ordering index I varies from 0 to N–1.

4) Allocation Matrix (AM)

It is binary entries and the semantics:

$$AM[R,C]=\begin{cases}1, & \text{if a connection is allocated from input } R \text{ to output } C\\ 0, & \text{otherwise}\end{cases}$$

At the beginning of time slot *L* in a cycle, all entries of the allocation matrix are set to zero. Then a sequence of *N* diagonal patterns is applied to the request matrix in the order specified by the pattern sequence matrix PM. That is, the diagonal pattern with index *PM*[0, *L*] is applied first followed by diagonal pattern *PM*[l, *L*] . . . *PM*[*N*–1, *L*]. As these diagonal patterns are overlaid on the request matrix, the entry *AM*[*R*, *C*] is set to 1 at the *I*-th point in the sequence if the following conditions are true.

- *RM*[*R*, *C*] = 1
- Input *R* and output *C* are still available for allocation (i.e., they have not been allocated to a different connection by a previously applied diagonal in the current time slot)
- *SM*[*R*, *C*] = *K*. where *PM*[*l*, *L*] = *K*

The above scheduling procedure is repeated for each cycle of *N* successive time slots. That is after a cycle has been completed with the use of column *N–1* of the pattern sequence matrix.

The basic 2DRR algorithm provides a fairness guarantee that each of the N^2 input/output queues will receive at least one opportunity for service during every cycle of *N* time slots. However, few input and output node could not be permissioned in some timeslots because the basic 2DRR use only value of PM to running scheduling. It occur scheduler tightly and throughput delay.

2.2. The Repetitive two Dimensional Round Robin (Re-2DRR)

Re-2DRR based on the basic 2DRR. The Re-2DRR creates Sub-AM if AM is not usable because of empty sending packet. If Sub-AM is not better than AM, scheduling algorithm retry creating Sub-AM by another SM, but that retrying have a limit. All created Sub-AM is not better than AM, the Re-2DRR chooses either AM or Sub-AM.

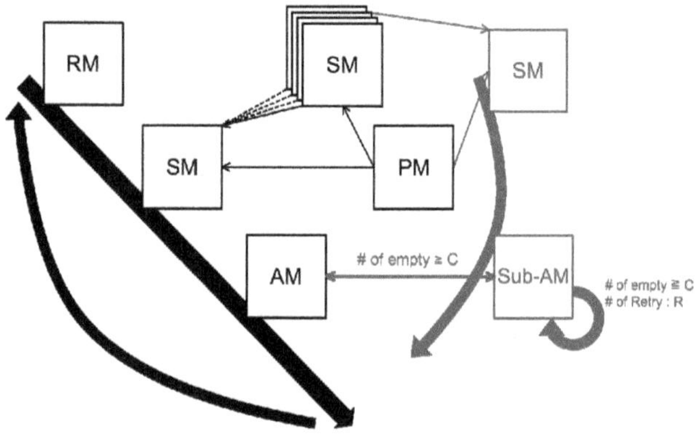

Figure 2. *Re-2DRR Scheduling Algorithm*

Fig.2 is Re-2DRR Scheduling Algorithms figure. The black color part shown the basic 2DRR scheduling work, and the red color part is the Re-2DRR scheduling works.

In the Re-2DRR scheduling algorithm, two thresholds are used. The first threshold is the number of empty sending packet for decision of available AM (threshold "C") and the second threshold is the upper limit of retrying to create Sub-AM (threshold "R"). The scheduler works more effectively by setting two thresholds optionally.

The Re-2DRR can operation flexibly by changing that two threshold. In threshold C, it changing probability of operating Re-2DRR. And threshold R is changing probability of algorithm chose Sub-AM and number of making Sub-AMs. In table 1 show a variation of the Re-2DRR operation results by N=4.

We recognize the operation of making Sub-AM is burdened with implementation. And the Re-2DRR is making for high throughput at all port in packet switch communications.

Table 1. Result of Re-2DRR in simulation (N=4)

C	R	Making Sub-AM	Sending by Sub-AM	End Time	Ave Packet Wait Time
1	1	18833	4315	277192	138556
	2	33922	5494	277004	138433
	3	49911	6227	277325	138635
	4	61212	6655	276782	138430
2	1	8465	1159	277082	138483
	2	15763	1472	277196	138536
	3	23608	1527	277161	138560
	4	29519	1593	277045	138485
3	1	4042	257	277077	138554
	2	8284	334	277278	138651
	3	12703	363	277351	138692
	4	16608	386	277230	138545

3. System to Assume

In this paper we define three specific systems. It is make more packet loading.

3.1. Less than N Port Have More Packet Load

It is less than N port have more packet loading. It like Fig.3 (a). In Fig.3 (a) mean a communication of Input 1 to Output 1 (point of red) use more packet traffics.

This traffic is estimated to be about some node use big data communication temporary.

3.2. Static N Port Have More Packet Load

This specific system is have more packet load at number of N communications. Example in Fig.3 (b) mean static number of 4 input to number of 4 output (place of red) have more packet loading.

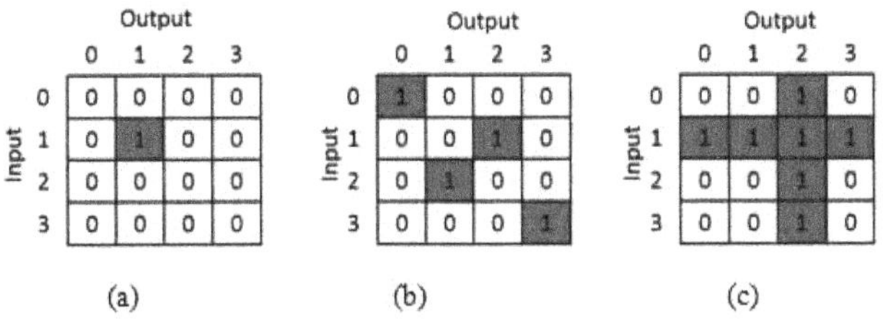

Figure 3. A place of more packet load

This traffic is estimated to be about number of N nodes and number of N nodes make static communication and use a big data.

3.3. One to All and All to One Port Have More Packet Load

This specific system is like a broadcast communication. In Fig.3 (c) mean input 1 to all output, and all input to output 2 have more packet load.

4. Improvement

In this paper, we improve portion of Re-2DRR. And we regarded two methods.

4.1. Selectable Sub-AM Group

In Re-2DRR, if Sub-AM worse than AM about the number of empty packets, scheduler make more another one Sub-AM for R times. This method improve about portion of making Sub-AM. If AM have many empty packet, this algorithm making the number of G Sub-AMs. After that, scheduler checking the better in Sub-AM group and select the best Sub-AM. If AM is better than Sub-AM groups Sub-AMs after made Sub-AM group, that algorithm send by AM.

In this method suppression a repeat making Sub-AM operation.

In Fig.4, the black color is same of Re-2DRR. The red color is this method point.

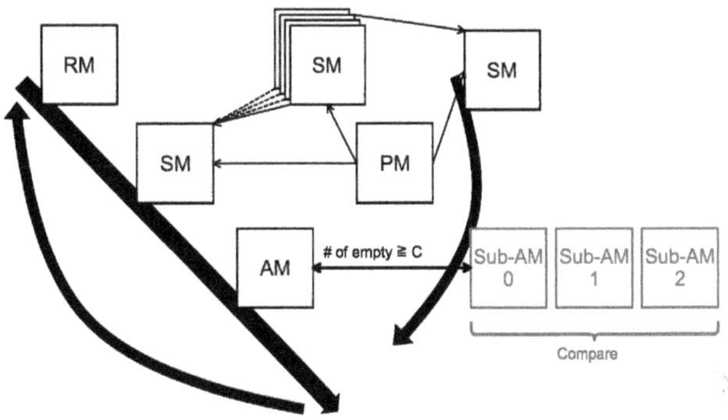

Figure 4. Selectable Sub-AM group

4.2. Make Priority Port

The basic Re-2DRR is choose AM or Sub-AM about the number of empty packet. This method is making priority port in operation of checking and choosing SM or Sub-SM of the basic Re-2DRR.

This method algorithm is choosing AM or Sub-AM preferentially about a set priority. For example in Fig.5, it is example of AM or Sub-AM. And place of yellow are priority ports in this time. This method algorithm choosing (b), because place of yellow is priority ports have permission of sending packet. So this method algorithm don't need the threshold of C, because this method just judge by priority port.

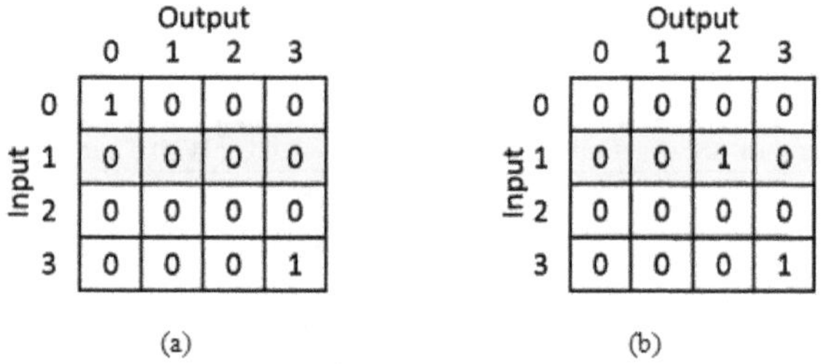

Figure 5. *Example of priority port*

5. Validation

To validate proposed two methods on Re-2DRR, several numerical tests are performed. We compared proposed selectable Sub-AM group on Re-2DRR, setting priority port on Re-2DRR and basic Re-2DRR. Numerical tests are performed with *N* x *N* matrix (*N*= 4). The throughput and the finish time of all sending packets are compared. The throughput is average waiting time of all packets in packet switch buffer. *C* and *R* is the threshold in Re-2DRR. *C* is the number of empty sending packet for decision of available AM and *R* is the upper limit of retrying to create Sub-AM. *G* is the threshold in the method of selectable Sub-AM group about the number of Sub-AM in Sub-AM group. The method of making priority port isn't need *C*.

Table 2, 3, 4, 5, 6, 7 and 8 show the comparison of results by basic Re-2DRR and two method on Re-2DRR. Table 2 is the results on more treble packet load to (1, 1) port. Table 3, 4 and 5 are the results on the number of *N* port (in this time N is 4: (0, 0), (1, 1), (2, 3) and (3, 2) ports) have more treble packet load. Table 4 is the results about each four ports average of packet waiting time. And table 5 is the results about four ports maximum of packet waiting time. Table 6, 7 and 8 are the results on input 1 to all output and all input to output 2 have more treble packet load. Table 7 is the results about each seven ports average of packet waiting time. And table 4 is the results about seven ports maximum of packet waiting time.

In table 2, Sub-AM group (*C*:1 *G*:4) and Sub-AM group (*C*:1 *G*:3) results close to Re-2DRR (*C*:1 *R*:4) and Re-2DRR(*C*:1 *R*:3) results except for Make Sub-AM group. The basic Re-2DRR don't making Sub-AM groups, so need extravagant making Sub-AM operation. However, method of Sub-AM group on Re-2DRR made Sub-AM group in advance. It mean the method of Sub-AM group in Re-2DRR can working by less making Sub-AM operation. The (1, 1) ports throughput of method of making priority port on Re-2DRR is more desirable than those of the others. But another values are increasing. But Priority (*R*:3) keep values increasing and keep high (1, 1) ports throughput.

In table 3, the method of making Sub-AM group on Re-2DRRs results are close to the basic Re-2DRR. And it shows the method of making Sub-AM groups making Sub-AM operation are less than the basic Re-2DRRs making Sub-AM operation. However the method of making priority port on Re-2DRR is not have enough effects. This method can't cause empty packet sending, because it give very high priority to setting four priority ports at (0, 0), (1, 1), (2, 3) and (3, 2). There are get big priority area, so that method increasing chose AM. In table 6, 7 and 8, this method setting seven priority port at same of more packet load ports, which is get more big priority area. It is block to making Sub-AM. Priority (*R*:4) limit in table 6, 7 and 8 is setting priority at input 1 about (1, 0), (1, 1), (1, 2) and (1, 3). It mean setting priority area narrowing. In conclusion, the method of making priority port on Re-2DR R have a just effect on one priority port like table 2.

Table 2. *Comparison on (1, 1) port have more packet load*

	Make Sub-AM	Send by Sub-AM	End Time	Ave Wait Time	Make Sub-AM group	(1, 1) Ave Wait	(1, 1) MAX Wait Time
Re-2DRR (*C*:1 *R*:4)	543976	6908	398402	1561.236	-	2667	4456
Re-2DRR (*C*:1 *R*:3)	414737	6042	399563	1564.182	-	2677	4516
Sub-AM group (*C*:1 *G*:4)	546784	6077	394756	1553.451	136696	2643	4735
Sub-AM group (*C*:1 *G*:3)	418731	5916	397935	1560.104	139577	2662	4541
Priority (*R*:4)	1134177	136500	396138	1670.850	-	1106	2876
Priority (*R*:3)	583186	115229	397203	1659.550	-	1560	4093

Table 3. *Comparison on the number of N port have more packet load*

	Make Sub-AM	Send by Sub-AM	End Time	Ave Wait Time	Make Sub-AM group
Re-2DRR (*C*:1 *R*:4)	332910	67320	423527	1993.703	-
Re-2DRR (*C*:1 *R*:3)	257648	55580	424641	1995.891	-
Sub-AM group (*C*:1 *G*:4)	386220	39035	423077	1989.144	96555
Sub-AM group (*C*:1 *G*:3)	285531	36749	425153	1998.776	139577
Priority (*R*:4)	90322	73489	440118	2047.618	-
Priority (*R*:3)	90400	73511	445007	2065.108	-

Table 4. Comparison on the number of N ports have more packet loads average of packet waiting time

	(0, 0)	(1, 1)	(2, 3)	(3, 2)
Re-2DRR (*C*:1 *R*:4)	2649	2659	2668	2661
Re-2DRR (*C*:1 *R*:3)	2656	2676	2647	2654
Sub-AM group (*C*:1 *G*:4)	2653	2659	2670	2653
Sub-AM group (*C*:1 *G*:3)	2661	2692	2687	2647
Priority (*R*:4)	2403	2589	2767	2582
Priority (*R*:3)	2466	2593	2780	2612

Table 5. Comparison on the number of N ports have more packet loads maximum of packet waiting time

	(0, 0)	(1, 1)	(2, 3)	(3, 2)
Re-2DRR (*C*:1 *R*:4)	4794	4646	4628	4620
Re-2DRR (*C*:1 *R*:3)	4480	4739	4519	4660
Sub-AM group (*C*:1 *G*:4)	4663	4651	4597	4468
Sub-AM group (*C*:1 *G*:3)	4940	4773	4547	4574
Priority (*R*:4)	4813	4954	4713	4938
Priority (*R*:3)	4783	4636	4877	4811

Table 6. Comparison on input 1 to all output and all input to output 2 have more packet load

	Make Sub-AM	Send by Sub-AM	End Time	Ave Wait Time	Make Sub-AM group
Re-2DRR (*C*:1 *R*:4)	1857306	99209	796028	2991.344	-
Re-2DRR (*C*:1 *R*:3)	1430890	95902	799003	2998.931	-
Sub-AM group (*C*:1 *G*:4)	2162800	96774	802024	3007.809	540700
Sub-AM group (*C*:1 *G*:3)	1640709	95880	807698	3024.896	546903
Priority (*R*:4)	0	0	801634	3122.378	-
Priority (*R*:3)	0	0	806794	3133.948	-
Priority (*R*:4) limit	73350	3689	799421	3103.385	-

Table 7. Comparison on input 1 to all output and all input to output 2 have more packet load s average of packet waiting time

	(1,0)	(1,1)	(1,2)	(1,3)	(0,3)	(2,2)	(3,2)
Re-2DRR (*C*:1 *R*:4)	3851	3946	3894	3797	3836	3900	3880
Re-2DRR (*C*:1 *R*:3)	3552	3653	5250	3171	3333	3339	3740
Sub-AM group (*C*:1 *G*:4)	3352	3550	5264	3557	3706	3618	3169
Sub-AM group (*C*:1 *G*:3)	3519	3691	5320	3280	3376	3433	3744
Priority (*R*:4)	3910	3860	3905	3892	3908	3944	3954
Priority (*R*:3)	3859	3861	3951	3961	3973	3968	3901
Priority (*R*:4) limit	3803	3899	3892	3909	3910	3955	3844

Table 8. Comparison on input 1 to all output and all input to output 2 have more packet loads maximum of packet waiting time

	(1,0)	(1,1)	(1,2)	(1,3)	(0,3)	(2,2)	(3,2)
Re-2DRR (*C*:1 *R*:4)	9169	9423	9351	9460	8808	8458	8395
Re-2DRR (*C*:1 *R*:3)	8111	8143	8892	7378	7935	8032	8462
Sub-AM group (*C*:1 *G*:4)	8185	7961	9095	8018	7906	8011	7502
Sub-AM group (*C*:1 *G*:3)	8018	8424	9499	7938	8008	8400	8808
Priority (*R*:4)	8451	8753	9262	8659	9320	9339	9033
Priority (*R*:3)	8549	8936	9376	9054	8881	9117	8881
Priority (*R*:4) limit	8520	8728	8915	8648	8712	8934	8678

6. Conclusion

A new two method on Re-2DRR is proposed in this paper. The proposed method of making Sub-AM group on Re-2DRR is designed for less making Sub-AM operation. It mean more easer working and implementation. And the method of making priority port on Re-2DRR is designed for the high throughput in one specific priority port communications.

Acknowledgements

This work is supported in part by JSPS KAKENHI Grant Number 24500046.

References

[1] M. Takajo, S. Kimura and Y. Ebihara, "A Proposal of Grouped Two-Dimensional Round Robin Schedulers for Multiaccess Communications," The Transactions of the Institute of Electronics, Information and Communication Engineers B, Vol. J82-B, No. 4, 1999, pp. 560-568.

[2] Craig Partridge et al., "A 50-Gb/s IP Router," IEEE/ACM Transactions of Networking, Vol. 6, No. 3, 1998, pp. 237-248.

[3] T. Tsuda, "Multimedia Communication System," The Institute of Image Information and Television Engineers, Vol. 45, No. 1, 1991, pp. 31-34.

[4] K. Nishimura, T. Mori and Y. Ishibashi, "Video-on-Demand with Multiple Readouts," The Institute of Image Information and Television Engineers, Vol.48, No. 3, 1994, pp. 287-294.

[5] ITU-T: ITU-T Recommendation I.371, 1993, pp.2-4.

[6] R. O. LaMaire, "Two-Dimensional Round-Robin Schedulers for Packet Switches with Multiple Input Queues," IEEE/ACM Transactions on Networking, Vol. 2, No. 5, 1994, pp. 471-482.

[7] M. J .Karol, M. G. Hluchyj and S. P. Morgan, "Input versus output queueing on a space-division packet switch," IEEE Trans. Commun., Vol. COM-35, 1987, pp. 1347-1356.

[8] J. Wong, J.p. Sauve, and J.S. Field, "A Study of Fairness in Packet Switching Networks," IEEE Trans. Commun., col.COM-30, No.2, 1982, pp. 346-353.

[9] E. L. Hahne, "Round-Robin Scheduling for Mac-Min Fairness in Data Networks," IEEE Journal on Selected Areas in Communications, Vol. 9, No. 7, 1991, pp. 1024-1039.

[10] K. Omori, M. Yoo , T. Yokoyama, "A Packet Switch Scheduler based on 2DRR for High-Throughput," The 75th National Convention of IPSJ, 1L-4, 2013, pp. 205-206.

Hospital information systems: A survey of the current situation in Iran

Mohsen Pourali[1, *], Abbas Ghodrat Panah[2]

[1]Financial department, Mehr Hospital, Mashhad, Iran
[2]Accounting group, Attar University, Mashhad, Iran

Email address:
Mohsen.poorali@gmail.com (M. Pourali), Sg_abbasgh@yahoo.com (A. G. Panah)

Abstract: The main objective of hospital information systems (HIS) is to support hospital activities at practical, tactical and strategic levels. Computer based hospital information systems use computer hardware and software to collect, store, process, review and establish link with administrative data related to all hospital activities and to satisfy all the needs of clients. Considering the assessment and poll conducted in 2010 as well as the collected comments of physicians, hospital personnel, managers, researchers and computer engineering experts, HIS software in Iran consist of 10 organizational components and 10 service providing components with respect to domestic conditions. Study of HIS software providing companies in Iran during 2010 and their comparison with current status (2013) suggested that the number of HIS software manufacturing companies has experienced a 35% growth and the number of outstanding and desirable HIS sub-systems in Iran shows a 142% growth while the percentage of acceptable and rejected sub-systems has decreased by 18% in spite of the 35% growth in the number of companies.

Keywords: Computer Based Hospital Information Systems, Organizational Components, Service Providing Components, Evaluation of HIS

1. Introduction

Hospital information system also known as HIS is referred to as health information system which is an integrated information system for management, storage, and retrieval of patients' information.

The objective of these systems is to provide support for hospital activities at practical, tactical and strategic levels. In computer based HIS, computer software and hardware are used to collect, store, process, review and establish link with administrative data in all hospital activities and to satisfy the needs of clients. The fact is that nowadays a hospital may not still continue to carry out the paperwork procedure of outpatients or inpatients in its traditional style, therefore establishment of HIS seems a necessity in order to increase accuracy and expedite the provision of services to patients, paperwork and circulation of documents in the hospitals and rapid file retrieval for various purposes such as research and studies of relevant students while facilitating access to medical documents. HIS resolves all the aforesaid problems associated with various medical wards in a hospital thus transforming the hospital from a traditional organization into a modern medical center.

In fact, the HIS is not merely restricted to medical issues. Hospitals are certainly formed of clinical and para-clinical divisions that have together with the support unit constituted an integrated unit that seeks a specified objective. Support units that are serially linked to the medical wards are all in line with provision of services to the patients. Support systems in hospitals are called Management Information Systems (MIS). Since support and treatment cycles supplement one another to enlarge the service provision cycle in the hospitals, a Hospital Information Management System (HIMS) has also been established which manages the entire medical and support cycles as well as all the activities in the hospitals.

Application of hospital information system in Iran was first introduced in 1999 as it was decided to initiate it for the very first time as a pilot project in the hospitals of Shahroud, Mashhad, Yazd and Zanjan. Having made this decision, the executive procedures of HIS project commenced in 1999 at Imam Hossein Hospital of Shahroud through conducting of preliminary studies and review of existing domestic and overseas experiences. The hardware platform was equipped during the first phase of the project in 2000 while admission and discharge stages were launched in the second phase and then, the mutual link between inpatient wards of para-clinical departments, patient invoice and identification code, completion of patient discharge stages, insurance and physicians fee schedule, and the clinical information of patients were covered by the hospital electronic system until the fifth phase in September 2001. As a result, the first electronic hospital of Iran was operationalized as a national pilot project in 2000 at the Imam Hossein 313-bed hospital of Shahroud [1].

In 2003 and following a call for Iranian experts working in countries of United Arab Emirates and Canada, Astan Ghods Razavi was first to apply the first HIMS software with trade name "Green Hospital Information System" at the newly founded 320-bed Razavi Hospital of Mashhad which included a perfect hospital information management system that provides integrated coverage of the entire medical and support cycles and activities while all the parts of the aforesaid software were installed and initiated in 2005.

2. Structure and Facilities of HIS Software in Iran

While each hospital is considered an independent organization for provision of healthcare services, it is also influenced by domestic, regional and national healthcare regulations. Accordingly, hospital information systems are software systems that are highly influenced by domestic and local rules both in terms of design and assessment. Hence, it is observed that some software are manufactured in some place in the world and universally applied in other countries but this has not been the case with hospital information systems and may not be. Thus, assessment and evaluation of hospital information systems must be carried out in accordance with domestic standards either for procurement, ranking or design.

Considering the assessment and poll conducted by the Bureau of Statistics and Information Technology of the Ministry of Healthcare and Medical Education in 2010 through compilation of comments made by physicians, hospital staff, managers, researchers and computer engineering experts, the HIS software in Iran should include the following organizational components and service providing elements [4]:

2.1 Organizational Components

The organizational components consist of:

2.1.1. Admission Information Sub-System

This system is responsible for electronic documentation and admission of the patient as the first sub-system that provides services to the clients of the medical unit.

2.1.2. Outpatient Information Sub-System

While maintaining its integrity with HIS software of inpatient wards, this system must record and preserve the outpatient clients and information files.

2.1.3. Hospital Ward Information Sub-System

This sub-system must be able to cover the capabilities required for intensive care units and also be capable of establishing links with human resources, electronic medical record and electronic nursing record sub-systems.

2.1.4. Pharmacy Information Sub-System

This sub-system must be capable of recording the inpatient and outpatient information of medicines in addition to management of medicine storehouses.

2.1.5. Laboratories Information Sub-System

This sub-system is equipped with recording and provision of tests results for inpatient and outpatient while maintaining an integrated link with electronic medical record.

2.1.6. Radiology Information System

In addition to recording and providing radiology test results of inpatients and outpatient, this sub-system must be directly linked to the picture archiving communication systems (PACS).

2.1.7. Operation Room Information System

This sub-system must be capable of managing the operation room with regards to admission of patients and also be able to record the required data during the surgery.

2.1.8. Medical Document Information System

Preparation of precise and perfect information and statistics on status, quantity and quality of the services provided at the clinics, para-clinics and medical wards to be used by the state organizations engaged in the area of healthcare, managers and decision makers of hospitals are among the capabilities of this Sub-System.

2.1.9. Discharge Information System

Discharge Information System calculates the fee of medical services provided in the medical wards.

2.1.10. Hospital Nutrition Sub-System

It is used to mechanize the link between functions of nutrition department with prescriptions of the treating physician related to nutrition. In some HIS software, the aforesaid sub-system manages the meals of staff, patient escorts and those of other clients in addition to management of meals for patients.

The link between organization components is presented in Figure 1 [5].

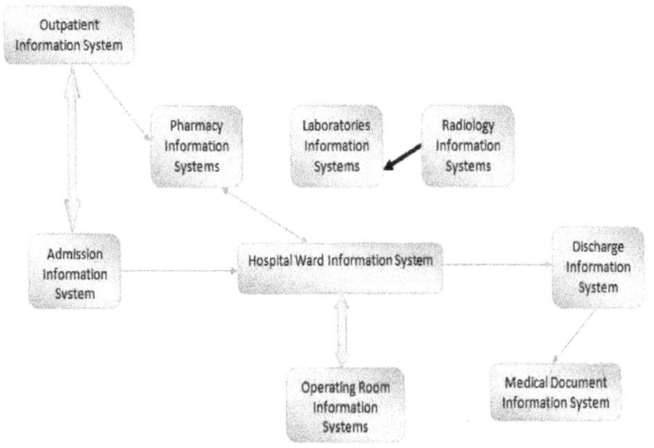

Figure 1. *The link between organizational components*

2.2. Service Providing Components

The service providing components consist of:

2.2.1. Electronic Medical Record

The electronic medical record is one of the hospital requirements the data from which are used by the entire hospital wards including medical wards, clinics and para-clinics. Although the medical information of each individual are recorded at different wards of the hospital, integrity of information in the medical record increases the efficient operation and usefulness of medical data while these information may be used in case of following referrals of patient. Some government authorities in Iran such as the Social Security Organization and some of HIS manufacturers such as Farasoo Company have already paved the way for submission of information of electronic medical record to the patient for use in other medical centers while maintaining confidentiality.

2.2.2. Electronic Nursing Record

This one deals with recording and archiving of information from patient's clinical (nursing) reports and is used similar to the medical electronic record in order to provide the data required for diagnosis and treatment. Physicians and nurses are the main beneficiaries of this system. The difficulties of using electronic nursing records in Iran include the statutory problems and the necessity for manuscript reports which has led to failure in use and entry of precise and perfect data of nurses in the HIS software due to double entry and time-consumption.

2.2.3. Bed Management Information System

Management of hospital beds calls for integrated and efficient relation between medical, admission and discharge units which is a facility provided by this sub-system.

2.2.4. Personnel and Scheduling Information System

Personal, employment, professional position and rank of personnel may be recorded via this sub-system. It also manages the schedules of medical and support personnel and is effectively linked to wage and salary system.

2.2.5. Decision Making Support Sub-System

One of the most efficient applications of using HIS software is its contribution to decision making. Diagnosis and treatment decision-support systems are currently being applied in HIS software of Iran.

2.2.6. Terminology Service

Supporting the coding systems for consistency with international organizations and unification of individuals' understanding of medical diagnoses and procedures is one of the most significant components in hospital information systems. Clinical diagnoses coding (ICD10), Clinical Procedures Coding (CPT) and Medical Laboratory Observations Coding (LOINC) are currently used in majority of HIS software of Iran.

2.2.7. Communication Service

The communication service establishes an infrastructure for transfer of data between organizational and service providing components at inter-hospital communication level in case the databanks of these two components are separated so that safe and secure transfer of data may become possible. Standard data transfer protocols such as HL7 are also underlined in the area of healthcare in case of external transfers which is also provided in some of the HIS software of Iran.

2.2.8. Telemedicine Service

Telemedicine is the application of information and telecommunications technology in order to provide remote medical services. Web-based systems have facilitated this external feature while most HIS software in Iran are equipped with this inter-hospital facility.

2.2.9. Resource Management Information Sub-system

Inventory of goods and healthcare commodities is one of the most fundamental resources of hospitals as the necessity for control of inputs and outputs, consumption, deterioration or expiration of goods is only decided in storehouse systems. In case of some HIS software that has incorporated the integrated data of support systems, other inventory of goods and commodities may also be controlled which prevents repetitive data entry and re-recording of data.

2.2.10. Security Service

Observance of information security and access limit of users are essential objectives taking into account the integrity if information in HIS software. The link between organization components is presented in Figure 2 [5].

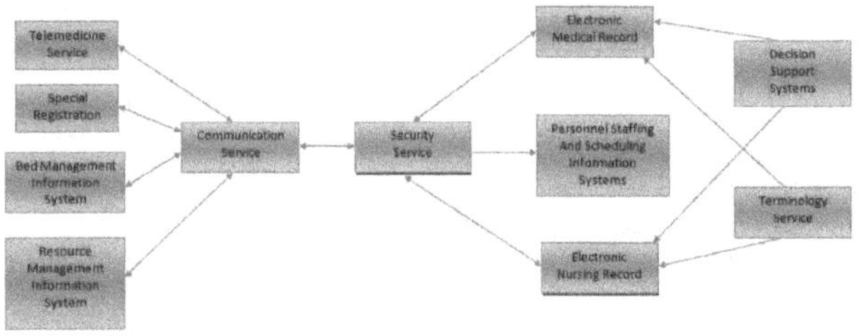

Figure 2. *The link between service providing components*

The link between organization components and service providing components is presented in Figure 3 [5].

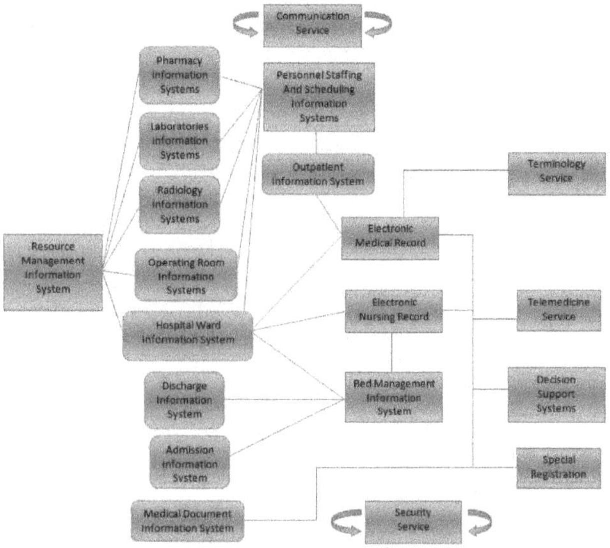

Figure 3. *The link between organizational and service providing components*

3. Current Status of HIS software in Iran

According to the study conducted by the Bureau of Statistics and Information Technology of Ministry of Healthcare and Medical Education in 2010 [3], the status of HIS software in Iran comprises 20 HIS software manufacturing companies (Table1).

Scores one, two and three have respectively been allocated to favorite, acceptable and rejected statuses. As the conducted assessment reveals, electronic medical records and discharge with 1.3 and 1.4 averages are the most favorite sub-systems while telemedicine and communication service are the most inadequate sub-systems with averages of 2.5 and 2.7, respectively.

Based on the assessment, an average of 6.7% of companies falls into favorite category while 5.9% and 7.5% of companies are categorized as acceptable and rejected, respectively.

Table 1. *List of 20 HIS software and their relevant scores*

Components	Rejected	Acceptable	Favorite	Variance	Average	Sum
Electronic Medical Record	2	17	1	0.2	2.1	41
Electronic Nursing Record	7	9	4	0.6	2.2	43
Personnel Staffing and Scheduling Information System	12	4	4	0.7	2.4	48
Decision Support Systems	8	12	0	0.3	2.4	48
Terminology Service	7	0	13	1	1.7	34
Security Service	1	15	4	0.2	1.9	37
Communication Service	17	0	3	0.5	2.7	54
Telemedicine Service	13	4	3	0.6	2.5	50
Resource Management Information System	6	3	11	0.8	1.8	35
Bed Management Information System	7	7	6	0.7	2.1	41
Admission Information Sub-System	6	6	8	0.7	1.9	38
Outpatient Information Sub-system	10	1	9	1	2.1	41
Hospital Ward Information System	8	6	6	0.7	2.1	42
Pharmacy Information System	5	6	9	0.7	1.8	36
Laboratories Information System	6	6	8	0.7	1.9	38
Radiology Information System	9	9	2	0.5	2.4	47
Operation Room Information System	9	7	4	0.6	2.3	45
Medical Document Information System	3	0	17	0.5	1.3	26
Discharge Information System	3	2	15	0.6	1.4	28
Hospital Nutrition System	10	4	6	0.8	2.2	44
Average	7.5	5.9	6.7			

The most recent status of HIS software in Iran according to the study conducted by the Bureau of Statistics and Information Technology of Ministry of Healthcare and Medical Education in 2013 [2], the status of HIS software in Iran comprises 27 HIS software manufacturing companies (Table2).

Table 2. *List of 27 HIS software and their relevant scores*

Components	Rejected	Acceptable	Favorite	Outstanding	Variance	Average
Electronic Medical Record	6	4	10	7	1.23	2.33
Electronic Nursing Record	9	5	5	8	1.56	2.56
Personnel Staffing and Scheduling Information System	14	2	3	8	1.85	2.81
Decision Support Systems	15	9	1	2	0.78	3.37
Terminology Service	1	9	11	6	0.70	2.19
Security Service	0	4	3	20	0.56	1.41
Communication Service	10	2	6	9	1.72	2.48
Telemedicine Service	13	4	3	7	1.67	2.85
Resource Management Information System	6	2	5	14	1.54	2.00

Components	Rejected	Acceptable	Favorite	Outstanding	Variance	Average
Bed Management Information System	4	1	12	10	1.04	1.96
Admission Information Sub-System	2	5	6	14	1.00	1.81
Outpatient Information Sub-system	5	6	2	14	1.53	2.07
Hospital Ward Information System	7	7	4	9	1.49	2.44
Pharmacy Information System	4	6	8	9	1.16	2.19
Laboratories Information System	2	5	9	11	0.92	1.93
Radiology Information System	6	7	7	7	1.26	2.44
Operation Room Information System	6	8	5	8	1.33	2.44
Medical Document Information System	1	5	4	17	0.86	1.63
Discharge Information System	3	5	7	12	1.11	1.96
Hospital Nutrition System	8	0	7	12	1.67	2.15
Treatment Accounting Information System	5	5	10	7	1.14	2.30
Average	6.05	4.81	6.10	10.05		

Scores one, two and three have respectively been allocated to favorite, acceptable and rejected statuses. As the conducted assessment reveals, security and medical records systems with 1.63 and 1.4 averages are the most favorite sub-systems while telemedicine and decision-support are the most inadequate sub-systems with averages of 3.37 and 2.85, respectively.

Based on the assessment, an average of 10.5 % of companies falls into excellent category while 6.10%, 4.81% and 6.05% of companies are categorized as favorite, acceptable and rejected, respectively.

Comparatively speaking and considering the following table, the numbers of HIS software manufacturing companies and favorite and excellent HIS software have grown by 35% and 142% from 2010 to 2013, respectively (Table 3).

Table 3. *Overview of number of HIS software and their status in 2010 and 2013*

	Rejected	Acceptable	Outstanding and Desirable	No. of Companies
2010 Assessment	7.45	5.9	6.65	20
2013 Assessment	6.05	4.81	16.14	27
Deviation	(1.40)	(1.09)	9.49	7
Deviation Percentage	%(18.82)	%(18.48)	%142.75	%35

4. Discussion and Conclusion

In this article we reviewed the current status of Hospital Information Systems in Iran. Our study included the comparison of characteristics of about 20 information systems. Based on the assessment, an average of 10.5 % of companies falls into excellent category while 6.10%, 4.81% and 6.05% of companies are categorized as favorite, acceptable and rejected, respectively. Considering the assessment and poll conducted in 2010 as well as the collected comments of physicians, hospital personnel, managers, researchers and computer engineering experts, HIS software in Iran consist of 10 organizational components and 10 service providing components with respect to domestic conditions. Study of HIS software providing companies in Iran during 2010 and their comparison with current status (2013) suggested that the number of HIS software manufacturing companies has experienced a 35% growth and the number of outstanding and desirable HIS sub-systems in Iran shows a 142% growth while the percentage of acceptable and rejected sub-systems has decreased by 18% in spite of the 35% growth in the number of companies.

References

[1] D., Zeydanloo. Hospital Information System. The Center for Research, Development and Policy Making of Faculty of Medical Sciences of Shahid Beheshti University, 2012.

[2] H., Riazi, S., Abedian, A., Bitaraf. Performance Assessment of Hospital Information Systems. The Bureau of Statistics and Information Technology of the Ministry of Healthcare and Medical Education, 2013.

[3] Anonymous, Results of Performance Analysis of Hospital Information System Software. The Bureau of Statistics and Information Technology of the Ministry of Healthcare and Medical Education, 2010.

[4] Anonymous, Framework of Performance Assessment of Hospital Information Systems. The Bureau of Statistics and Information Technology of the Ministry of Healthcare and Medical Education, 2010.

[5] Christoph Schlachter. New Business Models for E-Healthcare and the role of trust. Master thesis submitted to the Department of Informatics University of Zurich, Zurich, Switzerland, 2004.

Area and depth investigation of Anzali pond using satellite imageries and group method of data handling neural network

Farshad Parhizkar Miandehi[1,*], Asadollah Shahbahrami[2]

[1]Electronic and Computer Faculty, Islamic Azad University of Zanjan, Zanjan, Iran
[2]Engineering faculty, University of Guilan, Rasht, Iran

Email address:
Farshad.parhizkar@gmail.com (Farshad P. M.), shahbahrami@guilan.ac.ir (Asadollah S.)

Abstract: Analysis of changes in natural resources is one of the fundamental issues in remote sensing. Several research studies regarding the process of changes in natural resources using satellite imageries and image processing techniques have been done. Anzali pond is one of the important ecosystems in Iran that under the impact of some factors such as drought has the gradual drying trend over the last years. This study measures the area of basin surface and predicts the process of changes in the climate of the pond neighborhood during the next years, using GMDH neural network. Satellite imagery and meteorological data is used for this analysis. The final results represent reduction in area from 82 km^2 in 1998 to 51 km^2 in 2010. The average depth of the pond decreased to less than 4m in 2010 from 9m in 1998. The main reason for this reduction is diversion of rivers, sediment entering and changes in land use around the pond. If this trend continues, the amount of pollutants and toxins will reach to warning and this is a serious threat for animals and pond dwellers.

Keywords: Anzali Pond, Remote Sensing, Image Processing, GMDH Neural Network

1. Introduction

Investigating the conditions of natural ecosystems such as ponds, forests, grasslands and lakes is one of the significant issues in every country which is usually performed by remote sensing technology. Assessment or evaluation of land use changes and developments are a process that leads to understanding of how humans interact with the environment. A fundamental issue in pond evaluation is to consider changes in terms of area and depth [1].

The depth of the pond depends on the area of it. Therefore, calculation of area for forecasting the depth is essential. Several studies have been conducted about the Urmia lake in Iran about determination of influential factors on the reduction of volume and area of the Urmia Lake using visual analysis of satellite imageries and meteorological data [2]. In similar research studies, the environmental risk is determined through characterization of texture of the lake using image processing techniques [3]. In 2007, a study was done on the pond that utilized satellite imageries for estimating the masses collected on the pond surface [4]. In another work, changes in appearance of the pond, using satellite imageries and texture sampling were identified [5].

A pond is a shallow body of water separated from a sea by a low sand bank or reefs that have many advantages including flood control, water quality maintenance, wildlife habitat and erosion control. Anzali pond is one of the most important ecosystems in the north of Iran and in terms of ecological and economical sustainability has regional and international significance. Therefore, evaluation of the pond changes is essential. The Anzali pond lies in a location about 40 km from the north of Rasht in the southwest Caspian Sea.

The similarity in the texture of the pond margin is one of the most substantial issues such as the similarity between canebrake, rice cultivated land and aquatic plants, that makes it difficult to calculate the area. In this study, reaching to an appropriate formula, first, the solid part is separated from the aqueous part. Next, the area of the pond is calculated between1991 to 2010. By measuring the area and having influential factors such as sediment entering, input rivers, amount of rainfall as well as evaporation. The table of affecting factors on the pond is created and finally, using neural networks, an appropriate estimation for the future conditions of the pond according to changes in the area and depth, is estimated.

The structure of this paper is as follow:

In section 2, some primary definitions are expressed. The third section includes the proposed method and the method of calculating the area from satellite images. Next, changes in the depth and area in the future years is forecasted using neural network. Finally, in section 4 the final results are discussed.

2. Definitions and Procedures

2.1. Remote Sensing

Natural phenomena of the earth surface changes rapidly and these changes during the human life are very salient. In recent decades, using remote sensing technology for detection of these alteration, have aroused researchers' interest. Monitoring and evaluating regions such as coastal areas like the lakes and ponds as the ecological environments have been focused. Evaluating these regions is one of the essential issues in national development and natural resources management. In recent years, evaluating and detecting changes in the lakes, ponds and shorelines/coastlines became one of the important issues. Due to dynamic nature of shorelines managing this kind of ecologic environment needs correct information during specific time intervals. In this situation remote sensing technology plays a substantial role for obtaining information from phenomena on the earth surface. Multi-spectral satellite imageries have many advantages such as numeral interpretation and availability.

2.2. GMDH Neural Network

Group method of data handling (GMDH) algorithm is a self-organizing approach by which gradually complicated models are generated based on the evaluation of their performances on a set of multi-input-single-output data pairs (x_i, y_i) $(i=1, 2, \dots M)$. The GMDH was firstly developed by Ivakhnenko [6] as a multivariate analysis method for complex systems modeling and identification.

GMDH can be used to model complex systems without having specific knowledge of the systems. The main idea of GMDH is to build an analytical function in a feed forward network based on a quadratic node transfer function [7] whose coefficients are obtained using regression technique. In recent years, the use of such self-organizing network leads to successful application of the GMDH type algorithm in a broad range area in engineering, science, and economics.

3. The Proposed Procedure

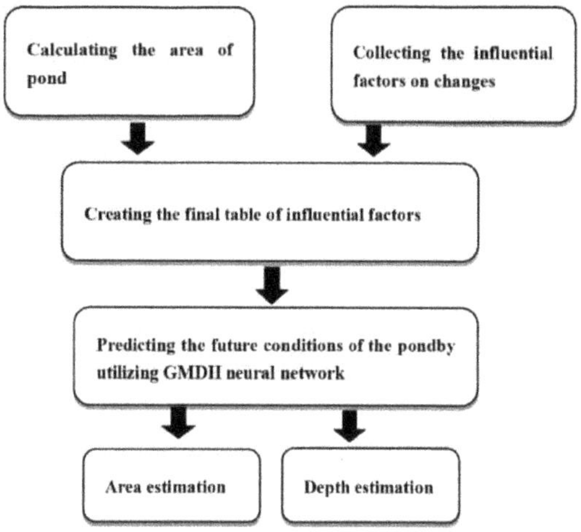

Figure 1. *The flowchart of proposed procedures*

As shown in Figure 1, first the area of pond has been calculated by using image processing techniques. Next, the table of influential factors was created according to meteorological data. In the next step, GMDH neural network was used in order to predict the future conditions of the pond's depth and area calculated based on these input data.

3.1. Measuring the Area of the Pond by Using Image Processing Techniques

Calculating the area was performed by using remote sensing and image processing techniques. In this study, the Quick bird satellite imageries were applied. In some images, noise caused some errors in calculation of the area where image processing techniques solved this problem. Next, in segmentation part, the area of the pond was separated from the ground. Finally, the area is measured by counting the pixels of pond surface and considering the image scale. For classifying pixels into two classes of water and ground, this study used spectral features of water. It means that by considering the water spectrum and taking into account the image spectral bands, through allocating precise image coefficients, the water part can be separated from the ground part. Then by counting the number of pixels in water part, area of the pond is measured.

In this method, the area is measured by dividing the number of pond pixels in $1km^2$to the total number of pixels in the same part. This method is a type of unsupervised classification and this strategy is relevant to determination of changes in the pond.

Furthermore, the pixels were classified into water and ground classes, applying the following Equation 1. In this equation B_2, B_4 , and B_5 are second, fourth and fifth band, respectively.

If ((B4 > B2) and (B5> B2))

Then 0 else 255

Figure 2 depicts the separation of water part from ground in 1991.

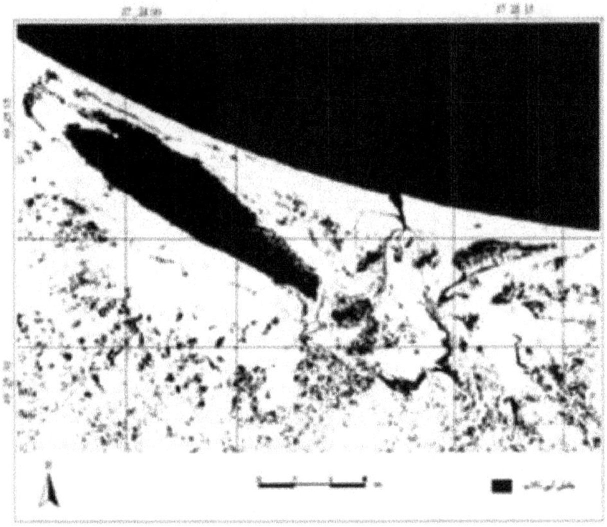

Fig. 2. Separation of water part from ground in 1991.

3.2. Modeling Using GMDH-Type Networks

The classical GMDH algorithm can be represented as set of neurons in which different pairs of them in each layer are connected through a quadratic polynomial and thus produce new neurons in the next layer. Such representation can be used in modeling map inputs to outputs. The formal definition of the identification problem is to find a function *f*, so that it can be approximately used instead of actual one, *f*, in order to predict output *y^* for a given input vector

$$(x_1,\ x_2, x_3,\dots,\ x_n\ ) \quad (1)$$

close as possible to its actual output *y* . Therefore, given *M* observation of multi-input-single-output data pairs so that

$$Y_i = \text{f}\ (x_{i1}, x_{i2}, x_{i3}, \dots, x_{i4}) \quad (2)$$

It is now possible to train a GMDH-type neural network to predict the output values

The problem is now to determine a GMDH-type neural network so that the square of difference between the actual output and the predicted one is minimized, that is

$$\sum_{i=1}^{M}(y_i^2 - y_i)^2 \to minimization \quad (3)$$

General connection between inputs and output variables can be expressed by a complicated polynomial of the form

$$Y_i = \alpha_0 + \sum_{i=1}^{n}\alpha_i x_i + \sum_{i=1}^{n}\sum_{i=1}^{n}\alpha_{ij}x_i x_j + \sum_{i=1}^{n}\sum_{i=1}^{n}\sum_{i=1}^{n}\alpha_i x_i x_j x_k \quad (4)$$

The coefficient α_i in Equation 5 are calculated using regression techniques [7, 8] so that the difference between actual output, *y*, and the calculated one, *y^*, for each pair ofx_i, $x_j$as input variables isminimized. Indeed, it can be seen that a tree ofpolynomials is constructed using the quadratic form given in Equation 5 whose coefficients are obtained in a least-squares sense. In this way, coefficients of each quadratic function $G_i$are obtained optimally fit the output in the whole set of input-output data pair, that is

$$\frac{\sum_{i=1}^{M}(y_i - g_i)^2}{Mn} \to Minmization \quad (5)$$

By using GMDH and the relevant values, the formulas of every regression related to the factors are calculated according to the Table 1.

3.2.1. Calculation of Changes in Depth of Pond

Table 1. *Function obtained from GMDH on each of the influential factors from 1991 to 2010*

Influential factors on water changes	Linear regression formula
The area	y = -0.071x + 206.34
Amount of rainfall	y = -8.6803x + 18587
Water entering	y = -6.705x + 15350
Sediment entering	y=35543x+18.339
evaporation	y=19198x+9.12543

Table 2. *Dependent and independent values for implementation of neural network in order to predicting the height of water in pond.*

Meteorological data	constants	variables
Rainfall- independent	B1	X1
Water entering- independent	B2	X2
Temperature- independent	B3	X3
Sediment- independent	B4	X4
Height- dependent	Y	

Y=1298.19+0.00033X1+0.00011X2- 0.5904X3+2.6502X4

Table 3. *Data needed for GMDH neural network*

year	Sediment entering (ton)	Volume of water enteringMillion m^3	Rainfall (mm)	Evaporation(MM)	Area (Km^2)
1991	974.44	1600	1095	1100	57.84
1993	990.759	1700	1246	950	58
1998	1073.616	3100	1154	1020	81.87
2001	1175.728	1900	1324	900	66.9
2005	1273.572	1800	1257	850	66.5
2006	1273.189	1700	1425	800	66
2007	1273.158	2000	1326	900	64.5
2008	1272.214	1900	1411	800	62.09
2009	1271.144	1800	1324	1000	60.39
2010	1291.52	1700	1264	900	56.91

For predicting the depth, meteorological data and height of the pond are independent and dependent values. By investigating the data and values according to Table 3, the coefficients and equation are obtained. The determination coefficient is about 0.74.

3.2.2. Calculation of Changes in the Surface of Area

Table 4. Dependent and independent values for implementation of neural network in order to predict the area of pond.

Meteorological data	constants	variables
Rainfall- independent	B1	X1
Water entering- independent	B2	X2
Temperature- independent	B3	X3
Area- dependent	Y	

Y=3104.01+10.1X1+0.15X2-45.13X3

For predicting the area changes with GMDH method, meteorological data and area are considered as independent and dependent values. After investigating the data and values according to table IV, the appropriate equation and formula is reached. This coefficient is about 0.89.

4. Discussion & Conclusion

Determination of climate changes in natural ecosystems is one of the vital issues in remote sensing. Anzali pond is one of the important ecosystems in north of Iran that has have severe reduction in area and depth of pond.

This study used satellite imageries and meteorological data for evaluating the area and depth of Anzali pond during 1991 to 2010. A GMDH neural network method was applied for investigating these criterions. Climate changes especially in recent years lead it to be dried. If serious decisions are not made to prevent sediment entering and changes in land use of pond surrounding, the amount of pollutant and toxins will reach to warning phase. This situation can be end angered the aquatics and birds. The depth decreased between 4 and 5m and the area of the pond also has reduction about $25km^2$. It is suggested that for the future work, a better estimation of pond position can be achieved through combining image processing techniques with other textual features like GLCM features such as entropy and mean.

The results of this research indicate a decrease in the area of about 25 km^2 and the average depth reduced about 5m between 1991 and 2010. By examining the obtained coefficients, it is understood that the trend of reduction in depth and area has increased in recent years. The main reasons for this reduction are excessive entry of industrial and non-industrial sediments to the pond, land use changes and diversion of input rivers to the pond for irrigation of agricultural lands.

Maintaining this procedure can endanger the life of birds, fishes and animal spices with extinction. The increase in pollutants and toxins are serious threats for residents of the pond. Therefore some crucial decisions should be taken for resolving the crisis.

Generally, in this paper:

First, the soil part was separated from aqueous part by using image processing techniques on satellite images. Next, the area is calculated by counting the pixels of the pond surface. For measuring the depth of the pond, the table of influential factors on the pond changes was created. Finally, by utilizing GMDH neural network, an appropriate formula for estimating the area and depth changes was estimated.

Acknowledgement

The authors would like to thank Guilan weather station for providing meteorological data that have been utilized in this research study.

References

[1] S.L., Ozesmi, E. M., Bauer. "Satellite Remote Sensing of Wetlands. Wetlands Ecology and, Management", Vol.10, pp.381-402, 2002.

[2] M. Abbaspour, and Nazaridoust, "Determination of Environmental Water Requirements of Lake Urmia, Iran: an Ecological Approach", International Journal of Environmental Studies, Vol.64, pp.161-169, 2007.

[3] E. De Roeck, K, Jones, "Integrating Remote Sensing and Wetland Ecology: a Case Study on South African Wetlands", pp.1-5, 2008.

[4] T. Qulin, Y. Shao, S. Yang, Q. Wei, "Wetland Vegetation Biomass Estimation Using Landsat-7 ETM+ Data", Geoscience and Remote Sensing Symposium, Vol.4, pp. 2629 – 2631, 2003.

[5] G. Zhaoning, G. Huili, Z. Wenji, L. Xiaojuan, H. Zhuowei, "Using RS and GIS to Monitoring Beijing Wetland Resources Evolution", Geoscience and Remote Sensing Symposium IEEE International, Vol.23, pp.4596 – 4599, 2007.

[6] J. Harken, and J. Gerjevic, Using Remote Sensing Data to Study Wetland Dynamics in Iowa. Grant (Seed) Final Technical Report, University of Northern Lowa, 2004.

[7] A.G., Ivakhnenko, "Polynomial Theory ofComplex Systems", Systems. Man &Cybernetics. IEEE Transaction, Vol.SMC-1, pp.364-378, 1971.

[8] S.J. Farlow, et al., Self-organizing Method inModeling: GMDH type algorithm, MarcelDekker Inc., 1984.

[9] A. Darvizeh, N. Nariman-Zadeh, and H. Gharababei, "GMDH-Type NeuralNetwork Modelling of Explosive CuttingProcess of Plates Using Singular ValueDecomposition", Systems Analysis Modelling Simulation,Vol.43, pp.1383-1397, 2003.

APLSSVM: Hybrid Entropy Models for Image Retrieval

Li Jun-yi[1], Li Jian-hua[1], Zhu Jin-hua[2], Chen Xiao-hui[3]

[1]School of Electronic Information and Electrical engineering, Shanghai JiaoTong University, Shanghai, China
[2]College of Network Communication Zhejiang Yuexiu University of Foreign Languages, Zhe Jiang, China
[3]Information Engineering School, Yulin University, Yulin, Shanxi, China

Email address:
leejy2006@163.com (Li Jun-yi)

Abstract: Aiming at properties of remote sensing image data such as high-dimension, nonlinearity and massive unlabeled samples, a kind of probability least squares support vector machine (PLSSVM) classification method based on hybrid entropy and L_1 norm was proposed. Firstly, hybrid entropy was designed by combining quasi-entropy with entropy difference, which was used to select the most "valuable" samples to be labeled from massive unlabeled sample set. Secondly, a L_1 norm distance measuring was used to further select and remove outliers and redundant data from the sample set to be labeled. Finally, based on originally labeled samples and screened samples, PLSSVM was gained through training. Experimental results on classification of ROSIS hyperspectral remote sensing images show that the overall accuracy and Kappa coefficient of the proposed classification method reach 89.90% and 0.8685 respectively. The proposed method can obtain higher classification accuracy with few training samples, which is much applicable to classification problem of remote sensing images.

Keywords: Remote Sensing Image, L_1 Norm, Active Learning,
PLSSVM (Probability Least Squares Support Vector Machine), Hybrid Entropy

1. Introduction

Classification of remote sensing images means to make each pixel point region in the image belong to a category in several categories or one among several special elements. The classification results is to divide image space into several sub-regions, and each sub-region presents a practical land object [1-2]. In actual classification of remote sensing images, there are usually massive unlabeled samples, while the proportion of labeled samples is very small. Thus, it is very difficult to look for the information in need of labeling from these massive unlabeled samples. Besides, the cist used to label these samples is very high. Active learning algorithm is a new method for sample training. It is different from passive learning algorithm where samples are selected randomly [3-4]. In the process of machine learning, learners can actively choose the data most beneficial to improving properties of a classifier, automatically mark and add them in training samples for learning so as to effectively avoid excessive manual intervention and reduce the number of labeled samples.

The core of active learning algorithm is that which strategic selection function is used to select the most "valuable" sample for labeling from unlabeled samples. Since the evaluation criteria for "value" are different, multiple active learning algorithms appear. Literature [4] selects the samples for labeling which current classifier cannot confirm the category mostly. Generally, this is called uncertain sampling. This method can fully select the samples beneficial to the classifier, and gain better results than random algorithm. But it has large randomness, so only sub-superior samples set can be picked out. In addition, outliers and redundant data may be easily chosen [7]. The introduction of quasi-entropy can reduce sampling randomness to some extent. Literature [8] proposes a heuristic active learning algorithm which selects the most possible misclassified samples based on committee. This algorithm chooses the most possible misclassified samples of current classifier during every sampling and eliminates the samples more than a half in the space so as to gain faster convergence speed than mainstream selection algorithm. Literature [9] randomly selects unlabeled samples from uncertain misclassified samples on the verification set for labeling. This algorithm owns better accuracy rate than standard algorithm. But, these algorithms still probably choose outliers and redundant data, and calculation complexity is high. The introduction of entropy difference can help pick up misclassified samples more conveniently. In order to get more refined sample set, hybrid entropy is gained through fusing quasi-entropy and entropy difference. Since the algorithm may result in selecting outliers and redundant data, L_1 norm distance measurement is used to choose these data and eliminate them.

This paper proposes an active learning algorithm based on hybrid entropy and L_1 norm. This algorithm improves selection function from two aspects: 1) the most "valuable' samples are selected with hybrid entropy, and a rough sample set to be labeled is gained; L_1 norm distance measurement is used to choose and eliminate possible outliers and redundant data; 2) remote sensing image data usually own such features as high dimension, nonlinearity and massive data, so support vector machine ca be used to analyze and treat them. But traditional support vector machine classification method only takes into account of two extreme cases during deciding sample classification, i.e. the label for the sample belonging to the category is +1 and the label for the sample which does not belong to the category is -1. However, in practical application, due to the existence of uncertainty and influence of external factors, every sample has different division methods. Especially form some problems, due to sample randomness and fuzziness, they cannot be classified into a class explicitly, but can only classified into a class according to certain probability or certain membership degree. So, it is improper to empress class information only with $\{-1,+1\}$ [10]. Thus, for the samples selected on the basis of active learning algorithm, PLSSVM is adopted as the classifier to classify and identity hyperspectral remote sensing images.

2. Plssvm

Aiming at classification inaccuracy and uncertainty of traditional support vector machine as well as defects of interference samples, Literature [10] designs PLSSVM to classify the samples which cannot be explicitly classified into a class according to certain probability. In this way, sample classification has qualitative interpretation and quantitative evaluation. Posterior probability of sample x belonging to each class is:

$$\begin{bmatrix} 1 & -p(1|2) & \cdots & -p(1|c) \\ -p(2|1) & 1 & \cdots & -p(2|c) \\ \vdots & \vdots & & \vdots \\ -p(c|1) & -p(c|2) & \cdots & 1 \end{bmatrix} \cdot (p_1, p_2 \cdots, p_c)^T = (0,0,\cdots,0)^T, \quad (1)$$

Where, c is the number of classes; $p(c|1)$ is posterior probability that sample x belongs to the cth class under the condition where sample x belongs to the first class. Similarly, $p(1|c)$; p_m is posterior probability that sample x belongs to the mth class $(m=1,2,\cdots,c)$.

Formula (1) can be regarded as c equation sets used to solve c unknown variables p_m. Through solving Formula (1), in output probability modeling of multi-classification problem, decision function of p_m of sample x in each class can be gained, i.e. take the class with the largest posterior probability as the sample. The class that x belongs to is as follows:

$$y(x) = \arg\max_{m=1,2,\cdots,c}(p_m). \quad (2)$$

3. Active Learning Based on Hybrid Entropy and L_1 Norm

Labeled sample set $L=\{(x_1,y_1),(x_2,y_2),\cdots,(x_l,y_l)\}$ from unknown distribution and an unlabelled sample set $U=\{x_{l+1},x_{l+2},\cdots x_n\}$ are given. Overall sample set is $\chi = L \cup U$. There are c classes. $x_i \in R^d$ ($i=1,2,\cdots,n$; d refers to the number of dimensions of samples) and $y_i \in \{1,2,\cdots,c\}$ is the label of sample x_i. The system adopts labeled sample set L as the training set to gain initial PLSSVM classifier, and actively selects some samples with large information quantity from unlabelled sample set U according to a strategy. Then, experts label them and add them in the training set. Thus, new PLSSVM classifier is obtained. After repeated cycles, classification results will finally reach the threshold value of an evaluation index or specified cycle times.

A. Sample selection strategy based on hybrid entropy

The classifier may easily make mistakes during judging the most uncertain sample classification, thus leading to low classification accuracy rate. Therefore, uncertainty is an important factor that experts should consider when selecting the samples to be labeled. Sample uncertainty algorithms can be based on Shannon entropy, posterior probability and the nearest boundary etc. The algorithm based on Shannon entropy has gained good results in many applications, but it cannot select the optimal samples so that calculation complexity is high during training the set. Thus, optimization selection standard (i.e. quasi-entropy with high quality factor) is needed to measure sample uncertainty. Literature [11] points out that quality factor of $-p^a (0<a<1)$ convex function is higher than that of $p\log p$. If the quality factor is larger, quasi-entropy is more sensitive to probability distribution evenness near the minimum value, and the shape of minimum value of quasi-entropy is shaper. So, quasi-entropy surpasses Shannon entropy in terms of significance index of minimum value. Therefore, quasi-entropy with high quality factor replaces Shannon entropy. Assuming posterior probabilities that sample x_i belongs to every class are $p_1, p_2, \cdots p_c$, and $\sum_{m=1}^{c} p_{im} = 1$ is met, uncertainty measure of sample x_i can be expressed as

$$\lambda_i = \sum_{m=1}^{c} f(p_{im}) \quad (3)$$

Where, $f(p_{im}) = -p_{im}^a$; λ_i has the following properties:

Property 1: when posterior probability distribution is most even (i.e. all p_m are equal), λ_i is the minimum and equal to $cf(1/c)$. This is also the situation where uncertainty is the largest.

It can be known from Property 1 that when posterior probabilities p_m that sample x_i belongs to every class are equal, sample uncertainty is the largest, and the value of quasi-entropy λ_i is the smallest. So, quasi-entropy can be sued to figure out uncertainty measurement value of each sample. If quasi-entropy value of samples is smaller, the information quantity is larger.

In information entropy, the samples which may be easily misclassified can be expressed with the absolute value of differences of two absolute values:

$$d_i = |H(p_{\max}) - H(p_{\sec})|,$$
$$H(p_{\max}) = -p_{\max} \log p_{\max}, \tag{4}$$
$$H(p_{\sec}) = -p_{\sec} \log p_{\sec},$$

Where, $p_{\max}$ is the maximum posterior probability that sample x_i belongs to every class; $p_{\sec}$ is the second largest posterior probability that sample x_i belongs to every class.

Entropy difference distance metric function of density functions $p_{\max}$ and $p_{\sec}$ of the two posterior probabilities have the following characteristic [12]

$$\|p_{\max} - p_{\sec}\|_{L_1} = \sum |p_{\max} - p_{\sec}| \le \frac{1}{2} \tag{5}$$

Where, $\|p_{\max} - p_{\sec}\|_{L_1}$ is standard Minkowski L1 norm distance measurement, then

$$|H(p_{\max}) - H(p_{\sec})| \le \|p_{\max} - p_{\sec}\|_{L_1} \tag{6}$$

This characteristic shows retrieval results of Entropy difference distance metric is included in retrieval results of L_1 norm distance measurement, and the retrieval range narrows.

It can be seen from Formula (4), when posterior probability of samples changes slightly, and the change in entropy value will also be small. When entropy difference value is smaller, the possibility that sample x_i belongs to some two classes is close, i.e. this sample may be misclassified most easily, and the information quantity is also the largest.

According to analysis of quasi-entropy and entropy difference, the following conclusions can be drawn: if quasi-entropy value is smaller, sample uncertainty is larger; entropy difference value is smaller, the sample may be misclassified more easily. If the values of quasi-entropy and entropy difference are smaller, information quantity is larger and there are larger impacts in classification effects. In massive data sets, the sample size selected purely by quasi-entropy or entropy difference strategy is also large. In order to pick out more refined samples and reduce labeling cost, quasi-entropy and entropy difference are fused to gain a new sample selection measurement strategy - hybrid entropy.

$$u_i = \lambda_i d_i. \tag{7}$$

M samples with the highest information quantity are worked out according to Formula (7), i.e. M samples with the smallest u_i value.

B. Sample similarity measurement based on L_1 norm

The samples selected by hybrid entropy may have outliers and redundant data. These data make little contributions to classification accuracy of the classifier and even will affect its classification accuracy. Therefore, L_1 norm distance measurement will be adopted to work out similarity among samples. Outliers and redundant data will be removed according to similarity value.

Literature [13] adopts L_1 norm, L_2 norm and quadric expression to compare data retrieval properties. The testing results show these distance measurement methods differ little in retrieval property. L_1 norm distance measurement is more robust than L_2 norm distance measurement, and L_1 norm distance measurement is the most simplest in calculation. So, L_1 norm distance measurement is adopted to calculate similarity among samples to be labeled.

$$s_{hj} = \sum_{k=1}^{d} |x_{hk} - x_{jk}|, \quad (h, j = 1, 2, \cdots, v), \tag{8}$$

Where, x_{hk} and x_{jk} are the kth attribute in the hth and jth samples; v is the number of samples.

Assuming mean space distance of samples of the same class is θ, $a = \theta/100$, $\beta = \theta$. If $s_{hj} < a$, sample x_j is judged to be redundant information and eliminated; if $\min s_{hj} > \beta$, sample x_j is judged to be an outlier and deleted. Then, the remaining samples are selected and submitted to experts for labeling. This deletes outliers, eliminates redundant data, further narrows scale of sample set to be labeled and reduces cost of manual labeling.

4. Algorithm Steps

Input: labeled sample set is expressed as L and unlabelled sample set is expressed as U; the number of samples is expressed as M; ending condition is expressed as S; the parameter is expressed as *a*.

Algorithm process:

1) Train classifier PLSSVM with labeled sample set;
2) Carry out a~g repeatedly until ending condition S is met;
   a) Posterior probability that unlabeled sample set U belongs to each class is calculated with classifier PLSSVM;
   b) Calculate quasi-entropy λ_i and entropy difference d_i of unlabeled samples according to posterior probability gained, Formula (3) and (4);
   c) Calculate hybrid entropy u_i according to Formula (7);

d) Select m samples with the smallest u_i value and add them in the sample set to be labeled;
e) Calculate similarity of M samples according to Formula (8), eliminate the samples meeting $s_{hj} < a$ and $\min s_{hj} > \beta$, and make the remaining samples form new sample subset A;
f) Submit A to experts for labeling and add labeled samples in L;
g) PLSSVM. Utilize L to train classifier PLSSVM again.

Output: train sample set L finally labeled and gain classifier PLSSVM.

5. Experiment and Analysis

A. ROSIS hyperspectral experimental data

ROSIS hyperspectral experimental data come from Literature [14]. Spectral region is 0.43~0.86 μm, with 610×340 pixel, 103 wave bands and 1.3 spatial resolution. Besides, training region and testing region actually measured synchronously are provided. The training samples include 9 classes of land objects: bituminous pavement (548 pixel), tree (524 pixel), brick (514 pixel), shadow (231 pixel), pitch roof (375 pixel), bare land (532 pixel), metal plate (265 pixel), grit (392 pixel) and grassland (540 pixel). Testing samples include 9 classes of land objects: bituminous pavement (6592 pixel), tree (3064 pixel), brick (3682 pixel), shadow (942 pixel), pitch roof (1330 pixel), bare land (5029 pixel), metal plate (1345 pixel), grit (2099 pixel) and grassland (18675 pixel). ENVI4.7 software is utilized to transform original data corresponding to the regions ROSIS hyperspectral image training sample and testing sample are interested in to ASCII data so as to process data in Matlab 7.8 environment.

B. Calcification results of remote sensing image and analysis of results

Active learning algorithm is adopted to select training samples for the classifier and to construct two types of APLSSVM, expressed as APLSSVM1 and APLSSVM2 in this paper. In the experiment process, parameter setting is as follows: kernel function of PLSSVM adopts polynomial kernel function; the optimal values of penalty parameter C and kernel parameter γ are confirmed with cross validation method, a=0.6 and M=100.

1) Based on the same initial sample set, change the number of newly-added training samples, evaluate effects of the number of newly-added training samples on classification accuracy of two type of APLSSVM; the ending condition S is that the difference between adjacent two classification accuracies is less than 0.002 or the number of iteration times reaches 15. This indicates high classification accuracy can be gained when PLSSVM is used to process remote sensing images; when the number of newly-added training samples is less than 300, classification accuracy of APLSSVM1 boots rapidly with the rise in the number of labeled samples; when the number of newly-added training samples exceeds 300, classification accuracy of APLSSVM1 basically tends to be stable and maintains about 90% with the rise in the number of labeled samples; for APLSSVM2, its classification accuracy increases slowly with the rise in the number of labeled samples; to reach the same classification accuracy with APLSSVM1, APLSSVM2 needs more labeled samples, which will consumes more time and energy of experts. So, the cost is expensive.
2) In the experiment, given training samples serve as the initial sample set. Under the condition where the number of newly-added training samples is the same, classification effects of two APLSSVM classifiers and passive PLSSVM classifier are compared. APLSSVM1 and APLSSVM2 selects newly-added training samples for labeling through iteration of active learning algorithm; passive PLSSVM directly selects samples of the same number as newly-added samples for training. The number of training samples the three classifiers select is: original sample set + 300 newly-added samples. The ending condition S is that the number of iterations reaches 3. Table 1, Table 2 and Table 3 are confusion matrix and Kappa coefficient corresponding to each figure.

It can be seen that APLSSVM2 and passive PLSSVM classify most grassland into bare land, and the misclassification phenomenon is serious; APLSSVM1 performs relatively well in this aspect and can well classify the two types of land objects; misclassification accuracy of other land objects approaches for the three classifiers.

The following can be gained according to Table 1-3:

User's accuracy: among all kinds of land objects, user's accuracy differs mostly for bare land. User's accuracy of APLSSVM1 is 80.04%, up over 30% compared with user's accuracy of APLSSVM2 and passive PLSSVM. According to confusion matrix in Table 2 and Table 3, APLSSVM2 and passive PLSSVM misclassify most grassland into bare land. Thus, the proportion of grassland in bare land samples exceeds a half. For pitch roof, the largest user's accuracy of APLSSVM2 is 83.90%, followed by APLSSVM1 (70.29%), and passive PLSSVM has the smallest user's accuracy (65.58%). For the three classifiers, user's accuracy differs little among other land objects.

Table 1. *Confusion matrix obtained by APLSSVM 1*

	Bituminous pavement	Tree	Brick	Shadow	Pitch roof	Bare land	Metal plate	Grit	Grassland	User's accuracy/%
Bituminous pavement	5416	5	166	0	115	9	0	25	11	94.24
Tree	0	2747	3	0	0	13	0	0	465	85.10
Brick	273	0	3196	0	11	50	5	379	41	80.81
Shadow	26	1	0	942	0	0	2	0	0	97.01

	Bituminous pavement	Tree	Brick	Shadow	Pitch roof	Bare land	Metal plate	Grit	Grassland	User's accuracy/%
Pitch roof	418	0	36	0	1201	2	53	5	0	70.29
Bare land	23	201	0	0	0	4799	0	0	973	80.04
Metal plate	0	2	0	0	0	35	1281	0	0	97.19
Grit	405	0	251	0	3	0	2	1687	0	71.85
Grassland	31	94	28	0	0	121	2	3	16901	98.38
Producer's accuracy/%	82.16	90.07	86.85	100	90.30	95.43	95.24	80.37	91.90	Overall accuracy=89.90% Kappa=0.8685

Table 2. *Confusion matrix obtained by APLSSVM 2*

	Bituminous pavement	Tree	Brick	Shadow	Pitch roof	Bare land	Metal plate	Grit	Grassland	User's accuracy/%
Bituminous pavement	5717	0	240	0	129	4	0	31	13	93.20
Tree	0	2889	0	0	0	12	0	0	703	80.16
Brick	135	0	3172	0	3	18	0	380	30	84.86
Shadow	27	0	0	942	0	0	1	0	0	97.11
Pitch roof	209	0	17	0	1193	0	0	3	0	83.90
Bare land	10	59	3	0	0	4958	1	0	5115	48.87
Metal plate	0	1	0	0	0	0	1287	0	0	99.92
Grit	345	0	206	0	1	0	0	1675	0	75.21
Grassland	19	76	24	0	0	9	1	4	12796	98.97
Producer's accuracy/%	88.47	95.50	86.62	100	89.97	99.14	99.77	80.03	68.59	Overall accuracy=81.56% Kappa=0.7691

Table 3. *Confusion matrix obtained by passive PLSSVM*

	Bituminous pavement	Tree	Brick	Shadow	Pitch roof	Bare land	Metal plate	Grit	Grassland	User's accuracy/%
Bituminous pavement	5341	5	146	1	111	5	0	24	21	94.46
Tree	0	2805	2	0	0	15	0	1	981	73.74
Brick	284	0	3174	0	9	51	9	373	79	79.77
Shadow	3	1	0	841	0	0	2	0	100	88.81
Pitch roof	411	0	24	0	1107	4	51	3	88	65.58
Bare land	19	84	2	0	0	4801	0	0	5253	47.26
Metal plate	0	2	0	0	0	35	1181	0	98	89.74
Grit	402	0	208	0	3	0	1	1596	78	69.76
Grassland	32	67	26	0	0	18	1	2	12477	98.84
Producer's accuracy/%	82.27	94.63	88.61	99.88	90	97.40	94.86	79.84	65.07	Overall accuracy=78.48% Kappa=0.7305

Producer's accuracy: producer's accuracy of grassland differs most greatly. Producer's accuracy of APLSSVM1 is 91.90%, up over 20% compared with producer's accuracy of APLSSVM2 and passive PLSSVM. According to confusion matrixes in Table 2 and Table 3, nearly 1/3 grassland samples are misclassified into bare land. Producer's accuracy of other land objects approaches for the three classifiers. Overall accuracy and Kappa coefficient: since overall accuracy takes into account of corresponding weight relationship of each class, it is relatively objective; since Kappa coefficient considers the prelateship between user's accuracy and producer's accuracy, it has become classification accuracy evaluation index of remote sensing images together with overall accuracy. Based on analysis of Table 1-3, overall accuracy and Kappa coefficient of APLSSVM1 are the highest, followed by APLSSVM2. Passive PLSSVM performs most poorly.

Experiment results show, APLSSVM1 over considers sample uncertainty and samples which may be easily misclassified, and eliminates outliers and redundant data from samples to be selected. Finally, more refined training sample set is gained. Therefore, under the same number of training samples, APLSSVM1 has higher classification accuracy than other classifiers.

6. Conclusions

a) Hybrid entropy gained through fusing quasi-entropy and

entropy difference can measure sample uncertainty and avoid sample misclassification. Sample selection strategy based on hybrid entropy can choose more refined samples and reduce the cost of manual labeling.

b) Sample similarity measurement method based on L_1 norm can screen out outliers and redundant data, which further reduces the scale of sample set to be labeled and cost of manual labeling.

c) Compared with heuristic active learning algorithm which selects the most possible misclassified samples based on committee, active learning algorithm based on hybrid entropy and L_1 norm can pick out more valuable samples to be labeled and gain high classification accuracy with few training samples.

d) PLSSVM owns both qualitative explanation and quantitative evaluation during classifying uncertain samples, suitable for classifying remote sensing image data.

e) For remote sensing image data with massive unlabelled samples, active learning can help find out the most valuable information from massive unlabeled samples. Compared with passive PLSSVM which selects samples randomly, APLSSVM owns higher classification accuracy.

References

[1] WANG Yuan-yuan, CHEN Yun-hao, LI Jing. Application of model tree and support vector regression in the hyperspectral remote sensing [J]. Journal of China University of Mining & Technology, 2006.35(6):818-823.

[2] CHEN Shao-jie, LI Guang-li, ZHANG Wei, et al. Land use classification in coal mining area using remote sensing images based on multiple classifier combination [J]. Journal of China University of Mining & Technology, 2011, 40(2):273-278.

[3] HAMANAKA Y, SHINODA K, TSUTAOKA T, et al. Committee-based active learning for speech recognition [J]. IEICE Transactions on Information and Systems, 2011, 94(10):2015-2023.

[4] ZHANG L J, CHEN C, BU J J, et al. Active learning based on locally linear reconstruction[J]. IEEE Transactions on Pattern Analysis and Machine Intelligence, 2011, 33(10): 2026-2038.

[5] SUN Z C, LIU Z G, LIU S H, et al. Active learning with support vector machines in remotely sensed image classification[C]//QIU P H. YIU C. ZHANG H. et al. Proceedings of the 2nd International Congress on Image and Signal Processing. Piscataway: IEEE Computer Society. 2009: 1-6.

[6] TUIA D. RATLE F. PACIFICI F. et al. Active learning methods for remote sensing image classification [J]. IEEE Transactions on Geoscience and Remote Sensing, 2009, 47(7): 2218-2232.

[7] CHEN Y, HE Z. Blind separation using a class of new independence measures[C]//IEEE. Proceedings of IEEE International Conference on Acoustics, Speech, and Signal Processing. Piscataway: IEEE Signal Process, 2003: 309-312.

[8] LONG J, YIN J P, ZHU E. An active learning method based on most possible misclassification sampling using committee [J]. Lecture Notes in Computer Science. 2007. 4617: 104-113.

[9] BRUZZONE L, PERSELLO C. Active learning for classification of remote sensing images[C]//IEEE. Proceedings of IEEE International Geoscience and Remote Sensing Symposium. Piscataway: IEEE In-corporated, 2009: 693-696.

[10] GAO Y, WANG X S, CHENG Y H, et al. Fault diagnosis using a probability least squares support vector classification machine [J]. Mining Science and Technology, 2010, 20(6) : 917-921.

[11] CHEN Yang. Properties of quasi-entropy and their application [J]. Journal of Southeast University: Natural Science Edition, 2006, 36(2): 221-225.

[12] COX I J, MILLER M L, MINKA T P, et al. The bayesian image retrieval system, PieHunter: theory, implementation, and psyehophysieal experiments [J]. IEEE Transactions on Image Processing, 2000, 9(1): 20-37.

[13] JOHN R S. Integrated spatial and feature image systems: retrieval, analysis, and compression [D]. New York: Columbia University, 1997.

[14] WEI L, SAURABH P. JAMES E F. et al. Locality-preserving dimensionality reduction and classification for hyperspectral image analysis [J]. IEEE Transactions on Geoscience and Remote Sensing, 2012, 50(5): 1185-1198.

Sparse spectral hashing for content-based image retrieval

Li Jun-yi, Li Jian-hua

School of Electronic Information and Electrical engineering, Shanghai JiaoTong University, Shanghai 200240, China

Email address:
leejy2006@163.com (Li Jun-yi), ljh888@sjtu.edu.cn (Li Jian-hua)

Abstract: In allusion to similarity calculation difficulty caused by high maintenance of image data, this paper introduces sparse principal component algorithm to figure out embedded subspace after dimensionality reduction of image visual words on the basis of traditional spectral hashing image index method so that image high-dimension index results can be explained overall. This method is called sparse spectral hashing index. The experiments demonstrate the method proposed in this paper superior to LSH, RBM and spectral hashing index methods.

Keywords: Hashing Index, Sparse Dimensionality Reduction, Laplacian Image

1. Introduction

There are often hundreds of visual features extracted from images. These high-dimension features give rise to huge difficulties for machine learning algorithms such as image similarity study and semantic analysis. To solve this problem, index technology of image high-dimension features becomes a research hotspot in recent years.

Although multi-dimension technology represented by R Tree and KD Tree have gained certain progress, the researches show that time expenditure of most multi-dimension index structures is exponential order, unsuitable for high-dimension situation (such as dozens of dimensions). Besides, the query efficiency is even lower than that of sequential scanning of original data. Meanwhile, how to guarantee data Semantic Hashing [8] (i.e. similarity calculated in index space keeps consistent with original high-dimension space) becomes a hot issue.

In this aspect, LSH(Locality Sensitive Hash) index method [5,6] is proposed. LSH maps high-dimension features into embedded subsapce through a group of hash functions to reach high-dimension index purpose. In LSH, hash functions must meet the following conditions: after harsh function mapping, conflict probability of any two high-dimension data is in direct proportion to the distance of data points among original high-dimension space. Since LSH generates index coding based on probability model, it is hard to gain stable results in actual applications. In addition, with the rise in coding digits, LSH accuracy rate improves slowly. Different from random index of LSH, some index technologies based on machine learning are put forward, such as RBM (restricted Boltzmann machine RBM) [8] and stump Boosting SSC[9]. RBM utilizes two-layer unoriented graphics model to generate RBM random index and present exponentially distributed data. Researches show RBM will gain better index properties than LSH[11]. But, due to complexity of RBM, accuracy and efficiency cannot be ensured at the same time, "Boosting" is a technique to enhance generalization ability of machine learning method. It repeatedly constructs weak classifiers through giving training data different distribution weight, and then weak learning devices are combined to generate strong classifiers to gain machine learning results. Researches show Boosting-based index method is also more effective than LSH index coding, but slightly weaker than RBM[11]. But, Boosting is still faced with the problems of high complexity and low high-dimension index efficiency.

To overcome the above problems, Spectral Hashing (SH) index technology based on spectral analysis is proposed [11]. SH introduces eigenfunction for high-dimension data sample. Binary coding is directly conducted for high-dimension data dimension reduction through Principle Component Analysis (PCA). SH can not just improve index efficiency, but also can keep consistent between sample distance calculated in index space and original high-dimension space. But, SH method applies PAC to reduce dimension for original space in index coding process so that all high-dimension features (or visual words) participate in coding. In practice, generally semantics implied in an image is represented only with several distinctive features, rather than introducing other unrelated features in image expression

Based on such consideration, this paper introduces Sparse Principle Component Analysis (SPCA) in SH index coding process and puts forward corresponding global optimization solution to establish explainable binary coding for large-scale image data and fulfill image index. This paper calls such method Sparse Spectral Hashing (SSH) index.

2. SSH

2.1. Relevant Definitions and Hypotheses

A training set composed of N images $\{(x_i): i = 1, 2, \dots N)\}$ is given, where x_i means d-dimension eigenvector of the ith image, and d means the number of visual words in the training set. Θ is the index function of d-dimension vector x_i mapped to m-dimension Hamming space vector y_i from Euclidean space. Θ can be defined as follows:

$$\Theta : x_i \in R^d \rightarrow y_i \in \{-1,-1\}^m \quad (1)$$

A good index function Θ must have the following characteristics: 1) Θ is semantic hash function. In other words, if Euclidean distance between vector x_i representing the ith image and vector x_j representing the jth image is very close, corresponding result after they pass Θ index is also very close to Hamming distance; 2) the index result gained by Θ is efficient. In other words, original data of the whole image data set are mapped by Θ, relatively few coding digits are needed to express original high-dimension image data; 3) the mapping process of Θ index coding can be explained. For every image, just a few visual words used to distinguish semantics are needed for expression.

Favorable index coding should be efficient and keep similarity of the data indexed in original space [11]. In other words, the probability that the result of a bit in index coding is 1 and -1, and each bit is not correlated. SH coding defines the following objective function and constraint conditions to gain the index results:

$$\begin{aligned} &\min imize : trace(Y^T L Y) \\ &subject : \mathrm{Y(i,j)} \in \{-1,-1\} \\ &Y^T 1 = 0 \\ &Y^T Y = I \end{aligned} \quad (2)$$

Where, $L = D - W$ is Laplacian matrix; $W \in R^{N*N}$ is similarity matrix, $W(\mathrm{i,j}) = \exp(-\| x_i - x_j \| / \varepsilon^2)$; D is diagonal matrix, with diagonal element of $D(i,i) = \sum_j^N W(i,j)$. $Y(i,j) \in \{-1,1\}$ makes sure index coding is binary coding; $Y^T 1 = 0$ makes sure the probability that index coding is 1 and -1 is 50%, while $Y^T Y = I$ make sure every bit of index coding is not correlated.

Solving Equation (2) is a NP problem. SH relaxing index coding result is binary condition so that Equation (2) is solvable. That is, SH converts solving Equation (2) to solving the minimum eigenvalue of Laplacian matrix L. After solving Equation (2) is converted to dimensionality reduction problem of Laplacian eigenmap, PCA is directly introduced in SH to carry out dimensionality reduction for original data.

However, in PCA dimensionality reduction process, every dimension of original data participates in dimensionality reduction in the form of linear combination. It is hard to gain physical interpretation of this process. For given image training set, over-completed visual words can be usually gained. An image can be fully expressed only with several visual words, i.e. an image is usually related to a limited number of visual words. For example, visual words related to colors may be more suitable for expressing rainbow, while visual words related to shapes are more suitable for expressing automobile.

This paper uses SPCA[12] in SH index to replace PCA, transforms traditional PCA to non-convex regression form to gain SPC so that index coding is more interpretable. This algorithm in this paper is called SSH index. Since SPCA is a non-convex algorithm, convex optimization algorithm is thus adopted to gain globally optimal solution of SPC.[4]

Assuming SPC p of Laplacian matrix L is a d-dimension vector, the following optimization problem can be gained through giving a constraint to cardinality of p and removing unrelated limiting conditions [12]:

$$\begin{aligned} &\min imize : p^T L p + \rho Card^2(p) \\ &subjectto : p(i) \in \{-1,1\} \\ &p^T 1 = 0 \end{aligned} \quad (3)$$

Where, $Card(p)$ means cardinality of p; parameter ρcontrols sparse degree. Solving Equation (3) is still a NP problem. However, we can find out corresponding positive semidefinite convex optimization problem [4]:

$$\begin{aligned} &\min imize : trace(LP) + \rho 1^T |P| 1) \\ &subjectto : p(i) \in \{-1,1\} \\ &p^T 1 = 0 \end{aligned} \quad (4)$$

Where, $P = pp^T$, every element of $|P|$ is the absolute value of corresponding elements in matrix P. Equation (4) can be solved through recursion [4].

The above paper gives SSH solving process. The vector after Euclidean space dimensionality reduction can be transformed to vector of Hamming space through directly taking threshold value. But, a problem is still not solved, i.e. how does the images outside training set index and code? In recent years, there have been some methods to solve this problem [2]. Main thought is to transform the eigenvector to eigenequation. Through assuming every original eigenvector belongs to a manifold subspace and obeys multi-dimension even distribution, this problem can be solved through eigenequation of weighted Laplace-Beltrami operators [11].

2.2. Binary Index Coding of SSH

For given training set including N images $X \in R^{Nxd}$,

mapping function Θ maps d-dimension X of Euclidean space to m-dimension Y of Hamming space. The process of solvingΘis divided into two steps:

1) Solve m sparse principle vectors through Formula (4), and map $X \in R^{Nxd}$ to $B \in R^{Nxm}$.

Calculate covariance matrixΣ of X. its SPC p can be solved through convex optimization stated previously. Update Σaccording to Formula (5).

$$\Sigma = \Sigma - (p^T \Sigma p) pp^T \quad (5)$$

Repeat this process for m times and gain m SPC $\{p_1, \cdots, p_m\}$. These principal component vectors serve as column vectors of the matrix and gain matrix M. eigenmatrix B after dimensionality reduction of $N \times m$ is thus gained through $B = X \times M$.

2) Map Euclidean space matrix B to Hamming space matrix Y.

Define the jth vector of matrix B as $B_{(:,j)}$, and δ_j^k can be defined as follows:

$$\delta_j^k = 1 - e^{-\frac{\varepsilon^2}{2}\left|\frac{k\pi}{B_{(:,j)}^{\max} - B_{(:,j)}^{\min}}\right|^2} \quad (6)$$

Where, $k = 1,...N$; $B_{(:,j)}^{\max}$ and $B_{(:,j)}^{\min}$ refer to the maximum value and the minimum value of $B_{(:,j)}$;ε is a constant. For each column vector $B_{(:,j)}$, N δ_j^k can be solved. Thus, $N \times m$ $\delta_j^k (k = 1,...N; j = 1,...m)$ can be gained. Sort δ_j^k, take the first m δ_j^k and express them as $\{\delta_1^{\min}, ..., \delta_m^{\min}\}$.

Assuming binary coding corresponding to x_i is $y_i \in \{-1,1\}^m$, the jth mapping value $y(i,j)$ can be solved according to the following function:

$$y(i,j) = \Theta(\delta_j^{\min}, B(i,t)) - \sin(\frac{\pi}{2} + \frac{k\pi}{B_{(:,t)}^{\max} - B_{(:,t)}^{\min}} B(i,t)) \quad (7)$$

Where, $\delta_j^{\min}$ is the jth minimum value of $\{\delta_1^{\min}, ..., \delta_m^{\min}\}$, which is solved through the t column of k and B; $B_{(:,j)}^{\max}$ and $B_{(:,j)}^{\min}$ refer to the maximum value and the minimum value of $B_{(:,t)}, i = (i,...N), j = (1,...m)$. Transform it to binary coding through regarding 0 as the threshold value.

3. Experiment

Before you begin to format your paper, first write and save the content as a separate text file. Keep your text and graphic files separate until after the text has been formatted and styled. Do not use hard tabs, and limit use of hard returns to only one return at the end of a paragraph. Do not add any kind of pagination anywhere in the paper. Do not number text heads-the template will do that for you.

Finally, complete content and organizational editing before formatting. Please take note of the following items when proofreading spelling and grammar:

3.1. Experimental Data set and Feature Expression

This paper compares properties of SSH index algorithm on two image data sets (Oxford5k and MCG-WEBV) as well as E2LSH, RBM and SH.)

Oxford5k: including 5062 11 landmark images of University of Oxford. This data set provides the standard answer of artificial labeling. In this experiment, after SIFT local features are extracted from each image, K-means clustering algorithm is used to gain 300 visual words to express original image data.

MCG-WEBV: this data set contains 80031 videos of YouTube website with the highest click rate from December 2008 to February 2009. This data set provides 828-dimension vectors extracted from key frames of videos. 3814 images are drawn randomly in this experiment.

This paper takes 1.5% of original mean Euclidean distance as neighbor threshold value which serves as the standard [11]. F1 and AUC serve as measurement standards.

3.2. Experimental Results

Table 1 and Table 2 show index results of two data sets. m means digits of index coding. The boldface means the best result under each index coding digit. It can be seen that as a random mapping index algorithm, index property of E2LSH changes little as the rise in the number of index digits. SSH obtains the best results on F1 and AUC measurement standards.

Table 1. *Experimental results of Oxford5k data set*

m	F1				AUC			
	SSH	*SH*	*E2LSH*	*RBM*	*SSH*	*SH*	*E2LSH*	*RBM*
2	0.2135	0.2134	0.1055	0.2088	0.5088	0.5085	0.5085	0.5085
4	0.2135	0.2135	0.1055	0.1791	0.5088	0.5088	0.5085	0.5043
8	0.2136	0.2136	0.1055	0.1595	0.5097	0.5097	0.5085	0.4933
16	0.2493	0.2286	0.1055	0.1649	0.5980	0.5520	0.5085	0.4991
32	0.3579	0.3273	0.1046	0.1054	0.7246	0.6928	0.5085	0.4812

Table 2. Experimental results of MCG-WEBV data set

M	F1				AUC			
	SSH	SH	E2LSH	RBM	SSH	SH	E2LSH	RBM
2	0.4003	0.3826	0.0664	0.3255	0.6312	0.6117	0.6073	0.5971
4	0.4960	0.4688	0.0664	0.3227	0.7299	0.7197	0.6073	0.5482
8	0.5652	0.4481	0.0664	0.3161	0.7671	0.6998	0.6073	0.5475
16	0.5489	0.0611	0.0664	0.3112	0.7432	0.6075	0.6073	0.5486
32	0.3706	0.0027	0.0664	0.3040	0.6792	0.5975	0.6073	0.5503

4. Conclusions

This paper introduces SPCA in traditional SH and designs global optimal solution so that high-dimension image index coding become more effective and interpretable. Besides, this paper also discusses image index coding mode outside the training set. Experimental results show SSH is superior to other similar algorithms.

References

[1] M. Belkin and P. Niyogi. Towards a theoretical foundation for Laplacian-based manifold methods. Journal of Computer and System Sciences, 74(8):1289 - 1308, 2008.

[2] Y. Bengio, J. Paiement, P. Vincent, O. Delalleau, N. Le Roux, and M. Ouimet. Out-of-sample extensions for lle, isomap, mds, eigenmaps, and spectral clustering. In Proceedings of Advances in Neural Information Processing Systems (NIPS), page 177, 2004.

[3] S. Berchtold, C. Bohm, H. Jagadish, H. Kriegel, and J. Sander. Independent quantization: an index compression technique forhigh-dimensional data spaces. In Proceedings of International Conference on Data Engineering (ICDE), pages 577 - 588, 2000.

[4] A. D, a' rAspremont, L. E. Ghaoui, M. I. Jordan, and G. G. Lanckriet. A direct formulation for sparse PCA using semidefinite programming. Proceedings of Advances in Neural Information Processing Systems (NIPS), 2004.

[5] M. Datar, N. Immorlica, P. Indyk, and V. Mirrokni. Locality-sensitive hashing scheme based on p-stable distributions. In Proceedings of Annual Symposium on Computational Geometry, pages 253 - 262. ACM, 2004.

[6] Q. Lv, W. Josephson, Z. Wang, M. Charikar, and K. Li. Multi-probe LSH: efficient indexing for high-dimensional similarity search. In Proceedings of International Conference on Very Large Data Bases (VLDB), pages 950 - 961, 2007.

[7] R. Salakhutdinov and G. Hinton. Learning a nonlinear embedding by preserving class neighbourhood structure. In AI and Statistics, 2007.

[8] R. Salakhutdinov and G. Hinton. Semantic hashing. International Journal of Approximate Reasoning, 50(7):969 - 978, 2009.

[9] G. Shakhnarovich, P. Viola, and T. Darrell. Fast pose estimation with parameter-sensitive hashing. In Proceedings of IEEE International Conference on Computer Vision (ICCV), page 750, 2003.

[10] Y. Tao, K. Yi, C. Sheng, and P. Kalnis. Quality and efficiency in high dimensional nearest neighbor search. In Proceedings of International Conference on Management of Data (SIGMOD), pages 563 - 576. ACM, 2009.

[11] Y. Weiss, A. Torralba, and R. Fergus. Spectral hashing. In Proceedings of Advances in Neural Information Processing Systems (NIPS), pages 1753 - 1760, 2009.

[12] H. Zou, T. Hastie, and R. Tibshirani. Sparse principal component analysis. Journal of Computational and Graphical Statistics, 15(2):265 - 286, 2006.

On heijunka design of assembly load balancing problem: Genetic algorithm & ameliorative procedure-combined approach

Zhi Zhuo Hou[1], Hiroshi Katayama[2], Reakook Hwang[3]

[1]Department of Industrial and Management System Engineering, Graduate School of Creative Science and Engineering, Waseda University, Tokyo, Japan
[2]Department of Industrial and Management System Engineering, Faculty of Science and Engineering, Waseda University, Tokyo, Japan
[3]Samsung Economic Research Institute, Seoul, Korea

Email address:
breathlesc@ruri.waseda.jp (Zhi Zhuo Hou)

Abstract: Mixed-model straight/U-shaped assembly line has been recognized as a relevant component of Just-In-Time (JIT) production line system. For this system, "Heijunka" design is also challenged as both the task assignment and the production sequence affect the workload imbalance among workstations. In this context and recognizing uncertain task time environment that is often observed in actual manufacturing scene, this research addresses the Line Balancing Problem (LBP) and the Product Sequencing Problem (PSP) jointly and proposes a mathematical model with stochastic task time which is subjected to normal distribution. The objectives of this model are to maximize line efficiency and to minimize the variation of work overload time. A Multi-objective Genetic Algorithm (MOGA) and an Ameliorative Structure of Multi-objective Genetic Algorithm (ASMOGA) with Priority-based Chromosome (PBC) are applied to solve this problem. At last, this research conducts an experimental simulation on a set of benchmark problems to verify the outperformance of the proposed algorithm.

Keywords: Mixed-Model Assembly Line, Load Balancing, Multi-Objective Genetic Algorithm, Ameliorative Procedure

1. Introduction

This research focuses on load balancing, which is an important concept of resource management in operational systems. The study aims to equalize or reduce imbalance of workload among resources in processing systems. This objective is important because fair assignment of workload on each resource enables high utilization of fixed assets. This can be achieved through task assignment procedure. Due to the trend towards a larger scale complex structure of processing systems, this concept becomes one of the most critical issues in operations and production management. The pay back of swollen fixed cost of existing configurations is highly depending on the utilization of resources in such systems. For this reason, this research highlights load balancing problem for assembly line production systems.

Assembly line is a typical flow-line production system that normally consists of sequence of workstations. These workstations are connected by material transport system such as belt conveyors. The transport system moves the products along the line at constant speed where products are evenly distributed. At each workstation, a group of trained workers repeatedly perform predetermined tasks on a partially finished product in fixed time called cycle time. These tasks are the elementary components of precedence graph which represents relation of tasks of assembly line production system. Namely, each task is subjected to sequence constraints and performs a compulsory operation to complete a final product.

Assembly line systems are categorized by two features: The first feature is layout configuration: Straight-shaped Assembly Line (SAL) and U-shaped Assembly Line (UAL). Most of the new assembly lines tend to be arranged in terms of UAL rather than SAL since UAL can be more flexible to work across both sides of the line while workers can only work on adjacent sections in case of SAL. Consequently, UAL has been viewed as an integral component of JIT production principle.

The second feature is capability of manufacturing variety: Single-Model Assembly Line (SMAL) and Mixed-Model Assembly Line (MMAL). In the early days, companies mainly employed SMAL to produce a volume of single products. However, it is difficult to satisfy the various requirements of customers. Hence MMAL was developed to meet such high level of demands.

This study deals with the Mixed-model Straight/U-shaped Assembly Line (MMS/UAL) due to the advantages mentioned above. Comparing to SAL, the optimal design of MAL needs to handle both LBP and PSP, which are closely interrelated. The optimization of LBP highly depends on PSP, which, in turn, is affected by LBP. Especially for MMS/UAL, the workload of a workstation is not only related to the assigned tasks, but also depending on the model sequence processed at this workstation. Regarding this point, load balancing problem is extended in terms of multi-decision criteria design problem. "Heijunka" criterion, one of the new multi-decision criteria, has been developed to solve this situation. "Heijunka" is Japanese word meaning level equalization. It is one of the LEAN tools used by manufacturing companies, but can be applied to any operations framework.

Two objective functions are considered in this "Heijunka" design for both LBP and PSP: 1) maximizing line efficiency and 2) minimizing the maximum of work overload ratio. In order to define the mathematical model with both two objectives, task times are assumed to be stochastic variables that subjects to normal distributions. Since there are numerous uncertain factors in real-life applications (such as workers' skill level, mentation, task complexity, machine breakdowns and non-JIT etc.), deterministic task times may be quite unrealistic even in full-automatic assembly lines. Under this stochastic assumption, both the objectives are obliged to be normally distributed. The procurement objective 1) is to maximize the mean and to minimize the variance of line efficiency variable. On the other hand, objective 2) is proposed for leveling the variance of work overload times among workstations based on the idea of "Heijunka".

In this research, an approach for this multi-criteria MMS/UAL model is developed by utilizing MOGA.

For computational complexity, line balancing and model sequencing are both known to be of the NP-hard class of combinatorial optimization problems, so the mixed-model straight/U-shaped line balancing and sequencing problem is also NP-hard. Many meta-hierarchical design procedures for this sort of problem is proposed to actualize significant improvement. Within these approaches, GA is known as a stochastic search algorithm that mimics the process of natural selections and genetic mutations. The implementation of genetic operators makes GA very effective in performing global search, while most of conventional heuristic methods usually hard to overcome local search. Since the task precedence graph among different models are actually integrated, a PBC is advanced to encode the solution of this problem into a chromosome efficiently. In addition, to improve the performance of MOGA, an ASMOGA is presented. In order to optimize the outcomes of GA, the evaluation method is proposed as the weight mapping function of line efficiency and work overload time, and the selection operator is considered as roulette wheel selection procedure.

At last, experimental simulation on the objective problems are conducted by comparing the performance of MOGA and ASMOGA. Furthermore, the attained performance of straight lines and the performance of U-lines are compared to confirm the improvement.

The structure of this dissertation is organized as following: section 2 describes the assembly load balancing problem by constructing the mathematical model of the problem and illustrates the procedure of task assignment; section 3 proposes a genetic algorithm for solving this problem; section 4 provides the experimental results on a set of benchmark problems; section 5 concludes this paper.

2. Assembly Line Load Balancing Problem

As mentioned before, two objectives of maximizing line efficiency and minimizing work overload time are proposed for both LBP and PSP in MMU/SAL system. Since calculating the value of both objectives highly relies on line organization, an elaborate task assignment procedure for both straight line and U-shaped line is necessary. Therefore, Chapter 2 proposes a detailed mathematical model and a proper approach of task assignment.

2.1. Mathematical Model

2.1.1. Notations

1) Indices:

i task index, $i = 1, \dots, I$

j workstation index, $j = 1, \dots, J$

m production model index, $m = 1, \dots, M$

k chromosome index, $k = 1, \dots, popSize$

r_{ik} priority index of task *i* at chromosome *k*, $i = 1, \dots, I, k = 1, \dots, popSize$

2) Parameters:

c cycle time

θ maximum load time; $\theta = 0.8c$

q_m production quantity of product model m;

I_j vector that represents the task index of workstation j; $I_j = \{\text{vector of } i \,|x_{ij} = 1\}$

I_m vector that represents the task index of model m; $I_m = \{\text{vector of } i \,|z_{im} = 1\}$

t_i operation time of task i; $t_i \sim N(\mu_i, \sigma_i^2)$

T_j workload of workstation j; $T_j = \sum_{i \in I_j} t_i$, $T_j \sim N(\mu_T, \sigma_T^2)$

μ_T mean of T_j; $\mu_T = \sum_{i \in I_j} \mu_i$

σ_T^2 variance of T_j; $\sigma_T^2 = \sum_{i \in I_j} \sigma_i^2$

$f_{T_j}(x)$ probability density function of T_j ; $f_{T_j}(x) =$

$\frac{1}{\sqrt{2\pi}\sigma_T}\exp\left(-\frac{(x-\mu_T)^2}{2\sigma_T{}^2}\right)$

$F_{T_j}(x)$ cumulative distribution function of T_j; $F_{T_j}(x) = P(T_j \le x) = \int_{-\infty}^{x} f_{T_j}(x)dx$

η line efficiency; $\eta = \frac{1}{J\times c}\sum_{j=1}^{J} T_j = \frac{1}{J\times c}\sum_{i=1}^{I} t_i$

μ_η mean of η; $\mu_\eta = \frac{1}{J\times c}\sum_{i=1}^{I}\mu_i$

σ_η^2 variance of η; $\sigma_\eta^2 = \frac{1}{(J\times c)^2}\sum_{i=1}^{I}\sigma_i^2$

P_j work overload probability of workstation j; $P_j = P\{T_j > c\} = 1 - P\{T_j \le c\} = 1 - F_{T_j}(c)$

P_{Max} maximum of P_j; $P_{Max} = max\{P_j | j \in J\}$

V_k fitness value of chromosome k, $V_k = \mu_\eta - \sigma_\eta^2 - P_{Max}$

$pre(i)$ set of predecessors of task i

$suc(i)$ set of successors of task i

3) Decision Variables:

$$x_{ij} = \begin{cases} 1, if\ task\ i\ is\ assigned\ to\ workstation\ j \\ 0, otherwise \end{cases}$$

$$z_{im} = \begin{cases} 1, if\ task\ i\ is\ an\ element\ of\ model\ m \\ 0, otherwise \end{cases}$$

2.1.2. Formulations

1) Objective functions:

$$\text{Max } \mu_\eta \qquad (1)$$

<Maximize mean of line efficiency>

$$\text{Min } \sigma_\eta^2 \qquad (2)$$

<Minimize variance of line efficiency>

$$\text{Min } P_{Max} \qquad (3)$$

<Minimize the maximum probability of work overload times>

2) Subject to:

$$x_{ij} = 0\ or\ 1\ \ i = 1, \dots, I; j = 1, \dots J \qquad (4)$$

$$\sum_{j=1}^{J} x_{ij} = 1\ i = 1, \dots, I$$

<Each task must be assigned to one and only one workstation>

$$z_{im} = 0 \text{ or } 1\ i = 1, \dots, I; m = 1, \dots M \qquad (5)$$

$$\sum_{m=1}^{M} z_{im} = 1\ i = 1, \dots, I$$

<Each task must belong to one and only one product model>

$$\sum_{j=1}^{J} j(x_{pj} + x_{ij} \le 0) \qquad \forall p \in pre(i) \qquad \text{(6: Straight Line)}$$

<All the predecessors for task *i* are assigned to the same or to an earlier workstation>

$$\sum_{j=1}^{J} j(x_{pj} + x_{ij} \le 0) \text{ or } \sum_{j=1}^{J} j(x_{sj} + x_{ij} \le 0)$$

$$\forall p \in pre(i), \forall s \in suc(i) \qquad \text{(7: U-shaped Line)}$$

<All the predecessors or all successors for task *i* are assigned to the same or an earlier workstation>

2.2. Task Assignment

The mixed-model assembly line studied in this paper consists of a set of workstations which are arranged along a straight/U-shaped conveyor that automatically moves at a constant speed. Different products with similar characteristics are launched onto the conveyor according to the product sequence at a fixed rate. Tasks are moved through the workstations sequentially and processed into finished products after leaving the last workstation. During the period of manufacturing, there are several different products processed at different workstations. After a lapse of time called cycle time, each product enters the next workstation and the worker returns back to the upstream boundary of the workstation to manufacture the next product.

2.2.1. Problem Description

For load balancing, it concerns the assignment of a set of tasks to different workstations regarding some special objectives, such as minimizing the number of workstations for a given cycle time (Type 1), minimizing the cycle time for a given number of workstations (Type 2), maximizing the line efficiency by minimizing both the cycle time and the number of workstations (Type E), or optimizing a certain objective for a given combination of cycle time and number of workstations (Type F). Since the objective of this paper is to maximize line efficiency and minimize workload variation simultaneously with given task properties and workstation properties, the type of this problem will be Type F. Examples for both straight and U-shaped assembly line load balancing problem are used to demonstrate the assignment.

(1) Line properties: quantity of workstations $J = 4$; cycle time $c = 15$; maximum workload $\theta = 0.8c = 12$.

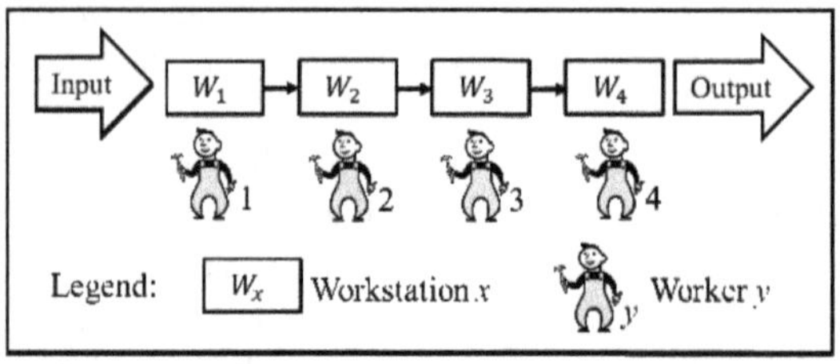

***Figure 1.** Straight Assembly Line*

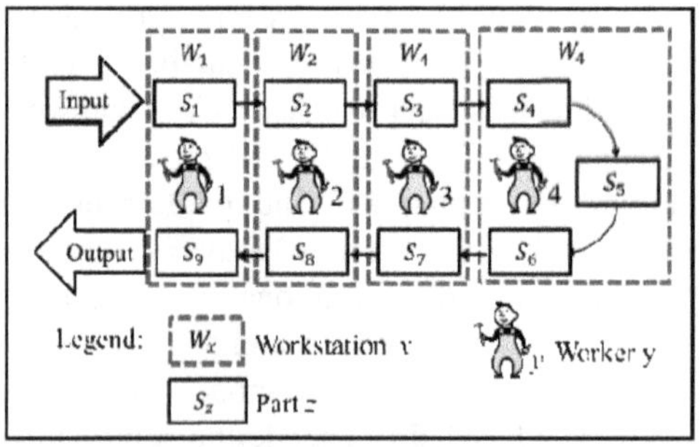

***Figure 2.** U-shaped Assembly Line*

As shown in Figure 1 and Figure 2, the layout of U-shaped lines is significantly different from straight line. U-shaped lines allow the forward and backward task assignment. For instance, the first task and the last task must be placed at the last workstation, which is impossible for a straight line. Besides, there are two kinds of workstation in U-lines: 1) Crossover workstation, where tasks are able to be allocated to both the front and back part of workstations and operators can work at both sides. 2) Regular workstation, where the difference between front and back part of the workstations does not exist. As for the U-shaped line in Figure 2, workstation 1, 2, 3 are crossover workstations while workstation 4 is regular workstation. Furthermore, not all the parts of a workstation need to be assigned with tasks. The parts assignment depends on the product sequence as shown in Figure 3 illustrated in the following head.

(2) Task properties: task quantity I = 11; task time $t_i \sim N(\mu_i, \sigma_i^2)$; one PBC $r_{ik}\,(i = 1, \ldots, I, k = 1)$; task precedence diagram; quantity of products M = 3.

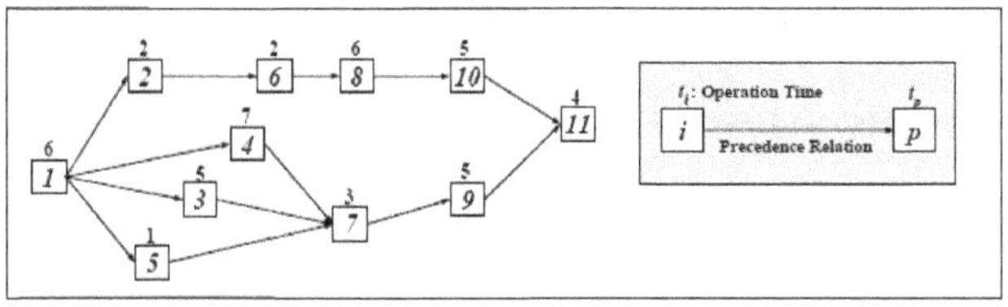

Figure 3. Task Precedence Diagram

Because of the technical requirements, each product has its own precedence relationships among tasks called precedence diagram. Generally, these diagrams of different products can be combined into a single precedence diagram. For instance, Figure 3 illustrates the precedence diagrams of 3 kinds of products, in which each node represents a task and each arrow connecting two different nodes indicates their precedence relationship.

Since the difference between straight line and U-shaped line is not negligible, the sequence of assignment for both lines is quite different: For straight line, task 1 must be assigned to the first workstation and task 11 must be assigned to the last workstation, the sequence of searching available tasks starts with task 1 and ends with task 11(From first to last); For U-shaped line, task 1 and task 11 must be assigned to the first workstation, the sequence of searching available tasks starts with task 1 and task 11 (From two edges to middle).

Table 1. Task Time

i	1	2	3	4	5	6	7	8	9	10	11	Total
μ_i	6	2	5	7	1	2	3	6	5	5	4	46
σ_T^2	2	1	3	4	2	3	2	5	1	2	3	2

Different from deterministic mathematical model in other researches, task times are assumed to be stochastic in this literature. As described in Table 1, time of task 1 is subject to normal distribution of N (6, 2). Since determining the workload of workstation with random task times is extremely hard, this paper presumes that the mean of task time is the actual task time during the procedure of assignment.

Table 2. Task Priority & Product ID (A Chromosome)

i	1		2		3		4		5		6		7		8		9		10		11	
r_{i1}	7	2	2	3	10	2	4	2	5	3	8	3	9	1	6	3	11	1	1	2	3	1

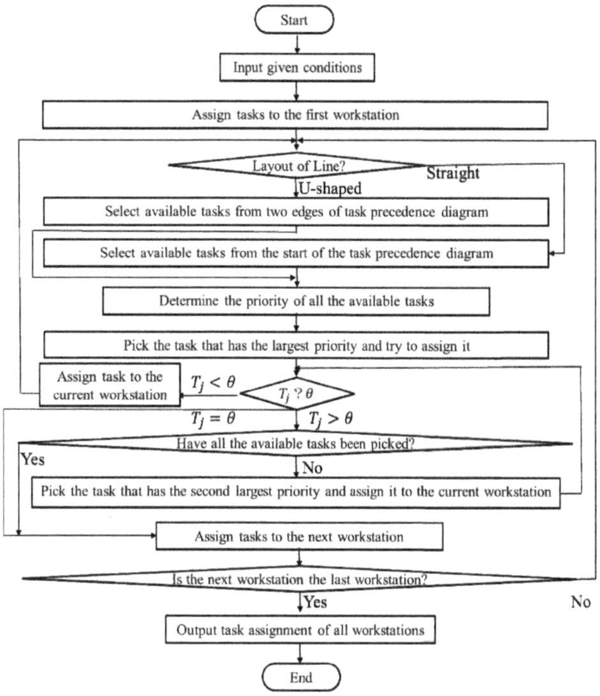

Figure 4. Regular Structure for Task Assignment

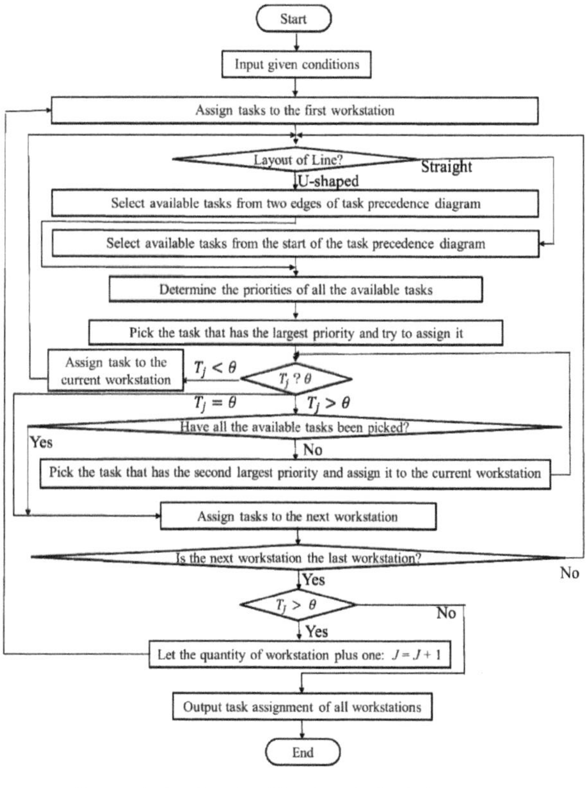

Figure 5. Ameliorative Structure for Task Assignment

Each task has a priority value which is randomly generated as shown in Table 2, which represents a chromosome of GA. These priorities are different from each other because the same priorities probably lead to a tie of task assignment.

Besides, product sequence is determined by the priority number of tasks: When the conditions of priorities (r_{i1} = {7,2,10,5,8,9,11,6,1,3}) and quantity of products (M = 3) are given, the ID of product is able to be deducted by calculating the function of $\{mod(r_{ik}, M) + 1\}$. For example, $\{r_{11} = 7, M = 3\}$ → task 1 represents product 2 (7 mod 3 + 1 = 2). In this analogy, the product sequence of this chromosome is {2,3,2,2,3,3,1,3,1,2,1} and the quantities for each product are $\{q_1 = 3,\ q_2 = 4,\ q_3 = 4\}$.

2.2.2. Assignment Procedure

Two kinds of assignment procedure are proposed as shown in Figure 4 and Figure 5: 1) Regular structure for MOGA and 2) Hierarchical ameliorative structure for ASMOGA. This ameliorative structure is originally developed by Katayama.

The assignment sequence for workstations is from the first workstation to the last workstation. For straight line, the first task is obliged to be assigned to the first workstation while both the first and the last task are obliged to be assigned at the first workstation of U-shaped line. After assigning first task to first workstation (or first and last task to first workstation), available tasks are selected to be candidates according to the task precedence diagram. Task with the largest priority is about to be assigned before other available tasks. This select-assign process does not stop until the load of this workstation exceeds the maximum workload θ. When this excess occurs, the task that has the second largest priority is selected to replace the task that has the most priority. The rest assignment of workstations can be done in the same manner. At last, the workload of final workstation has an inevitable probability of exceeding the maximum workload. To cope with this excess, this ameliorative structure lets $J = J + 1$ (if $T_J > \theta$), then reassigns the tasks until $T_J \leq \theta$. And this procedure is also the difference between the regular structure and the ameliorative structure.

The results of assignment for the examples of Chapter 2.2.1 are proposed as shown in Figure 6 and Figure 7. This assignment is based on both regular structure and ameliorative structure.

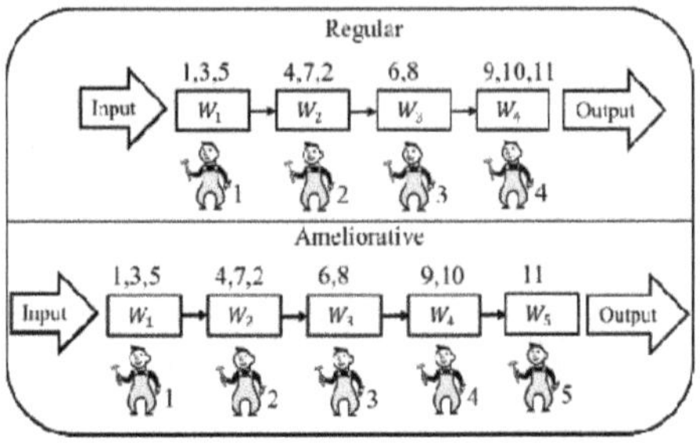

Figure 6. *Regular & Ameliorative Structure for Straight Line Assignment*

For the example of straight line, the assignment results for regular structure are different from those for ameliorative structure. The workload of last workstation in the regular assignment actually exceeds the maximum workload time. Hence, the amount of workstation is about to be 5 according to the ameliorative assignment structure.

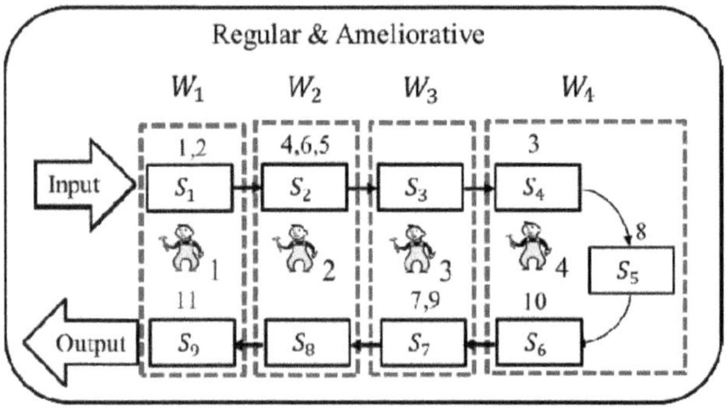

Figure 7. *Regular & Ameliorative Structure for U-shaped Line Assignment*

For the example of U-shaped line, the assignment results for both structures are same. Tasks are assigned to all the parts on workstations 1 and 4 while workstation 2 and 3 do not have all the parts assigned.

3. Genetic Algorithm Design

3.1. The Procedure of Genetic Algorithm

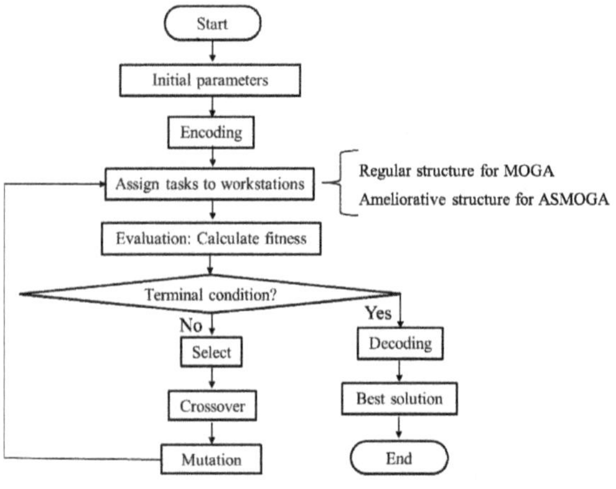

Figure 8. *Process of Genetic Algorithm*

The multi-objective problem formalized in the previous section cannot be easily solved by traditional mathematical techniques. This forces researchers to employ faster and more effective algorithms such as genetic algorithm. GA, which is differing from conventional search techniques, starts with an initial set of random solutions called "population". Each individual in the population is called a "chromosome", representing a solution to the problem at hand. A chromosome is a string of symbols; it is usually, but not necessarily, a binary bit string. The chromosomes "evolve" through successive iterations, called "generations". During each generation, the chromosomes are evaluated, using the measures of "fitness". To create next generation, new chromosomes called "offspring" are formed by selecting current chromosomes which are called "parents" according to the fitness values. Chromosomes have higher fitness are more likely to be selected. Consequently, new selected offspring are formed by either merging two parents using a "crossover" operator or modifying a current parent using a "mutation" operator under a given probability. After several of generations, the algorithm converges to the best chromosome, which hopefully represents the optimum or sub-optimum solution of the problem.

This section proposes a MOGA with PBC and an ASMOGA with PBC to deal with the mixed-model straight/U-shaped assembly load balancing problem. As shown in Figure 6, the process for both algorithms are same, except that the task assignment is distinguished from regular structure and ameliorative structure.

3.2. Encoding and Decoding

3.2.1. Encoding

Encode the parameters of problem into chromosomes is a key issue for the genetic algorithm. Gen *et al.* (1997) developed priority-based GA. This method is proposed to handle the difficulty of how to produce an efficient encoding that satisfies all the constraints of actual world. Recall that a gene contains two kinds of information: 1) The locus that represents the position of a gene located within the structure of chromosome; 2) The allele that represents the value taken by the gene. In this research, the initial generation are formed by randomly reproducing chromosomes which have both locus and allele. The locus is used to denote the task ID, and the allele is used to denote the priority and product ID, as shown in Table 3. Table 3 states a generation consists of 10 chromosomes. Within each chromosome, there are 11 priority values for each task. Furthermore, the product ID is conceived by the method mentioned at Chapter 2.2.1.

Table 3. *Population*

i	1		2		3		4		5		6		7		8		9		10		11	
r_{i1}	7	2	2	3	10	2	4	2	5	3	8	3	9	1	11	3	6	1	1	2	3	1
r_{i2}	2	3	7	2	11	3	5	3	4	2	9	1	8	3	10	2	1	2	3	1	6	1
r_{i3}	6	1	5	3	4	2	2	3	1	2	3	1	10	2	11	3	8	3	7	2	9	1
r_{i4}	10	2	7	2	2	3	4	2	5	3	11	3	9	1	1	2	10	1	8	3	3	1
r_{i5}	3	1	9	1	4	2	10	2	5	3	8	3	7	2	4	3	6	1	5	3	1	2
r_{i6}	5	3	11	3	10	2	4	2	3	1	2	3	1	2	9	1	8	3	7	2	6	1
r_{i7}	4	2	6	1	10	2	2	3	5	3	3	1	9	1	7	2	11	3	8	3	1	2
r_{i8}	9	1	2	3	5	3	7	2	3	1	6	1	1	2	11	3	4	2	10	2	8	3
r_{i9}	1	2	8	3	3	1	10	2	6	1	7	2	5	3	4	2	2	3	9	1	11	3
r_{i10}	8	3	2	3	10	2	11	3	9	1	3	1	5	3	4	2	1	2	6	1	7	2

3.2.2. Task Assignment

In address to calculate the fitness value of chromosome, a known task assignment is necessary. Like mentioned at Chapter 2.2.2, assignment results for each chromosome of each generation is able to be achieved by the assignment procedure.

3.2.3. Decoding

Decoding, a reverse process of encoding, is used to convert chromosomes into understandable solutions. After the terminal condition is satisfied, a chromosome with the best fitness is decoded into the best solution. The decoding method of this paper is converting the priority-based chromosome into the information of actual task assignment. This information consists of the status of workstations which are supposed to have the optimal line balance and product sequence. After obtaining the information of task assignment among workstations, the parameters of mathematical model defined in the Chapter 2.1 can be easily figured out. At last, the problems of line balancing and product sequencing are considered to be solved by outputting the final solution

3.3. Evaluation

Fitness evaluation is used to calculate and check the value of the objectives. In this case, the study considers the standards of evaluation function as all the three objective functions simultaneously.

The first fitness standard (f_1) maximizes the mean of line efficiency:

$$f_1(\mu_\eta) = \mu_\eta = \frac{1}{J \times c} \sum_{j=1}^{J} T_j = \frac{1}{J \times c} \sum_{i=1}^{I} t_i \quad (8)$$

The second fitness standard (f_2) is to minimize the mean of line efficiency:

$$f_1(\sigma_\eta^2) = \sigma_\eta^2 = \frac{1}{(J \times c)^2} \sum_{i=1}^{I} \sigma_i^2 \quad (9)$$

The third fitness standard (f_3) is to minimize the maximum value of work overload probability of workstation j:

$$f_3(P_{Max}) = P_{Max} = max\left\{P_j = 1 - \int_{-\infty}^{x} \frac{1}{\sqrt{2\pi}\sigma_T} \exp\left(-\frac{(c-\mu_T)^2}{2\sigma^2} dc \,\middle|\, j \in J\right\}\right. \quad (10)$$

The evaluation function consists of the three factors:

$$F(V_k) = V_k = f_1(\mu_\eta) - f_2(\sigma_\eta^2) - f_3(P_{Max}) = \mu_\eta - \sigma_\eta^2 - P_{Max} \quad (11)$$

The above $F(V_k)$ is the objective function combining μ_η, σ_η^2 and P_{Max} of the k-th chromosome. Since $f_1(\mu_\eta)$ is a maximization function, $f_1(\sigma_\eta^2)$ and $f_3(P_{Max})$ are both minimization functions, the evaluation function converts these functions into maximization functions. By this analogy, all the fitness of individual chromosome can be evaluated.

3.4. Selection

When the search of GA proceeds, the population undergoes evolutional change according to fitness, and relatively good chromosomes are survived while relatively bad solutions are died in order that the offspring composed of good solution are reproduced for offspring. To distinguish solutions, a principle of Darwinian natural selection is necessary. Generally, selection provides the driving force to the evolution.

This paper uses roulette wheel selection, a method to reproduce a new generation that is proportional to the fitness of each individual. The basic idea of this selection is to determine the cumulative selection probabilities for each chromosome by fitness. A roulette wheel is formed by these probabilities. After spinning the wheel population-sized times, a same-sized generation is reproduced. The procedure of selection can be described as five steps:

Step 1: Evaluate the fitness value of the chromosome v_k of current population

$$F(V_k) = V_k\,,\ k = 1, \ldots, popSize \quad (12)$$

Step 2: Calculate the total fitness for the current population:

$$Total = \sum_{k=1}^{popSize} F(V_k),\ k = 1, \ldots, popSize \quad (13)$$

Step 3: Calculate the selection probability p_k for chromosome v_k:

$$p_k = \frac{F(V_k)}{Total},\ k = 1, \ldots, popSize \quad (14)$$

Step 4: Calculate the cumulative selection probability q_k for chromosome v_k:

$$q_k = \sum_{n=1}^{k} p_k,\ n = 1, \ldots, k \quad (15)$$

Step 5: Generate a random number $r \in [0,1]$, and select chromosomes

1) if $r \le q_1$, then select the first chromosome v_1; $k = 1, \ldots, popSize$.

2) else, select the kth chromosome v_k when $q_{k-1} < r \le q_k$; $k = 1, \ldots, popSize$.

3.5. Crossover Operator

A cross over operator called Weight Mapping Crossover (WMX) is proposed to diversify the chromosome as shown in Figure 6. This crossover operator combines the features of two parent whose corresponding random value is less than crossover rate P_c.

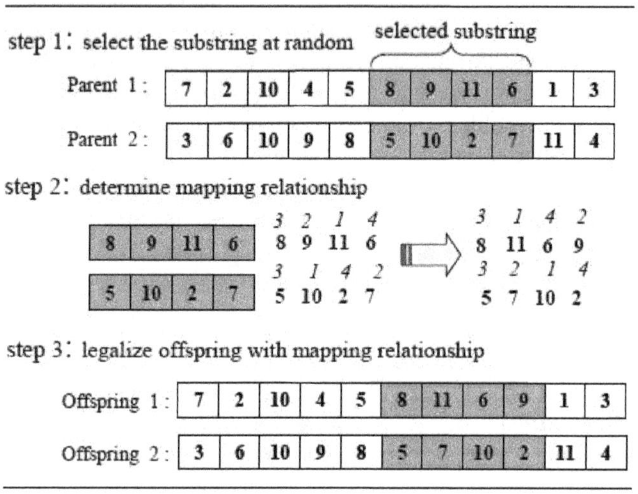

Figure 9. *Two Point-based Weight Mapping Crossover Operator*

3.4. Mutation Operator

Swap Mutation used in this algorithm is described as Figure 7. Two positions are randomly selected and their contents are swapped. This mutation operator arbitrarily alters two components of a selected chromosome and increases the variability of the population. Each chromosome undergoes a random change when the corresponding random rate is less than mutation rate P_m.

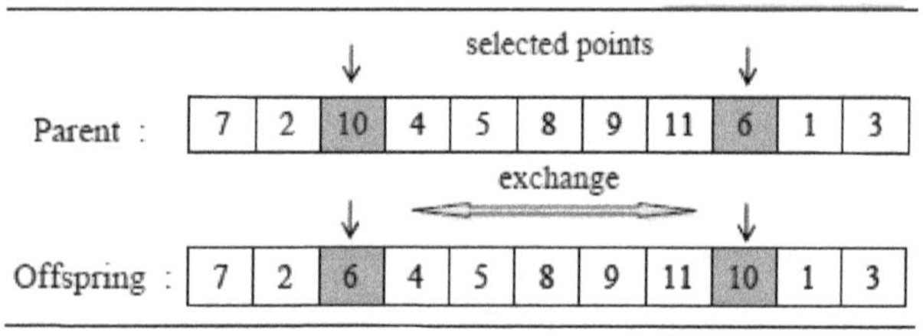

Figure 10. *Swap Mutation Operator*

4. Numerical Experiment

In this numerical experiment, the test problems are described using the well-known benchmark problems of Thomopoulos, Kim and Arcus to compare MOGA with ASMOGA. Besides, a comparison between straight lines and U-lines is conducted to confirm the outperformance of U-lines. The following parameters are applied to GA throughout the simulations:

Population size: *popSize* = 10
Maximum generation: *maxGen* = 100
Crossover probability: P_c = 0.25
Mutation probability: P_m = 0.25
Terminating condition: Reach the last generation defined at start

The algorithm is coded in C# and the experiments are implemented on a Core i7 3.00GHz PC. To illustrate how ASMOGA of U-lines improves the performance of load balancing by using an ameliorative structure on a set of numerical examples, two tables and a figure are listed.

As shown in Table 4 and Table 5, the workstations of line are supposed to be increased according to whether the workload of last workstation is bigger than the cycle time. Also, the product sequence for each problem is obtained by the function mentioned at Chapter 2.2.1. At the last column of these tables, the quantities for individual product is enumerated. Furthermore, Figure 8 illustrates the best results for both MOGA and ASMOGA (Jackson 11 tasks). Based on these results, the theory that the proposed ASMOGA can improve the load balancing can be confirmed.

Next, another comparison is conducted to describe the advantages of U-shaped line as shown in Table 5. U-shaped line is able to obtain improvements at line efficiency and workload variance concurrently.

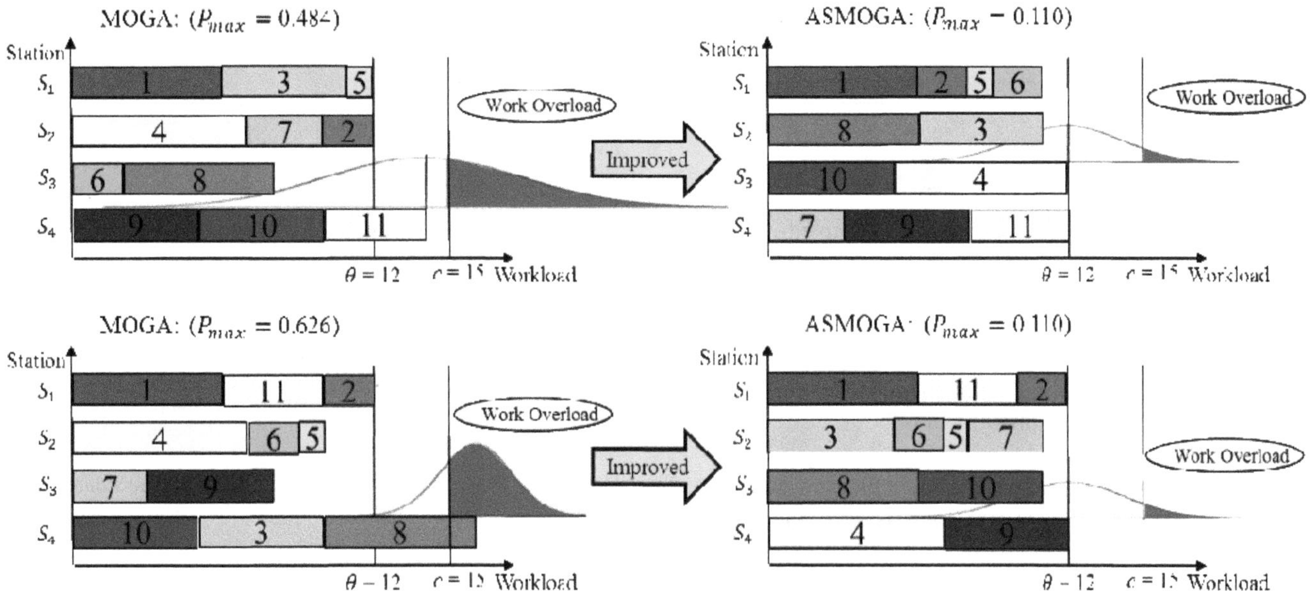

Figure 11. Best Results from the MOGA and ASMOGA

Table 4. Result of Straight Line

Problem	I	M	c	J	J'	MOGA μ_η	MOGA σ^2_η	MOGA P_{Max}	ASMOGA μ_η	ASMOGA σ^2_η	ASMOGA P_{Max}	$q_1, q_2, \ldots, q_M$
			3	3	4	73.2%	0.022	27.1%	76.6%	0.013	11.0%	6,7,6
Thomopoulos	19	3	3	3	4	69.5%	0.090	18.8%	70.7%	0.009	6.5%	6,7,6
			4	3	4	67.9%	0.108	23.5%	72.0%	0.010	12.8%	6,7,6
			138	6	7	70.8%	0.054	26.2%	75.0%	0.031	18.9%	15,16,15,15
Kim	61	4	205	6	7	73.3%	0.049	30.1%	78.2%	0.029	23.1&	15,16,15,15
			324	12	14	68.8%	0.102	27.6%	77.7%	0.047	14.5%	15,16,15,15
			27	12	15	66.6%	0.129	42.5%	71.7%	0.103	28.2%	22,23,22,22,22
Arcus	111	5	33	15	18	69.7%	0.113	57.3%	70.6%	0.097	25.7%	22,23,22,22,22
			34	27	33	71.5%	0.098	66.7%	73.4%	0.084	20.5%	22,23,22,22,22

Table 5. Results of U-shaped Line

Problem	I	M	c	J	J'	MOGA μ_η	MOGA σ^2_η	MOGA P_{Max}	ASMOGA μ_η	ASMOGA σ^2_η	ASMOGA P_{Max}	$q_1, q_2, \ldots, q_M$
			3	3	4	74.5%	0.017	11.0%	79.0%	0.011	7.8%	6,7,6
Thomopoulos	19	3	3	3	4	73.8%	0.018	6.5%	75.0%	0.010	8.4%	6,7,6
			4	3	4	77,8%	0.021	12.8%	82.3%	0.015	10.1%	6,7,6
			138	6	7	76.9%	0.047	18.9%	81.1%	0.028	17.7%	15,16,15,15
Kim	61	4	205	6	7	73.7%	0.036	23.1&	82.5%	0.023	25.9&	15,16,15,15
			324	12	13	81.1%	0.047	14.5%	85.5%	0.035	16.4%	15,16,15,15
			27	12	16	75.3%	0.114	28.2%	77.6%	0.087	36.3%	22,23,22,22,22
Arcus	111	5	33	15	19	66.6%	0.086	25.7%	69.6%	0.093	24.7%	22,23,22,22,22
			34	27	35	79.7%	0.102	20.5%	81.3%	0.075	18.8%	22,23,22,22,22

Table 6. Straight Line vs U-shaped Line from ASMOGA

Problem	I	M	c	J	J'	Straight			U-shaped			$q_1, q_2, \dots, q_M$
						μ_η	σ_η^2	P_{Max}	μ_η	σ_η^2	P_{Max}	
Thomopoulos	19	3	3	3	4	76.6%	0.013	11.0%	79.0%	0.011	7.8%	6,7,6
			3	3	4	70.7%	0.009	6.5%	75.0%	0.010	8.4%	6,7,6
			4	3	4	72.0%	0.010	12.8%	82.3%	0.015	10.1%	6,7,6
Kim	61	4	138	6	7	75.0%	0.031	18.9%	81.1%	0.028	17.7%	15,16,15,15
			205	6	7	78.2%	0.029	23.1&	82.5%	0.023	25.9&	15,16,15,15
			324	12	13	77.7%	0.047	14.5%	85.5%	0.035	16.4%	15,16,15,15
Arcus	111	5	27	12	16	71.7%	0.103	28.2%	77.6%	0.087	36.3%	22,23,22,22,22
			33	15	19	70.6%	0.097	25.7%	69.6%	0.093	24.7%	22,23,22,22,22
			34	27	35	73.4%	0.084	20.5%	81.3%	0.075	18.8%	22,23,22,22,22

5. Conclusion

This paper studies the load balancing of mixed-model straight/U-shaped assembly line problem. This problem is one of the most classic researches of production management system. The objective of the problem is to maximize the line efficiency and to minimize the work overload imbalance simultaneously for a given combination of cycle time and number of workstations. To solve this problem, the variable notations and the mathematical formulations are employed to obtain a model of problem. Then a multi- objective genetic algorithm with priority-based chromosome is developed and structured in terms of a hierarchical ameliorative design to find a near-optimal solution. To evaluate the performance of this algorithm, two sets of experiments are conducted respectively. One is comparison of MOGA with ASMOGA, and another is the comparison of straight line with U-line. As the result of numerical experiments, it was revealed that the proposed approaches can solve these multi-objective problems more quickly than conventional heuristic methods.

For future researches, I wish this proposed method could make a certain contribution toward more research areas such as logistics, SCM and further scheduling problems.

Acknowledgements

This research was supported by my research advisor Professor Hiroshi Katayama and Professor Katayama's former PhD student Dr. Reakook Hwang. I would like to acknowledge and to thank them for giving me the opportunity to research on assembly line projects and for their constant help and support during the whole realization of this paper.

References

[1] Chen R., Lu K. and Yu S., "A hybrid genetic algorithm approach on multi-objective of assembly planning problem [J]", *Engineering Applications of Artificial Intelligence*, Vol. 15 No. 5, pp. 447-457, 2002.

[2] Gen, M. and Cheng, R., *Genetic algorithm & engineering design*, New York: Wiley, 1997.

[3] Hwang, R. K. and Katayama, H., "A Multi-decision Genetic Approach for Workload Balancing with Mixed-Model U-shaped Assembly Line Systems", *International Journal of Production Research*, Vol. 47, No. 14, pp. 3797-3822, 2009.

[4] Hwang, R. K., *A Study on Load Balancing Problem Solving by Genetic Algorithm -Case Analyses on Assembly Line and Multiprocessor Systems-*, Tokyo: Waseda University Doctoral Dissertation, 2009.

[5] Hwang, R. K. and Katayama, H., "Integrated procedure of balancing and sequencing for mixed-model assembly lines: a multi-objective evolutionary approach", *International Journal of Production Research*, Vol. 47, No. 21, pp. 6417-6441, 2010..

[6] Hackman, S. T., Magazine, M. J. and Wee, T. S., "Fast, Effective Algorithms for Simple Assembly Line Balancing Problems", *Operations Research*, Vol. 37 No. 6, pp. 916-924, 1996.

[7] Kara. Y., Ozcan, U., and Peker, A., "Balancing and Sequencing mixed-model just-in-time U-lines with multiple objectvies", *The International Journal of Advanced Manufacturing Technology*, Vol. 32, No. 11-12, pp.1218-1231., 2007.

[8] Katayama, H., "An integrated management procedure of multi-item mixed-line production system-its hierarchical structure and performance evaluation", *International Journal of Production Research*, Vol. 36, No. 10, pp. 2633–2651, 1998.

[9] Kim, Y. K., Kim, J. Y. and Kim, Y., "An endosymbiotic evolutionary algorithm for the integration of balancing and sequencing in mixed-model U-lines", *European Journal of Operational Research*, Vol. 168, No. 3, pp. 838-852, 2006.

[10] Miltenburg, J., "Balancing and scheduling mixed-model U-shaped production lines", *International Journal of Flexible Manufacturing Systems*, Vol. 14, No. 2, pp. 119–151, 2002.

[11] Scholl, A., *Balancing and Sequencing of assembly lines 2nd ed.*, Hedelberg, Germany: Physisca Press, 1999.

[12] Ponnambalam S. G., Aravindan P. and Naidu G. M., "Multi-objective genetic algorithm for solving assembly line balancing problem", *International Journal of Advanced Manufacturing Technology*, Vol. 16.No. 5, pp. 341-352, 2000.

A user interest model based on the analysis of user behaviors

Zhu Jinghua

College of Network Communication, Zhejiang Yuexiu University of Foreign Languages, Shaoxing, China

Email address:
uem@163.com

Abstract: Understanding the users' interest is the base for the industralization of website. In order to provide individualized service better for the users, on the basis of analyzing the users' browse behavioral characteristics and according to the users' retention time in the page, and users' click frequency to the hyperlink and page, a model of computer user interest degree is established, and a neutral network is proposed to describe their correlation, and the reasonableness and effectiveness of this model are verified through experiment. The experiemtn result shows aathat this model can accurately find out the page that the users are interested in.

Keywords: Individualization, User Browse Behavior, User Interest Degree, RBF Network

1. Introduction

With the application and development of network technology globally, network is influencing people's work and lifestyle in various aspects. However, the existing information system has significant defect, such as scattered resources, concentrated retrieval, the information provided to all users is the same and there is response only in case of demand. For the ordinary users, the "information disorientation" and "information overload" on the internet have become increasingly serious problems. The key to solve these problems is to transform the Internet from passively accepting the browsers' request to activley perceiving the information demand of browsers' [1], so as to achieve the individualized active information service of Internet system to the browser.

In order to achieve the individualized service, first it is needed to trace and learn the users' interest and behavior, depict the relation between users' characteristics and the users. It is an important direction in the current individualized service research to analuze and capture the user interest according to the browse behavior or browse contents[2]. Radial basis function (RBF) neutral network, with its profound physiological basis, simple network structure, rapid learning ability and excellent approximation performance, is also well applied in the recommendation of webpage individualization[3]. A method of to calculate the users' interest in the webpage is given in this paper through the analysis on the users' browse behavior, and several important characteristics are grapsed to describe the users' browse behavior, and RBF is used to describe their correlation.

2. Characteristic Extraction of User Access Behavior

A lot of researches show that the users' interest in the webpage is closely related with their browse behavior on such webpage. Users visit a webpage usually with a certain hobby, and different users have different interests and hobbies. The users' access path contains the users' interest in a website and the shifting of user interest. Literatures [4] point out that many actions of uses can imply their hobby, fo example inquiry, browsing webpage and articlee, labeling bookmark, feeding back information, clicking mouse, dragging scroll bar, advance and retreat. [5] point out that the retention time, access frequency, saving, edition, modification and other actions of the users during access can reveal their interest. However, these articles do not quantitatively estimate how these behaviors reflect the users' interest.

Superficially, there are many browse behaviors that can decide the users' interest to the webpage, but through analysis, we find that there are three behaviors playing the key role: borwse time in webpage (the browse behaivor is classified according to the specific time interval, and an individualized recommendation model is established in the method of clustering [6]), the link clicked under a webpage (forecast the users' next behavior, calculate the webpage weight and recommend the webpage by collecting the information of users' browse behavior and through a certain mechanism), and the click frequency of a webpage (how users use mark and collection to further analyze the user's browse and search behaviors when using the browser[7]). There are three reasons: a. inquiry, edition, modification and other behaviors must increase the webpage browse time and page turning times (after page turning, what is positioned is still the same URL, so the manifestation is still to increase the webpage browse time), so it can be indirectly reflected through the webpage browse time. b. The page implementing the actions like saving and labeling bookmark, if really concerned by users, will be called for many times in the future for rebrowse, so it can reflect the access times. c. If the users retrieve based on the site, and there are more links making the users interested in the site, there will be more user click links, and the webpage is more important.

Table 1. Link click condition

Site		Site 1		Site 2
Page	Page 1	Page 2	Page 3	
Existing links	8	6	6	6
Clicked links	4	3	2	2

2.1. Method of Determining Page Weight According to the Users' Retention in the Page

Assume that there are n hyperlinks in a page accessed by the users, in which the accessed hyperlinks are respectively $\{H_1, H_2 \cdots, H_i\}$, the retention time is $\{T_1, T_2 \cdots, T_i\}$, and T(P) represents the weight of page P determined based on the users' retention time. Let a is the effective time of user retention in the current page, then the recurrence formula to calculate the page weight is:

$$T(P) = a + \sum (T_i / n) \quad (1)$$

This formula considers that the child nodes have some characteristics of the parent node, and some child nodes are even the embodiment of the parent node, so the interest in child nodes increases, which can be seen as the contribution to the interest strength of the parent node.

Actually, the length to browse the webpage is always closely associated with the total information in the webpage. In consideration of this situation, the above formula can be changed as:

$$T(P) = \frac{[a + \sum (T_i / n)] * B_i}{\sum B_i * \sum T_i} \quad (2)$$

Where B_i represents the information amount in page i, i.e. the multiple of the ratio between the webpage length and total browse length by the ratio between the number of byte of the webpage and the totla information.

2.2. Judge the Users' Interest Degree According to the Users' Link to the Hyerlink in the Webpage

Let that users obtain the URL of a site through the retrieval to a key word, and the browse to each page in this site is Page A→B→C→ ··· →N, and then the link is from this site to other sites $S_1, S_2, \cdots, S_i$, and the calculation formula of the weight is:

$$R(P) = (1 - J_1) \sum m_{i1} / c_{i1} + (1 - J_2)[\sum \sum m_{ji} / c_{ji}] \quad (3)$$

Where J represents the information disorientation rate when the users enter a new site each time. Because hyperlink is different from the traditional information carrier, there are different hyperlinks in the hypertext, which indicate to different contents, users are easy to follow the hyperlink when browsing the webpage and will be disoriented in the complex network information space of Internet, do not know their position in the information space, cannot return to a node and forget the original retrieval objective.

As shown in Table 1, the weight calculation formula of site 1 is:

$$R(S_1) = (1 - J_1) \times (4/8 + 3/6 + 2/6) + (1 - J_2) \times (2/6)$$
$$= (1 - J_1) \times (4/3) + (1 - J_2) \times (1/3)$$

Where J_1 and J_2 are the information disorientation rate when the users enter a new site each time that should be given according to the statistics. According to the formula above, the weight formula to calculate each specific webpage 1 in the website i is:

$$R(I) = m_{i1} / c_{i1} \quad (4)$$

2.3. The Method to Determine the Webpage Weight According to the Users' Click Rate to the Webpage

If a user is interested in a webpage, then he weill spend more time in browsing the webpage and will frequently access this webpage, and this is a method to measure the user interest quantitatively. However, the user's click frequency cannot accurately reflect the users' interest, because with the accumulation of time, the users must have more clicks to a webpage.

Table 2. Link click condition

Time	Click condition (time)	
	Page A	Page B
1st week	192	18
2nd week	58	42
3rd week	15	85
4th week	8	102

As shown in Table 2, the total click of Page *A* is 273, more than that of Page *B* 247, but in the 4th week, it is obvious that users are more interested in Page *B*, so the users' click rate can more reflect the change and strength of change.

The click rate can be described with the following formula:

$$C(P) = m / M \quad (5)$$

Where m is the access time of the node, and M is the total access time in all nodes.

3. Modeling and Verification

According to the characteristics of the user access behavior extracted above, the calculation method of determining the users' interest degree according to the users' browse behavior is given. The following formula is constructed:

$$W(CRT) = f[C(P), R(P), T(P)] \quad (6)$$

Where W is the users' interest in webpage P obtained through weight calculation.

Webpage interest degree means the degree of interest of unders in a webpage, which is expressed with the real number between 0 and 1, where 0 and 1 respectively reflect no interest and maximum interest.

Literautre [3] uses the characteristics of strong daptability and learning ability of neutral network to train the extraction of users' different demands, the users are classified into different clusters, and then are applied in the individualized recommendation of webpage to improve the problem of informaiton overlod on the electronic commerce website, in which the most common neutral network is BP network, also called multi-layer feed-forward network. When BP network is used for the function approximation, the weight value is adjusted with negative-gradient descent method. This method of weight value adjustment has its limitation and has the disadvantages of low convergence method and being extremely small locally, while radial neutral network is superior to BP network in the aspects of approximation ability, classification ability and learning speed. In this paper, with the characteristics of self-adaptive determination of radial based network (RBF network), no relation between output and initial weight value and high efficiency, a model based on RBF is designed.

The basic idea of RBF-based network model is: first, $(GS_1, \ldots, GS_j, \ldots, GS_h)^T$ is taken as the input vector of the network and GV $=(gv_1, \ldots, gv_k, \ldots, gv_p)$ as the target vector to train RBF network and get a well trained RBF network, and according to the actual condition of the network, $GV'=(gv'_1, \ldots, gv'_k, \ldots, gv'_p)$ is output, and the calculation accuracy of the target vector is compared, and then the parameters are adjusted, so that GV and GV' approach to each other as faras possible.

The specific steps to establish the determination method of RBF network-based model are as follows:

Step 1: Initialization. Let the input vector of RBF network is $(GS_1, \ldots, GS_j, \ldots, GS_h)^T$, GV is the target vector, and set the parameters of RBF such as the number of neuron in the hidden layer.

Step 2: Train the neutral network N;

Step 3: Adjust the parameters with the result of test data, so that the actual output of network approaches to GV as far as possible, let the actual output is $GV'=(gv'_1, \ldots, gv'_k, \ldots, gv'_p)$.

We the newrbe command int eh MATLAB statistical tool to train the RBF network model, and then call sim and test whether the network model is reasonable with the test set.

The calling format of newrbe is:

net=newrbe(P, T, spread)

Where, spread is the distribution density of the radial base function, the larger spread is, the smoother the network forecast value performance will be. P and T respectively represent the input vector and target vector in the training sample, newrbe can create an accurate RBF network, that is to say, the network creation process is also a training process, and the error of the network created is 0.

Table 3. *Evaluation of pre-forecast interest degree*

Interest degreE	Numerial expression
Very interested	(0.8,1.0]
Relatively interested	(0.6.0.8]
Ordinary	(0.4,0.6]
Not very interested	(0.2,0.4]
Very uninterested	[0.0,0.2]

In this paper, 80% of the smaples are taken as the trianing smaple, and the remaining 20% samples are taken as the test smaple. The test code is:

Y=sim(net, P_test)

In this paper, spread=9 is taken, and the forecast error at this moment is 0.

In order o verify the effect of RBF network model forecast user to the interest in webpage, we ask the users to give the pre-forecast interest degree when browsing the webpage, as shown in Table 3:

In Table 4, SPSSS statistical analysis software is adopted for relevant analysis, and the method of distance analysis is adopted to determine the similarity, and a similarity matrix is obtianed (aa represnets the estimated value)

Table 4. *Similarity matrix result*

Correlation between Vectors of Values				
	1: 10	2: 30	3: 60	4: aa
1: 10	1.000	.960	.955	.943
2: 30	.960	1.000	.977	.969
3: 60	.955	.977	1.000	.995
4: aa	.943	.969	.995	1.000

The difference between the estimated value and calculated value is compared in the experiemnt. In the test, the number of webpages browsed by users increases from 10 to 60, the distribution density of radial base function spread is 9, and RBF network model is used to respectively calculate the corresponding result, which is compared with the pre-forecasted interest degree. The result is as shown in

Figure 1, in which the transver coordinte represents the number of the webpage browsed by users (extract 10 pages at random, and sort them according to the value of page interest degree from small to large), and the longitudinal represents the interest degree. It can be seen from the figure that first, with the increasing of number of webpges browsed by the users, the extimated more and more approaches to the calculated value, and the change trend tends to beconsistent (this phenomenon can be found in the similarity matrix in Table 4), indicating that the capturing of users' interest in webpages is more and more accurate with the increasing of webpage browsing; second, when the interest degree is repatively low and high, the estimated value approaches to the calcualted value relatively; when the interest degree is between 0.3 and 0.7, there is a great error, and the reasons for the above phenomena might be the following: users are very sensitive to the webpge that they are very interested and uninterested in, the subjective scoring is relatively accurate, while for the scoring to the webpages that they are not so interested in, there might be a great deviation, and in this way, compared with the forecasted value, there is a significant error. When there is a large data volume, the neutral network model trained can more reflect the real state, so the calculated value and pre-forecasted interest value approach to each other very much.

4. Conclusion

It is very significant to find out the interesting user access mode, interesting webpages and user interest migration etc. from the log dta record for the auxilairy design of website and strategic decision making of elecronic commerce. In this method, how the users' browse behavior reflects the users' interest is quantitatively analyzed and estimated. Several important characteristics of user browse behavior are extracted, it is proposed to use RBF network model to describe the correlation between these characteristics and the users' interest degree, and the reasonablenes of this model is verified through experiment. However, as the users' browse behaviors are different and because of the randomness of user browse, it is difficult to extract all characteristics of user behavior. The method to expect the user interest in this paper is just a relatively reasonable calcultion method, if it is required to more accurately judge the users' interest degree, it is required to consider the correlation between the user browse behavior and page more, and consider how to mine the high-quality log data.

Acknowledgements

This work is supported by Zhejiang Province Education Department projects (No. Y201330252).

References

[1] Enrique Frias-Martinez, Sherry Y. Chen, Xiaohui Liu. Investigation of Behavior and Perception of Digital Library Users: A Cognitive Style Perspective[J]. International Journal of Information Management , 2008(28): 355-365.

[2] Zhang Haitao, Jing Jipeng, Method of Determining Webpage Level According to User Browse Behavior [J]. Intelligence Journal, 2004, 23(3): 303-306.

[3] Cheng Chih Chang, Pei-Ling Chen, Fei-Rung Chiu, et al. Application of Neural Networks and Kano's Method to Content Recommendation in Web Personalization[J]. Expert Systems with Applications, 2008.

[4] A. Georgakis, H. Li. User Behavior Modeling and Content Based Speculative Web Page Prefetching[J]. Data & Knowledge Engineering, 2006(59): 770-788.

[5] Wang Jimin, Peng Bo, Analysis on Click Behavior of Search Engine Users [J]. Intelligence Journal, 2006(2): 154-162.

[6] Feng-Hsu Wang, Hsiu-Mei Shao. Effective Personalized Recommendation Based on Time-Framed Navigation Clustering and Association Mining [J]. Expert Systems with Applications, 2004(27): 365-377.

[7] Mrugank V Thakor, Wendy Borsuk, Maria Kalamas. Hotlists and Web Browsing Behavior - an Empirical Investigation [J]. Journal of Business Research, 2004(57): 776-786.

[8] Zeng Chun, Xing Chunxiao, Zhou Lizhu, Technical Overview of Individualized Service [J]. Software Journal , 2002(10): 1952-1961.

[9] Shuchih Emest Changa, S Wesley Changchiena. Assessing Users' Product-Specific Knowledge for Personalization[J]. Expert Systems with Applications, 2006(30): 682-693.

[10] Shu-Hsien Liao, Chih-Hao Wen, Artificial Neural Networks Classification and Clustering of Methodologies and Applications Literature Analysis From 1995 to 2005[J]. Expert Systems with Applications, 2007(32): 1-11.

[11] Huang Xiaoyuan, Tian Peng, Securities Selection Decision-making Tools based on Neutral Network[J]. Application of Systematic Engineering Theory Method, 1995(2): 60-65.

[12] Tan Qiong, Li Xiaoli, Shi Zongzhi, A Method to Realize the Individualzied Service of Search Engine[J]. Computer Science, 2002, 29(1): 23-25.

Speed control of a DC motor using Controllers

Md Akram Ahmad, Pankaj Rai

Electrical Engineering Department, BIT Sindri, Dhanbad, India (Vinoba Bhave University Jharkhand)

Email address:
akram14407@gmail.com (A. Ahmad), pr_bit2001@yahoo.com (P. Rai)

Abstract: This paper describes the speed control of a separately excited DC motor using conventional controllers (PID, IMC) and Fuzzy Logic controller based on Matlab Simulation program. A mathematical model of the process has been developed using real plant data and then conventional controllers and Fuzzy logic controller has been designed. A comparative analysis of performance evaluation of all controllers has been done.

Keywords: PID Controller, IMC, FLC, DC Motor

1. Introduction

DC motors are widely used in industrial applications, robot manipulators and home appliances, because of their high reliability, flexibility and low cost, where speed and position control of motor are required. This paper deals with the performance evaluation of different types of conventional controllers and intelligent controller implemented with a clear objective to control the speed of separately excited DC motor.

PID controllers are commonly used for motor control applications because of their simple structures and intuitionally comprehensible control algorithms. Controller parameters are generally tuned using Ziegler-Nichols frequency response method [1]. Ziegler-Nichols frequency response method is usually used to adjust the parameters of the PID controllers. However, it is needed to get the system into the oscillation mode to realize the tuning procedure. But it's not always possible to get most of the technological plants into oscillation [2].

In process control, model based control systems are mainly used to get the desired set points and reject small external disturbances. The internal model control (IMC) design is based on the fact that control system contains some representation of the process to be controlled then a perfect control can be achieved. So, if the control architecture has been developed based on the exact model of the process then perfect control is mathematically possible [3].

Fuzzy logic control (FLC) is one of the most successful applications of fuzzy set theory, introduced by L.A Zadeh in 1973 and applied (Mamdani 1974) in an attempt to control system that are structurally difficult to model. Since then, FLC has been an extremely active and fruitful research area with many industrial applications reported [4]. In the last three decades, FLC has evolved as an alternative or complementary to the conventional control strategies in various engineering areas.

Analysis and control of complex, nonlinear and/or time-varying systems is a challenging task using conventional methods because of uncertainties. Fuzzy set theory [5] which led to a new control method called Fuzzy Control which is able to cope with system uncertainties. One of the most important advantages of fuzzy control is that it can be successfully applied to control nonlinear complex systems using an operator experiences or control engineering knowledge without any mathematical model of the plant [6].

2. DC Motor

Direct current (DC) motors convert electrical energy into mechanical energy through the interaction of two magnetic fields. One field is produced by a magnet of poles assembly, the other field is produced by an electrical current flowing in the motor windings. These two fields result in a torque which tends to rotate the rotor.

2.1. Modeling of Separately Excited DC Motor

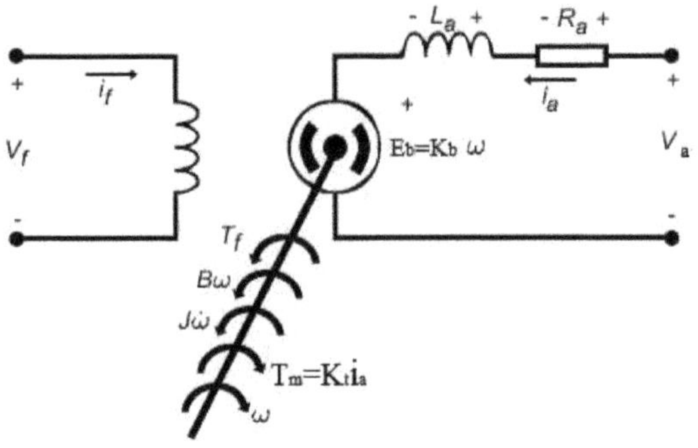

Figure 1. Separately excited DC motor model

The armature voltage equation is given by:

$$V_a(t) = R_a\, I_a\,(t) + L_a.\frac{d\ I_a\,(t)}{dt} + E_B(t) \quad (1)$$

Equation for back emf of motor will be

$$E_B(t) = K_b\ \omega(t) \quad (2)$$

Now the torque balance equation will be given by:

$$T_m(t) = \ K_t.\ I_a\,(t) \quad (3)$$

$$T_m(t) = J\ \frac{d\omega(t)}{dt} + B\omega(t) \quad (4)$$

Where,
K_t = Torque constant (Nm/A)
K_b = back emf constant (Vs/rad)
Let us combine the upper equations together:

$$V_a(t) = R_a.\, I_a\,(t) + L_a.\frac{d\ I_a\,(t)}{dt} + K_b\ \omega(t) \quad (5)$$

$$K_t.\ I_a(t) = J\ \frac{d\omega(t)}{dt} + B\omega(t) \quad (6)$$

Taking Laplace Transform of (5) & (6), we get

$$V_a(s) = R_a.\, I_a(s) + L_a.\, I_a(s) + K_b\ \omega(s) \quad (7)$$

$$K_t.\ I_a(s) = J\omega(s) + B\ \omega(s) \quad (8)$$

If current is obtained from (8) and substituted in (7) we have…

$$V_a(s) = \omega(s)\frac{1}{K_t}[L_a.\, Js^2 + R_a.\, J + L_a.\, B(s) + K_b.\, K_t] \quad (9)$$

Then the relation between rotor shaft speed and applied armature voltage is represented by transfer function:

$$\frac{\omega(s)}{V_a(s)} = \frac{K_t}{(JL_a s^2 + (JR_a + BL_a)s + (K_t K_b + BR_a)} \quad (10)$$

This is the transfer function of the DC motor.

Consider the following values for the physical parameters [7,8]

Armature inductance (L_a) = 0.5 H
Armature resistance (R_a) = 1Ω
Armature voltage (V_a) = 200 V
Mechanical inertia (J) = 0.01 Kg.m2
Friction coefficient (B) = 0.1 N-m/rad/sec
Back emf constant K_b = 0.01 V/rad/sec
Motor torque constant K_t= 0.01N.m/A
Rated speed = 1450 rpm
Based on the data book, the transfer function is as

$$\frac{\omega(s)}{V_a(s)} = \frac{2}{s^2 + 12s + 20.02} \quad (11)$$

3. Proportional-Integral-Derivative (PID) Controller

PID controllers are probably the most widely used industrial controller. In PID controller Proportional (P) control is not able to remove steady state error or offset error in step response. This offset can be eliminated by Integral (I) control action. Integral control removes offset, but may lead to oscillatory response of slowly decreasing amplitude or even increasing amplitude, both of which are error, initiates an early correction action and tends to increase stability of system.

Ideal PID controller in continuous time is given as

$$y(t) = K_p\left(e(t) + \frac{1}{T_i\int_0^t e(t)dt} + T_d\frac{de(t)}{dt}\right) \quad (12)$$

Laplace domain representation of ideal PID controller is

$$Gc(s) = \frac{Y(s)}{E(s)} = K_p(1 + \frac{1}{T_i s} + T_d s) \quad (13)$$

3.1. Tuning of PID Controller

Ziegler and Nichols proposed rules for determining values of K_p, T_i *and* T_d based on the transient response characteristics of a given plant. Closed loop oscillation based PID tuning method is a popular method of tuning PID controller. In this kind of tuning method, a critical gain K_c is induced in the forward path of the control system. The high value of the gain takes the system to the verge of instability. It creates oscillation and from the oscillations, the value of frequency and time are calculated. Table 1 gives experimental tuning rules based on closed loop oscillation method [2,9].

Table 1. *Closed loop oscillation based tuning methods*

Type of Controller	K_p	T_i	T_d
P	$0.5K_c$	∞	0
PI	$0.45K_c$	0.83T	0
PID	$0.6K_c$	0.5T	0.125T

From the Closed loop oscillation method, $K_c = 13$ and T = 2 sec, which implies $K_p = 7.8$, $T_i = 1$ and$T_d = 0.5$

Usually, initial design values of PID controller obtained by all means needs to be adjusted repeatedly through computer simulations until the closed loop system performs or compromises as desired. These adjustments are done in MATLAB simulation.

4. Internal Model Control (IMC)

The theory of IMC states that "control can be achieved only if the control system encapsulates, either implicitly or explicitly, some representation of the process to be controlled".

The Internal Model Controller is based on the inverse of the process model we are trying to control. If we cascade the process transfer function with a controller which is the exact inverse of the process, then effectively the gain becomes unity and we have perfect set-point tracking [10]. The main feature of internal model controller is that the process model is in parallel with the actual process.

Figure (2) shows the scheme of IMC. Internal model controller provides a transparent framework for control system design and tuning.

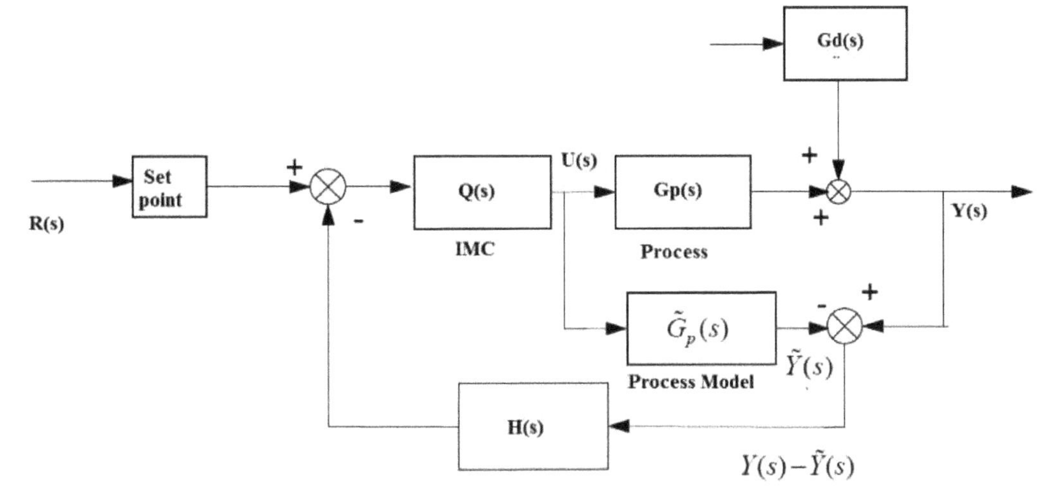

Fig 2. Internal module control scheme

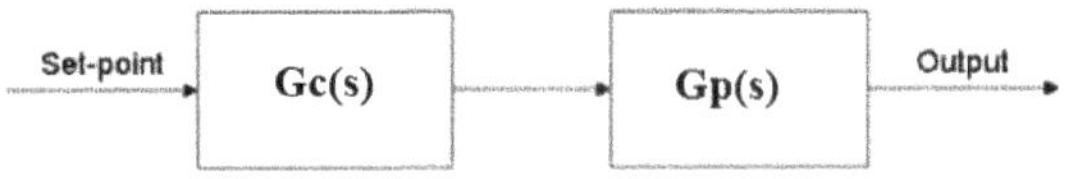

Fig 3. Equivalent Block diagram of IMC

A controller $G_c(s)$ has been used to control the process $G_p(s)$. Suppose $\widetilde{Gp}(s)$ is a model of $G_p(s)$[10].

Where

$$G_c(s) = \frac{Q(s)}{1-\widetilde{Gp}(s).Q(s)} \quad (14)$$

And if

$$G_p(s) = \widetilde{Gp}(s) \quad (15)$$

the model is an exact representation of process, then it is clear that the output will always equal to set point. Notice that this ideal control performance is achieved without feedback.

4.1. Design of IMC

Designed the IMC controller as

$$G_{IMC}(s) = Q(s) = [\widetilde{Gp}(s)]^{-1}G_f(s) \quad (16)$$

Where $G_f(s)$ is a low pass function defined as

$$G_f(s) = \frac{1}{(1+\lambda s)^n} \quad (17)$$

Here we consider 2nd order low pass filter (n = 2).

Thus, $G_f(s) = \frac{1}{(1+\lambda s)^2}$,

Where λ is closed loop time constant[10].

Now,

$$G_p(s) = \frac{K_t}{(J_m L_a s^2 + (J_m R_a + B_m L_a)s + (K_t K_b + B_m R_a)}$$

$$= \frac{2}{s^2+12s+20.02} = \widetilde{Gp}(s) \quad (18)$$

A good rule of thumb is to choose λ to be twice fast as open loop response.

λ=0.9 implies, $G_f(s) = \frac{1}{(1+0.9s)^2}$

Thus, $Q(s) = [\widetilde{Gp}(s)]^{-1}G_f(s)$ becomes,

$$Q(s) = \frac{s^2+12s+20.02}{1.62s^2+3.6s+2} \quad (19)$$

Hence, from equation (14)

$$G_c(s) = \frac{Q(s)}{1-\widetilde{Gp}(s).Q(s)}$$

Implies,

$$G_c(s) = \frac{s^2+12s+20.02}{1.62s^2+3.6s+0} \quad (20)$$

5. Fuzzy Logic Controller (FLC)

Table 2. Linguistic variables.

NB	NM	NS	Z	PB	PM	PS
Big negative	Medium negative	Small negative	Zero	Big positive	Medium positive	Small positive

Table 3. *Rule base for fuzzy logic controller.*

e \ ce	*NB*	*NM*	*NS*	*Z*	*PS*	*PM*	*PB*
NB	NB	NB	NB	NB	NM	NS	Z
NM	NB	NB	NB	NM	NS	Z	PS
NS	NB	NB	NM	NS	Z	PS	PM
Z	NB	NM	NS	Z	PS	PM	PB
PS	NM	NS	Z	PS	PM	PB	PB
PM	NS	Z	PS	PM	PB	PB	PB
PB	Z	PS	PM	PB	PB	PB	PB

The fuzzy controllers are designed with two input variables, error and change of error and one output variable. The Mamdani based fuzzy inference system uses linear membership function for both inputs and outputs [11]. For the fuzzy logic controller the input variables are error $(e)$and rate (change) of error (Δe), and the output variable is controller output(Δy). Triangular membership functions are used for input variables and the output variable. Each variable has 7 membership functions. Thus, there were total 49 rules generated. The universe of discourse of error, rate of error and output are [-120, 120], [-120,120] and [-180,180] respectively. The rule base framed for DC motor is tabulated in Table 3[12].

The structure of the rule base provides negative feedback control in order to maintain stability under any condition. Linguistic variables for error, rate of error and controller output are tabulated in table 2[13].

Fig 4, 5 and 6 shows membership functions of different variables implemented in FIS editor in MATLAB toolbox.

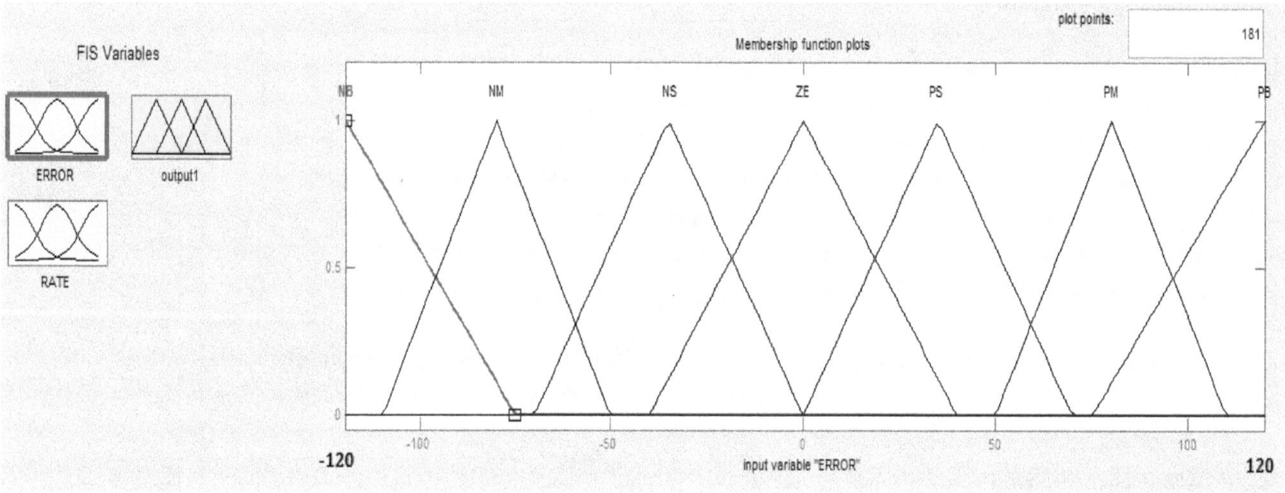

Fig 4. *Membership functions for input-1(error)*

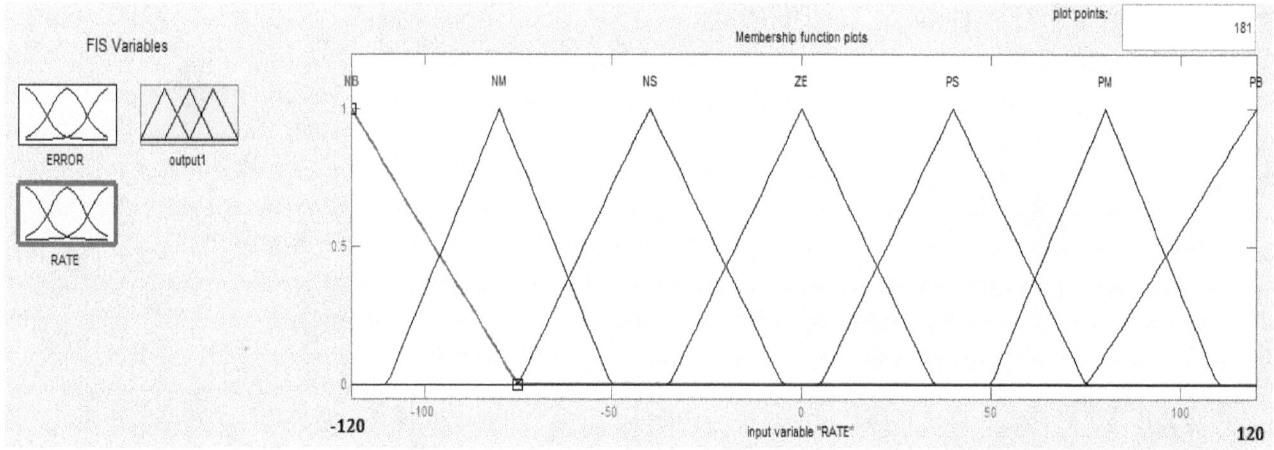

Fig 5. *Membership functions for input-2(change of error)*

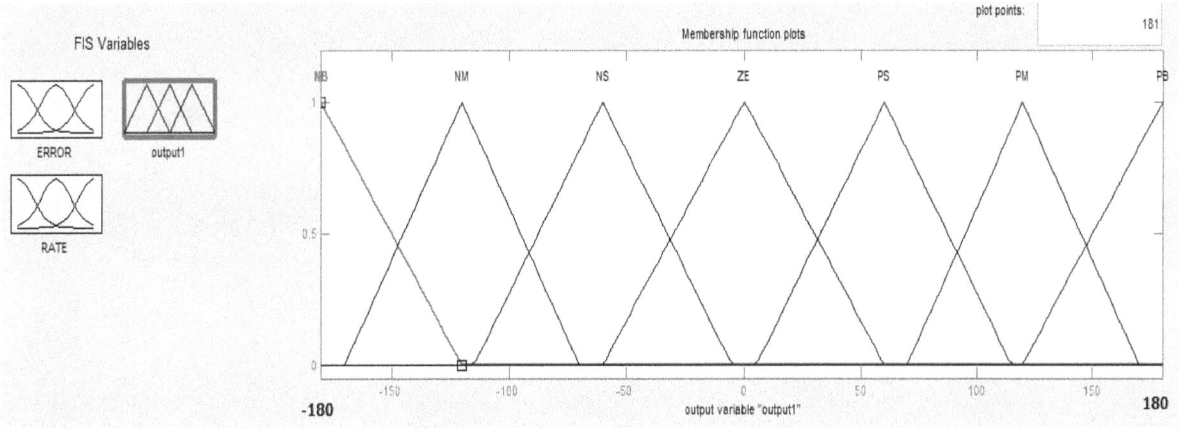

Fig 6. Membership functions for output.

6. Simulation

The simulations for different control mechanism discussed above were carried out in Simulink in MATLAB and simulation results have been obtained.

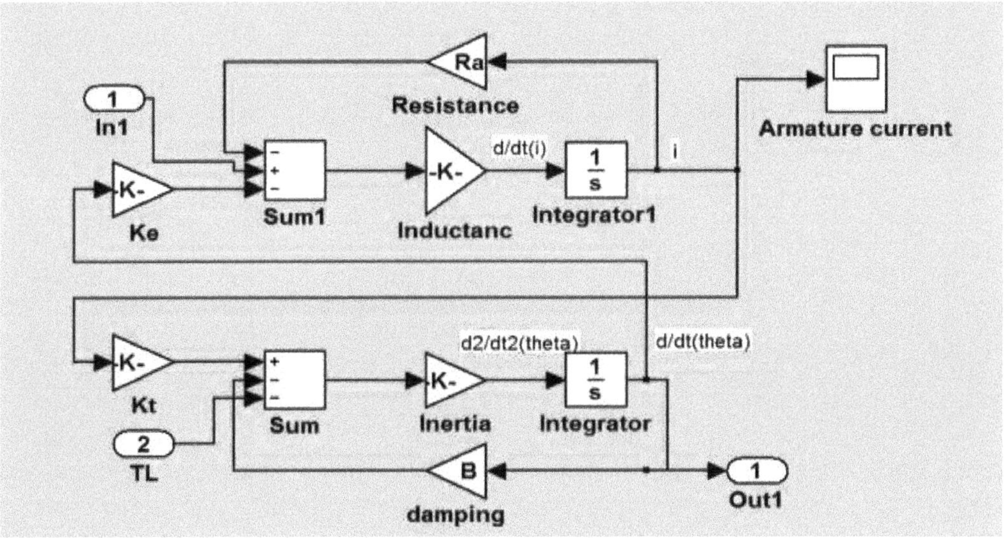

Fig 7. Simulink model of DC motor

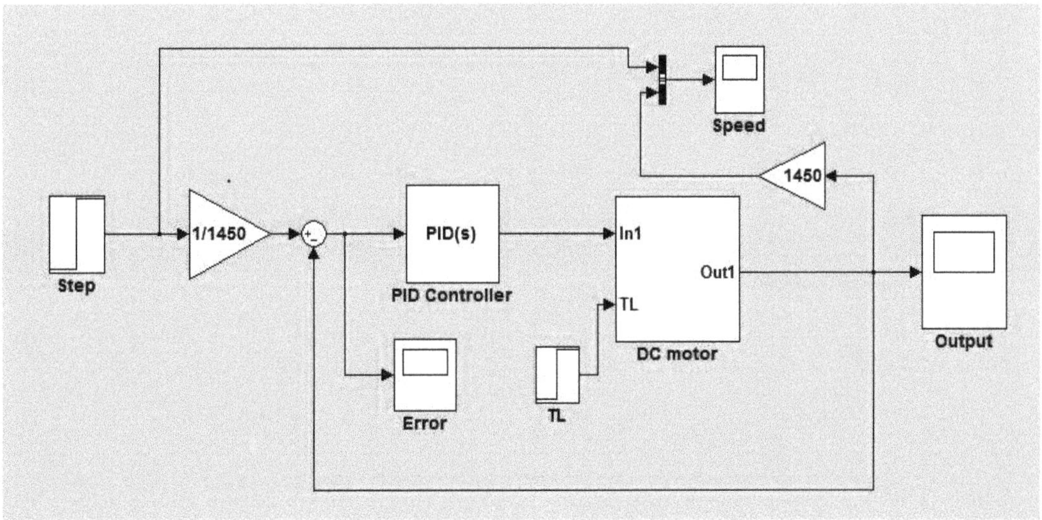

Fig 8. PID Controller Simulink model

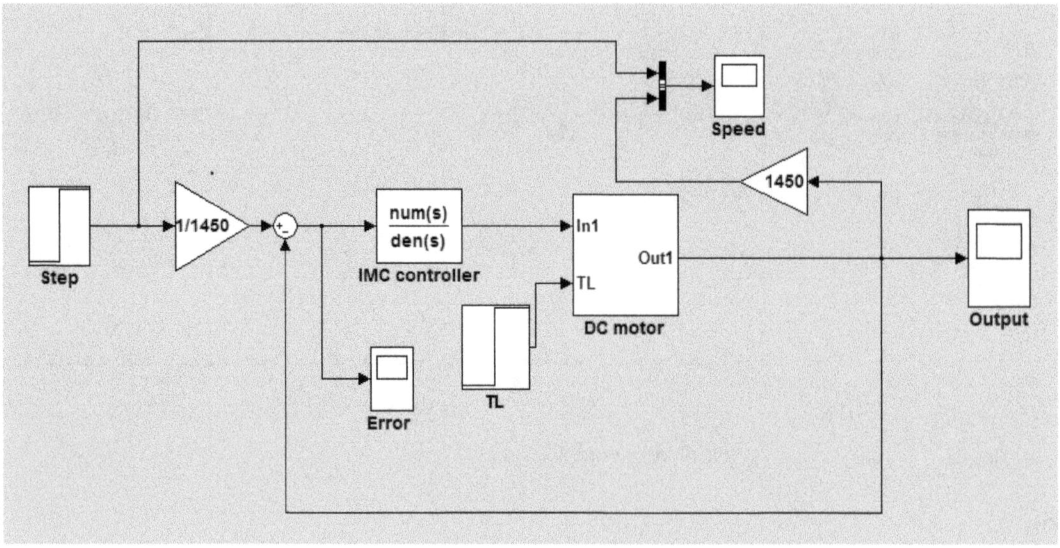

Fig 9. *IMC Controller Simulink model*

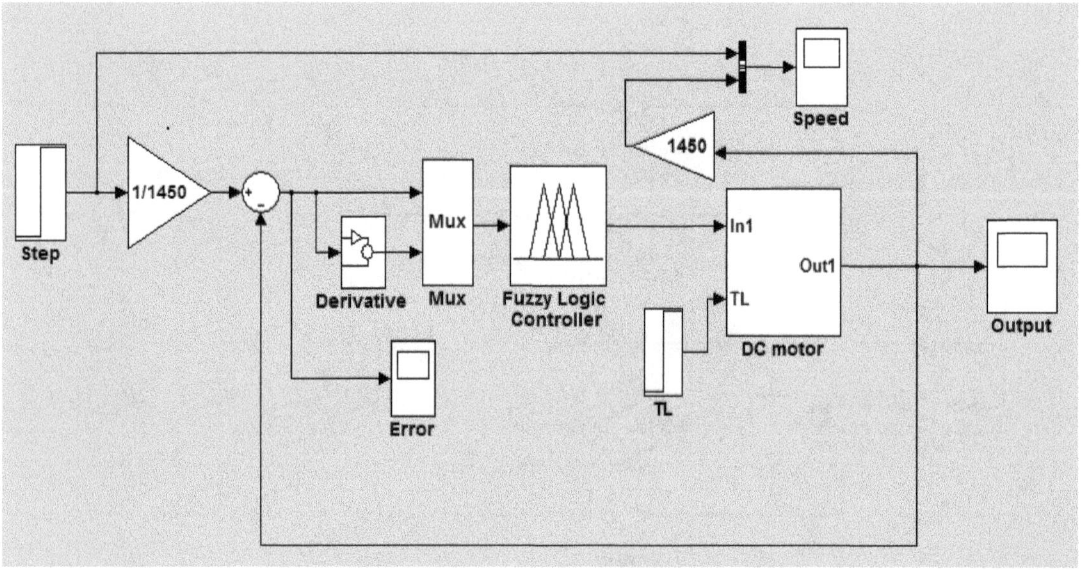

Fig 10. *Simulink model of FLC Controller*

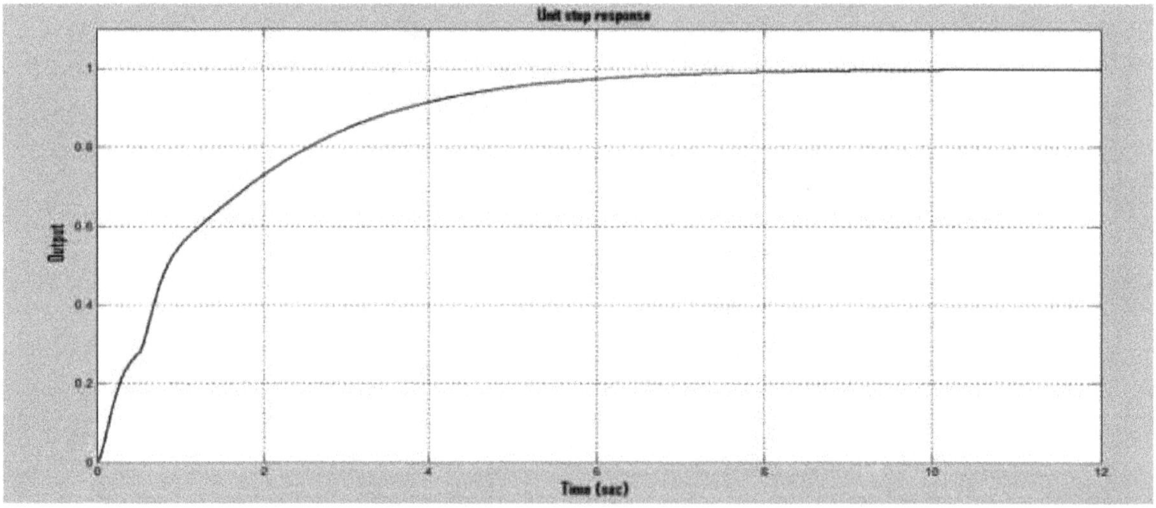

Fig 11. *Unit step response of PID Controller*

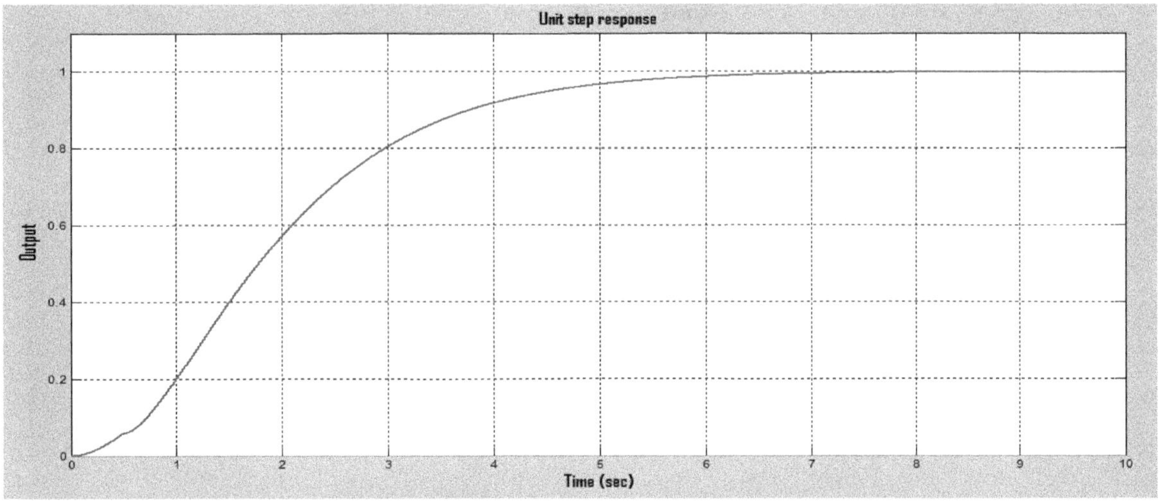

Fig 12. Unit step response of IMC

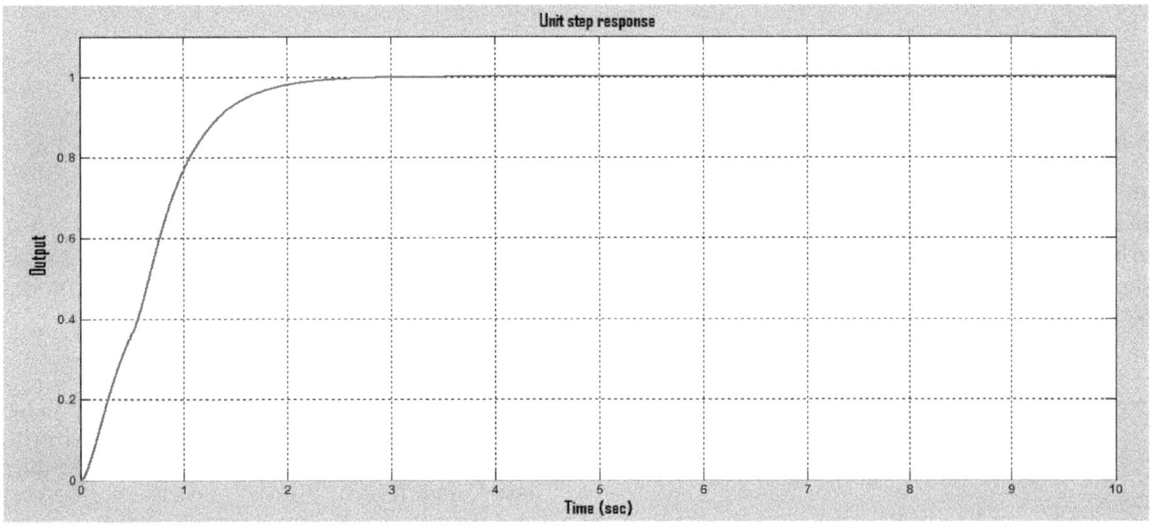

Fig 13. Unit step response of FLC

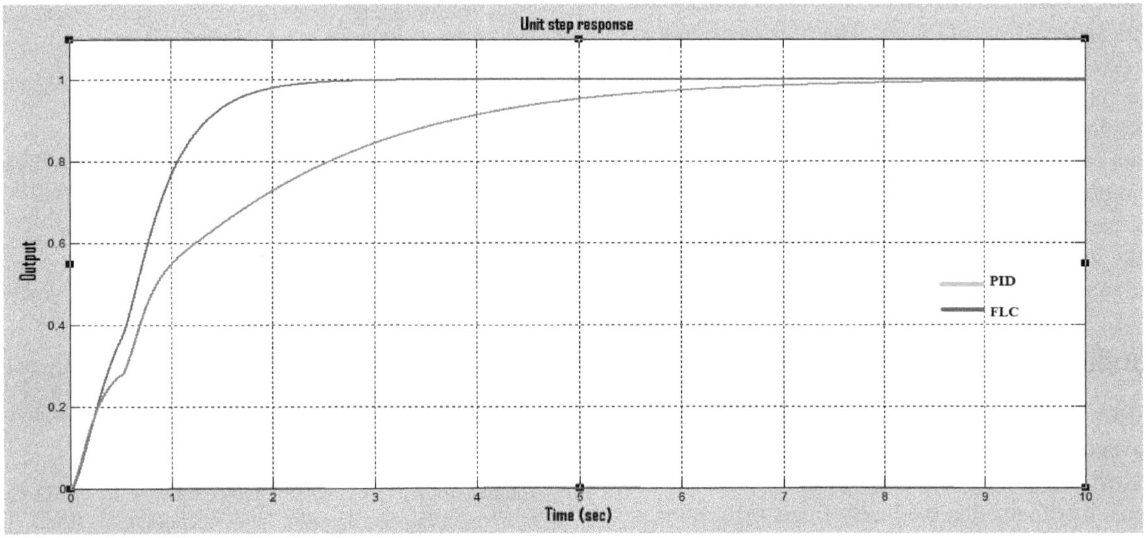

Figure 14. *Comparison of unit step response of PID and FLC controllers*

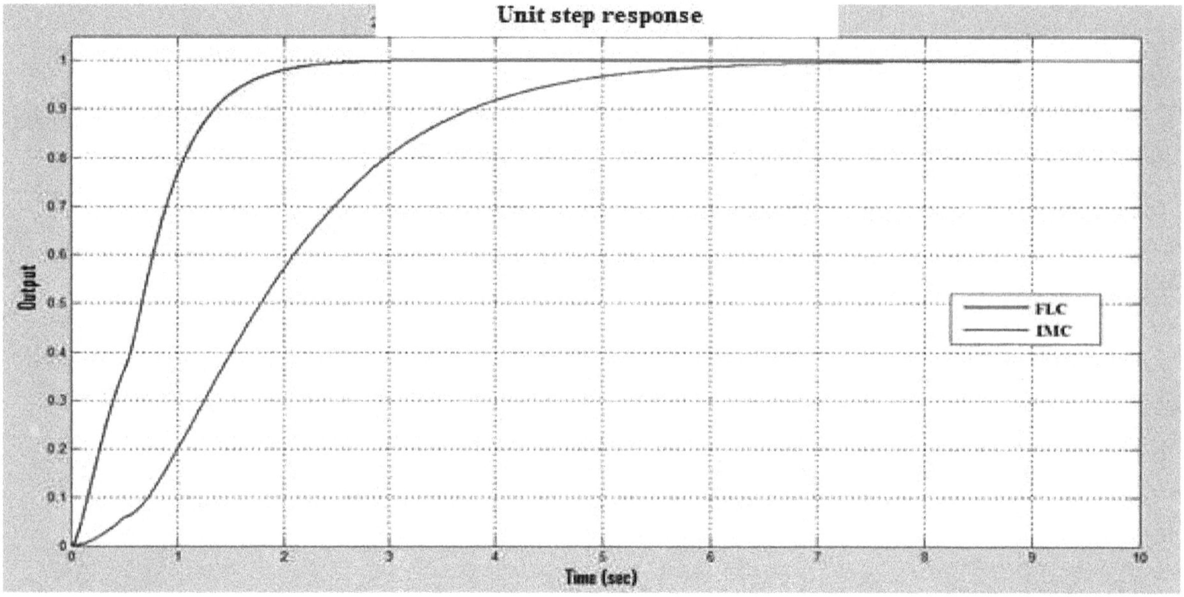

Fig 15. Comparison of unit step response of IMC and FLC controllers

7. Result and Discussion

To evaluate the performance of the different controllers, the maximum overshoot, the settling time and the rise time of step response has been analyzed.

Table 4 shows the comparison of parameters calculated from unit step response

Table 4. Comparison of different parameters in controllers

Controllers	Maximum Overshoot (%)	Settling time (sec)	Rise time (sec)
PID	2.1	7.2	3.65
IMC	0	6.9	2.5
FLC	0	2.3	1.8

The feedback controller (PID controller) gives 2.1% peak overshoot with settling time of7.2 sec. The peak overshoot is in a higher side. To compensate the high peak overshoot, model based controller (internal model controller) was designed. The internal model controller (IMC) reduces the peak overshoot to 0% and reduces the settling time to 6.9 sec. To further improve the response, Fuzzy logic controller having seven membership functions has been designed. The designed fuzzy logic controller gives a peak overshoot of 0% (no overshoot) and reduces the settling time to 2.3 sec.

8. Conclusion

In this paper, comparative studies of performance of different conventional controllers and fuzzy logic controller has been studied. According to the comparison of results of the simulations, it is found that the Fuzzy Logic Controller is better than conventional controllers namely PID and IMC.

Hence it is concluded that the proposed Fuzzy Logic Controller provides better performance characteristics and improve the control of DC motor.

References

[1] Husain Ahmed and Gagansingh, “Controlling of D.C. Motor using Fuzzy Logic Controller”, Conference on Advances in Communication and Control Systems 2013 (CAC2S 2013)

[2] Katsuhiko Ogata, “Modern Control Engineering”. 5thedition 2010.

[3] M.Saranya and D.Pamela, “A Real Time IMC Tuned PID Controller for DC Motor”, International Journal of Recent Technology and Engineering, ISSN: 2277-3878, Volume-1, Issue-1, April 2012

[4] H.X.Li and S.K.Tso, "Quantitative design and analysis of Fuzzy Proportional- Integral- Derivative Control- a Step TowardsAutotuning", International journal of system science, Vol.31, No.5, 2000, pp.545-553.

[5] Zadeh, L. A., Fuzzy Sets. Information and Control, 8, 338-353, 1965.

[6] Assilian, S. and Mamdani, E.H., An Experiment in Linguistic Synthesis with a Fuzzy Logic Controller. International Journal of Man-Machine Studies, 7(1), 1-13, 1974.

[7] K.Venkateswarlu and Ch. Chengaiah “Comparative study on DC motor speed control using various controllers” Volume 1 , Issue 6 / Dec 2013

[8] AlokRanjan Singh and V.K. Giri “Design and Analysis of DC Motor Speed Control by GA Based Tuning of Fuzzy Logic Controller” International Journal of Engineering Research & Technology (IJERT), Vol. 1 Issue 5, July – 2012

[9] KiamHeongAng, Gregory Chong and Yun Li, "PID Control System Analysis, Design, and Technology," IEEE Trans., Control Syst. Technol., vol. 13, no. 4, pp. 559-576, Jul2005.

[10] Zhicheng Zhao, Jianggang Zhang and MingdongHou, “An adaptive IMC-PID control scheme based on neural network," presented at the IEEE conference, 2009.

11] AlokRanjan Singh and V.K. Giri "Compare and simulation of speed control of DC motor using PID and Fuzzy controller" VSRD International Journal of Electrical, Electronics & Communication Engineering, Vol. 2 No. 10 October 2012

12] Larsen P.M., Industrial application of Fuzzy Logic Control,academic press, inc., may, 1979.

[13] Zadeh L.A., Fuzzy relation Equations and Applications to Knowledge Engineering, Kluwer AcademicPublishers, Holland, 1989

The Operation of the Cross-Border e-commerce Logistics in China

Xiaojun Liu, Dongyan Chen, Jieshan Cai

Department of Logistics and Information Management, Zhuhai College of Jilin University, Zhuhai, China

Email address:
Lxj02041820@163.com (Xiaojun Liu), 604995293@qq.com (Dongyan Chen), 670902983@qq.com (Jieshan Cai)

Abstract: According to the cross-border e-commerce background, the article is analyzed its operation on the cross-border e-commerce logistics in china. Firstly, this paper illustrates the operation characteristics of cross-border e-commerce logistics, then analyzes some aspects of the cross-border e-commerce logistics, like operations, logistics cost management and so on. Secondly, this paper analyzes existing problems in cross-border e-commerce logistics from the development of electronic commerce logistics cross-border in China. Finally, some suggestions were put forward on cross-border e-commerce logistics operation from the two aspects of macro level of cross-border e-commerce and micro level of cross-border e-commerce enterprise.

Keywords: Cross-Border e-commerce Logistics, Logistics Operation Model, e-commerce Logistics, Cross-Border e-commerce

1. The Background and Meaning of Research Project

In recent years, the cross-border e-commerce develops rapidly in China. It has involved people's life. Cross-border electronic commerce refers to a more advanced form of the application process of electronic commerce; it means that the both sides of trade in different areas or country can realize the transaction by using Internet or some platform with related information. Cross-border e-commerce also has the form of electronic commerce, such as B2C, B2B, C2C and so on. B2C and B2B are the main forms. Import and export in international trade usually involves international payment, customs release of import and export, international transportation, transportation insurance and so on. The safety and risk control also should be considered at the same time. These make differences between cross-border electronic commerce and the electronic commerce. As for the middle and small-sized enterprises, the cross-border electronic commerce is much thought highly of, it can provide many chance about overseas market. The rapid development of cross-border electronic commerce bring logistics a huge potential market, but in the aspect of cross-border e-commerce logistics, however, third party logistics companies in China have not provide the professional and individual logistics service to cross-border e-commerce. Cross-border e-commerce enterprises have not entered into a professional track of the operation of logistics, and explore a logistics operation mode that is suitable for the cross-border e-commerce.

As a result, the study of cross-border e-commerce logistics has significance.

Table 1. *Points of some scholars in China*

Author	Publish Date	Main Points
Xiangming Meng, Qianhui Tang	2014	Discuss the strategies of promoting the sound development of Chinese cross-border e-commerce [1].
Shuyan Cao, Zhenxin Li	2013	To develop the third party logistics with cross-border e-commerce [2].
Yongxing Wang	2013	Improve the logistics services of cross-border e-commerce [3].
Chao Mu	2013	Optimize customs' supervision of the cross-border e-commerce logistics [4].
Juan Liu	2012	Innovate the logistics services of cross-border e-commerce [5].

Cross-border e-commerce logistics as a new area is developing rapidly and this trend is drawing people's attention. But cross-border e-commerce logistics in the logistics academia still a new topic and deserve to explore and study. The Table 1 shows some opinions of scholars in China.

Cross-border electronic commerce developed early in the foreign country, especially in developed country in Europe and America, such as eBay of America. The logistics in some developed countries has faster development and more advanced. Table 2 shows some situations after the study of a part of scholars abroad.

Table 2. Points of some scholars abroad

Author	Publish Date	Main Points
Abbas Asosheh, Hadi Shahidi-ejad ,ourieh Khodkari	2012	The logistics mode of cross-border e-commerce that base global supply chain[6].
Nuray Terzia	2011	The e-commerce can increase the volume of international trade. In the long term, the development of e-commerce will bring great benefits for the developing countries in the international trade [7].
Ying Wang, Dayong Sang	2005	To develop the third party logistics with cross-border e-commerce [8].

2. Main Problems in the Development of the Chinese Cross-Border e-commerce Logistics

2.1. Supportive Policies of Chinese Cross-Border e-Commerce Logistics are not Enough

Cross-border electronic commerce began late in China but with a rapid development. There are not related supportive policies in China. But cross-border electronic commerce attracts more and more attentions because it is the new growth point in foreign trade of China. In this year, some department included Commerce Department have published a policy, About the Suggestions of Supporting Cross-border Electronic Commerce Retail Export, which is a specific measure with pertinence to solve the problems the retail export met in customs inspection and quarantine, revenue and other aspects. It is no doubt that this policy can break the ice in the export, and it is a rare chance to all retail export enterprises.

2.2. The Speed of the International Logistics's Development and the Demand of the Cross-Border e-commerce are not Matching at Present

The developed speed of cross-border electronic commerce in China makes people surprised. In 2011, the volume of trade in Chinese cross-border electronic commerce is about 1.6 trillion yuan. In 2012, it is about 2 trillion yuan, and it is about 3.1 trillion yuan in 2013. The trade scale growth faster. Take Yiwu City in Zhejiang Province as an example, the daily shipments of cross-border delivery reaches 20000 votes in the first half of this year. In term of logistics enterprises, the third party logistics companies engaged in cross-border electronic commerce is less, most of them is international express corporation to accomplish logistics distribution services, such big logistics quantity is not enough if it only depends on international express corporation, especially in the rush season for shopping, it is a normal phenomenon that express overstocks and blasting warehouse, which make an obstacle to the development of cross-border electronic commerce logistics.

2.3. Incomplete Foundation Facilities of Chinese Logistics

Logistics appeared late in China, the whole logistics environment is relatively poor, all kinds of supporting facilities are still to be perfected. There is also less transportation junction connected with different transportation modes. Cross-border electronic commerce involves cross-border warehousing, tax assessment, transportation and so on. In order to reduce the consumption, be faster and lower cost during transportation as far as possible. These both require establishing a efficient, effective and reasonable logistics system, and need more advanced and perfect logistics facilities. But which depend on international small packet and international express (much time of transportation, high cost) is contrary to the features that cross-border electronic commerce is convenient and efficient. It restricts the further development of cross-border electronic commerce. Good cross-border electronic commerce logistics system and foundation facilities need to be built.

2.4. Lack of Professional Services Provided by the Third Party Logistics

There are a lot of third party logistics companies in China, but the large-scale of them with higher professional level are less, such as DEPPON. Most of logistics companies provide logistics services just in China, even the electronic commerce services are just for the electronic commerce in China. As for the international express services, it uses a way as normal express without providing a full range of professional logistics service professionally for the cross-border electronic commerce. At present, only UPS, DHL, EMS provide international express services to the cross-border electronic commerce in China. Therefore, the professional third part logistics service is so necessary, it is beneficial the great development of Chinese cross-border electronic commerce and enable Chinese cross-border electronic commerce be in an invincible position in the international market.

3. The Suggestions of Operation About the Chinese Cross-Border e-commerce Logistics

3.1. The Logistics Strategy Alliance of the e-commerce Company

In the electronic commerce company's view, the self-run logistics will increase logistics costs of enterprises. It is a logistics operation mode that hard for the electronic commerce companies to make a decision. However, in the term of the scale economic effects, it is possible for cross-border electronic commerce companies to collaborate in logistics with each other and establish logistics strategy alliance. Many cross-border electronic commerce companies can work together to build a logistics warehousing center in China and a logistics distribution center abroad, members of the alliance can transport the goods to the logistics warehousing center in China. After overseas buyers place the order, according to the instruction, logistics center transport the goods to the distribution center abroad. And then, according to the delivery instruction, the distribution center abroad distributes the goods to overseas buyers. Figure 1 shows the operation of logistics strategy alliance.

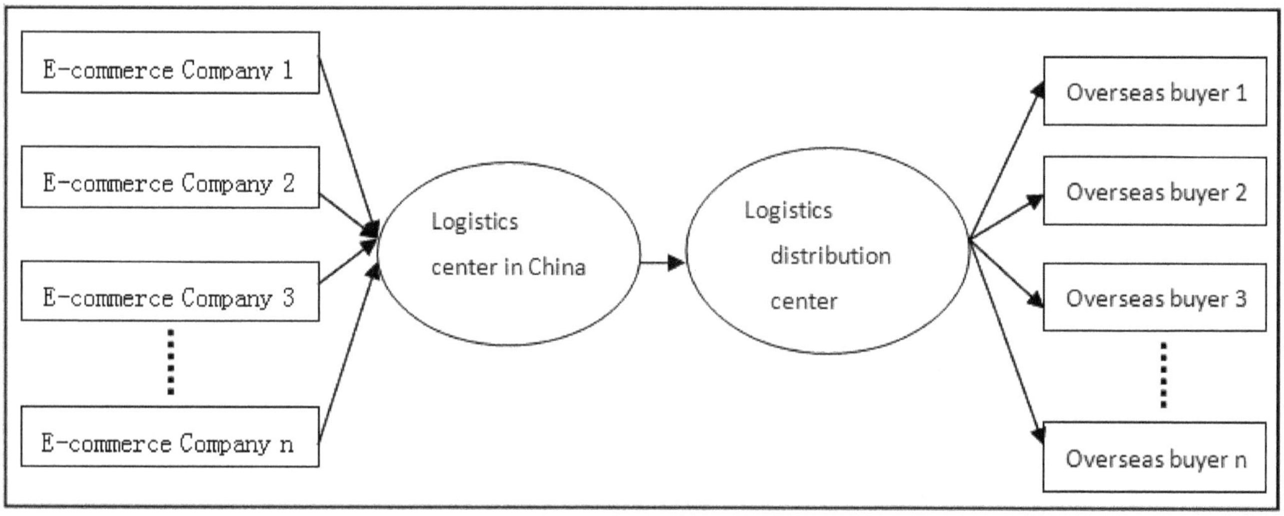

Figure 1. *The operation of logistics strategy alliance*

3.2. Select Overseas Warehousing

Overseas warehousing is based on the actual demand of cross-border electronic commerce companies. The two main ways of warehousing are the self-run storage and outsourced storage. Outsourced storage is the form of logistics operation that the cross-border electronic commerce company used today. By the way of overseas warehousing services provided by the professional supplier in overseas warehousing and help the cross-border electronic commerce company provide delivery services of the products and finish transactions. In the term of cost, it is the form of logistics operation that meets the demand of the cross-border electronic commerce company. As for some cross-border electronic commerce companies with large scale, it is not only to think of the cost, but also need to consider customer experience, customer satisfaction, market opportunity, commodity management, inventory control and so on. Consequently, companies with large-scale transaction can choose overseas warehousing as their form of operation.

3.3. The Third Party Logistics Company Provide Professional Logistics Services

The third part logistics company is a professional logistics service provider. It can provide all-around and high-quality services for customers. It is a prevalent phenomenon that there are many third party logistics companies in China. But little third party company can provide professional logistics services for the cross-border electronic commerce. There are differences between the cross-border electronic commerce and the cross-border electronic commerce domestic. Cross-border electronic commerce is a cross-border trade and its transaction processes and logistics operations are more complicated. In the whole process, it involves the process of international transportation, customs declaration and inspection and so on, it is not convenient for the operation of cross-border electronic commerce. If there are professional logistics service providers, and they can finish the work on transportation, warehousing, overseas distribution, customs declaration and inspection and so on. Not only the efficiency of logistics operation can be promoted, but also the cost of the cross-border electronic commerce can be reduced and customer satisfaction on shopping can be increased.

3.4. To Perfect the Logistics Infrastructure Construction in China

The logistics infrastructure in china is being perfect. By reasonable planning, the logistics infrastructure can truly play a promoting role for china's logistics development. From the perspective of cross-border e-commerce, logistics infrastructure can be improved by planning the logistics network and building the logistics nodes. The first one is to planning the logistics network reasonable, which can form a comprehensive transportation network system to coordinate with other transportation modes. From the perspective of logistics system, it involves the division of different modes of transportation, and optimizes the distribution of transport resources. The second one is to strengthen the construction of logistics nodes, as an important part of logistics, it is a must for us to develop the logistics nodes which has comprehensive functions. By doing this, it can enhance the operational efficiency of logistics.

.5. To Perfect the Legal Mechanism of Cross-Border e-Commerce Logistics in China

As an emerging industry, cross-border e-commerce is still acking the relevant laws and regulations. A good legal nvironment is beneficial to promote the development of ross-border e-commerce logistics, it is also good for the levelopment of china's cross-border e-commerce and helpful o improve the logistics operation efficiency of cross-border -commerce. At present, the Chinese laws don't have any elevant regulations about cross-border e-commerce logistics peration specification, cross-border e-commerce logistics ustoms clearance procedures, cross-border electronic ommerce tax regulations, cross-border e-commerce logistics varehouse management and cross-border e-commerce ogistics enterprises related measures for the administration. As the rapid development of cross-border e-commerce, laws nd regulations become an indispensable part of it. Laws and egulations have certain protection effect about both ross-border e-commerce enterprises and related logistics nterprise or consumers, and makes the emerging markets, merging industries rapid and sound development.

3.6. To Strengthen Policy Support of China's Cross-Border e-commerce Logistics

Supporting of policy is very important for the developing cross-border e-commerce logistics. Supporting of policy also provides a good opportunity and plays a good role in promoting the international competitiveness for the cross-border e-commerce logistics. In China, there is no enough policy supporting of the emerging industries. The departments of government should introduce some policies such as financial supporting, process simplifying, Cross-border e-commerce logistics tax breaks and so on to supporting the development of cross-border e-commerce. For example, in September 2013, by the ministry of commerce jointly with the national development and reform commission (NDRC), and the general administration of customs of the people's bank of nine departments jointly formulate the "About Supporting for Cross-border E-commerce Retail Sales Suggestions Policy", which puts forward the supporting for cross-border e-commerce retail export policy and export inspection, foreign exchange settlement and specific measures. This is a good start. It would bring more logistics enterprise welfare if providing more policy supporting in the future. This logistics enterprise will more competitive in the international competition.

4. Conclusion

E-commerce has come into our daily life, with the arrival of the economic globalization; e-commerce also realizes the globalization. The emergence of cross-border e-commerce makes people have a wonderful online shopping experience of globalization.

References

[1] Xiangming Meng, Qianhui Tang, "The present situation of Chinese cross-border trade e-commerce and the analysis of strategies," Journal of Shenyang University of Technology(Social Sciences),vol.2, 2014, pp120-125.

[2] Shuyan Cao, Zhenxin Li, "The research of the cross-border e-commerce third-party logistics model," Electronic Commerce, vol.3, 2013, pp23-25.

[3] Yongxing Wang, "Simply analyze the logistics strategies of the e-commerce B2C cross-border e-commerce," Practical Electronics, vol.6, 2013, pp15-18.

[4] Chao Mu, "The operation model of cross-border e-commerce in Qianhai Shenzhen-Hongkong Modern Service Industry Cooperation Zone," Logistics Technology, vol.11, 2013, pp409-411.

[5] Juan Liu, "The rise of the cross-border e-commerce with the small-volume trade and the discussion of the problems in the development——the e-commerce of the post-financial crisis era and the innovation of the logistics services," vol.2, 2012, pp89-92.

[6] Abbas Asosheh,Hadi Shahidi-Nejad, Hourieh Khodkari, "A model of a localized cross-border e-commerce," Business, vol.4, 2012, pp136-145.

[7] Nuray Terzia, "The impact of e-commerce on international trade and employment," Procedia.Social and Behavioral Sciences, vol.24, 2011, pp745-753.

[8] Ying Wang, Dayong Sang, "Multi-agent framework for third party logistics in e-commerce," Expert Systems with Applications, vol.1, 2005, pp431-436.

Permissions

All chapters in this book were first published by Science Publishing Group; hereby published with permission under the Creative Commons Attribution License or equivalent. Every chapter published in this book has been scrutinized by our experts. Their significance has been extensively debated. The topics covered herein carry significant findings which will fuel the growth of the discipline. They may even be implemented as practical applications or may be referred to as a beginning point for another development.

The contributors of this book come from diverse backgrounds, making this book a truly international effort. This book will bring forth new frontiers with its revolutionizing research information and detailed analysis of the nascent developments around the world.

We would like to thank all the contributing authors for lending their expertise to make the book truly unique. They have played a crucial role in the development of this book. Without their invaluable contributions this book wouldn't have been possible. They have made vital efforts to compile up to date information on the varied aspects of this subject to make this book a valuable addition to the collection of many professionals and students.

This book was conceptualized with the vision of imparting up-to-date information and advanced data in this field. To ensure the same, a matchless editorial board was set up. Every individual on the board went through rigorous rounds of assessment to prove their worth. After which they invested a large part of their time researching and compiling the most relevant data for our readers.

The editorial board has been involved in producing this book since its inception. They have spent rigorous hours researching and exploring the diverse topics which have resulted in the successful publishing of this book. They have passed on their knowledge of decades through this book. To expedite this challenging task, the publisher supported the team at every step. A small team of assistant editors was also appointed to further simplify the editing procedure and attain best results for the readers.

Apart from the editorial board, the designing team has also invested a significant amount of their time in understanding the subject and creating the most relevant covers. They scrutinized every image to scout for the most suitable representation of the subject and create an appropriate cover for the book.

The publishing team has been an ardent support to the editorial, designing and production team. Their endless efforts to recruit the best for this project, has resulted in the accomplishment of this book. They are a veteran in the field of academics and their pool of knowledge is as vast as their experience in printing. Their expertise and guidance has proved useful at every step. Their uncompromising quality standards have made this book an exceptional effort. Their encouragement from time to time has been an inspiration for everyone.

The publisher and the editorial board hope that this book will prove to be a valuable piece of knowledge for researchers, students, practitioners and scholars across the globe.

List of Contributors

Bai Li
School of Control Science and Engineering, Zhejiang University, Hangzhou, 310027, China
School of Advanced Engineering, Beijing University of Aeronautics and Astronautics, Beijing, 100191, China
Department of Chemical Engineering, National Tsing Hua University, Hsinchu, 30013, Taiwan

Yoshihisa Banno, Kouichi Taji and Kyohei Seta
Department of Mechanical Science and Engineering, Graduate School of Engineering, Nagoya University, Furo, Chikusa, Nagoya, 464-8603, Japan

Yuji Harata
Division of Mechanical Systems and Applied Mechanics, Faculty of Engineering, Hiroshima University, 1-4-1, Kagamiyama, Higashi-Hiroshima, 739-8527, Japan

Navid Khalili Dizaji and Nazila Masoudi
Department of Mechatronics Engineering, Tabriz Branch, Islamic Azad University, Tabriz, Iran

Aidin Sakhvati
Department of Electrical Engineering, Tabriz Branch, Islamic Azad University, Tabriz, Iran

Tahar Latreche
Magistère in Civil Engineering, B.P. 129 Salem Lalmi, 40003 Khenchela, Algeria

Ali Moradmard and Mohammad Tahghighi Sharabiani
Department of Computer Engineering, Islamic Azad University, Zanjan Branch, Zanjan, Iran

Elham Mahdipour and Masoumeh Bagheri
Computer Engineering Department, Khavaran Institute of Higher Education, Mashhad, Iran

Elham Mahdipour, Rahele Shojaeian Razavi and Zahra Gheibi
Computer Engineering Department, Khavaran Institute of Higher Education, Mashhad, Iran

Aalia Hemmati and Sima Emadi
Computer Engineering department. Islamic Azad university of Meybod, Yazd, Iran

Farshad Parhizkar Miandehi, Erfan Zidehsaraei and Mousa Doostdar
Department of Computer Engineering, Zanjan Branch, Islamic Azad University, Zanjan, Iran

Vahid Nouri
Department of Computer Engineering, Islamic Azad University, Mashhad Branch, Mashhad, Iran
Mohammad Reza Akbarzadeh
Department of Electrical Engineering, University of Neyshabur, Neyshabur, Iran

Tootoonchi, Alireza Rowhanimanesh
Departments of Electrical and Computer Engineering, Center of Excellence on Soft Computing and Intelligent Information Processing (SCIIP), Ferdowsi University of Mashhad, Mashhad, Iran

Zahra Madankan and Noushin Riahi
Computer Engineering Department, Engineering Faculty, Alzahra University, Tehran, Iran

Akbar Ranjbar
Electronic Engineering Department, Engineering Faculty, Shahed University, Tehran, Iran

Reakook Hwang
Industry & Strategy Department I, Samsung Economic Research Institute, Seoul, Korea

Koichi Murata
Department of Industrial Engineering and Management, College of Industrial Technology, Nihon University, Chiba, Japan

Hiroshi Katayama
Department of Industrial and management Systems Engineering, Faculty of Science and Engineering, Waseda University, Tokyo, Japan

Koichi Murata and Seiichiro Isobe
Department of Industrial Engineering and Management, College of Industrial Technology, Nihon University, Chiba, Japan

Nao Watanabe
Large Motors and Drives Department, Discrete Automation and Motion Division, ABB K.K., Tokyo, Japan

Reakook Hwang
Industry & Strategy Department I, Samsung Economic Research Institute, Seoul, Korea

Hiroshi Katayama
Department of Industrial and management Systems Engineering, Faculty of Science and Engineering, Waseda University, Tokyo, Japan

Cheng Zhao, Myungryun Yoo and Takanori Yokoyama
Department of Computer Science, Tokyo City University, Tokyo, Japan

Young Su Yun
Division of Management Administration, Chosun University, Gwangju, Korea

Wang Funing
Ningdong Power Plant, Gouhua Power Group, Ningdong town, Ningxia, P. R. C.

Kai Pingan
Energy Research Institute, Development and Reformation Committee of State, Beijing, P. R. C.

Petr Kadera and Pavel Vrba
1Czech Institute of Informatics, Robotics and Cybernetics, Czech Technical University in Prague, CZ-169 00, Prague, Czech Republic

Petr Novak
Czech Institute of Informatics, Robotics and Cybernetics, Czech Technical University in Prague, CZ-169 00, Prague, Czech Republic
Christian Doppler Laboratory for Software Engineering Integration for Flexible Automation Systems, Vienna University of Technology, A-1040, Vienna, Austria

Vaclav Jirkovsky
Czech Institute of Informatics, Robotics and Cybernetics, Czech Technical University in Prague, CZ-169 00, Prague, Czech Republic
Rockwell Automation Research and Development Center, CZ-150 00, Prague, Czech Republic

Hassan Salmi, Abdelmajid Badri and Mourad Zegrari
EEA&TI Laboratory, Faculty of Sciences and Techniques, Hassan II Casablanca University, Mohammedia, Morocco

Babak Darabinejad
Department of Computer Engineering, Mehrarvand International Institute of Technology, Abadan, Iran

Seyed Rasoul Mousavi Fayyeh
Department of Computer Engineering, Science and Research Branch, Islamic Azad University, Tehran, Iran

Hooman Sanatkar and Saman Haratizadeh
Faculty of New Sciences and Technologies, University of Tehran, Tehran, Iran

Lee Jeongeun and Rhee Kyonggu
Department of Accounting, Dongeui University, Busan, Korea

Farzam Saeednia
Department Of Electrical Engineering, Kazerun Branch, Islamic Azad University, Kazerun, Iran
Shapour Khorshidi
Air-Sea Science and Technology Academic Complex, Shiraz, Iran

Mohssen Masoumi
Department Of Electrical Engineering, Jahrom Branch, Islamic Azad University, Jahrom, Iran

Mohammad Hadi Yousofi
Department of Mechatronics, Postgraduate School, Islamic Azad University of Kashan, Kashan, Iran

Habib Yousofi
School of Medicine, Kashan University of Medical Sciences, Kashan, Iran

Sayyed Amir Mohammad Razavi
Department of Electrical and Computer, Islamic Azad University of Kashan, Kashan, Iran

Maryam Parhizgar and Farhad Mortezapour Shiri
Department of Computer Engineering, Sience and Research Branch, Islamic Azad University, Qazvin, Iran

Kazunori Omori, Myungryun Yoo and Takanori Yokoyama
Information Engineering, Tokyo City University, Tokyo, Japan

Mohsen Pourali
Financial department, Mehr Hospital, Mashhad, Iran

Abbas Ghodrat Panah
Accounting group, Attar University, Mashhad, Iran

Farshad Parhizkar Miandehi
Electronic and Computer Faculty, Islamic Azad University of Zanjan, Zanjan, Iran

Asadollah Shahbahrami
Engineering faculty, University of Guilan, Rasht, Iran

Li Jun-yi and Li Jian-hua
School of Electronic Information and Electrical engineering, Shanghai JiaoTong University, Shanghai, China

Zhu Jin-hua
College of Network Communication Zhejiang Yuexiu University of Foreign Languages, Zhe Jiang, China

Chen Xiao-hui
Information Engineering School, Yulin University, Yulin, Shanxi, China

Li Jun-yi and Li Jian-hua
School of Electronic Information and Electrical engineering, Shanghai JiaoTong University, Shanghai 200240, China

Zhi Zhuo Hou
Department of Industrial and Management System Engineering, Graduate School of Creative Science and Engineering, Waseda University, Tokyo, Japan

Hiroshi Katayama
Department of Industrial and Management System Engineering, Faculty of Science and Engineering, Waseda University, Tokyo, Japan

Reakook Hwang
Samsung Economic Research Institute, Seoul, Korea

Zhu Jinghua
College of Network Communication, Zhejiang Yuexiu University of Foreign Languages, Shaoxing, China

Md Akram Ahmad and Pankaj Rai
Electrical Engineering Department, BIT Sindri, Dhanbad, India (Vinoba Bhave University Jharkhand)

Xiaojun Liu, Dongyan Chen and Jieshan Cai
Department of Logistics and Information Management, Zhuhai College of Jilin University, Zhuhai, China

Index

Printed in the USA
CPSIA information can be obtained
at www.ICGtesting.com
JSHW052005011124
72840JS00003B/28